Political Science:
A Comparative
Introduction

3rd edition

Political Science: A Comparative Introduction

Rod Hague
and
Martin Harrop

palgrave

Published 2001 by
PALGRAVE
Houndmills, Basingstoke, Hampshire RG21 6XS and
175 Fifth Avenue, New York, N.Y. 10010
Companies and representatives throughout the world

PALGRAVE is the new global academic imprint of
St. Martin's Press LLC Scholarly and Reference Division and
Palgrave Publishers Ltd (formerly Macmillan Press Ltd).

ISBN 0–312–29460–3

This book is printed on paper suitable for recycling and
made from fully managed and sustained forest sources

Cataloging-in-Publication data is available from the
Library of Congress

Printed and bound in Great Britain by
Antony Rowe Ltd, Chippenham, Wiltshire

Summary of contents

Contents

List of illustrative material

For or against

Country and regional profiles

Preface

This edition retains the purpose of its predecessors. We have sought to provide a wide-ranging, contemporary and clearly written introductory text for courses in comparative politics, and for non-country-specific first-year introduction to politics courses. In achieving this broad objective, however, we have made substantial modifications for this new, revised and updated edition. The result, we hope, is a book that is both clearer in approach and crisper in execution.

The most obvious development is the inclusion of two new chapters: on political communication (Chapter 7) and authoritarian rule (Chapter 3). The chapter on political communication is designed to reflect the undoubted importance of not just the mass media but also, more generally, of perceptions, images and attitudes, to the political process. While the existing chapter on political culture addresses this agenda from one perspective, a communications approach offers an additional take. The communication chapter also offers a more coherent location for sections on public opinion and the mass media that were previously scattered about the text.

The chapter on authoritarian rule serves a dual purpose. It offers both a contrast with democracy (what know they of democracy who only democracy know?) and also a perspective on the tribulations of twentieth-century politics to which our current era is, in part, a reaction. In our view, some historical perspective is essential even for a subject and a text which is focused on the present; in any case, the claim that we live in an exclusively democratic world can be refuted with the single word, China. This chapter on authoritarian politics has also involved some relocation, and a side-effect is, we believe, improved organization of Part I as a whole.

The distinction between established democracies, authoritarian rule and new democracies now serves as the basic organizing device within chapters. We believe this gives a more straight-forward and political structure to the book. Yet we must of course remain sensitive to diversity within each category. Thus, although generally we use 'authoritarian' simply as a synonym for 'non-democratic', we recognize that some scholars prefer to distinguish between 'authoritarian' and 'totalitarian' rule. And in the detailed discussions of authoritarian politics within the chapter, we do counterpose authoritarian and totalitarian (especially communist) rule. Because many new democracies are still successor regimes, we locate our discussion of them in each chapter after the section dealing with authoritarian rule.

Similarly, many a soldier now marches under the democratic banner. We have adopted the distinction between established and new democracies because we feel the contrast in the previous edition between established and transitional democracies already had a 1990s feel to it. This time, we focus less on the mechanics of transition and pay more attention to the contemporary challenges facing new democracies. Throughout the book, we have sought to avoid conveying the impression that new democracies are acorns whose only destiny is the oak tree of established democracy; after all, backsliding and stalling are not unknown. Indeed, we have devoted more space in this edition to semi-democracies, a form which by its nature floats rather ambiguously between the poles of authoritarianism and democracy.

In addition to these major changes, we have taken the opportunity to restructure three existing chapters. The state in a global context (Chapter 4) now focuses more directly on the linkage between the international and the national. The comparative approach (Chapter 5, repositioned to Part 1) now gives more space to broader perspectives within the field. And the policy process (Chapter 17) now links more directly with our three-part distinction between authoritarian regimes, established democracies and new democracies. All other chapters have been reviewed with the aim of keeping the book contemporary in content and clear in expression. We have also updated the references, aware that many users are at least as interested in our sources as our conclusions!

We have made some changes to presentation, too, again with the goals of clarity and coherence in mind. The exhibits have gone, incorporated into the main text where appropriate. In their place emerge a smaller number of 'for or against' debates intended to stimulate classroom discussion. We hope users – students as well as instructors – will let us know their views on this new feature.

As is the way with web sites, ours too has moved. It is now at:

http://www.palgrave.com/politics/hague

It remains, as usual, to thank the many people who have helped us. Our major debt is to Shaun Breslin, our co-author on the last edition and our adviser on this one. Although 'HHB' (as it was known) now returns to its original incarnation as 'H&H', Shaun's contribution continues to enliven this version, even though he is no longer included in the list of authors. We must also thank Charles Polidano for his assistance in updating the bureaucracy chapter and our publisher Steven Kennedy, and his speedy reviewers, whose advice and encouragement helped us with what turned out to be major revisions. We are also most grateful to Vipa Tiranutti for her careful work on the references and the index and to Keith Povey for his patient copy-editing.

Finally, we would like to thank the numerous teachers and students from around the world who have provided corrections and encouragement, whether to the publisher or direct to the authors. We continue to welcome all feedback, not least because some errors of fact or interpretation are bound to have crept into this revised edition. Please contact Martin Harrop at

Department of Politics
University of Newcastle
Newcastle upon Tyne
England
NE1 7RU

e-mail Martin.Harrop@ncl.ac.uk

Rod Hague
Martin Harrop

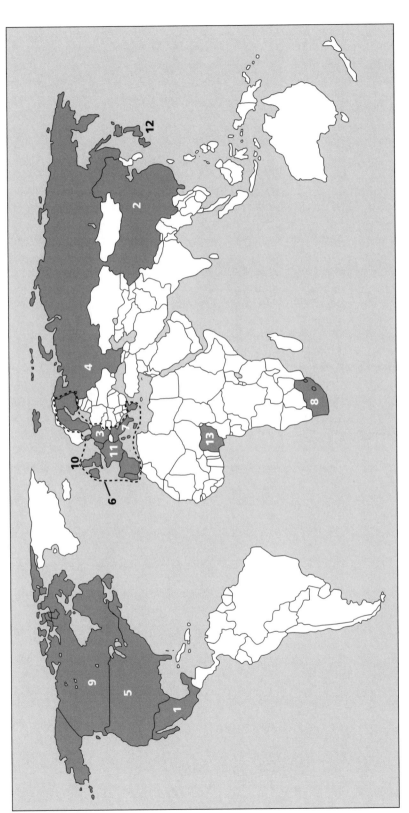

Countries featured in Country Profiles are shaded on map

Map of the World

PART 1

FOUNDATIONS

In this part we set out the foundations of comparative government and politics. Chapter 1 introduces the core concepts of the subject and the classification of governments adopted for this book. The next two chapters develop our classification: Chapter 2 focuses on democracy while Chapter 3 examines authoritarian alternatives. Chapter 4 assesses the global context within which all states, democratic or authoritarian, now operate while Chapter 5 explores the strategies and techniques involved in studying politics comparatively.

Politics and government

In this book we examine how politics is organized in countries around the world. We focus on how nations solve the core political problem of making collective decisions. But we cannot jump straight into these issues. For just as what astronomers 'see' in the sky depends on the type of telescope through which they peer, so too does any interpretation of politics depend on the concepts through which we approach the topic. Indeed, in politics it often seems as though everyone has their own telescope – and claims that their own instrument is the best!

This point illustrates a key fact about studying politics. Major concepts remain at the forefront of discussion in a way that does not normally apply to more scientific disciplines. Political analysis is far more than mere opinion; yet even so, conclusions vary with the analyst rather more than is comfortable for those who advocate a strictly scientific approach to the subject. *Comparative* politics, based on a range of countries, is especially suited to the task of revealing contrasting perspectives on our subject matter. So in this chapter we discuss some central concepts of the discipline, not so much to establish 'correct' definitions as to introduce our own interpretations.

Politics

To start at the beginning: what is politics? We can easily list, and agree on, some examples of political activity. When the American president and Congress start their annual tussle over the federal budget, they are clearly engaged in politics. When protesters caused turmoil outside a World Trade Organization conference in Seattle in 1999, they were clearly making a political point of some description. When Chechnya declared its independence from Russia in 1995 its action was obviously political. The heartland of politics, as represented by such examples, is clear enough. However, the boundaries of the political are less precise. When one country invades another, is it engaged in politics or merely in war? Would politics occur if resources were unlimited? Is politics restricted to governments or can it also be found in families, universities and even seminar groups?

A crisp definition of politics – one which fits just those things we instinctively call 'political' – is impossible. Politics is a term with varied uses and nuances. Perhaps the nearest we can come to a capsule statement is this: politics is the activity by which groups reach binding collective decisions through attempting to reconcile differences among their members. Four significant points inhere in this definition:

- Politics is a *collective activity*, involving people who accept a common membership or at least acknowledge a shared fate. Robinson Crusoe could not practise politics.
- Politics presumes an initial *diversity of views*, if not about goals then at least about means. Were we all to agree all the time, politics would be redundant.
- Politics involves *reconciling such differences*

through discussion and persuasion. Communication is therefore central to politics.

- Political decisions become *authoritative policy* for a group, binding members to decisions that are implemented by force if necessary. Politics scarcely exists if decisions are reached solely by violence, but force, or its threat, underpins the process of reaching collective decisions.

> **Definition**
> Miller (1991, p. 390) defines **politics** as 'a process whereby a group of people, whose opinions or interests are initially divergent, reach collective decisions which are generally accepted as binding on the group, and enforced as common policy'. For Miller, the political process typically involves elements of persuasion and bargaining, together with a mechanism for reaching a final decision.

The necessity of politics arises from the collective character of human life. We live in groups that must reach collective decisions: about sharing resources, about relating to other groups and about planning for the future. A family discussing where to take its vacation, a country deciding whether to go to war, the world seeking to limit the damage caused by pollution – all are examples of groups seeking to reach decisions which affect all their members. As social creatures, politics is part of our fate: we have no choice but to practise it.

So although the term 'politics' is often used cynically, to criticize the pursuit of private advantage under the guise of the public interest, politics is in fact an inescapable feature of the human condition. Indeed, the Greek philosopher Aristotle (384–322 BC argued that 'man is by nature a political animal'. By this he meant not just that politics is unavoidable but rather that it is the essential human activity; political engagement is the feature which most sharply separates us from other species. For Aristotle, people can only express their true nature as reasoning, virtuous beings through participating in a political community.

Members of a group rarely agree, at least initially, on what course of action to follow. Even if there is agreement over goals, there may still be a skirmish over means. Yet a decision must be reached, one way or the other, and once made it will commit all members of the group. Thus politics consists in pro-

cedures for allowing a range of views to be expressed and then combined into an overall decision. As Shively (1995, p. 11) points out,

> political action may be interpreted as a way to work out rationally the best common solution to a common problem – or at least a way to work out a reasonable common solution. That is, politics consists of public choice.

By debating the options, the quality of the final choice should improve and the participants to the discussion should become both better informed and more committed to the agreed course of action. All collective decisions result from politics but the best politics produces good, well-executed policy.

Of course, politics consists of more than the disinterested pursuit of the collective good. Members of a group will share some interests but not others. Deciding to go to war is one thing; agreeing on who should be conscripted is quite another. Introducing a pension for senior citizens is one thing; working out whose taxes should be increased to foot the bill is another. A decision will affect all, and even benefit all, but not everyone will gain equally. Most often a course of action will produce both winners and losers. Here perhaps we arrive at the essence of the subject: politics is about reaching decisions which impinge on both the shared and the competing interests of the group's members. Indeed some authors *define* political situations as those in which the participants mix common and competing interests. 'Pure conflict is war', writes Laver (1983, p. 1). 'Pure cooperation is true love. Politics is a mixture of both.'

So one aim of politics is compromise: to reach agreements acceptable to all even if the first choice of none. But another object is more ambitious: to reconcile special interests in the pursuit of the common good. Thus, Allison (1996, p. 389) suggests politics arises when people say 'I have a right to that' rather than merely 'I will have that'. The British political theorist Bernard Crick (1992, first pub. 1962) advances this view with particular vigour. He asks: 'why call a struggle for power "politics", when it is simply a struggle for power?' Crick prefers to define politics as the 'activity by which differing interests within a given unit of rule are conciliated by giving them a share in power in proportion to their importance to the welfare and the survival of their community'. Crick's definition is somewhat idealistic; it seems to dismiss the possibility of politics occurring at all in dictatorships. But he is surely right to stress that politics involves negotiation, bargaining and compromise.

Once reached, political decisions bind all the group's members. In Easton's famous definition (1965a and b), 'politics is the authoritative allocation of values'. Public authority – ultimately, force – is used to enforce collective decisions. If you break the rules, the government may put you in prison; at any rate, it is the only body with the authority to do so. A defining feature of a government is its ability to uphold the right to use force, a feature that gives political study unique significance. You may play no part in shaping the laws of your country but you are expected to abide by them. And even if you leave one country, you will be subject to the government of another. From government there is no escape. You cannot – in the contemporary world – choose a life without government.

Government and governance

Groups must not only reach decisions on their common affairs, they must also work out how such decisions are to be reached. The question of who decides raises the question of government. Nearly all large societies develop special institutions for making and enforcing collective decisions. These bodies are the government. The government may be elected, appointed, inherited or imposed but it usually provides the structure within which the activity of politics takes place; it provides the framework for politics. In popular usage, 'the government' refers just to the highest echelon of political appointments: in other words, to presidents and department heads, prime ministers and cabinet members. But in a broader sense the government consists of all those organizations charged with the task of reaching decisions for the community.

We must distinguish between government and governance. An old word enjoying renewed popularity, governance refers to the activity, process or quality of governing. This term directs our attention not so much to the structures of government as to the task of governing itself: to the policies which are made and to the effectiveness with which they are carried out. At least in established democracies, government is to some extent giving ground to governance. That is, collective decisions are less often made by a single leader (say, the president) or by a single group (say, the cabinet). Rather, policies emerge from consultations between many affected interests, outside as well as inside government. Further, policies are often modified when they are put into effect: those who implement policy take part in governance if not government. Governance – the task of managing complex societies – involves the coordination of many public and private sector bodies; it is the ability to get things done without the capacity to command that they are done. In short, government is only one actor, and not always the leading one, in governance (Rhodes, 1996). But the governance theme does not just apply to established democracies. Many international agencies also suggest that effective governance is crucial to economic development in new democracies. In an influential report, the World Bank (1997, p. 1) argued that 'the state is central to economic and social development, not as a direct provider of growth but as a partner, catalyst and facilitator'.

Definition

A **government** consists of institutions responsible for making collective decisions for society. More narrowly, government refers to the top political level within such institutions. **Governance,** by contrast, refers to the process of making collective decisions, a task in which government may not play a leading, or even any, role. In international relations, for example, no world government exists to resolve problems but many issues are resolved by negotiation – a case of governance without government.

And it is the field of international relations which offers the best current examples of governance. The reason for this is clear: there is no world government, no institution making enforceable decisions for the world as a whole. Even so, many aspects of global relations are regulated by agreement. One example is the internet, a massive network of linked computers beyond the control of any one government. Yet standards for connecting computers and data to the internet are agreed; thus we can speak of the governance, but not the government, of cyberspace (Loader, 1997). Similarly, international institutions have emerged to formulate rules in many other areas: for instance, the World Trade Organization works to reduce trade barriers between its member states. However, such organizations are certainly not governments; they have limited powers, especially in enforcement, and they lack a police force to enforce their will. So the emerging pattern, in international and perhaps also in national politics, is rules without rulers, governing without government. In a word: governance (Rosenau, 1992).

The state and sovereignty

Statehood is now the dominant principle of political organization. Oceans aside, the world is parcelled up into separate states which, through mutual recognition, form the international system. The state is a unique institution. It stands above all other organizations in society. The state can legitimately use force to enforce its will and citizens must accept its authority as long as they continue to live within its borders. As Edelman (1964, p. 1) writes,

> the state benefits and it threatens. Now it is 'us' and often it is 'them'. It is an abstraction, but in its name men are jailed, or made rich on defense contracts, or killed in wars.

Understanding, and therefore developing the potential to control, the powers embedded in the state are prime tasks for students of comparative politics. But what exactly is the 'state' and how does it differ from government? The state is the more abstract term, referring to the ensemble formed by government, population and territory. The French state, for example, is more than its government; it also encompasses the people and the territory of France. To bring out the distinction between government and state, we can note that all countries have someone who serves as head of state but that this person is not usually head of the government as well. European monarchs are examples: they symbolize the state but leave prime ministers to control the levers of power. In short, the state defines the political community of which government is the executive branch.

> **Definition**
> Sometimes used to mean the same as government, the **state** is better understood as a political community formed by a territorially defined population which is subject to one government. The Montevideo Convention of 1933 regarded the capacity to enter relations with other states as one of four core features of states. The others were: a permanent population, a defined territory and a government (Rosenau, 1989, p. 17).

A central feature of the state is its capacity to regulate the legitimate use of force within its boundaries. The Russian revolutionary Lenin (1870–1924) expressed the link between the state and violence in describing states as 'bodies of armed men'. And it is certainly true that when the power of the state is turned on its own people, gruesome brutality results. But although the state can and does employ coercion, it is of course far more than just a band of hoodlums. Because the state is based in a fixed territory, it has a long-term incentive to increase the wealth of its people and therefore of itself. To use Olson's phrase, states are 'stationary' rather than 'roving bandits' and behave better as a result (Olson, 2000). Most importantly, the state claims not just the capacity but also the right to employ force. As the German sociologist Max Weber (1864–1920) noted, the exclusive feature of the state is its integration of force with authority: 'A state is a human community that (successfully) claims the monopoly of the legitimate use of physical force within a given territory' (Gerth and Mills, 1948, p.78). Any state must successfully uphold its claim to regulate the authorized use of coercion within its domain. When the state's monopoly of legitimate force is threatened, as in a civil war, its continued existence is at stake. While the conflict continues, there is no legitimate authority. Society becomes stateless.

It would be a mistake to regard the territorial state as a constant feature of human history. Rather, the tidy division of the contemporary world into states itself helps to define the modern era which is the focus of this book. Before modern states emerged in the sixteenth and seventeenth centuries, governance operated through a patchwork of weaker institutions, including loosely integrated empires, independent cities, monarchs, churches, powerful landowners and tribes (Spruyt, 1994). In medieval Europe, from which the modern state was eventually to emerge, feudalism provided an important model of social organization. Under feudalism, society was arranged as a hierarchy of personal relationships between lords, knights and serfs. Central authority was limited and notions of citizenship and legal rights applying to all did not exist. Politically, monarchs were weak figures, sharing secular power with feudal lords and spiritual authority with the Church. Local lords were responsible for raising an army as needed. Administration and the economy operated locally, with little national regulation. As Marx wrote of feudal lords, their estate *was* their state.

In its contemporary form, the state emerged in Europe from the embers of this feudal system. First in England and France, then in Prussia, Russia and elsewhere, monarchs succeeded in subordinating the landed aristocracy. Military forces came under the undisputed command of the crown. Warfare, taxation and statemaking went together, for in its origins the European state was a war machine (Porter, 1994). As kings fought to acquire territory and population from other monarchs, royal bureaucracies developed to extract the resources needed for war and also to administer (for example to pay and equip) the military. Finer (1997, p. 16) maintains that 'the raising and maintaining of military forces is the overwhelmingly most important reason for the emergence of the civil bureaucracy' which is such an important part of the modern state. With the growth of bureaucracy, local patterns of administration and customary justice became more uniform, easing the development of national markets and, later, the transition from agricultural to industrial economies.

As states themselves developed, so did the need for their theoretical justification. Here sovereignty proved to be the crucial innovation. In discussing the state, we must therefore unpack this notion. The French philosopher Jean Bodin (1529–96) played a major role here, defining sovereignty as the untrammelled and undivided power to make laws. Comparable developments occurred elsewhere. In England, for instance, the conservative jurist William Blackstone (1723–80) observed that 'there is and must be in every state a supreme, irresistible, absolute and uncontrolled authority, in which the

right of sovereignty resides'. In the work of scholars such as Blackstone and Bodin, we observe an attempt to justify the emerging power of the central state against the backdrop provided by decentralized feudalism.

By supporting the idea of a single point of ultimate authority for society, early advocates of sovereignty made possible later debates about the relationship between the sovereign and society. Reflecting eighteenth-century revolutions in France and the United States, the concept of sovereignty was reformulated for the democratic era, coming to express the doctrine that the state represented the collective will of the entire community. Louis XIV's 'L'état, c'est moi' gave way to the American constitution's 'We the people'. Thus, as democracy gained ground, so too did the belief that elected parliaments acting on behalf of the people, rather than unelected monarchs acting as God's representative on earth, are the true source of sovereignty. We arrive at the modern era in which the state becomes the core political unit by virtue of its integration of force and authority.

Definition
Sovereignty refers to the ultimate source of authority in society. The sovereign is both the highest and the final decision-maker within a community.
Internal sovereignty refers to law-making power within a territory.
External sovereignty describes international recognition of the sovereign's jurisdiction over its territory. The phrase 'the sovereign state' reflects both dimensions.

Sovereignty refers to the fount of authority in society and specifically to the body with law-making powers. Contemporary discussions of sovereignty distinguish between internal and external aspects. The law-making body within the state possesses *internal* sovereignty – the right to make and enforce laws applying within its territory. *External* sovereignty is the recognition in international law that a state has jurisdiction (that is, authority) over a territory. By implication, the state is answerable for that jurisdiction in international law. External sovereignty is important because it allows a state to claim the right both to regulate affairs within its boundaries and to participate as an accepted member of the international system. In this way, the development of the international system of states has strengthened the authority of states in the domestic sphere; indeed, internal and external sovereignty are two sides of a single coin.

Although the origins of the modern state lie in Europe, the form has now spread throughout the world. The end of empire multiplied the number of independent states. The United States achieved independence from Britain in the eighteenth century, Latin American countries broke free from Spanish and Portuguese control in the nineteenth century and Asian and African colonies achieved statehood in the twentieth century, mostly after the Second World War. Within Europe itself the number of states continued to increase in the twentieth century. This growth resulted from the fall of the Austro-Hungarian and Ottoman Empires after the First World War and then from the collapse of the Soviet empire in the early 1990s. By 2000, membership of the United Nations (an association of states, despite its name) stood at 189, of which 34 had joined since 1990 (Figure 1.1).

Yet many of these newer states remain weak or 'soft', lacking the hard core which characterizes the strong states of Western Europe. Where the powerful European states were forged in war and territorial struggle, most of the newer states were born as the haphazard offspring of decolonization. Especially in Africa, postcolonial states lack a precolonial national tradition on which to draw. The form of statehood has sufficed to secure external sovereignty and the international recognition flowing from it, but internally many new states lack strong governing institutions. Borders are arbitrary, ethnic commitments overwhelm national identities and the writ of the government may not extend much beyond the capital. Some African states are not 'internally pacified'; local leaders or warlords provide whatever governance exists (Sorensen, 1997). Despite the USA's status as the world's leading power, within its own borders the federal administration occupies a less privileged position than does the national government in, say, Britain, France or Germany. Two hundred years of independence have not sufficed to give the United States the profound sense of statehood embedded in European countries with their history of monarchical and even absolute rule.

At the start of the twenty-first century, even the most secure states continue to evolve. Territorially-based states must confront multinational corporations, financial flows and ecological problems which show no respect for national boundaries. In response to these realities of interdependence, most states are now involved in a network of international organizations and agreements, which compromises sovereignty. This process has gone furthest in the European Union, a loose federation of countries developed in the homeland of the modern state. Of course, within the EU, member states continue to operate; indeed, they are the Union's indispensable building blocks. But nearly all states, within and beyond the EU, increasingly work through global and especially regional relationships that dilute the traditional strength of sovereignty.

Even within countries, the state became less dominant in the final quarter of the twentieth century. Government gave ground to governance and identifying a sovereign power became more difficult. As the danger of world war receded, as governments reduced their involvement in economic production and as some public welfare services came to be viewed as unaffordable, so the role of the state began to evolve from direct involvement in society to coordinating the work of other groups. These trends were most obvious in countries making the transition from communism to democracy but they were also apparent within established democracies. Just like American presidents, most states today must rely on their power to persuade. The state

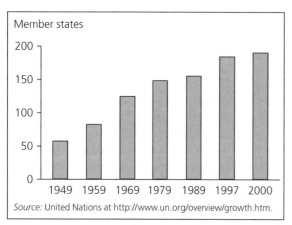

Member states

Source: United Nations at http://www.un.org/overview/growth.htm.

Figure 1.1 Number of states belonging to the United Nations, 1949–2000

remains a unique and important institution but the idea of sovereignty has become an inadequate guide to understanding how it goes about its tasks of leadership, coordination and persuasion.

The nation

Nationality is a difficult but crucial term. It is both distinguishable from and related to the state. While one can apply to become a citizen of a specific state, a nation is usually conceived not as an association one joins but as a group into which one is born. A nation defines a people, not a voluntary association. Indeed, the very word 'nation' comes from the Latin, *nasci* – 'to be born'. Yet seeking to reduce the idea of a nation to a shared ancestry, or indeed to any other single factor, is a fruitless exercise. A shared language, for example, is often taken as evidence of a common nationality but, if so, it is a misleading guide. Switzerland is indisputably a single nation even though French, German and Italian are spoken there. Similar claims that nationality can be reduced to a shared history or common ethnicity are equally misleading. Even territory is not a perfect marker: Irish people who seek their living overseas do not necessarily cease to belong to the Irish nation or people, even though they have left the territory of the Irish state. Since nations are 'imagined communities', a nation can really only be defined as any group which upholds a claim to be regarded as such (Schöpflin and Hosking, 1997).

Definition

A **nation** is a people centred on a defined territory that seeks political expression of its shared identity, usually through a claim to statehood. **Nationalism,** the key ideology of the twentieth century, is the doctrine that nations are entitled to self-determination. The significance of nationalism is that it offers one answer to a question beyond the reach of democracy: who are 'the people' who are to govern themselves?

Yet nationality and statehood *are* related, and in two ways. First, nations, like states, are creatures of the modern world; their emergence owed much to the need to provide a common identity for people newly subject to direct rule from a remote capital city (Hechter, 2000). In Europe, for example, national identities provided a broader but no less powerful substitute for the network of local obligations existing under feudalism. Second, national loyalties today often emerge not from the need to strengthen an existing state but rather from opposition to its rule by a territorial group within its domain. Even though national claims to statehood do not always succeed, the idea of nationhood typically implies a claim to some measure of self-government. Thus, to describe French-speaking Canadians as a separate nation indicates a demand for some form of statehood. In a similar way, to refer to the indigenous people of the Americas as Indian 'nations' (as opposed to 'ethnic groups') suggests a claim for a measure of self-government. So whether nations operate as adjuncts or opponents of states, the two ideas are bound together by their political character. As Hechter (2000) points out, nations emerge from the attempt of spatially concentrated and culturally distinct peoples to attain political self-determination.

Nationalism is simply the claim that nations do have a right to self-determination – to govern themselves. The British philosopher John Stuart Mill (1806–73) was an early advocate of this position. He argued that 'where the sentiment of nationality exists in any force there is a *prima facie* case for uniting all the members of the nationality under the same government, and a government to themselves apart.' The principle of national self-determination also provided a justification for redrawing the map of Europe with the final collapse of the Austro–Hungarian empire in 1918. The United Nations Covenant on Civil and Political Rights (1966) offers further support to national self-government:

> all peoples have the right to self-determination. By virtue of that right they freely determine their political status and pursue their economic, social and cultural rights.

As Tivey (1981) points out, nationalism has become the common ideology of the modern world, serving in particular as the gravedigger of empires.

Where a sense of nationhood has been successfully harnessed to the state, as in France or Poland, a single political community of enormous significance

– the nation-state – has emerged. But using nationality as an adhesive to integrate states carries dangers in a world where international migration has increased national diversity within countries (Pesic, 1994). For better or worse, multinational states are becoming the norm. Even Germany, once a country where nationality was inherited rather than acquired, has become more diverse through accepting immigrants and asylum-seekers. In such circumstances, the risk of civil conflict increases. A particular danger is that civil and political rights will only be granted to people with the 'correct' national qualifications. The result is a two-tier society, with endemic conflict between majorities and minorities. For instance, in its early post-communist history, Latvia only granted citizenship to people fluent in the native language, a filter that left the once-dominant Russians in a difficult and marginal position. Israel is a Jewish state in which the minority Arab population (about 15 per cent of the total) continues to suffer outsider status. The contemporary challenge is to find ways in which national groups can co-exist within the framework of a single state. So far, the American experience with 'hyphenated Americans' – immigrants who retain their ancestral loyalties while also embracing the American creed – has proved difficult to repeat elsewhere.

Power

Power is the currency of politics. Just as money permits the efficient flow of goods and services through an economy, so power enables collective decisions to be made and enforced. Without power, a government would be as useless as a car without an engine. Power is the tool that enables rulers to achieve collective goals. How then should the concept of power be understood?

One measure of power is simply the ability of a community to achieve its aspirations. In this sense, describing the United States as a powerful country simply means that it has the capacity to achieve many of its objectives. Notice that the emphasis here is on power *to* rather than power *over* – on the capacity to achieve goals, rather than to exercise control over other countries or people. This 'power to' approach is associated with the American sociol-

ogist Talcott Parsons (1967). He interpreted power as the capacity of a government to draw on the obligations of its citizens so as to achieve collective purposes such as law and order and protection of the environment. As with energy supplies, so too with political systems: the more power they deliver, the better. The more powerful the government, the more effective it will be at achieving the goals of the community. For Parsons, then, power is a collective resource. The German-born political theorist Hannah Arendt (1906–75) made a similar point when she defined power as 'not just the ability to act but the ability to act in concert' (1966, p. 44). A group whose members are willing to act together possesses more power – greater capacity to achieve its goals – than a group dominated by distrust and suspicion (Putnam, 2000).

Definition

Power is the capacity to produce intended effects. In politics, power can be viewed benignly, as the capacity of a community to shape its own destiny (power *to*). Power can also be seen as the ability of an individual or group to get its way against opposition. From this second perspective, we can say that A exerts power over B when A alters what B does (power *over*).

Parsons' view of power has exerted some influence but remains incomplete. Power, like politics, also has a hard edge. Politics is more than a technical task of implementing a vision shared by a whole society. It is also an arena of conflict over which goals to pursue. Politics is substantially a matter of whose vision triumphs, a point which must be reflected in any definition of power. From this widely adopted perspective, power consists of the ability to get one's way, to impose one's opinions, to overcome opposition. The underlying view of power here assumes conflict rather than consensus. In Dahl's famous definition (1957), power is a matter of getting people to do what they would not otherwise have done.

But what about actors who are so powerful that they prevent opposition from arising in the first place? Is this not the most subtle form of control of all? A president who controls the media so tightly that the public never learns about his theft of state assets will not face opposition on that score. A nuclear power station that leaks radioactivity will not face objections from the local community if residents do not even realize they have been contaminated. Powerful actors, including the mass media, can certainly influence the agenda of politics. Through their control of information, they can affect not the decisions which are reached but the topics which are raised. Measuring power by simply observing who has most sway over decisions ignores the difficult but still important question of who decides which issues come up for decision in the first place.

To deal with this point, Lukes (1974) seeks to broaden the notion of power. Lukes suggests that power is exercised over people whenever their interests are ignored, even if these people are unaware that their interests have been affected. For Lukes, A exerts power over B when A affects B in a manner contrary to B's interests. So, the manager of the leaky nuclear plant has exercised power over the local inhabitants because their interests have been damaged by the release. Whether the residents are aware of the pollution is immaterial. Similarly, the influence of advertisers over consumers does not depend on consumers' awareness that they are so affected. On a smaller scale, the outside observer can often notice parents exerting power over their children in ways that are not apparent to the children themselves. Whether or not we regard these cases as examples of power, we must accept that manipulating people's knowledge and attitudes is the most efficient way to control them.

Authority and legitimacy

Authority is a broader notion than power. Where power is the capacity to act, authority is the right to do so. Authority exists when subordinates acknowledge the right of superiors to give orders. So a general may exercise power over enemy soldiers but he does not have authority over them; this is restricted to his own forces. Yet authority is more than voluntary compliance. To acknowledge the authority of rulers does not mean you agree with their decisions; it means only that you accept their right to make decisions and your own duty to obey. Relationships of authority are still hierarchical. In politics, the exercise of authority is usually based on an underlying structure of power.

> **Definition**
> **Authority** is the right to rule. Strictly, authority is the right to act, rather than the power to do so. However, authority creates its own power so long as people accept that the authority-figure has the right to make decisions. A **legitimate** system of government is one based on authority: that is, those subject to its rule recognize its right to make collective decisions.

The German sociologist Max Weber (1957, first published 1922) provided a path-breaking analysis of the bases of authority. He distinguished three ways of validating political power (Box 1.1). The first type is by reference to the sanctity of *tradition*. This authority is based on 'piety for what actually, allegedly or presumably has always existed'. Traditional rulers do not need to justify their authority though they are certainly willing to enforce it. Rather, obedience is demanded as part of the natural order. For example, monarchs rule because they always have done so; to demand any further justification would itself challenge traditional legitimacy. Traditional authority is usually an extension of patriarchy – that is, the authority of the father or the eldest male. Weber offers several examples of paternal relationships:

> patriarchy means the authority of the father, the husband, the senior of the house, the elder sibling over the members of the household; the rule of the master and patron over the bondsmen, serfs, and freed men; of the lord over the domestic servants and household officials, of the prince over house- and court-officials. (Gerth and Mills, 1948, p. 296)

While such illustrations may seem old-fashioned, in reality traditional authority remains the model for many political relationships, especially in non-democratic countries. In the Middle East, 'government has been personal, and both civil and military bureaucracies have been little more than extensions of the leader' (Bill and Springborg, 2000, p. 152). The leader takes care of his followers and so on down the chain. The relationship is presented as familial but in practice is based on inequality: the strong look after the weak in exchange for their loyalty. When entire political systems operate on the principle of traditional, patriarchal authority, they are termed 'patrimonial'.

Charismatic authority is Weber's second form of authority. Here leaders are obeyed because they inspire their followers, who credit their heroes with exceptional and even supernatural qualities. Where traditional authority is based on the past, charismatic authority spurns history. The charismatic leader looks forward, convincing followers that the promised land is within reach. A key point here is that, contrary to popular use, charisma is not for Weber an intrinsic quality of a leader. Rather, charisma refers to how followers perceive such figures: as inspirational, heroic and unique. So there is little point in searching for personal qualities that distinguish charismatic from ordinary leaders; rather, the issue is the political conditions which bring forth a demand for charismatic leadership. Generally, such leaders emerge in times of crisis and upheaval. Jesus Christ, Mahatma Gandhi, Martin Luther King and Adolf Hitler are prominent examples. The role of Ayatollah Khomeini in transforming Iran after the fall of the Shah in 1979 is a more recent illustration. Charismatic authority is short-lived unless it can be transferred to a permanent office or institution. 'It is the fate of charisma,' wrote Weber (1957, p. 129), 'to recede with the development of permanent institutional structures.' This process is called the 'routinization' of charisma. Unusually for charismatic leaders, Ayatollah Khomeini succeeded in establishing a theocratic regime in Iran, dominated by the Islamic clergy, which continued after his death in 1989.

The third base for authority in Weber's scheme is called *legal-rational*. Here obedience is owed to principles rather than to people, resulting in government based on rules rather than allegiance to individuals. Unlike charismatic and traditional powers, legal-authority authority inheres in a role or a position, not in an individual. Indeed, a major virtue of legal-rational authority is that it limits the abuse of power. Because it derives from the office rather than the person, we can speak of officials 'going beyond their authority'. Setting out the extent of an office-holder's authority reveals its limits and so provides the opportunity for redress. In this way, legal-rational authority is a foundation of individual rights. Weber believed legal-rational authority was

BOX 1.1

Weber's classification of authority

Type	Basis	Illustration
Traditional	Custom and the established way of doing things	Monarchy
Charismatic	Intense commitment to the leader and his message	Many revolutionary leaders
Legal-rational	Rules and procedures – the office, not the person	Bureaucracy

becoming predominant in the modern world and certainly it is the dominant form in established democracies. Indeed Weber's homeland of Germany is the best example of a *Rechtsstaat*, an entire state based on law.

We must introduce one final concept here: legitimacy. Broadly, legitimacy is a similar idea to authority. The difference lies in the context of use: the term 'legitimacy' is normally used in discussing an entire system of government, whereas 'authority' often refers to a specific position. When the authority of a government is widely accepted, we describe it as 'legitimate'. Thus we speak of the legitimacy of a regime (system of government) but the authority of an official. Legitimacy, we should note, is much more than mere legality. Legality denotes whether a rule was made correctly – that is, following regular procedures. By contrast, legitimacy refers to whether people accept the validity either of a specific law or of the entire political system. Regulations can be legal without being legitimate. For example, the majority black population considered South Africa's apartheid 'laws' to be illegitimate, even though these regulations were made according to the country's then racist constitution. The same could be said of many laws passed by communist states: properly passed and even obeyed but not accepted as legitimate by the people. While legality is a topic for lawyers, political scientists are more interested in legitimacy: in how a regime gains and sometime loses public faith in its right to rule. Legitimacy is judged in the court of public opinion, not in a court of law. It is a crucial concept in understanding both the stability and the effectiveness of governments.

Classifying governments

Our final task in this chapter is to introduce our classification of governments. Classification is one of the oldest and most important tools of comparative politics. Consider, to begin with, the famous and still-relevant grouping of the 158 city-states of Ancient Greece developed by the Greek philosopher Aristotle. Greek city-states were small communities showing considerable variety in their forms of rule. These settlements provided an ideal laboratory for Aristotle, who sought to understand their political diversity not just for its own sake but also for a more practical purpose: to discover which type of government seemed to offer the best combination of stability and effectiveness. In undertaking his task, Aristotle produced the earliest known example of systematic analysis in comparative politics.

Aristotle based his scheme on two dimensions (Box 1.2). The first was the number of people involved in the task of governing: one, few or many. This dimension captures the breadth of participation in a political system. His second dimension, perhaps more subjective but certainly no less important, was whether rulers governed in the common interest ('the genuine form') or in their own interest ('the perverted form'). The significance of this second aspect is that a political system is likely to be more effective and stable when rulers govern in the long-term interests of the community, rather than in the narrow interests of a particular social group. Indeed, a core task of institutional design is to ensure that government is not captured by partial interests but remains sensitive to the shared interests of the whole community.

Cross-classifying the number of rulers (one, few or many) with the nature of their rule (genuine or perverted) yields the six types of government shown in Box 1.2. It is worth outlining each cell in this highly influential table. In the case of rule by a single person, Aristotle took kingship as the genuine form and regarded tyranny as is its perverted equivalent. For government by the few, Aristotle distinguished between aristocracy (which he defined as rule by the

---

BOX 1.2
Aristotle's classification of governments

	RULE BY		
	One	Few	Many
Genuine	Kingship	Aristocracy	Polity
FORM			
Perverted	Tyranny	Oligarchy	Democracy

Source: Aristotle (1962 edn) book 3, ch. 5.

---

virtuous) and its base form, oligarchy (rule by the rich). And within the category of rule by the many, Aristotle separated the ideal form 'polity' – broadly equivalent to rule by the moderate middle class, exercised through law – and the debased form of 'democracy', which he interpreted unsympathetically as government by the poor in their own self-interest.

Modern classifications continue to be informed by Aristotle's work. For this book, the distinction between democratic and non-democratic systems remains the starting-point. Not surprisingly, however, Aristotle's categories now need to be supplemented to produce a classification more sensitive to the modern world (Box 1.3). In particular, given the recent diffusion of democracy, it is helpful to distinguish between *established democracies* where the democratic way is entrenched (e.g. the USA) and *new democracies* where older, pre-democratic traditions still exert influence (e.g. many postcommunist countries).

We will develop this distinction in the next chapter, but the difference, in brief, is this. In an established or consolidated democracy, the voters' verdict is the accepted method of changing rulers. Elections themselves are free and fair, and the constitution, written or unwritten, provides an accepted framework for political competition. In essence, democracy is taken for granted. By contrast, in a new democracy, the new regime has not become the only game in town. Elections may deliver a government but its authority remains contested. Traditional power-holders – generals, bureaucrats, party bosses or even religious leaders – seek to

---

BOX 1.3

The classification of governments used in this book

Type of government	Central characteristics	Examples
Established ('consolidated') democracy	Representative and limited government operating through law provides an accepted framework for political competition.	Australia, Canada, France, Germany, India, Italy, Netherlands, New Zealand, Norway, Sweden, United Kingdom.
New democracy	Representative institutions are adopted but the influence of pre-democratic regimes and traditions is still felt. Law, tolerance of opposition, media freedom, individual rights and a market economy are not fully entrenched.	Many postcommunist countries in East Europe and many postmilitary states in Africa and Latin America.
	Note: Where democratic and authoritarian features coexist on a long-term, non-transitional basis, we use the term **semi-democracy**.	In Russia's semi-democracy, an elected president governs in an authoritarian style but with some consideration to the elected legislature.
Authoritarian rule	Rulers stand above the law and are free from effective popular accountability. The media are controlled or cowed. Political participation is usually limited and discouraged. However the rulers' power is often constrained by the need for tacit alliances with landowners, industrialists and the military.	The most common form of rule in history. Examples include military governments, ruling monarchies (still found in the Middle East) and postcommunist regimes in Central Asia where elections do little more than ratify the president's existing personal power base.
	Note: In the special case of **totalitarian states**, participation was compulsory but controlled as the government sought total control of society, justified by an ideology that sought to transform both society and human nature. These regimes placed heavy reliance on party members, the secret police and other informers as agents of social control.	Communist and fascist regimes subscribed to totalitarian thinking but the model was rarely fully implemented, except for a time in the Soviet Union. More recently, Iran after the Islamic revolution of 1979 showed totalitarian characteristics.

---

protect their old privileges. Even elected politicians may not operate within the rule of law. The regime still betrays a transitional, contested and uncertain character. This category of new democracy is particularly current because of the collapse of military and communist rule in the final decades of the twentieth century, yielding a considerable number of new democracies whose practical operation still reflects a non-democratic past.

It is crucial to recognize that no law dictates that all new democracies must grow into established democracies. 'Backsliding' is not unknown, as with the collapse of the Weimar Republic in Germany in the 1930s or the occasional military coups which still occur in Africa today. Certainly, 'new democracy' is a temporary designation; a country cannot be a new democracy for ever. We require an additional term to cover countries where democratic consolidation does seem to stall, yet without a reversal to authoritarian government. Here we can usefully speak of *semi-democracy:* a half-way house between democracy and authoritarianism in which both principles co-exist in a continuing and sometimes stable balance. A president may be democratically elected but govern in an authoritarian fashion, as in Russia. Or a dominant party may weight the electoral balance in its favour, for example by influencing the media or hemming opposition parties about with restrictions, as with Singapore's ruling People's Action Party. From the perspective of the opening decade of the twenty-first century, it seems likely that many new democracies, particularly in poorer countries remote from the democratic heartlands of West Europe and North America, will park themselves in the lot of semi-democracy. Over the course of this book, we will examine the varied and murky ways in which semi-democracies operate.

With authoritarian government, we return to firmer ground. We use the term *authoritarian rule* to cover any form of non-democratic government. The key feature of such regimes is that they deny the mass of the population any effective control over its rulers. Rulers stand above the law; dissent which goes beyond carefully monitored boundaries is punished, often aggressively. Institutions of representation, such as elections and legislatures, are weak, while the institutions of power, such as the bureaucracy and the military, are strong. As Aristotle recognized, non-democratic regimes take several forms, and we will examine their contemporary variety in Chapter 3. We should note, in particular, that 'soft authoritarian' regimes – where rulers possess some legitimacy and hard power remains sheathed – shade into semi-democracy. We must also mention here one particular form of hard authoritarian rule: the *totalitarian governments* of the twentieth century which sought total control over

their populations in an attempt to construct a new order of society, whether fascist or communist. Such governments demanded the active support of the people, not merely the passive acquiescence with which most authoritarian rulers rest content. Totalitarian regimes can certainly claim to belong in a category of their own, and some commentators present authoritarian and totalitarian systems as separate types (Linz, 2000). For simplicity, however, we will include all forms of non-democracy in the broad category of authoritarian rule, making further distinctions within the category as required.

Key reading

> **Next step:** *Crick (2000, first pub. 1962) remains a lively and argumentative introduction to politics.*

Other excellent guides to politics include Dahl (1991) and Shively (1995). Governance is covered by Rosenau (1989) and R. Rhodes (1996). On the state, Hall and Ikenberry (1989) is a good starting-point, Dunleavy and O'Leary (1987) is comprehensive, while van Creveld (1999) traces the state's rise and alleged fall. Nationalism is examined historically by Breuilly (1993) and Hechter (2000). Boulding (1989) and Lukes (1974) provide contrasting perspectives on power; see Lukes (1986) for an edited collection. Watt (1982) provides an introduction to authority. Good accounts of politics in the developing world, such as Clapham (1985) and Bayart (1993), are probably the best sources on authoritarian rule. Jackson and Rosberg (1982) is the key account of personal rule in black Africa. Most texts on political ideologies, such as Heywood (1998) and Ball and Dagger (1995), cover communism and fascism.

CHAPTER **2** | # Democracy

We live in an increasingly democratic world. Between 1975 and 1995 the number of democracies more than doubled; as a result, most people in the world now live under tolerably democratic rule. In its current upsurge, democracy has expanded beyond its core of West Europe and former colonies in North America, Australia and New Zealand. Democracy now embraces South Europe (for example Spain), East Europe (for example Poland), Latin America (for example Argentina), more of Asia (for example Taiwan) and parts of Africa (for example South Africa). Democratization in the late twentieth century proved to be a political earthquake, producing a massive, and possibly irreversible, shift in the world's political landscape. Fukuyama (1989), for one, argues that the great conflict of ideas which dominated European and then world politics for 200 years after the French revolution has ended. Democracy, and its ally the market economy, has triumphed.

As democracy has spread, so it has become more varied in its operation. Understanding the forms taken by democracy in today's world is therefore a central task. In this chapter, we examine the established democracies of Europe and its former colonies, with their emphasis on representative and limited government. We then discuss the newer democracies created from the ashes of communist and military rule, focusing on the problems of establishing new political systems in difficult domestic

conditions. Finally, we assess those awkward semi-democratic regimes – Russia is an example – that straddle the border between democratic and authoritarian government. But to begin we must explore the origins of democracy itself. And that task must take us back to the fifth century BC to the world's most influential example of self-government: ancient Athens.

Direct democracy

Democracy is a form of government offering a workable solution to the fundamental political problem of reaching collective decisions by peaceful means. But democracy is also an ideal and an aspiration. So we cannot understand democracy simply by looking at examples for judged against the democratic ideal even the most secure 'democracies' are found wanting. Indeed, the tension between high ideals and prosaic reality has itself become part of the democratic condition (Dahl, 1989, p. 30). So what, then, is the core principle of democracy? The basic idea is self-rule: the word itself comes from the Greek *demokratia*, meaning rule (*kratos*) by the people (*demos*). Thus democracy – in its literal and richest sense – refers not to the election of the rulers by the ruled but to the denial of any separation between the two. The 'model' democracy is a direct democracy, a form of self-government in which all adult citizens participate in shaping collective decisions, in a context of equality and open deliberation. In a direct democracy, state and society become one.

The birthplace of democracy is ancient Athens. Between 461 and 322 BC, Athens was the leading *polis* (city-state) of ancient Greece. *Poleis* were small independent communities; Athens, one of the larger examples, had about 40 000 citizens. Especially in the earlier and more radical decades of this period, the Athenian *polis* operated on the democratic principle summarized by Aristotle as 'each to rule and be ruled in turn' (Box 2.1). This principle applied across all the institutions of government within the city-state. All citizens could attend meetings of the assembly, serve on the governing council and sit on citizens' juries. Because ancient Athens continues to provide the archetypal example of direct democracy, we will look at its operation in more detail (Figure 2.1).

History has judged there to be no more potent symbol of direct democracy than the *Ekklesia* (People's Assembly) at Athens. Any citizen aged at least 20 could attend assembly sessions and there address his peers; meetings were of citizens, not their representatives. The assembly met around 40 times a year to settle issues put before it – including the recurring issues of war and peace which were central to the *polis*'s prospects and prosperity. In Aristotle's phrase, the assembly was 'supreme over all causes'; it was the sovereign body, unconstrained by a formal constitution or even, in the early decades, by a body of written law.

But the assembly did not exhaust the avenues of participation in the Athenian democracy. Administrative functions were the responsibility not of professional public servants but of an executive council consisting of 500 citizens aged over 30,

> **BOX 2.1**
> ## Aristotle's characterization of democracy
>
> 1. All to rule over each and each in his turn over all.
> 2. Appointment to all offices, except those requiring experience and skill, by lot.
> 3. No property qualification for office-holding, or only a very low one.
> 4. Tenure of office should be brief and no man should hold the same office twice (except military positions).
> 5. Juries selected from all citizens should judge all major causes.
> 6. The assembly should be supreme over all causes.
> 7. Those attending the assembly and serving as jurors and magistrates should be paid for their services.
>
> *Source:* Aristotle, *The Politics*, Book VI.

chosen by lot to serve for a one-year period. Through this device of rotation, the council exemplified the principle of government by, and not just for, the citizens. Hansen (1991, p. 249) suggests about one in three citizens could expect to serve on the council at some stage in their life, an astonishing feat of self-government entirely without counterpart in modern democracies.

A highly political legal system provided the final leg of Athens's complex democracy. Juries of several

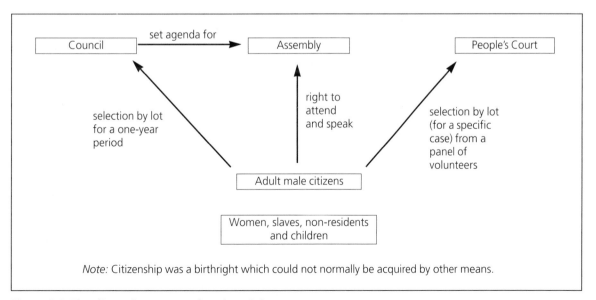

Figure 2.1 The direct democracy of ancient Athens

hundred people, again selected randomly from a panel of volunteers, considered lawsuits which citizens could – and frequently did – bring against those considered to have acted against the true interests of the *polis*. The courts functioned as an arena of accountability through which top figures (including generals) were brought to book.

Thus the scope of the Athenian democracy was extraordinarily wide, providing an all-encompassing political framework within which citizens were expected not just to live but also to develop their true qualities. For the Athenians, politics was intrinsically an amateur activity, to be undertaken by all citizens to develop both themselves and the broader *polis*. As Dahl (1989, p. 18) writes,

> In the Greek vision of democracy, politics is a natural social activity not sharply separated from the rest of life . . . Rather political life is only an extension of, and harmonious with, oneself.

Of course, we should not blind ourselves to the serious flaws in Athens's 'little democracy'. First, citizenship was restricted to a small élite: it was a birthright of males whose parents were both citizens themselves. The vast majority of adults – including women, slaves and foreign residents – did not qualify. Women played no significant public role and critics allege that slavery was the platform which freed citizens to devote time to public affairs (Finley, 1985). Second, participation was not in practice as extensive as the Athenians liked to claim. Most citizens were absent from most assembly meetings even after payment for attendance was introduced. Third, Athenian democracy was hardly an exercise in lean government. A modern management consultant would no doubt conclude that the system was elaborate, time-consuming and expensive: an over-complex method of governing a small, rural society. Its applicability to a modern world in which people must spend their working hours serving the market, rather than the state, is debatable. Finally, the principle of self-government did not always lead to decisive and coherent policy. Indeed, the lack of a permanent bureaucracy eventually contributed to a period of ineffective government, leading to the fall of the Athenian republic after defeat in war. Finer (1997, p. 368) suggests that Athenian democracy was a dead-end in that its functioning depended on

a small city state which not only precluded expansion but was inherently vulnerable to predators: 'the *polis* was doomed politically if it expanded and doomed to conquest if it did not. It had to succumb and it did.'

Yet for over 100 years, Athenian democracy survived and prospered. It provided a settled formula for rule and enabled Athens to build a leading position in the complex politics of the Greek world. Athens proves that direct democracy is, in some conditions, an achievable goal. Above all, Athens was crucial in establishing the democratic principle. It continues to provide a standard against which modern democracies are, right or wrong, sometimes still judged. As Dahl (1989, p. 30) writes, 'thus a conflict was created between representative democracy and earlier conceptions of democratic government that were never wholly lost.' Indeed, authors who value the rich collective life of the *polis* even interpret Athens as a beacon for the future rather than a residue from the past (Arendt, 1958). Certainly, Finer was correct in acknowledging the Athenian contribution to Western politics:

> The Greeks invented two of the most potent political features of our present age: they invented the very idea of citizen – as opposed to subject – and they invented democracy.

Representative and liberal democracy

The contrasts between the classical democracy of ancient Athens and the modern democracies of today's world are profound. Most obviously, citizenship today is extended to the vast majority of the adult population; no longer does citizenship imply an elite status. But two other contrasts are equally important. First, today's democracies are representative rather than direct. The principle is no longer self-government but elected government. Where the Greeks viewed elections as an instrument of aristocracy – as a means of selecting qualified people for technical tasks but an unfortunate departure from self-government – we regard elections as a central feature of our own democracies. Second, modern democracy is based on a liberal philosophy in which the role of the state is restricted by the constitution, producing a distinction between public and private that would have been unacceptable in classical Athens where citizens who lived an entirely private life were dismissed as *idiotes*. Today's democracies are liberal democracies and it is the constitution as much as the legislature that is 'supreme over all causes'. In this section, we examine how these modern concepts of representation and liberalism were grafted on to the original democratic idea.

Consider, then, how the modern era substituted representation for rotation as the chief instrument of democracy. Institutions of representation were not of course a creation of the modern era. In Europe, medieval monarchs had summoned the various estates of the realm – notably lords and commoners – to help with their twin tasks of raising revenues and prosecuting wars. Such assemblies certainly reduced royal autonomy, eventually producing in England an influential model of a mixed or balanced constitution, but they did not constitute a democracy. The members of such assemblies were summoned or self-appointed rather than elected. But the American Declaration of Independence of 1776 ('all men are created equal') and the French Declaration of the Rights of Man and the Citizen of 1789 ('men are born and remain free and equal in their rights') ushered in the modern era. In the nineteenth century, stimulated not just by the American and French revolutions but also by the diffusion of power brought about by mass literacy and industrialization, the notion of turning ancient institutions into representative bodies elected from a wide franchise rapidly gained ground. In particular, representation emerged as the perfect solution to the problem of reinventing democracy for large states. As some Americans put it, representation 'substituted the few in the room of the many'. One of the first authors to graft representation on to democracy was the British-born pamphleteer and international revolutionary Tom Paine. In the *Rights of Man* (first published 1791/2), Paine wrote:

> The original simple democracy . . . is incapable of extension, not from its principle, but from the inconvenience of its form. Simple democracy was society governing itself without the aid of secondary means. By ingrafting representation upon democracy, we arrive at a system of government capable of embracing and confederating all the

various interests and every extent of territory and population.

Scalability has certainly proved to be a key strength of representative democracy. Where Athenians thought that the upper limit for a republic was the number of people who could gather to hear a speaker, representative government allows even massive populations (such as 970 million Indians or 276 million Americans) to exercise some popular control over their rulers. And there is no upper limit. In theory, the entire world could become one giant representative system. Adapting Tom Paine's phrase, representative government has proved to be a highly convenient form.

Representation also resolves another democratic dilemma: how to combine popular preferences with expert judgment. In a direct democracy, open deliberation provides the solution: people learn about the issues through discussion that is central to the decision-making task (Bohman and Rehg, 1997). Through debate and listening to experts, the citizens themselves become proficient in the topics placed before them. But in a representative government, this intensive method does not work. The population is too large, its interest in politics is too intermittent and the issues are too numerous. Instead, representative government limits the popular voice to determining *who* governs and allows these (presumably expert) politicians to decide *what* policies should be followed. It was for this reason that James Madison, an architect of the American constitution, believed a representative system was superior to, and not just more practical than, direct democracy. Representation, he thought, served to 'refine and enlarge the public views, by passing them through the medium of a chosen body of citizens, whose wisdom may best discern the true interest of their country'.

This new theory of representative democracy, with its restricted role for the voters, rapidly gained ground as the first wave of democracies emerged in the nineteenth century. Eventually, the theory received its most systematic exposition from Joseph Schumpeter (1883–1965), an Austrian-born economist who became an academic in the United States. Schumpeter conceived of democracy as nothing more than party competition. Like many democrats in the modern era, he accepted that élite rule was both inevitable and desirable. He wanted to limit the contribution of ordinary voters because of his jaded view of their political capacity: 'the typical citizen drops down to a lower level of mental performance as soon as he enters the political field. He argues and analyzes in a way that he would recognize as infantile within the sphere of his real interests. He becomes a primitive again' (1943, p. 269). Reflecting this jaundiced opinion, Schumpeter argued that elections should not be construed as a device through which voters elect representatives to carry out their will; rather, the role of elections is simply to produce a government. From this perspective, the elector becomes a political accessory, restricted to selecting from broad packages of policies and leaders prepared by rival parties. Representative democracy is merely a way of deciding who shall decide:

> The deciding of issues by the electorate [is made] secondary to the election of the men who are to do the deciding. To put it differently, we now take the view that the role of the people is to produce a government . . . And we define the democratic method as that institutional arrangement for arriving at political decisions in which individuals acquire the power to decide by means of a competitive struggle for the people's vote. (Schumpeter, 1943, p. 270)

We turn now to the second distinctive feature of modern democracy: its liberal character. If representation is a device for restricting popular influence over the rulers, liberal democracy is a compromise which seeks to combine the authority of democratic governments with limits on the scope of their action. The core feature of liberal democracy is limited government. The goal is to secure individual freedom – including freedom from unwarranted demands by government itself. Limited government is protective, seeking to defend both the population from its rulers and minorities from a tyrannical majority (Held, 1996). This concern reflects the historical task of containing royal power and aristocratic privileges, and in particular entrenching religious freedom, but it also reflects successful attempts by the wealthy to protect their property into the democratic era. The outcome qualifies the operation of the democratic principle itself. In place of the all-

encompassing scope of the Athenian *polis*, modern liberal democracies are governments of laws rather than men. Even elected rulers are subject to constitutions that almost always include a statement of individual rights. In theory and sometimes in practice, citizens can use domestic and international courts to uphold these rights when they are threatened even by an elected government. So in a sense liberalism has disarmed democracy.

Both the representative and liberal elements of modern democracy dilute the original principle of self-rule. We find in contemporary democracies a form of rule in which decision-making is the responsibility of governments rather than the governed and in which the public sphere is limited by protecting the rights of citizens in general and of property-owners in particular. The dilution is considerable but the outcome is a flexible and scalable political system which is coming to dominate the world.

Waves of democratization

How then were these priniciples of representative and liberal democracy implemented in the transition to democracy? When and how did modern established democracies emerge? Here we explore the emergence of democratic institutions rather than ideas, a task for which Huntington's metaphor of waves of democratization is useful (Box 2.2):

> A wave of democratization is a group of transitions from nondemocratic to democratic regimes that occur within a specified period of time and that significantly outnumber transitions in the opposite direction during that period . . . Three waves of democratization have occurred in the modern world. (Huntington, 1991, p.15)

The first modern democracies emerged in the 'first long wave of democratization' between 1828 and 1926. During this *first wave* nearly 30 countries established at least minimally democratic national institutions, including Argentina, Austria, Australia, Britain, Canada, France, Germany, the Netherlands, New Zealand, the Scandinavian countries and the United States. Many of these fledgling democracies were later overthrown by fascist, communist or military dictatorships during Huntington's 'first reverse wave' from 1922 to 1942. However, democracy did consolidate in the earliest ninineteenth-century democratizations, including the United States and the United Kingdom. We will examine these two early transitions in more detail, not least because the USA remains the leading example of liberal democracy while Britain usefully illustrates representative democracy.

The transition to democracy in the United States was rapid but it was a transition nonetheless. The American republic, it is important to note, was not conceived as a democracy. Rather, the founders had thought of political leadership in classical terms, as the duty of a disinterested, leisured gentry. They deliberately employed indirect election – in which voters elect people who in turn select individuals to higher office – as a device to contain popular influence. The phrase 'we the people' which opens the American constitution was certainly not intended to refer to the entire adult population; indeed, the suffrage was originally restricted to white male property-owners. But the idea of actual rather than virtual representation – in other words, the proposition that citizens could only be represented fairly by those of their own sort – quickly gained ground in the new republic. The result was a swift extension of the suffrage to nearly all white males (Wood, 1993, p. 99). As early as 1830, just 40 years after ratification of the constitution, property qualifications had been withdrawn and nearly all states selected members of the Electoral College (which chooses the president) via direct popular ballot. Yet even though democratic values soon predominated, their implementation proved to be a long-term project. Senators continued to be chosen by state legislatures until 1913, women were not offered the vote on the same terms as men until 1919 and the black franchise was not fully achieved until the Voting Rights Act of 1965.

Even today, we must regard the USA as the clearest example of a *liberal* democracy in which limited government is entrenched by design. The founding fathers wanted, above all, to prevent tyranny, including tyranny by the majority. James Madison wrote that 'the accumulation of all powers Executive, Legislative and Judicial in the same hands . . . may justly be pronounced the very definition of tyranny'. To prevent any government – and especially elected

---

BOX 2.2

Huntington's three waves of democratization

Wave	Period	Examples
First	1828–1926	Britain, France, USA
Second	1943–1962	India, Israel, Japan, West Germany
Third	1974–1991	Southern and Eastern Europe, Latin America, parts of Africa

Note: The first wave was partly reversed between 1922 and 1942 (for example, in Austria, Germany and Italy) and the second wave similarly between 1958 and 1975 (for example, in much of Latin America and postcolonial Africa)

Source: Huntington (1991).

---

ones – from acquiring too much power, the constitution set up an elaborate system of checks and balances between the institutions of government (Figure 2.2). Because power is so fragmented, the danger of any particular faction manipulating public authority for private ends is much reduced. Power checks power to the point where it is often difficult for the government to achieve even needed reforms. The constitution contained the seeds of democracy but its philosophy was to place government under law before government by all the people. American government was liberal before it was democratic and many would argue that liberalism remains its guiding principle.

In Britain, too, we can identify a period of liberalization before the onset of democratic reform though the final outcome was a more representative, and less liberal, democracy. By the eighteenth century, the power of the monarch was checked by the authority of parliament even though the rights of the individual citizen were never stated as clearly in Britain as in the USA. The widening of the suffrage also occurred more gradually. Each step eased the fears of the propertied classes about the dangers of democracy, thereby facilitating further reform. A series of reform acts in the nineteenth century gradually extended the suffrage; after the Third Reform Act of 1884, working-class men formed a majority of the electorate (Table 2.1).

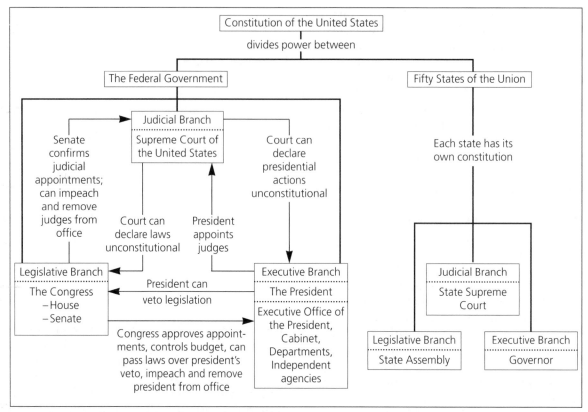

Figure 2.2 Liberal democracy: the US constitutional system

However, as in the United States, female suffrage was not achieved until after the First World War. In tandem with the extension of the suffrage, other aspects of the electoral system were gradually reformed: the secret ballot was introduced in 1870, single-member districts of roughly equal size became the norm and limits were placed on candidates' expenses. As the House of Commons acquired the aura of democratic legitimacy, so not just the monarchy but also the non-elected House of Lords retreated into the political background. Like the United States, the implementation of democratic procedures in Britain continued well into the twentieth century but the battle of principle was fought and won in the nineteenth.

If the USA emphasizes limited government, Britain gives priority to the representative element of modern democracy. Where American democracy diffuses power across institutions, British democracy focuses it on a single governing party. Representation operates through parties that retain a tight hold on their own members of parliament. The governing party wields extensive powers until the voters offer their verdict at the next election. Except for the government's sense of self-restraint, the institutions that limit executive power in the United States – such as a codified constitution, the separation of powers and federalism – are absent. Instead the electoral rules normally ensure a secure majority of seats to the winning party. Far more than the United States, Britain exemplifies Schumpeter's model of democracy as the outcome of party competition. 'We are the masters now', trumpeted a Labour MP after his party's triumph in the British election of 1945; similar thoughts must have occurred to many Labour MPs elected after their party's equally emphatic victory in 1997. From a comparative perspective, a governing party in Britain is still given an exceptionally free hand.

Huntington's *second wave* of democratization began in the Second World War and continued until the 1960s. Like the first wave, some of the new democracies created at this time did not consolidate: for example, elected governments in several Latin American were quickly overthrown by the military. But established democracies did emerge after 1945 from the ashes of defeated dictatorships, not just in West Germany but also in Austria, Japan and Italy. These postwar democracies were introduced by the victorious allies, usually with the support of domestic partners, as the Cold War division between Western and communist blocs became entrenched. Yet despite their partly imposed character, these second-wave democracies did establish firm domestic roots, helped by an economic recovery which was itself nourished by American aid. Postwar democracy also consolidated successfully in the new state of Israel and in the former British dominion of India. Yet second-wave democracies did differ somewhat in character from those of the first-wave; liberal traditions were somewhat weaker and parties proved to be even stronger. In several of these new democracies, a single party such as Congress in

India, the Christian Democrats in Italy, the LDP in Japan and Labour in Israel, dominated national politics for a generation. In the Federal Republic of Germany, similarly, parties were viewed as the carriers of democracy in a political system whose governing institutions had been discredited by their toleration of Nazi rule.

The *third wave*, finally, began in 1974. To date, its main – and highly diverse – elements are: (1) the end of right-wing dictatorships in South Europe (Greece, Portugal and Spain) in the 1970s, (2) the retreat of the generals in much of Latin America in the 1980s and (3) the collapse of communism in the Soviet Union and East Europe at the end of the 1980s. This third wave has transformed the global political landscape: the predominance of democratic forms in today's world itself places added pressure on those non-democratic regimes that survive. Yet we must be careful here to distinguish democratic forms from democratic substance. Within the third wave, it is only the South European group that provides consistently secure cases of democratic consolidation, aided by membership of the European Union and economic development. Elsewhere, in East Europe and Latin America, many third-wave democracies have not yet fully consolidated, if indeed they are ever to do so at all. The category of new democracy – and also of semi-democracy – remains central to understanding these fledgling regimes.

New democracies

Just as the earliest modern democracies represented a severe dilution of the Athenian vision of self-rule, so too are many new democracies developing a further compromise with their own authoritarian histories. Certainly, the distinctions between most new democracies and the early democracies such as the United States and the United Kingdom remain important.

Many new democracies do seem to have consolidated by one crucial test: a peaceful transfer of power through elections. For example, the South Korean presidential election of 1997 witnessed the first peaceful transfer of power to the centre-left in the country's history. Similarly, Wiseman (1995, p. 4) notes that 'in thirteen African states changes of government through the ballot box had actually taken

Table 2.1 The British electorate as a percentage of the adult population, 1831–1931

Year	Electorate (per cent of population age 20+)
1831	4.4
1832	First Reform Act
1832	7.1
1864	9.0
1867	Second Reform Act
1868	16.4
1883	18.0
1884	Third Reform Act
1886	28.5
1914	30.0
1918	Vote extended to women over 30
1921	74.0
1928	Equal Franchise Act
1931	97.0

Note: In 1969, the voting age was reduced from 21 to 18.

Source: Adapted from Dahl (1998), fig. 2.

place by 1995'. Peaceful transfers have also become almost routine in East Europe and parts of Latin America. Yet even when elections have succeeded in the delicate task of replacing a governing elite, most new democracies remain distinctive; the question is not whether they will consolidate but what exactly they are consolidating into. The difficulties facing new democracies can be grouped into two related clusters: the political problems associated with an illiberal inheritance and the economic problems caused by the combination of limited development and extreme inequality.

Consider first the political problems facing new democracies. Reflecting an authoritarian legacy, liberal ideas and institutions often remain weak. As Luckham and White (1996b, p. 7) point out, the development of democracy requires more than just competitive elections:

> It also requires the enforcement of legal restraint on state power, protection of civil rights, the establishment of relatively uncorrupt and effective bureaucracies, and the imposition of democratic control over potentially authoritarian forces such as the military and the security services.

Such contrasts between new and established democracies may decay with the passage of time but they are unlikely to disappear for the foreseeable future.

Definition

A democracy has consolidated when it provides an accepted framework for political competition. As President Havel noted in Czechoslovakia after communism's collapse, **democratic consolidation** requires more than creating appropriate institutions: 'we have done away with totalitarianism but we have yet to win democracy.' The standard definition comes from Przeworski (1991, p. 26):

> Democracy is consolidated when under given political and economic conditions a particular system of institutions becomes the only game in town and when no-one can imagine acting outside the democratic institutions.

To the extent that democratic consolidation requires substituting a government of laws for one of men, the task is still incomplete. Ruling communist parties and military councils brooked no interference from the judiciary and played little heed to constitutions, including statements of human rights. State officials operated with little concern for the citizen. The agencies of repression – the military, the intelligence services and the police – were as strong as the mechanisms of representation were weak. In general, building a *liberal* democracy on these weak foundations is a greater challenge than was the case for the United States, constructed on a constitution that at least asserted equality.

In the post military democracies of Latin America, for instance, the generals still possess considerable prestige deriving from their historical role as providers of order to unstable societies. This status is often still reflected in a guaranteed budget, seats in the legislature and virtual exemption from civil law. Even excluding the special case of the military, civil justice in much of Latin America remains underdeveloped. Lower courts are often inefficient and corrupt and many cases do not arrive there because the police are themselves corrupt or because ordinary people regard the courtroom as the prerogative of the wealthy. The concept of individual rights simply has no meaning in urban slums. In post-communist states, too, any national traditions of rule by law were dulled during the totalitarian experience. Ruling communist parties were above the law and public officials continue to regard their position as an opportunity to obtain private advantage. The combination of an inadequate number of laws, plus systematic evasion and inadequate enforcement of those that do exist, is a difficult base from which to consolidate democracy. In Africa, too, the limited penetration of the state through its territory inevitably limits the impact of a transition from authoritarian to democratic rule at national level. So in many new democracies, the tradition of power revolving around individuals – whether communist party bosses, the 'big men' of African politics or the arrogant generals and landowners of Latin America – tends to subvert attempts to consolidate the democratic framework.

The economic difficulties of new democracies are even more obvious: a combination of poverty and inequality exacerbated by severe decline in the early years of the new order. Even in many of the larger and more developed new democracies, living standards remain well below Western levels. In the USA, gross national product per head had reached

Country profile **MEXICO**

Population: 96m.

Gross domestic product per head: $7700.

Form of government: a federal and presidential republic.

Legislature: the 500 members of the Chamber of Deputies, the lower house, are elected for a five-year term. The 128 members of the Senate are elected for a three-year period, with four Senators per state.

Executive: the president, directly elected for a non-renewable six-year term, heads both the state and the government, choosing the members of the Cabinet.

Judiciary: headed by the Supreme Court of Justice, the judicial system mixes American constitutional principles with the civil law tradition. In practice, both judicial independence and police enforcement of law have been weak.

Party system: dominated by the Institutional Revolutionary Party (PRI) until the 1990s. Other major parties are the conservative National Action Party (PAN), which formed part of Fox's Alliance for Change in the 2000 elections, and the left-wing Revolutionary Democratic Party (PRD).

Electoral system: 300 members of the Chamber represent single-member districts, the other 200 are elected by the list system of proportional representation. The Senate also operates a mixed electoral system.

'Yes, it can be done,' shouted the crowds in Mexico City as they celebrated the downfall of the PRI after the presidential election of 2000. After 70 years in power, the PRI not only lost a presidential election for the first time but also no longer controlled either house of the national legislature. The world's oldest ruling party had suffered an historic reverse, defeated by a centre-right coalition led by Vicente Fox. This peaceful transfer of power decisively confirmed Mexico's status as a new democracy. For students of comparative politics, Mexico offers a remarkably successful example of democratization.

The PRI had been founded in 1929 in the decade following the radical Mexican revolution. Gradually, however, socialist principles were diluted as the PRI established a classic semi-democracy based on patronage networks. The PRI distributed favours while repressing opposition and manipulating election results. In the 1950s and 1960s, the PRI seemed to have discovered what one observer described as 'the perfect dictatorship'. However, three problems recurred:

- Continuing poverty for those excluded from the PRI network, reflected in periodic revolts.
- Increasing opposition from the expanding urban middle class created by economic growth.
- Occasional economic crises when the PRI placed its political objectives before sound economic policy.

With the political effectiveness of the PRI machine decaying, President Salinas (1988–94) initiated economic reforms, including privatizing major firms and opening the economy to international competition, not least through NAFTA. In contrast to the Soviet Union, where Gorbachev had initiated political reform before restructuring the economy, liberalization in Mexico preceded political change. As the PRI lost direct control of economic resources, so its powers of patronage declined and voters became free to support opposition parties, especially in the cities. Independent trade unions began to form outside the once-enveloping embrace of the PRI system. But the PRI also introduced political changes that served to enliven the previously moribund opposition. By the 1990s, the PRI no longer felt able to manipulate election results. In 1997, it lost its majority in the Chamber of Deputies after relatively fair elections; and the decisive election in 2000 was overseen by an independent election commission. As with several ruling parties, the PRI's fall was partly self-induced: its leaders recognized that the tools needed to guarantee their party's continued grip on power were hindering the country's further development.

Mexico's gradual moves to democracy seem to have avoided what Baer (1993, p. 64) describes as 'the dilemma of all reforms from above, particularly in ageing regimes: how to avoid unleashing a revolution from below'. However, it remains to be seen how far, and at what speed, democracy will consolidate in Mexico. The PRI remains a significant force, controlling half of the country's 32 states. Mexico's continuing problems – peasant revolts and urban squalor, drugs and crime, corrupt judges and incompetent police – mean that it remains premature to place the country in the same political category as its NAFTA partners, the USA and Canada.

Further reading: Camp (1999), Cornelius (2000), Lawson (1997).

$31 500 by 2000; in the new democracy of neighbouring Mexico, the equivalent figure was just $7700. Starker contrasts apply in Europe: German product per head is more than six times the figure for its postcommunist neighbours, the Czech Republic and Hungary. Relative poverty often goes hand in hand with greater inequality; many new democracies retain a large agricultural sector, where sharp contrasts continue between a rich, powerful élite and a poorly educated, and often powerless, population. Conflicts between landowners and dependent peasants are endemic in much of Latin America, for instance. As Vanhanen (1997) notes, such conditions favour neither the diffusion of power resources, nor the development of mutual toleration and compromise, which foster democratic consolidation. Further, the ex-communist states in East Europe, in particular, suffered enormous economic dislocation in the transition from the old order. As planned economies began to be dismantled in tandem with democratization, unemployment soared. Throughout the postcommunist world, the 1990s was a decade of deep economic decline in which the real suffering of the many was exacerbated by the ostentatious affluence of a few. Only at the start of the twenty-first century did economic growth return to most postcommunist democracies.

Lower levels of affluence in new democracies are important partly because a long research tradition claims that economic well-being is the key to democratic consolidation. In *Political Man* (1983, first pub. 1960), Lipset famously concluded that 'the more well-to-do a nation, the greater the chances that it will sustain democracy'. He showed that stable democracies scored highest on such measures as income per person, literacy and the proportion of the population living in cities. Following Aristotle, Lipset believed that a large middle class opposed to extremism was conducive to democracy. More recent research confirms the correlation between affluence and stable democracy, even though there are exceptions such as poor but democratic India. Summarizing the research stimulated by Lipset's work, Marks and Diamond (1992, p. 110) describe the connection between affluence and democracy as 'one of the most powerful and stable relationships in the study of comparative national development'.

Crucially, the economic and political weaknesses of new democracies are linked. The absence of a liberal political framework itself inhibits economic advance. Weak legal systems restrict economic development because corporations lack confidence that commercial disputes can be resolved fairly and promptly through the courts. Close personal connections develop between politicians in need of money and well-placed business executives who value political influence. These semi-corrupt networks preclude the development of a clear framework for market regulation. In practice, dominant firms that survive the transition from the previous regime can often see off competitive threats, preventing the development of a level playing field in which the most efficient companies can prosper. Scared off by corrupt and slow-moving bureaucrats, foreign investors are inclined to go elsewhere, especially as population and market size are relatively small in new democracies. As a result, both economic and democratic development slow, held back by the incomplete penetration of liberal ideas and institutions.

We should mention one final factor affecting the consolidation of third-wave democracies: the timing of their transition. To be born into a world which is already democratic increases the pressures on new democracies to consolidate quickly but provides a more supportive environment which will probably assist the final outcome. The first democracies of modern times were not so much adopting a new political order as inventing it. Innovation was a leisurely, even evolutionary, process of adapting old ideas to large states. By contrast, third-wave democracies were delivered into a world where democratic ideas were already becoming predominant; as a result, they are expected to mimic established examples without the economic resources and gradual development which helped the countries of the first wave. Both domestic and international audiences expect the process of developing democracy to be collapsed into a decade or two. In the first wave, democracy could be an outcome but in the third wave it has to be an intention. As Hollifield and Jillson (2000, p.11) suggest,

The latest transitions to democracy have occurred with dizzying speed, giving the societies involved little time to prepare for the leap to representative government. Whereas democracies in West Europe, the United States and the former British dominions had a gestation period of one or two centuries, in the third wave democratization has come virtually overnight. This has led to a great deal of improvisation and many setbacks.

At the same time, democracies of the third wave have one clear advantage over their predecessors: a favourable global and regional context. Leading actors such as the United States and the European Union, and sympathetic institutions such as the World Bank, began to promote democracy once the Cold War conflict ended. Often, a favourable regional context also eased transition. Greece, Portugal and Spain – and more recently Poland, Hungary and the Czech Republic – undoubtedly benefited from their position close to the heartland of European democracy. In a similar way, Mexico's transition from semi-democracy owes something to its trading links with the USA, consolidated through NAFTA. Indeed Diamond (1997, p. 39) suggests that 'the greatest regional force for democratic consolidation in the Americas may well be the move towards regional free trade'. The general prognosis for new democracies is far from bleak though the political and economic contrasts between new and old democracies are likely to remain fundamental.

Semi-democracy

The final concept to explore in this chapter is that of semi-democracy. This term lacks the theoretical purity of either democratic or authoritarian rule; its task is more descriptive. Semi-democracy denotes forms of government which, in practice, blend both democratic and authoritarian elements. In a semi-democracy, democratic legitimacy is not wholly lacking; rather, it is acquired and exploited in dubious ways and often remains contested. The hybrid is not new but it is becoming more prevalent. Indeed, in a world dominated by democratic ideology, semi-democracy is a more likely outcome than a return to authoritarianism for new democracies that do not consolidate fully. Semi-democracies do not always lack legitimacy; the dominant leaders can use ethnic diversity, fear of political instability or the demand for economic development as reasons for departing from the liberal aspects of established democracies.

The crucial point is that we should not think of democracy and authoritarianism just as whole systems of government. Rather, each principle can provide pockets of power that can coexist, sometimes indefinitely, within the one political system; once set, semi-democracy is a strong amalgam. Crouch (1996, p. vii), for instance, shows how Malaysia's 'repressive-responsive' regime combines democratic and authoritarian features in a manner that 'provides the foundation for a remarkably stable political order'. Similarly, Borón (1998, p. 43) refers to the 'faulty democracies' of Latin America in which rulers, once elected, govern in an authoritarian style, showing little concern for mass poverty or legal niceties. In these conditions, suggests Borón, democracy 'endures but does not consolidate'.

> **Definition**
>
> A **semi-democracy** blends democratic and authoritarian elements in stable combination. Although rulers are elected, often helped by control of the media, they govern with little respect for individual rights and often harass opposition or even non-official groups. By contrast, a **new democracy** is one that has not yet had time to consolidate; that is, democracy has not become the 'only game in town'. In practice, new democracies and semi-democracies show similar characteristics but a new democracy is transitional while a semi-democracy is not. Assuming a new democracy does not return to authoritarian rule, it can develop either into an established democracy or into a semi-democracy.

In understanding the operating methods of semi-democracies, it is useful to distinguish two variants. In the first type, an elected party or leader sets the framework for political competition, governing in an illiberal fashion. In Russia, for example, the president not only takes the lead in seeking to impose solutions to national problems but more significantly is expected to do so. President Yeltsin, in particular, ruled in a personal way which inhibited the development of government institutions (Gill and Marwick, 2000). In such conditions, opposition can survive but not flourish. One way of achieving this control is through semi-competitive elections. 'Democratic despots' use control over money, jobs, contracts, pensions, public housing, the media, the police, the electoral system, the courts and, if needed, the election count to deliver success. Egypt and Tunisia are examples of countries where elections have long been semi-competitive. Note, however, that such methods are often combined with effective governance and a favourable disposition toward a dominant ruler or party. For example, Singapore's People's Action Party may manipulate elections in its favour but during its tenure Singapore has become a richer country, on a per person basis, than Britain.

Opposition can also be kept under control by intimidation. Semi-democracies are highly illiberal regimes in which policies are pushed through with scant concern for their impact on particular groups or communities. Individual rights are violated and 'independent' bodies such as the media are carefully monitored. An elected president, such as Fujimori in Peru, may revise the constitution through an autogolpe (self-coup) which consolidates his grip on power. Semi-democratic regimes are willing to rough up their opponents and harass dissidents, tactics that often come wrapped in a nationalist cloak. Kenya under President Moi is an example of such oppressive rule. Institutions such as the assembly and the judiciary are cowed by the dominant force. Ordinary 'citizens' may have a vote and their rights are tolerably secure when the interests of the regime are not at stake. But citizens are sensitive to the sound of gunfire. They know when to lie low. This form of semi-democracy is sometimes called an illiberal or electoral democracy (O'Donnell, 1996).

Definition

In an **autogolpe** (self-coup), elected civilian presidents extend their powers beyond those granted under the constitution. For example, in 1992 the Peruvian President Alberto Fujimori suspended the constitution, the judiciary and Congress before introducing a new constitution (subsequently ratified by referendum) permitting him to stand for re-election. The president was re-elected in 1995 and 2000 but resigned later in the year following allegations of corruption. Typically, an autogolpe transforms a new democracy into a semi-democracy.

In a semi-democracy based on a dominant party or individual, power is concentrated in a few hands. But there is another form of semi-democracy in which elected rulers have too little power. Here elected rulers are puppets rather than despots. In this version, 'power may be shifted to the military, bureaucracy or top business groups' (Case, 1996, p. 439). Thus elected politicians must continue to battle against military, ethnic, religious and regional leaders seeking to maintain their established privileges. Such conflicts are signs of an unconsolidated democracy in which elections are established but do not function as definitive statements of who should exercise final decision-making power. In Thailand, Turkey and Pakistan, among others, the military stands as a guardian of the nation, exerting a 'silent veto' over civilian decisions (Gills, Rocamora and Wilson, 1993, pp. 21–8). Such semi-democracies are sometimes called supervised or even façade democracies.

In some postsoviet republics, too, the power élite shows little respect – indeed considerable contempt – for elected authority. The communist party may have reformed, and many state-owned enterprises may have been sold to the private sector but the same people continue in power. The group that ruled under communism continues to govern, prospering by selling state assets to itself on the cheap: piratization rather than privatization. In such circumstances, the president is merely the mouthpiece of a dominant and corrupt élite, and elections are just plebiscites to confirm the élite's choice of top leader. Real power comes from patronage and from deals with regional and ethnic power brokers or even with criminal gangs. In this type of semi-democracy ('quarter-democracy' might be more accurate), power gives the capacity to take elected office but elected office does not add much power.

The ways of semi-democracy are a sobering reminder to those who take a naive view of the 'triumph of democracy'. Simplistic counts of the number of democracies do not tell the whole story. As quantity has increased, quality has fallen. Why is it, then, that so many new democracies turn out, on closer inspection, to be only semi-democratic? There are two answers, the optimist's and the pessimist's. The optimist's view is that semi-democracy is merely transitional, a temporary staging post in the world's pilgrimage from authoritarian rule to established democracy. This is certainly a possibility. After all, nearly all Western democracies passed through a stage of competitive oligarchy, meaning that the

FOR OR AGAINST
'ASIAN DEMOCRACY'

Many Asian leaders reject aspects of the Western democratic tradition. They claim to be building a distinctive form of 'Asian democracy'. For example, the rulers of Malaysia and Singapore explicitly reject the Western interpretation of liberal democracy based on individual rights. They favour an approach that gives more weight to Asian values, including respect for authority, avoiding public conflict and accepting the primacy of the group. Democracy is defined in almost familial terms, with the elected leader adopting a paternal style. The state leads society, and democracy therefore depends less on the independent groups and associations which provide the foundation for Western democracy. The institutional consequences of 'Asian democracy' include a subservient media and judiciary. In addition, the police and security forces become more aggressive in their approach to criminals and dissenters.

The case for
The attempt to develop non-Western models of democracy derives in part from the natural cynicism of former subjects to their colonial 'masters'. Asian leaders reject what they see as imperialist attempts to 'universalize' Western democracy. Dr Mahathir, Prime Minister of Malaysia, condemns Western democracies 'where political leaders are afraid to do what is right, where the people and their leaders live in fear of the free media which they so loudly proclaim as inviolable'. A former foreign minister of Vietnam exposed Western hypocrisy more bluntly: 'Human rights? I learnt about human rights when the French tortured me as a teenager'. Further, the Asian model has delivered economic growth by allowing leaders to focus on long-term modernization free from electoral pressures. Thus Prime Minister Goh of Singapore suggests that

> our government acts more like a trustee. As a custodian of the people's welfare, it exercises independent judgement on what is in the long-term economic interests of the people and acts on that basis. Government policy is not dictated by opinion polls or referenda.

The case against
Critics allege that 'Asian democracy' is simply an excuse for failing to move beyond semi-democracy. Putzel (1997, p. 253) roundly declares that 'claims for "indigenous forms of democracy" appear to be no more than justifications for authoritarian rule'. And Brzezinski (1997, p. 5) suggests that 'the "Asian values" doctrine is nothing but a rationalization for a certain phase of historical development'. By this he means that through accidents of history Western societies have more experience with protecting individual freedom. Asia, Brzezinski suggests, is still playing catch-up, both economically and politically. And the financial crisis that engulfed East Asia in 1997 will require most countries in the region to reduce the state's role in the economy, yielding a rather more liberal form of democracy. Finally, a Western human rights activist argues that democracy and human rights are inherently universal:

> There is nothing special about torturing the Asian way. Rape is not something that is done an Asian way. Rape is rape, torture is torture and human rights are human rights. (Vatikiotis 1995, p. 98)

Assessment
The debate on Asian democracy will not be resolved easily. It mixes analysis, ideology and colonial memories in an explosive combination. But two points are clear. The first is that Asia has never been a single category. China is authoritarian, Indonesia largely so, Singapore is a semi-democracy and Japan is a second-wave democracy. Second, rather than referring to 'Asian' democracy, it might be more useful to consider the kind of democracy best suited to economic development. The Western model may be appropriate for developed countries while the 'Asian' approach is more effective in countries which are still growing their industrial capacity.

Further reading: Bell *et al.* (1995).

contest for power became open and legitimate before the vote became universal. Even in the United States, democracy took decades to establish. Also, a fully developed and open economy may prove to be incompatible with semi-democracy, which often operates 'crony capitalism' – that is, political leaders distort market allocations to bolster their own support. Recognizing this problem, the leaders of Mexico's PRI in effect arranged their own downfall.

But it is prudent to consider a more pessimistic account of semi-democracy: that it is a stable method of governing poor and unequal societies, particularly in a postcommunist era when blatant dictatorship has become unacceptable. When poverty coincides with extreme inequality, and when ethnic divisions are strong, the prospects of creating a democratic community of equals are slender. Further, semi-democracy is usually sufficient for the ruling élite to meet the conditions of aid set by the World Bank, the IMF and donor governments. While these international bodies may welcome democracy, in practice they give higher priority to economic reform. Perhaps the heart of the matter is that semi-democracy is a tacit, but not unstable, compromise between domestic élites and international organizations. For such reasons, Case

(1996, p. 464) concludes that semi-democracy is not 'a mere way station on the road to further democracy'.

Key reading

> **Next step:** *Dahl (1989) is a magisterial account of democracy by a scholar who spent his professional life studying the subject.*

Other useful assessments of democracy include Held (1996) and, for a more straightforward introduction, Dahl (1998). Two excellent readers on the global resurgence of democracy are Diamond and Plattner (1996) and Hadenius (1997). Democratization has spawned an outstanding literature: Huntington (1991) is influential, O'Donnell, Schmitter and Whitehead (1986) is an excellent work, Potter *et al.* (1997) is a good text while Pridham (1995) is a collection of classic articles. Gill (2000) overviews the process of transition. For democratization in the developing world, see Luckham and White (1996a). Bratton and van de Walle (1997) and Joseph (1998) examine Africa, Peeler (1998) considers Latin America. Bell *et al.* (1995) discusses illiberal democracy in Asia while Gill and Marwick (2000) review Russia's stillborn democracy. Agüero and Stark (1998) is an excellent survey of post-transition Latin America.

Authoritarian rule

Brooker (2000, p. 1) writes that 'non-democratic government, whether by elders, chiefs, monarchs, aristocrats, empires, military regimes or one-party states, has been the norm for most of human history.' As late as 1981, Perlmutter (p. xi) could still claim that 'the twentieth century is the age of political authoritarianism' and certainly that century will be remembered more for the brutal dictatorships it spawned – including Hitler's Germany, Stalin's Russia, Mao's China and Pol Pot's Cambodia – than for the democratic transition at its close (Hobsbawm, 1994). Even today, studying non-democracies remains far more than an historical exercise. China's nominally communist ruling élite continues to govern a quarter of the world's population. Other non-democratic regimes are still internationally significant: for example, Saddam Hussein's Iraq and the ruling families in oil-rich Middle East states. And as terms such as 'postmilitary' and 'postcommunist' imply, an authoritarian legacy continues to influence and inhibit the development of new democracies in the contemporary world.

As the geographical location of these examples suggests, the 'triumph of liberal democracy' is rather a Western conceit. In most of the Middle East and Asia, the battle for democracy has a long time to run – if it has even begun. In these regions, as in most of Africa and much of Latin America, traditions of allegiance to personal rulers constitute an indigenous form of politics far removed from the Western emphasis on government by law. Beyond its Western homeland, liberal democracy is often seen as a soulless foreign import – the political dimension of 'Mcworld' – and a product ill-suited to developing economies. For those in the West, studying authoritarian rule broadens horizons culturally as well as historically.

We should consider one final reason for studying authoritarian rule: to provide a comparative perspective on democracy itself. Examining non-democracies is the only convincing answer to the question, 'What know they of democracy whom only democracy know?' Students of democracy often express disappointment at the quality of today's democracies, at least when compared to the shining beacon of ancient Athens. Yet a more positive assessment emerges when modern democracies are placed against the dark tones of twentieth-century tyrannies. So this chapter will cast further light on democracy by allowing us to assess Churchill's oft-quoted judgment that 'democracy is the worst form of government except for all those other forms that have been tried from time to time'.

We begin by examining what are sometimes called 'simple' or 'traditional' authoritarian regimes – those that existed before the rise of the modern state. We then turn to twentieth-century authoritarianism, focusing on communist, fascist and military rule, before discussing contemporary non-democratic regimes.

Traditional authoritarian rule

We must resist equating all authoritarian rule with twentieth-century tyranny. The power of most traditional non-democratic leaders was neither unlimited nor arbitrary. Nor were authoritarian regimes of past times inherently unstable: hereditary monarchies, for example, offered a clear solution to the problem of succession which is often held out as the major weakness of non-elected governments. Until the massive expansion of the state in the modern era, non-democratic government often provided a settled political framework within which life could be lived. Rulers lacked direct means for controlling their subjects and were forced to administer their kingdoms and empires indirectly, calling on the services of local leaders (Finer, 1997). In practice, national figures governed by making deals with these notables. We should note that this pattern of rule is still found in many countries where the penetration of the state remains limited; for this reason, 'traditional authoritarianism' is best regarded as a way of governing rather than as a historical period.

We must also recognize that many of the original words developed to describe authoritarian rule did not convey the negative connotations they now possess (Box 3.1). Today, such words as 'tyrant' and 'dictator' have become little more than terms of abuse but their initial meaning was more neutral and precise. In ancient Greece, for instance, a 'tyrant' was simply a ruler of a *polis* who had acquired his position by unconstitutional means, typically using deception or force. Indeed, the Athenians themselves fondly remembered a supposed golden age of peace and prosperity under the tyrant Peisistratus. Certainly, Aristotle teaches us that the comparative merits of tyranny and democracy should be assessed, not assumed. Similarly, the term 'dictator' was originally used in the republic of ancient Rome not to convey a position of unlimited power but rather to describe a constitutional role of crisis leader (Neumann, 1957). In times of war a British prime minister probably exercises at least as much freedom of action as a Roman dictator yet today we would shrink from using the word 'dictator' because of the term's critical undertow.

Traditional authoritarian regimes encompassed enormous variety. They included the bureaucratic empires of Ancient Rome, Imperial China, Egypt, Mesopotamia, and the Aztecs and Incas; the feudal systems of West Europe in the Middle Ages; and the absolutist monarchies or empires, such as Tsarist Russia and Ottoman Turkey, which did not disintegrate until early in the twentieth century.

While empires have special operating problems deriving from their scale, Finer (1997, p. 38) suggests that 'palace politics' is the characteristic

---

BOX 3.1

Authoritarian rule: traditional terms

Absolutism	Originally a theological term referring to God's independent power to decide who should be saved. In politics, the term developed at the end of the eighteenth century to describe rulers subject to no legal constraints. An absolute ruler is sovereign in theory but not all-powerful in practice, a combination which characterized European monarchs during the Age of Absolutism (1648–1789).
Autocracy	An autocrat is a single ruler not beholden to the ruled. A similar notion to absolute rule.
Despotism	In classical Greek, a despot ruled in the manner of a master over his household slaves. In modern use, the term connotes absolute and even arbitrary rule. However, the French philosopher Voltaire (1694–1778) referred to 'enlightened despots' such as Frederick the Great of Prussia.
Dictatorship	The original 'dictators' were magistrates in classical Rome who were given unrestricted powers during a temporary emergency. In modern use, the term bears a similar meaning to autocracy. It is also used as an antonym to democracy.
Monarchy	Originally 'rule by the one', monarchy today refers to hereditary kings and queens whose powers are often only symbolic.
Oligarchy	Rule by the few.
Tyranny	In ancient Greece, a tyrant was a ruler whose power was acquired by force or deception. In modern use, the term refers more to the form of rule than to the manner of its acquisition. Today, tyranny implies a coercive and unlimited dictatorship.

Sources: Bogdanor (1991), McLean (1996).

---

mode of traditional authoritarianism, though the political strength of the palace also depends on other bodies, notably the church, the bureaucracy and the military. In palace politics, the officers of state are nothing more than servants of the ruler; the Keeper of the King's Purse and Minister of Finance are one and the same position. Thus, the palace is the original 'home office'. Because allegiance is owed to the ruler rather than to rules, palace politics is based on personal relationships. Politics becomes soap-opera: a never-ending but ultimately repetitive story of feuds, factions and intrigue. Courtiers, clerics, clerks and wives all compete in a never-ending battle for access to, and favours from, the central figure. Formal positions mean far less than obtaining the ear of the leader. Even when the ruler's position is usurped by an upstart, the political flavour remains constant, showing that even this extremely personal form of politics can provide a stable formula for rule. Finer's examples of pure 'palace-type political systems' include ancient Egypt, the Roman empire and some eighteenth-century absolute rulers in Europe, such as the court of Louis XIV in France. In most such cases, the ruler's authority was based on tradition or religion – as with the 'divine right of kings' in Europe and the 'mandate of heaven' claimed by Chinese Emperors.

Weber's notion of patrimonial authority provides a related perspective on authoritarianism. A patrimonial ruler exercises authority in the same way that a male head of household rules, but also provides for, his family (Gerth and Mills, 1948, p. 296). Again, the central feature is rule by a single person rather than by law. Whether that ruler is termed chief, emir, emperor, monarch, president or sultan is secondary. The leader is the sun around which all other planets revolve. More recent readings of traditional authoritarianism in contemporary regimes resemble both Finer's and Weber's accounts. Linz's (2000) category of 'sultanistic regime', in which personal rulers maintain their authority through a judicious mixture of bribes and vengeance, is compatible with both interpretations. So too is the idea of 'personal rule' which Jackson and Rosberg (1982) apply to modern African politics.

Palace politics can provide stable governance, particularly in simple agricultural societies where the penetration of the state remains limited. However, in larger and more bureaucratic states and empires, more organized decision-making develops. A council meeting may become the formal decision-making site though in reality the leader may still rely heavily on an inner core of trusted courtiers. But even in this developed form the danger of traditional authoritarian rule is that it becomes insular and introverted – too much politics and not enough government. Further, the court is in effect a tax on society: money comes in from the authority of officials to grant licences and take bribes. Such a political economy discourages economic development and is increasingly unpopular with international agencies; with good reason, contemporary sultans rightly regard both with suspicion. Even so, in Africa and the Middle East, presidents and ruling families continue to practise personal rule; 'pre-modern' rule lives on. For instance, Bill and Springborg (2000, p. 160) report that, in the Middle East,

> political systems grew out of tribal constellations and the personalism that prevailed in the family and clan has had a pervasive and protracted influence. The Middle Eastern leader has led by virtue of his personal relations with his followers. Formal organizations and institutions have rarely effectively intervened.

These authors give King Abdul Aziz Ibn Saud (leader of the Saudi state from its inception in 1902 until his death in 1953) as a twentieth-century exemplar of a traditional authoritarian leader. The King ran his kingdom as a gigantic personal household, using marriage as an important political tool. In total, he took 300 wives drawn from all the powerful families in the state. Immensely informed about the rivalries within his territory, the King followed a policy of divide and rule: 'two things I will not stomach: first a rebel and second the feigned loyalty of two persons inwardly leagued against me'. He was in a position to control the political and personal fortunes of all the leading figures, and did so. The carrot was used more than the stick, but the ruler's monopoly of both devices enabled him to combine sympathy to those who acknowledged his power with ruthlessness towards those who schemed against him. Ibn Saud adopted a similar dual approach to his dealings with ordinary people, spending several hours a day listening to individual complaints while forcefully thwarting any attempts they might make to develop organized representation.

Like most traditional authoritarian rulers, the King was more concerned with protecting his position than developing his kingdom. Politics came before policy. Such developments as education (or more recently television and the internet) are always perceived as a threat by traditional rulers who are concerned, above all, to maintain the population's dependence on the leader's patronage. Thus, the King eventually stumbled when the exploitation of oil reserves increased inequality, corruption and social tensions within the country. Yet Ibn Saud built and governed a nation which his family continues to rule in a manner that exemplifies traditional authoritarian rule – its virtues as well as its vices – through the ages (Kostiner and Teitelbaum, 2000).

Authoritarian rule in the twentieth century

The twentieth century raised the political stakes. Unlike their traditional counterparts, modern dictators could exploit the economic resources of the industrial revolution, the communications facilities of national media and the political resources of an extended state to mobilize their people in the service of large-scale war or even the systematic murder of sections of their own population. Authoritarian leaders were no longer just masters of their palace; their decisions now impinged directly on ordinary people. The outcome might be a welfare state or a warfare state; either way, politics played on a wider canvas.

Reflecting these developments, a new terminology of authoritarianism developed. Traditional terms had referred to *who* rules: for example, monarchy was rule by the one while oligarchy was rule by the few. But the new concepts referred more to *how* rule was organized – specifically, to the scope, style and objectives of the regime (Box 3.2). Even the word 'authoritarian' is a modern notion, referring in ordinary language to a heavy-handed, non-consultative form of rule. In most political analysis, as in this chapter, the phrase 'authoritarian rule' covers any type of non-democratic regime – traditional or modern, communist or fascist, civilian or military.

On occasion, however, we will use 'authoritarian' in a second sense: as a contrast to totalitarian dictatorship. As defined by Linz (2000, p. 4), a totalitarian system is 'a regime form for completely organiz-

ing political life and society'. For example, during the Cold War communist and fascist states were described – indeed, condemned – as 'totalitarian' in that they both aimed for total penetration and control of society in an attempt to transform it. Both communist and fascist rulers sought, or at least claimed to seek, a reconstruction of human nature and society: communist states claimed to be aiming for a classless utopia while fascist governments sought national revival through submission to a dominant leader. One result of such all-encompassing regimes was what Perlmutter (1981, p. xi) terms the 'conspicuous politicial innovations' of twentieth-century authoritarianism, namely:

the unopposed single party, the party-state, political police, the politburo, revolutionary command councils, storm troops, political youth movements, cadres and gulags, propaganda machinery and concentration camps.

BOX 3.2

Authoritarian rule: twentieth-century terms

Authoritarian rule
(1) Any form of non-democratic rule. (2) Those non-democratic regimes which, unlike totalitarian states, do not seek to transform society and the people in it. Many military governments were authoritarian rather than totalitarian.

Communist states
Political systems in which the communist party monopolized power, leading to an all-encompassing bureaucratic state. In theory, the object was to implement Marx's vision of a classless society; in practice, the party sought to protect its position through complete control of society.

Fascism
An anti-liberal doctrine that glorified the nation and advocated a warrior state, led by an all-powerful leader, to which the masses would show passionate commitment and submission. Advocated by Mussolini in Italy and, supplemented by Aryan racism, the basis for National Socialism in Nazi Germany.

Totalitarian states
Any regime that seeks total control of society with the theoretical aim of transforming it. Communist and fascist states are oft-cited examples. However, the term is often criticized as a Cold War device for condemning communist states by linking them with disgraced fascism.

See also: p. 14.

Clearly, such bold aspirations were far removed from the traditional authoritarian regime, with its overriding commitment to maintaining the ruler's power base. Totalitarian rulers demanded active popular support for their goals whereas authoritarian rulers remained content with passive obedience. So although totalitarianism is sometimes dismissed as a political science model rather than an historical reality, the term does capture one distinctly twentieth-century style of non-democratic rule (Sartori, 1993). Below, we will describe communist and fascist rule in more detail before turning to the large number of military governments – usually authoritarian rather than totalitarian – which ruled many developing countries for part of the century's second half.

Communist states

The 1917 October Revolution in Russia was a decisive event of the twentieth century. It signalled the international advent of a regime, an ideology and a revolutionary movement which sought to overthrow the capitalist democracies of the West. Although communism failed to become a governing force in the affluent West, communist power did expand dramatically in Eastern Europe and Asia. The Union of Soviet Socialist Republics (USSR) – effectively, a new Russian empire – was formed in 1924, extending from the Ukraine in the West to the central Asian republic of Kazakhstan in the East (Table 3.1, Map 3.1). By area, the USSR became the largest country in the world with further expansion when the Baltic states of Estonia, Latvia and Lithuania were forcibly incorporated into the Soviet Union in 1940. After the Second World War East European countries such as Hungary, Poland and Romania became Soviet satellites. Germany became a nation divided between the Federal Republic in the west and the communist Democratic Republic to the east. In Asia, the Chinese revolution of 1949 established an additional if distinctive communist state. During the Cold War, several developing countries such as Benin and the Congo also declared their Marxist allegiance though it is doubtful whether their communist commitment was ever more than nominal. Even so, until the communist order collapsed in the late 1980s and early 1990s such regimes accounted for more than 1.5 billion

Table 3.1 Postcommunist states	
State	Population, 2000 (million)
Eastern European states formerly under the control of the Soviet Union	
Albania	3.5
Bosnia–Herzegovina	3.8
Bulgaria	9.8
Croatia	4.3
Czech Republic	10.3
Hungary	10.1
Former Yugoslav Republic of Macedonia (FYROM)	2.0
Poland	38.6
Romania	22.4
Serbia and Montenegro	10.7
Slovakia	5.4
Slovenia	1.9
States formed from the Soviet Union	
Armenia	3.3
Azerbaijan	7.7
Belarus	10.4
Estonia	1.4
Georgia	5.0
Kazakhstan	16.7
Kyrgyzstan	4.7
Latvia	2.4
Lithuania	3.6
Moldova	4.4
Russia	146.0
Tajikistan	6.4
Turkmenistan	4.5
Ukraine	49.2
Uzbekistan	24.8

Source: CIA at http://www.cia.gov.

people – about one in three of the world's population.

Communist states were marked by sharp discrepancies between ideology and practice. In his theoretical writings, Karl Marx (1818–1883) had envisaged an equal, classless and stateless utopia in which goods would be distributed from each according to their ability to each according to their need. In

Map 3.1 Postcommunist East Europe

Marx's theoretical vision, the state would be converted 'from an organ superior to society to one completely subordinate to it'. For practical revolutionaries, though, the initial problem was more immediate: how to overthrow the existing capitalist order. Here Vladimir Lenin (1870–1924), the Russian revolutionary, made a pivotal contribution. He argued that the communist party must serve as a vanguard organization, leading the workers into political activity that would itself further enhance their revolutionary consciousness. By assuming the party understood the true interests of the working class better than the workers themselves, Lenin provided the decisive rationale for the monopoly position which communist parties created for themselves once power was achieved.

In reality, ruling communist parties dominated society. They were strongly authoritarian, brooking no opposition, stage-managing elections, acting above the law, modifying constitutions as they saw fit, determining all major appointments to the government, controlling the media and spying on their populations. Far from disappearing as anticipated by Marx, the communist state became an all-embrac-

ing, all-powerful presence operating under the party's guidance. Economies were brought under public control as part of the push to industrialize; the elaborate 5-year plans produced in the Soviet Union were undoubtedly the most ambitious, detailed and comprehensive attempts at economic planning the world has ever seen. The party controlled and the state implemented; together, this new form of party-state snuffed out independent organizations, creating a social wasteland of distrust in which true political beliefs could only be expressed safely within the family (and sometimes not even there). Not only was active opposition suppressed but explicit support – in the form of demonstrations, party-led meetings and the voting-booth – was required. This insistence on active if ritual support was one factor distinguishing totalitarian from merely authoritarian regimes.

As communist states retreat into history, we should be careful to avoid stereotyping their characteristics. Economically, many communist regimes industrialized successfully and delivered a rough equality of welfare to the mass of the population, even though the party élite remained economically

FOR OR AGAINST

AUTHORITARIAN RULE AS A RECIPE FOR ECONOMIC DEVELOPMENT

Can authoritarian rule be defended as an effective method for economic development? If so, we will have a powerful critique of democracy's claims to be universally the best form of government since we would nearly all prefer to eat under a dictator than to starve in a democracy. In addition, we could reasonably anticipate that democracy is unlikely to deepen in poor countries over the long term if the cost is slower economic development.

The case for

Sorensen (1993, p. 65) points out that 'In the twentieth century there was no case of successful economic development without comprehensive political action involving enormous state intervention in the economy.' The reason is clear: industrialization requires massive investment in infrastructure such as transport, communications and universal education; initially, these can only be funded by the state. And authoritarian rulers can generate the surplus needed for investment precisely because they can resist short-term pressures for immediate consumption. Simply put, they can ignore the squeals of those whose consumption is reduced by the need for investment.

Consider some examples. The communist revolution in Russia initiated a remarkably rapid transformation from a rural to an industrial society. Similarly, communist China has achieved twice the rate of economic growth of democratic India – and surely reduced net human suffering in the process. Between 1960 and 1985, authoritarian Indonesia, Singapore and South Korea were among the fastest-growing economies in the world. In parts of Latin America, too, technocrats operating under more or less authoritarian governments have succeeded in imposing coherent economic policy on unruly societies. Even some military rulers have initiated worthwhile modernization: for example, General Nasser's reforms in rural Egypt mean that nearly all Egyptians now have access to safe water, a considerable achievement.

The case against

A few non-democratic regimes may initiate

economic development but the vast majority do not. Many traditional rulers, such as the ruling families in the Middle East, resisted modernization for as long as they could. Other dictators, for example Nigeria's military 'lootocrats', set back economic development by decades. Overall, statistical assessments of the link between form of government and economic developments show no clear relationship (Inkeles, 1990). If industrialization really does require foregoing immediate consumption, rulers should attempt to persuade the people of the need for sacrifice, not impose dictatorial solutions. Besides, even if non-democratic rule can lead to industrialization, that hardly excuses the abuses of power and human rights which are an inherent risk of authoritarian regimes. For example, China's path of communist modernization involved the brutality of the Great Leap Forward, in which around 40 million people died in five years as a result of a bungled experiment in forced collectivization. Who is prepared to say that the eventual achievement of high economic growth justified such a massive human price?

Assessment

It may well be that in the twentieth century economic development could be achieved by a stable authoritarian élite capable both of extracting resources for investment and of providing state leadership for emerging private industries. But in the twenty-first century, globalization has given developing countries access to new sources of capital through multinational corporations, overseas banks and agencies such as the World Bank. To access these resources, developing countries benefit from convincing lenders that their economy is market-based and that their politics takes the form of a tolerably liberal democracy. The twentieth century may prove to have been the pinnacle of 'the developmental state' led by authoritarian rulers; in the new century, markets and democracy may go together for developing as much as for developed countries.

Further reading: Johnson (1987), Robinson and White (1998), Sorensen (1997).

as well as politically privileged. Nor were communist states all of a piece. One distinction lay between the Soviet Union and the rest. Russia lacked any pre-communist tradition of either liberalism or democracy and, in the era of the USSR, it approximated the totalitarian model of complete state dominance and party control. But in East European countries, where communism had generally been imposed by force of Soviet arms, domestic leaders could sometimes soften Moscow's orders so as to respect national traditions. This lighter touch permitted some independent organizations to survive – for instance, the Catholic Church in Poland. China followed an even more independent path. There, the road to power took the form of a protracted guerilla struggle by the People's Liberation Army (PLA), based on an ideology of anti-Japanese nationalism as much as the Marxist class struggle. With the triumph of the communist revolution in 1949, both aspects – the political weight of the army and the significance of Chinese nationalism – were carried into power.

A second distinction is between early and late communism. Once the initial thrust to industrialize had been achieved, many communist states settled into the banal routines of middle age. The Soviet Union is again a striking example. Under Stalin's brutal dictatorship, Russia achieved forced industrialization, and the collective ownership of agriculture, during the 1930s. But after the tyrant's death in 1953, a programme of 'de-Stalinization' followed. Nikita Khrushchev, the new party secretary, famously denounced Stalin in his 'secret speech' to the party élite in 1956. Terror ceased to be a routine political tactic; the Soviet Union came to offer a more predictable and less centralized environment for its citizens. The regime accorded greater weight to technical experts (e.g. in the military and bureaucracy), implicitly limiting the extent to which authority resided in the party alone. The party lost its reforming drive and instead became a club – the only club – for ambitious careerists. Some Western commentators even detected the onset of pluralism (diffusion of power) in the mature USSR (Hough and Fainsod, 1979) while others prefer to interpret late socialism in the Soviet Union as post-totalitarian (Linz 2000, p. 6).

Yet the attempt to transform communist rule into more rational and orderly governance eventually proved its undoing. State-led planning was more appropriate for industrializing than for developed economies; it seemed incapable of delivering the advanced products and services found in the West. 'Advanced socialism' proved to be a contradiction that eventually became apparent to the ruling party itself. In the more industrial communist states of Russia and East Europe, communism reached a dead end; the party lacked a mission and continued to rule only because it had done so in the past. In such circumstances, reform was always likely to escalate into revolution. When Mikhail Gorbachev became General Secretary of the Soviet party in 1985, his intention was modernization but the outcome was dissolution. In East Europe communist rule fell apart in 1989 once the Soviet leader made it clear that the USSR would no longer intervene militarily to protect the puppet rulers of its satellite states. The following year, the Soviet Union itself dissolved into 15 constituent republics. In Russia itself, the communist party was outlawed, a humiliating fate for what was once the most powerful party on earth. Even where nominally communist rule still survives, as in China and Vietnam, most economic development now occurs outside the state sector. In the twenty-first century, communism's major significance lies in its legacy for successor regimes. As an ideology, a system of rule and a method of economic organization, communism is finished.

Fascist states

Although we can still observe the consequences of communism in the twenty-first century, fascism's challenge was confined to the period bordered by the two great wars. It began with the emergence of revolutionary groups (*fascia*) in Italy during the First World War and ended with Germany's military defeat in 1945. It is certainly true that fascist elements could continue to be found in Spain under General Franco and even Portugal under Salazar, two dictators whose right-wing rule continued well into the 1960s. But these were conservative authoritarian regimes based on army and church; they sought merely to recover traditional national glories rather than to build a new self-consciously modern order (Linz, 2000). Even in its interwar heyday, fascist regimes were rarer on the ground than were communist states. Mussolini's leadership of Italy, lasting from 1922 until he was deposed in 1943, is the main example but even this dictatorship was fascist more by bombastic declaration than by institutional reality. In Hitler's Germany, the Nazi party espoused an ideology that certainly included fascist principles but these elements blended with crude Aryan racism to form national socialism. Yet the fascist worldview cannot be ignored; it represents an important nationalist response to the rise of communism. Its significance for the twentieth century – and for six million European Jews in particular – was profound.

What, then, was the doctrine which these interwar European regimes claimed to manifest? Fascism lacked the theoretical sophistication of communism; it offered an ideological impulse rather than a coherent model of government. Fascism was an extreme glorification of the nation, often defined in racial terms. The notional purpose was to create an all-embracing nation to which the masses would show passionate commitment and submission. An autocratic ruler (führer or duce) and a single party would personify the state. State and nation were to become one. As Mussolini put it, 'everything in the state: nothing against the state: nothing outside the state'. Fascism was an attempt to use the power of the state, as revealed by the First World War, to revive the countries defeated in that conflict. Religion, liberalism, parliamentary democracy, even capitalism, were condemned as weak distractions from the key task of national revival. A strong, self-sufficient, war-like nation could mobilize the population more effectively – and in a more modern way – than any other type of regime. Fascism, not liberalism, was the defense which proud nations should adopt against the communist threat. In short, fascism was the twentieth-century doctrine of nationalism taken to extremes (Eatwell, 1996).

In power, fascist regimes governed very differently from ruling communist parties, even though both forms are grouped under the totalitiarian label. Certainly, fascist states were committed to mobilizing the population in an organized effort at national rebirth, just as communist regimes were notionally committed to constructing a classless society. And both ideologies gave primacy to politics: nothing could compete with the authority bestowed on the supreme fascist leader, just as ruling communist parties dominated their own societies. But fascism lacked the organized character of communist rule; it produced a movement rather than a method of governing. It favoured the risky 'leader principle' in which governance depended on a single individual rather than a well-developed party. Yet Hitler, for one, never showed much interest in administration, preferring to leave his underlings to fight out their bureaucratic battles among themselves. Where communist states often ran on auto-pilot, with an anonymous party functionary in nominal charge, fascism – a doctrine of constant movement and change – never developed comparable routines of rule. Fascist parties were essentially personal vehicles through which the leader managed his rise to power; unlike communist parties, they lost significance once the state was won. And in power, neither Mussolini nor even Hitler achieved the domination of society found in communist party states. Mussolini did not abolish the Italian monarchy while Hitler preferred to exploit rather than nationalize German industry. For all its impact on the twentieth century, fascist practice often seemed to present politics as theatre: marches, demonstrations, symbols and speeches. Facism's death in 1945 preceded that of its communist bogeyman.

Military governments

Like communism and fascism, military government was primarily a twentieth-century phenomenon. As Pinkney (1990, p.7) writes,

the involvement of soldiers in politics is not new, and can be traced back at least as far as Roman times. The phenomenon of military government, in the sense of a government drawn mainly from the army and using the army as its main power base, is much newer and belongs essentially to the last 50 years.

However, the contrasts between military regimes, on the one hand, and communism and fascism, on the other, are acute. Most military coups came later in the century, between the 1960s and 1980s, and, more significantly, they occurred in developing countries in Latin America, Africa and parts of Asia where the state had not achieved the penetration found in its European heartland. Where fascism and communism sought to exploit the power of the modern state, many military coups (especially in smaller African countries) were made possible precisely because the state remained simple and underdeveloped. An ambitious general just needed a few tanks, driven by a handful of discontented officers, to seize the presidential palace and the radio station. Yet because the state's penetration through society remained limited, life after the coup would continue unchanged outside the capital. Lacking the economic resources and governance tools of modern states, most military rulers were modest in their policy aspirations. 'The state in uniform' lacked the grand objectives of both communist and fascist regimes; in some cases, ruling generals sought little more than to steal money from the government – and to prevent civilian participation while they did so. Military government was always authoritarian and sometimes brutal, not least during Latin America's phase of repressive army rule from the mid-1960s to the mid-1970s. Nonetheless, most military regimes lacked the totalitarian goals of fascism and communism.

> **Definition**
> A **military coup** is a seizure of political power by the armed forces or sections thereof. The term conjures up images of a violent, secretive and unwelcome capture of power against the opposition of civilian rulers. In fact, most coups replaced one military regime with another, many involved little if any loss of life and some were more or less invited by the previous rulers.

In many of the newly-independent countries created in the wave of decolonization in the 1950s and 1960s, generals soon seized power from civilian rulers – and then from other generals. Sub-Saharan Africa is the major example. Here, 68 coups occurred between 1963 and 1987 (Magyar, 1992, p.233). As late as 1987, half the countries of Africa were under military control. But military takeover was not restricted to new states. In Latin America, where colonies won independence in the nineteenth century, only Mexico and Costa Rica were immune from military government in the postwar period. The most important factor in explaining this clustering in time was the Cold War. During this period, many developing countries became pawns on a global chessboard dominated by the United States

and the Soviet Union. Each superpower sought allies and did not enquire closely into the background, civilian or military, of a country's rulers. Governing generals might lack support in their own country but they could survive through the political, economic and military backing of a superpower. Simple contagion, both from one country to another and within a single country over time, was another major factor. Once the army had seized power in all the surrounding states, it was natural for generals in the remaining island of civilian rule to wonder whether they should follow the trend.

> **Definition**
> The **Cold War** refers to the competition between the United States and the Soviet Union which lasted from the late 1940s to the collapse of the Soviet Union in 1991. Falling short of open war, the Cold War often reached a high intensity of confrontation, particularly before détente began in the late 1960s. The Cold War was a conflict between superpowers, reinforced by conflicting ideologies and heightened by the capacity of each side to destroy the other. Its end, brought about by communism's fall, was an event of the first magnitude. It released the waves of globalization, regionalization, nationalism and democratization which characterize the politics of the twenty-first century.

Inclusionary and exclusionary regimes represented the two extremes of military rule (Remmer, 1989). In the former, the military leaders did try to build a base of support among the political class – and even, on occasion, the wider population – often by exploiting the population's respect for a strong leader. Civilian politicians were represented in a cabinet and the bureaucracy continued to make important decisions. The modernizing regime of General Abdel Nasser in Egypt was an example. Nasser came to power in a coup in 1952, became president in 1956 and remained there until his death in 1970. Inclusionary military regimes often underwent a process of civilianization, becoming instances of presidential rather than military government. This was again the case in Egypt, which turned into a state dominated by the bureaucracy rather than the military. Another example of a military leader broadening his support was Colonel Juan Peron in Argentine. He came to power in a coup in 1943 and

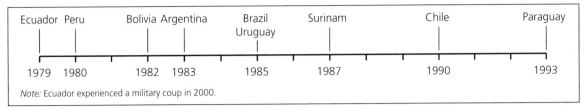

Note: Ecuador experienced a military coup in 2000.

Figure 3.1 The ending of military rule in Latin America

undertook a populist programme of state-led industrialization based on a strong trade union movement and a commitment to social welfare for the urban working class.

But most military governments were exclusionary rather than inclusionary; in classic authoritarian fashion, the generals sought to prevent popular participation in politics. Take General Pinochet's bloody rule of Chile between 1973 and 1989. Pinochet suppressed all potential sources of popular opposition. He exterminated, exiled or imprisoned thousands of labour leaders and left-wing politicians, concentrating power in the hands of his ruling military clique. The standard institutional form of an exclusionary regime was the junta (council), a small group made up of the leader of each branch of the armed forces. In Chile, for instance, Pinochet himself acted as chief executive while a classic four-man junta representing the army, navy, air force and national police performed legislative functions. In some extreme cases in Africa, exclusionary (mis)rule by army despots transformed weak states into collapsed states. Public authority disintegrated, society became divided into competing clans, military bands roamed the country and people survived by subsistence and barter. In Uganda, for example, the tyrant Idi Amin Dada (who had seized power in a coup in 1971) 'destroyed a state that was still being made, a state groping with rudimentary tasks of broadening its authority over an uncertain territory, against a background of scarce resources and unrefined administration' (Khaidagala, 1995, p.35). The eventual result was civil war.

Just as military governments prospered during the Cold War, so they shrivelled after its close. As Wiseman (1996, p.4) writes, 'authoritarian African political leaders [such as the armed forces] were more strongly placed to resist the pressures of African democrats when they could turn to outside pressures to help them stay in power.' By the 1990s,

conditionality ruled the roost. Aid and technical assistance flowed to civilian regimes that adopted democratic forms and offered at least some protection to civil rights. International bodies such as the World Bank stipulated market-based economic policies that did not sit comfortably with military rule. And just as contagion accelerated the diffusion of military coups in the 1960s and 1970s, so also did it encourage generals to return to their bases in the 1980s and 1990s. In Latin America even before the Cold War ended, and later in most of Africa, the military withdrew from formal rule, transforming the pattern of government around the world. The last Latin American generals were back in their barracks by 1993 (Figure 3.1).

For now at least, military governments – like communist states – are known mainly for their impact on successor regimes. The problem today is that long periods of army rule led to an interweaving of civilian and military power. In many Latin American countries, senior officers became accustomed to seats in the cabinet, to a high level of military expenditure, to running the security agencies independently of civilian control, to making money from defence contracts and to exemption from civilian justice. Some of these privileges were entrenched before military rulers could be persuaded to relinquish their occupancy of the state. In Chile, for instance, General Pinochet ensured military autonomy was secured in the new constitution before handing power to civilians in 1980. The armed forces were exempted from prosecution in civilian courts and retained the role of guarantors of the 'institutional order' and 'national security' (Luckham 1996, p.149). Similarly, Ecuador's armed forces were guaranteed 15 per cent of the country's oil revenues until 2010. Such conditional transitions, characteristic of Latin America, helped the shift to, but weakened the depth of, the postmilitary regime. They form a difficult legacy for new democracies.

Country profile NIGERIA

Population: 122m
Gross domestic product per head: about $345 but with marked inequality.
Main groups: Hausa-Fulani in the north, Yoruba in the southwest and Ibos in the southeast. These groups make up about 65 per cent of the population.
Religions: Muslim 50 per cent, Christian 40 per cent, traditional religions about 10 per cent.
Form of government: a presidential republic. Civilian rule was reintroduced in 1999 following 15 years of military rule.
Territorial basis of power: federal, with the number of states increasing from 12 in 1967 to 36 in 2000.

In February 1999, Olusegun Obasanjo was elected civilian president of Nigeria in elections considered to have been fair if hardly flawless. Hardly a world-shattering event, we might think, except that for the previous 15 years, as for most of its history since achieving independence from Britain in 1960, Nigeria had been governed by the military. And Nigeria is, potentially, an important country: it is the largest African country by population and possesses substantial petroleum reserves. Nigeria's transition from military to civilian rule is an important event within Africa and a significant one beyond.

Military rule under General Sani Abacha, Head of the Provisional Ruling Council from 1993 until his death from a heart attack in 1998, had been corrupt, sordid and self-serving. Nigerians called his regime a 'lootocracy'; it consisted of little more than theft of public assets for personal benefit. One of Abacha's tricks was to starve the country's oil refineries of resources so that a petrol shortage resulted, even in a country with massive reserves of crude oil. He would then grant import licences for refined gasoline to his business friends. Abacha laundered many of his gains through London bank accounts but other members of his family preferred to deal in cash. After the General's death, his wife was caught fleeing to Saudi Arabia with 38 suitcases full of foreign currency while one of his sons was intercepted carrying the astonishing sum of $100m in notes.

The transition to civilian rule was remarkably smooth, raising hopes that Nigeria would begin the road to recovery after decades of misrule. Yet so far the results have been limited, providing evidence not just of the long-term damage inflicted by the military within Nigeria but also of the deeper problems facing many African states. Nigeria's economy remains in poor condition. The industrial sector declined in the 1990s, with some figures suggesting that manufacturing output was even lower in 1997 than in 1982. In the oil-producing Niger Delta, wealthy executives of multinational companies extract the vital commodity while local people subsist in absolute poverty and complete squalor amid a degraded environment.

The infrastructure which might permit rapid economic recovery has also decayed. The electricity supply is irregular while corruption scares off many foreign investors; Nigeria is probably the most corrupt country in the world. Developments in telecommunications, potentially a large market, are slowed by confused policy-making and by engineers who first install telephone lines and then cut them if the customer refuses to pay protection money. The civil service is massively over-staffed, with many illiterates appointed to posts which require documents to be processed. Military equipment is also in a poor condition; the navy has more admirals than seaworthy ships.

Ethnic conflict, superimposed on provinces operating in a federal framework, also holds back postmilitary recovery. Reflecting the colonial policy of divide and rule, the federal government became an arena for conflict between regions and ethnic groups, leading to civil war in 1967. Even today, divisions between Hausa-Fulani, Yoruba and Ibos are entrenched. A gain for one group is defined as a loss by the others, with the result that the interests of the country at large are subordinated to conflicts between North and South and between Muslims and Christians.

The transition to civilian rule has thrown Nigeria's continuing difficulties into sharper relief. An aimless continuation of the status quo is perhaps the most likely prognosis but neither national disintegration, nor even another phase of military rule, can be ruled out.

Further reading: Diamond, Kirk-Greene and Oyediran (1997), Holman and Wallis (2000).

Authoritarian rule today

In the twenty-first century, authoritarian regimes form a more diverse group than ever before; no longer are their ranks dominated by military governments and communist party states. Instead, we are presented with a varied collection including Afghan Talibaan, Chinese communists, Pakistani generals, Iranian clerics, Iraqi despots, Saudi princes and assorted authoritarian presidents in some of the smaller states of Central Asia, Africa and Latin America. These rulers have little in common beyond their rejection of Western democracy. It is tempting to dismiss this ragged band as twentieth-century left-

overs, soon to fall victim to the double embrace of democracy and capitalism. But such a judgment is certainly premature, involving a risky bet on yet another wave of democratization. Treating contemporary authoritarian rule as exceptional also betrays a Western bias which regards non-democracies as unusual or residual.

In this section, we will outline some authoritarian regimes in two of the least democratic regions of the non-Western world: Asia and the Middle East (Map 3.2). We will travel from east to west, reviewing in turn rule by the communist party in China, by the military in Pakistan, by Islamic clerics in Iran and by Saddam Hussein in Iraq (Table 3.2). In both Asia

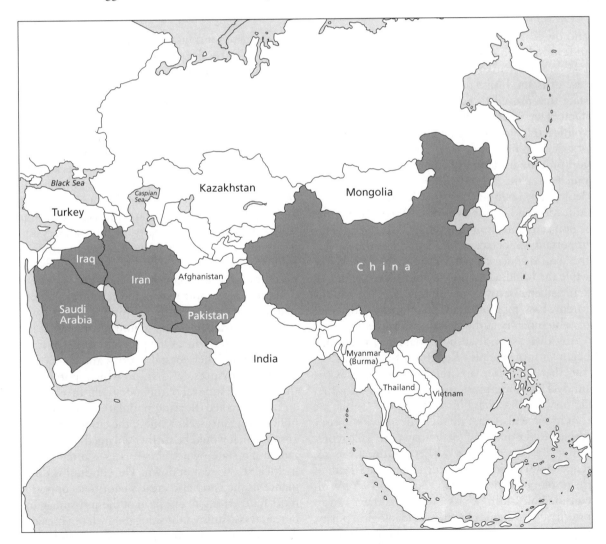

Map 3.2 Asia and the Middle East, highlighting states discussed in this chapter

Table 3.2 Some authoritarian regimes in Asia and the Middle East

Country	Form of government	Head of state	Population (million)	Area (sq km)	Gross national product per head ($)
China	Communist party state	President Jiang Zemin	1261.8	9 572 900	3 800
Iran	Disputed theocracy (rule by clerics)	President Mohammad Khatami	65.6	1 648 000	5 300
Iraq	Personal dictatorship	President Saddam Hussein	22.7	434 924	2 700
Pakistan	Military rule	General Parvaiz Musharraf	141.6	796 100	2 000
Saudi Arabia	Ruling family	King Fahd Abdul Aziz	22.0	2 200 518	9 000

Note: For a discussion of Saudi Arabia, see p. 33–4.

and the Middle East, conditions remain generally unfavourable to democracy. For instance, religion takes non-Christian forms which, especially in the case of Islam, limits the separation of church and state that proved to be the foundation for liberal democracy in the West. Similarly, the dominant political tradition in Asia and the Middle East is one of guardianship and personal rule, not the Western compromise of democracy constrained by law. In much of Asia, several other conditions inhibit democracy, including poverty, inequality, limited education and ethnic divisions. Of course, neither region is uniformly authoritarian: Asia includes the important democracies of India and Japan, as well as the semi-democracies of Singapore and Malaysia, while the Middle East also contains Israel, a democratic albeit assertively Jewish state. Yet Asia and the Middle East still provide an exceptionally wide range of contemporary authoritarian governments.

Any discussion of authoritarianism today must begin with the People's Republic of China (PRC). Together with Vietnam, the PRC exemplifies the survival of communist rule into the twenty-first century. In understanding contempory China, we should remember that the PRC never wholly conformed to the model of totalitarian party rule represented by, say, the early Soviet Union. Even so, remarkable changes have occurred since the death of the revolutionary leader Mao Zedong in 1976. With considerable skill, Mao's successors have given priority to economic growth over ideological purity, reducing the state's role in direct economic production and creating a somewhat more predictable legal

environment for transactions that are not politically sensitive. Today the propaganda slogans include 'to get rich is glorious' and even 'some get rich first', an astonishing contrast to the theme of 'politics in command' adopted during Mao's Great Leap Forward of 1958.

China's political system may no longer be communist in any traditional sense but it remains deeply authoritarian. The party is above the law because the party makes the law. Local mayors retain a strong role in economic development through licensing and regulation; they, not market forces, determine 'who gets rich first'. The party, the bureaucracy and even the army has a role in most economic transactions. So far, China's transformation involves the decentralization of economic, and to some extent political, power more than a shift towards a Western market economy operating within the rule of law.

In decentralizing, the communist party has created new tensions. One problem is the contrast between the richer coastal regions and the poorer internal provinces, a divison which potentially threatens the survival of the state itself. In addition, an impoverished 'floating population' of over 150 million migrants seeks work in the cities, a resentful group which would be further enlarged if the many remaining state-owned enterprises – often highly inefficient – were shut down. The continuing dominance of the party also creates enormous opportunities for corruption: one head of the anti-smuggling bureau was dismissed for smuggling while a previous director of the anti-corruption office took bribes. And the tentative opening of the economy to international influences has contributed to a freer flow of information while still leaving overseas companies dissatisfied with the continuing bureaucratic restrictions placed on them.

Yet despite these challenges the Chinese party continues as guardian of society, claiming to represent the long-term 'best interests' of all the people. As with many other Asian states, economic growth and above all political stability still provide rulers with a measure of legitimacy. There remains a widespread belief that China should develop, politically as well as economically, in its own way, and not import Western models. In any case, the regime continues to suppress independent organizations such as Falun Gong, a spiritual movement whose members are quickly detained and sometimes killed when they engage in public demonstrations. Those who might seek to challenge the party's supremacy need little reminder of the Tiananmen Square massacre in 1989, when the People's Liberation Army eventually turned its tanks and guns on the people (Nathan, Hong and Smith, 1999).

Where the PRC provides a continuing example of communist rule in Asia, Pakistan offers one of the few contemporary instances of military government. Throughout its post-colonial history, military and civilian rule have oscillated in this large, poor, unequal and substantially feudal Islamic state. The current military government, the fourth since Pakistan was created from the partition of India in 1947, dates from a coup in 1999 which followed several years of ineffective civilian rule and, in particular, military frustration at a setback in the long-running conflict with India over Kashmir. Together with the bureaucracy, Pakistan's army has long seen itself as the guardian of the national interest – and the common weal is indeed a concept remote from the workings of civilian politics. Strong divisions between provinces (which, unlike India, have never been overcome by a dominant party) have led to a paralysis in national policy-making. Money has become the core political currency, with political allegiances simply bought and sold. In these circumstances, it is neither difficult nor even implausible for the army to present itself as national guardian. Even so, military rule has lacked both the merciless exploitation of the population by the military despots in Myanmar (Burma) and the ruthless modernization adopted by General Suharto

in Indonesia during the 1970s and 1980s. Rather, Pakistan provides a continuing example of a political system in which the military supervises domestic politics, exerting a silent veto even when civilian rulers are nominally in charge (Rais, 1997).

If Pakistan's military government is unusual in the modern world, Iran provides a unique form of authoritarianism: government by clerics. Iran's theocracy was a creation of the revolution of 1979, the last great insurrection of the twentieth century. In this revolution, Ayatollah Khomeini, a 76-year old cleric committed to Islamic fundamentalism overthrew the Shah of Iran, a pro-Western absolute monarch committed to economic development. The revolutionaries advocated an Islamic republic free from foreign domination – 'neither East nor West' was the slogan. In power, the ayatollahs (religious leaders) created a unique Islamic state in which they governed directly rather than by overseeing secular rulers. The post-revolutionary constitution did incorporate a directly-elected presidency and assembly (Majlis), features that allow Brooker (2000, p. 244) to classify Iran as a mere 'semi-dictatorship' But the real power lay with the clerics, expressed in part through a 12-member Council of Guardians which certifies that all bills and candidates conform with Islamic law. In their strict enforcement of traditional and sexist Islamic codes, the ayatollahs permeated society in a manner reminiscent of totalitarian regimes. The Interior Ministry still makes extensive use of informants while the state employs arbitrary arrests and even assassination as a form of terroristic control. These are classic signs of totalitarianism. But rule by ayatollahs has not delivered economic growth, even in a country with considerable oil reserves, and Iran's politics has turned into a ruthless battle between the now-traditional clerics and liberal reformers, led by a president elected for an initial four-year term in 1997. In a country where two-thirds of the population is under 25, it seems unlikely that religious leaders will be able to resist further reform indefinitely (Schirazi, 1998).

Our final example of contemporary authoritarian rule is Saddam Hussein's Iraq. If post-revolutionary Iran was in some respects a totalitarian state which has now moved in an authoritarian direction, Iraq under Saddam Hussein has followed a reverse journey. Since the 1960s Saddam has accumulated more and more power in the hands of himself, his immediate family and the numerous security forces which spy on each other, on potential opponents and on the population. As with other totalitarian regimes, Saddam has ruled through terror; criticism of the president is punishable by death. Deserting the military can lead to amputation; some doctors who refused to carry out such penalties have been executed. Minorities such as the Kurds, and also the Shi'ite Muslim majority, have been systematically repressed. Like Hitler, the Iraqi president has constructed an elaborate cult around his own personality and used his country's considerable economic resources as a resource for political projects, including both a war against Iran launched in 1980 and the invasion of Kuwait ten years later. The President's son oversees the Special Republican Guard consisting of around 25 000 Saddam loyalists and also runs a smuggling operation which gives his father sufficient funds to buy off potential opponents.

Saddam's rise to total power resembled Stalin's career in Russia more than Hitler's in Germany. Just as Stalin rose to power within the Soviet communist party, so Saddam operated within the alliance of the military and the Arab Ba'ath Socialist Party, an alliance which had originally seized power in 1968. Ba'ath means 'renaissance' and the party's advocacy of a pan-Arab unity enabled Saddam to claim leadership of the Arab world, just as communist ideology created an environment in which Stalin could practise his terror. However, it was not until 1979 that Saddam finally assumed the offices of party leader, head of state and chairman of the military Revolutionary Command Council. Saddam's hold on power, despite international sanctions that have led to widespread malnutrition among his country's children, is a tribute to the dictator's ruthless skill. He has exploited divisions among domestic opponents and within the international community. It is as well to conclude by observing that his dictatorship is a most untypical example of the broad and diverse category of authoritarian government, past or present.

Key reading

> **Next step:** *Linz (2000, first pub. 1975) is the classic defence of the distinction between authoritarian and totalitarian regimes.*

A useful current source on non-democracy, distinguishing between party, military and personal regimes, is Brooker (2000). Classic works on totalitarianism include Arendt (1966, first pub. 1951) and Friedrich and Brzezinski (1965); Sartori (1993) and Gleason (1995) are more recent reviews of this disputed concept. For Hitler, see Bullock (1990); for Stalin, Tucker (1990); and for Saddam Hussein, Karsh and Rautsi (1991). On military governments, Finer (1988, first pub. 1962) is an influential and accessible study; see also Nordlinger (1977). For twentieth-century authoritarianism, see Perlmutter (1981 and 1997). Jackson and Rosberg (1982) remains the key account of personal rule in Africa, while Chebabi and Linz (1998) examine sultanistic regimes. Nathan, Hong and Smith (1999) consider the dilemmas of reform in China, while Schirazi (1998) charts the declining weight of Islam in Iranian politics.

The state in a global context

States have always faced outwards as well as inwards. The origins of the modern European state lie in the requirement by monarchs to raise men and taxes from within their territory in order to wage wars. And the theory of sovereignty which underlies the modern system of states also blends the domestic and the international: a government's claim to exercise authority over its territory is confirmed by its acceptance into the club of nations. So rather than conceiving of states as independent entities, each entire unto itself, we should recognize the intimate links between the national and the international. We must raise the question of how relations between countries impinge on politics within them.

In this chapter, we focus on four aspects of the global environment: (1) international organizations, (2) regional bodies such as the European Union, (3) humanitarian intervention in the domestic affairs of states and (4) the global economy, including multinational corporations. One theme will be the greater impact of the international environment on weak than on strong states. Weak states – and most countries in the world are both small and poor – must accept both the external setting, and their vulnerability to it, as a given. The task of their leaders is to manage external influences as best they can. By contrast, powerful states, notably the United States, can influence the international setting while also retaining some autonomy from it. In addition, we will raise the broader question of whether bodies such as international organizations represent not so much constraints on states but rather the migration of state authority to the global level. Even if this is the case, we will suggest that the legitimacy accorded to established democracies will not easily be replicated by any international body.

International organizations and the state

The international environment contains numerous international organizations which we can conveniently divide into two groups. The first and more significant is intergovernmental organizations (IGOs) – bodies whose members are states (Box 4.1). The original example, founded in 1865, is the International Telecommunications Union (ITU), a body which now has 750 employees, 188 government members and over 550 associate members, including about 500 corporations. Other IGOs include the United Nations and the North Atlantic Treaty Organization. The second type consists of international nongovernmental organizations (INGOs, usually called NGOs). These are institutions whose members are individuals or private groups drawn from more than one country. Examples are the International Red Cross, Greenpeace and (just to show that some of these bodies are anything but new) the Catholic Church. In general, NGOs exert less influence than IGOs but they are important in some weak states which rely heavily on aid agencies for basic supplies and services.

We will consider IGOs first. IGOs are established by treaty and usually operate by consent, with a permanent secretariat to service the organization. They consist of universal bodies such as the United Nations, which all countries can apply to join;

regional organizations such as the European Union; and single-purpose institutions which perform a specific function. Example of this last group include the International Atomic Energy Agency, which oversees the civilian use of nuclear energy, and the International Postal Union.

The impact of IGOs on nation states is a matter of controversy. One perspective is that IGOs have become important political actors, exerting significant influence over their member governments. After all, setting up an IGO creates a body with its own employees and agenda. IGOs may be created by states – indeed, they may be the state 'gone global' – but, like children, they grow up to develop their own interests and perspectives. If IGOs are irrelevant, asks Keohane (1994), why do they last so long and increase in number? Furthermore, even though most IGOs lack an enforcement mechanism, most states do comply with IGO decisions. Backsliding is unusual. The mechanisms of IGO governance – conferences, discussions, treaties and statements – are characteristic of modern politics and an appropriate response to a world which lacks a global government to address global problems. IGOs may be less visible than states, and certainly lack the legitimacy of direct election, but these points hardly justify the conclusion that IGOs are politically insignificant.

A more critical reading of IGOs is that they are mere decoration designed to conceal the continued pursuit of national self-interest. The argument is that IGOs do not govern states; rather, dominant states govern through IGOs (Robinson, 1996). The 1991 Gulf War, for instance, was won by American forces protecting their country's oil supply. The United Nations label, secured by President Bush, was a convenient brand under which the USA could continue to pursue its national self-interest. More generally, the developed West put in place the entire postwar international system, including its trading regime, to benefit its own economic interests (Webber, 1997). Firm proof of IGO influence, measured by changes in what members do or by the ability of IGOs to resolve major disputes, is hard to come by. As a rule, strong states only comply with IGO recommendations because they just commit themselves to what they are already doing (Downs, Roche and Baroom, 1996). So what we might call a realist position is that states, especially the leading

---

BOX 4.1

Main abbreviations used in Chapter 4

EU	European Union
FTA	Free trade association
IGO	Intergovernmental organization
NGO	Nongovernmental organization
MNC	Multinational corporation
NAFTA	North American Free Trade Association
NATO	North Atlantic Treaty Organization
UN	United Nations
WTO	World Trade Organization

---

ones, remain dominant, only agreeing in IGOs to what is in their national interest. IGOs bend to the will of their most powerful members; at most they are arenas through which states influence each other, not powerful actors in their own right.

A compromise might be this. While realists are surely correct to suggest that strong states retain most of their traditional autonomy, it is also the case that IGOs have several advantages for all states. IGOs provide information and advice. They are useful for endorsing unpopular policies, providing national governments with both a conscience and a scapegoat: 'of course, we don't want to close your steel mill but the European Union insists on it'. In addition, membership of universal organizations, especially the UN, confirms to all and sundry (including domestic opponents) that national rulers have acquired statehood and sovereignty. Joining the UN reduces vulnerability to external threats since the UN Charter expresses the principle of non-interference in domestic affairs. Thus UN membership is both a reflection and a tactic of political consolidation. In all these ways, IGOs help states. Further, IGOs can lead states to appreciate the extent of their common interests and reduce suspicion between them through achieving concrete results beneficial to all. IGOs prosper because they are functionally useful: everyone gains from a world telephone network and from safer nuclear power plants (Mitrany, 1965; Jacobson, 1985). In particular, IGOs are necessary for addressing complex issues which cannot be solved by single states using traditional military means: 'you can't shoot the ozone hole'. Thus, the point is not whether IGOs possess *power over* states but is, rather, that an effective IGO enhances its members' collective *power to* achieve shared goals.

Given that IGOs affect states to some degree, the next question is: in what ways? How does the network of IGOs alter governance within states? At the very least, belonging to several hundred IGOs – as most West European states do – complicates the task of governance (Table 4.1). States must arrange to pay their subscriptions, attend meetings, identify their national interests, consult with interest groups back home, initiate some proposals, respond to others and implement agreements. They must build coalitions behind their own proposals and against those which threaten their own objectives. These activities dilute the distinction between domestic and foreign policy. As Dehousse (1997, p. 40) writes, 'the time when "foreign policy" concerned only foreign ministries has gone for good. Most ministries now attempt to conduct an external policy of their own.' An international dimension is present in many, perhaps most, of their activities.

So IGOs increase fragmentation within national governments. In part this is because a club-like spirit often develops among ministers in 'their' IGO. For

example, finance ministers – never popular at home – are among friends at bodies such as the International Monetary Fund. Back home, ministers stoutly defend the interest of their IGOs against attacks from other ministers (Bayne, 1997). Thus IGOs splinter the always fragile unity of national executives. Andeweg (1997, p.77) develops this point in discussing the impact of the EU on its members:

> European integration contributes to the fragmentation of national governments. Dutch Ministers of Agriculture, for example, have been eager to transfer powers from The Hague to Brussels. After all, in the European Council for Ministers, they meet only other Ministers of Agriculture, who are all convinced of the importance and needs of that particular sector, whereas in their national cabinets they confront ministers with other portfolios and considerably more scepticism.

Especially in the European Union, many issues are settled at sectoral level – such as agriculture, finance or transport – leading some authors to question whether it is still sensible to think in terms of the position of 'a national government' at all. In a few cases, different ministries of the same government have been known to advocate contradictory positions in EU negotiations!

Given that IGOs tends to fragment national political systems, we must ask which governing institutions gain, and which lose, from interdependence (Box 4.2). Among the winners are the executive and the bureaucracy. These bodies provide the representatives who attend IGO meetings and conduct negotiations and they therefore occupy pole position. Protective interest groups also benefit, since they provide their government with the expertise it needs to formulate a sensible negotiating position on specialist matters. So although IGOs lead to a more fragmented executive and bureaucracy, they also enhance the overall position of these core institutions against other bodies. More surprisingly, perhaps, the judiciary is also growing in significance as a result of IGO activity. IGOs contribute to the more judicial character of domestic politics partly because national judges often incorporate international agreements into their own decision-making and partly because some IGOs themselves adopt a

---

Table 4.1 Countries with most memberships of intergovernmental organizations

Country	Memberships
France	441
United Kingdom	396
Germany	392
Netherlands	375
Denmark	373

Note: Countries with fewest memberships are those whose sovereignty is in dispute (for example Taiwan), very small countries (for example Liechtenstein) or impoverished developing countries devastated by internal conflict (for example Mozambique).

Source: adapted from Shanks, Jackobson and Kaplan (1996); data from 1992.

BOX 4.2

The impact of IGOs on national politics: some winners and losers

Winners	Losers
Executive	Legislature
Bureaucracy	Parties
Judiciary	
Protective interest groups	

---

highly judicial style, issuing judgments on the basis of reviewing cases.

So much for winners; what of losers? The biggest domestic loser from international integration is probably the legislature, which may only learn of an international agreement after the government has signed up. In some countries, Australia for one, international treaties are an executive preserve. Thus, the more treaties a government signs, the more it can bypass the assembly. Parliaments are of course aware of their second-class position in international affairs and many have set up specialized committees of scrutiny in an attempt to cover lost ground. In Europe, for instance, the parliaments of all EU member states have now established European Affairs committees, even though these bodies inevitably tend to be reactive. Political parties, too, seem to have fallen behind. Like assemblies, their natural habitat appears to be the state, not the international conference. Party groupings have developed in the EU but these are loose groupings which lack the cohesion and drive of national parties.

As unofficial bodies, NGOs generally exert less influence over national governments than do intergovernmental organizations. However we cannot ignore NGO impact on national governments particularly in developing countries where state authority is collapsing. This particular influence arises from the position some NGOs have achieved as executors of IGO, especially United Nations, policy. By the mid-1990s, over 10 per cent of all public development aid was distributed through NGOs, compared to less than 1 per cent in 1970 (Weiss and Gordenker, 1996). About 10 super-NGOs, including CARE, Save the Children and Oxfam, dominate

the distribution of aid in complex emergencies. In acting as UN subcontractors, NGOs in some respects become substitute governments. For instance, NGOs coordinated primary education in northern Sri Lanka after civil war started there in 1987. In other cases the international community sets up NGOs to perform specific tasks within countries. De-mining in Afghanistan is an example. As a channel for distributing aid and implementing associated policy, NGOs possess clear attractions to outside donors. They are more efficient and less corrupt than many domestic governments, especially administrations whose failure contributed to the crisis in the first place. They are also more sensitive to local conditions than are multilateral military forces. All this gives NGOs considerable political clout in the least developed countries on which aid is concentrated. As Mortimer (1997, p. 18) notes, such engagements

> often leave NGOs to take decisions with grave political or even military implications, which involve taking sides in a local struggle. The decision in 1994 to provide food and water to refugee camps on the Rwanda–Zaire border, controlled by the perpetrators of Rwandan genocide, is a clear example.

The role of NGOs as substitute states is one factor lying behind Fernando and Heston's assertion (1997, p. 8) that 'NGO activity presents the most serious challenge to the imperatives of statehood in the realms of territorial integrity, security, autonomy and revenue'. If such a claim can be made about NGOs, it certainly also applies to IGOs, which have complicated the task of governance within states and to an extent altered the distribution of influence within them.

Regional organizations and the state

Regional bodies are a specific form of IGO in which neighbouring countries join together for common purposes, most often to increase trade. Like other IGOs, their members are governments but their organizational development is highly variable, ranging from the elaborate architecture of the EU to simple free trade agreements. Regional organizations merit special attention because they have grown greatly in number and significance, especially since the end of the Cold War. Once countries found they could no longer shelter under the skirts of a superpower, they turned to their neighbours to find a means of responding to the new pressures of a world economy in which international trade played a growing part. As Gamble and Payne (1996a, p.249) write,

> the turn to regionalism at the end of the 1980s coincided with the breakdown of the oldest regionalism in the global political economy, the division between the capitalist and the socialist worlds which developed after the Russian Revolution.

The cornerstone of regional integration is established states that are capable of making and implementing agreements with other countries. As Hurrell (1995) notes,

> It is no coincidence that the most elaborate examples of regionalism have occurred in regions where state structures remain relatively strong and

where the legitimacy of both frontiers and regimes is not widely called into question.

The European Union is a good example: strong states have come together, pooling some sovereignty, to create a regional body with unique powers. By contrast, when a country faces severe internal tensions, it is unlikely to be able to build regional alignments. For example, the postsoviet republics which formed the Commonwealth of Independent States in 1991 were so preoccupied with domestic difficulties that they had little spare capacity to develop their association. So, as with IGOs, we can treat regional organizations as (a) the displacement of state power on to the international arena, (b) international bodies with the potential to affect decision-making among their member states, or (c) both, as in the case of the EU.

One specific problem which regional developments pose for national governments is managing the domestic political implications of creating the new zone. The political set-up costs can be considerable. Establishing a free trade area may offer economic gains to a member country as a whole but the losers within each state will still complain and the general gains from increased trade are less visible

---

BOX 4.3
50 years of the European Union

1951 Treaty of Paris signed by France, West Germany, Italy, Belgium, the Netherlands and Luxembourg. This set up the European Coal and Steel Commission (ECSC) which included a supranational High Authority.

1957 The ECSC members sign the Treaty of Rome, establishing the European Economic Community (EEC) and Euratom.

1965 The Merger Treaty combines the ECSC, EEC and Euratom.

1973 Britain, Denmark and Ireland join the EEC.

1979 The European Monetary System (EMS) is agreed, linking currencies to the European Currency Unit (ECU). First direct Europe-wide elections to the European Parliament held.

1981 Greece joins the EEC.

1986 Spain and Portugal join the EEC. Signing of the Single European Act, to streamline decision-making and set up a single market by 1992.

1992 Treaty of Maastricht launches provisions for economic and monetary union (EMU) and replaces the EEC with the European Union from 1993.

1994 Austria, Finland and Sweden join the EU.

1997 Treaty of Amsterdam agrees to extend the Union's role in justice and home affairs, to increase the authority of the European Parliament and to address the problem of unemployment.

1999 Launch of European Monetary Union, irrevocably linking 11 (now 12) national currencies to the euro. The euro is launched as a virtual currency.

2000 Treaty of Nice agrees (subject to ratification) on institutional reforms to prepare for enlargement. These modifications include a reallocation of member states' voting power and a modest reduction in the range of issues requiring unanimous agreement.

2002 National currencies are withdrawn within the eurozone.

Note: Nomenclature of the 'European Union' has varied over time, reflecting institutional and constitutional developments. For a map, see p. 154.

than the damage caused to specific jobs, corporations and industries. Further, a free trade zone in itself is unlikely to inspire groups within a country to make sacrifices for some abstract national 'efficiency gain'. As an American Secretary of Commerce put it, 'people see only lay-offs, not pay-offs'. Of course, one way to solve this problem is by creating a sense of identity with the larger region. For instance, the European Union has made strenuous efforts to develop a European identity, paralleling the efforts of early nation-builders to create loyalties to new states. Yet so far regions lack the emotional pulling-power of established nations.

The case of the North American Free Trade Association (NAFTA) illustrates these problems. NAFTA is a remarkable attempt to eliminate, over 15 years, trade tariffs between two developed states, the USA and Canada, and a developing economy, Mexico. NAFTA's combined market of 380 million people gives the association global significance. As with the EU, both establishing and maintaining NAFTA caused domestic political difficulties, particularly in the USA. In negotiating the compact, the American administration faced opposition from domestic producers and unions which feared that free trade with Mexico would cause a migration of jobs to low-cost assembly sites (the *maquiladora* industries) on the Mexican side of the border. In a famous phrase, the independent politician Ross Perot referred to the 'great sucking sound' of jobs being pulled down to Mexico. The intensity of this debate within America illustrates the inherent problem of selling free trade areas to doubtful populations in democracies.

Similar problems have affected the European Union even though the EU is undoubtedly the most developed regional organizations in the world today. Although the EU has acquired at least a partially federal character, pooling some of the sovereignty of its member states, the journey towards integration has proved difficult, especially as public opinion in many countries has turned more instrumental (Box 4.3). The effort to establish a common currency is one illustration of the problems which EU initiatives cause within member states. The Maastricht Treaty of 1991 committed members (except Britain and Denmark) to establish a common European currency by 1999. To achieve this, member states had to ensure that their economies 'converged'. In

practice, this meant each government had to reduce its budget deficit to a maximum of 3 per cent of gross domestic product. However, deficit reduction caused considerable domestic opposition in many European states. For instance, when President Chirac called a general election in France in 1997, he described it as a referendum on the government's attempts to cut back the budget deficit in order to meet the Maastricht criteria. His government lost. Although the common currency project succeeded, further deepening of political integration within Europe remains in doubt, especially with the continuing pressures to extend membership to candidate countries to the East (e.g. Poland) and the North (e.g. Estonia). The EU will probably continue as a unique hybrid, combining elements of a genuine federation with a flexible intergovernmental alliance.

Definition

The **democratic deficit** is a phrase widely used in discussions of the European Union. Implicitly, the term denotes the failure of the EU to develop the legitimacy which is accorded to established democracies. Laffan (1999) notes five aspects to the deficit: (1) the EU's founding treaties have not been directly ratified by its citizens, (2) citizens are unclear how the EU reaches its decisions, (3) detailed policy-making is led by technicians rather than politicians, (4) citizens feel remote from the EU and (5) the EU lacks European-wide institutions such as media and political parties that animate national political debate. Yet for all the debate about the deficit, the EU has gone further than any IGO in developing democratic mechanisms (Dahl, 1999).

Excluding the European Union, and a few South American states such as El Salvador which have adopted the American dollar as their own currency, the domestic implications of regional blocs have so far been limited. Impact is restricted because the characteristic form of regional integration is the free trade area. Through this device, states attempt to gain the economic advantages of larger and more open markets without sacrificing their political sovereignty. Thus modern regions tend to be looser arrangements than classic federations, which involved the participating units (such as the American states) pooling their sovereignty in a new central authority. While the European Union has inspired regional moves elsewhere, these other regions have not so far sought to replicate the EU's unique semi-federal status (Box 4.4). Indeed, Alesina, Spolaore and Wacziarg (1997) suggest that once a free market is secured, there is no reason for further moves toward political integration. Regional free trade agreements may need only the most minimal supporting organization.

Like other IGOs, most regional organizations lack the legitimacy that only democratic election can provide; even more than the EU, they suffer a 'democratic deficit'. Thus the elaborate architecture of the European Union may prove to be a false model for the rest of the world. Certainly, it seems unlikely that the turn to economic regions at the end of the twentieth century will result in political federations of the type created a century or two earlier. But even free trade areas may deepen the predominant political form of its leading member. Participation in NAFTA has surely contributed to democratization in Mexico just as the prospect of joining the EU encourages candidate countries to pass the political tests imposed by the Union. Economic motives yield political effects.

Humanitarian intervention and the state

In placing the contemporary state in a global context, human intervention is a central issue.

BOX 4.4
Examples of regional organizations

Grouping	Abbreviated title	Date established	Purpose	Members
Nordic Council	–	1952	To promote regional economic, cultural and environmental cooperation	Denmark, Finland, Iceland, Norway, Sweden
Benelux Economic Union	–	1958	To develop closer economic cooperation and integration	Belgium, Luxembourg, The Netherlands
European Union	EU	1958*	Wide-ranging cooperation and integration	15 members
Association of Southeast Asian Nations	ASEAN	1967	To provide economic, social, and cultural cooperation among non-communist countries	Brunei, Indonesia, Malaysia, Philippines, Singapore, Thailand and now Vietnam
Asia–Pacific Economic Co-operation	APEC	1989	To promote trade and investment in the Pacific Basin	19 member states from the Asia Pacific including Australia, Canada; China, Japan, Mexico, New Zealand, South Korea, Taiwan and the United States
Commonwealth of Independent States	CIS	1991	To coordinate relations among members and to provide a mechanism for the orderly dissolution of the USSR	12 former members of the USSR
Southern Cone Common Market	Mercosur	1991	To increase regional economic cooperation	Argentina, Brazil, Paraguay, Uruguay and two associates, Chile and Bolivia
North American Free Trade Association	NAFTA	1994	To create a free trade area between its members	Canada, USA, Mexico

* Originally established by the Treaty of Rome as the European Economic Community.

When the international community forcibly interferes in a state's domestic affairs, national sovereignty is clearly violated. Just as the dissolution of the Cold War encouraged the emergence of regional coalitions, so too did it free an emerging international community to authorize several such interventions, usually on humanitarian grounds. Examples include Iraq (to protect the Kurds), Rwanda (to deter genocide) and Somalia (to distribute emergency aid). Whatever the success or future of these operations, they must cause us to question the continuing vitality of national sovereignty. Has the autonomy of a state now become conditional on its good behaviour, as judged by an emerging international community? Are states now prisoners of global norms? (Box 4.5).

The development of support for humanitarian intervention is reflected in changing conceptions of the United Nations. The UN's orginal purpose, as set out in its Charter (1945), is

> to maintain international peace and security, and to that end: to take effective collective measures for the prevention and removal of threats to the peace.

The Charter's focus is clearly on conflicts between states, not within them. The principle of non-intervention was explicitly enshrined in the Charter, partly to ease American entry into the UN. And for most of its history the focus of UN activity has been on keeping the peace in (or after) disputes between countries. Jackson (1989, p. 17) even likens the state system, as reflected in the UN's Charter, to a traditional club which assumes 'members are honourable fellows. Provided members conform to club rules in their outward conduct, their private lives are their own. Even skeletons in closets are their own affair.'

Yet despite the limits of its charter the UN has become more involved in domestic disputes. The turning-point came with Security Council authorization for a US-led military expedition to expel Iraq from Kuwait in the Gulf War (1991). Of course, this was a traditional international dispute but it did seem to open the prospect of a role for the UN in creating a new world order. The pace of UN operations quickened. By 1995, 60 000 blue helmets were deployed in 16 operations around the world. And of 11 UN operations set up between 1992 and

---

BOX 4.5
Where the national meets the international: definitions

Absolute sovereignty
The notion that each state has unqualified jurisdiction over its territory and people.

Conditional sovereignty
A state's sovereignty is made subject to its observing principles such as protecting the rights of its people. To embrace conditional sovereignty is to reject the idea that the state is the final source of authority within its borders.

Humanitarian intervention
Intervention in another country's domestic affairs (whether invited or not) with the aim of reducing immediate human suffering

International community
A fashionable term referring to an embryonic transnational society which is said to be emerging in the era of global interdependence, especially since the end of the Cold War.

1995, nine were in response to internal civil conflicts. The motive was humanitarian intervention usually following the failure of states amid civil war and ethnic violence (Box 4.5). Again, we see how the impact of external forces is focused on the weakest states in the developing world; powerful states would neither require nor countenance foreign interference.

For all its theoretical significance, humanitarian intervention has a poor record in practice. One problem is that the same Western public which demands intervention in response to images of suffering also wants its own forces withdrawn as soon as the project turns messy. In addition, the developing world often views UN intervention as recolonization: 'whose disaster is it anyway?' Further, the UN is unsuited to running, as opposed to legitimizing, military operations. It is an underfunded, decentralized and generally ineffective body. As a result, the willingness of the international community to consider intervention in the affairs of states is not matched by the means to give effect to its purpose. For this reason, initial optimism about building a new world order has given way to realism, even cynicism. For example, by presidential direc-

HUMANITARIAN INTERVENTION BY THE INTERNATIONAL COMMUNITY

Is the international community justified in forcibly interfering in the domestic affairs of states? The entire history of the state system is based on non-intervention, a tradition that was reinforced during the Cold War by the division of much of the world into two opposed armed camps. But the collapse of communism has opened up new possibilities for intervention. So is the international community now justified in intervening in another state's affairs – by force if necessary – to reduce acute human suffering?

The case for

All governments should reduce human suffering when they are able to do so. Whether that suffering occurs inside or beyond a state's boundaries is irrelevant; the value of a human life is the same everywhere. This view is anything but new: in the seventeenth century, the Dutch jurist Hugo Grotius (1583–1645) had argued that sovereignty was not the highest law. Hoffman (1995, p. 35) is among those who has recently reinforced this opinion: 'the state that claims sovereignty deserves respect only as long as it protects the basic rights of its citizens. When it violates them, the state's claim to sovereignty falls.' Oxfam adopts a similar position: 'we do not accept that the principle of sovereignty should block the protection of basic rights, including the right to emergency relief and safety' (Harriss, 1995, p. 3). Sovereignty, it is argued, does not entitle a state to decline humanitarian aid, since the result is added suffering for the people who are the tangible expression of that state. Also, when the state has failed, as several have done in Africa, arguably there is no sovereignty left to violate.

The case against

By itself, ethics makes poor politics. At issue is not the principle of intervention but its likelihood of success. There is simply no world force capable of providing effective humanitarian intervention. Instead, an international consensus has to be built behind intervention on each occasion and such agreements soon disintegrate when problems arise in the field. Somalia is an example (Mayall, 1996, p. 9). When television images of starvation generated a public demand for the international community to 'do something', the UN authorized military intervention to support the distribution of aid. The project was a disaster. An inadequate number of troops was despatched in 1992 after a long delay to carry out an unfamiliar humanitarian mission with insufficient local knowledge in a hostile situation. After a local warlord killed 20 Pakistani soldiers serving with the UN, and a captured American pilot was paraded in public, the United States decided to 'bring the boys back home'. The entire UN mission folded in 1995. The lesson of Somalia is clear: without improved implementation, humanitarian intervention remains an idea better-suited to the seminar room than to the real world.

Assessment

If the principle of intervention is accepted, the next – and more difficult – steps will be practical. Will powerful states ever permit the emergence of a global military force? Should intervention be subcontracted to regional bodies, as with NATO's air-strikes into Bosnia to enforce the 1995 Dayton Peace Agreement? In addition, the international community will need to work out when, and not just whether, intervention is justified. For example, van Eijk (1997) suggests any humanitarian intervention must pass seven specific tests. These are: (1) human rights must be threatened, (2) no alternative solution is available, (3) intervention must receive wide international support, (4) intervention must be justified to the UN in advance, (5) the extent of intervention must be minimized, (6) intervention must be able to make a constructive contribution and (7) intervention must last no longer than is required. Establishing that a potential intervention passes all these tests is itself a time-consuming process.

Further reading: Held (1995), Hoffman (1995), van Eijk (1997).

tive, American involvement in UN operations is now restricted to short-term operations where a clear US interest is at stake.

Yet despite the practical difficulties experienced by UN missions, something *has* changed. The more interventions there are, successful or not, the less convincing the traditional idea of national sovereignty becomes. Slowly the notion of international society, of a community of states sharing the values of democracy and human rights, gains strength. Even Boutros Boutros-Ghali was emboldened to say, when Secretary General of the United Nations, that 'the time of absolute exclusive sovereignty has passed; its theory was never matched by reality' (United Nations, 1992). Absolute sovereignty may eventually be replaced by conditional sovereignty: that is, by the idea that a state's membership of the world system depends on good behaviour towards its own citizens.

A further step towards sidestepping state sovereignty has been taken by setting up international courts to try individuals directly for their alleged crimes, even if these were committed in the name of the state. These tribunals are an additional tangible expression of declining commitment to state sovereignty. Proposals for a permanent International Criminal Court to deal with future cases of genocide, war crimes and crimes against humanity will, if adopted, constitute a further change. Of course, the Nuremberg trials after the Second World War had established that individuals are responsible for their own acts in war. That view itself departed from the notion of treating states as the only subjects of international law. However, in the 1990s, the International Court of Justice set up new tribunals, the first since Nuremberg, to try people from Rwanda and former Yugoslavia suspected of genocide and other war crimes. One innovation of these new tribunals is that they indicted suspects who were not already in custody. However bringing these suspects to justice proved politically difficult. International snatch squads are not yet accepted and their use can stimulate a damaging reaction in the suspect's own community. Yet failing to capture indicted suspects, such as Radovan Karadzic in Serbian Bosnia, makes the international community appear weak. So far, the efforts made are typical of the uncertain and often ineffective way in which the international community has intervened in national

politics. This is one reason why even though non-intervention may be declining as a *principle*, it will continue to dominate *practice*.

The global economy and the state

The final aspect of the global context we must examine for its impact on states is the global economy. The 'global economy' is a convenient phrase to describe the growing trend for economic activity to operate between countries (e.g. international trade) and even beyond them (e.g. currency trading). Particularly since 1945, international trade has grown apace while production and especially finance have broken free of national restraints, providing a prime example of the much-touted idea of globilization (Box 4.6). Today, money washes round the world in far greater quantities than is needed to support trade. Foreign direct investment (FDI) – directly-owned investment by firms outside their home country – has also expanded dramatically and now accounts for about a fifth of the world's stock of investment (Williams, 1997). IGOs such as the International Monetary Fund and the World Trade Organization are important players in seeking to regulate global economic trends (Box 4.7). So how

---

BOX 4.6
What is globalization?

Waters (1996, p.3) defines globalization as 'a process in which the constraints of geography on social and cultural arrangements recede and in which people become increasingly aware that they are receding'. This has two implications. The first is a decline in the significance of territory in human affairs or, to put the point more dramatically, the annhiliation of space. The second is that the concept of globalization is in itself evidence of a trend. As Waters comments, '"globalization" can hardly be said to have begun before people realised the earth was a globe'.

Although the world has become more integrated since 1945, it would be wrong to suppose that globalization is entirely novel. As Krasner (1994, p. 13) comments, 'Globalization is not new ... challenges to the authority of the state are not new ... Transnational flows are not new.' Further, since globalization is a continuing process, we should not imply that we inhabit a world which is fully global.

BOX 4.7
Intergovernmental organizations and the world economy

IGO	Full title	Function
IMF	International Monetary Fund	To promote international monetary stability and cooperation
IBRD	International Bank for Reconstruction and Development ('World Bank')	To promote economic recovery and development
WTO	World Trade Organization	To supervise and promote international trade

Note: The WTO was founded in 1995 to replace GATT (General Agreement on Tariffs and Trade) which, like the IMF and the World Bank, had been established at Bretton Woods (Jackson, 1998).

does an increasingly interdependent global economy affect politics within national boundaries? As with other aspects of the global environment, impact varies between the rich and poor states. The global economy presents states in the developed world with a reasonably favourable balance of opportunities and threats. But the least developed countries remain in a dependent, postcolonial position, surviving by exporting basic foodstuffs or minerals in competition with other equally poor states. We will therefore assessing the global economy's impact on the developed and developing worlds separately, beginning with the affluent established democracies.

Perhaps the main influence of today's open trading world on established democracies has been to modify their policy agendas. For thirty years after the Second World War, the major domestic concern was extending the scope and levels of welfare provision, using the resources provided by the postwar economic boom. From the 1980s, however, rulers in many established democracies placed greater emphasis on economic competitiveness (Cerny, 1990). International competition remorselessly exposes economic weaknesses that could be covered up in an era of national markets and state-owned monopolies. But in a process of competitive deregulation, public ownership has now been reduced by privatization, budget deficits have been cut back, corporate and individual tax rates have been reduced and opaque share trading and corporate reporting requirements have been modified in line with international (in practice, mainly American) standards (for more on this changing agenda, see Chapter 17).

Two key channels through which external

economic forces exert influence in established democracies are multinational corporations (MNCs) and global financial flows. Consider MNCs. The balance between MNCs and governments raises, in modern form, the age-old question of the relationship between economic and political power. In its current form, the logic governing the relationship is simple: capital is mobile, labour less so and states not at all. Companies can move their factories between countries, but states, by definition, are fixed in space. As a result, countries (and regions within them) must compete to provide an attractive home for foreign direct investment. Providing an environment which is at least as business-friendly as that provided by competitor states is clearly a major challenge for governments, producing potential for competitive deregulation and tax competition. Consider the shopping list of a typical MNC: it will look for low costs and taxes, the ability to take profits out of the country, weak or pliable labour unions, light and predictable regulation, a workforce with relevant skills, a stable political and business environment and efficient transport and communication. If a government fails to supply sufficient items from this shopping list, it risks losing jobs and access to fresh technology. But the issue is not just about attracting new investment: MNCs can also obtain government money just by hinting that they might move existing plants elsewhere. When Ford threatened to stop making Jaguar cars exclusively in the UK, the British government found enough money to prevent the company from starting a production line in its American factories.

However, unlike the vulnerable states of the developing world, the relationship between the governments of established democracies and MNCs is far from one-sided. MNCs must sell their products in the affluent and sophisticated markets of the developed world. Aware of their attractions, host governments can strike a deal. For instance, local MNC production may be subject to a requirement that local factories of the MNC buy a certain share of their resources from suppliers in the host country. And if the labour market is already tight, governments may only be interested in MNCs which can raise the quality of employment. In addition, states can join together in an alliance such as the European Union to create a larger market which gives the member states more bargaining power with MNCs than they would possess separately. As with many political relationships, each side needs the other, with the balance varying over time.

International financial flows are the second major way in which markets constrain policy-making in the established democracies. Governments fund their debt by borrowing, often from overseas. The less confidence financial markets possess in a country's government or economy, the higher the rate of interest they will demand for lending to that country. For example, the German government could traditionally borrow money at lower cost than the British government, reflecting greater confidence in the deutschmark than in the pound. One advantage of the single European currency for weak member economies is that they can, in effect, shelter behind the deutschmark. In similar fashion, the global financial system also influences currency values. The weight of money in the financial market is far greater than that in the vaults of central banks. If the market believes that a currency is overvalued, funds will move out of that currency, causing a decline in its value. The outcome may be an unwanted devaluation for those governments that seek to maintain a fixed exchange rate. Sweden is a classic example. In 1992, international markets temporarily lost confidence in the Swedish economy, due to a large and growing budget deficit. Desperately trying to stave off a devaluation, the government dramatically increased short-term interest rates, made radical cuts in its budget, increased value added tax and cancelled two days' paid national holiday. The measures failed to restore international confidence and the krona was allowed

to float. There can be little doubt that the world financial markets have encouraged fiscal discipline within states, encouraging governments to reduce budget deficits and to limit the size of pre-election give-aways. For better or for worse, good housekeepers are rewarded while spendthrifts are punished.

A final effect of economic globalization on established democracies is to increase economic inequality within their borders. Unskilled workers in developed countries face downward pressure on incomes from the low-wage economies of the developing world. Similarly, firms are willing to pay more to recruit and retain managers who can increase corporate profitability. So the developed world has experienced a pattern long familiar in poorer countries: even as average incomes increase, so does the inequality of its distribution. In the United States, the income of the richest fifth of the population increased by 34 per cent between 1977 and 1988. By contrast, the poorest fifth faced a 10 per cent reduction. In Britain, economic inequality in 1997 was greater than at any time since 1887.

Inequality has increased at the level of the region as well as the individual. Core regions possess the location and skills needed to prosper from increases in trade; peripheral regions find themselves trapped in a cycle of decline. For Thomas (1997), 'it is no longer enough to think only in terms of rich and poor states; we need to consider groups or classes of rich and poor people which crosscut state boundaries'. Eventually, we may find that the categories 'rich' and 'poor' apply less to countries than to sectors and regions, producing massive new problems of political management for governments increasingly hemmed in by global constraints. In such circumstances, the role of governments in moderating domestic conflict will be as crucial as ever but whether they will still have the means to redress market outcomes remains to be seen.

Most developing countries find themselves in a more exposed position in relation to external economic forces. For better or worse, the impact of the global economy is far greater than for developed states. Partly, this weakness arises from the dependence of many developing countries on a single product or market for their exports. For example, Nigeria's exports consist overwhelmingly of oil; most of Mexico's exports go to the USA. Many commen-

Country profile **THE PEOPLE'S REPUBLIC OF CHINA**

Population: officially estimated by the 2000 census at 1265 m, the largest in the world. Probably even higher as many second children remain unregistered so families can comply with one-child regulations.

Gross domestic product per head: $3800 using international estimates. Although China is only the 129th richest country in income per head, its economy is the second largest in the world after the USA.

Form of government: an authoritarian regime dominated by the Chinese Communist Party (CCP).

Assembly: a large unicameral National People's Congress, now including some representatives from Hong Kong. The Congress extends to some loyal non-party representatives (for example from national minorities) and real debate is increasing. However, the CCP remains dominant.

Executive: The premier formally heads the cabinet, the State Council. Leading state officials (including the premier) also serve on the Politburo (political bureau) of the CCP. The Head of State, President Jiang Zemin, also holds the top position of General Secretary within the party.

Judiciary: judges of the Supreme People's Court are appointed by the National People's Congress. The Supreme People's Procurate is charged with supervising the legal system to prevent abuses of power, a thankless task.

Electoral system: direct elections take place at the lowest levels of organisation (e.g. to county level congresses) but indirect election is usual at higher levels. Members of the National People's Congress are chosen from lower-level congresses, mass organisations, workplaces, universities and so on.

Party system: the CCP is the only significant party. Some minor parties are permitted but only if they do not challenge communist dominance.

In 1978, the CCP embarked on a series of economic reforms that radically transformed the Chinese economy, setting it on course to become the largest in the world some time this century. The old state planning system was gradually dismantled, allowing market forces, previously condemned as a capitalist evil, to assume an important role. As a result of these reforms, China's economy has grown rapidly; in the 1990s at an average of 9 per cent a year. Even when growth slowed at the end of the decade in the wake of the Asian financial crises, it still exceeded the world average. At the start of the new century, China accounted for 12 per cent of gross world production although income per head remained lower even than in Russia.

This remarkable growth has in large part been achieved by integration with the global economy. In the mid-1980s, China abandoned its policy of disengagement. Initially, economic contacts were restricted to four Special Economic Zones, so as to control the influence of overseas corporations. As foreign investment flooded in, generating rapid growth, so the remainder of the country opened to international contacts. Nevertheless, the coastal areas still dominate China's international economic relations, accounting for 80 per cent of all inward investment. China's success in attracting investment in no small part results from low wages and high tax breaks.

As China opened to the outside world, so it sought to limit external access to its own economy in order to protect domestic producers. But in 1999 China signed a deal with the USA which should pave the way for China's entry into the World Trade Organization (WTO), thus opening China's domestic market to overseas companies. While joining the WTO will bring new jobs in some sectors, it will also increase unemployment in the countryside and in China's large remaining state-owned sector. And rising unemployment will exacerbate social tensions. In the countryside, mechanization and the introduction of the profit motive resulted in the loss of six million jobs per year, on average, in the 1990s. Many of the rural unemployed have migrated to the cities in search of work.

Substantial income disparities exist between coastal areas and the interior, and between urban and rural dwellers. There is also considerable resentment at the extent of corruption and the fact that the main beneficiaries of reform appear to be the party-state cadres themselves – many of whom are on the boards of new companies. In 1999, 10 000 political protests were reported to the national government as the losers from the reform process vented their anger. Even such a fast-growing economy has significant social problems – indeed, many of them emerge from growth itself or at least from its uneven distribution. With such a large and diverse society, it makes little sense to talk of how China – all of China – has integrated into the global economy.

Further reading: Lardy (1998), Lieberthal (1995), Manion (2000).

tators argue that through such concentrated trade patterns the economies of the least developed countries are locked into dependence on rich countries. The result is unbalanced development, a pattern that explains why a politician in Venezuela felt able to denounce oil, his country's major natural resource, as 'the devil's excrement'. Dependency theorists argue that what has emerged is not a neutral global economy but rather a new form of economic colonialism in which the developed world shapes the structure of client economics in the developing world. This is not development but rather what Frank (1969) once called 'the development of underdevelopment'.

The IGOs which have emerged to regulate the global economy according to the liberal principle of free trade are particuarly influential in vulnerable developing economies (Box 4.7 on p. 57). The ability of IGOs to grant or withhold loans gives them an oversight role over the least solvent states which amounts to veto power. A crucial test of the skill of the leaders of such countries is their ability to negotiate with these economic IGOs. It is true that middle-income developing countries can increasingly access private capital from overseas, thus bypassing the IGOs. Yet even here, as for the developed states, the IGOs remain important in providing an international seal of approval for a government's economic policies, thus lowering the cost of borrowing from any overseas source, private as well as public.

Consider, by way of example, the impact of the World Trade Organization (WTO). Its function is to provide a way of resolving trade conflicts between member states and to seek further reductions in tariffs and other barriers to trade. In practice, this means that members gain preferential access to each others' markets. With most countries requiring access to lucrative North American and European markets, membership of WTO is highly desirable. But in order to join, as Russia and China want to do, states must meet specific conditions. In essence, the price to governments of entering the global economy is to open their domestic market. Thus the WTO has leverage not just over its 120 members but also over the 70 or so states which have yet to join.

Certainly, the weaker the finances of a developing country, the more leverage international agencies

can exert. IGO impact has been particularly strong in those countries most affected by the 1980s debt crisis. This problem arose when Western banks increased lending to developing countries which then failed to meet repayments. Although some larger states had regained international credit worthiness by the mid-1990s, many of the least developed states remained in massive debt. As late as 1995, the developing world as a whole owed $1.5 trillion; interest payments stood at $232 billion per year. So the least developed states remain unable to bargain about the terms of any further financial aid. Bodies such as the World Bank and the IMF are generally willing to provide additional support but this debt restructuring is conditional on domestic economic reform, often including privatization, lower trade tariffs and more transparency in allocating government contracts. For example, the international community (led by the IMF and Japan) offered a $16 billion loan to the Thai government in 1997. The conditions attached to the loan were extensive and specific, including (1) halving the country's trade deficit, (2) balancing the budget, (3) speeding up privatization, (4) allowing foreign ownership of banks and (5) letting the currency float.

> **Definition**
> **Conditionality** is the practice of attaching strings to aid. Political conditionality might include a requirement to legalize opposition and hold competitive elections. Economic conditionality often takes the form of a specified **structural adjustment programme,** typically involving privatizing state companies, introducing more competition and opening domestic markets to overseas companies.

Governments which build domestic political support by using the economy to reward their supporters find the injunction to reduce their control of the economy striking at the heart of their power. In effect, the international agencies require such countries to restructure their politics as well as their economy. Partly for this reason, Dr Mahathir, Prime Minister of Malaysia, likens the international political economy to 'a jungle of ferocious beasts' and claims that the IMF is willing 'to subvert our economy' in order to prove the validity of its own theories. However, Mahathir's assault on international agencies is largely a political tactic to increase his own domestic support. A few governments, such as Egypt in 1988 and Jordan in 1990, have sought to fight back by abandoning IMF restructuring and the aid linked to it. Politically, these states were unwilling to relinquish control over state-owned enterprises or to offer a larger role to MNCs. Significantly, though, both Egypt and Jordan later returned to domestic restructuring. Rather than fighting the IGOs head-on, a more subtle political strategy is to accept the conditions of the loan but, once the money is in the bank, to disregard those promises involving heavy political costs. As long as the loan is repaid, no one will agonize over the small print, a point of which Thailand's policy-makers were doubtless fully aware when they accepted the 'onerous' conditions of their 1997 loan. Alternatively, countries can simply lie about the extent of their financial reserves in order to secure loans, as Russia did successfully to the IMF in 1996.

Attacks by developing countries on such bodies as the WTO have not gone unsupported by groups in the developed world. To date, the most prominent example of a backlash is the 'battle in Seattle' in 1999, when a WTO conference was marked by violent protests outside the conference hall. Over 5000 anti-globalization protestors marched through the streets and over 500 were arrested as police in riot gear fired tear-gas canisters and plastic bullets. The activists included union members, environmentalists, students and indigenous people. The conference itself ended in acrimony, with many developing countries objecting to what was seen as American attempts to impose its own agenda. It is clear from the Seattle debacle that IGOs such as the WTO suffer from a democratic deficit which limits their legitimacy with the general public. But it is also highly likely that a WTO which streamlines its procedures, shows more sensitivity to developing countries and holds smaller conferences will continue to succeed in promoting trade.

In any case, it is not only IGOs which impose conditionalities on vulnerable countries. Since the end of the Cold War, individual states – including established democracies such as the UK – have subjected bilateral aid to specific conditions. During the Cold War, competition between the American and Soviet superpowers gave developing countries considerable leverage; a promise of cooperation with one superpower was often enough to gain financial support with no questions asked. But the end of the Cold War diminished the strategic value of small states and Africa in particular suffered strategic marginalization. Donor governments can now afford to attach conditions to aid, strings which may take the form of pressure for political change. For example, sanctions may be imposed on countries with poor human rights records (for example, China) or corrupt governments (Kenya). States which have invaded other countries (Iran), which sponsor international terrorism (Syria), which are ruled by undemocratic means (Libya) or which are still under communist control (North Korea, Cuba) find themselves isolated from, or entirely without influence within, the international system. Thus dominant countries can directly affect the political situation confronting national leaders in poorly regarded developing states. The worst cases become pariah states, kept out of the international community altogether.

Key reading

Next step: *Waters (2000) is an accessible introduction to the debate about globalization.*

Kegley and Wittkopf (2000) provide an excellent introduction to world politics. Blake and Walters (2001) is also a good introduction, particularly to development and underdevelopment. On international organizations, Kratochwil and Mansfield (1994) is a useful reader, while Boli and Thomas (1999) examine non-governmental organizations specifically. Mayall (1996) covers the UN's new interventionism. On regionalism, Gamble and Payne (1996b) is a good survey; see also Hettne (1999). Stubbs and Underhill (1999) is a helpful edited collection on international political economy. On globalization, Hirst and Thompson (1996) is a good place to start. Strange (1994) has generated considerable debate on how much power national governments retain in a global world, while Smith, Solinger and Topik (1999) combine theory and case studies in examining the same theme.

The comparative approach

In this chapter, we examine the nature of comparative politics and the main research strategies used in its execution. This exercise is by no means straightforward. The content and boundaries of comparative politics are poorly defined, partly because the 'field' is an ambiguous compound of method, subject area and its own intellectual history. As Evans (1995, p. 2) says, comparative politics has 'a messy centre'. Broadly (and breadth is really the point), the goal of comparative politics is to encompass the major political similarities and differences between countries. The task is to develop some perspective on the mixture of constants and variability which characterizes the world's governments and the political contexts in which they operate. Sometimes an awareness of diversity provides the starting point for a comparative enquiry. As Mackenzie wrote, 'political science has its beginning when an observer notes that another people is not governed as we are and asks the question, "why?"' (Rose, 1991). For instance, the democratic/authoritarian distinction used in this book draws attention to an aspect of variation between countries. In other cases, comparative understanding emerges from considering a thesis about similarities. A brave scholar advances a 'universal' proposition: say, that government is giving way to governance, that class voting is declining or that legislatures are concentrating more on committee work. But whether the initial focus is on differences or similarities, the task of comparative politics is to provide understanding of constants, variations and trends in national government and politics.

Given this definition of comparative *politics*, the comparative *approach* is simply the family of strategies and techniques which advance understanding within the field. Grander definitions are of course available. With justification, the comparative approach can be regarded as the 'master strategy' for drawing inferences about causation in any area of study. After all, experiments and statistical analysis designed to uncover relationships of cause and effect necessarily involve a comparison between observations, whether of individuals, social groups or countries. In other words, all explanatory research is by nature comparative (Holland, 1986). But in politics the reverse does not apply; in reality, only a small portion of comparative political research focuses on explanation. Objectives are often more modest if still challenging: to describe and to comprehend but not necessarily to explain. To identify trends in judicial activism, electoral systems or political participation is itself a worthwhile exercise; the task of encompassing cross-national similarities and differences is demanding enough without imprisoning ourselves in a straitjacket called explanation. In any case, identifying what is happening is a precondition of explaining why it is occurring. King, Keohane and Verba (1994, p. 44) are surely right in saying that 'good description is better than bad explanation'.

We proceed in this chapter from the general to the specific. We begin by assessing the major levels of analysis in comparative politics – institutions, states and societies – before turning to the overall advantages and difficulties of comparison. We then examine the major techniques used in the field: case studies, focused comparisons and statistical analysis.

Comparing institutions, societies and states

When we engage in comparative politics, what is it that we compare? In one sense, the answer is obvious: comparative politics adopts the country as its core unit. But although comparisons across countries are indeed the focus of this book, only a few chapters (such as those discussing democracy and authoritarian rule) take entire national governments as their level of analysis. Within a focus on countries, we face a choice between three different levels of analysis: the institutions of government, the social context of politics or the state as a whole (Box 5.1). Nor are decisions about the appropriate emphasis merely technical; in fact, the recent history of comparative politics is a story of shifts in the favoured level. So as we examine each of these three traditions of enquiry, we will also be covering the intellectual development of the subject.

Comparing institutions

Since government is the heart of the body politic, studying governing institutions will always be a central activity of political science. As Rhodes (1995, p. 43) writes,

If there is any subject matter at all that political scientists can claim exclusively for their own, a subject matter that does not require acquisition of the analytical tools of sister fields and that sustains their claim to autonomous existence, it is of course, formal political structures.

But how exactly should an 'institution' be understood? The term is often left undefined but its core reference is to the major organizations of national government, particularly those defined in the constitution. The legislature, executive and judiciary are the classic trio. But the use of the term often extends outward in two directions. The first extension is to other governing organizations which may have a less secure constitutional basis, such as the bureaucracy and local government. And the second extension is to other important political organizations which are not formally part of the government, notably political parties. However, as we move away from the heartland of constitutionally mandated structures, so the term 'organization' tends to supplant the word 'institution'. Implicitly, therefore, an emphasis on institutions in political analysis connects with the origins of the subject in constitutional studies and asserts the unique character of those organizations charged with the task of governance.

Definition

An **institution** is a well-established body, often with public status, whose members interact on the basis of the specific roles they perform within the organization. In the study of politics, the core meaning of an institution is an organ of government mandated by the constitution. **Institutional analysis** presumes that organizations shape the behaviour of their members while **institutionalization** is the process by which organizations acquire the capacity to do so. Means by which institutions influence their members include creating clearly defined roles (that is, expectations), standard operating procedures, a shared culture and rules governing conduct.

BOX 5.1
Levels of analysis in comparative politics

Level	Forms	Example
Institution-centred	The organizations of government and the relationships between them	The balance between president and congress in the USA
Society-centred	How social factors influence individual behaviour in politics	Voting behaviour
State-centred	The priorities of the state and their impact on society	Building the welfare state; regulating for economic competitiveness

The starting-point of institutional analysis is that roles matter more than the people who occupy them. It is this assumption that enables us to discuss presidencies rather than presidents, legislatures rather than legislators and the judiciary rather than judges. Put differently, the capacity of institutions to shape the behaviour of their members means that politics, just like other social sciences, is more than a branch of psychology. Of course, institutions are impossible without people; indeed, organizations are little more – but no less – than accepted rules for interaction between their members. Even so, institutions can usefully be conceived as possessing a history, culture and memory of their own, sometimes embodying founding values and traditions but more often simply growing 'like coral reefs' through 'slow accretion' (Sait, 1938). The value of institutions in political affairs is that their long-term commitments are more reliable than are those of any single employee, thus building up trust. For instance, giving a central bank the duty of curbing inflation will be more credible in financial markets than assigning the task to an elected politician whose time horizon does not extend beyond the next election (Majone, 1996, p.43). For such reasons, institutions are sometimes incorporated within law as possessing their own rights and duties.

An institutional approach implies a certain approach to political analysis. As members of institutions, people acquire interests such as defending the organization against predators and ensuring their own personal progress within the structure. Politics is not just a conflict between social forces or political ideologies; rather, it is as much about people defending the interests of the organization they work for. In short: institutions define interests. As March and Olsen (1984, p. 738) conclude in their influential restatement of the institutional approach,

> The bureaucratic agency, the legislative committee and the appellate court are arenas for contending social forces but they are also collections of standard operating procedures and structures that define and defend interests. They are political actors in their own right.

Further, institutions bring forth activity which takes place simply because it is expected, not because it has any deeper political motive. When a legislative committee holds hearings on a topic, it may be more concerned to be seen to be doing its job than to probe the topic itself. So, much political action should be understood by reference to its significance within the organization, an objective that is separate from its ostensible purpose. Similarly, when a president visits an area devastated by floods, he is not necessarily seeking to direct relief operations or to achieve any purpose other than to be seen to be performing his duty of showing concern. The activity in itself achieves the goal of meeting expectations arising from the actor's position within the institution (Peters, 1999).

Comparing societies

In the 1960s and 1970s the focus of comparative politics moved away from the institutional level. Decolonization spawned many new nations in the postwar era where the formal institutions of government proved fragile. What matters the judiciary if the president simply dismisses judges who make unpalatable judgments? Nor were the institutions of government of particular importance in communist states where the ruling party was the real wielder of power; in practice, 'governing' institutions were the party's servants. Studying institutions seemed to have become a somewhat introverted concern of scholars interested in established democracies only. The failure of newly designed democratic institutions to take root in former colonies led naturally to a concern with the social foundations of democracy. Why did democracy consolidate in the West but not, say, in Africa?

In addition, a more technical factor contributed to a declining interest in institutions. The Second World War had stimulated new developments in social science techniques (e.g. attitude surveys) which younger scholars were keen to apply to politics. The 'old-fashioned' analysis of constitutions and government institutions did not lend itself to statistical treatment, in contrast to sample surveys of political attitudes and behaviour in the wider society. So the study of institutions fell out of favour as researchers used the comparative method in a search for generalizations about the political attitudes and behaviour of individuals.

In this shift to a more society-centred approach, Easton's systems model of the political system

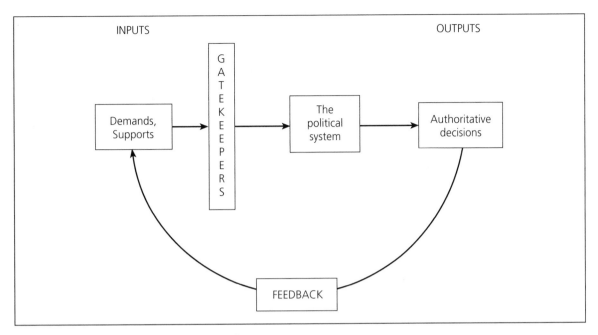

Figure 5.1 Easton's model of the political system

proved highly influential (1965a and b). Although few political scientists explicitly use Easton's framework today, his work still forms part of the vocabulary of political analysis. 'The political system' has become a widely used phrase among political scientists. Easton conceived the essence of politics as lying in its relationship with the wider society (Figure 5.1). His political system consists of all those institutions and processes involved in the 'authoritative allocation of values' for society. Specifically, the political system takes inputs from society, consisting of demands for particular policies and expressions of support. The political system then converts these inputs into outputs – enforceable policies and decisions. These outputs then feed back to society so as to affect the next cycle of inputs. Although inputs are regulated by gatekeepers, such as parties and interest groups (which bias the system in favour of certain demands and against others) Easton's model viewed the political system as a mechanism for converting demands from society into concrete policies. The real driver was the inputs rather than the institutions. Indeed, the institutions of government were reduced to little more than a 'black box' in an abstract diagram. In practice, Easton's model also proved to be too static, premised on the achievement of equilibrium between inputs and outputs.

Society-centred analyses formed part of the behavioural revolution in politics, an approach which offers a useful contrast with institutional analysis. The central tenet of behaviouralists was that 'the root is man' rather than institutions (Eulau, 1963). People are more than badges of the institution they work for; they possess and indeed will create some freedom to define their own role. The higher the position in an organization, the more flexibility the occupant possesses, including the ability to reshape the institution itself. This assumption that political analysis should begin with individuals rather than organizations proved to be particularly attractive in the United States, a country whose governing institutions were, after all, a conscious creation of the Founding Fathers. Organizations were not ignored altogether but the study of assemblies, for instance, moved away from an emphasis on formal procedures toward a focus on 'legislative behaviour'. Thus, researchers investigated the social backgrounds of representatives, their individual voting records and how they defined their own roles within the institution (Wahlke *et al.*, 1962). In the study of the judiciary, too, scholars began to take judges rather than courts as their level of analysis, using statistical techniques to assess how the social background and political ideology of justices shaped their legal judgments (Schubert, 1972).

The disregard of institutions by much society-centred analysis of the 1960s now seems extreme but its effect in broadening horizons represents a permanent and positive legacy for comparative politics. Note, for example, that the parts of this book examining the relationship between politics and society take up more space than the sections dealing with government institutions. Comparative government is now irreversibly embedded in comparative politics.

Comparing states

In the 1980s, however, attention returned to the state. 'Bringing the state back in' became a strong rallying-cry in comparative politics (Evans, Rueschemeyer and Skocpol, 1985). Partly, this reflected a belated recognition that the state is the single central concern of political study. In addition, statistical and behavioural studies largely ran out of steam, becoming increasingly technical and failing to engage with political change. Yet the new focus on the state represented more than a return to descriptive studies of government institutions; rather, the state as a whole, rather than its specific manifestations, provided the level of analysis. The focus lay not so much on institutional detail but on the state as an active agent, shaping and re-shaping society.

Where society-centred analysis saw the state as embedded in society, the state-centred approach saw society as part of a configuration defined largely by the state itself. The state acts autonomously and is not just imprisoned by social forces. In particular, the state is seen as using its administrative capacity and monopoly of legitimate force to bring about fundamental social changes. For example Skocpol (1985) showed how successful revolutionaries such as the Russian Bolsheviks and Iranian mullahs used their control of the state to produce total transformations of society. Even in the Western world, the large-scale role of the state has enabled it to initiate social and economic changes. The state has facilitated industrialization while leading the development of mass education and modern welfare states.

State-centred analysts suggest that the uses to which public power has been put by those charged with its exercise cannot be understood by routine analysis of specific institutions. Rather, the state itself must provide the level of analysis. The interests of the state can be identified and analysed without declining into institutional detail, just as a country's 'national interest' is a useful guide to its foreign policy even though that policy is in practice the work of many hands. The state-centred perspective carries implications of a ruling élite, albeit one nested in political rather than economic structures. Thus Block (1977) refers to 'state managers' who seek to sustain the conditions of economic growth in their own interests, even though they are not directly the lackeys of the capitalist class.

In a comparative context, of course, it is clear that the power of the state is a variable rather than a constant. For example, in communist countries, the state was an overarching influence, pervading virtually all aspects of life. In established democracies, the state is less dominant. In much of the developing world, the state is less important still; its writ may not run far beyond the capital city and a few major towns. In addition, the power of the state varies even within the democratic world, as the somewhat-faded distinction between strong and weak states still makes clear (Dyson, 1980). For example, France and Japan are normally taken as strong states. In these countries, state intervention is regarded as legitimate in many areas of life – including the economy. The leading role of the state is acknowledged, if not always welcomed, by élites and indeed the general population. 'Interests of state' were a trump-card in political argument. By contrast, in weak states such as the United States, the state remains the servant of society and of many of the individuals within it; we could even debate whether the national government rules the rest of the world more decisively than it controls its own population.

While state-centred analysis offers a broader framework for understanding major political developments than can institutional analysis, its applicability varies not just across countries but also over time. Given the diminished status of the public sphere in many democracies in the twenty-first century, broad generalizations about state leadership of society carry less conviction; as a result, comparative politics may witness a revived interest in finer-grained institutional analysis.

The advantages of comparison

What is to be gained by comparing politics in different countries? Why compare across nations? The answer is that a comparative approach broadens our understanding of the political world, leading to improved classifications and giving potential for explanation and even prediction (Box 5.2). We discuss each of these strengths in turn.

The first strength of a comparative approach is straightforward: it enables us to find out more about the places we know least about. In 1925 Munro described the purpose of his textbook on foreign governments as aiding 'the comprehension of daily news from abroad'. Background information about foreign governments not only helps to interpret new developments, it also helps with practical political relationships. British ministers have a mediocre track-record in negotiations with their European partners partly because they assume that the aggressive tone they adopt in the Commons chamber will also work in European meeting rooms. Their assumption is incorrect, showing ignorance of the consensual political style found in many European democracies. Similarly, American students often puzzle at how the British parliamentary system can deliver stable government when the prime minister, unlike their own president, is constantly at the mercy of a vote of confidence in the Commons. Reflecting the weakness of American parties, the power of a governing party in Britain to command the legislature is understated. Through comparison, say Dogan and Pelassy (1990), we discover our own ethnocentrism and the means of overcoming it.

A second advantage of comparison is that it improves our classifications of politics. For instance, once constitutions have been grouped into written and unwritten, or electoral systems into proportional and non-proportional, we can search for the factors which predispose countries to have one type rather than the other. Similarly, once we classify executives into presidential and parliamentary types, or party systems into two-party or multi-party, we can look at the consequences of each. But without variation, and some sort of measurement or classification of it, we have nothing to explain. In short, comparative politics turns constants into variables, thereby providing the raw material for explanation.

The potential for explanation is the third advantage of a comparative approach. Comparative researchers seek to understand a variety of political systems not just for the sake of it but in order to formulate and test hypotheses about the political process. Comparative analysis enables us to develop and scrutinize such questions as: Do first-past-the-post electoral systems always produce a two-party system? Are two-chambered assemblies only found under federalism? Are revolutions most likely after defeat in war? As these questions illustrate, an hypothesis suggests a relationship between two or more factors or variables: for example, between electoral and party systems, or between war and revolution. Verified hypotheses are valuable not just for their own sake but because they are essential for explaining the particular. Consider a specific question: why did a major socialist party never emerge in the United States? An obvious answer is because the USA was built on, and retains, a strongly individualistic culture. This answer may seem to be particular but in fact it is quite general. It implies that other countries with similar values would also lack a strong socialist party. It also suggests that countries with a more collective outlook will be more likely to have a party of the left. These comparative hypotheses would need to be confirmed before we could claim a full understanding of our original question about the USA. So explaining the particular calls forth the general; only theories can explain cases.

Generalizations, once validated, have potential for prediction. This is our fourth reason for studying politics comparatively. If we find that proportional representation (PR) does indeed lead to coalition government, we can reasonably predict at least one

---

BOX 5.2

The advantages of comparison

1. Learning about other governments broadens our understanding, casting fresh light on our home nation.

2. Comparison improves our classifications of political processes.

3. Comparison enables us to test general hypotheses about politics.

4. Comparison gives us some potential for prediction and control.

effect of introducing PR to countries such as Canada which still use the plurality method. Equally, if we know that subcontracting the provision of public services to private agencies has raised quality and lowered costs in one country, we can advise governments elsewhere that here is an idea at least worth considering. Or authoritarian rulers might look to China for clues on how non-democratic rulers can reduce their control over the economy while retaining their own hold on political power. Lesson-drawing provides some capacity to anticipate and even to shape the future (Rose, 1993).

The difficulties of comparison

The breadth inherent in the comparative approach to politics brings its own dangers and difficulties (Box 5.3). But Sartori (1970) has warned against the dangers of over-conscious thinking leading to the dead-end conclusion that all comparisons suffer overwhelming difficulties. In any case, many of the problems identified in the literature presuppose that explanation is the sole function of comparison. When due weight is given to description as well as explanation, some methodological difficulties fade away.

Knowledge requirements

By definition, any comparative study involves at least twice as many countries as does a study of a single country. A statistical analysis, perhaps examining the relationship between democracy and economic development, might draw information from all the countries of the world. Clearly, the knowledge requirements for research in comparative politics can be substantial. One common solution is to form a team of researchers, each expert in at least one of the countries included in the study. In this way, knowledge deficits can be reduced. However, such collaboration is hardly a practical proposition for an individual student with no funding (though e-mail provides a convenient device through which politics students in one country can contact those in another for information).

Fortunately, the idea that knowledge requirements increase directly with the number of cases is a misunderstanding, albeit an understandable one. In comparative research, the prime focus should be the comparison between countries, rather than the countries themselves. It is often unnecessary and perhaps even undesirable for the comparative scholar to possess the depth of understanding acquired by the expert on a single country; breadth is at least as valuable as depth. For example, identifying a transition away from British-style plurality electoral systems, and speculating on the reasons for such a trend, does not call for in-depth knowledge of how the electoral system operates in each particular country. Similarly, we can draw conclusions about democratization in Latin America without understanding the intricacies of transition in every case. And those who debate the relative merits of presidential and parliamentary government cannot possibly read all that has been written about the operation of these systems of government in every country where they have been tried. The task in comparative politics is to draw on specialist knowledge so as to produce new and more general observations. The skill resides not in knowing all there is to know but in knowing what needs to be known – and in being able to find it out.

Same phenomenon, different meanings

In comparing political behaviour across countries, we should remember that the meaning of an action depends on the conventions of the country concerned. When British MPs vote against their party

---

BOX 5.3
The difficulties of comparison

1. By definition, comparative research demands knowledge of more than one political system.
2. The 'same' phenomenon can have different meanings in different countries. This makes it difficult to compare like with like.
3. Relationships between countries mean they cannot be regarded as independent, further reducing our ability to test theories.
4. There are not enough countries in the world to allow theories to be tested precisely.
5. The countries or other cases selected for study may be an unrepresentative sample, limiting the general significance of the findings.

in the House of Commons, their acts are far more significant than when American legislators do the 'same' thing in the less partisan Senate. To take another illustration, Western observers were sometimes shocked by the apparent indifference with which military coups were greeted in developing countries. They failed to recognize that coups had become a regular – and fairly peaceful – mechanism for the circulation of élites. In a sense, coups had become the 'functional equivalent' of elections in the West – and should have been compared accordingly.

This problem of the meaning and significance of action is particularly important in politics because politics is largely conducted in terms of coded language and symbolic behaviour. Our reaction to a 'terrorist' differs from our response to a 'freedom fighter', just as, in the West, 'Islamic fundamentalist' implies something different from 'religious leader'. Even more neutral terms such as bureaucracy, the state, social solidarity and left and right are viewed more positively in most of continental Europe than in the United States. To understand how political discourse varies across countries is not merely a preliminary to a comparative project; it is itself an under-used form of comparative research (Howarth, 1995). At the very least, practitioners of comparative politics should be aware that comparing like with like is not always straightforward; it requires sensitivity to each of the countries under scrutiny.

Definition
Countries must be compared against a common concept but the meaning of that concept may itself vary between countries. One response to this difficulty is to compare political activities by their underlying function rather than their ostensible purpose. Different institutions are **functionally equivalent** when they fulfil the same role within the political system: for instance, elections and revolutions can each serve as devices for replacing the governing élite (Myers and O'Connor, 1998).

Interdependence

Although 189 'independent' states belonged to the United Nations by 2000, in reality, far fewer cases are available to the student of comparative politics.

Countries learn from, copy, compete with, influence and even invade each other in a constant process of interaction. Even the states which provide the units of our subject did not develop separately; rather, the model of statehood diffused outwards from its proving ground in Europe. As Dogan and Pelassy (1990, p. 1) say, 'there is no nation without other nations'. The major transitions of world history – industrialization, colonialism and decolonization, democratization, marketization – unfolded on a world stage; in that sense we have one world system rather than an assortment of independent states (Wallerstein, 1979). Specific institutional forms also reflect diffusion: the communist model was often imposed by force of Soviet arms, the presidential system in Latin America was imported from the United States while the ombudsman was a device copied from Sweden. The development of supranational and intergovernmental bodies also creates denser connections between states as well as creating more complex patterns of governance. However, a natural comparative design is to examine how member states respond to the demands of international organizations of which they are all members (for example the European Union). But it is clear that any comparative study which assumes that cases are independent – and much statistical analysis proceeds on precisely this basis – treads on thin ice.

Too many variables, too few countries

This is a major problem for those who conceive comparative politics as analogous to the experimenter's laboratory, in which researchers patiently seek to isolate the impact of a single variable. Even with 189 sovereign states, it is impossible to find a country which is identical to another in all respects except for that factor (say, the electoral system) whose effects we wish to detect. This means that comparison in political science can never become a full equivalent of the experiments conducted in the natural scientist's laboratory. We just do not have enough countries to go round, a difficulty termed the 'small-N' problem ('N' is the statistician's term for 'number of cases').

To make the same point from another angle, we will never be able to test all the possible explanations of a political difference between countries. For example, several plausible reasons can be invoked to 'explain' why France and Italy once possessed the two strongest communist parties in the democratic world. Perhaps the strength of communism was a reaction against the power of the Catholic Church. Or perhaps sympathy to communism arose because the ruling élite had been slow to integrate the working class into democratic politics, again a feature of both countries. So here we have two potential explanations, both broadly consistent with the facts, but no way of isolating whether or which one of the two is decisive. Our ideas resist precise testing; lacking the ability to re-run national histories, we just run out of countries.

Selection bias

This problem arises when the choice of what to study, or even how to study it, produces unrepresentative results. It is an inherent risk when any one study covers only a few out of many possible countries. The danger often arises as an unintended consequence of a haphazard process of country selection. For example, we choose to study those countries which speak the same language, or which have good exchange schemes, or in which we feel safe. Large, powerful countries are studied more intensively than small, powerless ones. One result is that the findings of comparative politics are weighted toward established democracies, a rare form of government in the expanse of human history. One virtue of designs covering a large number of countries is that they reduce the risk of selection bias. Indeed, if the study covers all current countries, selection bias disappears – at least as long as generalization is restricted to the contemporary world.

But, alas, the problem may just resurface in another form, through an unrepresentative selection of variables rather than countries. The difficulty here is best approached through an example. Much statistical research in comparative politics relies on existing data collected by governments and international bodies with different interests from our own. Their priorities tend to be financial, economic, social and political – in that order. So financial and economic variables may receive more attention than they justify, and politics runs the risk of becoming a branch of economics. Thus a large body of research examines the relationship between changing economic conditions and the popularity of national governments as reported in regular opinion polls. This work has produced worthwhile findings but its sheer quantity reflects the ready availability of statistical information more than the intrinsic significance of the topic for the development of comparative politics.

A final and important example of selection bias comes from examining only positive cases, thus eliminating all variation in the phenomenon we seek to explain. As King, Keohane and Verba (1994, p. 129) note, 'the literature is full of work that makes the mistake of failing to let the dependent variable vary; for example, research that tries to explain the outbreak of wars with studies only of wars, the onset of revolutions with studies only of revolutions, or patterns of voter turnout with interviews only of nonvoters.' When only positive cases of a phenomenon are studied, the conclusions drawn are inherently suspect. Skocpol's (1979) study of revolutions in France, Russia and China is a case in point. Her research design allowed her to identify the features common to her revolutions, such as the declining international and domestic effectiveness of the old regime. However, she was unable to say how often a failing regime was followed by a revolution. She had selected on the dependent variable and was restricted to positive cases. She was therefore unable to assess how far government ineffectiveness and revolutions covaried.

Definition

Selection on the dependent variable occurs when only similar (usually positive) cases of a phenomenon are selected. By eliminating variation, there is no contrast left to explain; we are left with variables that do not vary. For example, a study of countries which have democratized successfully can tell us nothing about the conditions of successful democratization. Those conditions can only be identified through a comparison with failed democratizations (the **dependent variable** is simply the phenomenon we seek to explain – for example, whether democratization succeeds or fails).

History plays a trick on us by selecting on the dependent variable through evolution. For instance, in our discussion of the origins of the modern European state, we noted that their emergence owed much to the efforts by monarchs to mobilize men and materials for war. However this tells us nothing about how many monarchs failed in the task, with the result that their proto-states disappeared into the waste-bin of history (Przeworski, 1995, p. 19).

Comparative techniques

In this section we turn from strategy to techniques. We examine some of the main methods used in comparative politics: case studies, focused comparisons and statistical analysis (Box 5.4). These techniques range from intensive scrutiny of one or a few countries (case studies and focused comparisons) to the more systematic analysis of variables drawn from a larger number of examples (statistical analysis). With case studies and focused comparisons, the object is to provide a detailed account of a few examples falling into a wider category: a study of a specific military coup, say, or an examination of a particular revolution. The focus is on how the factors at work in the example interact to form a particular configuration or conjuncture. By contrast, statistical analysis examines the relationships between political variables applying across cases: say, the impact of economic inequality on political instability or the relationship between the affluence of a country and whether is it democratic (Ragin, 1994a, p. 302). Much discussion of methodology is premised on variable-oriented research although case analysis is used more often in comparative research.

Case studies

A case is an instance of a more general category. To conduct a case study is therefore to investigate some-

thing which has significance beyond its boundaries. For instance, lawyers study cases which are taken to define a legal principle with wide applicability. A project turns into a case study only when it becomes clear what the study is a case *of*. As Scarrow (1969, p. 7) pointed out, case studies make a contribution to general knowledge of politics if 'the analysis is made within a comparative perspective which mandates that the description of the particular be cast in terms of broadly analytic constructs'. In other words, a single case can offer a detailed illustration of a theme of wider interest, whether we take the United States as an example of presidential government, Canada as an illustration of federalism or Finland as a case of coalition government. Thus cases are deliberately chosen, or can at least be written up, as examples of broader phenomena. Because case studies locate their findings in a wider context, they are a tool of comparative politics, even though only one example is examined.

In the absence of overarching theory, case studies are the building blocks from which we construct our understanding of the political world (Yin, 1994). We usually proceed by comparing cases rather than by making deductions from first principles. In consequence, much comparative political analysis takes the form not of relating cases to abstract theory, but simply of drawing analogies between the cases themselves. How did the process of state-building differ between postcolonial states of the twentieth century and the states of early modern Europe? What are the similarities and differences between the Russian and Chinese revolutions? Reflecting this pragmatic approach, Khong (1992) suggests that much political reasoning, especially in foreign policy, is by analogy. Decision-makers and analysts look for earlier crises which resemble

---

BOX 5.4
Major techniques in comparative politics

	Number of cases	Case- or variable-centred?	Strategy
Case studies	One	Case	Intensive study of a single instance with wider significance
Focused comparisons	A few	Case	Intensive comparison of a few instances
Statistical analysis	Large or all	Variable	Quantitative assessment of the impact of variables

the current one, so that lessons can be learned and errors avoided.

Reflecting the tendency for comparative politics to move from cases to theory, rather than vice versa, some of the most important examples in comparative politics are best conceived as archetypal cases. The idea here is that in comparative politics a case often generates the category of which it is then taken, in a somewhat circular way, as representative. Take the French Revolution. We will suggest that this episode altered the whole concept of revolution, reconstructing the idea as a progressive, modernizing force. In this way, the French Revolution made possible all the modern revolutions which followed. To regard the French experience of 1789 as just a representative 'case' of a wider category would understate its significance. It was not just a prototype (an early model) but also an archetype (a defining case). In similar fashion, the American presidency does far more than illustrate the presidential system of government; it is the model which influenced all later attempts to create similar systems, notably in Latin America.

Case studies are a strategy for selecting a topic more than a technique for conducting research. In practice, they are normally multi-method, using the range of techniques in the political scientist's toolkit: reading the academic literature, examining secondary documents (for example newspapers), searching for primary material (for example unpublished reports) and ideally conducting interviews with participants and other observers. Scholars of cases engage in 'soaking and poking, marinating themselves in minutiae' (King, Keohane and Verba, 1994, p. 38). Case studies aim to provide a description which is both rounded and detailed, a goal which the anthropologist Clifford Geertz (1993, first pub. 1973) famously defined as 'thick description'.

Leaving aside archetypal cases, there are two ways in which cases can generate wider significance. Either a case can be useful because it is representative – a typical, standard example of a wider category – or else it can be selected because it is deviant or unusual in some way, helping us to understand exceptions to the rule. Of these two approaches, the representative case is more common. It is the workhorse of case study designs, as useful as it is undramatic. Often researchers will use their own country

as a representative case. For example, researchers may be interested in female political participation throughout the democratic world but choose to study the phenomenon in their own country in detail. The home country is the research site but the hope is that the results will contribute to a broader, cross-national debate. Of course, no country is exactly like any other but a collection of representative case studies will at least provide the raw material for subsequent generalizations.

By contrast, the purpose of a deviant case study is to cast light on the exceptional and the untypical: the countries which remain communist, or which are still governed by the military, or which seem to be immune from democratizing trends. For example, Rhodes (1994) sought to explain why Britain did not develop a powerful central bureaucracy until the middle of the nineteenth century, much later than most other countries of Western Europe. His answer was that Britain's island character and secure borders meant that it had no need of the large standing army required by continental countries. Consequently, Britain did not require the bureaucracy needed to provide administrative support to the army. As this illustration shows, deviant cases are often used to tidy up our understanding of exceptions and anomalies. In the same way, we could examine India as an exception to the thesis that democracy presupposes prosperity or as a deviant case of a country still employing the plurality method of election. Normal science, suggests Kuhn (1970), proceeds in exactly this way, with researchers seeking to show how apparent paradoxes can be resolved within a dominant intellectual tradition. While deviant cases always attract interest, the danger is that they become over-studied; the exceptional is always more exotic than the typical.

We should mention here a sub-design within the broader category of deviant cases. In a prototypical case a topic is chosen not because it is representative but because it is expected to become so: 'their present is our future' (Rose, 1991, p. 459). Studying an early example may help us to understand a phenomenon which is growing in significance elsewhere. Later in this book we will look at new public management in New Zealand, since that country has travelled furthest down the road of bureaucratic reform. In the nineteenth century, de Tocqueville (1966, first pub. 1835) studied America because of his interest in the new politics of democracy; 'my wish has been to find there instruction by which we may ourselves profit'. Today, Europeans still look to the United States as a forerunner of trends, especially in the economy, which are expected to cross the Atlantic in due course. Of course, prototypical cases carry a danger: what if the prototype turns out to be a dud? The design, by its nature, involves a bet on an uncertain future. Also, innovators are by nature unrepresentative; they often possess unusual enthusiasm and experience additional difficulties to those confronting their imitators. Yet by the same token, the prototypical case study does offer opportunities for lesson-drawing: later adopters can learn from the mistakes of the innovator (Rogers, 1971).

Focused comparisons

Focused comparisons fall between case studies and statistical analysis. They are 'small N' studies which concentrate on the intensive comparison of an aspect of politics in a small number of countries. Most often, the number of countries is either two, a paired or binary comparison, or three, a triangular comparison. The emphasis is on the comparison at least as much as on the cases; otherwise, the design would be a multiple case study rather than a focused comparison.

To illustrate the technique, consider three examples of paired comparisons. First, in a classic study, Heclo (1974) compared the origins of unemployment insurance, old age pensions and earnings-related supplementary pensions in Britain and Sweden. In both countries, he concluded, the bureaucracy was the main agency of policy formulation in these areas. Second, Kudrle and Marmor (1981) compared the growth of social security programmes in the United States and Canada. They argued that the presence of elements of left-wing and Tory paternalistic ideology in Canada explained its higher levels of spending and programme development. Third, Lipset (1990) also compared the political cultures of the United States and Canada, tracing contemporary contrasts back to America's origins as a revolutionary society committed to individual freedom.

Small-N studies such as these have proved to be the success story of comparative politics in recent decades (Collier, 1991). Focused comparisons

remain sensitive to the details of particular countries and policies while also forcing the intellectual discipline inherent in the comparative enterprise. The dimensions of comparison must be addressed, similarities and differences sorted out and some effort made to account for the contrasts observed. Focused comparisons work particularly well when a few countries are compared over time, examining how they vary in their response to common problems such as the transition to democracy. Unlike some comparative work, focused comparisons remain sensitive to history. If it is difficult to produce a poor case study, it is virtually impossible to deliver an uninteresting report using focused comparison.

How should countries be selected for a focused comparison? The normal strategy is to select broadly similar cases, seeking to account either for a phenomenon shared among countries (e.g. the development of the welfare state within Scandinavian states) or for specific differences in otherwise similar cases (e.g. why did Britain manage a more peaceful transition to democracy than did Germany?) This latter strategy is called a 'most similar' design. In such a strategy, we seek to compare countries which are as similar as possible in, say, their history, culture and political institutions, so that we can clearly rule out such factors as explanations for the particular difference of interest. For instance, Kudrle and Marmor's study (1981) sought to explain why social security programmes are more developed in Canada than in the United States, two countries which are similar in many other ways. Similarly, Berglund (1990) sought to explain Finland's distinctive pattern of unstable coalitions, a large communist vote and relatively low turnout by setting his country in a Scandinavian context. As Berglund (1990, p. 11) notes,

> Few countries are more suitable for systematic, comparative analysis than the four Nordic countries, Denmark, Finland, Sweden and Norway. The similarities between them are numerous and there is a great deal of substance to the many references . . . to the existence of a historical and cultural community in Northern Europe.

However, more often than not many factors will remain as possible explanations for an observed difference and there will be no decisive way of distinguishing between them. The problem of too many variables and too few countries cannot be sidestepped; in practice, the value of a focused comparison will often lie in the journey rather than its destination.

A 'most different' design, by contrast, seeks to test a relationship by discovering whether it can be observed in a range of different countries. If so, our confidence that the relationship is real, and not due to both factors depending on an unmeasured third variable, will increase (Peters, 1998). Thus, our confidence that proportional representation leads to coalition government increases with the number of countries in which this pattern is found.

Definition

A **most similar** design takes similar countries for comparison on the assumption, as Lipset (1990, p. xiii) puts it, that 'the more similar the units being compared, the more possible it should be to isolate the factors responsible for differences between them'. By contrast, the **most different** design seeks to show the robustness of a relationship by demonstrating its validity in a range of contrasting settings (Przeworski and Teune, 1970).

Statistical analysis

Although statistics can enter into many studies, including case studies, our focus here is on the use of statistical analysis as a primary research strategy. In such variable-oriented research, the object is to explore the covariation between variables, at least some of which are usually measured quantitatively. One variable is dependent – that which we seek to explain. The others are independent or explanatory – those factors which we believe may influence the dependent variable (Box 5.5). Examples of statistical work in comparative politics include tests of the following hypotheses:

- the more affluent a country, the more likely it is to be a consolidated democracy
- the more educated a population, the higher the proportion of post-materialists within it
- the higher a person's social status, the more likely he or she is to participate in politics

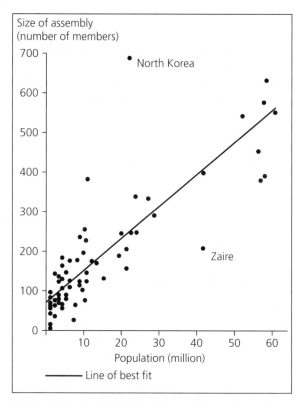

Figure 5.2 Population and assembly size from fig. 14.1 (p. 29), showing the line of best fit and highlighting two outliers

As a straightforward illustration of the statistical approach, consider the relationship between a country's population (independent) and the number of members in its national assembly (dependent). A scatterplot, as in Figure 5.2, displays all the information about these two variables for the countries surveyed. Clearly, the larger the population, the larger the assembly. However, the content of the graph can be summarized by calculating a regression line which gives the best fit to the data. This line, also shown in the figure, is defined by an equation linking the variables. Given such an equation, we can use the population of any particular country to predict its assembly size; indeed, these predictions can easily be made from the regression line using a ruler. We can then observe, and seek to explain, deviant cases (called outliers in statistics) for which special explanations can be sought, thus providing a link to case analysis. In our example, North Korea's Supreme

---

BOX 5.5
Dependent, intervening and independent variables

Type of variable	Definition	Example
Dependent variable	The factor we seek to explain	Party voted for
Independent variable	The factor believed to influence the dependent variable	Social class
Intervening variable	A factor through which the independent variable influences the dependent variable	Attitudes to party leaders

---

People's Assembly is far larger than would be expected for a country with a population of just 23 million. Conversely, Zaire has a high negative residual – a smaller assembly than would be anticipated, given its population.

Such a methodology is useful but carries two main dangers. The first is that a strong correlation between two variables may arise simply because both depend on a third, unmeasured variable. In principle, the solution to spurious correlation is simple: include all relevant variables in the analysis, for statistical techniques can effectively control for such problems. In practice, not all the relevant variables will be known; so spurious correlation is a continuing danger. For example, the relationship between proportional representation (PR) and multi-party systems might arise because both factors emerge in divided societies, not because PR itself increases the number of parties. Or ethnic minority status might be correlated with low turnout simply because ethnic minorities are concentrated among the poor.

Secondly, even if a relationship is genuine, the direction of causation remains to be established. Suppose we find that democracies have higher growth rates than authoritarian regimes. Is this because democracies facilitate economic growth or because a high rate of growth fosters a stable democracy? A case can be made both ways, and by itself a correlation will not tell us the answer. In interpreting an equation, we always run the risk of repeating the error made by the child who asked its parent to stop the trees from waving their branches because they were making the wind get up. In general, correlations obtained by non-experimental methods can never finally prove a relationship of cause and effect. However, even a spurious correlation may be a useful if risky basis for prediction.

Yet even accepting these limits to statistical analysis, we should retain the genuine benefits which it can provide. As Peters (1998) wisely says, 'statistical analysis may not be everything but it is certainly something'. In particular, the ability to predict, even with the limited accuracy typically found in comparative politics, is well worth having. And even simple descriptive statistics – how many semi-presidential executives are there? what was the probability that an authoritarian regime in 1980 would become democratic by 1990? – are essential means for comprehending the variability of the political world. Indeed, straightforward counting is probably the most under-used statistical technique in comparative politics. Statistics may be an exercise in simplification but, precisely for that reason, they help us with our core task of interpreting politics at a comparative level. As King, Keohane and Verba (1994, p. 42) rightly say, 'simplification has been an integral part of every known scholarly work'.

Key reading

Next step: *Peters (1998) is a thorough and balanced discussion of comparative techniques by an experienced practitioner.*

Dogan and Pelassy (1990) is a challenging account of the comparative approach, more philosophical than Peters but insightful even so. For general overviews, Lijphart (1971), Rose (1991), Collier (1991), Keman (1993) and Mair (1996) are all worth reading. King, Keohane and Verba (1994) explore how qualitative designs can lead to valid causal inferences; they have much to contribute to comparative research design. Dogan and Kazancigil (1994) mix comparative approaches and examples in a stimulating way. For the institutional approach, see Peters (1999), and for the state-centred approach Evans,

Rueschemeyer and Skocpol (1985). On specific techniques, Yin (1994) is a useful account of case studies. For focused comparisons, see Ragin (1994a) and Ragin, Berg-Schlosser and de Meur (1996). On statistics, Lewis-Beck (1995) is our recommended introduction; Jackson (1996) is a more advanced treatment. Pennings, Keman and Kleinnijenhuis (1999) look at statistical methods in comparative politics specifically.

PART **2**
POLITICS AND SOCIETY

The relationship between politics and society has always preoccupied political thinkers. Government does not operate in isolation, unaffected by the society of which it forms part. This part locates politics in a broader social framework. Chapter 6 looks at the attitudes of people toward government, Chapter 7 discusses communication flows between politics and society while Chapter 8 examines how people participate in the political process.

Political culture

? Different
funous
of
p.c.

'The strongest is never strong enough unless he succeeds in turning might into right and obedience into duty.' So wrote Rousseau in the eighteenth century, and rulers the world over have taken his saying to their hearts. For instance, the cult of Lenin in the Soviet Union required two- and three-year-olds to sing nursery songs about Lenin; four- and five-year-olds to decorate his portrait; and six-year-olds to lay flowers at his statue (Tumarkin, 1997). Attempts to foster loyalty to the regime were not of course restricted to communist states; they are found in all countries. Civics classes in American high schools and the deference to authority encouraged in many Asian countries are other ways in which states have tried to transform might into right, obedience into duty. To study how people view their country's politics is to investigate political culture. The notion of political culture does not refer to attitudes to specific actors such as the current president or prime minister; rather it denotes how people view the political system as a whole, including their belief in its legitimacy.

Political culture in established democracies

As with many themes in comparative politics, polit-ical culture has been studied most intensively in the context of established Western democracies. The classic study is Almond and Verba's *The Civic Culture* (1963). Based on surveys conducted during 1959–60 in the USA, Britain, West Germany, Italy and also Mexico, this landmark investigation sought to identify the political culture within which a liberal democracy is most likely to develop and consolidate.

Almond and Verba's argument is based on a distinction between three pure types of political culture: the parochial, subject and participant. In the parochial political culture, citizens are only indistinctly aware of the existence of central government – as with remote tribes whose existence is seemingly unaffected by national decisions made by the central government. In the subject political culture, citizens see themselves not as participants in the political process but as subjects of the government – as with people living under a dictatorship. In the more familiar participant political culture, citizens believe both that they can contribute to the system and that they are affected by it.

> **Definition**
> Pye (1995, p. 965) defines **political culture** as 'the sum of the fundamental values, sentiments and knowledge that give form and substance to political processes'. The building blocks of political culture are therefore the beliefs, opinions and emotions of individual citizens toward their form of government.

Almond and Verba's core idea was that democracy will prove most stable in societies where subject and parochial attitudes provide ballast to an essentially participant culture. This mix is termed the 'civic culture' (Figure 6.1). In this ideal combination, citizens are sufficiently active in politics to express their preferences to rulers but not so involved as to

[handwritten margin notes at top: "But does not have the power to 'over-throw' the government = disequilibrium to the system. Just enough to influence it."]

refuse to accept decisions with which they disagree. Thus the civic culture resolves the tension within democracy between popular control and effective governance. In Almond and Verba's study, Britain, and to a lesser extent the United States, came closest to this ideal. In both countries citizens felt they could influence the government but often chose not to do so, thus giving the government a measure of flexibility.

Of course, times move on. In the decades following Almond and Verba's study many liberal democracies hit turbulent waters: Vietnam and student activism in the 1960s, the oil crisis of the 1970s, the anti-nuclear movement and the rise of ecology groups in the 1980s, privatization and cutbacks to the welfare state in the 1990s. As Almond and Verba (1980) noted in an update of their original work, such events left their mark on Western political cultures. In Britain and the USA trust in government declined. In 1964, three-quarters of Americans said that they trusted the federal government 'to do the right thing'; by 1996, only a third did so. In Britain, the proportion trusting the government to put country before party fell from 39 per cent in 1974 to 22 per cent in 1996 (Figure 6.2). These figures show a shift away from the civic culture towards a more sceptical and instrumental attitude to politics. Declining turnout, particularly in the USA, also suggests a move away from the participant culture which Almond and Verba regarded as the corner-stone of democracy (Putnam, 2000).

[handwritten margin note: "? Voting Turn out"]

Yet in America as in other established democracies, governments continued to govern. In most of the democratic world rulers were able to privatize public corporations and reduce welfare provision without

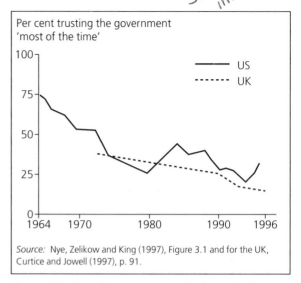

Per cent trusting the government 'most of the time'

Source: Nye, Zelikow and King (1997), Figure 3.1 and for the UK, Curtice and Jowell (1997), p. 91.

Figure 6.2 Trust in government in the United States and the United Kingdom, 1964–96

threatening the stability of the political system itself. Such discontent as emerged focused more on the performance of governing institutions and leaders than on the democratic process itself. Thus, Norris (1999a, p.227) finds that between 1981 and 1997 confidence in the legislature, civil service and the police fell in most democracies surveyed but that popular support for democratic principles remained high. Today's 'disillusioned democrats', as Norris calls them, may be cynical but they remain committed to democracy's ideals.

So whether or not stable democracy needs the precise balance expressed in Almond and Verba's notion of the civic culture, it certainly appears that established democracies possess, and perhaps require, a bank of political capital which can sustain them through bad times. As Machiavelli (1469–1527) noted in *The Prince*, 'the prince should have the people on his side; if the contrary is true, there is no help in adverse moments'. Inglehart (1988, p.1221) makes a similar point:

> Even when democracy has no answer to the question, 'what have you done for me lately?' It may be sustained by diffuse feelings that it is an inherently good thing. These feelings may in turn reflect economic and other successes that one experienced long ago or learned about second hand as part of one's early socialization.

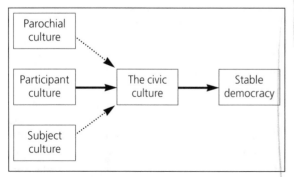

Figure 6.1 Almond and Verba's theory of the civic culture

[handwritten note at bottom: "The system can compensate"]

FOR OR AGAINST

THE SIGNIFICANCE OF POLITICAL CULTURE

To what extent can a country's political culture explain the form and stability of its system of government? Political scientists have debated this question with vigour; the answers given reveal contrasting ideas about how best to approach comparative politics.

The case for

For its advocates, political culture provides the setting of all political activity. We can no more understand a country's politics without looking at its culture than we can understand a game of soccer without knowing the rules. As Abraham Lincoln said, 'public sentiment is everything. With public sentiment nothing can fail. Without it nothing can succeed.' More specifically, a society's political culture narrows the range of acceptable attitudes towards democratic and authoritarian rule. Western countries show a cultural bias toward democracy: the virtues of democracy are not so much promoted as presupposed, thus reinforcing democratic stability. By contrast, in Islamic states such as Iran the cultural skew is different: democracy is taken to be materialistic, unprincipled and American, thus excluding liberal democracy from mainstream discourse. Of course, cultures do not emerge from nowhere; they reflect a country's history and traditions. And there lies the essential importance of political culture: it is the means by which a country's history influences its current politics and through which a form of government perpetuates itself. To dismiss the significance of political culture would be to deny the importance of history itself.

The case against

What could be more superficial than to say that a system of government continues because it is in tune with a country's political culture? Such an 'explanation' is just idle speculation if there is no independent evidence of what the values of people living in the country actually are. Many descriptions of a 'political culture' are often little more than an exercise in stereotyping which invariably ignores diversity within the country concerned. How can we define an 'American' political culture which is common to Alabama, California, Massachusetts and Utah? Even when hard evidence of political attitudes does exist, references to political culture re-describe the problem rather than provide a real explanation. That is, the key issue is not showing how a country's form of government reflects its values but understanding how those norms arose in the first place, a problem which takes us away from the platitudes of political culture towards real encounters with a country's history, economy and international relations. In particular, descriptions of political culture tend to be static as well as simplistic, lacking sensitivity to how a culture continually evolves in response to political experience. As Steinbach (1992, p.120) writes, 'political scientists neglect the historical preconditions of a political culture that, after all, represents the outcome of a process rather than the sum of attitudes and values.'

Assessment

Political culture is a seductive term, offering easy explanations for why states vary in their forms of government. The difficulty is that the concept seems almost too simple to apply; who does not enjoy comparing Americans with Canadians or Swedes with Norwegians? Yet the fact is that surveys do reveal sustained differences across nations in political attitudes – for example, the proportion of the population favouring state intervention to reduce income inequality is far higher in many European countries than in the United States (Lipset, 1996). Critics of political culture who dismiss such findings as 'predictable' engage in the same stereotyping of which they accuse their opponents. Political culture may never be the final word in comparative political analysis but, carefully handled, it can be a useful spring-board.

Further reading: Almond and Verba (1980), Barry (1988), Huntington (1996), Lipset (1983).

In a more recent study using Italy as his laboratory, Putnam (1993) extends the analysis of political culture to show how a supportive social environment directly enhances the performance as well as the stability of a political system. In their original work, Almond and Verba had portrayed Italy as a country whose people felt uninvolved in, and alienated from, politics. Putnam revisits Italy's political culture but pays more attention to diversity within the country. He shows how cultural variations within Italy influenced the effectiveness of the 20 new regional governments created in the 1970s. Similar in structure and formal powers, these 20 governments nonetheless varied greatly in performance. Some (such as Emilia-Romagna in the North) proved stable and effective, capable of making and implementing innovative policies. Others (such as Calabria in the South) achieved little. What, asks Putnam, explains these contrasts?

Definition

Social capital refers to a culture of trust and cooperation which makes collective action possible and effective. As Putnam says, it is the ability of a community, to 'develop the "I" into the "we" '. A political culture with a fund of social capital enables a community to build political institutions with a real capacity to solve collective problems. Where social capital is scarce, even an elected government will be viewed as a threat to individual interests.

Putnam finds his answer in political culture. He argues that the most successful regions have a positive political culture – that is, a tradition of trust and cooperation which results in high levels of what he terms 'social capital'. By contrast, the least effective governments are found in regions lacking any tradition of collaboration and equality. In such circumstances, governments can achieve little and the stock of social capital, already limited, will deflate further. But where does social capital itself come from? Like Almond and Verba before him, Putnam's answer is historical. Somewhat controversially, he attributes the uneven distribution of social capital in modern Italy to events deep within each area's history (Morlino, 1995). The more effective governments in the North draw on a tradition of communal self-government dating from the twelfth century. The least successful administrations in the

South are burdened with a long history of feudal, foreign, bureaucratic and authoritarian rule. Thus, Putnam's analysis illustrates how political culture can be used as the device through which the past is taken to influence the present.

Postmaterialism in established democracies

One factor which helps to account for changes in political culture, at both mass and élite level, is postmaterialism. This notion is a useful example of the way in which political scientists have sought to incorporate change into the analysis of political culture.

From the late 1940s to the early 1970s, the Western world witnessed a period of unprecedented economic growth. 'You've never had it so good' became a cliché that summarized the experience of the postwar generation. This era was also a period of relative international peace, permitting a cohort to grow up with no experience of world war. In addition, the newly-instituted welfare state offered increased security to many Western populations against the scourges of illness and unemployment. According to Inglehart (1971, 1997), this combination of affluence, peace and security led to 'a silent revolution' in the political cultures of Western democracies. He suggests that the emphasis on economic achievement as the main priority is making way for an emphasis on the quality of life:

> in a major part of the world, the disciplined, self-denying and achievement-oriented norms of industrial society are giving way to the choices over lifestyle which characterize post-industrial economies.

From the 1960s, a new generation of postmaterialists emerged – young, well-educated people whose concerns centre on lifestyle issues such as ecology, nuclear disarmament and feminism. Where pre-war generations valued order, security and fixed rules in such areas as religion and sexual morality, postmaterialists de-emphasize political and religious authority. They place more emphasis on self-expression and flexible rules. Postmaterialists are élite-challenging advocates of the new politics rather than élite-sustaining foot-soldiers in the old party battles. They are more attracted to single-issue groups than to the broader packages offered by political parties. A loaf of bread does not satisfy postmaterialists; it must also be wholemeal and additive-free!

Based on extensive survey evidence, Inglehart shows that the more affluent a democracy, the higher the proportion of postmaterialists within its borders. The United States was in the vanguard. In the early 1970s, American postmaterialists were concentrated among yuppies – young, upwardly mobile urban professionals, especially those in the wealthiest state of all, California. Three decades later, this baby-boom generation retains a relatively progressive outlook despite its unparalleled affluence. In Europe postmaterialism came first to, and made deepest inroads in, the wealthiest democracies such as Denmark, the Netherlands and Germany. The affluent Scandinavian countries (except Norway) have been unusually receptive to postmaterialist ideas (Knutsen, 1990). Postmaterialism is less common in poorer democracies with lower levels of education: for example, Greece, Ireland, Spain and Portugal.

Definition

Postmaterialism is a commitment to radical 'quality of life' issues (such as the environment) which can emerge, especially among the educated young, from a foundation of personal security and material affluence. Postmaterialists participate extensively in politics but they are inclined to join élite-challenging promotional groups rather than traditional political parties (Inglehart, 1997).

It seems likely that postmaterial values will become more prominent in the future. When Inglehart began his studies in 1970–71, materialists outnumbered postmaterialists by about four to one in many Western countries. But by 2000 the two groups were expected to be of similar size (Abramson and Inglehart, 1992), a major transformation in political culture. One reason for this changing balance is that education is the best single predictor of postmaterialism. Indeed 'postmaterialism' may be largely reducible to the liberal outlook induced by higher education, especially in the arts and social sciences, and then sustained through participation in the 'knowledge economy' (Farnen and Meloen,

2000). Certainly, educational standards are continuing to rise throughout the world, giving a further and probably irreversible push to postmaterialism. Demographic trends are also favourable. Since post-materialism is least prevalent among the oldest and least educated generations, it may become more widespread as these older cohorts die.

However the real impact of postmaterialism may turn out to be on élites rather than the mass public. Postmaterialists are an active, opinion-leading group and already postmaterialism's shock troops are moving into positions of power, securing a platform from which their values can directly affect government decisions. So far the 1960s generation has retained touches of radicalism even as it secures the seductive trappings of office. For example, Bill Clinton (born 1946, the first president to be born after the war) offered a more liberal agenda to the American people than did his predecessor in the White House, George Bush (born 1924). These two men belonged to different parties, to be sure, but they also represented contrasting generations. A similar claim can be made about Britain by comparing Tony Blair (born 1953) with his predecessor John Major (born 1943) or even about Germany by comparing Gerhard Schröder (born 1944) with the previous Chancellor Helmut Kohl (born 1930). Younger leaders may not be fully-fledged postmaterialists but their outlook does appear to be more optimistic than that of the preceding generation with its direct experience of world war.

Political culture in authoritarian states

In the mature democracies of the West, political culture contributes to the stability of government, offering diffuse support to those charged with the task of ruling. Authoritarian rulers, by contrast, face characteristic problems arising from their unwillingness to confront the challenges of the ballot box. Lacking the legitimacy which flows from free election, such rulers must find other ways of responding to the political culture of the societies they govern. Broadly speaking, their options are three-fold: to ignore, to manipulate or to seek to transform the existing political culture. Each approach merits separate discussion even though in practice non-democratic rulers often mix these strategies.

1. *Ignoring political culture* Disregarding the political culture of the wider society is the tactic favoured by most authoritarian governments. Military rulers, for example, ride to power on a tank and show little concern for the niceties of political culture. Their task is to protect their own back against others who seek to replace them. Far from seeking to draw support from the wider culture, military rulers typically seek to isolate the mass population from engagement with government, thus shrinking the political arena. In extreme cases, tyrants (civil or military) demand the submission of the populace, not its support. Yet it is a tribute to the power of political culture that such repressive survival strategies rarely succeed over the long term. In practice, naked power only prospers when wrapped in legitimacy's clothes.

2. *Manipulating political culture* The second approach is to exploit the political culture by selectively emphasizing its authoritarian elements. This strategy can be more effective over the long term. An authoritarian government which is congruent with cultural values may prove to be more stable than a democratic regime which remains unnourished by the wider culture (Eckstein, 1998a). For instance, traditions of deference, and of personal allegiance to powerful individuals, are a cultural resource which many leaders in Asia and Latin America have exploited to the full to sustain their power. Loyalty to the national leader is presented as a natural outgrowth either of the submission of the landless peasant to the powerful landowner or of the unforced obedience of the child to the parent. The ruler is father and/or chief patron to the nation, providing security and stability but not full democratic accountability. In pre-democratic Mexico, for example, scholars suggested that 'underlying values were fundamentally authoritarian in the sense that Mexican children learned in the family to accept the authority of their fathers and they later transferred this acceptance of authority to political leaders, including the president' (Turner, 1995, p.209).

3. *Seeking to transform political culture* The most interesting approach to political culture in non-democratic regimes is to seek to reshape the country's values. By definition, totalitarian regimes were transformative in outlook. In Hitler's Germany, for instance, all textbooks had to conform to Nazi ideology and pupils were trained in arithmetic using examples based on 'the Jewish question'. But it was communist regimes which made the most systematic and long-lasting effort at reworking political culture. Their starting-point was that the state must transform the way people think and behave. As Meyer (1983, p. 6) comments, communist revolutions were intended to be cultural revolutions. The ultimate goal was to create through education and persuasion a new communist man and woman who would live in a classless, atheist society, free from the poisons inhaled under capitalism.

Take the Soviet Union and China as examples. In both countries the new communist rulers sought to increase mass participation in politics. Mass campaigns ensured that everyone became involved in politics. Yet the anticipated transformation of political culture never came about. Mass participation took on a purely ritual form, based on passive obedience to power rather than active commitment to communism. Fear created citizens who outwardly conformed but in reality adopted strategies designed to ensure their own survival: 'two persons in one body' (White, 1979, p. 11). So while totalitarian reconstructions of political culture rarely succeeded in the manner intended, they often strengthened negative attitudes to politics which continue to hold back the development of participatory cultures in post-communist countries.

Political culture in new democracies

In established democracies, political culture provides a bank of support that can sustain the system through lean times. However, newer democracies lack this goodwill reservoir; their support needs to be earned. So in a new democracy attitudes to the political system depend more on its current performance. In particular, a new democracy which literally delivers the goods will engender supportive attitudes capable of sustaining it in the future. As Diamond and Lipset (1995, p. 751) write, 'for the long-run success of democracy, there is no alternative to economic stability and progress'. Two examples of successful democratic consolidation, Germany and Spain, confirm this point. West

Germany's success in translating its economic miracle of the 1950s and 1960s into favourable attitudes to its new democracy was testament to the power of economic performance to reshape political cultures. In a similar if less dramatic way, the consolidation of the new democracy in Spain in the final quarter of the century owed much to economic development which had been inhibited – though not prevented – under the authoritarian rule of General Franco. Economic and political liberalization marched hand in hand. So it is important to recognize that political culture is itself shaped by a nation's economic performance and its history.

Compared to these success stories, postcommunist and postcolonial political systems have experienced difficulty in delivering the performance needed to strengthen democratic commitment. Consider the postcommunist countries. In the giddy moment of revolution in 1989, expectations ran away with themselves. With a measure of freedom achieved, the people expected affluence to follow, seemingly unaware of the magnitude of change needed to transform an inefficient state-run economy into a vibrant free market. Anticipating effortless wealth, many in East Europe simply encountered long-term unemployment. As de Tocqueville noted long ago (1954 edn., first pub. 1856), dashed expectations are politically more damaging than outright fatalism. Initial reserves of goodwill were soon in danger of running dry as factories closed, infrastructure decayed and the welfare safety-net provided by communism disappeared. Far from delivering affluence, the new 'democratic' system seemed to deliver insecurity and poverty to many, and wealth, often acquired in dubious ways, only to a few. As one frustrated politician said, 'When people had security, they wanted freedom; now they have freedom, they want security.'

By the start of the twenty-first century, however, post-communist states had clearly diverged in the development of their political cultures. Several East European countries, for example Poland, had witnessed considerable economic recovery after the initial melt-down of the early and mid-1990s. The population had begun to learn that over the longer term, democracy could deliver an improved standard of living for most, if not all, the people. Prospective membership of the European Union offered a further stimulus to embracing a democratic culture. As one Hungarian intellectual wrote, 'the élite have caught the train and are heading westwards. They are learning the common Euro-American value system the way a puppy learns to bark' (Lloyd, 1998).

In the central Asian republics, however, political leaders saw no reason to imitate Western models. Impoverished, even pre-industrial economies declined rather than developed and authoritarian rule seemed the surest means of maintaining political stability in such challenging conditions. In any case, the precommunist heritage simply offered weak foundations on which to build a democracy; Tismaneanu (1995) describes the political cultures of the Asian republics, such as Kazakhstan and Uzbekistan, as 'antidemocratic, anti-liberal and ethnocentric'. With Russia and China as powerful neighbours, regional politics in Asia were also less favourable to constructing a democratic culture than was the case in East Europe. In these circumstances, it would have required an astonishing economic transformation to induce a democratic orientation in either the political élite or the general population. Such agricultural societies may need a generation of industrialization, quite possibly state-led, before a democratic culture can emerge.

In several ways, the problems faced by an earlier generation of leaders in creating democratic cultures in newly-independent African states resemble those confronting leaders of the postcommunist world. For countries emerging from colonial status in the 1950s and 1960s, just as in the postcommunist world of the 1990s, the problem of excessive expectations proved difficult to control. In much of Africa, the successful struggle for independence stoked the fires of popular expectation. Yet like the Central Asian republics, most ex-colonies remained poor agricultural societies. And in Africa as well as central Asia indigenous cultures also contained a strong element of deference towards the personal (though not unlimited) authority of traditional rulers, most of whom had little sympathy for the Western import of parliamentary democracy. But the postindependence generation of leaders faced an additional problem: the distinctive difficulty of arbitrary borders inherited from colonial rulers. The postcolonial state was typically weaker than the postcommunist state, with limited penetration into the countryside, and provided only a limited focus for public attention. In Almond and Verba's terms, large parts of the postcolonial world faced the problem of parochial political cultures. The initial task was to nationalize rather than to democratize the political culture; in short, to build a country before attempting to construct a democratic culture.

Élite political culture

Although the impact of mass political culture on political stability has been debated widely, the significance of élite political culture has been addressed less often. Yet in countries with a parochial or subject political culture, élite political culture is primary. Even where mass attitudes to politics are well-developed, as in consolidated democracies, it is still the views of the élite which exert the most direct effect on political decisions. As Verba (1987, p. 7) writes, the values of political leaders can be expected to have both 'coherence and consequences'; for instance, leadership has proved central to recent democratic transitions. In this section, we examine élite political culture, again focusing on its consequences for political stability.

Élite culture is far more than a representative fragment of the values of the wider society. Throughout the world the ideas of élites are distinct from, though they overlap with, the national political culture. For instance, leaders in democracies generally take a more liberal line on social and moral issues. Stouffer's (1966) famous survey of American attitudes to freedom of speech, conducted in 1954, confirmed this point. Stouffer showed that most community leaders maintained their belief in free speech for atheists, socialists and communists at a time when the public's attitudes were much less tolerant. By the 1980s, surveys revealed a striking increase in the American public's support for free speech (Weissberg, 1998). Nonetheless, it was crucial to the cause of free speech in the United States that a majority of the political élite remained committed at a time when the principle was under strong attack from Senator Joe McCarthy's anti-communist witch-hunt (Fried, 1990). In a similar way, many leaders of postcommunist countries accept the need for a thorough transition to a market economy even while mass culture finds more reas-

surance in the equality of poverty practised under communism.

> **Definition**
> **Élite political culture** consists of the beliefs, attitudes and ideas about politics held by those who are closest to the centres of political power. The values of élites are more coherent and consequential than are those of the population at large.

One reason for the liberal and sophisticated outlook of political leaders is their education; in most democracies, politics has become virtually a graduate profession. The experience of higher education nurtures an optimistic view of human nature, strengthens humanitarian values and encourages a belief in the ability of politicians to solve social problems (Astin, 1977). Indeed the contrast between the values of the educated élite and the least educated section of the population is a source of tension in many political cultures.

In assessing the impact of élite political culture on stability, three dimensions are crucial:

- Does the élite have faith in its own right to rule?
- Does the élite accept the notion of a national interest, separate from individual and group ambitions?
- Do all members of the élite accept the rules of the game, especially those governing the transfer of power? (Figure 6.3).

A major component of élite political culture is the rulers' belief in their own right to rule. The revolutions of 1989 in Eastern Europe illustrate how a collapse of confidence among the rulers themselves can lead to the fall of regimes. As Schöpflin (1990) points out,

> an authoritarian élite sustains itself in power not just through force and the threat of force but, more importantly, because it has some vision of the future by which it can justify itself to itself. No regime can survive long without some concept of purpose.

In the initial phase of industrialization, communist rulers had good reason to believe their new planned economies were producing results. But by

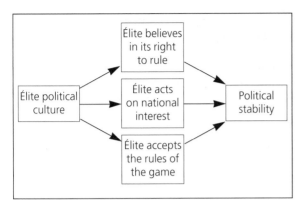

Figure 6.3 How élite political culture affects political stability

the late 1980s progress had given way to decline: planned economics had reached a dead-end. As even nominal support from intellectuals faded, so party officials began to lose confidence in their own right to rule. As disintegration loomed, so they began to line their own pockets by stealing from the state. The system became, if it was not already, corrupt. In the end, communist rule was toppled so easily because it had already been weakened from within. Communist rulers were aware that they had become a barrier to, rather than a source of, progress. Élite values had ceased to underpin the system of government.

A more recent example of élite political culture sustaining non- or semi-democratic government is rule by experts. Latin America provides the best recent instances of technocratic culture. The 'Chicago boys' or 'techno-boys' are a cohort of European- or American-trained graduates (mainly in economics or engineering) who influenced economic policy-making in much of the continent, notably Chile, in the final decades of the twentieth century. These technocrats distrust nationalist language, give priority to growth over its distribution, believe there is one best economic policy – and that they alone know what it is. When supported by a strong political leader, these specialists are able to impose harsh monetary remedies on countries whose financial discipline has too often taken second place to political requirements. Because the authority of these specialists derives in part from their faith in their own prescriptions, Centeno and Silva (1998, p.3) are surely justified in concluding

that, 'an élite culture links all of the different historical apparitions of expert rule' on the continent. Rule by experts provides an instance where the technical, de-politicized views of an educated élite come to dominate the political agenda.

For long-term stability, the political élite must accept and act on some interpretation of the national interest. At issue here is the attitude of rulers to the government posts they hold. Is public service seen as just that – a way of serving the national interest? Some national bureaucracies, from France to Pakistan, have seen themselves as guardians of the nation even to the point of protecting their country from 'mere politicians'. Latin America's technocrats are again an example: they assume that their assessment of the country's long-term economic interests must come before the preferences of specific social groups. Often, however, the state is seen by its ruling élite as a seam of scarce resources to be mined for the benefit of the rulers, their family, their constituents and their ethnic group. In much of the developing world, where economic resources are scarce and state institutions are weak, this approach predominates. In postcommunist countries, too, officials who survived the collapse of the old order often gained personally from acquiring public assets through corrupt privatizations. The élite rediscovered a role: defrauding the public purse while flying the flag of transition to a market economy. It would of course be naive to suppose that politicians anywhere are guided solely by the national interest. However, at a minimum, élite values should not condone self-interested behavior which threatens the collective interest. When exposed, corruption should generate criticism rather than a mere shrug of the shoulders.

Perhaps the most critical dimension of élite political culture is the attitudes which politicians hold to the rules of the game. A range of possibilities exists here. Is élite competition absolute, as in countries such as Northern Ireland where gains to one side (Protestant or Catholic) were traditionally viewed as losses by the other? In such circumstances there is little common ground on which compromises can be sought and found. The considerable achievement of the peace process in Northern Ireland was to silence the guns despite the continuing distrust – indeed, hatred – between the two sides. Alternatively, is strong party conflict moderated by agreement on the rules of the competition, as in Britain and New Zealand?

The consequences of these attitudes to the political game are highly significant. As an example of unmoderated conflict, consider America's Watergate scandal, during which President Nixon's Republican supporters engaged in such illegal acts as break-ins and phone-taps against their Democratic opponents. This unhappy episode reflected the President's own stark view of politics: 'us' against 'them'. Nixon was willing to dispense with the normal rules to ensure that his enemies 'got what they deserved'. A democracy where such a culture prevailed among the élite would have limited prospects of survival.

By contrast, when party or group leaders are willing to compromise to allow the expression of other interests and values, the prospects for political stability improve. Lijphart (1977) argued that an accommodating attitude among group representatives in divided societies such as Austria and the Netherlands provided a recipe for stable government in the 1950s and 1960s. Then, religion still strongly divided these countries; however, party politicians representing the various communities accepted the right of each social group to a fair share of state resources. The major groups – in the Dutch case, Catholic, Protestant and secular – were left free to distribute these resources almost as their leaders wanted. An attitude of 'live and let live' successfully contained explosive divisions and showed the importance of élite values in contributing to democratic stability. Indeed, this culture of compromise and accommodation has outlasted the social divisions it was originally intended to remedy, and perhaps acts now more as a brake on progress than as a guarantee of stability.

Political socialization

Political socialization is the means through which political culture is transmitted across the generations. It is a universal process. To survive, all societies must pass on the skills needed for people to perform political roles, varying from voting at an election to governing the country. The key point about socialization is that it is largely an uncontrolled and uncontrollable process. No matter how much rulers

try (and try they do), they find themselves unable to dominate either the process or the content of socialization. By its nature, therefore, socialization serves to replicate the status quo. As a result, political culture becomes a stabilizing force, providing a major barrier against planned change.

> **Definition**
> **Political socialization** is the process through which we learn about politics. It concerns the acquisition of emotions, identities and skills as well as information. The main dimensions of socialization are what people learn (content), when they learn it (timing and sequence) and from whom (agents). Most studies of political socialization derive from the primacy model – the assumption that what we learn when young provides a lens through which we interpret later experience.

Learning a political culture is very different from acquiring an academic skill, such as a knowledge of history. Formal education involves assimilating and learning how to use information transmitted from teacher to student in an educational setting. Political socialization is more diffuse, indirect and unplanned. It involves the development of political emotions and identities (what is my nation? my religion? my party?) as well as the acquisition of information. Political socialization takes place through a variety of institutions – the family, the peer group, the workplace – as well as formal education. It is as much influenced by the context of communication as its content. For example, children's attitudes toward politics will be influenced as much by their experience of authority at home and at school as by what parents and teachers say their views should be.

The primacy view of political socialization is that basic political loyalties are formed when young. Childhood learning is 'deep learning' because it provides a framework for interpreting information acquired in adulthood. Core political identities are developed in early childhood, when the family is the crucial influence on the child. In late childhood, these attachments are supplemented by a marked increase in information. The main effect of adolescence is to refine the child's conceptual understanding, building on information already obtained. These three stages of socialization – early childhood,

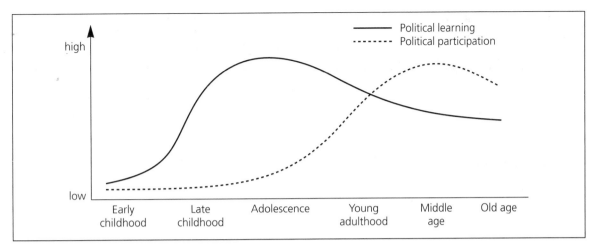

Figure 6.4 Political learning and participation across the life cycle

late childhood and adolescence – prepare the child for political participation in adult political life (Figure 6.4). Adult experiences will modify but not usually transform the outlook secured when young. The primacy model of socialization approach works best during stable eras, for example the USA during the 1950s, because approaches to politics among the older generation will still be relevant to youngsters growing up.

One example of the primacy model is Pye's (1985) analysis of Asian political cultures. Pye argues that

> the cornerstone of powerbuilding in the Asian cultures is loyalty to a collectivity. Out of the need to belong, to submerge one's self in a group identity, is power formed in Asian cultures.

But what is the origin of this need to belong and conform? Pye suggests that the answer lies in the experience of childhood. The Asian child finds unquestioned love and attention from the family: the child respects and does not question parental authority, leading to similar deference to political rulers later in life. This acceptance of benevolent leadership is supposedly characteristic of 'Asian democracy'.

Even when political authority disintegrates, and children grow up amid change and disorder, childhood experiences still colour later life. Consider the distressing case of Africa's child soldiers. Although the United Nations Convention on the Rights of the Child prohibits conscription of children under 15, boys and girls have fought in guerrilla armies in several African countries: for instance, Uganda, Liberia, Mozambique, Ethiopia and the Sudan. Estimates suggested there were about 200 000 child soldiers worldwide at the start of the 1990s. Children make good fighters; they are quick learners, more obedient than adults, less likely to run away, easier to confuse and more willing to fight without drugs. They can be fooled into thinking that adorning themselves with charms or special paint will protect them from enemy bullets. If they are first forced to kill their own relatives or set fire to their own village, they know they can never go back home but must throw in their lot with the roving guerrillas. Such socialization to violence clearly presents an overwhelming task of 're-socialization' when public order is finally restored. Once children have learnt to kill with casual brutality, can they later learn to respect others, to give and receive affection and to listen to their conscience? The primacy model, and indeed common sense, suggests there will be limits to what can be achieved – and that a generation of orphaned, hardened killers will remain available to prospective warlords (Machel, 1996).

Although most research on political socialization has focused on children, we must remember that the process is lifelong; basic political outlooks mature in response to events and experience, and political learning does not stop at childhood's end (Conover and Searing, 1994). Indeed we can contrast the

Country profile **GERMANY**

Population: 82m.

Gross domestic product per head: $22 100 (much lower in former East Germany).

Form of government: a parliamentary federal republic.

Legislature: the 669-member Bundestag is the lower house. The smaller and weaker upper house, the Bundesrat, represents the 16 federal Länder (states).

Executive: the Chancellor leads a cabinet of between 16 and 22 ministers. A President serves as ceremonial head of state.

Judiciary: the Federal Constitutional Court is an influential arbiter of constitutional questions, including disputes between the national and state governments.

Electoral system: the Bundestag is elected through an additional member system which has now been adopted in over 20 countries.

Members of the Bundesrat are nominated by the Länder; hence, the Bundesrat is never dissolved.

Party system: the leading parties are the SPD (Social Democrats) and the CDU (Christian Democrats). These have governed in coalition with the smaller FDP (Free Democrats) and now the Greens, in office with the SPD since 1998.

The Federal Republic of Germany boasts the third largest economy in the world. Its skilled employees, based in capital-intensive factories, produce manufactured goods for sale at premium prices throughout the world. Germany's exports have exceeded its imports each year since 1955 and the country's 'economic miracle' supports extensive public services; both contributed to the growth in the legitimacy of the Federal Republic founded in 1949 upon the ashes of Hitler's Third Reich. Only in the later 1990s, as unemployment passed the four million mark, did the German economic model and its generous welfare system begin to experience stress.

Germany has been a leading player in the development of the European Union. Its political commitment to a United Europe has not wavered and it has been willing and able to support its objectives with hard cash. Because Germany naturally views European developments through the lens of its own system of government, the country's political institutions are of continental significance

Seeking to avoid the political instability of the Weimar Republic (1919–33), which had contributed to the Nazi seizure of power, the framers of the postwar constitution made the Chancellor the key figure in the new system of government. The Chancellor determines government policy, appoints Cabinet ministers, heads a staff of 500 and can only be removed from office when parliament also demonstrates a majority for a named successor. Within a parliamentary framework, Germany offers a distinctive form of 'Chancellor democracy'. Most of

the Republic's six chancellors have been strong figures, further enhancing the status of the office (p. 243). For example, Helmut Kohl (Chancellor, 1982–98) was the dominant force behind the rapid, peaceful and expensive unification of Germany following the dramatic opening of the Berlin Wall in 1990. Though unification has proved costly for Western Länder, and required massive restructuring in the former German Democratic Republic, the result is the largest country in West Europe – and a state which is strategically positioned at the heart of the European continent.

For students of political culture, the country's postwar history shows how the legitimacy of a political system can flow from successful economic performance. Between 1959 and 1988 the proportion of Germans expressing pride in their political institutions increased from 7 to 51 per cent. Over a similar period, support for a multiparty system grew from 53 to 92 per cent. Although this success story has not been repeated so easily in the former East Germany, and a slush-fund scandal tarnished the reputation of Helmut Kohl after he left office in 1998, the emergence of a supportive public in the Federal Republic since 1949 offers hope to other transitional countries seeking to build a democratic culture on an authoritarian history.

Further reading: Conradt (2001), Fuchs (1999), Helms (2000).

primacy model with an alternative recency model – the idea that current information carries more weight just because it is contemporary. The proposition here is that what we see on television today matters more than submerged childhood memories; in other words, adult reality packs more punch than childhood myths. In the eighteenth century, Montesquieu (1949, first pub. 1748) observed that

> we receive three educations: one from our parents, another from our teachers, and a third from the world. The third contradicts all the first two teach us.

The recency approach undoubtedly carries some plausibility. Adult experiences of such major events as war or depression surely leave their mark, helping to shape the political outlook of a generation. But in our time such crises have become exceptional. Minor events continue to come and go but they are viewed through – rather than overriding – established perspectives.

Religion and political culture

No discussion of political culture is complete without an assessment of religion. As a source of basic values, religion is an important component of political culture in many countries. Indeed, most ancient civilizations did not, and non-Christian religions do not, draw a sharp distinction between religious and political authority; rather, the ruler embodied both the spiritual and secular authority. As Jenkinson (1991, p.67) says, 'in the ancient civilizations of China, Egypt, Babylonia, Assyria, Persia and South and Central America, the combination of priest and ruler seems to have been a consistent feature'. The ruler might claim either to be divine himself or alternatively to be God's representative on earth; in either case, laws were treated as divine commands and crime and sin were not distinguished. In contemporary Islamic states, politics and religion are fused; rulers are expected to implement religious values since the Koran requires all Muslims to 'bring about the good and forbid the wrong'. Throughout history, political culture has been woven from the fabric of religion.

In comparison with other religions, Christianity was highly distinctive in developing the idea of the church as a religious community served by a priesthood claiming to exercise spiritual authority independently of secular power (Madeley, 1991, p.92). The biblical proposition, 'render therefore to Caesar the things that are Caesar's and to God the things that are God's', expressed this idea of distinct spheres for politics and religion, the former responsible for the human body and the latter for the human soul. By separating secular and religious authority in this way, the Christian tradition created the conditions for a fateful conflict between them. Indeed the very idea of the modern state emerged in its European heartland during the seventeenth century precisely from conflicts between the standard-bearers of religious and secular power: namely, the Catholic (literally, universal) Church and the strengthening authority of territorial monarchs. The outcome of this conflict, as expressed in the Peace of Westphalia of 1648, was the principle of 'to each prince his own religion', a policy which confirmed the supremacy and autonomy of secular rulers within their own domain. Thus conflicts unleashed by Christianity's partition of religious and secular authority led to the idea of territorial sovereignty which underpins the modern state.

Definition

Compared to political ideologies, **religion** has three linked qualities: transcendence, sacredness and ultimacy. 'Transcendence' refers to faith in a supernatural reality. 'Sacredness' describes those aspects of the world which are placed above the secular by virtue of their religious significance. 'Ultimacy' denotes a belief that religion answers ultimate questions about the meaning of life (Comstock *et al.*, 1971).

As the principle of religious tolerance gradually became entrenched within European states following the reformation, so religion became a matter of individual conscience rather than princely choice. This 'privatized' view of religion received an early decisive statement in the American Bill of Rights (1791): 'Congress shall make no law respecting an establishment of religion, or prohibiting the free exercise thereof.' Slowly, religion became just one element of political culture and a declining one at that. Religion was interpreted as a leftover from an earlier, pre-scientific era. Religion meant underdevelopment; modern meant secular. The Church represented the past but the secular state shaped the present and the future. Indeed the state's expansion in the twentieth century itself contributed to further secularization, as welfare states, especially in northern Europe, supplanted the role of the churches in providing welfare to the needy. In the extreme case, communist states attempted to build a political culture from which religion was completely excised; religion was dismissed as an opiate for those unfortunates who had been forced to endure the evils of capitalism. Since religion had no role in bringing the people to socialism, it was suppressed in communist states.

> **Definition**
> The diminished space occupied by religion in political, social and personal life is termed **secularization**, a phenomenon which many observers viewed as inherent to the modern world, at least until the final decade of the twentieth century (Weigel, 1990).

From today's perspective, this dismissal of religion as pre-modern was distinctly premature; its role in contemporary political culture is far from residual. As Weigel (1990) claimed, 'the unsecularization of the world is one of the dominant social facts of life in the late twentieth century'. In East Europe, postcommunist states permitted the expression of religious traditions which communism had failed to dislodge. In Africa, popular religions drawing on a range of cultural traditions have threatened the cosy relationships between official churches and the government (Haynes, 1996). And in the United States, which always remained a nation of believers despite the constitutional separation of church and state, the Christian right became a major political force in the 1980s, reflecting 'a yearning for a society where biblical precepts and saintly men would govern society' (Peele, 1984, p. 81). Drawing on the strong moral tone of American political culture, the leaders of the new Christian right in the USA initiated a counter-movement against the 'unholy' trinity of secularism, postmaterialism and liberalism. A quarter of a century on from its emergence, America's 'new' religious right has become an established electoral force which Republican candidates in particular must avoid offending.

In the developing world religion has become the culture of the dispossessed and is a major device through which those who feel distanced from society can articulate their frustration. Especially for poor people in highly unequal societies, religion is a powerful voice of political protest. Consider, for instance, liberation theology, a radical movement within the Catholic Church in Latin America in the 1970s and 1980s. Historically, the Catholic hierarchy in Latin America had supported conservative ruling élites, reflecting the traditional pattern of mutual aid between church and state (Medhurst, 1991, p. 190). Yet stimulated by the Second Vatican Council (1962–5), called by Pope John XXIII to renew the Church's role in the modern world, many Latin American theologians began to stress the importance of active commitment to the poor and oppressed. A few priests even drew on the Catholic tradition of the just war to contemplate the overthrow of capitalism, a position that established a remarkable link between liberation theology and Marxism. In retrospect, there can be little doubt that progressive Catholicism contributed to Latin America's shift toward democracy in the 1980s (Sigmund, 1993).

Today, the most dramatic evidence of the continued importance of religion is the resurgence of Islam. In the Middle East and North Africa, Islam predominates; in a postcommunist world it has become the major challenge to Western liberalism. 'Islam' is the Arabic word for 'submission' to the will of God (Allah); the religion originated with the prophet Mohammed in the seventh century. The central tenet of Islam, which sets it at odds with Western liberalism, is that religion should govern all aspects of life. Yet there are of course internal theological divisions within Islam, notably between Shi'ite and Sunni Muslims. The Shi'ites, especially in Iran, strictly affirm that religion is the foundation of human life and that nothing, including law, is independent of it. In contrast to Christianity, religion and political culture merge, creating a single basis for authority and, in extreme cases, a contemporary form of totalitarianism. In the years following the Iranian revolution of 1979 these ideas were implemented with vigour; the *ulama* (the clergy) ruled directly, rather than through advising secular rulers. Today, revolutionary fervour in Iran has cooled and more liberal rulers are seeking some autonomy from the mosque. By contrast, Sunni Muslims have always allowed space to secular rulers and law; Sunni Islam is diverse, flexible and accommodating. And Sunni Muslims, it is important to note, form a clear majority of the world's Islamic population

Islam rejects foreign domination. The slogan 'neither East nor West' became a clarion call of the Iranian revolution and played a substantial role in the revival of Islam elsewhere. Today strong Islamic movements in developing countries are often a form of protest by people who have suffered most, but gained least, from economic growth linked to the West (Keddie, 1991, p. 304). The Islamic revival has provided a rallying cry behind which people in many developing countries can protest against the continued influence of the West on their societies. Islam is a non-Western view of the world that is always prone to becoming anti-Western. It demonstrates the continuing power of religion to shape the political culture of the dispossessed. In particular, Islam illustrates the extent to which religion, like other forms of political culture, operates internationally, responding to inequalities between, and not just within, nations (Esposito, 1997).

Global political culture?

Most discussion of political culture has focused on its role within the state but this tradition now needs supplementing. Like many aspects of politics, culture must be viewed from a global perspective. As the example of religion confirms, ideas and images know no boundaries; they travel faster than products and arguably have more impact.

In a major essay, Huntington (1996) argues that culture based on civilizations rather than countries will be the dominant source of world conflict in the twenty-first century. He notes that the old bases of international conflict – between communism and capitalism, between the Soviet Union and the United States – are exhausted. But the end of the Cold War, Huntington suggests, does not mean the end of cultural conflict. Rather the focus will shift from a battle of ideologies to 'a clash of civilizations', an irreducible division between the major cultural groupings of the world. These groupings are supernational but subglobal (Box 6.1). Between the con-

tradictory worldviews they represent there is little common ground or room for compromise. As globalization proceeds, interaction and friction between civilizations will intensify, producing a high potential for conflict. Huntington notes, for example, how cultural kinship influences the choice of sides in contemporary conflicts: 'in the Yugoslav conflicts, Russia provided diplomatic support to the Serbs ... not for reasons of ideology or power politics or economic interest but because of cultural kinship' (1996, p. 28). Huntington is also doubtful of pragmatic efforts to switch civilizations; he suggests that the reason Australia failed to reinvent itself as an Asian country is simply that it's not. The same problem underlies Turkey's efforts to join the European family: critics claim that Turkey just does not share European culture.

Huntington's analysis appeals because it takes the analysis of political culture into the international realm. However, commentators make three criticisms: (1) Huntington understates the vitality of the nation state, (2) he mixes culture and religion in the confusing idea of a 'civilization', and (3) he ignores the ability of some civilizations to evolve in response to contact with others (Kirkpatrick, 1993). Thus the clash of civilizations may be less strident than he suggests.

But even if we were to reject all Huntington's conclusions, there are certainly aspects of political culture operating on a regional, if not a global, scale.

BOX 6.1
The clash of civilizations?

Huntington divides the civilizations of the world into six or seven main groups. These are:

1. Western
2. Japanese
3. Islamic
4. Hindu
5. Slavic-Orthodox
6. Latin American
7. (possibly) African

Such divisions pose special problems for torn countries located on the fault-lines between cultures. Mexico (situated between the West and Latin America) and Turkey (on the border between the West and Islam) are examples of such 'split' countries.

For example, the postwar effort to build a united Europe was led by a multinational élite with a strong commitment to the European idea. This project was nurtured by the continent's shared experience of war and a desire to prevent its recurrence. In Asia, efforts at building regional institutions have been helped by cultural factors, not least the shared desire to catch up with the West. The Confucian tradition is also common to several countries in the region, contributing to the flow of business across national boundaries. Yet we should be wary of postulating a global culture entirely disconnected from national anchors. Today's 'global' culture is primarily a Western product. American culture, in particular, has proved to be uniquely exportable: 'Macworld' is a place where we can eat American food, watch American movies, and write books using American software. Global culture is not neutral between civilizations; it inevitably reinforces the strength of the leading power.

Key reading

> **Next step:** *Pharr and Putnam (2000) is an important comparative study of political culture in established democracies, focusing on increasing dissatisfaction with the performance of government.*

Norris (1999a) is a useful supplement to Pharr and Putnam. For work examining the concept of political culture more directly, Almond and Verba's *The Civic Culture* (1963) remains an excellent starting point but it needs to be supplemented by the follow-up, *The Civic Culture Revisited* (1980), edited by the same authors. Eckstein *et al.* (1998) apply Almond and Verba's ideas to the interesting example of postcommunist Russia, as does Petro (1995). Putnam (1993) is another influential study, using modern Italy as a case but with more general significance. On élite political culture, a comparative study focused on attitudes to equality is Verba (1987). The key source on postmaterialism is Inglehart (1971, 1990, 1997). A standard text on political socialization is Dawson, Prewitt and Dawson (1977). Nye, Zelikow and King (1997) examine the declining faith of Americans in their federal government. Eatwell (1997) is a collection focused on the political cultures of European countries. On the developing world see Diamond (1993). Haynes (1998) is an accessible introduction to religion and politics. Huntington (1993, 1996) is the source on the clash of civilizations.

Political communication

Society, and with it politics, is created, sustained and modified through communication. Without a continuous exchange of information, attitudes and values, neither society nor politics would be possible. As Williams (1962, p.11) writes, 'What we call society is not only a network of political and economic arrangements, but also a process of learning and communication.' In similar vein, Habermas (1978) suggests that democracy can best be understood as a form of communication in which citizens inform, educate and become reconciled to each other in the process of reaching collective agreements. For Habermas, as for many others, democracy *is* a form of political communication.

Certainly, the main business of politicians is communication; their task is to signal their agendas, policies and strategies to other players of the political game. Indeed, in public affairs words often speak louder than actions. When America's Federal Reserve Board raised interest rates in 1999, the stock market soared, even though higher interest rates would normally have led to lower share prices. The reason? Investors were more reassured by Chairman Alan Greenspan's verbal statement that no further rises should be needed than they were disappointed by the actual increase itself. Even when politicians do act, their actions convey meanings that transform their behaviour into communication. When President Truman authorized the US Air Force to drop atom bombs on Hiroshima and Nagasaki in

August 1945 he was also signalling to Japanese opponents his willingness to continue using these new weapons of mass destruction on civilian populations. The Japanese got the message and quickly surrendered. In short, political activity is invariably a form of communication and the analyst's first task is always to interpret ('decode') the message so that its underlying themes ('sub-texts') become apparent.

Once the message itself is understood, the 'transmission model' offers a useful guide to research (Figure 7.1). This traditional account interprets communication as consisting of who says what to whom, through which media and with what effects. The model distinguishes five aspects to any communication: a sender (who?), a message (what?), a channel (how?), a receiver (to whom?), and a presumed impact (with what effects?). For example, a local party (the sender) might distribute a leaflet (the channel) advocating voting at a forthcoming election (the message) to its own supporters (the receivers), with the result that turnout increases (the impact). This simple model is often criticized as one-directional – that is, it fails to recognize that most communication involves continuing interaction between the participants – and for paying too little attention to the multiple meanings embedded in most political communication. Yet despite these weaknesses the transmission model usefully breaks down the process of communication into component parts. In this way, it assists empirical research.

Sender ⇨ Message ⇨ Channel ⇨ Receiver ⇨ Impact

Figure 7.1 The transmission model of political communication

Development of the mass media

To understand contemporary trends in the communications media, we must begin not by discussing such johnny-come-latelys as the internet but by placing the mass media in a historical context. The story of the expansion of mass communication is intimately linked to the growth of the state itself, especially in the nineteenth and twentieth centuries. A history of politics must also be, in part, a history of communication (Table 7.1).

Two preliminary points should be made. First, the impact of each new medium, from writing through printing to television, has generated more controversy than consensus. The impossibility of isolating pure media 'effects' means there is more sense in asking in what ways, rather than to what extent, specific media have altered politics. Second, we must beware of 'technological determinism' – that is, of using technical advances as our sole explanation of innovations in communication. Typically, new media have emerged in response to a recognized social need. For instance, the telegraph, the telephone and the internet were each consciously developed to improve communication across distance. If communication technologies have transformed the social and political world, it is because the world has been ripe for change (Williams, 1989).

Leaving aside our natural facility for speech, writing was the mother of all communications innovations. According to Ong (1982), the invention of writing in the early civilizations of the Near East in the fifth millennium BCE changed everything. Ong suggests that 'by separating the knower from the

Table 7.1 The development of communication media

Date	Development
Fifth millennium, BCE	Writing systems develop in the earliest urban civilizations of the near East, notably Phoenicia.
About 750, BCE	The first modern alphabet, based on sounds rather than symbols, emerges in Greece.
1450, CE	In Mainz, Johannes Gutenberg invents printing with movable metal type. Book production is aided by new techniques for the mass manufacture of paper.
Nineteenth century	Compulsory primary education introduced, and mass literacy achieved, in Western states.
	The telegraph – a way of sending information across wires using electric signals – permits international dissemination of news, decisions and instructions (e.g. by the British empire to its colonies).
Later nineteenth century and early-twentieth century	Popular newspapers emerge, often with mass circulation. New railway networks allow national distribution.
1930s	Radio's golden age. For the first time, politicians broadcast directly into electors' homes.
1950s–1960s	Television becomes the most popular, and usually the most trusted, broadcast medium in Western countries. Election campaigns are soon fought on, and not just reported by, television. American entertainment programmes are widely exported.
1970s–1980s	The television audience begins to fragment, with an increase in the number and commercialization of channels, distribution by cable and satellite and widespread use of video.
1990s–2000s	Internet access reaches more affluent and educated groups in Western societies, representing a further opening of international communication.

known', writing permitted the development of abstract concepts, objectivity and the accumulation of detailed, accurate knowledge. Certainly, the long-term political impact of writing has been profound. It permitted the record-keeping which is a foundation of the modern state; without writing, states could not have developed as they did. Writing also made possible the transmission of both information and values over large distances, as with the spread of Christianity through monastries and church schools in early Europe and indeed the diffusion of information through the internet today (Mann, 1986, p.335). However, the bridge to the era of modern communication was provided not by writing but by Gutenberg's fifteenth-century invention of printing to paper using movable type. This innovation enabled written knowledge to reach a wider, if not initially a mass, market.

Yet it was not so much the invention of writing and printing, but rather the later extension of literacy to the wider population, which marked off the current era of both communication and politics. Mass literacy in a common language was central to the successful development of contemporary states, facilitating administration of large areas and encouraging the development of a shared national identity. By the end of the eighteenth century, 'signing literacy' had reached about 80 per cent in innovative Sweden. Other European countries, and New England, achieved mass literacy in the nineteenth century, following the introduction of compulsory primary education. Mass literacy was a function, an achievement and an affirmation of the modern state, just as it remains an aspiration for many countries in the developing world today.

In particular, widespread literacy in a shared language made possible the popularization of newspapers, the key development in political communication during the nineteenth and early twentieth centuries. Originally, newspapers had been small-circulation party journals containing lengthy editorials and dreary reports of politicians' speeches. But advances in printing (e.g. the steam press) and distribution (e.g. the railway) opened up the prospect of populist and profitable papers funded by advertising. Paradoxically, by growing away from their party roots, papers became more popular and thus politically more important. While American newspapers remained mainly local, the press in more compact countries such as Britain and Japan became truly national, building enormous circulations which still survive. Newspaper owners became powerful political figures, not just for the impact of their party endorsements but also for their willingness to use their journals to promote favoured causes. Control over the means of mass communication had become, as it remains, a major political resource.

Definition

Mass media refer to methods of communication that can reach a large and potentially unlimited number of people simultaneously. Television and newspapers are the most important; others are posters, radio, books, magazines and cinema. An e-mail to a friend is personal, not mass, communication, but sending a message to all members of a newsgroup is an example of mass communication.

Although newspapers remain important channels of political communication, their role was of course supplanted by broadcasting in the twentieth century. Cinema newsreels, radio and then television enabled communication with the mass public to take place in a new form: spoken rather than written, personal rather than abstract and, on occasion, live rather than reported. Oral communication reasserted itself, though now in a form which could escape the confines of the small group. Significantly, the two major ideologies founded in the twentieth century – communism and fascism – each consciously sought to mobilize popular support through exploiting these new media: mass media would be used to control mass man (and woman) in the manner dramatically portrayed in George Orwell's *1984*. While such visions ultimately proved to be fanciful, the broadcast media – like newspapers earlier – did serve as agents of national integration. In most countries, a small number of national channels initially dominated the airwaves, providing a shared experience for a dispersed population.

In the Western world, a major impact of the broadcast media was to force politicians to learn new communications techniques. A public speech to a live audience encouraged expansive words and dramatic gestures but a quieter tone was now needed for transmission direct to the living room. The task was to converse rather than to deliver a speech; to talk to the millions as though they were individuals. President Franklin Roosevelt's 'fireside chats', broadcast live by radio to the American population in the 1930s, exemplified this new, informal approach. The impact of Roosevelt's somewhat folksy idiom was undeniable. He talked not so much *to* the citizens but *as* a citizen – and was rewarded with his country's trust (Barber, 1992). In this way, broadcasting transformed not just the reach but also the tone of political communication.

The media: contemporary trends

In the first decade of the new century, the three major trends in communications are commercialization, fragmentation and globalization (Box 7.1). The combined political effect of these developments is to reduce national political control over broadcasting, permitting consumers either to choose their own political programming or increasingly to escape from political content altogether. If the mass media performed a nation-building function in the twentieth century, their emerging effect in the new century is to divide the traditional national audience, perhaps contributing thereby to declining political participation.

1. *Commercialization* means that communication is increasingly treated as the important business it has become. The American Federal Communications Commission estimates that worldwide revenues from the mass media exceeded $1 trillion per year by the start of the 1990s; the figure rises each year (Tracey, 1998, p.8). Commercialization also allowed the new media moguls, such as Rupert Murdoch, to build transnational broadcasting networks, achieving on an international scale the prominence which the newspaper barons of the nineteenth century had achieved at national level. In the Americas, Canada excepted, broadcasting had always been commercially led, but in West Europe commercialization was an important and controversial political development. The first television stations in Europe had been national and publicly owned; for instance, the British Broadcasting Corporation (BBC). Such stations were controlled by public supervisory boards, funded by a special licence fee, and they adopted a public service ethos which aimed to educate and inform, rather than merely to entertain, the viewer. However in the 1970s and 1980s new commercial channels were introduced and advertising was added to many public stations (though not to the BBC). These developments threatened previously cosy links between parties and broadcasters and represented a shift to conceiving the viewer in less political terms, as a consumer rather than a citizen. In this increasingly commercial environment, Tracey (1998) claims that public service broadcasting has become nothing more than 'a corpse on leave from its grave'. Since governing parties no longer pay the piper, their influence over the tune has inevitably declined.

2. *Fragmentation* means that consumers are increasingly able to watch, listen to and read what they want, rather than what they are given. Distribution of programmes by cable, satellite and the internet allows viewers to receive a greater range of content, local and overseas as well as national (Figure 7.2). With the widespread use of video recorders, content became separated from the channels through which it is distributed. Unlicensed pirate stations further complicate the picture (Soley, 1998). The result is a more splintered audience; during the 1990s, for instance, the audience share of the big three American television networks – ABC, CBS and NBC – dropped by a third. The political implications of this fragmentation will be substantial. The media may cease to be agents of national

---

BOX 7.1

Contemporary trends in mass communication

Trend	Definition
Commercialization	The decline of public broadcasting and the rise of for-profit media
Fragmentation	The increased range of channels and an enhanced ability to consume programmes on demand (e.g. videos)
Globalization	Improved access to overseas events and media in 'the global village'

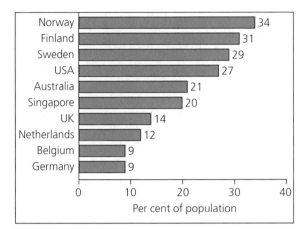

Sources: *Financial Times*, 6 July 1999; and United Nations Development Programme, *Human Development Report* (Oxford and N.Y.: Oxford University Press, 1999), figure 2.4, p. 63.

Figure 7.2 Countries with highest proportions of internet users, 1998

integration, functioning instead to bring together groups with narrow interests both within and across countries. Freedom of speech – including the freedom to express racist and sexist views – may emerge by default, due to the practical impossibility of regulating the babble of sounds emerging from diverse media. Reaching viewers with remote controls, video recorders and more entertainment options will become more difficult, forcing political parties to invest greater sums in paid advertising. Politicians will have to communicate in a manner, and at a time, of the voters' choosing. They will have to continue their migration from television news to higher-rated talk-shows. The sound-bite, never unimportant, will become more vital as politicians learn to articulate their agenda in a 30-second commercial. In short, just as the balance within the media industry has shifted from public service to private profit, so within political communication itself will the emphasis move from parties to voters. Politicians rode the emergence of new media with considerable success in the twentieth century but they will find the going tougher in the new millennium.

3. *Globalization*, finally, is represented by the metaphor of a global village. The world has been compressed into a television screen. In 1776 it took 50 days for news of the English reaction to the American Declaration of Independence to get back

to the United States. In 1950 British reaction to the outbreak of the Korean War was broadcast in America in 24 hours. With advances in satellite broadcasting, reports filmed in Britain now take a mere 25 seconds to reach American TV screens – and vice versa. We now take for granted the almost immediate transmission of newsworthy events around the world. During the war in Kosovo in 1999, television stations worldwide were supplied by NATO with video footage of high-tech weapons hitting specified objectives. At the same time, Serbia offered pictures of civilians 'taken out' by missiles destroying wrong targets. The prime impact of the global village has been to encourage more open and informed societies – it is now harder than ever for governments to isolate their populations from international developments. Even communist states found it difficult to jam foreign radio broadcasts aimed at their people. Reflecting on communism's collapse, Eberle (1990, pp. 194–5) claimed that 'the changes in Eastern Europe and the Soviet Union were as much the triumph of communication as the failure of communism'. Recent technological developments also facilitate underground opposition to authoritarian regimes. A small group with a fax machine and internet access now has the potential to draw the world's attention to political abuses, providing source material for alert journalists. Burma's military rulers, China's communist government and Saudi Arabia's ruling families have all suffered from overseas groups in this way. Not even the most dictatorial government can control global information flows, the speed and detail of which have served to raise the political cost of domestic repression.

The media in established democracies

The media possess a natural vitality in consolidated democracies, where freedom of expression is legally protected. In this section, we examine the political significance of the major media – television and newspapers – and discuss what has become one of the key relationships within the political élite: that between politicians and journalists.

In nearly all established democracies, television has become the pre-eminent mass medium. Television

THE POLITICAL SIGNIFICANCE OF THE INTERNET

The internet is a network of physical connections which, in conjunction with software standards ('the world wide web'), allows computers to communicate with each other. In the 1990s, the internet became one of the most talked-about communications channels, not just because of its explosive growth but also because it permits the dissemination of any kind of data: text, images, speech and video. But will the internet prove to have long-term political significance?

The case for

By 1999, there were over 150 million internet users worldwide, about half in the United States though the highest penetrations were in Scandinavia. Because the rate of diffusion is exceeding previous innovations such as radio and television, we can expect internet use to spread rapidly in the developed world, especially among the better-educated (Table 7.2). The internet goes much further than any previous medium in overcoming distance, paying scant regard to national boundaries and cultures. During the war in Kosovo in 1999, for instance, it was as easy for users to access the views of the Yugoslav, American or British governments – or of all three. Thus the web will weaken the hold of states over their populations and will fragment political communication, allowing virtual communities with specialized interests to exchange information and ideas in a manner which overwhelms national boundaries. State censorship will become impractical; if a government wants its economy to benefit from e-commerce, it must pay the political price of allowing internet users to access sources of information beyond its control. Governments may be unable to monitor, let alone tax, this enhanced economic activity; the net will bring about the final triumph of business over politics. And the regulation of the internet itself will remain in the hands of technical committees rather than states, a leading case of governance without governments.

The case against

The long-term political impact of the internet is exaggerated. Users can 'travel the world', but how many Americans, in particular, will do so, given the predominance of American sites? In any case the sites which will attract most visitors will be those

Table 7.2 Time taken from inception for new media to reach 50 million households in the USA

Medium	Years
Radio	38
Television	13
Cable	10
Internet	5*

*estimate for 1995–2000.

Source: *Financial Times*, 28 July 2000, citing Morgan Stanley Dean Witter.

from governments, corporations and institutions which are already best-known. In that sense, the internet will remain a secondary medium. Nor can a computer network overcome differences of language or culture; secondary nets for languages other than English are recreating rather than bypassing linguistic divisions. And for all the talk of electronic democracy, official referendums by internet are nowhere to be found. Note, too, that in the past, newspapers, radio and television all improved coverage of far-off affairs but none succeeded in displacing the state; why should the technical act of linking computers together prove to be any different?

Assessment

Firm judgments are premature. If previous innovations offer any lessons, it is that projections of their impact often proved wildly inaccurate. Some people thought radio would change the world; others said the telephone would never catch on. But two points are clear. First, technology does not determine content. The messages which travel round the internet will reflect forces beyond the net itself. Second, access to the internet requires a telecommunications infrastructure which barely exists in many developing countries. At the end of the twentieth century, most people in the world had never made a telephone call, let alone surfed the net.

Further reading: Kamarck and Nye (1999b), Norris (1999b), Sunstein (2001).

is a visual, credible and easily-digested format which reaches nearly every household, providing the main source of political information (Table 7.3). In election campaigns, for instance, the television studio has become the main field of battle. The party gladiators participate through appearing on interviews, debates and talk-shows; the spectators participate through watching and, ultimately, voting. Local party activists, once the assault troops of the campaign, are now mere skirmishers. Television has ceased to cover the campaign; it has become the campaign. Of course, the political significance of television goes far beyond elections. Much larger, if still declining, numbers watch the evening newscasts and it is here, in deciding what to cover and what to leave out, that television producers exert most influence (Box 7.2). Through their assumptions about newsworthiness, editors resolve their daily dilemma of reducing a day's worth of world news to half an hour (or less) on the evening news. Because news programmes focus on the exceptional, their content is invariably an unrepresentative sample of events: for example, policy fiascos receive more attention than policy successes. Similarly, corruption is a story but integrity is not. Necessarily, television is a distorting mirror on the world – and the more compressed news coverage becomes, the less accurate its lens must be.

Despite the primacy of television, it would be wrong to discount the political significance of the second mass medium, newspapers. The print media remain important in politics, not least because they are free of the tight regulation still applied to national broadcasters. In nearly all democracies, newspapers are freer with comment than is television; indeed, in an age when news provision has become dominated by television, interpretation and evaluation have become prime functions of the press. Television tells us what happened; at their best, newspapers can place events in context. A television programme can only cover one story at a time whereas newspapers can be scanned for items of interest and can be read at the user's convenience. For such reasons, quality newspapers are the trade press of politics, read avidly by politicians themselves.

Further, newspaper circulations remain extensive in many democracies. In Japan, Britain and Scandinavia, most adults still read a daily newspaper

---

BOX 7.2

Some tests used by journalists to determine newsworthiness

1. Will the story have a strong impact on viewers?
2. Does the story involve violence, conflict, disaster or scandal? ('if it bleeds, it leads')
3. Is the story current and novel?
4. Does the story involve people with whom our audience is already familiar?
5. Is the story relevant in other ways to our particular audience?

Source: Graber (1997), pp. 106–8, based on studies in the USA.

(Table 7.3). In Japan, unusually, the public still relies more on the national press than on television for its information and some studies indicate that Japanese newspapers exert more influence over the electorate's agenda (Feldman, 1993, p.24). In Britain and Scandinavia, newspapers retain at least some loyalties to the parties from which they originally emerged. When a national British paper switches its party support, as the best-selling *Sun* did to Labour in 1997, the shift commands attention elsewhere in the media, illustrating how newspapers remain significant political players in their own right. Newspapers also influence television's choice of topics: a story appearing on TV's evening news often begins life in the morning paper. In short, in countries with a lively press tradition newspapers retain a political significance greatly in excess of their circulation.

What is the media's impact on how people vote in elections in liberal democracies? This remains a matter of controversy. In the 1950s, before television became pre-eminent, the reinforcement thesis held sway (Klapper, 1960). The argument here was that party loyalties were transmitted through the family and that, once developed, such identities acted as a political sunscreen protecting people from the harmful effects of propaganda (Box 7.3). People saw what they wanted to see and remembered what they wanted to recall. In Britain, for example, it was argued that party identification determined choice of newspaper more than papers influenced how people voted; at most, the press reinforced existing dispositions. The reinforcement theory therefore contended that exposure to the media tended to

Table 7.3 Media penetration and campaign coverage on television

	TV sets per 1000 people, 1996	Newspaper circulation per 1000 people, 1996	Campaign coverage on television		
			Paid political ads?	Free time to parties?	Leader debates?
Australia	554	297	Yes	Yes	Yes
Austria	518	294	Yes	Yes	
Belgium	463	160	Yes	Yes	Yes
Canada	**714**	159	Yes	Yes	Yes
Denmark	592	311	No	Yes	Yes
Finland	605	**547**	Yes	No	Yes
France	591	218	No	Yes	Yes
Germany	564	311	Yes	Yes	No
India	27	61	No	Yes	
Ireland	411	153	No	Yes	Yes
Italy	524	104	Yes	Yes	No
Japan	**684**	**580**	Yes	Yes	Yes
Netherlands	514	305	No	Yes	
New Zealand	521	223	Yes	Yes	Yes
Norway	460	**593**	Yes	Yes	Yes
Sweden	499	446	Yes	No	Yes
United Kingdom	516	332	No	Yes	No
United States	**805**	212	Yes	No	Yes

Notes: The three largest figures in each column are shown in **bold**. Newspaper readership is normally at least twice circulation. The figure for television penetration in India is for 1994.

Sources: Unesco Statistical Yearbook (Paris: Unesco, 1998) at http://www.unesco.org; and LeDuc, Niemi and Norris (1996b) table 1.7 (updated).

strengthen existing attitudes rather than convert people from one viewpoint to another. This thesis was a useful counter to unqualified assertions of media power. It was also consistent with early postwar surveys showing that few people actually changed their voting intention during election campaigns. Indeed, it remains the case that the more information people possess about politics, the less likely they are to alter their views in response to new information. The *cognoscenti* are inoculated against

change by their existing stock of knowledge; it is the least informed and interested who are most influenced by new messages (Zaller, 1992).

Although the reinforcement theory proved its value half a century ago, it is an inadequate guide to the role of the media today. Party loyalties are now weaker, and television more pervasive, than in the 1950s. For this reason, the agenda-setting view of media impact has gained ground. In an election campaign, media coverage directs our attention to the candidates and the issues, even if it does not add greatly to our knowledge or determine our reactions. More generally, the media help to shape political culture though their influence on day-to-day discussion. Thus the significance of agenda-setting goes far beyond elections; it provides a useful notion for thinking about media effects as a whole. Walter Lippman's (1922) view of the press is applicable to the media generally: 'It is like a beam of a searchlight that moves restlessly about, bringing one episode and then another out of the darkness and into vision.'

Recognizing the influence of the media, governments and parties make enormous efforts to influence both the amount and the tone of their coverage by the media. Governing parties, in particular, devote considerable attention to informing, cultivating and seeking to manipulate the journalists whose reports achieve national coverage. The humble government press office, now populated by highly-paid spin doctors, has never been more important.

It is worth considering the balance between government (say, a White House spokesperson), and the media (say, a White House correspondent) for this relationship is increasingly central to the character of élite politics in modern, communication-rich democracies. The game is classically political, mixing shared and competing objectives. The government needs coverage and the media must fill its space, creating a shared interest in news. But the government seeks favourable coverage while journalists are after a big story, objectives that are rarely consistent since, as every reporter knows, good news rarely makes the headlines. The game is further complicated by competition among the journalists themselves, giving the administration leverage it can exploit by placing stories with preferred correspondents. But as with so many political relationships, the game of government-media relations is repeated each day, allowing long-term norms of acceptable behaviour to develop. A spokesperson who gives out misleading information, or no information at all on a significant topic, will have less credibility with the media in future. So briefers accept that it pays to be accurate and even-handed in distributing information; the facts must be correct if not necessarily complete. Equally, competition among journalists is reduced because they learn to hunt as a pack.

> **BOX 7.3**
> ## Reinforcement and agenda-setting theories of media impact
>
> According to the **reinforcement** theory, the media conserve but do not change the political attitudes and behaviour of the electorate. Political outlooks are too entrenched to be swayed by media reports. The reinforcement theory, also referred to as the 'minimal effects' model, was based on three mechanisms:
>
> 1. Selective perception – people watch and read material which agrees with their existing views.
> 2. Selective interpretation – people interpret information so as to render it consistent with current opinions.
> 3. Selective recall – people tend to forget information that runs counter to their prior beliefs and values.
>
> By contrast, the **agenda-setting** theory maintains that the media (and television in particular) influence what we think about, though not necessarily what we think. The media frame the agenda: 'to the extent that the mass media have influenced their audiences, it has stemmed not only from what is said but more significantly from what is not said' (Lazarsfeld and Merton, 1996, p.18; First pub. 1948).

Correspondents know it is more important for their own careers not to miss the story that everyone else has than it is to obtain exclusives. Thus, in practice, stable routines develop which reduce the game of government-media relations to a few well-understood ground-rules. The outcome is not so much collusion as contained competition (Maltese, 1994).

> *Definition*
> A **pseudo-event** is a press conference, photo-opportunity or other occurrence which would not take place but for the coverage it generates. Estimates suggest that in the United States most television news stories are pseudo-events. The dominance of pseudo-events shows how news is not so much discovered as manufactured in the continuous interplay between government and media.

Of course, the government invariably has a head start over opposition parties in media presentation. Statements by presidents and prime ministers are always more newsworthy than those made by their political opponents. Journalists have no option but to cover a prime ministerial press release, even if they are fully aware of the party-political motives underlying its timing. Many a prime minister has arranged a prestigious overseas trip in the run-up to an election, keen to exploit the domestic impact of a handshake with, say, the American president. Coverage of opposition parties is inevitably a lower priority for the media (Miller *et al.*, 1990).

Public opinion

Especially in democracies, politics is a battle for influence over the important but imprecise terrain of 'public opinion'. Sir Robert Peel, twice Prime Minister of Britain in the nineteenth century, defined public opinion as 'that great compound of folly, weakness, prejudice, wrong feeling, right feeling, obstinacy and newspaper paragraphs'. Many modern politicians are equally cynical about public opinion but this does not prevent them from being interested observers of it.

Definition

Public opinion refers to the aggregate views of the politically relevant population on the politics of the day. Key dimensions of public opinion are: reach (what proportion of the population forms the 'public'?), salience (how much does an issue matter to people?), direction (what is the public's preference on an issue?) and momentum (is an issue, party or candidate gaining or losing support?)

In democracies public opinion extends to virtually the entire adult population. Nearly all adults have the vote, their views are represented in frequent polls and elected politicians have an incentive to study the findings. Even here, though, a minority underclass exists which rarely votes, lives in no-go areas for pollsters and does not follow politics at all. Public opinion does not encompass the politically excluded. In authoritarian regimes, of course, national politics engages far fewer people, even as spectators, and therefore public opinion shrinks.

Given that public opinion is an important element of democratic politics, how exactly does it exert its influence? In a sense public opinion pervades all policy-making, forming part of the environment within which politicians work. Thus public opinion sits in on many government meetings even though it is never minuted as a member. In such discussions public opinion usually performs one of two roles, acting either as a prompt ('public opinion demands we do something about traffic congestion') or as a veto ('public opinion would never accept restrictions on car use'). So as Qualter (1991, p. 511) writes, 'while public opinion does not govern, it may set limits on what governments do'.

Public opinion is never all-powerful, even in liberal democracies. Four factors limit its influence:

- The impact of public opinion declines as issues become more detailed. Voters are more concerned with goals rather than means, with objectives rather than policies. 'What policies politicians follow is their business; what they accomplish is the voters' business' (Fiorina, 1981). A few important objectives preoccupy the public but most policies are routine and uncontroversial. In detailed policy-making, organized opinion matters more than public opinion.
- The public is often surprisingly ill-informed, and this, too, limits its impact. Most Americans, for example, are unable to name their members of Congress. Similar findings from other democracies confirm the ignorance of large sections of the public, especially on foreign policy issues remote from ordinary life. Limited knowledge is another reason why public opinion functions more often, and more appropriately, as an agenda-setter than as a policy-maker.
- Public opinion can evade trade-offs but governments cannot though they sometimes try. The public may want lower taxes and increased public spending but rulers must make a choice. So even in the most democratic of countries, government by public opinion remains a distant dream – or nightmare.
- Politicians respond to their perceptions of public opinion but these interpretations can be systematically inaccurate, derived as they are from the distorting lens of interest groups and the selective telescope of the media (Herbst, 1998). Politicians typically respond to mobilized opinion rather than public opinion.

The idea of public opinion has gained further currency as opinion polls, citizen juries and focus groups have developed to study it. Indeed there are few areas in politics where a concept is so closely linked to how it is measured. In modern democracies, public opinion is both measured by, and partly composed of, reports of investigations into its content (Box 7.4). Consider opinion polls, the best-established and most accurate method of identifying what people believe and profess. Although the public itself remains resolutely sceptical of polls, their accuracy is now well-attested, at least in predicting election outcomes. In the United States, the average error in predicting the major parties' share of the vote at national elections between 1950 and 1988 was a mere 1.5 per cent, an impressive figure even if not always accurate enough for the television networks to pick the right winner on election night. Precision is similar in other democracies. Counter-intuitive it may be, but 1000 people carefully selected for an opinion poll can accurately represent the whole population. A well-chosen sample will certainly provide a more reliable guide to public opinion than the self-selected readers who answer write-in polls in magazines, the listeners who call radio discussion shows or the voters who contact their representative about their pet topic. In fact, a major virtue of opinion polls is that they capture the views of the many bored and uninterested electors who would otherwise be left out of the debate.

Opinion polls contribute to the democratic process in three ways. First, they bring into the public realm the voices of people who would otherwise go unheard. They are the only form of participation, apart from the ballot box itself, in which all count for one and none for more than one. Second, polls are based on direct contact by interviewers with the public; they get behind the group leaders who claim to speak 'on behalf of our members'. Third, polls enable politicians to keep in touch with the popular mood and they give some insight into the reasons for election results. In short, opinion polls oil the wheels of democracy.

Yet it would be wrong to overstate the value of opinion polls in defining the 'mood of the people'. Just like students taking a test, interviewees answer but do not set the questions. Party officials and journalists in the capital city commission polls and set the pollsters' agenda. The concerns of the political élite, caught up in the intricacies of day-to-day politics, contrast with those of ordinary people. People may never have thought about a topic before answering questions on it. They may give an opinion when they have none; or agree to a statement because it is the easiest thing to do ('yea-saying'). Thus Ginsberg (1986) suggests that élites use polls to 'pacify or domesticate opinion' by reducing citizens to passive respondents who voice opinions in response to a narrow range of topics selected by the élite itself. Certainly, one danger of opinion polls is that they construct, and even shape, public opinion at the same time as they measure it.

Because opinion polls do not give respondents a chance to discuss the issue before expressing their views, the technique is criticized by advocates of deliberation. Where, ask the critics, is the equivalent of the vigorous debate which preceded the moment of decision in the Athenian assembly? To be useful, it is argued, public opinion must have been shaped in the press of collective discussion, not simply measured through individual questionnaires.

BOX 7.4
Measuring public opinion

An **opinion poll** is a series of questions asked in a standard way of a systematically-selected sample of the population. The term usually refers to short surveys on topical issues for the media. Polls are usually conducted face-to-face or by telephone (Mann and Orren, 1992).

A **sample survey**, though conducted using similar methods as opinion polls, involves a more detailed questionnaire, often conducted for government or for academic researchers (Broughton, 1995).

In a **deliberative opinion poll**, or **citizens' jury**, people are briefed by, and can question, experts and politicians on a given topic before opinions are measured. The technique seeks to measure what public opinion would be if the public were fully informed about the specific issue through discussion (Fishkin, 1991).

Where opinion polls, conventional or deliberative, yield statistical results, a **focus group** is a moderated discussion among a small group of respondents on a particular topic. A focus group is a qualitative tool, often used to explore the thinking and emotions lying behind people's attitudes, including those expressed in polls. A favourite tool of party strategists, the technique is more open-ended than an opinion poll with its pre-set questions and answers (Greenbaum, 1998).

Building on this line of thought, scholars have developed the idea of a deliberative opinion poll or citizen jury (Fishkin, 1991). This technique involves exposing a sample of electors to a range of viewpoints on the selected topic, perhaps through presentations by experts and politicians, followed by discussion. Once the issues have been thoroughly aired, and only then, a measure of opinion is taken. As Fishkin (1991, p.1) explains,

> an ordinary opinion poll models what the public thinks, given how little it knows. A deliberative opinion poll models what the public would think, if it had a more adequate chance to think about the questions at issue.

This technique can therefore be used to anticipate how opinion might develop on new issues and is particularly useful on issues with a large technical content, for example nuclear energy or genetic testing. Though not widely used, citizens' juries are an ingenious attempt to overcome the problem of ill-informed replies which bedevils conventional polls investigating public opinion.

The media in authoritarian states

Far from acting as the fourth estate, casting its searchlight into the darker corners of government activity, the media in authoritarian states are subservient to political power. In such regimes, official television stations and subsidized newspapers reproduce the regime's line, critical journalists are harassed and the entire media sector develops an instinct for the limits of the permissible. In short, journalists are cowed into blandness and self-censorship becomes an understandable reflex. If democracy thrives on the flow of information, authoritarian rulers survive by limiting free expression, leading to journalism which is subdued even when it is not subservient.

In her study of sub-Saharan Africa before the wave of liberalization in the 1990s, Bourgault (1995, p.180) identified several means used by authoritarian leaders to limit independent journalism. These included: broad libel laws, endless states of emergency, licensing of publications and journalists, heavy taxation of equipment, a requirement to post bonds before a new publication could be launched,

restricted access to newsprint and the threat of losing government advertising. Sub-Saharan Africa also demonstrates the lack of resources which holds back the development of the media sector – and authoritarian states are most often found in relatively poor countries. A shortage of resources limits journalistic initiative and increases vulnerability to pressure; impoverished journalists may even be reduced to publishing favourable stories in exchange for money.

Pressures from authoritarian leaders on the media are by no means restricted to Africa. In post-communist Central Asia, journalists continue to practise the delicate art of coexisting with non-democratic rulers. Large parts of the media, including news agencies and printing presses, often remain in state hands, giving the authorities leverage over the media. In Belarus, a leading independent paper even has to be printed overseas, in Lithuania. The state also typically retains ownership of a leading television channel. Foley (1999) reports that

> from Kazakhstan to Kyrgyzstan and Tajikistan to Belarus and Ukraine, the story is a dismal one: tax laws are used for financial harassment; a body of laws forbids insults of those in high places; compulsory registration of the media is common. In Azerbaijan, as in Belarus, one-man rule leaves little room for press freedom.

The justification for restricting the freedom of the media typically refers to an over-riding national need: for social stability, nation-building or economic development. A free press, like a competitive party system, is presented as a recipe for squabbling and disharmony. Many of these 'justifications' for controlling the media may just be excuses for continuing non-democratic rule. Even so, we should not assume that the Western idea of a free press has universal appeal. Islamic states, in particular, stress the media's role in affirming religious values and social norms. A free press is seen as an excuse for licence; why, the question is asked, should we import Western, and particularly American, ideas of freedom if the result is just scandal-mongering and pornography? In some Moslem societies, the result is what Mernissi (1993, p.68) terms 'TV Islam', a strange brew of dull religious programming and inoffensive American movies.

In totalitarian states, the media had a more

positive role to play in seeking a transformation of political culture. The means of communication were therefore brought under tighter control than in authoritarian systems. Unrelenting penetration of mass communication into everyday life was a core component of the totalitarian system. 'It is the absolute right of the state to supervise the formation of public opinion', said Joseph Goebbels, Hitler's Minister of Propaganda. It is significant however that neither communist nor fascist regimes regarded the media, by themselves, as a sufficient means of ideological control. Communist states supplemented mass propaganda with direct agitation in places where people gathered together; fascist regimes valued direct control through public meetings over impersonal broadcasts.

In communist states, the dual dimensions of political communication were propaganda and agitation. Propaganda explained the party's mission and instructed both the élite and the masses in the teachings of Marx, Engels and Lenin. To achieve their propaganda objectives, ruling communist parties developed an elaborate media network with radio, posters, cinema and television all reinforcing each other. Even art had to become 'socialist art', playing its part in the revolution of hearts and minds.

BOX 7.5
Limiting the damage: China and the internet

As an example of how authoritarian governments seek to limit media freedom, consider the following rules introduced by the Chinese government in 2000 to regulate internet content providers. Website providers in China are required:

- to obtain the approval of the government before cooperating with businesses overseas
- to avoid content that subverts the power of the state, harms the country's reputation, or reduces the prospects of reunification with Taiwan
- to avoid content that supports banned cults [notably Falun Gong]
- to record the content of their site
- to record all visitors to their site over the preceding 60 days
- to hand over such records to the police on demand

Source: *Financial Times*, 3 October 2000.

Communist societies were short of many things but propaganda was not one of them. Where propaganda operated through the media, agitation operated at local level. Agitation sought to mobilize the masses behind specific policies such as increased production. The party sought to place an agitator in each factory, farm, military unit and other public bodies. Together, propaganda and agitation dominated the flow of information; their combined effect would be all the greater because, in the nature of a total regime, no dissenting voices could be permitted.

Definition
Propaganda is communication intended to promote a particular cause by changing attitudes and behaviour; today, the term also implies the absence of a balanced perspective. The word is religious in origin: in the seventeenth century, the Catholic Church established a College of Propaganda to propagate the faith. Propaganda was an important feature of communication in totalitarian regimes, with their aim of transforming political culture. It has also been important to democracies in times of war, both externally to mislead the enemy and internally to protect domestic morale.

The communist experience remains important today as a real-life experiment in attempting to use the media as a tool for influencing the public. So what was the impact of such propaganda? Communist propaganda may have helped with agenda-setting, disguising local problems such as accidents, poverty or pollution which could be hidden from people in other parts of the country. Propaganda may also have scored some success in highlighting achievements such as the shift to an industrial society. And, just as advertising by parties in democracies is often aimed at their own activists, so communist propaganda may have been internalized by party members. It is noteworthy that even in China, where greater tolerance and freedom is now permitted, the ruling communist party has kept close control over the means of mass communication (Box 7.5).

But on the whole the communist experience revealed the limits of media power. A cynical public was not easily fooled. Grandiose statements were too often contradicted by the grim realities of immediate experience. In any case, as communist states became inert, so propaganda became empty ritual. Eventually, the main function of propaganda became that of showing the population that the party still ruled; whether the propaganda was convincing almost ceased to matter. Propaganda became less a mechanism of conversion and more a symbol of control. Like the drizzle nothing could be done about it so it was ignored.

The media in new democracies

An assessment of the position of the media in new democracies depends heavily on the point of contrast. When the comparison is with the preceding regime, media independence seems to be one of the main hallmarks of the new order. Censorship gives way to a multitude of new publications peddling everything from serious news to virtual pornography. The old are bemused, just as the young are amused, but everyone can see that the climate has changed. Indeed, an increasing spirit of media adventure is one of the first cracks to appear in pre-democratic structures; journalists are quick to sense that authoritarian rulers are losing the will to repress.

Yet even after several years as a new democracy, the position of the media usually remains weaker than in established democracies. Governing parties continue to exert influence over broadcasting media, political entrepreneurs use ownership of newspapers to maximize their influence and journalists themselves remain poorly trained and insecure in employment. In postcommunist Europe, the rapid entry and equally rapid exit of foreign capital from the media industry contributed to this instability (Kettle, 1997). Far from becoming the fourth estate, the media in most new democracies remain pawns in a political game swirling above them.

In many newly-democratic regimes, the impulse of leaders is still to manipulate and even control the media despite their rhetorical commitment to free speech (Milton, 2000). Indeed, the freedom of the media is one test, rarely clear-cut, of whether a political system *is* democratic. Russia is an example of a postcommunist, semi-democratic state where pressures on the media, from powerful business people as well as politicians, remain intense. This influence derives precisely from the centrality of television to political communication in Russia. As in many poor countries, broadcasting is the main way of reaching a large, dispersed and impoverished population for whom free television has more appeal than paid-for papers. The television audience in Russia for nightly news programmes matches that for the Super Bowl in the United States (Mickiewicz, 1999). For good reason, then, Moscow's politicians compete intensely for control of a pluralistic, but far from independent, television system. The leading Russian banks own many private television stations, which dutifully propagate their masters' interests, while the public television stations – ORT and RTR – suffer direct political interference.

Vladimir Putin's success in the presidential election of 2000 owed much to his control of public television, whose news broadcasts in the final days of the campaign portrayed his opponents as sympathetic to gays and Jews. However, even the President was unable to suppress the surge of media criticism that followed an explosion abroad a Russian submarine, with loss of all 118 lives on board, a few months later. While Putin's election demonstrates beyond doubt that the Russian media are subject to political influence that can alter election outcomes, the Kursk disaster showed that such influence is markedly less complete than in the communist era.

While the existence of substantial media freedom is a major achievement of many postcommunist polities, it would be wrong to suppose that the postcommunist media are now as free as in consolidated democracies. There is little tradition, even from the precommunist era, of holding rulers to account through independent media scrutiny. Even where political domination of the media does not continue, journalistic standards remain low, reflecting decades in which reporters appointed by the party did little more than reproduce party platitudes. Easy editorializing still takes priority over the hard graft of news-gathering (Dempsey, 1993, p. 281). In Poland, for instance, journalists are traditionally expected to be teachers and preachers rather than professional reporters (Goban-Klas, 1997). Entrenching the freedom of the media to investigate and criticize public conduct is inevitably a gradual affair, requiring restraint by political rulers and, as often as not, the support of independent courts.

Key reading

Next step: *Barber (1992) is a lucid history of the media and politics in the United States.*

Communication may be central to politics but the definitive contemporary treatment of the topic is still to be written. Williams (1962) is one of the originators of the academic study of communication and his short book is still relevant to students of politics. Mann's history of power (1986) includes considerable material on communication and its impact. Most modern studies focus on the media rather than communication generally. Graber (1997) usefully covers the media in contemporary American politics. Semetko (1996) is a helpful comparative overview of the media in democracies; Kuhn (1997) focuses on West Europe. On public opinion, Glynn *et al.* (1998) is a wideranging collection, while Splicahl (1999) offers an erudite overview. Mann and Orren (1992) and Broughton (1995) cover opinion polls in the USA and Britain respectively. Greenbaum (1998) discusses focus groups; Fishkin (1991) looks at citizen juries. Away from the Western world, Bourgault (1995) is an informed account of the media in sub-Saharan Africa, principally before democratization. Mickiewicz (1999) contains fascinating material on television in Russian politics, while Milton (2000) is a more general study of the media in postcommunist states.

CHAPTER **8** | # Political participation

An environmentalist lying in front of workers building a new road, a citizen contacting a legislator about a missing social security cheque, a revolutionary plotting the violent overthrow of a despised regime – all are examples of individual participation in politics. This chapter examines general citizen involvement in politics; we reserve participation through elections to the next chapter.

Patterns of participation differ greatly between democratic and authoritarian governments (Box 8.1). Indeed, such contrasts follow from the nature of these regimes. In established democracies, voluntary participation is the norm. People can choose whether to get involved (for example by voting or abstaining) and how to do so (for example by joining a party or signing petitions). The main exception to the voluntary nature of participation is compulsory voting, found in a handful of democracies such as Australia and Belgium. In authoritarian regimes, by contrast, participation is diminished in quality if not quantity. Most non-democratic rulers hang a 'keep out' sign over the political sphere and formal participation by ordinary people is often limited to rigged elections. In totalitarian regimes, however, participation takes a different form again: both extensive and regimented. It involves the expression of support for, but not the selection of, government personnel and policy. Its main function is to mobilize the people behind the regime's effort to transform society, whether towards a communist or fascist ideal. In this chapter, we examine political participation in democratic and non-democratic settings before turning to the less orthodox forms of participation represented by violence and revolution.

Participation in established democracies

The most striking fact about political participation in established democracies is how far it falls short of a participatory ideal. Voting in national elections is normally the only activity in which a majority of citizens engages. However, throughout the democratic world anything beyond voting is the preserve of a minority of activists. Indeed the activists are outnumbered by the apathetics – people who neither vote nor even follow politics through the media. Further, even the activists seem to be reducing their

BOX 8.1
Patterns of participation across regimes

Participation:	Established democracies	Authoritarian regimes	Totalitarian regimes
Amount	Medium	Low	High
Character	Voluntary	Manipulated	Regimented
Purpose	To influence who decides and what decisions are made	To protect rulers' power, and to offer a democratic facade	*In theory:* to transform society *In practice:* to demonstrate rulers' power

involvement in formal politics, with party membership and turnout in decline in many democracies (Mair and van Biezen, 2001).

In a renowned analysis, Milbrath and Goel (1977, p. 11) divided the American population into three groups, a classification which has since been applied to other democracies. Their categories were: (1) a few *gladiators* (about 5–7 per cent of the population) who fight the political battle, (2) a large group of *spectators* (about 60 per cent) who watch the contest but rarely participate beyond voting, and (3) a substantial number of *apathetics* (about one-third) who are withdrawn from politics (Figure 8.1). Milbrath's labels were based on an analogy with Roman contests at which a few gladiators performed for the mass of spectators but some apathetics did not even watch the show.

Definition

Political participation is activity by individuals formally intended to influence either who governs or the decisions taken by governments. Citizens can be classified both by the extent of their political involvement (e.g. gladiators, spectators and apathetics) and by the form their engagement takes (e.g. conventional, unconventional or both).

Early postwar investigations, such as Milbrath and Goel's, viewed participation as one-dimensional; the idea was that everyone could be arrayed at some point along a single scale of political activity. However, later research showed that people are politically active in different ways, allowing specialization to occur within the broad category of participation. In a study based on a national sample of Americans interviewed in 1967, Verba and Nie (1972) confirmed the existence of Milbrath's gladiators, active in all ways, and of his apathetics who did not participate at all. But the in-betweens fell into more specialized groups. One large category contained those who always voted but virtually never did anything else. Another group consisted of 'parochial participants' – people who contacted officials on individual problems but were otherwise inactive. Thus people vary in *how,* and not just in *how much,* they participate in politics. This diversity becomes especially clear when we extend the analysis of participation to include protestors – those who specialize in direct action such as boycotts and marches. In

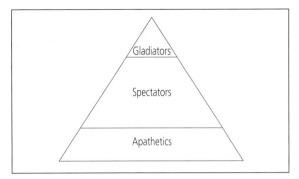

Figure 8.1 Patterns of participation in democracies

Britain, whether a person engages in such radical acts tells us little about whether he or she votes a lot or a little; the two forms of participation appear to be unconnected (Parry, Moyser and Day, 1992, p. 58). So participation in liberal democracies may be limited in extent but it is also multi-dimensional; people select the form as well as the extent of their political involvement.

In every country political activists are anything but a cross-section of society. In most liberal democracies, participation is greatest among well-educated, middle-class, middle-aged white men. Furthermore the highest layers of political involvement show the greatest skew. As Putnam (1976, p. 33) says,

> The 'law of increasing disproportion' seems to apply to nearly every political system; no matter how we measure political and social status, the higher the level of political authority, the greater the representation for high-status social groups.

What explains this bias in participation towards upper social groups? Two main factors are at work: political resources and political interest. First, the members of high-status groups are equipped with relevant political resources. These include education, money, status and communication skills. Education gives access to information and, we trust, strengthens the ability to interpret it. Money buys the luxury of time for political activity. High status provides the opportunity to obtain a respectful hearing. And communication skills such as the ability to speak in public help in presenting one's views persuasively.

Second, high-status individuals are more likely to be interested in politics. No longer preoccupied with daily struggles, they can take satisfaction from engagement in collective activity. The wealthy are also more likely to be brought up in a family, and attend a school, which encourage an interest in current affairs. Reflecting the normal pattern of political socialization, adult participation echoes these early influences. So upper social groups show an interest in politics and can afford to put these concerns into practice.

We can apply this dual framework – based on political resources and political interest – for understanding participation bias to the question of why women are still under-represented at higher political levels. In 2000, women made up just 14 per cent of the world's legislators, double the figure of twenty-five years earlier but still a large under-representation (Table 8.1). As a group, women still possess fewer political resources than men. They have less formal education (though this difference has reversed among the young in many established democracies). Further, interest in formal politics is sometimes limited by childbearing and homemaking responsibilities. In addition to these underlying factors, male pre-eminence in politics tends to pereptuate itself. Some women lack the confidence needed to throw themselves into the hurly-burly of formal, male-led politics while many still face the high hurdle of discrimination from sexist male politicians. These gatekeepers claim that women are 'unsuited' to politics – and then use the scarcity of women in high office to prove their point!

We should also note three institutional factors linked to female representation in national parliaments:

- *The electoral system.* Women do best under the party list version of proportional representation, a method that allows party officials to select a gender-balanced set of candidates. When New Zealand switched to a more proportional system in 1996, the proportion of women legislators increased from 21 to 29 per cent.
- *Quotas.* These ensure women make up a certain proportion of a party's candidates or, more radically, of its elected representatives. In Norway, for example, the leading parties introduced quotas as early as 1973. Quotas are easily applied with party list PR but even in constituency-based electoral systems it is possible to require both genders to be included on a district short-list.

Table 8.1 Female representation in national parliaments

	Year	Women MPs %
Sweden	1998	43
Denmark	1998	37
Finland	1999	36
Netherlands	1998	36
Norway	1997	36
Germany	1998	31
New Zealand	1999	29
Australia	1998	22
Canada	1997	20
Britain	1997	18
Mexico	1997	18
World average	**2000***	**14**
USA	1998	13
Ireland	1997	12
France	1997	11
Italy	1996	11

* Based on the most recent election in all countries for which data are available, including many not shown in this table.

Note: In bicameral assemblies, figures are for the lower house.

Source: Inter-Parliamentary Union (2000).

- *Turnover of legislators.* Low turnover, as in the United States Congress, creates a recruitment bottleneck which enables men, once elected, to remain in post for decades.

Definition

Political exclusion refers to those people who through occupying a marginal position in society are effectively excluded from participation in collective decision-making. Migrant workers, criminals, drug addicts and those who do not speak the native language are examples of groups confronting this difficulty.

The emphasis of research on political participation is on explaining what distinguishes the gladiators from the spectators. But we must also examine those who participate least, not just those who are most engaged. So what about the apathetics, the people who do not participate at all? This group raises the emerging problem of political exclusion. The apathetics who do not participate are, in effect, excluded from the normal means by which citizens collectively shape their society (Verba, Scholzman and Brady, 1995). A typical non-participant would be an unemployed young man with no qualifications, inhabiting a high-crime inner-city neighbourhood, often from a minority culture and perhaps not even speaking the dominant language. Usually such people are not on the electoral roll, often they do not watch the news on television and rarely do they read a national newspaper. Their political activity, if any, is often irregular and spasmodic, as with riots. Just as higher social groups possess both the resources and the interest to overparticipate, so a shortage of resources and lack of interest in the remote goings-on of national politics explain the underparticipation of those near the bottom of increasingly unequal Western societies. The emergence of a two-tier political system, characterized by a majority which at least votes at national elections combined with a non-participating underclass, is a growing challenge to the assumption of political equality on which democracy is based.

Participation trends in democracies

In 1996, 325 000 Belgians, 3 per cent of the country's population, marched through Brussels in a peaceful protest against an inadequate public investigation into a sexually motivated child murder. This White March (white was worn as a symbol of purity) was an example of 'new politics'. In Belgium as in many other Western democracies, new politics has mounted a major challenge to the 'official' system. It is a style of participation which deliberately seeks to distance itself from established channels, thereby questioning the legitimacy as well as the decisions of the government. Advocates of new politics are willing to consider nonconformist forms of participation: demonstrations, sit-ins and

sit-downs, boycotts and political strikes. In some democracies, including West Germany and Italy, unorthodox participation in the 1960s and 1970s extended further, to include violent activities such as terrorism and kidnapping.

These newer modes of participation are usually in pursuit of broad, not class-based, objectives: for example, nuclear disarmament, feminism and the environment (Box 8.2). New politics is concerned with making statements and expressing identities, as with the gay movement, not just with achieving precise regulatory objectives, as with traditional interest groups. If political parties exemplified old politics, informal single-issue movements define new politics. Tarrow (1998) even speaks of the emergence of a 'movement society' in which new politics becomes the normal mode of participation as traditional parties lose weight.

At one level, the whole rationale of new politics is to threaten the dominance of existing élites. It provides a 'people's challenge' to the iron triangles of government, protective interest groups and mainstream parties. So at first glance the contrast between new and old politics seems to confirm the multi-dimensional character of participation, with older generations concentrating on orthodox politics and younger people more attracted to new politics. Yet beneath the surface the distinction is muddied. Except for their youth, the unconventional activists of the 1960s resembled the orthodox activists of an

---

BOX 8.2

Old and new politics

	Old politics	New politics
Organization	Formal	Informal
Attitude to political system	Supportive	Critical
Vehicle of participation	Parties,	Single-issue groups
Style of participation	Orthodox	Unconventional
Concerns	Interests	Values
Breadth	National	Global
Motives	Instrumental	Expressive
Typical age	Middle-aged	Younger

earlier era: well-educated, articulate people from middle-class backgrounds. And more than a few leaders of the new politics are switching to orthodox politics as they age; many a protest activist of the 1960s had turned into a party leader by the century's end. A prominent example here is Joschka Fischer, whose appointment as Germany's Foreign Minister in 1998 led to the republishing of press photographs showing him assaulting a policeman during demonstrations thirty years earlier. For all the ideological differences between new and old politics, one function of new politics has been to provide a training ground for future national leaders.

Definition

Social movements are defined by Tarrow (1998, p. 4) as 'collective challenges by people with common purposes and solidarity in sustained interaction with élites, opponents and authorities'. Unlike parties, social movements do not seek state power. And unlike interest groups, they do not operate through detailed engagement with government. Rather, they aim to bypass the government through a self-help ethos or, alternatively, by seeking publicity through the media.

Established democracies hold no monopoly over new politics. Hiding under the label of 'new social movements' (NSMs), new politics also became a significant feature in many authoritarian states, notably in the 1970s and 1980s. In Latin America, encouraged by development agencies and radical Catholicism, social movements sought to carve political space for themselves by asserting their identity as indigenous peoples, gays, feminists and ecologists (Escobar and Alvarez, 1992). As in the established democracies, NSMs arose more from opposition to the state than from any desire to become part of it. In contrast to Western democracies, however, new politics in less developed countries was also the territory of the poor, as people facing acute problems of daily life organized to improve their conditions. The urban poor organizing soup kitchens, the inhabitants of shanty towns lobbying for land reform, the mothers pressing for information on their sons who 'disappeared' under military rule – all were examples of this flowering of popular political activity. However, the reluctance of these movements to engage with formal politics

limits their long-term national significance. Local and small-scale in origin and character, NSMs often lack policy sophistication, particularly on national economic issues. Indeed the democratic transition has taken some wind from their sails. In Uruguay, for example, 'democracy brought, by a curious twist, the disappearance of many grass-roots movements that had been active during the years of dictatorship' (Canel, 1992, p. 290).

Participation in authoritarian regimes

With the exception of totalitarian regimes, authoritarian rulers typically seek to limit mass engagement in politics. They prefer to build a moat between state and society, securing their own position. Because political participation is viewed as a threat to the position of those in power, the tendency is to restrict its extent and to control its expression. And because authoritarian regimes lack an accepted mechanism for replacing the government, rulers invariably fear that even the most innocuous forms of participation might spiral into a threat to the regime itself. But non-democratic rulers also discover that the political costs of oppression can sometimes exceed its benefits, providing opportunities for groups such as students to test the limits of the acceptable in a continuing game of cat-and-mouse with the authorities. Even in authoritarian systems, the boundaries are negotiated; repression can alternate with a degree of tolerance, depending on the political balance within the ruling élite itself.

In this section, we will use military governments to illustrate the general pattern of limited and controlled participation in authoritarian settings. We will also consider patron–client networks, a form of participation which is particularly common in authoritarian regimes and which provides an effective device for rulers seeking to manipulate rather than prevent popular involvement with politics.

To begin with military regimes, most such governments adopted what Remmer (1989) calls an 'exclusionary approach' to popular participation. The generals discouraged mass involvement in politics because they feared its consequences for their own position. Chile between 1973 and 1989, under General Pinochet, was an extreme case. He sought

FOR OR AGAINST

BOWLING ALONE

'Americans of all ages, all stations in life, and all types of disposition are forever forming associations . . . Thus the most democratic country in the world now is that in which men have in our time carried to the highest perfection the art of pursuing in common the objects of common desires' (de Tocqueville 1954, p. 513, first pub. 1835).

In influential publications, Putnam (1993, 2000) questions whether de Tocqueville's thesis about the United States is still correct. Putnam claims that 'something has happened in America in the past two or three decades to diminish social engagement and civic connectedness', with damaging consequences for the quality of politics. He suggests that Americans now spend more time watching Friends than making them. Is Putnam right? If so, does his thesis also apply to other democracies?

The case for
Putnam marshals considerable evidence from the USA to illustrate his theme. For instance:

- Between the early 1960s and 1990 voter turnout declined by nearly a quarter (and by rather more among young electors).
- Between 1973 and 1993 the proportion of Americans claiming to have attended a public meeting in the last year fell by more than a third.
- Between 1974 and 1989 the proportion of people engaged in regular volunteer work dropped by a sixth.
- Between 1960 and 1994, the proportion agreeing with the survey statement 'most people can be trusted' fell from a half to a third.

More significantly, Putnam also explains why he judges such findings important. He believes that social participation creates social capital. It nurtures commitment to the common good, allows networks to develop from which new projects can emerge, permits individuals to develop their skills, knowledge and understanding, and generally encourages the give-and-take which is a hallmark of democracy. What kind of 'democracy' awaits, he asks, if most people are now 'bowling alone'?

The case against
All arguments that 'things are not what they were' are suspect. Golden ages are more often tricks of memory than historical realities. Even in the 1950s, commentators were bemoaning the rise of the 'lonely crowd', 'mass society' and the 'inner-directed personality' (Riesman, 1950). It is much more likely that social activity has changed its form rather than its extent. As Putnam himself recognizes, some types of group, such as crime-watch groups, health clubs, support groups (e.g. of crime victims) and public interest groups have grown. For instance, member-ship of the American Association of Retired Persons grew from 400 000 in 1963 to 33m in 1993. With the advent of the telephone and e-mail, people can associate with like-minded individuals elsewhere in the country rather than face-to-face. As a result, they depend less on old-fashioned neighbours. There is no reason to suppose that this change reflects any loss of 'social capital'. Indeed, the ability to join, benefit from and then leave highly specific and instrumental networks in response to changing indi-vidual needs may increase the 'efficiency' of social relationships compared to a time when people had long-term relationships with just a few people.

Assessment
Even if social participation is declining in the USA, it is difficult to see what can be done to reverse the trend. Any political implications need political solu-tions. If America is to solve its turnout problem, for instance, the solution surely lies in improved registra-tion procedures, not in persuading people to invite their neighbours to a barbecue. In any case, in Europe (where television never became as all-con-suming as it once was in the USA), social participa-tion does not seem to have declined to the same extent. America may lead the world but sometimes the world declines to follow.

Further reading: Pharr and Putnam (2001), Putnam (1993, 2000), Rueschmeyer, Rueschmeyer and Wittrock (1998).

not just to govern without popular involvement but aimed also to suppress all potential sources of popular opposition. He exterminated, exiled or imprisoned thousands of labour leaders and left-wing politicians, concentrating power in the hands of his own military clique. Pinochet himself acted as chief executive while a four-man junta representing the army, navy, air force and national police performed legislative functions. The purpose of such an apparatus was to monitor political participation so as to identify threats to the military's position, for example from students or organized workers. As a result, and often as an intention, ordinary citizens were persuaded to keep their heads down and steer clear of any engagement with the bared teeth of military might.

However, not all military regimes were as brutal as Chile's. A few even adopted Remmer's 'inclusionary' approach to participation. That is, some military leaders tried to build a base of support among the political class – and even on occasion the wider population – usually by exploiting the population's respect for a strong leader. Such inclusionary regimes were often organized on presidential lines, based around a dominating personal ruler attempting to build a strong country (Munck, 1989). The modernizing regime of Abdel Nasser in Egypt was such a case. Nasser came to power in a coup in 1952, became president in 1956 and remained there until his death in 1970. He sought to broaden his political appeal beyond the military, though as a result his regime underwent a process of civilianization, becoming an instance of presidential and bureaucratic, rather than purely military, government. However, even in Nasser's Egypt (as in contemporary China) any political competition was confined to élite groups. As Lesch (2000, p.580) says,

> The government wanted to demobilize and depoliticize the public. The regime offered access to jobs, socioeconomic equity and national independence in return for which the public was expected to be politically quiescent.

We turn now to patron–client networks, a core technique used by authoritarian leaders to structure political participation. Clientelism, as this practice is often called, is a form of political involvement which differs from both voluntary participation in liberal democracies and the regimented routines of totalitarian states. Although patron–client relationships are found in all political systems, the developing world (and especially authoritarian regimes within it) offers the fullest expression of such relationships. Indeed in many developing countries networks of patrons and clients are often the main instrument for bringing ordinary people into contact with formal politics.

Patron–client relationships are informal hierarchies fuelled by exchanges between a high-status 'patron' and some (often many) 'clients' of lower status. The colloquial phrase 'big man/small boy' relationships conveys the nature of the interaction. Patrons are landlords, employers, political entrepreneurs or most often ethnic leaders. Indeed, the elusive notion of an ethnic group can be partly understood as a large patron–client network for distributing favours. Lacking resources of their own, clients gather round their patron for protection and security. Political patrons control the votes of their clients and persuade them to attend meetings, join organizations or simply follow their patron around in a deferential manner. For example in Sri Lanka patrons with access to the resources of the state largely decide how ordinary people vote (Jayanntha, 1991). Patrons exploit their local power-base to strike deals with ministers in the national government, offering the support of their clients in exchange for a share of the government's resources.

Definition

Clientelism is a term used to describe politics substantially based on patron–client relationships. These relationships are often traditional and personal, as in the protection provided to tenants by landowners in developing countries. But they can also be more instrumental, as with the resources which dominant parties in American cities provided to new immigrants in exchange for their vote. Where clientelism is common, it can pervade the political culture, affirming the inequality from which it springs (Clapham, 1982).

Participation through patronage is a device which appeals particularly in authoritarian settings because it links élite and mass, centre and periphery, in a context of inequality. Patronage networks act as political glue, binding the 'highest of the high' with the 'lowest of the low' through faction membership.

Such networks transcend, without nullifying, inequalities of power, wealth and status. Thus inequality provides the soil in which patron–client relationships flower. Poverty means the poor are vulnerable and need protection; inequality means the rich have the resources to provide help in exchange for political allegiance.

As with other aspects of politics, participation in totalitarian regimes formed a distinct pattern of mass participation, more extensive than democracies but also more regimented than authoritarian states. For the classic example, we must look back to communist regimes, particularly in their earliest, vigorous decades. At first glance, participation in communist states left established democracies in the shade. People in such states were far more active in politics than are citizens in contemporary democracies. Citizens sat on comradely courts, administered elections, joined para-police organizations and served on people's committees covering local matters. This apparatus of participation derived from the Marxist idea that all power at every level of government should be vested in soviets (councils) of workers and peasants. Marxist theory stressed self-government, so citizens in communist states had a wider menu of participation opportunities than their counterparts in democracies.

Definition

Regimented participation is élite-controlled involvement in politics designed to express popular support for the notional attempt by the rulers to build a new society. Its purpose is to mobilize the masses behind the regime, not to influence the personnel or policies of the government.

However, the quality of participation in communist states did not match its quantity. Although the party's desire for popular participation may originally have been genuine, the impulse to safeguard party control proved to be stronger. Communist élites sought to ensure that mass participation always strengthened, and never weakened, the party's grip; so party members guided all popular participation. At regular meetings of women's federations, trade unions and youth groups, party activists explained policy to the people. But the information flowed in one direction only: from top to bottom. So members of such groups eventually behaved the way

they were treated: as passive recipients rather than active participants. Except for careerist die-hards, cynicism soon replaced idealism. The outcome was that communist parties directed political participation to an extent unknown in the democratic world.

Eventually, some ruling parties did allow more participation but only in areas that did not threaten their monopoly of power. In particular, party leaders encouraged reforms that would revive ailing economies and so bolster the rulers' own position. Industrial managers were given more say in policy-making as political participation became more authentic on local, specific and economic matters. But crucially these reforms were not matched in the sphere of national politics. Because no real channels existed for airing grievances, people were left with two choices: either to shut up and get on with life or to express their views outside the system. For all the notional participation, communist governments chose to ignore the extent of popular resentment to their rule.

Participation in new democracies

A change in form of government always requires the politically active population to learn new habits. However, the transition from non-democratic to democratic rule is especially acute. Participation which was either deliberately limited or tightly controlled (or both) suddenly becomes voluntary but necessary: votes must be cast, parties organized, people recruited to political office. Cynicism must give way to a measure of engagement as enemies learn to live together. Creating democratic institutions is a short-term constitutional task but unlearning old assumptions about the limited role for voluntary participation is a long-term problem to which generational turnover is perhaps the only solution.

Consider postcommunist countries. In the communist world the old style of regimented participation quickly disintegrated as these regimes fell apart, partly in response to dramatic street protests in the capital cities. Once new and nominally democratic institutions had been created, the task was to consolidate the new order by developing structured forms of voluntary participation through parties, elections and interest groups. This has proved to be

Country profile **RUSSIA**

Population: 147m (and declining by about 800 000 per year).
Gross domestic product per head: $4000 (fell by over 40 per cent 1991–8).
Unemployment: about 30 per cent.
Form of government: federation of 21 autonomous republics.
Executive: formally semi-presidential but with a strong presidency. The

prime minister heads the Council of Ministers and succeeds the president if needed (no vice-president).
Assembly: the Duma (lower house) contains 450 members elected by an additional member system. The Federal Council (upper house) contains two members from each of 89 geographical units.
Judicial branch: based on civil law.

Headed by a Constitutional Court and, for civil and administrative cases, a Supreme Court. Substantial lawlessness.
Natural resources: massive reserves of oil, gas, coal, timber and minerals but many are difficult to exploit.
Environment: extensive pollution, deforestation and contamination (including local radioactivity).

Russia is a vast country with an imperial and authoritarian past. It is a place full of problems, potential and paradoxes. By area Russia is the largest country in the world, almost twice the size of the United States. The population includes 36 national groups with populations of at least 100 000. Russia's rulers have in the past been autocratic empire-builders, basing their imperial expansion on control of a serf society and (until the communist era) a rural economy. Thus Russia's experience with communist dictatorship represented a variant of a familiar authoritarian pattern. The communist party did, however, dominate society completely, more so than in nearly all other communist states. Internationally, the Union of Soviet Socialist Republics (USSR, 1922–91) formed what amounted to a Russian empire.

Of all the postcommunist states, Russia raises the most interesting questions about the relationship between participation and democracy. For many observers a country with Russia's autocratic past cannot expect to develop the voluntary participation underpinning established democracies. The country's history has bequeathed a political culture based on a fatalistic acceptance of strong leadership. This desire for a near-dictator was, it is claimed, reinforced by the economic decline and ethnic divisions of the early postcommunist years. Cynics suggest that Russia spent the twentieth century proving that communism did not work and intends to do exactly the

same with liberal democracy in the twenty-first century. Eckstein (1998, p. 377) concludes that

> It would be harder to think of a less likely case for successful democratization than Russia. Support for the idea of democracy is at best tenuous and instrumental, it has no strong roots in an accustomed central political culture and the social context is inhospitable to it in almost all respects.

Yet this assessment may be too gloomy. In any large country, attitudes to politics are neither simple nor uniform. Among younger generations, and in the Moscow region, support for democracy is firmer. The desire for effective government in postcommunist Russia may be a short-term response to social breakdown, not an indicator of deep-seated authoritarianism. Russia's past may be non-democratic but this does not prevent its people from learning from established democracies elsewhere. Further, by the mid-1990s Russia had succeeded in holding a series of reasonably free elections to both the presidency and the Duma. Whatever the future may hold for postcommunist Russia, it is surely too fatalistic to claim that an authoritarian past rules out the possibility of building democracy in Russia. The real question, perhaps, is just how democratic Russia's 'democracy' will prove to be.

Further reading: Danks (2001), Eckstein (1998b), Petro (1995).

a continuing task. The populations of many Eastern European states had experienced regimented participation under communist rule and seen mass participation on television during its collapse. However, they had little experience of voluntary participation as understood in the West. The same was true of political élites. In the Balkan states such as Bulgaria and Romania, as in the successor states to the Soviet Union, communist rule was itself a continuation of an authoritarian political tradition. Even in Czechoslovakia, Illner (1998, p.75) notes that 'more active participation was reduced again after the short period of post-1989 exhilaration and the traditionally detached attitudes of the population towards public involvement were continued'. A stable system of voluntary participation requires the relationship between state and society to be completely recast, a task requiring far greater skill than merely chopping up the rotting timbers of the communist state.

The problem is to build a 'civil society' regulated by law but remaining separate from the state. Such a society provides opportunities for people to participate in collective activities that are neither pro-state nor anti-state but simply non-state – an innovative idea in a postcommunist setting. Under communist rule, civil society had been demobilized. It had been stood down so that the rulers could directly control the individual: 'everyone was supposed to be the same – working for the state, on a salary, on a leash' (Goban-Klas and Sasinka-Klas, 1992). Any groups that did exist might well contain informers acting for the party; the mere possibility was enough to keep people on their guard. In short, civil society was flattened by the bulldozer of the communist party; public opinion was diminished as private opinion remained just that – private. Yet, as Diamond, Linz and Lipset note (1995, p. 28),

> civil society contributes in diverse ways to deepening, consolidating and maintaining democracy. It supplements the role of political parties in stimulating political participation and increasing citizens' political efficacy and skill.

The notion of a civil society played an important role in the critique of communist power developed by Eastern European dissidents in the 1980s. However, these thinkers naturally tended to see civil society as an enemy of, not a complement to, state power. To support civil society was to oppose the state. Konrad's view (1984, p. 66) was widely held: 'a society does not become politically conscious when it shares some political philosophy, but rather when it refuses to be fooled by any of them'. Anti-politics, as this cynical attitude came to be known, proved to be more destructive than constructive. It supplied a critique of communism but no basis for constructing postcommunist avenues of political participation. The fall of communism brought many political amateurs into politics for a brief period but in many countries traditions of paternalism and élite arrogance re-established themselves as the old rulers modified their line but maintained their grip. Building a participatory civil society from communism's legacy is a difficult and long-term task.

Definition

Civil society consists of those groups which are 'above' the personal realm of the family but 'beneath' the state. The term covers public organizations such as firms, labour unions, interest groups and even (on some definitions) recreational bodies. Such institutions form part of the collective life of society, and of democracy, but are voluntary in character and autonomous from the government. Italians put it this way: if the state is represented by the *palazzo* (the palace), civil society is found in the streets of the *piazza* (the square). Where a civil society is absent, as in totalitarian regimes, only two groups remain: rulers and ruled.

Despite the absence of a communist legacy, the story is similar in many of the African and Latin American countries seeking to nurture new avenues of participation following the retreat of the generals in the 1980s. Again, the act of overthrowing the old order did stimulate significant mass participation, at least in major cities, providing echoes of the original struggle for independence in the 1950s and 1960s. Wiseman (1995, p.5) suggests that

> the prodemocracy movements of most African states in the late 1980s represented a remarkable coming-together of political participation by a range of social groups. Prominent among them were church leaders and professional associ-

ations of lawyers, journalists, students and medical staff.

These bodies had always maintained some distance from the state; they formed the glimmerings of the civil society found in established democracies. Perhaps even more than in the communist world, mass political participation in strikes or street demonstrations was the key to political reform. In Benin, for instance, students marched out of classes in the national university in 1989 demanding payment of overdue scholarships. Later in the year civil servants and schoolteachers threatened a general strike for non-payment of salaries. These protests initiated a period of reform which culminated in the electoral defeat of President Kerekou in 1991 (Bratton and van de Walle, 1997, p. 1). Where Benin led the way, other African countries followed.

Yet the difficulties of entrenching voluntary participation in Africa remain subtantial. The core problem of poverty narrows horizons while illiteracy is another negative factor for voluntary participation. Further, the national government in many African states has limited functions and weak penetration outside the capital. National media barely exist so that even passive participation through following political news is impractical. Such participation as emerges, at least beyond voting in an occasional election, is likely to be directed towards informal politics in ethnic groups and contained through patron–client networks. These factors all suggest that voluntary participation in the new democracies of Africa is unlikely to match even the undemanding levels of consolidated democracies.

Similarly, in the poorer countries of Latin America, the development of voluntary participation is likely to be equally slow. Economic inequality and a strongman tradition (both in government and in the countryside) help to sustain patron-client relationships even in the new era of formal political equality. As in postcommunist states there is also some tradition of 'anti-politics' represented in new social movements. Born out of the struggle to survive under brutal authoritarian rule, these groups tend to remain outside the state rather than serving as channels for engagement with it. In short, political participation in new democracies is likely to remain more limited and controlled than in established democracies.

Political violence

The forms of participation we have examined so far operate within a peaceful framework. Yet when orthodox politics leaves conflicts unresolved, and sometimes even when it does not, the outcome can be violence – by the state against its own people, by citizens seeking to change government policy or by one social group (usually egged on by its leaders) against another. To appreciate the full repertoire of activities under the heading of political participation, we must also consider the role of violence in politics.

> **Definition**
> **Political violence** consists of 'those physically injurious acts directed at persons or property which are intended to further or oppose governmental decisions and public policies' (LaPalombara, 1974, p. 379). **Political terror**, a sub-category of political violence, occurs when such acts are aimed at striking fear into a wider population. Both violence and terror can be committed by as well as against the state. **Genocide**, in which the state is again usually implicated, is the deliberate extermination of a large proportion of a people, nation, race or ethnic group.

Perhaps the key point about political violence is that it must be viewed through the conventional lenses of political analysis, not through a distorting filter that regards violence as the preserve of irrational fanatics. As Clausewitz said of war, violence is 'a continuation of politics by other means'. The threat and use of force is a way of raising the stakes; it supports but rarely replaces conventional politics. Most political violence is neither random nor uncontrolled but tactical. When farmers block a road, when the secret police beat up a student activist, or even when terrorists blow up a plane, a deliberate political signal is usually embedded in the illegal act. Even when so-called 'uncontrolled' violence erupts between ethnic groups, the disturbances are usually initiated – though not carried out – by political leaders.

Campaigns of terror exemplify the use of violence for tactical political ends. To be effective, terror must be well-planned and directed – in other words, it must embody political skill. Such acts are intended to coerce a wider target into submitting to its aims by creating an overall climate of fear. To take an early example, the Reign of Terror unleashed throughout France after 1789 was a deliberate policy of the Jacobin revolutionaries. As Davies (1996, p. 706) notes,

> The Terror was not confined to the destruction of the revolution's active opponents. It was designed to create such an atmosphere of fear and uncertainty that the very thought of opposition would be paralysed. It produced a climate of spies, informers and unlimited suspicion.

It is precisely this desire to influence the wider political climate which converts casual brutality into political terror. Paradoxically, 'random' violence is a systematic technique for inducing anxiety among a broader population. Watching an aeroplane hijack unfold on television, viewers throughout the affluent world will say, and are intended to say, 'there but for fortune . . .'.

Just as it would be a mistake to conceive of political violence as separate from 'normal' politics, so it would be wrong to disassociate violence from the state. Violence is more commonly employed by the state than against it. As the monopolist of authorized coercion, states are well-positioned to terrorize their citizens, and over the course of the twentieth century many did so. Indeed, precisely because political violence is an organized technique, its practice increased with the growth of the state in the last century. Rummel (1997) coins the term 'democide' to describe a state that turns its weapons on its own people. He estimates that between 1900 and 1987, almost 130 million people were killed by the very institution intended to provide peace, law and order (Table 8.2). The cultural residue of officially sanctioned mass murder can be profound, with the emergence of traumatized, broken societies such as Rwanda (800 000 killed in 1994) and Cambodia (two million dead, 1975–9). Rummel's solution to democide? Democracies, he notes, rarely fight each other and hardly ever kill their own people. In a democracy, the ballot replaces the bullet; it is absolute power which creates the conditions for democide. Thus, the transition to democracy in the final decades of the twentieth century may reduce state-sponsored political violence and render the twenty-first century a time of relative peace in

Table 8.2 The ten most lethal governments, 1900–87

Country	Years	Rate[a] (%)	Total killed
Cambodia	1975–79	8.2	2 000 000
Turkey	1919–23	2.6	703 000
Yugoslavia	1941–45	2.5	655 000
Poland	1945–48	2.0	1 585 000
Turkey	1909–18	1.0	1 752 000
Czechoslovakia	1945–48	0.5	197 000
Mexico	1900–20	0.4	1 417 000
USSR	1917–87	0.4	54 769 000
Cambodia	1979–87	0.4	230 000
Uganda	1971–79	0.3	300 000
WORLD	1900–87	0.2	129 909 000

[a] per cent of its population that a regime murders each year, on average.

Note: Post-1987 democides include Armenia, Azerbaijan, Burundi, Bosnia, Croatia, Iran, Iraq, Rwanda and Somalia.

Source: Rummel (1997).

comparison with the barbarities of preceding decades.

To demonstrate the link between violence and the state, consider the extreme case of genocide. A well-organized state, with extensive penetration through society and a population accustomed to obeying authority, makes murder on a truly mass scale possible though not of course inevitable. The central African state of Rwanda is a recent example: in a few weeks in 1994, most of the minority Tutsi, and some Hutu considered to be sympathizers, were butchered. In total, about one in ten of the population died in the massacres. It is worth discussing the Rwandan tragedy in more detail since it reveals several characteristic features of genocide. For one thing, the butchery was far from a spontaneous outburst of ethnic hatred. Although sullen, machete-wielding Hutu peasants dutifully implemented the killings, fully aware of the property that might accrue to them in an over-populated country suffering severe economic problems, the orders came from government and military leaders. They told the peasants to 'clear the bush' and to 'to pull up the roots' (i.e. kill women and children too). The Rwandan case also illustrates that even though genocide may take only a few months, its origins are deep-rooted. In Rwanda, the traditional balance between Tutsi and Hutu had been upset by Belgian colonialists who elevated these ethnic groups into full-blooded 'tribes'. They further portrayed the Tutsi as an ethnic aristocracy, thereby starting the dynamic that enabled the majority Hutu to invoke the ideology of democracy to support their claim that they rather than the minority Tutsi should monopolize power. An effective system of local rule, also inherited from the colonial era, provided the administrative means to implement genocide. In the end, the Tutsi could not escape with their lives because they could not escape from the state (Prunier, 1997).

Revolution

Occasionally, political violence extends to the governing framework itself and the entire political order becomes a matter for dispute. When the existing structure of power is overthrown, leading to a long-term reconstruction of the political, social and economic order, we speak of a revolution. Revolutions are rare but pivotal events, inducing broad and deep alterations in society. The major instances – France, America, Russia, China, Iran – have substantially defined the modern world. We therefore conclude this chapter on participation with an assessment of the nature and causes of revolutions, focusing in particular on the French and Russian cases.

Although changes of the magnitude needed to qualify as a revolution usually require violence, it is debatable whether violence should be built into the definition of the term. The question here is whether a 'peaceful revolution' is a contradiction in terms. To 'revolve' is literally to move round, and the ancient world used the term 'revolution' in this modest sense, to refer to a circulation in the ruling group, howsoever induced. And recent experience certainly confirms that major political changes can occur without large-scale violence. The collapse of communism in Eastern Europe in 1989, leading to the fall of the Soviet Union in 1991, is an example of

major reform initiated by peaceful means, with Czechoslovakia's 'Velvet Revolution' a case in point. If a revolution is to be measured by its impact rather than the violence of its birth, 1989 certainly qualifies as a year of revolutions. Against this, the contemporary use of the term 'revolution' undoubtedly suggests transformation through violence, a change in meaning which reflects the modern world's experience of violent political transformations beginning with the seminal French Revolution of 1789. Stretching the term 'revolution' to include any major political change perhaps reduces the term's precision and value (Lachmann, 1997).

The French revolution

Our scrutiny of revolutions must begin with France in 1789, as this was the first and most important revolution of modern times. Indeed, it is no exaggeration to say that the modern concept of revolution developed from the French experience which revealed revolutions in their modern guise as agents of progress.

What, then, were the contours of this landmark episode? Before 1789, France still combined an absolute monarchy with feudalism. Governance was a confused patchwork of local, provincial and royal institutions. However, in the 1780s the stormclouds gathered: the old regime came under stress as the monarchy became virtually bankrupt and in 1788 a poor grain harvest triggered peasant revolts in the countryside and discontent in the cities.

The revolution was initiated after the Estates General was convened in May 1789 for the first time in over 150 years. An assembly was called in an effort to protect aristocratic privileges. However, the Third Estate, representing the people, withdrew and declared itself to constitute the National Assembly.

There followed a half-decade of radical reform in which, amid the enormous violence of The Terror, the old institutions were demolished and the foundations of a modern state laid down. The monarchy was abolished in 1791; two years later Louis XVI was executed. In the 1790s assorted attempts to build a constitutional monarchy, a republic and a parliamentary government on the foundations provided by the new order ended in failure. Eventually Napoleon instituted a period of authoritarian rule lasting from 1799 to 1814. Universal male suffrage was not adopted until 1848 and the conflict between radicals and conservatives embedded in the revolution remained important to French politics for the next two centuries.

Despite its mixed outcomes, the epochal significance of the French revolution cannot be doubted. It established the future shape of liberal democracy – popular sovereignty, a professional bureaucracy, a market economy and a liberal ideology. Politically it destroyed absolute monarchy based on divine right and curtailed the traditional powers of the aristocracy. Economically, by weakening aristocratic control over the peasantry, the revolution helped to create the conditions under which market relations could spread and capitalism would eventually emerge. Ideologically the revolution was strongly secular, fathering liberal ideas of individual rights enforceable through codified law. The revolution was also powerfully nationalist: the nation became the transcendent bond, uniting all citizens in patriotic fervour. The shockwaves of the French revolution reverberated throughout Europe as ruling classes everywhere saw their very existence imperilled.

Marx and the communist revolutions

The equation of revolutions with progress was further developed in Marx's theory of revolution, an account which exerted profound influence on both academic study and political practice. Karl Marx (1818–83) viewed revolution as inescapable. He argued that revolution involved the transformation of society from one mode of economic production to another – from feudalism to capitalism (as in France), or from capitalism to socialism (as, Marx hoped, in the future). The entire movement of history was inevitable and would culminate in the creation of a communist utopia.

Marx's theory was based on a materialist reading of history. He argued that the prevailing economic system always creates conflict in society between ruling and exploited classes. Members of the exploited class become increasingly alienated from the existing order and are drawn together by an emerging class consciousness. Once the exploited class achieves sufficient unity, it rises up and overthrows the ruling class. The distribution of power is transformed as the exploited class take its destiny into its own hands and begins a new historical epoch based on a new mode of production. Just as the French revolution enabled the new merchants and manufacturers to seize power from a dying aristocracy, so Marx believed that in capitalist societies the working class would eventually destroy the system which exploited them. Treated as a commodity, and enduring a declining standard of living, the working class would eventually fulfil its historic role as capitalism's gravedigger. The communist revolution would initiate a new, rational and progressive era of distribution according to need.

Marx succeeded in drawing attention not just to the economic factor in revolutions but also, more broadly, to the way revolutions can dispose of a political order which has become a fetter to progress. But his account also created paradoxes of its own. If a revolution is inevitable, should activists just sit back and wait for it to arrive? If capitalism must mature before it enters its phase of decline and becomes ripe for overthrow, why did the major communist revolutions of the twentieth century – in Russia in 1917 and in China ending in 1949 – occur in some of the weakest links in the capitalist chain? Part of the answer, surely, is that revolutionary situations may arise whenever, and for whatever reason, a state loses its legitimacy and governing effectiveness. And in both Russia and China, hard-nosed practitioners were on hand to seize the moment. Lenin and Mao Zedong did more than just lend a helping hand to abstract historical forces: they helped to make revolutions happen.

Countering Marx's determinism, Lenin (1870–1924) attached great significance to political organization in fomenting the Russian revolution. He developed the notion of the vanguard party, an élite body of revolutionaries which claimed to understand the long-term interests of the working-class better than that class itself. 'Give us an organization of revolutionaries and we shall overturn the whole of Russia', he declared in 1902. Without such a party, Lenin thought, the working class could only develop limited 'trade union consciousness'. However, critics allege that Lenin's notion of the vanguard party prepared the ground for the regimented participation demanded by the ruling party which became such a stultifying feature of communist states.

The Chinese revolution of 1949 deviated even more sharply from Marx's model. Mao Zedong (1893–1976) succeeded in 'adapting' Marxism to a peasant society without an established working class of any sort. Where Marx had regarded the peasantry as a reactionary class, Mao recognized the revolutionary potential of China's peasants. They were spurred into insurrection as their situation worsened after the arrival from 1839 of Western powers such as Britain and France. But nationalism also played a major part in the Chinese revolution. Downplaying the policy of class war, the communists built their policies around anti-Japanese sentiment. As such, the rise to power of the Chinese communists in 1949 can be seen as a victory for nationalist ideology. In relying on the peasantry and nationalism, Mao deviated sharply from Marx's original ideas, leading Schwarz (1960) to question whether Mao could sensibly be called a Marxist at all.

Social psychological and structural theories

France, Russia and China may be the most famous examples of revolutions but they hardly exhaust the category. In fact, the twentieth century vastly increased the world's stock of illustrations (Box 8.3). Confronting these examples, political scientists have sought to develop general explanations of revolution which extend beyond Marx's focus on class conflict. Here we will consider two such accounts: first the social psychological account associated with Gurr; and second, Skocpol's structural interpretation.

The social psychological theory focuses on individual motivations rather than social groups. It seeks to identify what inspires individuals to participate in revolutionary activity. Why do some people some-

---

BOX 8.3

A century of revolutions

Country	Date	Outcome
Mexico	1910	A populist revolution leading to rule by a dominant party, the PRI
Russia	1917	The first communist state
Turkey	1922	A secular nation-state built from the ruins of the Ottoman Empire
China	1949	The communist People's Republic of China, led by Mao Zedong
Iran	1979	An Islamic state led by Ayatollah Khomeini
Eastern Europe and the Soviet Union	1989/91	Collapse of communist rule

---

times feel so strongly about politics that they are willing to give time, energy and ultimately their lives to achieve change?

In his study of the French revolution, de Tocqueville (1966, first pub. 1856) had noted that grievances patiently endured become intolerable once the possibility of a brighter future crosses the population's minds. In the 1960s this insight was developed by advocates of the social psychological approach. One of the main exponents of this new school was Gurr (1980). He argued that relative deprivation was the key to revolutions. For Gurr, political instability only results from deprivation when combined with a belief that conditions are worse than they could and should be. The most explosive situation is when a period of rising expectations is followed by a decline in the ability of the regime to meet those demands. Such a situation creates a dangerous gap between expectations of continued improvement and the reality of decline. Davies (1962) sums up the implications of this approach: 'revolutions are most likely to occur when a prolonged period of economic and social development is followed by a short period of sharp reversal'. This hypothesis is known as the J-curve theory (Figure 8.2).

Davies suggests that relative deprivation helps to account for the Russian revolution of 1917. Although Russia became a military power in the nineteenth century, it remained a poor country with a serf economy and government dominated by an autocratic Tsar. However, the Tsar did institute important reforms between 1860 and 1904, including improved rights for the peasantry, the introduction of a modern legal system, state-sponsored industrialization and a general liberalization of society. But these reforms served only to induce relative deprivation; the peasants were legally free but most remained burdened by debt. Furthermore, expectations raised by political reforms were then dashed by the Tsar's inability to push ahead with further, more radical changes. Reform oscillated with repression in a perfect formula for fostering relative deprivation. Though an attempted revolution failed in 1905, the hardships imposed by Russia's involvement in the First World War created another revolutionary situation in 1917. This time the chance was taken. The Bolsheviks exploited the opportunity and established the world's first communist state.

Relative deprivation is certainly a background factor in many revolutions. Peasant frustrations, in particular, were involved in the French, Russian and Chinese revolutions. The contribution of the social psychological approach lies in demonstrating that how people perceive their condition is more important than the actual condition itself. Yet although the social psychological account provides insight into the conditions of political instability and violence, it seems incapable of explaining revolutionary progress and outcomes. Whose discontent matters? Why does discontent sometimes lead to an uprising but sometimes not? How and why do uprisings turn into revolutions? How is discontent channelled into organized opposition movements? Why is such

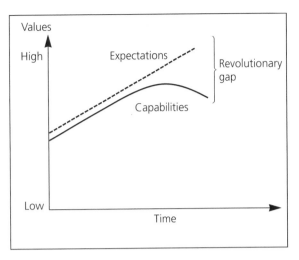

Figure 8.2 The J-curve theory of revolutions

opposition usually suppressed but sometimes not? Because relative deprivation has no answer to these questions, it is better regarded as a theory of political violence in general rather than of revolutions in particular.

Given the failings of the psychological approach, the study of revolutions turned away from broad psychological theories and returned to a more fine-grained historical examination of a small number of cases. Skocpol's (1979) influential discussion of the French, Russian and Chinese revolutions was an example of this fresher approach. For Skocpol, the causes of revolutions cannot be found in the motives of the participants. What matters are the structural conditions – the relationships between groups within a state and, equally important, between states. The background to revolution is provided by a regime that is weak internationally and ineffective domestically. The classic revolutions occurred when a regime had already lost its effectiveness and well-organized revolutionaries succeeded in exploiting peasant frustration with the old regime. In these circumstances the actual seizing of power can be quite straightforward. The real revolution begins as the new rulers develop and impose their vision on society and, in particular, opposition groups. Revolutions do not stop with the taking of power, as the social psychological theory seemed to imply, but only start at this point. Thus Skocpol says much about how discontent is mobilized into political activity and how that activity turns into a revolutionary transformation. Her achievement was to bring political, and especially state-centred, analysis back to the study of revolutions.

Key reading

> **Next step:** *Putnam (1993, 2000) is an interesting assessment of the decline of social participation in the USA, with an eye to its political impact.*

Rueschmeyer, Rueschmeyer and Wittrock (1998) apply Putnam's thesis of declining social participation to Europe, with mixed results. Milbrath and Goel (1977) is still a useful general text on participation, while Verba, Scholzman and Brady (1995) is a major study of participation in the USA, building on a generation's worth of previous research. For a comparable British investigation see Parry, Moyser and Day (1992). A major comparative study of unconventional participation is Barnes and Kaase (1979), summarized in Marsh (1990). Dalton and Kuechler (1990) is a good collection on social movements; see also Tarrow (1998). Escobar and Alvarez (1992) is an excellent collection on social movements in Latin America. The literature on participation in postcommunist societies is still fragmentary; on Russia, see Eckstein (1998b). For participation in African transitions, see Bratton and van de Walle (1997, ch. 4). Gilbert (1995) examines terrorism. On revolutions, see Skocpol (1979) for a classic analysis and Halliday (1999) for the links between revolutions and world politics.

PART 3

LINKING SOCIETY AND GOVERNMENT

This part examines major mechanisms through which society influences government. We begin with the main linking device in established democracies: elections. We then turn to interest groups where we discuss not only narrow sectional groups but also broader campaigning organizations seeking to promote their vision of the public group. And we conclude with an analysis of political parties, many of which originate in society but which, in power, are charged with directing the state and thereby leading society.

Elections and voters

On 27 April 1994, Primrose Ngabane, a 58-year-old black domestic employee, voted in South Africa's first non-racial election. To cast her ballot (she voted for the white-led National Party), she had to walk several miles, take a long bus journey and a group taxi, and queue outside the polling station for several hours (Reynolds, 1994, p. 1). Primrose Ngabane's commitment was typical of millions of people throughout the world who acquired the right to vote in the final quarter of the twentieth century. Democratization drew ordinary people into the political process via competitive elections. In countries like South Africa, this involved extending the right to vote to previously disenfranchized groups. In the postcommunist world, the democratic revolution took the form of adding significant choice to what had previously been charade elections. As a result of such changes, elections became more central to national politics in more countries than ever before.

To understand elections, we must unravel both the forces shaping individual choice and the role of elections in the political system. At the *individual* level, the task is to understand the forces shaping the voter's choice. Why, for instance, was Primrose Ngabane one of about 4 per cent of blacks to vote for the National Party, a party that had once enforced apartheid? Such questions involve the study of voting behaviour, a field of politics which,

with the arrival of the sample survey, has exploded since 1945. At the level of the *political system,* the task is to understand the wider significance of elections. What are their functions in the overall system of government? For example, the South African contest of 1994 was a classic example of a 'founding election', a high-turnout affair which helped to establish the legitimacy of a new regime.

> **Definition**
> An **election** is a competition for office based on a formal expression of preferences by a population. These opinions are then combined into a collective decision about which candidates have won.

Elections in established democracies

Elections in established democracies are genuinely competitive; they are 'free and fair' (Box 9.1). Such elections are the central instrument of liberal democracy. Through such contests rulers are called to account, and if necessary replaced. At least for the brief period of an election campaign voters really are the masters and politicians really are the supplicants. But we should not conclude that choosing rulers is the only function of elections in democracies. Even when elections are competitive, they can perform a range of other functions, including informing the people about national problems and even showing them the limits of their own political authority.

There are in fact two accounts of democratic elections: the bottom-up and top-down theories (Harrop and Miller, 1987). The bottom-up theory is the more orthodox; it stresses the extent to which competitive elections render governments accountable to the governed. The last election decides who

BOX 9.1
What is a free and fair election?

With the spread of democracy in the 1990s, election monitoring became a growth industry. In a report commissioned by the Commonwealth Parliamentary Association, two Canadian election officers (Gould and Jackson, 1995, p. 36) set out some standards by which elections can be judged. They suggest that the key test of a 'free and fair' election is whether 'the will of the majority of voters is expressed freely, clearly and knowledgeably, and in secret'. Specifically:

A free election respects human rights and freedoms, including:

- Freedom of speech
- Freedom of association
- Freedom to register as an elector, a party or a candidate
- Freedom from coercion
- Freedom of access to the polls
- Freedom to vote in secret
- Freedom to complain

A fair election takes place on a level playing field, including:

- Non-partisan administration of the election
- Constitutional protection of electoral law
- Universal suffrage and accessible polling places
- Balanced reporting by the media
- Equitable access to resources for campaigns
- Open and transparent counting of the vote
- Equitable and non-coercive treatment of parties, candidates and electors by the government, the police, the military and the judiciary.

Further reading: Abbink and Hesseling (1999), Kumar (1998).

BOX 9.2
A classification of elections in established democracies

1. Realigning ('critical') elections
These change the underlying strength of parties and redefine the relationships between parties and social groups. Full realignment, usually lasting for at least a generation, often takes place over two or three critical elections.

Example: American presidential elections in the 1920s and 1930s which forged the Democratic New Deal coalition.

2. Normal elections
Such elections express the balance of long-term party loyalties in the electorate as a whole. The party leading in party identification wins.

Example: Democratic presidential election victories in the USA.

3. Deviating elections
The natural majority party loses the election due to short-term factors, such as a faltering economy or an unappealing candidate.

Example: Republican presidential election victories in the USA.

4. Dealigning elections
The major parties lose support but no new cleavage emerges to supplant the existing system. Common in Western democracies.

Example: the British election of February 1974 in which the minority Liberals gained ground in a protest against the two major parties.

governs; the thought of the next election influences how they do so. Competition between parties forces them to respond to the views of the electors, attuning state to society. From this perspective, then, the key function of competitive elections is to channel communication upwards from voters through to parties and governments.

While the bottom-up account is the conventional picture, it has not gone unchallenged. Top-down theorists such as Ginsberg (1982) are more critical of the electoral process in democracies. Ginsberg argues that 'competitive elections are, in reality, devices for expanding the power of the élite over the population'. He suggests that elections incorporate potential dissenters into the political system, reduce popular participation to a mere cross on a ballot and encourage people to obey the state without limiting its autonomy. Like fast-food restaurants, elections give a feeling of choice to voters but the menu is restricted to a few variations on a conventional theme. So the top-down perspective suggests that choice and accountability are not the key functions of elections. Rather, their leading role is to increase the legitimacy of ruling élites; to add to the authority, effectiveness and stability of the state; and also to educate the voters about élite concerns. 'Since the nineteenth century,' notes Ginsberg, 'governments have ruled *through* elections even when they have sometimes been ruled *by* them.'

Our view falls between these two perspectives. Democratic elections are, we think, best seen as an *exchange* of influence between élites and voters. Elections are like a forge, in whose noise and glare rulers strive to shape power into authority. But rulers gain added authority only in exchange for responsiveness to voters; they do not win something for nothing. Equally, the voters gain influence over government decisions but only in exchange for obedience to decisions they only partly shape. Overall, democratic elections expand the authority of government while reducing the likelihood of that authority being misused. In that sense, they benefit both rulers and ruled.

Of course, democratic elections vary in significance. A few are political earthquakes, restructuring the party landscape for a generation or more. Many more produce barely a tremor on the body politic, simply returning the existing government to power for another term. One useful way of classifying elections in democracies is to categorize them by their impact. Box 9.2 overleaf outlines the main types of competitive election, as judged by their political consequences. Note that, in the nature of the case, history is the final arbiter. Many elections regarded as epochal by contemporary observers are soon forgotten.

Elections: scope, franchise and turnout

An electoral system is a set of rules for conducting an election. Normally we think of an electoral system in terms of the procedures for translating votes into seats. But there are three broader – and prior – issues. These are: the scope of elected office (which offices are elected), the extent of the franchise (who can vote), and turnout (who does vote). In discussing these topics we use established democracies for illustrations.

A key feature of an electoral system is its scope. Which offices are subject to election is almost as important as who has the right to vote. Compare the United States and Britain. The USA is unique in its massive range of elected offices, ranging from presi-

dent to dogcatcher. In total, the USA possesses more than 500 000 elected offices, a figure reflecting a strong tradition of local self-government. Britain would need over 100 000 elected positions to match the American ratio of posts to population. Yet in Britain, as in many non-federal democracies in the EU, voting has traditionally been confined to elections for the European and national parliaments and for local councils (however, the Labour government elected in 1997 did introduce elected parliaments to Scotland and Wales). Similarly, Australians engage in much more electing than New Zealanders.

Definition

A **second-order election** is one whose result is heavily influenced by voting in other first-order contests, normally occurring at the same time. For instance, a party's success in local elections is often affected by its popularity in more important national contests, thus degrading the link between successful local governance and election results. Similarly, the American notion of presidential **coattails** implies that elections for lesser offices are influenced by the contest for the White House. **Ticket-splitting**, or voting for different parties for different offices up for election at the same time, reduces the size of coattails.

Other things being equal, the greater the number of offices subject to competitive election, the more democratic a political system becomes. However, there are dangers in electionitis. One is voter fatigue, leading to a fall in turnout and the quality of choice. In particular, the least important elections tend to become second-order contests – that is, their outcomes reflect the popularity of national parties even though they do not instal a national government. For example, elections in EU member states to the European parliament become referendums on *national* governments, although their supposed purpose is to elect a member for the *European* parliament. The difficulty with such second-order contests is that they snap the link between performance in office and the voters' response (Anderson and Ward, 1996). In a similar way, effective local administrations may be thrown out for no better reason than the incompetence of their party colleagues at national level.

The franchise (who can vote?) is another impor-

Country profile **THE UNITED STATES**

Population: 273m.
Gross domestic product per head: $31 500.
Form of government: a presidential, federal republic.
Legislature: the 435-member House of Representatives is the lower house. The 100-member Senate, perhaps the most influential upper chamber in the world, contains two directly-elected senators from each state.
Executive: the president is supported by a massive apparatus, including the 350-strong White House Office, and the Executive Office of the President, numbering around 2000. The Cabinet is far less significant than in, say, Britain.
Judiciary: a dual system of federal and state courts is headed by the Supreme Court. This nine-member body can nullify laws and actions which run counter to the Constitution. America has a strongly legal culture.
Electoral system: the plurality method is still used; there is little pressure for, or possibility of, reform.
Party system: the Democratic and Republican parties show extraordinary resilience, despite periodic threats from third parties. Their survival reflects ideological flexibility, their entrenched position in law and the bias of plurality elections against minor parties.

The United States is the world's remaining superpower. This status is based partly on its 'hard power': a large population, a massive and dynamic economy and the capacity to deliver military force anywhere. Yet America's 'soft power' is also significant. Its leading position in the TMT sector – technology, media and telecommunications – is underpinned by a strong base in science and university education. Its culture, brand names and language have universal appeal. Above all, America retains a faith that it is 'bound to lead' (Nye, 1990). With the rise of Japan and the European Union, the United States may no longer dominate the world but it remains by far the most important power.

The internal politics of the United States is therefore of vital interest. Ironically, the world's No. 1 operates a political system intended to frustrate decisive policy-making. By constitutional design, power is divided between federal and state governments. The centre is itself fragmented between the executive, legislature and judiciary. American politics takes the form of 'hyper-pluralism' in which reforms are more easily blocked by interest groups than carried through by a disciplined party. The president, the only official elected by a national constituency, finds his plans obstructed by a legislature which is among the most powerful (and decentralized) in the world. Major reforms such as the New Deal require a major crisis, such as the depression, to bring forth that rare consensus which generates rapid reform. Except in such times of crisis, Washington politics is a ceaseless quest for that small amount of common ground on which all interests can agree.

Similar paradoxes abound in the American experience with elections. First, the United States has over 500 000 elected offices, more than anywhere else, yet turnout is low for most of them, including the presidency. Second, a premise of equality underlies elections yet Southern blacks were effectively denied the vote until the Voting Rights Act of 1965. Third, the 'log cabin to White House' ideal is widely accepted but money is increasingly necessary, though not sufficient, for electoral success. Fourth, many states use devices of direct democracy but there has never been a national referendum. Fifth, elections are expected to involve debates between candidates and parties but in many contests advertising by interest groups drowns the candidates' voices. Finally, elections should create legitimacy for the winner but the many confusions of the 2000 presidential election – including the fact that more electors voted for Al Gore than for George W. Bush – hardly contributed to the authority with which the eventual winner entered the White House.

Further reading: McKay (1997), Wilson (1997).

Table 9.1 Declining turnout at national elections, 1950s–1990s

Decline over 10%	Decline of 1–10%	No decline
Austria	Australia	Denmark
France	Belgium	Sweden
Japan	Canada	
New Zealand	Finland	
Switzerland	Germany	
United Kingdom	Ireland	
USA	Netherlands	
	Norway	

Note: Figures are based on a comparison between the first two elections in the 1950s and the last two elections before 2000. Most of the fall occurred in the late 1980s and the 1990s.

Source: adapted from Bentley, Jupp and Stedman-Jones (2000).

See also: Pharr and Putnam (2001).

tant element of the rules governing elections. In most democracies, the franchise now extends to nearly all citizens aged at least 18. However this wide franchise is fairly recent, particularly for women. Few countries can match Australia and New Zealand where women have been electors since the start of the twentieth century. In many countries, women did not win the vote until after the Second World War; in a few, Kuwait included, women remain disenfranchized. Through much of the democratic world, the most recent extension to the suffrage was the reduction in the 1960s or 1970s in the age qualification from 21 to 18. The main remaining exclusions are criminals, the insane and non-citizen residents such as guest workers. Yet in each of these areas there may still be room for further progress. Should the electoral process adopt techniques enabling people with even severe learning difficulties to express preferences? Is denial of the vote really an appropriate response to a criminal conviction? And, of growing importance as international mobility increases, why should non-citizen residents be denied the vote when such people live, work and pay taxes in their host country? (Weale, 1999).

A universal suffrage does not guarantee a full turnout. A wide variety of factors, at the level of both the electoral system and the individual, influence turnout (Box 9.3), producing significant variations across countries. More significantly, turnout is now declining in most established democracies, a trend which first became apparent in local elections but which spread to national contests towards the end of the twentieth century (Table 9.1). The democracy with the most serious problem of non-voting is the United States: in presidential elections barely one in two Americans of voting age casts a ballot. Even in the extraordinarily close contest of 2000, only 52 per cent of electors went to the polls. Lijphart (1997) even suggests that the United States should adopt compulsory voting (as in Australia) as a way round this problem. However, it is a moot point whether compulsory voting is a contribution to, or a denial of, democracy. An easier step might be to simplify registration. Unlike most European countries, registration in the United States is the responsibility of the individual rather than the authorities and must be arranged anew when citizens go to live in another state. Turnout is respectable among the registered; the problem lies in persuading some Americans to register at all.

BOX 9.3

Features of the electoral system and of individuals which increase turnout

Features of the electoral system	Features of individuals
Compulsory voting	Middle age
Proportional representation	Strong party loyalty
Postal voting permitted	High education
Weekend polling	Attends church
Elections decide who governs*	Belongs to a union
Automatic registration	Higher income

* Examples of elections which do *not* decide who governs are those to the American Congress and the European parliament.

Source: Franklin (1996).

Electoral systems: legislatures

Most controversy about electoral systems centres on the rules for converting votes into seats. Such rules are as important as they are technical. They form the inner workings of democracy, sometimes as little-understood by ordinary voters as the engine of a car but still a core component of the overall machine. In this section we examine the rules for translating votes into seats in parliamentary elections (Box 9.4).

The key distinction is between nonproportional systems and proportional representation (PR). Nonproportional systems are the simplest; they are based on the old idea of electing a person or people to represent a specific territory such as a Canadian riding, an American district or a British constituency. Parties are not rewarded in proportion to the share of the vote they obtain; instead, 'the winner takes all' within each district. These nonproportional systems take one of two forms: plurality or

---

BOX 9.4

Electoral systems: legislatures

PLURALITY AND MAJORITY SYSTEMS – *'winner takes all'*

1. Simple plurality – 'first past the post'
Procedure: Leading candidate elected on first and only ballot.
Where used: 13 countries (for example UK, USA, Canada, India, Thailand).

2. Absolute majority – alternative vote ('preferential vote')
Procedure: Voters rank candidates. If no candidate wins a majority of first preferences, the bottom candidate is eliminated and his or her votes are redistributed according to second preferences. Repeat until a candidate has a majority.
Where used: Australia (House of Representatives).

3. Absolute majority – second ballot
Procedure: If no candidate has a majority on the first ballot, the two leading candidates face a runoff.
Where used: Mali, Ukraine.

Note: In elections to France's National Assembly (lower house), all candidates receiving the support of more than 12.5 per cent of the electorate on the first ballot go through to the second round. The candidate with most votes wins this additional ballot.

PROPORTIONAL SYSTEMS – *seats obtained by quota in multimember constituencies*

4. List system
Procedure: The ballot is cast for a party's list of candidates though in most countries the elector can also express support for individual candidates on the list.
Where used: 24 countries (for example Israel, Scandinavia, most of continental Europe, including Eastern Europe, and most of Latin America).

5. Single transferable vote (STV)
Procedure: Voters rank candidates in order of preference. Any candidate needs to achieve a set number of votes (the quota) to be elected. Initially, first preferences only are counted. Any candidates over the quota at this stage are elected. Their 'surplus' votes (that is, the number by which they exceeded the quota) are then distributed to the second preferences shown on these ballot papers. When no candidate has reached the quota, the bottom candidate is eliminated and these votes are also transferred. These procedures continue until all seats are filled.
Where used: Irish Republic, Malta, some Australian states, Estonia (1990 only) – and Cambridge, Massachusetts.

MIXED SYSTEMS – *combining single-member seats with PR*

6. The Additional Member System (AMS) – also known as the Mixed Member System (MMS) and Mixed Member Proportional (MMP)
Procedure: Some seats are elected on a territorial basis by plurality and others on a party basis using PR. Usually the latter acts as a top-up to secure a proportional outcome overall. Electors normally have two votes, one for the territorial election and the other for the PR contest.
Where used: 11 countries (for example Germany, Hungary, Japan, Russia and New Zealand).

Note: the figures for the number of states employing each method are not based on all countries but just on the 53 democracies covered in Leduc, Niemi and Norris (1996a)

majority. In plurality (also called 'first-past-the-post') systems, the winning candidate is simply the one who receives most votes in a unit of territory. A plurality of votes suffices; a majority is unnecessary. Despite its antiquity and simplicity, the plurality system is rare and becoming rarer. It survives mainly in Britain and British-influenced states such as Canada, various Caribbean islands, India and the United States. However, because India is so populous, around half of the world's people living in democracies still use this first-past-the-post method (Lijphart, 1999).

The crucial point about the plurality method is the bonus in seats it offers to the party leading in votes. In Canada, for instance, the winning party's share of seats exceeded its vote share by between 13 and 25 points at the five elections between 1984 and 2000 (Table 9.2). To see how this bias operates, consider an extreme case in which the Reds defeat the Blues by one vote in every district. Despite the closeness of the vote, the Reds would win every seat. A theoretical example, of course, but one which demonstrates the inherent bias of a method which offers all the representation of a particular district to the one party which tops the ballot. The political impact of this amplifying effect is usually to deliver government by a single party with a clear majority in the assembly. In essence, the plurality method is a giant conjuring trick, pulling the rabbit of majority government out of the hat of a divided society. In Britain and Canada, for instance, a majority in the popular vote for a single party is exceptional but a secure parliamentary majority for the winner is customary. But the amplifier does not always work; plurality elections have not delivered majority government since 1989 in India's increasingly fragmented party system.

The other form of nonproportional system is the majoritarian method. As its name implies, this requires a majority of votes for the winning candidate, normally achieved through a second ballot. If no candidate wins a majority on the first round, then an additional ballot is held, usually a runoff between the top two candidates. Many countries in West Europe used majority voting before switching to PR early in the twentieth century. The system is also used in parts of East Europe. For democrats, the argument for a majoritarian system is intuitively quite strong: namely, that no candidate should be elected without being shown to be acceptable to a majority of voters.

There is another, and rather efficient, way of achieving a majority outcome in a single ballot within single-member seats. This is the Alternative Vote (AV), used for Australia's lower house, the House of Representatives (Box 9.4). AV takes into account more information about voters' preferences than simple plurality voting. AV is periodically recommended by electoral reformers in Britain, and in 1998 the Jenkins Commission, set up by the Labour government, advocated AV as the geographical part of its own proposal for a mixed member system.

We move now from nonproportional systems to proportional representation. PR is the norm in West, and now East, Europe; it also predominates in Latin America. The guiding principle of PR is to represent parties rather than territory. Thus PR is more recent than nonproportional systems; it was not widely adopted until the twentieth century. The basic idea is straightforward and plausible: parties should be awarded seats in direct proportion to their share of the vote. In a perfectly proportional system, every party would receive the same share of seats as of votes; 40 per cent of the votes would mean 40 per cent of the seats. Although the mechanics of PR are designed with this end in mind, in fact most 'PR' systems are not perfectly proportional. They usually offer at least a modest bonus to the largest party, though less than most nonproportional methods,

---

Table 9.2 The Canadian elections of 1993 and 2000

Party	1993		2000	
	Votes %	Number of seats	Votes %	Number of seats
Liberal	42	177	41	173
Conservative	**16**	**2**	12	12
New Democratic Party	7	9	9	13
Reform/Alliance	19	52	26	66
Bloc Québécois	14	54	11	37
Total	(98)	(294)	(99)	(301)

Note: The **bold** entries show the extreme bias against the Conservatives in 1993. Minor parties not shown.

and they also discriminate by design or practice against the smallest parties.

Since a single party rarely wins a majority of seats under PR, majority governments are unusual and coalitions become standard. Because PR usually leads to post-election negotiations in parliament about which parties will form the next government, it is best interpreted as a method of selecting parliaments rather than governments.

How does PR work? The most common method, by far, is the list system. The principle here is that the elector votes for a list of the party's candidates rather than for just a single person. The number of votes won by a party determines how many candidates are elected from that party's list. The order in which candidates appear on the slate (usually decided by the party itself) governs which people are elected to represent that party. For example suppose a party wins 10 per cent of the vote in an election to a 150-seat assembly. That party will be entitled to 15 MPs, who will be the top 15 candidates on its list. So list voting is party voting. This method therefore weakens the link between the representative and a particular constituency.

List systems vary in how much influence they give voters over which candidates they can vote for from a party's list. At one extreme stand the closed party lists used in Portugal, South Africa and Spain. Voters there have no choice over candidates; they simply vote for a party. This gives party officials at the centre enormous, perhaps excessive, control over political recruitment. At the other extreme lie the free party lists used in Switzerland and Luxembourg. In these countries electors can vote either for a party's list or for an individual candidate from the list. Most countries give voters at least some choice between candidates from a party's list, a procedure which in application gives some advantage to celebrities. However, the natural (because simplest) procedure is for electors to vote for a party's entire ticket.

How many representatives are elected for each constituency, a number known as the district magnitude, is a critical influence on how proportional PR systems are in practice (Lijphart, 1994). The more members per district, the more proportional the outcome can be. Where many members are elected per district, a party can win a seat with a small share of the vote. In a few countries, for example the Netherlands and Israel, the whole country serves as a single large constituency, permitting exceptional proportionality. In the Israel election of 1999, a total of 15 parties won seats in the 120-member Knesset. But where fewer members are elected per district, the voting threshold needed to win a seat can be demanding. For example, each of the 52 constituencies Spain uses for its national elections returns just seven members, thus producing a less proportional outcome overall. Indeed the Spanish Socialists have managed to win a majority of seats with just 40 per cent of the vote, confirming the boost which proportional systems with a small district magnitude give to the leading party (Gallagher, 1997, p. 116).

Definition
District magnitude refers to the number of representatives chosen for each electoral district under proportional representation. The more representatives to be elected for a district, the more proportional the electoral system can be. When the entire country serves as a single district, very small parties can win representation in parliament. By contrast, when only three or four members are elected per district, smaller parties often fail to win a seat even with a respectable vote. Thus the 'proportionality' of a PR system is not constant but varies with its district magnitude.

Most list systems add an explicit threshold of representation below which small parties receive no seats at all. Thresholds help to protect the legislature from extremists. The cut-off is 2 per cent in Denmark and 4 per cent in Sweden. Many Eastern European countries adopted somewhat larger thresholds, usually of 4 or 5 per cent, when they switched to PR for their postcommunist elections

Plurality and PR systems are usually considered alternatives, yet a hybrid form emerged after the war. The additional member system (AMS) seeks the best of both worlds (Shugart and Wattenberg, 2000). It combines the geographical representation of the plurality method with the party representation of PR. It achieves these objectives while also delivering a proportional outcome overall. Germany provides the model for this ingenious compromise. There, half the seats are filled by plurality voting in single-member seats, thus retaining the representative-constituency link, but the remaining seats are allocated to parties with the aim of producing a proportional result overall. Electors have two votes, one for a constituency candidate and one for a party list, but it is the party vote which determines the number of seats awarded to each party. Candidates from the party's list are then used to top up its directly-elected candidates until the correct number of seats is achieved. The compromise nature of AMS has encouraged other countries to experiment with similar methods. Twenty-five countries, covering about 16 per cent of the world's population, now use various forms of AMS for legislative elections. These include Japan, Mexico, Italy and New Zealand. AMS has also prospered in the postcommunist world, including Russia and has been adopted for Scottish and Welsh assemblies in the UK.

What is the relationship between electoral systems and party systems? This remains a matter of controversy. In a classic work, Duverger (1954) claimed that the plurality method strongly favored a two-party system while PR contributed to a multiparty system. At the time, the plurality system was associated with strong, decisive government and PR was found guilty by its association with unstable coalition governments. But in the 1960s a reaction set in against attributing weight to political institutions such as electoral systems. Writers such as Rokkan (1970) adopted a more sociological approach, pointing out that social cleavages had produced multiparty systems in Europe long before PR was adopted early in the twentieth century. PR did not cause a multiparty system; rather it was adopted because it was the only electoral system which would satisfy all the interests and parties of divided societies. More recently Lijphart (1994) has suggested a middle position. He believes that plurality systems nearly always deliver parliamentary majorities, just as Duverger claimed, but that electoral systems are only one of several influences on the number of parties achieving representation.

Much ink has also been used on a related issue: the question of which is the 'best' electoral system. In truth there is no such thing; different methods work best in different circumstances. For example, in countries with intense social divisions such as Northern Ireland and South Africa, PR will provide at least some representation for parties based on minority groups. In this way, the risk of majority

tyranny is reduced. But where regular changes of government occur under a majority system, as in Great Britain, this argument for PR loses some of its force. Over time, the swing of the pendulum gives each party its turn in office – proportional tenure without proportional representation. And as the pendulum swings, so each new government can implement its policies without needing to water them down through compromises with coalition partners. For better or worse, it is difficult to see a figure such as Margaret Thatcher emerging as a compromise coalition leader after an election fought under PR. It must be acknowledged, though, that the plurality method can thrust parties in and out of office in an erratic and exaggerated way. Canada is a good example. In 1984, the Conservatives won three-quarters of the seats on just half the vote. Nine years later they were decimated in an astonishing election which reduced them to just two seats despite retaining 16 per cent of the vote (Table 9.2).

Whatever their theoretical weaknesses, electoral systems tend to persist once established in the founding election. After all, parties elected by one system have no incentive to change to another. Yet although electoral reform is uncommon it is far from unknown: Japan, Italy and New Zealand each changed their electoral system in the 1990s. All three countries adopted the fashionable additional member system. In Japan, the object was to reduce the significance of money in elections by ending an unusual system that forced candidates from the same party into competition with each other. Yet factionalism and even corruption continue to inhibit real policy debate. Reformers in Italy wanted to escape from the unstable coalitions produced by PR and to encourage a small number of large parties that would alternate in power, British-style. Yet the first government produced under Italy's new electoral law lasted just eight months, hardly a model of political stability. In New Zealand, the motive was to reduce the unrestrained power of the single-party governments produced by the plurality method. Again, however, the first parliamentary term under the new system was hardly a great success. It was marked by a fractious and unstable coalition involving New Zealand First. In 1999, the electorate responded by voting New Zealand First not just out of office but almost out of parliament.

As these illustrations confirm, electoral reform

FOR OR AGAINST

THE PLURALITY METHOD ('FIRST PAST THE POST')

The debate between advocates of the plurality system and those who favour proportional representation (PR) has continued ever since associations dedicated to electoral reform emerged in continental Europe towards the end of the nineteenth century. Although many of the arguments are familiar, a recent exchange between a vigorous defender of the British plurality method (Michael Pinto-Duschinsky) and his several critics provides a useful summary.

The case for

For Pinto-Duschinsky (1999, p. 118), the point of elections is to deliver a government rather than a representative assembly. Voters should be able 'to hire and fire the executive,' a task for which the plurality method is well-suited. Governments form quickly in British-style systems whereas coalitions can take months to form after a PR election. Equally, it is common for voters in plurality elections 'to throw the rascals out' whereas leading parties often continue in power interminably in countries using PR. The problem with PR today is not too little stability but too much, leading to governance which offends no one and therefore achieves nothing. Further, coalition-making too often becomes an exercise in 'the distribution of patronage and contracts'. In any case, because the logic of coalition formation gives special influence to small, pivot parties such as the FDP and the Greens in Germany, 'proportional representation' does not, in fact, deliver power in proportion to votes. So advocates of PR are barking up the wrong tree: 'what is at stake is not mathematical "fairness" but democracy itself. When the people are unable to control the arrogance of power, there is no democracy.'

The case against

Bingham Powell (1999, pp. 127–31): 'Policy-makers should take account of the preferences of as many people as possible and, on average, PR systems produce governments and especially policies closer to the median voter.'

Lijphart (1999, pp. 133–6): PR is linked to higher turnout (about 10 per cent higher, on average), contributes to stable democracy in divided societies and avoids the possibility of 'seat victories for parties that are mere runners-up in vote totals – which is probably the plurality method's gravest democratic deficit.'

Vowles: 'In New Zealand in 1978 and 1981, an incumbent and highly unpopular government remained in power despite the opposition party winning pluralities of votes twice in a row. From a New Zealand perspective, advocacy of the plurality method based on its ability to better dismiss unpopular governments makes a good joke.'

Shugart (1999, pp. 143–7): The choice is less stark than Pinto-Duschinsky would have us believe. 'There is a middle ground in electoral systems, populated by electoral systems that are indeed "broadly proportional" yet enhance the probability that elections will revolve round two competing governmental options. They do so by either mixing both PR and plurality, as in Germany, or by using quite small multi-member districts with PR, as in Spain.'

Assessment

Pinto-Duschinsky performs a useful service in directing us to the impact of electoral systems on the quality of governance and away from the secondary issue of statistical 'fairness'. But 'the quality of governance' is not a self-evident term. Should governance in a democracy consist in giving a clear run to the leading party or in constructing policies to which most represenatives in the national assembly are willing to consent?

Source: Representation, vol. 36, no. 2 (1999), pp.117–55.

does not always deliver the desired effects at least in the short term. Over the medium term, however the impact may be more promising. Japanese debate now accepts the weaknesses of factionalism, New Zealand is becoming accustomed to coalitions and 2001 saw a transfer of power in Italy from a centre-left to centre-right government. Clearly electoral systems do make a difference.

Electoral systems: presidents

In comparison with parliamentary contests, the rules for electing presidents are straightforward. Unlike seats in parliament, a one-person presidency cannot be shared between parties; the office is indivisible. So PR is impossible. As Figure 9.1 shows, 61 of the 91 directly-elected presidents in the world are chosen by a majority system. And of these, most are selected by a majority run-off, meaning that if no candidate wins a majority on the first round an additional ballot is held. This second vote allows electors a choice between the top two candidates and ensures the winner receives a majority of votes in the decisive ballot. France is an influential example of this system. The next most common method is by plurality: the candidate with most votes on the first and only round wins. This technique saves the bother of two ballots but the winner may receive only a small share of the vote. To take an extreme illustration, General Banzer won the Bolivian election of 1997 with just 20 per cent support.

As Figure 9.1 also shows, almost a third of presidents manage to avoid the perils of direct election altogether. Many of these are chosen via indirect election where a special body (which may itself be elected) chooses the president, thus acting as a buffer against the whims of the people. The United States was once an example. The Founding Fathers opposed direct election of the president, fearing the dangers of democracy. Instead, they set up an electoral college with delegates selected by each state legislature as it saw fit. The delegates were expected to show wisdom beyond that of ordinary people. Today, of course, America has embraced direct election, with the electoral college surviving only as a relic of the eighteenth century.

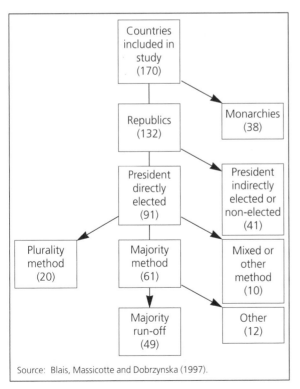

Source: Blais, Massicotte and Dobrzynska (1997).

Figure 9.1 Methods for selecting presidents

> *Definition*
> **Indirect election** occurs when officeholders are elected by a body which has itself been chosen by a wider constituency. Indirect election was widely used within communist parties as a device for limiting democratic expression; each level only elected the next level up. The device is also employed in elections to some upper houses of parliament. For example, the members of the French Senate are chosen by a local college comprising mayors, councillors and members of the National Assembly from the area concerned.

The presidential term is normally no shorter, and sometimes longer, than for parliament. The longer the term, the easier it is for presidents to adopt a broad perspective free from the immediate burden of re-election. But term limits are often also imposed, restricting the incumbent to one or two periods in office. The fear is that without such constraints presidents will be able to exploit their unique position to remain in office too long. Thus, the USA introduced a two-term limit after Franklin Roosevelt won four elections in a row between 1932 and 1944.

BOX 9.5

Methods for electing presidents: some examples

Country	Method of election	Term (years)	Re-election permitted?
Argentina	Electoral college	6	After one term out
Brazil	Run-off	5	After one term out
Finland	Plurality*	6	Yes
France	Run-off	7	Yes
Ireland	Single transferable vote	7	Two term limit
Mexico	Plurality	6	No
Russia	Run-off	5	Two term limit, then a term out
United States	Electoral college	4	Two term limit

* If no candidate wins a majority in the popular vote, selection is by an electoral college.

Source: Adapted from Jones (1995b).

As with other institutional fixes, term limits solve one problem at the cost of creating a new one: lame-duck presidents lose clout as they near the end of their term. For instance, the Korean financial crisis of 1997 coincided with the end of the president's non-renewable six-year tenure, adding to uncertainty. Also, presidents subject to term limits sometimes seek to alter the constitution in order to permit their own re-election. This has been a regular source of friction in much of Latin America. Box 9.5 gives examples of the restrictions which countries place on presidential re-election.

The timing of presidential elections is also important. When they are concurrent with elections to the assembly, the successful candidate is more likely to be drawn from the same party as dominates the legislature. This reduces the fragmentation which is an inherent risk of the presidential executive (Jones, 1995a).

Referendums

Elections are instruments of representative democracy; the role of the people is only to decide who will decide. Referendums, and similar devices such as the initiative and the recall, are devices of direct democracy, enabling voters to decide issues themselves. Yet in practice referendums do not always live up to their democratic pretensions. Sometimes they are nothing more than instruments of control by the élite. Napoleon, Hitler and other dictators used referendums (often called plebiscites in a non-democratic context) to boost their authority. Hitler's methods were so robust that even inmates of concentration camps and patients in Jewish hospitals were persuaded to support the Nazi position. Unsurprisingly, such experiences tarnished the image of referendums in the immediate post-war decades.

Slowly, however, referendums have come back into use. Of the 728 national referendums held in the world between 1900 and 1993, 65 per cent occurred after 1960. Their subject matter falls into three main categories:

- Constitutional issues (such as changing the electoral system in Italy and New Zealand).
- Territorial issues (such as the decision to join a federation or allow more autonomy to provinces).
- Moral issues (such as temperance, divorce and abortion).

Important referendums in the 1990s included those in South Africa in 1992 in which the white minority voted to end apartheid, and in East Timor in 1999, when the population turned out in number to vote for independence from Indonesia, despite the fear of attacks from pro-Indonesian militia. But few democracies make more than occasional use of the device. Heavy users are Australia, where amending the constitution requires approval through a referendum, Denmark, France, New Zealand and especially Switzerland. Between 1945 and 1980, most referendums in the Western world occurred in Switzerland (Lijphart, 1984).

Although the United States has never employed a referendum at national level, traditions of direct democracy are strong in many states and localities. Over the twentieth century, more than 1700 propositions were put to the voters in state-level referendums and initiatives (Magleby, 1994). The western states, especially California, account for many of these votes. For instance, Proposition 13 in 1978 limited property taxes in California and became the first of the modern taxpayers' revolts. California is also one of 15 American states to use the recall (Box 9.6). Adopted early in the twentieth century, the recall has achieved little. The normal tenure of elected officials is rarely cut short (Cronin, 1989).

Despite their democratic credentials, the results and impact of referendums can be influenced by governments. Even freely elected rulers often secure the desired result by controlling timing and wording. In 1997 the British government only held a referendum in Wales on its devolution proposals *after* a similar vote in Scotland, where support for devolution was known to be firmer. This trick of timing worked, just. In addition, referendums can be contained by limiting their impact. In Italy, referendums can only vote down existing laws; it is then parliament's job to introduce replacement bills. In more extreme cases, rulers can simply ignore the result of a referendum. In 1980, Sweden voted to decommission its nuclear power stations. It took almost twenty years for the first reactor to close. We should note also that referendums often reveal a reluctance by the voters to embrace change. In Switzerland, for example, the voters have consistently supported the country's international isolation, confirmed by what Kobach (1997) calls the 'thunderous rejection' of UN membership in a decisive referendum in 1986. The referendum is as much an instrument of conservatism as it is of democracy.

BOX 9.6
The referendum, initiative and recall

Referendum – a vote of the electorate on an issue of public policy such as a constitutional amendment.

Initiative – a procedure which allows a certain number of voters (typically around 10 per cent in American states) to initiate a referendum on a given topic.

Recall – allows a certain number of voters to demand a referendum on whether an elected official should be removed from office.

Source: Cronin (1989).

So referendums and other instruments of direct decision-making live uneasily in the house of representative democracy. Their main benefit is to provide a double safety-valve. First, a referendum allows a government to put an issue to the people when for some reason it is incapable of reaching a decision itself. Like a plumber's drainrods, referendums resolve blockages. Second, where the initiative and the recall are permitted, aggrieved citizens can use these devices to raise issues and criticisms that might otherwise go unheard. But these benefits are easily hijacked: by dictators seeking to reinforce their own position, by wealthy companies waging expensive referendum campaigns on issues in which they have an economic interest, and by illiberal majorities seeking to legitimize discrimination against minority groups. The world's experience with referendums suggests that proposals for direct democracy based on electronic voting should be approached with scepticism (Budge, 1996). Even though technology renders direct democracy possible in large societies through mechanical push-button voting, the possible is not always desirable.

Voting behaviour

Given that voters have a choice, how do they decide who to vote for? Although this is the most studied question in all political science, there is no single answer. The nature of electoral choice varies across voters, countries and time. As a broad summary, however, since 1945 electors in the established democracies have moved away from group and party voting towards voting on issues, the economy, leaders and party competence. Franklin (1992) describes this process as 'the decline of cleavage politics and the rise of issue voting'.

For two decades after the war, most studies of electoral behaviour disputed the intuitive proposition that voters do 'choose' which party to support. An influential theory of electoral choice, originally developed in the United States in the 1950s, argued that voting was an act of affirmation rather than choice (Campbell *et al.*, 1960). Voting was seen as an expression of a loyalty to a party, a commitment which was both deep-seated and long-lasting. This 'party identification', as it was termed, was acquired initially through one's family, reinforced through membership of politically uniform social groups (for example workmates) and confirmed by the traditional American requirement to register as a party supporter to be eligible to vote in its primaries. Electors learned to think of themselves as Democrats, Republicans or, in a minority of cases, as Independents. This view of the voter as a creature of habit is variously called the socialization, Michigan or party identification model. Mulgan (1997, p. 268) offers a good summary:

like sports fans cheering on their team, voters with strong partisan preferences welcome the opportunity to express their support and to share in the party's performance, even when they know their own support will not affect the outcome.

Definition
Party identification is a long-term attachment to a particular party which anchors voters' interpretations of the remote world of politics. Party identification is often inherited through the family and reinforced by the elector's social milieu. It influences, but is separate from, voting behaviour. The stability of party identification was used to explain the continuity of Western party systems in the 1950s and 1960s.

In Europe, where social divisions ran deeper, voting was seen as an expression of loyalty to a social group rather than a party. The act of voting affirmed one's identification with a particular religion, class or ethnic group. Thus electors thought of themselves as Catholic or Protestant, middle-class or working-

class; and they voted for parties which explicitly stood for these interests. Social identity anchored party choice. But whether the emphasis was placed on identification with the party (as in the USA) or with the social group (as in Europe), voting was viewed more as a reflex than as a choice. In reality, the electoral 'decision' was an ingrained habit.

Models of party and group voting assumed a stable rather than a volatile electorate. This approach was appropriate in the relatively static and apolitical 1950s but became less useful in the 1960s and 1970s. Those decades witnessed partisan dealignment – the weakening of the ties which once bound voters, social groups and political parties together. In the third quarter of the century, though only to a lesser extent since, the proportion of party identifiers declined in many established democracies (Box 9.7).

What caused this decline in party loyalties? Why did voters really begin to choose? One factor was government failure: the decay of party loyalties was not uniform but tended to be focused on periods of disillusionment with major parties (for example the USA during the Vietnam war). Another influence

---

BOX 9.7
Decline in party identification, 1970s–1990s

Decline over 10%	Decline of 1–10%	No decline
Austria	Australia	Belgium
Canada	Finland	Denmark
France	Japan	
Germany	Netherlands	
Ireland	New Zealand	
Italy	Norway	
Sweden	United Kingdom	
USA		

Note: Figures are based on a standard survey question asking people whether they 'think of themselves' as, for example, a Democrat or a Republican. Decline is measured between an initial survey (1967–78, depending on country) and a later survey (1991–98).

Source: Bentley, Jupp and Stedman Jones (2000).

See also: Dalton and Wattenberg (2000).

was the declining ability of social cleavages to fashion electoral choice. Class and religious identities were fundamental to the outlook of older generations but they became less relevant to young, well-educated people living in urban, mobile and more secular societies. Class voting, in particular, declined throughout the democratic world, allowing Dalton (1996, p. 324) to conclude that 'class-based voting . . . currently has limited influence in structuring voting choices'. Parties developed more of a catch-all character, and television, more neutral than the press, also loosened old loyalties. In addition, many younger voters were more attracted to single-issue groups than to the established parties, which were seen as slow-moving and part of the official system. All these developments led to an increase in electoral volatility and to the emergence of new parties with a more radical complexion, such as the Greens.

Definition

Partisan dealignment refers to the weakening of bonds between (a) electors and parties, and (b) social groups (for example classes) and parties. In most consolidated democracies, such links have declined in strength but they have not disappeared; electorates are dealigning rather than dealigned.

The decay of group and party voting has led political scientists to focus on the question of how voters do now decide. The contemporary emphasis is on four factors: political issues, the economy, party leaders and party image. Fiorina's theory (1981) of retrospective voting captures these themes. Retrospective voting means casting one's ballot in response to government performance; the phrase tells us much about the character of contemporary electoral behaviour. Electors do form a general assessment of the government's record – and, increasingly, they vote accordingly. A vote is no longer an expression of a lifelong commitment, rather it is a piece of business like any other. The elector asks of the government, 'what have you done for me (and the country) lately?' Retrospective voting helps to explain why economic conditions as reflected in unemployment and inflation figures have such a strong impact on the popularity of governments (Norpoth, 1996). More voters now proceed on the brutal assumption that governments

should be punished for bad times and perhaps also rewarded for economic advance. Rather than staying with parties come what may, more voters now judge by results; they are fairweather friends only.

In this new and more pragmatic era, electors assess the general competence of parties. Increasingly, they ask not just what a party proposes to do but also how well it will do it. Given that parties are less rooted in ideology and social groups, their reputation for competence in meeting the unpredictable demands of office is a crucial marketing asset. So party image becomes crucial. In particular, the electoral significance of the party leader is probably increasing, stimulated by television's dominant position in political communication (Mughan, 2000). Through its leaders and its conduct of the campaign, any serious party must convey the impression of being government-ready. A reputation for competence and credibility, not just a shopping-list of proposals aimed at the party's natural supporters, is the foundation of electoral success.

This trend provides the background in which political marketing, as plied by the new breed of spin doctors, has emerged. While these professionals may resort to paid advertising, their strategy is rarely that of a consumer goods company. Rather, political communication is a distinct form of marketing, largely because its wars are fought on the battleground of news reports rather than commercials. As the term 'spin doctor' implies, the art lies in gaining the most sympathetic treatment of the issues which are most favourable to one's party. The skill is to generate trust in one's own side – and especially to create doubts about one's opponents. Given volatile and sceptical voters, gaining and retaining credibility is the cardinal objective (Bowler and Farrell, 1992).

Elections in authoritarian states

Strange as it may seem, elections are not always competitive. Only the most extreme dictator dispenses with elections altogether; today, the appearance of choice must be preserved even if real freedom in the ballot booth is still denied. In authoritarian systems, elections are often corrupt affairs, with the winner known in advance and electoral malpractice playing its part in delivering the desired result. However, elections in authoritarian and even semi-democratic systems are more often 'made' than 'stolen' (Mackenzie, 1958). That is, the dice of resources, visibility and access to the media are so heavily loaded towards the current rulers that the desired result is manufactured without resort to electoral theft. In totalitarian regimes, by contrast, elections were acts of acclamation rather than choice, with just one official candidate presented to the voters – and enormous efforts made to ensure the entire electorate voted for the party's selection. So how do these less competitive forms of election work? How are they made and stolen?

The most common form of semi-competitive election is that controlled by a *dominant party or leader* (Box 9.8). Such elections mix choice and control in the characteristic fashion of an authoritarian or semi-democratic state. The ruling party uses all the advantages of office (and these include effective governance and a high-visibility leader) to ensure its re-election. Patronage is the party's key resource; it is used either to reward loyal voters directly, as with cash for votes, or to provide local notables with jobs, contracts, access, influence, status and money. In exchange, these local big men deliver the vote of dependent clients in their patch. In some developing countries, Morocco for one, votes are still bought and sold, with political entrepreneurs offering job lots to whichever party offers the best price. Since vote selling is a significant source of money for poor people, criticizing the practice is politically impossible in countries such as Morocco. Who can criticize electors who trade their vote for food?

In dominant party elections, rulers also exploit their control over both the media and the administration of the election. Opposition candidates find they are disqualified from standing; that electoral registration is inefficient in their areas of strength; that they are rarely permitted to appear on television; that they are harassed by the police; and that their leaflets and even their votes are mysteriously lost. The opposition loses heart because it knows its function is always to oppose but never to win. By contrast, the incumbent president will benefit from a unique visibility built over time from easy access to television, from the ability to use the state's coffers in his campaign and from calling in political credits carefully acquired during his tenure. Anticipating

the president's re-election, all the underlings will seek whatever advantage may accrue to them from helping his campaign, thus amplifying his victory. Why back candidates who are sure to lose?

Here, for example, is a description of President Fujimori of Peru in full campaign mode during his re-election campaign in 2000 making promises which impoverished communities would have difficulty in rejecting:

> Criss-crossing the country, making full use of military aircraft and helicopters, he has campaigned in every large Peruvian town and city this week, drawing huge crowds. Each day, he has made some new offer to the electorate: more support for the soup kitchens run by low-income women, new insurance schemes for mothers and babies, more paved roads and drinking water systems, internet connections for every Peruvian school. (Bowen, 2000)

Mexico's Partido Revolucionaria Institucional (PRI), one of the world's most successful vote-winning machines, was the classic example of a

---

BOX 9.8
Forms of semi- and non-competitive election

1. Dominant party or leader

This is a semi-competitive form, permitting a facade of competition. However, the ruling party (or the dominant ruler) exploits patronage, corruption, control of the media and when necessary ballot-rigging to ensure its own continued hold on power. It is a form characteristic of semi-democracies, for example Egypt and Singapore.

2. Candidate-choice

This is also a semi-competitive form; it allows some choice of candidates but not of party. It was found in the less totalitarian communist states (for example Poland) and in some one-party systems in the developing world (e.g. Kenya under KANU).

3. Acclamatory

This is a non-competitive form with only one candidate; any 'choice' is restricted to the nomination phase. It was found in totalitarian regimes, notably the Soviet Union.

party-based approach to semi-competitive elections. By winning 11 presidential elections in a row before its historic defeat in 2000, the PRI became a 'party of the state', giving it unique access to resources which it could pass out through its intricate patronage network. However, in Mexico as in the larger Latin American countries, semi-competitive elections slowly became harder to manage. Domestically, population shifts to the cities took voters away from rural areas where patrons were most powerful. Rising educational standards meant fewer illiterate voters remained to be manipulated while economic growth left fewer people feeling obliged to sell their vote. After the Cold War, Western observers and aid organizations became less forgiving of obvious fraud. Privatization of state corporations left fewer resources (jobs and contracts) to distribute to supporters. The media became a little more willing to expose corruption. As a result of such trends, the PRI in Mexico began to fight cleaner elections, creating the conditions for its own defeat in the 2000 presidential contest.

While semi-competitive elections preserve an illusion of choice, non-competitive contests were more brutal. They were found in one-party, especially communist, systems and there was no pretence that the ruling party could be defeated or even opposed through elections. Rather, their theoretical purpose was to confirm the party's continued support among the people. In practice, such elections demonstrated the party's power to get out the vote, strengthening its dominance over society.

Acclamatory elections were the purest form of non-competitive election. They allowed no choice at all, not even between candidates supporting the one party. They were a phenomenon of totalitarian dictatorships, notably the harshest communist regimes. In the Soviet Union, for instance, the official candidate was simply presented to the electorate for ritual endorsement. Even the ballot procedure was biased: voters who wanted to endorse the official candidate could place their slip directly in the box in full view of the supervisor. Only those who wanted to cross out the official name would need to proceed to the curtained-off area. Soviet elections were grim, ritualistic affairs, irrelevant to the real politics taking place within the party. They were an opportunity for the party's agitators to lecture the population on the party's achievements and to demonstrate their control by getting people out to vote on election day. Contemporary examples are confined to decaying communist dictatorships. In Cuba, for example, 601 candidates were put up for election to the National Assembly in 1998; there were exactly 601 seats to be filled.

Candidate-choice elections were a more liberal form of controlled election, characteristic of communist Eastern Europe in the 1970s and 1980s and of contemporary China. Such contests allowed more candidates than seats, particularly at local level, thus giving voters a small measure of choice. But all candidates supported the communist party; the 'choice' was between candidates committed to the same cause. However, as communist control began to weaken such elections could easily become an arena of opposition. In Poland, for instance, the communists introduced a reform which permitted Solidarity, the independent movement led by Lech Walesa, to contest one third of the seats in the parliamentary elections of June 1989. Solidarity won every one, signalling the end of communist rule. Through a series of reforms beginning in 1979, China also introduced a choice of candidates in local elections. The central party finds such a mechanism useful in testing whether local party officials retain the confidence of their communities. However, no opposition to the party's policy platform is permitted and the party retains control over candidate selection. There are few signs of elections in China threatening the party's control.

Elections in new democracies

Nothing seems to mark out a new democracy as clearly as the introduction of free, fair and competitive elections. And the first election following the withdrawal of the dictators is indeed a high turnout affair marking the launch of a new regime. The significance of such founding elections lies less in the result than in their capacity to legitimize the new order. Founding elections are both a referendum on, and a celebration of, democracy (Bogdanor, 1990). Examples of founding elections include South Africa in 1994 and the first postcommunist elections in most of East Europe in 1990. Throughout Africa, founding elections between 1990 and 1994 were marked by exceptionally high turnouts, convincing victories for the winners and, most important, the peaceful ejection of sitting presidents in 11 countries (Bratton, 1998). Democracy seemed to have arrived.

Definition

A **founding election** is the first election following the transition from authoritarian to democratic rule. Such watershed contests are a public affirmation of the new regime; they are normally high-stimulus, high-turnout events. By contrast, **second elections** are normally marked by lower turnout, some disillusionment and, in some cases, the return of electoral malpractice. The quality of second and subsequent elections is the better test of whether a new democracy has effected the transition to an established democracy.

However second and subsequent elections are a more convincing test of successful democratic consolidation. The broad coalitions which brought down the old rulers soon fall part; the heroes of the struggle – such as Nelson Mandela in South Africa – gradually depart; and popular euphoria gives way to a more realistic assessment of the long road ahead. In these more chastened circumstances, the question is whether elections continue to provide a fair, routine and accepted method of replacing unpopular rulers. Certainly, some new democracies are succeeding in making the transition to consolidation of the new order. Here, for example, is Levitsky's assessment of the 1999 election in Argentina:

> Perhaps the most striking change was the routine, even boring character of the election. In short, a central characteristic of the 1999 election – Argentina's tenth national election since the collapse of military rule in 1983 – was the unprecedented degree to which electoral politics had become routinized (Levitsky, 2000, p. 56).

Although Russia remains no more than a semi-democracy, Sakwa (2000, p. 85) writes in similar vein about its elections in the same year:

> The 1999 elections were no longer so much about a change of regime as about a change of leaders within the system. This is no mean achievement and suggests that the Russian political system is beginning to stabilize and mature.

Yet in many other new democracies quality seemed to decline between founding and second elections. Particularly in subsaharan Africa, opposition boycotts, manipulation by existing rulers and simple administrative incompetence came to the fore. International monitoring agencies have become increasingly critical of post-founding elections in many African countries. Rather than becoming the only game in town, the nature and significance of elections continues to be contested, suggesting that some new 'democracies' are moving towards semi-democracy rather than an established democracy. Further, existing rulers seem to have recovered their capacity to secure their own re-election, outcomes which suggest – even if they do not prove – electoral manipulation. As Bratton (2000, p. 65) notes, 'in a "big man" political culture, it is unclear whether the reelection of an incumbent constitutes the extension of a leader's legitimacy or the resignation of the electorate to his inevitable dominance.' Elections themselves are becoming entrenched but their significance as mechanisms of popular choice still varies greatly between new democracies.

The conclusion is that the existence of an established democracy must be judged against more demanding standards than merely holding regular elections. Regular elections are a necessary but not a sufficient condition of democracy. As Rose and Shin (2001, p. 331) point out,

> A spectre is haunting contemporary studies of democratization: conventional influences, such as the introduction of free elections, have not (or at least not yet) created political regimes that match the standards of established democracies.

First-wave democracies, such as Britain and the USA, established the rule of law and the principle of executive accountability to the legislature before they extended the vote to the general population. By contrast, many recent democracies introduced elections even though the idea of a government by laws rather than men (and women) has still to be accepted. In these circumstances, an election is at risk of becoming an agent of, rather than a constraint upon, the wielders of power. As Rose and Shin note, it is certainly possible 'for a new democracy to persist as a "broken-back" democracy, with free elections taking place in the context of deficiencies in the rule of law, civil society and/or accountability'.

Key reading

Next step: *LeDuc, Niemi and Norris (1996a) is an excellent comparative study of elections and voting, reviewing a wide literature.*

Katz (1997) reviews democracy and elections, while Farrell (2001) is a clear and current introduction to electoral systems; Shugart and Wattenberg (2000) look at additional member systems specifically. For the impact of electoral systems on party systems, see Lijphart (1994). Ginsberg (1982) is a stimulating top-down view of competitive elections. Dalton and Wattenberg (2000) is a comparative study of voting trends. On the United States see Asher (1988b) for presidential elections generally, and Pomper *et al.* (2001) for the 2000 election. Gallagher (1997) is the best short survey of electoral systems and voting in Western Europe. Denver (1994) and Norris (1997) are accessible accounts of voting behaviour in Britain. Bowler and Farrell (1992) is one of the few comparative studies of electoral strategies in an era of political marketing; for Britain, see Bartle and Griffiths (2001). On referendums see Gallagher and Uleri (1996) and Mendelsohn and Parkin (2001).

Interest groups

Interest groups (also called pressure groups) are 'organizations which have some autonomy from government or political parties and . . . try to influence public policy' (Wilson, 1990b). Interest groups presuppose formal organization and thus can be distinguished from acts of participation by individuals. They include bodies such as employers' organizations, trade unions, consumer groups as well as campaigning institutions seeking either to advance general causes (e.g. protection of the environment) or to influence policy in specific areas (e.g. gun control or abortion). Like political parties, interest groups inhabit the space between society and state, helping to link the two. But where political parties aspire to become the government, interest groups seek just to influence it. Reflecting this narrower focus, interest groups do not fight elections; indeed, many adopt a pragmatic and often low-key approach in dealing with whatever power structure confronts them.

Although many interest groups go about their work quietly, their activity is pervasive in democratic politics. Their staff are to be found negotiating with bureaucrats over the details of proposed regulations, pressing their case in legislative committee hearings, seeking to influence media coverage of their trade and not infrequently offering inducements along the way. In authoritarian systems, interests are articulated in a less public, more spasmodic

and sometimes more corrupt fashion. Interests are still expressed to government but often through individual firms or powerful individuals rather than through organized interest groups.

There is an intellectual puzzle about how interest groups succeed in developing in the first place. In *The Logic of Collective Action* (1968), Olson argued that people have no reason to join interest groups when the fruits of the group's efforts are equally available to non-members. Why should a worker join a union when the wage rise it negotiates goes to all employees? Why should a company pay a fee to join an industry association when the benefits the group obtains will help all the firms in that sector? However, the brute fact is that new groups do emerge and grow; the green lobby, for instance, has grown enormously in recent decades. Perhaps this is because members receive the selective benefits of developing their skills and meeting new people as well as contributing to a shared goal which is dear to their hearts (Moe, 1980).

Definition

A **free rider** leaves others to supply **collective goods** – that is, benefits such as unpolluted air that must be supplied to everyone if they are supplied at all. The possibility of free riding creates incentives not to join interest groups such as labour unions that negotiate benefits – for example, a safer working environment – that advantage members and non-members alike.

From a historical perspective, interest groups did develop in a predictable way. In the West, they emerged in a series of waves formed by social change (such as industrialization) and by the expansion of state activity (such as public welfare). Periods of social change raise new problems while an active government gives people more hope of, and gains

---

BOX 10.1
Waves of interest group formation in the United States

Period	Description	Examples
1830–60	Founding of first national organizations	YMCA and many abolitionist groups
1880–1900	Founding of many business and labour associations, stimulated by industrialization	National Association of Manufacturers, American Federation of Labor
1900–20	Peak period of interest group formation	Chamber of Commerce, American Medical Association
1960–80	Founding of many environmental and public interest groups	National Organization for Women, Common Cause

Source: Hrebenar and Scott (1997, pp. 13–15). See also Wilson (1973).

---

from, influencing public policy. Box 10.1 summarizes the development of interest groups in the United States. Most Western nations have followed a similar course, resulting in the mosaic of independent group activity which today makes up civil society. The sheer quantity of interest group activity today is a tribute not just to the complexity of modern society but also to the continuing role of the state in its regulation. Far from leading to a decline in interest groups, the contemporary era of privatization and 'small government' seems to have increased their number as more organizations jockey for favourable treatment from an expanding group of regulators.

The range and influence of modern interest groups raises awkward questions about the distribution of power in democracies. Consultation between government and interest groups is now constant and intimate. Favoured groups acquire insider status and thus the potential to influence decisions at an early stage. Often interest groups work in tandem with national governments in developing positions for bodies such as the European Union and the World Trade Organization. Despite only representing small minorities, interest groups are deeply entrenched in policy-making, certainly more so than many supposedly 'sovereign' parliaments. Interest group activity creates a system of functional representation operating alongside electoral representation. Here, then, is an important issue about all democracies: if legislatures have accountability without power, do interest groups possess power without account-

ability? Are interest groups, as Lowi (1969) contended, 'a corruption of democratic government'? Or does group access to policy-making simply express the right to organize in defence of specific objectives? In short, do interest groups help or hinder democracy?

Protective and promotional groups

When we think of 'interest groups', the bodies which first come to mind are protective groups formed to protect the material interests of their members; for instance, trade unions, employers' organizations, industry bodies and professional associations of lawyers or physicians. Sometimes called sectional or functional groups, such entities are founded to influence government and they have sanctions to help them achieve their goals. Workers can go on strike; medical practitioners can refuse to cooperate with a new prescription policy. Protective groups seek selective benefits for their members and insider status with relevant government departments (Box 10.2). Because they represent clear occupational interests, protective associations are often the most influential of all interest groups. But protective groups can also be based on local rather than functional, interests. Thus, geographic groups arise when the interests of people living in the same location are threatened, for instance by a new highway or a hostel for ex-convicts. Because of their negative

---

BOX 10.2

Protective and promotional groups

	Protective groups	Promotional groups
Aims	a group *of* – defends an interest	a group *for* – promotes a cause
Membership	closed – membership is restricted	open – anybody can join
Status	insider – frequently consulted by government and actively seeks this role	outsider – not consulted as often by government. Emphasizes public opinion and the media
Benefits	selective – only group members benefit	collective – benefits go to both members and non-members
Focus	mainly national – group aims to influence national government	more international – group may seek to influence bodies such as the EU and global public opinion.

---

stance – 'build it anywhere but here'- these are called 'Nimby' groups (Not In My Back Yard).

Of course, the members of protective groups can also lobby government themselves. For example, there is nothing to prevent a firm from approaching an executive department or a sympathetic legislator directly; such contacts are likely to yield a quicker result than working through an industry association. In many countries and sectors, such direct contacts are becoming more frequent. In the United States, an increasing proportion of all business lobbying is accounted for by corporations lobbying government directly rather than through their trade associations. McKay (1997, p. 250) reports that

> since the 1960s there is overwhelming evidence that individual firms have taken a more active part in public policy-making. Most major corporations now have Washington offices and employ professional lobbyists to advance and protect their interests.

Thus an interest group is just one of several channels of influence available to a firm or individual.

Protective groups are not the only type of interest group. Indeed, many groups founded since the 1960s are promotional rather than protective. Rather than protecting their members' material interests, promotional groups advocate ideas, identities, policies and values. Also called attitude, cause and campaign groups, promotional groups include pro- and anti-abortion groups; organizations combating pornography; and ecology groups. In the United States, revealingly, promoting the public interest is largely the responsibility of a legion of promotional bodies. For example, Common Cause (Gardner, 2000) describes itself as 'a nonprofit, non-partisan citizen's lobbying organization promoting open, honest and accountable government'. Because bodies such as the women's movement and the gay lobby emphasize public attitudes, they are also often classified as promotional, even though they work primarily for the benefit of particular groups.

Lacking both the resources and the access available to protective groups based on the economy, promotional groups typically use publicity as their stock in trade. Their target is society as much as government. Their membership is large but often passive and unstable, drawn from the general public rather than specialist industries. Promotional groups often raise funds by sometimes indiscriminate use of direct mail. When an American political scientist enrolled her four-month-old son as a member of Common Cause in an effort to discover the extent to which mailing lists are shared, Junior received 248 items of mail over the next 18 months, including 135 appeals for money (Scholzman and Tierney, 1986, pp. 94–5).

Promotional groups are most significant in established democracies, especially the USA with its participatory culture, open media and unique tradition of charitable giving. Promotional groups are far from new – consider nineteenth-century temperance or anti-slavery movements, for instance – but they are growing in weight. Indeed, the increasing influence of promotional groups since the 1960s, especially in the United States, constitutes a major trend in interest group politics. The relative significance of protective and promotional groups reveals much about the nature of politics and policy-making in any particular country.

Interest groups do not always lobby government directly. Often, they join together in federations or coalitions with other groups to increase their effectiveness. On the protective side, examples include the Federation of German Industry and the National Association of Manufacturers in the USA. The members of these 'peak associations', as they are termed, are themselves interest groups representing specific industries or manufacturing trades. Trade unions respond similarly: for example, the German Federation of Labor and America's AFL-CIO are coalitions of individual unions. Peak organizations are particularly significant from a political perspective. They are generally more attuned to, and seek more influence over, national government than do their members. They talk the language of policy as well as, or sometimes instead of, the language of industry. In some countries, peaks play an integral role linking government with their own members and, through them, with the wider society. For the peaks to acquire such a position, however, they must achieve some autonomy from, and preferably control over, a large group membership. As the frequency with which peak associations are called 'federation' or 'confederation' implies, such centralization is often lacking. Among promotional groups, collaboration tends to take the form of coalitions of existing groups or ad hoc cooperation on specific campaigns, for example among groups seeking better government or to reduce third world debt, rather than the creation of new peak associations.

Channels of access

How are interests communicated to political decision-makers? What are the channels through which this process takes place? Figure 10.1 sets out three of the regular mechanisms of interest group influence found in consolidated democracies: direct dealings with government, indirect influence

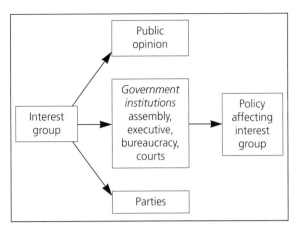

Figure 10.1 Channels of interest group influence

through political parties and indirect influence through public opinion. In this section, we will also look at specialist lobbying companies which help to pilot their interest group clients through these varied channels of access.

Direct dealings with government

Most interest group activity addressing government focuses on the bureaucracy, the legislature and the courts. In established democracies, the *bureaucracy* is the main pressure point. Interest groups follow power and it is in executive offices that detailed decisions are made. As Matthews (1989, p. 217) comments,

> the bureaucracy's significance is reinforced by its policy-making and policy-implementing roles. Many routine, technical and 'less important' decisions, which are nonetheless of vital concern to interest groups, are actually made by public servants.

The broad contours of policy, as set by elected politicians, are difficult for even the most powerful interest groups to control; shrewd protective groups therefore focus on the small print. On such matters, most established democracies follow a convention of discussion with organized opinion through consultative councils or committees; often the law requires such discussion. For instance, consultations are a central feature of the extraordinarily deliberative character of Swedish policy-making (Anton, 1969). Similarly, Denmark has been termed 'the consulting state' because of the extensive negotiations between the government and the country's 2000 or so national groups. Even in France where the higher bureaucracy prizes its autonomy, extensive dialogue takes place between groups and civil servants. As long ago as the 1970s there were no fewer than 500 councils, 1200 committees and 3000 commissions, all bringing together groups and the bureaucracy at national level.

Assemblies are an additional channel through which interests and demands can be voiced. However, while the bureaucracy is invariably a crucial arena for groups, the significance of the legislature depends on its political weight. A comparison between the United States and Canada makes the point. The American Congress (and especially its committees) is a vital part of the policy process; weak party discipline and strong committees combine to create an ideal habitat for lobby operations. Interest groups exert substantial influence over individual members of Congress and committee decisions, and large financial contributions by Political Action Committees (PAC) mean that it is politically difficult for legislators to spurn group demands. By contrast, party voting is normal in the Canadian parliament. In Canada, as in most Western democracies, lobbyists therefore concentrate their fire on the bureaucracy (Pross, 1993, p. 145).

> **Definition**
> A **class action** is a legal device initiated by complainants on their behalf and 'for all others so situated.' The mechanism, most often used in the USA, enables legal costs and gains to be shared among a large group and provides a lever by which interest groups can pursue their goals through the courts.

If interest groups feel ignored in the policy making process, they may still be able to seek redress in the *courts*. In the European Union, an interest group that is unsuccessful at home can take its case to the European Court of Justice. In the United States, business corporations routinely subject government statutes and regulations to legal challenge. Class actions (legal cases covering many people with the same grievance) are common in America. But the

USA has a strongly legal culture; in other countries the courts are growing in importance but remain a remedy of last resort. In Australia, for instance, the requirement for litigants to prove their personal interest in the case hinders legal action; an interest group cannot bring a case simply on the grounds that it is important to their members as a group.

Indirect influence through political parties

Because both interest groups and parties are devices through which society seeks to influence the government, there is in practice overlap between them. For example, Britain's labour movement historically regarded its industrial (trade union) and political (Labour Party) wings as part of a single campaign promoting working-class interests. In the contemporary world, environmental groups in many countries have spawned green parties. And postcommunist Europe has seen the emergence of specialized parties which are essentially disguised interest groups: for example, 'parties' defending pensioners, car-owners and ethnic minorities. The difficulty confronting narrow 'interest parties' is that when they achieve a share in office (as some do where coalitions are the norm), they come under pressure to adopt a wider, national perspective. In Germany, for instance, the Greens relinquished some traditional aspirations, for example the rapid ending of nuclear power, after joining a coalition government in 1998.

To avoid such conflicts with their traditional supporters, most interest groups seek to hedge their bets rather than to become, or develop intimate links with, a political party. Loose, pragmatic links between parties and interests are the norm. In the United States, business and organized labour gravitate towards the Republican and Democratic parties respectively but these are partnerships of convenience, not indissoluble marriages. The traditional maxim of the American trade union movement has been to reward its friends and punish its enemies, wherever these are found. Business shows at least as much pragmatism. Despite an ideological affinity with the Republican party, corporations still contribute heavily to the election coffers of many Democratic members of Congress. A hefty donation ensures a hearing when a company takes a problem to Congress. Most interest groups give more to incumbents; they do not waste money on no-hopers, even if these doomed candidates are standing for the 'correct' party. The theme is similar, if less explicit, in other countries. In Germany, for instance, the powerful Federation of German Industry (BDI) certainly enjoys close links with the Christian Democratic Union but wisely remains on speaking terms with the more left-wing Social Democrats. As a rule, protective interests follow power, not parties.

Indirect influence through the mass media

Press, radio and television provide an additional resource for interest groups. By definition, messages through the media address a popular audience rather

Table 10.1 Methods of political action used by European environmental groups	Groups often using action %
Public action	
Media contacts	86
Mobilizing public opinion	72
Conventional action	
Contacts with the executive	53
Contacts with parliament	53
Contacts with local government	45
Participation in government bodies	41
Formal meetings with the executive	36
Contacts with party leaders	11
Challenging actions	
Protest actions	25
Court actions	20
Non-cooperation with government	13

Note: Based on interviews in 1985/86 with 69 organizations in 10 West European countries.

Source: Dalton (1994), table 8.2.

than specific decision-makers. Thus the media are a central focus for promotional groups seeking to steer public opinion. Ecological groups mount high-profile activities, such as seizing an oil rig to prevent it from being sunk, to generate footage shown on television across the world. Promotional groups view the media as sympathetic to their cause (Table 10.1). Traditionally, the media are less important to protective groups with their more specialized and secretive demands. What food manufacturer would go public with a campaign opposing nutritional labels on foods? The confidentiality of the committee room is a quieter arena for fighting rearguard actions of this kind; going public is a last resort. But even protective groups are now seeking to influence the climate of public opinion, especially in political systems where assemblies are important. In the United States, most protective groups have learned that to impress Congress they must first influence the public. Therefore groups follow a dual strategy, going public and going Washington. Interest groups in other democracies are beginning to follow suit. Slowly and uncertainly, protective groups are emerging from the undergrowth into the glare of publicity.

Lobbyists

Specialized lobbying firms increasingly act as the hired guns of interest groups, helping their clients in some or all of their efforts to influence decision-makers, opinion leaders or even the general public. An interest group might hire a lobbying company to help with a campaign to oppose a particular bill or to organize an advertising campaign aimed at raising the group's awareness with the general public. Thus lobbying organizations are technicians of influence, helping interest groups to achieve their objectives. The 'lobby' is a term derived from the hall of Britain's House of Commons where people could, and indeed still do, approach members of parliament to plead their cause.

But what is the political impact of lobbying companies? Is it possible for wealthy interest groups simply to pay a fee to a lobbying firm to ensure a bill is defeated or a regulation deferred? On the whole, the answer is no. Such companies are inclined to exaggerate their own powers for commercial reasons but we should avoid falling victim to their own

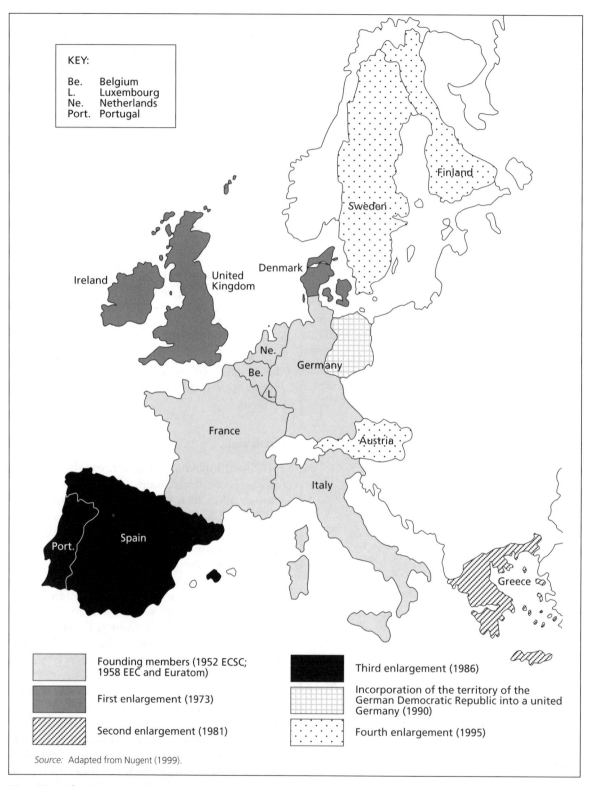

KEY:

Be.   Belgium
L.   Luxembourg
Ne.   Netherlands
Port. Portugal

Founding members (1952 ECSC; 1958 EEC and Euratom)

First enlargement (1973)

Second enlargement (1981)

Third enlargement (1986)

Incorporation of the territory of the German Democratic Republic into a united Germany (1990)

Fourth enlargement (1995)

Source: Adapted from Nugent (1999).

Map 10.1 The European Union

public relations. Most lobbying organizations can achieve little more than access to relevant politicians and, perhaps, bureaucrats. Often, the lobbyist's role is merely to hold the client's hand, helping a company to find its way around the corridors of power when the firm comes to town. Influence can rarely be purchased through a lobbyist but must come from the petitioning group itself. And impact depends first and foremost on the intrinsic strength of the case. To the experienced politician listening to yet another group presenting its case, integrity and conviction direct from the petitioner sing louder than the sophistication of a professional lobbying firm which is paid to talk.

Why then are lobbying companies growing in importance? Part of the answer lies in the increasing sophistication of public relations campaigns, with their growing focus on the public. Professional advisers come into their own in planning and delivering multi-faceted campaigns, with their mixture of advertising, mail-shots and market research as well as direct attempts to influence decision-makers. It is the growing complexity of such campaigns (many of which have only a marginal effect) which accounts for a large part of the undoubted increase in employment in the 'lobbying' industry. So it would certainly be wrong to invest lobbyists with more influence or even skill than they possess. However, even if they can just provide political access in exchange for their fee, perhaps that exchange in itself compromises the principle of equality which supposedly underpins democracy.

Conditions of influence

What gives some interest groups more influence than others? The answer depends on the sanctions the group can apply and on its legitimacy, membership and resources. The ability of a group to invoke *sanctions* reflects its usefulness to those in power. Thus protective groups (such as industry associations) have more impact than promotional groups (such as ecology movements). Since the re-election of governing parties depends partly on economic success, any protective group based on the economy can demand a hearing. Indeed, governments are likely to consider the impact of any proposals on the economy even without explicit attempts at influence

from protective groups. Multinational companies considering a new investment are in a particularly strong position to influence national governments. Such firms have the sanction of taking their investments (and their jobs) elsewhere. As economies become more open, so multinational corporations acquire a stronger bargaining position in direct dealings with government, supplementing the national trade associations which articulate the shared interests of their member firms.

The degree of *legitimacy* achieved by a particular group is also important. The aphorism 'What is good for General Motors is good for America' encapsulates this point. Interests enjoying high prestige are most likely to prevail on particular issues. Professional groups whose members stand for social respectability can be as militant on occasion, and as restrictive in their practices, as blue-collar trade unions once were. But lawyers and doctors escape the public hostility that unions attract. The high standing of such professions helps to explain why they have retained substantial independence in running their affairs.

Definition

Density of membership refers to the proportion of those eligible to join a group who actually do so. High density gives more authority and, in turn, a stronger bargaining position with government. The declining density of trade union membership in the final quarter of the twentieth century undoubtedly weakened labour's bargaining power (Table 10.2).

A group's influence also depends on its *membership*. This is a matter of density as well as sheer numbers. The nearly complete membership which many medical associations achieve among physicians adds to their clout. The highest penetrations are usually achieved when, as with many professional bodies, membership is a condition of practice. By contrast, low density reduces influence, especially when an occupation is fragmented among several interest groups. For instance, American farmers divide between three major organizations with lower total coverage than Britain's National Farmers' Union. In the European Union, breadth of membership is especially important for lobbying organizations. Groups which can demonstrate the support of national associations in all member countries will

Regional profile THE EUROPEAN UNION

Population of member states: 369m
Gross domestic product per head:
15 942 purchasing power units (by the same measure USA equals 22 422 and Japan equals 19 078).
Form of government: a unique regional body in which policy is made partly by European Union (EU) institutions and partly through negotiations among the member states, which retain considerable independence.
Executive: the Council of the European Union, composed of heads of gov-ernment, provides political drive. The powerful European Commission, divided into 17 directorates, initiates legislative proposals.
Assembly: the unicameral European Parliament has 626 members directly elected from each country for a five-year term. The number of MEPs from each country reflects its population. Though growing in significance, the Parliament still lacks full control over the Commission, the budget and even legislation.
Judicial branch: the influential European Court of Justice, composed of one judge from each member country, has successfully developed the constitutional underpinnings of federalism.
Members (founders in italic): Austria, *Belgium*, Denmark, Finland, *France*, *Germany*, Greece, Ireland, *Italy*, *Luxembourg*, *The Netherlands*, Portugal, Spain, Sweden, UK.

The European Union is the most developed example of regional integration in the world. Unusually among regional bodies, the EU has developed institutions resembling the architecture of national governments. It has a parliament (of sorts) and an influential Court of Justice. The heart of the EU, however, is the European Commission (an EU body) and the Council of Ministers (an intergovernmental body). The tension between these units – between the EU as a cohesive actor and the EU as an arena for negotiation between member states – is central to its functioning.

The EU's emergence owes much to Europe's long history of conflict. After the 1939–45 war, many European leaders set out to create a unified continent within which war would no longer be feasible. The goal was to build a United States of Europe. However, economic factors also played their part. European economies needed to be rebuilt after the war and then, to achieve the benefits of scale, integrated into a large, single market.

More recent members, notably Britain, have emphasized the economic basis of the Union while rejecting the idea of a federal Europe. Mrs Thatcher expressed this position in 1988: 'willing and active cooperation between independent sovereign states is the best way to build a successful European Community'. In developing this line, Britain has exploited the continental notion of subsidiarity to argue that decisions should be taken at the national level wherever possible.

The development of the EU has encouraged interest groups to adopt a Europe-wide perspective. About 3000 professional lobbyists were registered at EU headquarters by 1990, many just keeping an eye on developments for their clients. Over 500 European-wide interest groups exist, mainly federations of national groups. Around half are based on specific industries (for example, pasta makers). However many groups possess few resources and they experience difficulty in taking positions acceptable to all their members. Increasingly, therefore, national interest groups lobby directly in the EU, often working in partnership with their home government. Other lobbying comes from regional and local governments within member states. Outside bodies, such as Japanese trade associations and American multinationals, are also active. Most lobbyists focus on the Commission, a small body that relies heavily on interest groups for its information and expertise.

Further reading: Nugent (1999) and, on interest groups and the EU specifically, Mazey and Richardson (1998).

Table 10.2 Density of trade union membership (workers belonging to a trade union, 1997)

	Per cent	Trend 1985–97
Denmark	90	Up
Sweden	86	Up
Norway	71	Up
South Africa	41	Up
Italy	38	Down
Australia	35	Down
Germany	33	Down
UK	30	Down
Netherlands	29	Down
New Zealand	24	Down
Japan	24	Down
USA	14	Down
France	9	Down

Note: Figures for non-EU states are for 1995.

Sources: International Labour Office, *Labour Report* (1997) and Waddington and Hoffman (2001).

receive a cordial reception from the Commission. In all countries, members' intensity of support is also important since commitment determines how far the members of a group are willing to go in support of its objectives.

The organizational resources available to an interest group are important and here money clearly helps. The National Rifle Association (NRA) in the USA illustrates this point. With an annual budget of $40 million, the NRA employs 275 full-time staff. Despite public sympathy, the coalition of gun control groups cannot match the NRA's 'fire power'. Yet even in the USA, hard-up but skilful campaigners can generate free publicity and wide public sympathy. Ralph Nader's Crusade for Car Safety in the 1960s was an early example. He exposed a dangerous design fault in some General Motors models, a flaw that the manufacturer hoped to keep away from the public gaze. Thus, just as the impact of lobbying firms is often exaggerated, so is the significance of the money available to an interest group. As a rule, financial resources are rarely decisive; the

skill with which resources are used matters just as much. Here again, the NRA is an example. Its campaigning skills are legendary; in a matter of days it can blitz members of Congress with 'spontaneous' letters, faxes and e-mail from its 2.6 million members. However, neither money nor skill can transform the fundamental political environment confronting an interest group. Consider the NRA once more. The key problems preventing radical gun control in the United States are (1) the difficulty of passing any legislation opposed by a significant minority within Congress and (2) an ambiguous constitutional reference to the 'right of the people to keep and bear arms'. The NRA has exploited both factors but created neither.

Policy communities and issue networks

In the democratic world, many interest groups are in virtually daily contact with government. So the question arises, what is the nature of such relationships? This is the core issue in the study of interest groups, bearing on the question of whether groups express or subvert democracy. Here we review two interpretations of the relationship between groups and governments, based on the contrasting ideas of policy communities and issue networks. The 'community' interpretation sees this relationship as close and mutually supportive whereas the 'network' approach views the links as looser and more open to new voices. As we will see, many observers identify a trend in the governance of liberal democracies away from policy communities and towards issue networks.

The metaphor of a policy community views the relationship between interest groups and the state as warm and snug. The term implies that the actors involved in detailed policy-making in a particular sector (especially interest group leaders and senior public officials) form their own small village. Everyone knows each other, uses given names and tries not to upset each other. Over time, the participants develop shared working habits and common assumptions about what can be achieved. The actors learn to trust each other and to respect each other's key objectives. Shared interests predominate: for instance, the road builders and the Transport

Department seek ever larger highway projects. Business is done behind closed doors to prevent political posturing and allow a quiet life for all. As in all communities, insiders are sharply distinguished from outsiders. Everyone inside the community wants to keep outsiders where they belong: outside. The golden rule is never to upset the apple cart.

> ### Definition
> A **policy community** is a close-knit group, consisting primarily of civil servants and leaders of insider groups. The members of the policy community settle detailed issues in their policy area in a confidential and depoliticized atmosphere of trust, based on shared interests. Policy communities are also termed 'subgovernments'. An **issue network** is a contrasting depiction of the links between interest groups and government. It implies a looser and larger collection of players whose impact depends on what they know as well as whom they know. If a policy community has the intimacy of a village, an issue network shows the more impersonal character of a large town.

American political scientists used the term 'iron triangle' to describe policy communities. In the USA, the three points on the triangle were executive agencies or departments, interest groups and congressional committees (Figure 10.2). Such triangles became an exercise in mutual back-scratching: the *committee* appropriated funds which was spent by the *agency* for the benefit of *interest group* members. Thus, the Department of Agriculture, the relevant committees in Congress and farmer's groups

would collude on ever larger food subsidies. Every point on the triangle benefited. This was a game without losers – except for the taxpayer who rarely knew what was going on. Iron triangles were also called 'subgovernments', implying that policy was made in an independent compartment of power. The effect of a series of subgovernments was to fragment policy-making, deflecting the political aims of the majority party in Congress or even of the president (Ripley and Franklin, 1991).

To portray the links between groups and governments in terms of policy communities is to criticize the working of liberal democracies. Such communities may make policy by consensus but they still amount to little more than conspiracies against the taxpayer. It is therefore fortunate, perhaps, that policy communities are beginning to decay in many democracies. Today, policies are subject to closer scrutiny by the media; new consumer groups protest loudly when they spot the public being taken for a ride; and legislators are less willing to keep quiet when they see public money being wasted. Also as issues become more complex, so more groups are drawn into the policy process, making it harder to stitch together secret deals among a few insiders. In the United States, where this trend has gone furthest, the committee barons who used to dominate Congress have lost much of their power. The iron has gone out of the triangle; now influence over decisions depends on what you know as well as who you know.

Reflecting these trends, the talk now is of issue networks. These refer to the familiar set of organizations involved in policy-making: government departments, interest groups and legislative committees. However, an issue network does not imply the familial relationships suggested by the term 'community'. In an issue network, the impact of an interest group varies from issue to issue, depending on its expertise. As Heclo (1978, p. 102) put it,

the notions of iron triangles and subgovernments presume small circles of participants who have succeeded in becoming largely autonomous. Issue networks, on the other hand, comprise a large number of participants with quite variable degrees of mutual commitment ... it is almost impossible to say where a network leaves off and i' viron-ment begins.

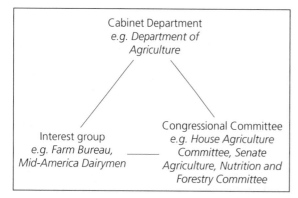

Figure 10.2 Iron triangles: how subgovernments operated in the USA

The emergence of issue networks reflects a shift to a more open policy-making style in which cosy deals are harder to sustain. Clearly, the idea of issue networks enables us to portray policy-making more positively. More interests participate in decisions, the bias toward protective groups is reduced, new groups can enter the debate and a sound point carries more weight. Interest groups come to be seen in a more democratic light.

Pluralism and corporatism

To appraise the political significance of interest groups we must now consider their function in the political system as a whole. This means broadening the debate beyond asking how policy is made in specific sectors: for instance, in agriculture, education or transport. In this section we move on to consider the overall role of interest groups in politics. Again, political scientists have developed two models: pluralism and corporatism. The contrast between the two models directs our attention to fundamental but again declining contrasts between the pluralistic politics of the United States and the more corporate politics characteristic of continental Europe. In a sense, therefore, this section addresses two ways of organizing a democracy.

Definition
Literally 'rule by the many', **pluralism** refers to a political system in which numerous competing interest groups exert strong influence over a responsive government. However each of these groups concentrates on its own area (for example education, medical care) so no single élite dominates all sectors. New groups can emerge easily, bringing further competition to the political marketplace.

The debate between pluralists and corporatists goes to the heart of a central question in politics: the relationship between society and the state. Pluralists see society dominating the state; corporatists view the state as leading society. At one level this difference is descriptive, reflecting contrasting assessments of the flow of influence between government and interest groups. But at a deeper level, the debate is ideological. Pluralists see the task of government as responding to interests expressed to it. Corporatists,

by contrast, favour an organized, integrated society in which the state offers leadership in pursuit of a vision shared with society.

The *pluralist* view dominated early postwar accounts of interest group activity. Its supporters see politics as a competition between a multitude of freely organized interest groups. These compete for influence over a government that is willing to listen to all the voices it can distinguish in the political din. In a pluralist system, the state becomes little more than an arena for competition between interest groups. The governing party is an arbitrator, not an initiator of change. For Bentley (1908), an American pioneer of this approach, 'when the groups are adequately stated, everything is stated. When I say everything, I mean everything.' All kinds of interest have their say before the court of government. Groups compete on a level playing field, with the government showing little bias either towards interests of a particular type, or to specific groups within that type. As interests emerge, new groups form to represent them; there are few barriers to entering the political market.

Because many people belong to more than one interest, the temperature of political conflict in a pluralist system remains low. Most groups restrict themselves to a single sector so there is healthy fragmentation across the range of government activity. Indeed the central tenet of pluralism is that no single dominant élite rules. Rather, different interest groups lead the way in each area of policy. So pluralism depicts a wholesome process of dispersed decision-making in which interest groups ensure government policies reflect the diversity of modern society. Dahl (1993, p. 706) summarizes the strengths of pluralism, suggesting that groups have

served to educate citizens in political life, strengthened them in their relations with the state, helped to ensure that no single interest would regularly prevail on all important decisions, and, by providing information, discussion, negotiation and compromise, even helped to make public decisions more rational and more acceptable.

Corporatism is a contrasting and more European approach to government–interest group relations. In a democratic setting, it refers to decision-making by negotiation between the government and a few

FOR OR AGAINST

THE USA AS A PLURALIST POLITICAL SYSTEM

Both as an ideal and as a description of how politics works, pluralism draws on American experience. But can American politics really be presented as an open competition between freely organized interests? Or is the entire decision-making process in the hands of an élite which, in effect, excludes consideration of any policies which would threaten its own values? Is American pluralism myth or reality?

The case for

In the USA, interest group patterns come closer to the pluralist model than anywhere else. As de Tocqueville (1954, first pub. 1856) wrote in the 1830s, 'in no country in the world has the principle of association been more successfully used, or applied to a greater multitude of objects, than in America.' Petracca (1992, p. 3) makes the point more succinctly: 'American politics is the politics of interests'. Nowhere else are interest groups so numerous, visible, organized, competitive or success-ful. Tens of thousands of groups, ranging from Happiness of Motherhood Eternal to the United Autoworkers of America, seek to influence policy at federal, state and local levels. Nor are such groups confined to corporate interests. Promotional groups are uniquely prominent in the USA. Over 500 groups focus on environmental protection alone. If one interest seems to be gaining the upper hand, others will form to counter its influence. Vigorous, indepen-dent and competitive media are always willing to listen to new groups with a story to tell. All this activity reflects Americans' constitutional right 'to petition the government for a redress of grievances'. Group activity also reflects the separation of powers. Weak parties and the separation of powers combine to ensure that American government is simply too fragmented to be anything more than an umpire of group demands.

The case against

All political systems generate myths and America's is pluralism. In reality, pluralist 'competition' operates within an unquestioned acceptance of broad American values favouring the free market and the pursuit of individual self-interest. The entire political discourse works within a narrow ideological range, shaping and limiting the demands expressed so as to benefit, in particular, corporate USA. Thus, in contrast to most other democracies, American parties emphasize personalities rather than policies. As a result, turnout has declined to the point where voters are an unrepresentative minority of society. Washington's intricate political games are dominated by middle-aged, middle-class, white male graduates, a group which forms only a small minority of a diverse population. In any case, some interest groups are wealthier and better organized than others so that the pluralist ideal of equal representation for all groups is far from reality. And, as the frequency of inner city disturbances reveals, some interests are left out of the debate altogether. As Schattschneider (1942) famously put it, some interests are organized into American politics – but others are organized out.

Assessment

The danger of the debate is that the word 'pluralism' becomes evaluative rather than descriptive. Those who favour the American way, see pluralism; those who are more critical, discern a hidden élite. But one conclusion, at least, seems clear. While overseas observers may interpret American politics as much ado about nothing, that view is not shared by the players themselves. To understand what happens in American politics (as opposed to what does not happen), it is necessary to to appreciate the vigorous competition between interest groups in American politics, even if the debate does take place in a limited framework.

Further reading: Dahl (1961), Domhoff (1983), Mills (1956), Polsby (1980).

powerful interest groups. Where pluralism implies competition between groups, corporatism implies coordination and planning. The privileged groups normally include peak associations representing industry and labour – for example, the Federation of German Industry and the German Federation of Trade Unions. Though formally accountable to their members, the main role of the 'peaks' in a corporate system is to carry their members with them after agreements have been struck with the government and other national groups. Hence, corporatism is a top-down approach. Issues such as price levels, wage increases, tax rates and pension entitlements are all settled in tripartite discussions among senior politicians, industrialists and union leaders and are often then presented as an agreed social pact or contract. The freewheeling practices of American pluralism are nowhere to be found.

Under corporatism, negotiations between the state and recognized groups take an administrative, technical form. Policy-making is depoliticized and electoral representation becomes less important. Policy is made in private negotiations in government ministries, not in the public debate of congresssional committee hearings. Corporatism also implies a hierarchy of groups, with the government dealing with the influential peak associations, which then pass decisions down the line. So in contrast to pluralism, which emphasizes an upward flow of preferences from group members to their leaders and then on to government, corporatism stresses the downward flow of influence. Corporatism therefore requires a high level of social and political organization, including compulsory membership of firms in employers' organizations and of employees in trade unions. The state retains a leadership or at least a coordinating role.

An example will add colour to this outline. Just as the United States is taken to exemplify pluralism, so Austria reveals many corporatist features (Fitzmaurice, 1991). At least until the mid-1990s, many of Austria's major economic and social decisions emerged through a system called Economic and Social Partnership. This brought all the major economic interests into an elaborate network which in turn connected to the government, the parties and the bureaucracy. At the pinnacle of this partnership stood the Party Commission. This was an entirely informal network which nonetheless made decisions affecting the whole working population. It set price limits, ratified wage increases and was an important forum for discussing economic policy. Final decision-making in the commission often ended as a face-to-face talk between just two people: the president of the Chamber of Commerce, representing capital, and the president of the trade union federation, representing labour. Except during war or other crises, it is inconceivable that a pluralistic country such as the United States, with its liberal philosophy, separation of powers, market economy and voluntary group membership could ever achieve such centralized decision-making.

Definition

In a democratic context, **corporatism** is a relationship between the state and interest groups in which major decisions on domestic matters emerge from discussion between the government and a few leading peak associations, usually representing capital and labour. In return for their influence, these favoured groups are expected to ensure the compliance of their members. This system is often called **liberal** or **societal corporatism** to distinguish it from the **state corporatism** of fascism (Schmitter and Lehmbruch, 1979). The fascist theory was that the economy should be organized by sector, with special committees ('corporations') planning each industry in response to national needs. In both forms, but especially in state corporatism, citizens are represented more through the workplace than the legislature.

Corporatism could work in Austria because all working people belonged to statutory and centralized chambers of commerce, labour and agriculture. In general, corporatism is most likely to take root where national interest groups possess a high density of membership and extensive authority over their members. The Scandinavian nations, Austria and the Netherlands fit these conditions well (Box 10.3). Scandinavia exhibits a tradition of compromise and consultation between government and interest groups which perhaps amounts to a 'Nordic model' (Arter, 1999). For example, Kvavik (1976) interpreted Norway in the 1970s as a 'cooptive polity' in which interest groups were brought into public policy-making and implementation in a distinctly non-pluralist way. Sweden also involves interest groups in a remarkably deliberative process of policy

---

BOX 10.3
Selected established democracies grouped by the extent of corporatism

Most corporatist
Austria
Denmark
Switzerland
Germany
Finland
Belgium
Ireland*

Many features of corporatism
Norway
Sweden
The Netherlands

A few features of corporatism
France
Italy

Least corporatist
Canada
United Kingdom
United States

* Ireland's social pact, beginning in 1987 and now called the Programme for Competitiveness and Work, gives tax cuts and a say in economic policy to trade unions in exchange for voluntary wage restraint. This scheme has so far proved consistent with rapid economic growth albeit with the risk of over-heating and inflation.

Source: Modified from expert assessments in Lijphart and Crepaz (1991)

---

formation, though without the assertive state leadership which is usually associated with corporatism. But one factor favouring corporatism was particularly important in Austria. The country had experienced bitter conflict between the wars; after 1945 both major groups, Catholic and socialist, sought negotiation and compromise. Corporatism was a form of consensus politics designed to forestall any repetition of social breakdown.

In the 1980s and 1990s, corporatism came under attack. Even in Austria, those who felt left out of the system began to voice their protest. The country's extreme right Freedom Party became one of the most successful populist parties in Western Europe, eventually becoming part of the government in a remarkable coalition with the establishment People's Party in 2000. This coalition symoblized a thawing of Austria's previously frozen corporate system. However, it was in the Anglo-American world (where corporatism was never more than half-hearted) that the heaviest blows were struck. As early as 1982 the American political economist Mancur Olson had claimed that corporatism was a form of political sclerosis, reflecting the gradual accumulation of power by sectional interests. Corporatism was viewed as harmful to both economy and society, because it invited excessive state intervention and over-reliance on the state. The carefully crafted consensus between government, capital and labour was

held to inhibit the continuous economic changes needed to remain competitive in an increasingly global economy.

Reflecting this intellectual sea-change, Margaret Thatcher and Ronald Reagan launched a political assault on the power of entrenched interests in Britain and the United States during the 1980s. While such attacks were focused on the privileges of organized labour, some large companies were also hit by more vigorous competition policy, more open markets and a growing emphasis on competitive tendering in the public sector. Structural change, particularly the decline of heavy industry with its strong unions, large companies and powerful trade bodies, accelerated the decay of corporatism. Writing on Scandinavia, Eriksen (1990) argues that 'the post-corporate state may represent a new order'. But it remains to be seen how far most European countries, with their long history of corporatist thinking and the inherent value they place on governing by consensus, have the desire, the ability or indeed the need to change their ways.

Interest groups in authoritarian states

The role played by interest groups in non-democratic states provides a sharp contrast to their position in established democracies. Authoritarian rulers see freely organized groups as a potential threat to their own power; hence, they seek either to repress organized groups or at least to tame them by incorporation within the power structure. In this section, we will examine the workings of these strategies in authoritarian regimes before turning to the special case of totalitarian states.

In the latter half of the twentieth century, many authoritarian rulers had to confront the challenge posed by the new groups unleashed by economic development. With urbanization, industrialization, cash-crop agriculture, monetary exchanges, formal education and the expansion of the media, conditions for the organized articulation of interests were created. A new generation of educated radicals emerged to lead labour unions and peasant leagues. How did rulers respond to these new conditions? One strategy was to seek to repress such groups completely. Where civil liberties were weak and many groups were new, this approach was feasible. For example, a strategy of repression was adopted by many military regimes. Military leaders often had their own fingers in the economic pie, sometimes in tacit collaboration with multinational corporations; the rulers' goal was to maintain a workforce that was both compliant and poorly paid. 'Trouble-makers' were quickly removed. Particularly in the countryside, the political class could rely on the support of traditional élites. Landowners rarely rejoiced when peasants began to organize; they preferred the 'divide and rule' strategy of dealing with individuals through traditional patronage networks. Thus, attempts to set up radical new organizations were crisply repressed. Although the generals may now have returned to their parade grounds, the exclusionary strategies they adopted are often followed, sometimes in less explicit form, by their civilian successors.

On the other hand, authoritarian rulers could seek to manage the expression of these new interests. That is, they could allow interests to organize but seek to control them, a policy of incorporation rather than exclusion. By enlisting part of the population, particularly its more modern sectors, into officially sponsored associations, rulers hoped to accelerate the push toward modernization. This approach was common in Latin America, where a corporate tradition entailed state licensing, regula-

tion and even funding of selected interest groups which were granted a monopoly of representation in their particular sphere. Before the pro-market economic reforms of the 1980s and 1990s, Mexico offered a particular working of this tradition. Its governing system was founded on a strong ruling party (the PRI) which was itself a coalition made up of labour, agrarian and 'popular' sectors. Trade unions and peasant associations had access to party leaders, who provided resources such as subsidies and control over jobs in exchange for political support. In effect, Mexico became a giant patron-client network – a form of corporatism for a developing country.

But Mexico's system, and many others like it, is now in rapid decline. It was over-regulated, giving so much power to civil servants and PRI-affiliated unions as to deter business investment, especially from overseas. As the market sector expanded, so the patronage available to the PRI diminished. In 1997, an independent National Workers Union emerged to claim that 'the old mechanisms of state control are exhausted', a point which was confirmed by the PRI's defeat in a presidential election three years later. But even when the PRI network was at its strongest, life could be hard in Mexico's highly unequal society. Hardship and discontent were endemic in remote provinces where traditional landowners still ruled the roost. Even in the organized sectors, workers and peasants regularly broke away from their associations. These independent movements then faced continual harassment from the combined forces of the state, the party, employers and officially favoured unions. Thus Mexico under the PRI's exclusive control exhibited both corporate techniques of policy-making and the repression which followed from the failure to incorporate all but a privileged section of the population into the PRI system.

The position of interest groups in communist states was even more marginal than in other non-democratic regimes. Independent interest groups did not exist for most of the communist era, a deliberate result of communist ideology. Communist states were party-led, not society-dominated. Groups served the party, not the other way round, and society was to be moulded, controlled and developed by the party élite. Interest articulation by freely organized groups was inconceivable.

Communist rulers sought to harness all organizations into 'transmission belts' for party policy. Trade unions, the media, youth groups, professional associations – all were little more than branches of the party, serving the great cause of communist construction.

However, the capacity to articulate interests did increase as communist regimes evolved. The use of coercion and terror declined while conflict over policy became more visible. Institutional groups such as the military and heavy industry had always carried weight but they became more important as economies matured and decisions became more technical. The more open struggle that developed in the 1970s and 1980s involved inputs from below; issues were no longer resolved by ruthless imposition. Sectional interests began to be openly expressed, particularly in Poland, Hungary and Yugoslavia. However one sharp contrast with Western pluralism remained: ruling communist parties tried to restrict interest articulation to safe technical matters. The party continued to crack down vigorously on dissent going beyond these confines. The objectives of the communist state remained beyond criticism. Thus 'socialist pluralism', to the extent that it existed at all, remained far more limited than its Western counterpart.

Even in reforming China, the Western notion of an 'interest group' still carries little meaning. The party continues to provide the framework for most formal political activity. 'Mass organizations' such as the All-China Federation of Trade Unions and the Women's Federation are led by party officials and transmit its policy. Private business is intertwined with the state sector and is not represented through traditional industry associations. Too many deals are done 'through the back door' to leave much role for policy-oriented interest groups. 'Rightful resistance' enables citizens to protest to higher authority about lower officials exceeding their legal powers but such appeals operate on an individual rather than a group basis. As Manion (2000, p. 446) concludes, 'the communist party basically monopolizes the function of interest aggregation'.

In fascist theory, as under communism, the state dominated partial interests. Indeed, the central premise of fascist thought was that the state must lead. But unlike communism, the fascist state sought to mobilize, rather than to destroy, group activity. In particular, it wanted to exploit, rather than take over, private industry. Fascism advocated a corporate relationship between state and industry (Brooker, 2000, p.156). Its thinking here drew on both the medieval tradition of occupational guilds and the Catholic notion of an interdependent society to postulate a politically appealing third way between capitalism and socialism. The economy would be arranged by industrial sector. Within each industry, special corporations (committees or chambers) composed of employers, employees, party and government would plan production, set wages and prices and resolve disputes. In this vertical arrangement, horizontal conflicts between business groups and labour unions would be overcome as both sides learned to serve national goals as defined by the supreme leader. Thus corporatism would secure the national interest by overriding class conflict. Such a system was formally implemented in Italy in the mid-1930s but in practice the 22 corporations established there had only token powers and minimal impact. Corporatism was even less significant in Nazi Germany. Indeed, the man charged by Hitler with introducing the format there claimed that after learning of his assignment, 'I did not sleep for several nights on account of the corporate system because I could not make head or tail of it' (O'Sullivan, 1986, p.133). In practice, industrial policy took the practical form of ensuring that large privately-owned manufacturers met the demands of an expansionist regime. The driving force was the political objectives of the Nazi state; corporate institutions took second place to the task of serving the war machine.

Interest groups in new democracies

The question of the role to be played by interest groups in new democracies remains open, intimately linked to the extent to which democracy itself consolidates. Certainly, the emergence of groups acting independently of the state was integral to the weakening of authoritarian rule. For instance, groups based around the green, peace and women's movements developed in some communist states in the 1980s, posing a challenge to party rule by their mere existence as non-party organizations. Eventually, some of these groups became the catalyst of regime change. In Poland, the trade union organization Solidarity (supported by the Roman Catholic Church) emerged in 1980 to assert the interests of Polish workers. Nine years later, Solidarity itself took the reins of government. However, groups such as Solidarity were not interest groups in the Western sense; they began as *de facto* opposition groups and then became broad social movements or popular fronts. They sought to replace rather than to influence communist rule. Their historical task was pivotal but short-term and went far beyond anything of which a narrow interest would have been capable. In the new democratic era, the groups which were the levers of regime change – including environmental and women's groups – have generally declined in strength. Similarly, the churches have paradoxically declined because their position as a 'semi-protected site of opposition' to communist rule is no longer needed in the new, freer order (Fitzmaurice, 1998, p. 174).

As popular fronts disappear and some institutional interests decay, so orthodox interest groups, with their detailed and routine demands, should take root in democracy's fresh soil. Ägh (1998, p. 22) suggests that the 'the chief actors of democratic transition are the parties, but those of democratic consolidation are the interest organizations and civil society associations, which provide the fine-tuning and effect the full accomplishment of democratization.' As yet, however, interest groups are not consistently developing in new democracies along Western lines, any more than political parties are growing into the mass membership organizations once found in West Europe. Certainly, some of the 'older' new democracies of Southern Europe – notably Spain and Portugal – have moved a long way toward the pattern of interest groups found in consolidated democracies. Yet even in Spain, Heywood (1995, p.243) notes 'the continuing primacy of the state over civil society' and that membership of voluntary associations is falling, not rising. Padgett (2000, p.166) reports that trade union membership has also declined in postcommunist Europe.

Even in eastern Germany, now formally part of the highly organized German economy, large firms are preoccupied with direct lobbying and small ones with survival, leaving little space for interest groups representing specific industries or general business values. Padgett concludes that 'nowhere in east/central Europe is even the semblanace of a stable, fully functioning interest group system' to be found. A similar story emerges from the post-military democracies of Latin America. Hagopian (1998, p. 238) considers that the rise of markets means that 'the corporate negotiating channels once open between unions and the state are being rendered obsolete'. Just as many newer democracies led the way in developing media-based rather than mass membership parties, so too do the direct links between companies and the government found there lead us to question whether the Western model of the traditional industry-wide interest group will ever become a potent force in new democracies.

Many new democracies witnessed a release of traditional social groups rather than interest groups. In the postcommunist world, groups based on ethnicity and nationality, long suppressed, have proved to be a potent force for (and response to) instability. National differences brought about the disintegration of Czechoslovakia, for example. In much of Africa, group politics in an era of post-military government continues to be based on ethnicity rather than interests generated through the workplace. Democratic or not, many poorer countries lack the complex economy needed to develop interest group patterns found in affluent established democracies. In addition, when such economic resources as are available are parcelled out on ethnic lines, or in any personal or unregulated way, incentives for orthodox interest groups to develop are limited.

Take Russia as an extreme and barely democratic case. The separation between public and private sectors, so central to the organization of interests in the West, has not emerged there. Instead private entrepreneurs compete for the wealth which can be extracted from the rusting hulk of state-owned industry. Ruthless business executives, corrupt public officials and jumped-up gangsters make deals in a virtually unregulated free-for-all. Certainly, individual financiers pull the strings of their puppets in government but the politics is personal rather than institutional. In such an environment interests are everywhere but interest groups are nowhere. To assume that new democracies will in due course replicate the group patterns of established democracies is not just a Western-centred view but also one which places a large bet on both economic development and democratic deepening in new democracies.

Key reading

> **Next step:** *Wilson (1990b) is a clear and straight-forward introduction to interest groups.*

Many of the best studies of interest groups continue to be about the United States; see the reader edited by Cigler and Loomis (1998), the collection by Salisbury (1992) and the text by Hrebenar and Scott (1997). On Britain, M. Smith (1995) is a brief, helpful introduction; Marsh and Rhodes (1992) is an influential account of issue networks. For a comparative perspective on interest groups in the Western world, see Thomas (1993) or Richardson (1993). On corporatism, Williamson (1985) is a helpful guide; for the relevance of the concept to the Nordic states, see Arter (1999). On postcommunist Russia see Cox (1993) and Sakwa (1996, ch. 8).

CHAPTER 11

Political parties

imperative
interest
articulation

'In this book I investigate the workings of democratic government. But it is not institutions which are the object of my research: it is not on political forms, it is on political forces I dwell.' So Ostrogorski (1854–1919) began his pioneering comparison of party organization in Britain and the United States. Ostrogorski was one of the first students of politics to recognize that parties were becoming vital in the new era of democratic politics: 'wherever this life of parties is developed, it focuses the political feelings and the active wills of its citizens' (Ostrogorski, 1902, p. liii).

Ostrogorski's supposition that parties were growing in importance was fully justified: the twentieth century proved to be the century of parties. In West Europe, mass parties battled for the votes of enlarged electorates. In communist and fascist states, ruling parties monopolized power in an attempt to reconstruct society and the people within it. In the developing world, nationalist parties became the vehicle for driving colonial rulers back to their imperial homeland. In all these cases, parties succeeded in drawing millions of people into the national political process, often for the first time. The mass party was *the* mobilizing device of the twentieth century.

In standing between the people and the state, parties became, and substantially remain, integral to politics in four main ways:

C#3   Q#1

- Ruling parties offer *direction to government,* performing the vital task of steering the ship of state.
- Parties function as agents of *élite recruitment.* They serve as the major mechanism for preparing and recruiting candidates for public office. If you want to lead your country, you must first persuade a party to adopt you as its candidate.
- Parties serve as agents of *interest aggregation.* They transform a multitude of specific demands into more manageable packages of proposals. Parties select, reduce and combine interests. They act as a filter between society and state, deciding which demands to allow through their net.
- To a declining extent, political parties serve as a *point of reference* for their supporters and voters, giving people a key to interpreting a complicated political world.

Definition

Political parties are permanent organizations which contest elections, usually because they seek to occupy the decisive positions of authority within the state. Unlike interest groups, which seek merely to influence the government, serious parties aim to secure the levers of power. In Weber's phrase, parties live 'in a house of power'.

In examining parties in established democracies, we should recognize their contrasting significance in West Europe, Australia and New Zealand, on the one hand, and the United States, on the other. In most consolidated democracies, and especially in West Europe, parties typically possess a large if declining dues-paying membership, a coherent ideology and strong discipline among their members of parliament. This European model of party reflects the impact on the entire party system of organized socialist parties emerging from outside the legislature, seeking representation for the working class. By contrast, in the USA, parties are weaker, especially outside Washington. In many parts of America, parties barely seem to exist between elections. Even presidential candidates impose themselves on a party more than they emerge from within its structures.

The question for early in the twenty-first century is whether we are witnessing a 'crisis of parties' and the export to the rest of the democratic world of the American format of weak, decentralized organizations. Old-style communist parties have virtually disappeared, social democratic parties are no longer fired by ideology, politicians increasingly communicate with electors through television, party membership is falling (and ageing), voters' loyalties are weakening and party income increasingly depends on state subsidies rather than members' subscriptions. No longer do parties seem to be energetic agents of society, seeking to bend the state towards their members' interests. Rather, they are in danger of becoming political pensioners, living off past glories and facing an uncertain future. If Ostrogorski were writing today, would he still interpret parties as a 'focus for the active wills' of the citizens?

Party organization

As Panebianco (1988) reminded us, internal organization is a key issue in the study of parties. How is power distributed within the party? What is the relationship between leaders, members and parliamentarians? The answer to these questions, Panebianco claims, must be historical. He places special emphasis on a 'genetic' account of party development, a term he uses to stress the importance of the party's 'founding moment' in dealing out the power cards between the elements of party organization. These 'continue in many ways to condition the life of the organization even decades afterwards'. In this section, we will examine a classification of parties based on their origins before turning to two specific issues: first, the relationship between the party inside and outside the legislature and second, how parties select their candidates.

Adopting Panebianco's historical approach leads to a three-fold distinction between élite, mass and catch-all parties (Box 11.1). *Élite* (or caucus) parties are 'internally created'. They are formed by cliques within an assembly joining together to reflect common concerns and then to fight effective campaigns in an enlarged electorate. The earliest parties were of this élite type: for example, the Conservative parties of Scandinavia and Britain that emerged in the nineteenth century. The first American parties, the Federalists and Jeffersonians, were also loose élite factions, based in Congress and state legislatures.

Mass parties are a later innovation. They originate outside the assembly, in groups seeking representation in the legislature for their interests and goals. The working-class socialist parties that spread across Europe around the turn of the twentieth century were prime examples of these externally created

---

BOX 11.1
Models of party organization

	Élite ('caucus') party	Mass party	Catch-all party
Emergence	19th century	1880–1960	After 1945
Origins	Inside the assembly	Outside the assembly	Developed from existing élite or mass parties
Claim to support	Traditional status of leaders	Represents a social group	Skill at governing
Membership	Small, élitist	Large card-carrying membership	Declining, leaders become dominant
Source of income	Personal contacts	Membership dues	Many sources, including state subsidy
Examples	19th-century liberal parties, many postcommunist parties	Socialist parties	Many modern Christian and Social Democratic parties in Europe

Source: Modified from Katz and Mair (1995).

parties. The German Social Democratic Party (SPD), founded in 1875 in hostile conditions, is the classic case. Such parties acquired an enormous membership and sought to keep their representatives in parliament on a tight rein. Stimulating élite parties to copy their techniques, these socialist parties exerted tremendous influence on European party systems in the twentieth century. In Germany, again, the Christian Democratic Union (CDU) was created after the Second World War to offer a broadly-based Christian alternative to the SPD. The United States, almost uniquely among consolidated democracies, never developed mass parties.

> ### Definition
> A **caucus** is a closed party meeting, usually held for strategy or nomination purposes. The term is often used in the context of legislative parties, where the caucus formed by a party's members of parliament in effect forms that party's top committee, as traditionally in Australia and New Zealand. Caucus (or élite) parties are those that originate in the legislature rather than the wider society.

The *catch-all* party, a term introduced by Kircheimer (1966), is the more recent form. Kircheimer used the phrase to describe the outcome of an evolutionary path followed by many parties, both élite and mass, in response to post-1945 conditions. Catch-all parties seek to govern in the national interest rather than as representatives of a single social group. They are dominated by their leaders who communicate with the voters through television rather than indirectly via a large, active membership. Catch-all parties seek electoral support wherever they can obtain it; their purpose is not to represent but to govern. The catch-all party is a response to a mobilized political system in which governing has become more technical and in which electoral communication is through the media. The transformation of several radical socialist parties into leader-dominated social democratic parties, as in Spain and the United Kingdom, is perhaps the most important example of a shift from mass to catch-all status. Another is the broadening of Christian Democratic parties (for example the CDU in Germany) from catholic defence organisations to broader catch-all parties of the centre-right. Indeed, the German notion of a *volkspartei* ('people's party')

with its wide spread of support captures the catch-all idea. America's parties, it might be argued, went straight from élite to catch-all status, missing out the mass stage.

We turn now to the relationship between the parliamentary party and the party organization. Parties are complex organizations, with legislators in the assembly and officials at party headquarters needing to develop a way of working together. The balance between the two wings clearly reflects a party's origins. In élite parties, with their origins in the assembly, the parliamentary party normally dominates, as with Britain's Conservatives. In the United States, to take another case, the parties in Congress are virtually independent of weak national party institutions. Members of Congress ask what their party can do for them, not what they can do for their party. By contrast, mass parties, especially socialist ones, traditionally sought to keep their parliamentary brothers and sisters on a stricter leash. Members of the legislative party simply formed one division of an advance occurring on a range of fronts. Other recently created external parties have also aimed to ensure that members of the legislature serve rather than dominate the wider party. For example, Germany's Greens (founded in 1980) originally sought to rotate members of the legislature midway through a parliamentary session. The purpose was to prevent legislators from losing touch with the wider party.

In practice, the relationship between the parliamentary and extra-parliamentary structures is one of interdependence; only rarely does one side completely dominate the other. In particular, the party leader, a strong figure in both the parliamentary party and the external organization, provides a bridge between the two worlds. Furthermore, as externally created parties come closer to power, so the autonomy of the parliamentary leadership tends to increase. The German Greens have formed part of a coalition government since 1998, a position which has inevitably led to further compromises with its founding ideals of democracy within the party.

We should, however, note that the party organization outside the assembly retains some useful 'power cards'. State financial aid normally goes to the party bureaucracy, not to the party in parliament. And only party officials can cope with increasingly technical tasks such as recruiting members and raising funds through mail-shots, or arranging for advertising during election campaigns. In particular, the media war of a modern election has reduced ordinary members of parliament to peripheral status; if they ever were big shots in the campaign, they are no longer. As politics becomes more professional, so the technicians in the extra-parliamentary organization regain some clout. This notion is captured in the idea of an 'electoral-professional' party centred around sophisticated media campaigns (Panebianco, 1988).

Candidate selection is the other crucial aspect of party organization. The questions here are: Who controls candidate recruitment? How does an ambitious politician go about winning a party's endorsement for election to the legislature? These are vital issues in parliamentary systems since those subsequently elected to the assembly form the pool from which top national leaders emerge. Given that candidates who are nominated for safe districts or who appear near the top of their party's list are virtually guaranteed a place in the legislature, it is the selectorate (selectors of candidates), not the electorate, which acts as gate-keepers to the house of power. Candidate selection is also an important area of transition in party practice, as ordinary members acquire more weight in selection procedures.

In most democracies, candidate selection is a decentralized procedure involving a major role for local parties and an increasing one for individual members. In countries using the plurality election system, the most common requirement for a prospective parliamentary candidate is to win selection by local constituency parties operating under the supervision of party headquarters. The major parties in Britain are examples of this approach. But even where party list proportional representation is used, a frequent format is national selection *after* consideration of suggestions from lower levels (for example the major parties in the Netherlands). In either case, then, nomination is certainly not the exclusive preserve of the party élite at the centre.

Mair (1994, p.15) notes that 'many parties now afford their ordinary members a greater voice in candidate selection than was once the case'. Israel is a striking example of dramatic democratization in candidate selection even in a country using party list PR (Hazan, 1997a, p.95). Israel's major parties have introduced the primary system previously associated with the United States, and party members now select all the candidates to be included on their party's national list at the general election. Members vote for up to 20 candidates from a long tally of hopefuls. Inevitably candidates with good name recognition score highest, driving politicians to publicity-seeking initiatives and reducing the coherence and effectiveness of the parties themselves. The result, Hazan concludes, has been to transform the Knesset from an assembly of parties into an assemblage of MKs (members of the Knesset). We see here clear evidence of the declining coherence of parties brought about by widening the selectorate and perhaps an argument against such an extension in the first place.

Definition

Primary elections enable a party's supporters to decide which candidate will represent their party at a subsequent general election. Primaries are widely used in the United States, where they were introduced to reduce the dominance of party bosses. Although many observers claim that the primary system takes too much control away from the party, destroying its cohesion, these nominating elections are now well-established in the USA.

It is not just the task of nominating candidates for the assembly which has broadened out. As Mair (1994) also notes, 'more and more parties now seem willing to allow the ordinary members a voice in the selection of party leaders'. Of course, parties in the USA have long selected their presidential candidates through party conventions and delegates to the convention are now mainly selected through primaries open to all registered supporters of the party (and in some American states even to all electors). In Canada both the Liberals and the Conservatives have used conventions for selecting their leaders since the 1920s. But the franchise for leadership elections is broadening in other countries too. In Britain, the three largest parties – Conservative, Labour and Liberal Democrat – all now give rank-and-file members at least some say in choosing their leader. The traditional method of giving members of parliament exclusive control over selecting their party's leader is in retreat, a trend which places more emphasis on the ability of candidates to reach out to a larger audience through the media. The broadening constituency for leadership elections contributes further to looser and more open party organizations.

The social base of parties

Since most modern parties emerged from outside the assembly to express group interests, they naturally acquired a specific social base which continues to influence their policies and outlook. West European parties, in particular, retain a secure foundation in the social structure which enables them not only to persist through time but also to exhibit remarkable continuity in their shares of the vote. As Bartolini and Mair (1990, p. 287) write, 'the twentieth century of mass politics in West Europe can be seen as a century of electoral stabilization, showing a fundamental bias toward stability'. Voters' loyalties may be weakening but they have not disintegrated. Most established parties in West Europe still have many core identifiers located in particular segments of society, which provide a solid, long-term grounding to their support. These links between parties and social groups usually develop at crucial points of conflict in a country's history. Such moments define

new social cleavages (that is, divisions) from which parties emerge and which they then reinforce, producing what was often called a 'frozen' party system (Lipset and Rokkan, 1967). So to explain the social base of parties, we must again don the historian's robes. Box 11.2 shows the three main cleavages from which most West European parties have emerged. As always, the American experience is distinctive.

The waves of social change described in Box 11.2 produce counter-currents which are powerful in their own right. Social change always creates losers as well as winners and the resulting tensions can lead to the emergence of extreme, often short-lived, protest or 'flash' parties. These parties can easily flourish in an unsettled society by proffering simple 'solutions' to irreversible changes. For example, although the main American parties do not show the strong social bases found in Europe, American history is still littered with the debris of political organizations offering a return to simple, home-spun, small-town – and white – values (Lipset, 1983). A twentieth-century example is George Wallace's campaign for the presidency in 1960. Fighting on a racially charged law-and-order ticket, Wallace won 13.5 per cent of the vote as candidate for his own American Independence party.

BOX 11.2

Major cleavages in the development of West European societies and their impact on parties

Stage	Definition	Party cleavages created by this revolution
National revolution	The original construction of the state as a territory governed by a single central authority	(a) Regional parties representing outlying territories vs. core parties representing the pre-eminent region (e.g. Liberal vs. Conservative in the United Kingdom). (b) Catholic parties representing traditional church control (e.g. over education) vs. secular (e.g. socialist) parties.
Industrial revolution	The emergence of urban societies based on manufacturing rather than extraction or agriculture	(a) Agrarian parties which defend rural interests (e.g. in Scandinavia). (b) A division between socialist parties representing the interests of the new urban working class and conservative parties representing employers' interests.
Postindustrial 'revolution'	The transition to societies in which education and knowledge replace capital and manufacturing as key resources	Green parties and a shift toward postmaterial values among many 'socialist' parties.

Sources: Lipset and Rokkan (1967) for the national and industrial revolutions; Inglehart (1997) for the postindustrial 'revolution'.

Another illustration of these movements of protest is the racist parties which emerged in many West European countries in the 1960s and the 1970s. Based on poorly educated segments of the urban working-class, these parties used the growth of immigrants and guest workers to 'explain' their supporters' sense of insecurity in a changing world. The most important example came from France where the National Front (FN), led by Jean-Marie Le Pen, remained a significant force until it was overwhelmed at the end of the century by the internal divisions which eventually afflict all such parties (Ignati, 1992, p. 1). At the start of the new century, the protest mantle passed to Austria's Freedom Party, whose leader Jörg Haider skilfully exploited dissatisfaction with the country's establishment parties. Most unusually for a protest party, the Freedom Party proved acceptable as a coalition partner in national government.

Definition

Protest parties exploit popular resentment against the government or the political system, usually by highlighting specific 'problems' such as high taxes or a permissive immigration or asylum policy. They are often short-lived **flash parties** which fall as quickly as they rise. Their leaders are typically populist but inexperienced, with activists operating on the margins of the law. France's National Front was a significant – and relatively long-lasting – example from the final quarter of the twentieth century.

We should end this section with a caveat. The links between society and parties are weakening as the conflicts of class and religion that fuelled party systems have softened. The anchors of voter loyalty are slipping. New generations of educated voters prefer to enter politics through single-issue cause groups, not political parties. Television and the internet allow for communication between leaders and voters without any need for party activists to serve as intermediaries, leading Seisselberg (1996) to postulate the emergence of new media-based 'personality parties' such as Silvio Berlusconi's Forza Italia. In the final quarter of the twentieth century, these factors led not just to the emergence of catch-all parties but also to a sharp fall in the membership of established parties (Table 11.1). Lacking a steady flow of young members, the average age of party

Table 11.1 Falling party membership in some European democracies, 1960–99

	Party members as a percentage of the electorate		
	Beginning of 1960s	Beginning of 1980s	End of 1990s
Austria	26	22	18
Finland	19	13	10
Belgium	8	9	7
Norway	16	14	7
Italy	13	10	4
Netherlands	9	3	3
Germany	3	4	3
UK	9	3	2

Sources: Mair (1994), table 1.1; Mair and van Biezen (2001), table 1. Figures for the final column are for 1997–9, depending on country.

members increased. By the late 1990s, the mean age of members of Germany's Christian Democratic Union, a major European party, had reached 54; Britain's Conservatives were just as elderly. The European mass membership party, based on mobilizing specific social groups, will certainly need to continue to adapt if it is to prosper – and perhaps even survive as a major force – throughout the twenty-first century. The American style of loose, flexible, open parties is still exceptional in the democratic world but may also serve as a prototype for developments elsewhere.

As parties' links with society have weakened, so they have come to depend more on the state for their sustenance. In particular, state funding of parties is now virtually universal in democracies (Katz, 1996, p. 130). In Austria, Denmark, Finland, Norway and Sweden, state funding for national parties is now their main source of revenue, reducing their incentive to recruit members. Only in the Netherlands, the UK and the USA do membership contributions clearly exceed funding from the public purse (Mair, 1994, p. 10). Since most state support goes to the leading parties, the effect is to reinforce the status quo. For these reasons, the state and the top levels of major parties are tending to converge into a single system of rule: the 'party state'. Given these tendencies, it is perhaps no wonder that the ordinary member feels remote from this process and has been drifting away from parties to the purer satisfactions of the single-issue group.

> **Definition**
>
> A **party system** denotes the interaction between the significant political parties. In a democracy, parties respond to each other's initiatives in competitive interplay. Also, all the parties in a country are influenced by the political and constitutional system of which they form part.

Party systems in established democracies

To understand the political significance of parties, we must go beyond examining them individually. Just as a football game consists of the play between two teams, so a party system consists of the interaction between competing parties. Competition speeds the take-up of innovations in party organization, fund-raising and election campaigning. Equally, legal regulation – particularly prominent in the United States – applies to all parties. It is a property of the party system as a whole. West Europe is the homeland of strong party systems operating in consolidated democracies. By contrast, Latin America is an example of a conti-

nent where party systems have traditionally been weak. Parties there have lacked strong roots in society, electoral systems have been unstable and some governments, civilian as well as military, have questioned the value of parties (Mainwaring and Scully, 1995).

The main feature of a party system is the pattern of competition within it. Like parties themselves, patterns of party competition persist over time, forming part of the operating procedures of a country's politics. Broadly, we can distinguish three distinct formats in democracies: (1) one party is a constant presence in government, (2) two major parties compete for sole control over the government, (3) a number of parties join together in a coalition. These three types are known as dominant party, two-party and multi-party systems respectively (Box 11.3). However, both dominant and two-party systems are now in decline and multi-party systems have become the most common configuration in consolidated democracies. The British and American model of two parties engaged in a permanent contest for power may still be influential but it is now rather unusual.

Dominant party systems

Here one party is a constant component of the executive, governing either alone or in coalition. A rare contemporary example is the African National Congress (ANC) in South Africa's young

---

BOX 11.3
Party systems in democracies

Type	Definition	Examples
Dominant party system	One party is constantly in office, either governing alone or in coalition	*Historic:* Japan (Liberal Democrats), India (Congress) *Current:* South Africa (African National Congress)
Two-party system	Two major parties compete to form single-party governments	Great Britain (Conservative and Labour), United States* (Democratic and Republican)
Multiparty system	The assembly is composed of several minority parties, leading to coalition government	Belgium, Netherlands, Scandinavia

* However, divided government means one party can control the presidency while the other has a majority in either or both houses of Congress.

FOR OR AGAINST

PARTIES AS VOTE-MAXIMIZERS

What are parties for? Their defining feature is to fight elections and many theorists assume, for simplicity, that the sole motive of parties is to maximize their vote. But how realistic is that assumption? Should parties be construed as seeking to influence government policy, rather than just maximizing their electoral support? This question of the fundamental goal of parties has caused controversy among political scientists seeking to construct theories of political competition in democracies.

The case for

The classic study of how parties compete is Anthony Downs's *An Economic Theory of Democracy* (1957), one of the most influential works of political science published since 1945. Downs assumes that in a political market, parties act in a rational, self-interested way. He defines a party as 'a team of people seeking to control the governing apparatus by gaining office in a duly constituted election'. And to maximize their control over the government, parties seek also to maximize their vote, even in a multi-party system:

> The more votes a party wins, the more chance it has to enter a coalition, the more power it receives if it does enter one and the more individuals in it hold office in the government coalition. Hence vote-maximizing is still the basic motive underlying the behaviour of parties. (Downs, 1957, p.159)

From this assumption, Downs deduces that as long as public opinion forms a symmetrical, bell-shaped distribution around the midpoint of a left-right scale (Figure 11.1), parties in a two-party system will converge at the midpoint of the ideological spectrum. A party may start out at one extreme but it will move toward the centre because more votes are to be won there than there is support to be lost through extreme supporters shifting to abstention. Evidence to support this prediction is legion: Bill Clinton and Tony Blair are just two examples of leaders who have won elections by steering their parties to the middle ground. Further, public funding for parties is now often in proportion to their electoral success, giving a further incentive for parties to maximize their vote.

The case against

Critics allege that Downs's vote-maximizing assumption is too extreme. It is often more accurate to see parties as office-seeking, a goal which may not require votes to be maximized at all. In the United States, for instance, George W. Bush won the presidency in 2000 despite losing the popular vote to Al Gore. In similar vein, the object of a party in a two-party parliamentary system is surely to win enough seats to form the next government; the size of its majority is secondary. For such reasons, Riker (1962, p. 33) distinguishes his position from Downs's as follows:

> Downs assumed that political parties seek to maximize votes. As against this, I shall attempt to show that they seek to maximize only up to the point of subjective certainty of winning.

More radically, parties may be modelled as seeking to influence public policy, rather than to obtain office or to maximize votes. For example, in European countries governed by coalitions (especially Scandinavia), the choice of partners is influenced by agreements over what policies the coalition will follow. If parties followed the goal of power above all else, why would they ever resign from coalitions over policy disagreements? Unlike private firms, parties are supported by volunteer activists who can walk away if they dislike their party's policy direction. De Swann (1973, p.88), a leading advocate of this 'policy-influencing' position, suggests that

> Considerations of policy are foremost in the minds of the actors . . . the parliamentary game is, in fact, about the determination of major government policy.

Assessment

Downs's vote-maximizing model may be simple but that is one of the functions of a model – to simplify. In any case, his assumptions seem to yield reasonable predictions: a recent study of 10 West European countries found that 'about half of the parties covered in the case studies used a strategy of vote maximization'. By contrast, only three parties acted as though policy influence were their main objective (Müller and Strøm, 1999, p.305). Even if counter-examples can be found, Downs's model is still useful as a yardstick against which actual party behaviour can be measured.

Further reading: Downs (1957), Green and Shapiro (1994), Müller and Strøm (1999), Riker (1962).

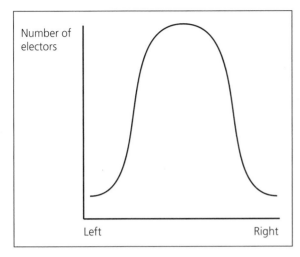

Figure 11.1 A bell-shaped distibution: parties converge at the centre

republic. The ANC benefits from memories of its opposition to apartheid, from its strong position among the black majority and from its use of office to reward its own supporters. By contrast, the opposition parties are weak and divided, with a smaller social base. Like the ANC, many other dominant parties were linked to the founding of a new nation. However, the very strength of a dominant party's position mean that factions tend to develop within it, leading to an inward-looking perspective, a lack of concern with policy and even corruption. The long-run result is electoral decline.

A more traditional, if now less clear-cut, instance of a dominant party is Japan under the conservative Liberal Democrats (LDP). The LDP did not engage in ballot-rigging or intimidation, devices used by dominant parties in semi-democracies. But the constant tenure in office of the LDP between 1955 and 1993 did lead to the corrupt meshing of state and party which characterizes such systems. The LDP used state patronage to reinforce its strength, passing out resources such as campaign funds to its candidates through party factions. Indeed, personalized factions within the ruling LDP became the main form of political competition, reducing the focus on policy choices and eventually increasing popular cynicism about the political process, particularly after the ending of the country's economic miracle in the 1990s. Today, the LDP continues as

the largest party but it is increasingly forced into coalition with other parties.

India provides our final instance of a dominant party losing its pre-eminence. Indian politics was led from 1947 by the Congress Party, a broad-based left-of-centre party which emphasized secularism in a nation riven by religious conflict (Mishra, 1994). Congress's pre-eminence owed much to its role in establishing an independent state. To maintain its dominant position, Congress relied on a pyramid of class and caste alliances to sustain a national organization in a fragmented society. However Congress is no longer able to dominate Indian politics; indeed, no single party has won a majority in a general election since 1984. Congress has lost ground partly because of growing religious tensions; in 1999, it came a poor second to the Hindu-based BJP and its allies. As its status has declined from dominant party to large party, so the shadow which Congress throws across Indian politics has shortened. One commentator described it as 'a carcass being picked over by careerists', a description which also fits many other 'dominant' parties.

Two-party systems

A two-party system is one in which two major parties of broadly comparable size compete for electoral support, providing a framework for political competition which limits the influence of third parties on the formation and policies of governments (Sartori, 1976). By itself, neither major party dominates; in combination, they form a strong party system.

Today, the United States is the surest example of a two-party system. Although the Republican and Democratic parties may be weak by European standards, a two-party system has been a constant feature of American history. The most obvious explanation for the resilience of America's two-party system lies in its plurality method of election. Winner-take-all in single member districts introduces a high hurdle against third parties achieving representation in Congress. Also, presidential contests are an electoral mountain which can only be conquered by major parties capable of assembling a broad national coalition. These features will probably sustain America's two-party system into the future despite the pressures toward fragmentation revealed in the periodic

Country profile **ITALY**

Population: 58m.

Gross domestic product per head: $20 200.

Form of government: parliamentary, with an indirectly elected president who can play a role in government formation.

Legislature: the Chamber of Deputies (630 members) and the Senate (315) are elected simultaneously by popular vote for a maximum of five years. A bill must receive the positive assent of both houses and (as in Australia) the Cabinet is equally responsible to both chambers, producing a strongly bicameral legislature.

Executive: the Prime Minister formally appoints, but cannot dismiss, the members of the large Cabinet. Coalition requirements limit the PM's choice. An 800-strong Office of the Prime Minister provides support, which has given PMs more influence over the machinery of government.

Judiciary: based on the civil law tradition, Italy has both ordinary and administrative judicial systems. A 15-member Constitutional Court has powers of judicial review.

Electoral system (1994): an additional member system, with three-quarters of both houses elected by simple majority and one-quarter by proportional representation.

Until 1992, Italy was a leading example of a dominant party system. The role of the Christian Democrats (DC) in several ways resembled the position of Japan's LDP. The DC was a leading player in all 47 Italian governments between 1947 and 1992. The DC was a patronage-based, Catholic catch-all party that derived its political strength from serving as a bulwark against Italy's strong communist party. Like Japan's LDP, the DC slowly 'colonized' the state, with particular ministries becoming the property of specific factions. The party used its control of the state to reward its supporters with jobs, money and favours, with little regard for the public purse. This patronage network spun across the country, providing a measure of integration between the affluent North and the backward South (LaPalombara, 1987). However the DC's rule was based on unstable coalitions with a range of partners; governments were short-lived and policy innovation rare.

Between 1992 and 1994, this party system fell apart in a meltdown without precedent in the democratic world. Still the largest party in 1992, the Christian Democrats (DC) had ceased to exist two years later. Its old sparring partner, the communists, had already given up the ghost, largely reforming as the Democratic Party of the Left (PDS) in 1991. Why then did this party-based system collapse? Donovan (1995, p. 3) suggests that five catalysts initiated the destruction of Europe's oldest ruling élite. These were: the collapse of communism; the success of the new Northern League in the 1990 regional elections, opening up the possibility of real political change; referendums on electoral reform in the early 1990s which revealed public hostility to the existing order; vivid attacks by Francesco Cossiga (President 1985–92) on the patronage power of the leading parties; and exposure of political corruption by a newly-assertive judiciary. Like many other dominant parties, the DC's reliance on patronage also came under pressure from the global economy and, in Italy's case, from EU pressures for a single open market.

Although the disintegration of the old system was decisive, Italy's new order is only now beginning to deliver more stable government. The election of 1994, the first fought under a new electoral system designed to reduce fragmentation, yielded a remarkable government of populist right-wing parties headed by media magnate Silvio Berlusconi. This government collapsed after seven months, the victim of traditional coalition infighting, to be replaced by an even more astonishing government of technocrats (experts, lawyers and academics). This crisis government contained no parliamentary representatives at all. The next election, in 1996, did produce signs of consolidation. Two major alliances emerged: the centre-left Olive Tree Alliance and the more right-wing Liberty Pole. The Olive Tree Alliance, committed to restoring the state's tottering finances, formed a government led by former academic Romani Prodi. But it was not until 2001, when Berlusconi's House of Freedom coalition won a majority in both legislative chambers, that stable government seemed to become a serious possibility.

Whatever the future may bring, Italy's old mass parties have disappeared for ever, replaced by the looser, leader-dominated parties which are characteristic of the new democracies founded in the 1990s. The rapid decline of the DC showed just how vulnerable and outdated its form of dominant party rule had become.

Further reading: Donovan (1995), Gundle and Parker (1996), Zariski (1993), Partridge (1998).

emergence of independent candidates. Certainly, the USA shows how weak parties, lacking the ideological cohesion and mass membership found in their West European counterparts, can nonetheless form a strong party system.

Britain is also often considered to exemplify the two-party pattern. Certainly, the Conservative and Labour parties regularly alternate in office, offering clear accountability to the electorate. However third parties have gained ground. In 1997, the centre Liberal Democrats won 46 seats (7 per cent), the highest for a third party in over 50 years. The Liberal Democrats now offer some limited support for the Labour government.

Like dominant party systems, two-party systems now appear to be in decline, sustained in large part by a plurality electoral system. Duverger's Law (1954) says that 'the simple majority single ballot [plurality] system favours the two-party system'. Thus the recent shift away from the plurality method, as in New Zealand and South Africa, has damaged the prospects of two-party systems. Electoral reform in the UK would strike a further blow at its two-party politics. Yet even where a favourable electoral regime continues, the two-party system has lost ground. Consider Canada. Traditionally dominated by the Conservatives and Liberals, the Conservatives were reduced to just two seats at the 1993 election. Two regional parties (the Bloc Québécois and the Reform party) emerged as the main opposition to the Liberals. The fragmentation of Canada's devolved political system proved stronger than the capacity of national parties to overcome regional differences.

Definition

Adversary politics was a phrase introduced by Finer (1974) to describe party competition in Britain's two-party system. Finer considered that the conflict between the Conservative and Labour parties took the form of 'a stand-up fight between two adversaries for the favour of the lookers-on'. This endless battle, he believed, caused ineffective governance. However, single-party government based on a secure parliamentary majority does permit radical change, as in Britain under both Margaret Thatcher and Tony Blair, even if it does reduce opposition to the impossible role of 'heckling a steam-roller'.

Multiparty systems

These are characterized by proportional representation, a system which normally precludes any single party from winning a majority of seats in the assembly. The result is government by coalition, a form that predominates in continental Europe and Scandinavia. As dominant and two-party systems decay, so multiparty systems are becoming the norm in democracies. It is therefore important to examine their character and functioning. In particular, how effective are multiparty systems in delivering sound governance?

Answers to this question have evolved over time, largely in response to variations in economic performance. Unlike Britain's two-party system, multiparty systems were once held to produce weak and unstable government with confused accountability to the electorate; if things went wrong, which party or parties in the coalition should be blamed? Further, the party composition of coalitions can change within a parliamentary term, reducing the link between elections and government formation. For instance, Finland averaged a government per year in the 30 years following 1945, far more than its number of elections. Sometimes, elections in multiparty systems are extremely slow in producing any government at all. After the Dutch election of 1972, six months elapsed before a workable coalition emerged. All this is far removed from the concentration of power in a single-party cabinet in Britain or even the focus of responsibility in the United States on the White House. Herbert Asquith, British Prime Minister 1908–16, expressed the English-speaking world's suspicion of coalitions when he wrote, 'Nothing is so belittling to the stature of public men, as the atmosphere of a coalition.'

But opinions of multiparty systems became more positive in the 1960s as the postwar recovery of continental economies took hold. In practice, coalition government did not lead to inconsistent, vacillating policies. In Scandinavia, for instance, coalitions were composed of parties with a similar ideological persuasion. Policy was formed by consensus. Coalitions came and went but without threatening continuity of policy. This contrasts with two-party systems, such as the United Kingdom, where each new government would set about reversing the policies of its predecessor. The claim was that the careful, cautious governance induced by multiparty coalitions was well-suited to complex societies with strong social divisions. Coalitions were seen as the anvil of democracy, a forge for manufacturing consensus.

However, the link between multiparty systems and weak government resurfaced in the 1990s. This reinterpretation reflected the tough 1990s agenda: cutting the government's budget deficit, privatizing state-owned companies and reducing welfare expenditure. The more parties there are in a government, it was now argued, the harder it became to reach agreement on such a reform programme. It was the traditional two-party systems, notably Britain and New Zealand, which pursued the new policies with most energy. Continental Europe tended to lag behind, leading to doubts about whether multiparty systems were sufficiently flexible to produce the rapid policy changes needed to adapt to a global economy. Blondel (1993), for one, argued that

'the consensus mode of politics is not well-equipped to lead to long-term strategic action ... its value appears to lie primarily in its ability to handle deep social cleavages rather than policy development.

Yet several continental countries are beginning to implement the reform agenda. The conclusion, perhaps, is that multiparty systems produce continuity of policy which is helpful when the economy is growing naturally, but are slower, though not necessarily less successful in the long run, at reviving economics which have fallen on hard times.

Parties in authoritarian states

In general, parties are less significant to authoritarian governments than to democracies. Either authoritarian rulers dispense with parties altogether, claiming there is no need for them in a country united behind its leader, or the ruler maintains a system of personal rule behind the façade of a one-party state. However, totalitarian regimes are as ever a special case. Especially under communism, parties were the central political instrument through which leaders sought, and sometimes achieved, total control over society. In this section, we will first examine the role of parties in non-totalitarian regimes before turning to the communist and fascist experience.

Some authoritarian regimes still get by with no parties at all. These are either pre-party or anti-party states. Pre-party states are most commonly found in the Middle East; for example, Saudi Arabia, Jordan and Kuwait. In these traditional monarchies, a ruling family dominates and parties have yet to emerge or be permitted. Pre-party states are rare in the modern world. In the more common anti-party state, by contrast, existing parties were banned when a new regime took over – military rulers were the main example. After seizing power, the generals often quickly abolished parties, claiming that the nation could no longer afford the bickering and corruption associated with them (an alternative tactic of military rulers was to ban all parties bar their own puppet organization).

Many civilian authoritarian rulers have found a one-party system useful but often just as a disguise for personal rule. Consider, for example, the African countries which achieved independence in the 1950s and 1960s. Once independence movements achieved power, the hero of the liberation struggle soon put a stop to party competition. One-party systems were established but they proved to be politically weak. The party lacked presence in the countryside, was riven by ethnic and regional divisions and became the personal vehicle of the country's hero-founder, used as a vehicle for distributing his patronage. For example when a coup overthrew Kwame Nkrumah in Ghana in 1966, his Convention People's Party simply disappeared with him. Thus, many of these one-party authoritarian regimes were governed more by personal rule than by a cohesive party. Many 'one party' states in the developing world became, in effect, no-party systems.

Leaving aside communist states, there are few cases of authoritarian rule where the political party is the true source of power. An example, bordering on semi-democracy, is Singapore's People's Action Party (PAP). This party has ruled the island since it achieved independence from Britain in 1959. Like many dominant parties, PAP was headed by a powerful leader, Lee Kuan Yew, who served as a father figure for the nation during his long tenure as Prime Minister from 1959 to 1990. Unusually, however, the party's dominance outlasted the departure of its founder. In 1997 PAP still won 81 out of 83 seats, leading the new Prime Minister to claim that the voters 'had rejected Western-style liberal democracy'. PAP continues to manipulate public opinion by limiting media freedom. It also runs smear campaigns against opposition figures; government-inspired libel and tax fraud suits have bankrupted several opposition politicians. PAP's attitude to the electorate blends threats against localities which seem likely to support the opposition with benevolence to districts which dutifully return its own candidates. But PAP also provides effective governance. Singapore is a classic example of the Asian developmental state in which a modern economy has been built on the foundations of tight political control. This commitment to economic development, enabling the country to by-pass the East Asian financial crash of the late 1990s, gives the PAP continued confidence in its right to rule.

Ruling parties in authoritarian systems face increasing problems in maintaining their power. International pressures for genuine democratization are growing and election observers are casting a more critical eye over traditional techniques for fiddling the electoral books. Just as important, economic pressures to reduce the public sector, stimulated by international organizations such as the World Bank, are reducing the supply of patronage on which dominant parties depend to buy support. Even ruling parties which have always been sympathetic to the private sector – such as Singapore's PAP – may eventually fall victim to their own economic success. As Lipset argued (1983, first pub. 1960), a wealthy and educated citizenry will eventually become frustrated with the tight control exercised by a single ruling party.

Although parties are usually weak in authoritarian regimes, communist states provide the limiting case of the power that a single ruling party can achieve in a non-democratic environment. If the mass party was the key innovation of the twentieth century, the device reached its most complete expression in the dominance which ruling communist parties exerted over society and state, most especially in the Soviet Union. The monopoly position of ruling communist parties was justified by Lenin's notion of the 'vanguard party' – the idea that only the party could fully understood the long-term interests of the

working-class. Armed with this doctrine, the Communist Party of the Soviet Union sought to implement its vision of a total transformation of society following the 1917 revolution.

In the communist model, the party's control was exerted through a variety of means. It acted as a watchdog over society, vetted appointments to all positions of responsibility, controlled the media and carried out agitation and propaganda activities. Initially, hardly any independent groups were permitted and civil society faded, leading to an absence of virtually any associations standing between the family and the state. As with all totalitarian regimes, coercion, and the fear of it, also helped ruling parties to achieve their goals. The secret police was the main instrument of repression, as with the feared NKVD (later KGB) in the Soviet Union. The KGB used a vast network of informers to identify, and then eliminate, 'class enemies' and 'poisonous weeds'. Where this system of social control operated fully, it provided the most systematic penetration of society that any political party anywhere has ever achieved.

Definition

Democratic centralism was a key feature of communist party organization. It was based on two principles. The first was that lower levels had always to accept the decisions made by higher levels (the centralism dimension). The second was that higher levels were elected by the level immediately below, thus forming a pyramid of indirect election (the democratic dimension). But only one person would be nominated for each election; and in reality this candidate was chosen from above. So in practice 'democratic centralism' was centralism without democracy.

The elaborate hierarchy that characterized the internal organization of communist parties served to strengthen top-down control (see Figure 11.2 for the Chinese case). At the base of the party stood many thousands of primary cells. At the pinnacle stood a ruling politburo (literally, political bureau) which directed the party's work. Behind a façade of elections to higher levels, the structure formed a rigid, centralized pyramid. Thus, the half dozen or so men who form the Standing Committee of the Chinese Communist Party (CCP) still exert enormous control over the country's political direction, even though the party itself no longer seeks to direct the

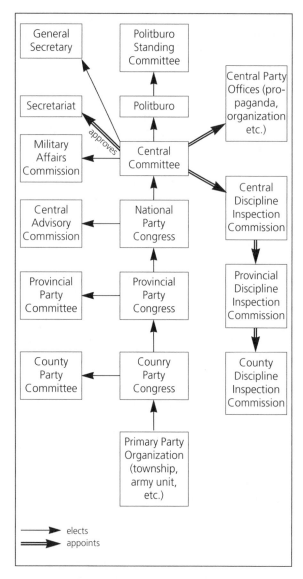

Figure 11.2 Organization of the Chinese Communist Party

command-and-control capability. Lacking a clear succession procedure and recognized limits to its authority, communist rule could always – though usually it did not – degenerate into personal dictatorship. In the Soviet Union, for example, Stalin's success in consolidating his control of the party in the 1920s enabled him to institute a personal despotism in which millions of people, including many from within the party itself, fell victim to the Great Terror of 1937–8.

Showing the limits of the concept of totalitarian rule, fascist parties never achieved communist levels of control of either state or society. In large measure, this weakness reflected the cult of the leader (*führerprinzip*) within fascism. The fascist party served its leader, not the other way round. For example, the party could not be a site of policy debate because policy was the leader's preserve. Where communist ideology venerated the party as the foundation of progress, fascist thinking was oriented to the leader as the personification of the state in Italy, and of the nation in Germany. The German experience, in particular, demonstrates the tangential role of the party within fascist regimes. The rise to power of the Nationalsozialistische Deutsche Arbeiterpartei (NSDAP, Nazi Party) owed much to Hitler's opportunistic political skills. Yet once Hitler achieved power in 1933, the Nazi Party became increasingly marginal. For rising politicians, the party became a stepping-stone to public office, where real power was to be found. Serving soliders were even prohibited from joining the party. And state officials had to swear an oath of loyalty to Hitler himself, not to his party. The feared SS (*Schutzstaffel* or 'protection units') began as the Nazi Party's security force but became a vehicle for Hitler's henchmen. The Fuhrer's method of administration – essentially, let the stronger man win – was based on people, not parties. The NSDAP was primarily a propaganda organization and even this function was eventually taken over by the government's own ministry. As Mommsen (1997, p.170) writes

> Many foreign observers, impressed by well-organized mass rallies, took it for granted that the NSDAP exerted an authoritative influence on decision-making; yet, in fact, it was increasingly condemned to political sterility.

economy and the population with the zeal of earlier decades. Manion (2000, p. 427) comments that 'for now, as in the past, the design of the communist party-state is a fair model of the organization of political power in China'.

Because internal elections were manipulated from above, in practice communist parties lacked authoritative selection procedures to their top posts. The result was considerable internal politicking as factions fought for control over the party's

Thus the significance of political parties in totalitarian states is not an issue which can be addressed without recognizing the fundamental contrasts between communist and fascist regimes. Under communism, the political party reached its twentieth-century apogee, with Lenin's notion of the vanguard party rationalizing communist command of both state and society. Under fascism, the party occupied a marginal position, becoming a vehicle of a dominating leader and eventually an appendage of a system of rule that was both personal and state-centred.

Parties in new democracies

The distinction between established and new democracies is vital in understanding the varying political significance of parties. Parties remain fundamental to the politics and government of consolidated West European democracies but their significance is much-reduced in the newer postcommunist and postmilitary democracies. In most new democracies, parties lack cohesion, a mass membership and even an ideology. To return to Ostrogorski's distinction, they are as much a political form as a political force – a vehicle for ambitious politicians as much as coherent actors themselves. Conaghan's description (1995, p. 450) of Ecuador's party system as 'populated by floating politicians and floating voters' resonates through much of the newly-democratic world. Further, most new democracies, as in East Europe, have rejected the model of a two-party system based on the plurality method in favour of a multiparty system based on proportional representation. PR offers representation in the assembly to more parties and minority interests, a valued feature in low-trust societies. But there are few incentives for parties to combine into the larger groupings which could perform the traditional function of putting policies together into overall packages to be presented to the electorate.

The soft character of parties in new democracies is well-illustrated in postcommunist states. The many new parties that emerged in the aftermath of communism's collapse are not becoming the mass organizations that developed in West Europe early in the twentieth century following its own era of democratization. Rather, postcommunist parties are typically of the élite, caucus type, lacking a mass membership and strong extra-parliamentary structures. It is not that postcommunist states are lacking in new parties. As the national movements which initially seized power from the communists began to split, many new parties appeared, representing specialized interests such as the countryside, peasants and ethnic minorities. Postcommunist countries are short of many things but they do not lack for parties. But expectations that new postcommunist party systems would settle down into a few Western-style mass membership parties, linked to social cleavages, have proved false. Even the largest of the new parties tend to be classic 'internal parties' – that is, loose coalitions of a few deputies in the national parliament. The deputies find value in a party label for fighting elections but otherwise these parties lack clear ideology. Few of them have acquired strong organization. As Steen (1995, p. 13) says about the Baltic countries, 'the parties are more like campaigning institutions before elections than permanent institutions propagating ideology'. In that respect, postcommunist parties follow the American rather than the West European model and the contrast with the tight control exerted by their communist predecessors could hardly be sharper.

The failure of postcommunist parties to penetrate society reflects a suspicious political culture. It remains difficult to enthuse electors who were denied a political voice under, and sometimes also before, communism. In addition, newly-founded parties do not possess the same incentives to build a mass organization as confronted West European socialist parties a century earlier. Parties in the Czech Republic, Poland, Hungary and Slovakia already receive generous state subsidies, eliminating the financial need to build a dues-paying membership. Why should leaders expand their party's membership if the result is simply to build a potential threat to their own position? After all, the mass media already exist in postcommunist states to provide a channel of communication with the electorate. So large numbers of local activists are unnecessary. And since voting has already extended to the whole population, there is no need for socialist parties to emerge to demand the suffrage for an excluded working class. A mass membership, and the organization to go with it, is simply unnecessary in postcommunist conditions.

> *Definition*
> **Successor party** is the term used to describe the new parties which formed in postcommunist states from the old ruling communist parties. The Social Democrats in the Czech Republic and Poland are examples. Reflecting their organization and membership, several successor parties achieved a remarkable electoral recovery in the mid-1990s. Ideologically, they accepted the end of communism but they did question the speed of transition to a full market economy.

For such reasons, Kopecki (1995, p. 515) suggested that 'parties in East-Central Europe are likely to develop as formations with loose electoral constituencies, unimportant membership and a dominant role for party leaders'. They will be élite parties rather than mass parties, led by political entrepreneurs unconstrained by a large party membership. Five years on, Lewis (2000, p. 6) confirmed the accuracy of Kopecki's prediction: 'parties have developed hesitantly and incompletely throughout much of East Europe – and in some countries to no great extent at all'. And Kitschelt *et al.* (1999, p. 396) suggest that there may even be advantages in the political flexibility of soft party structures:

The absence of sunk costs in large membership organizations enables East European democracies to enjoy the 'advantages of backwardness' and frees its politicians from devoting their energies to fighting armies of party functionaries who attend to empty organizational shells.

Ironically, the organizational weakness of the new parties allowed the communist successor parties to stage an unpredicted comeback in several countries. In the early to mid-1990s, successor parties won presidential or parliamentary elections in Poland, Hungary and Russia. The living corpse of communism rose from its uneasy grave, brought back to life in a popular protest against the mass unemployment of the early postcommunist era. This political rebirth, surely the most astonishing in the history of parties, owed much to the communists' inheritance – of money, property, facilities, people and expertise. The popular perception of the successor parties as orderly and purposeful proved electorally crucial in a chaotic environment. Yet the success of the successor parties itself proved to be temporary, a product of economic decline in the aftermath of communism's collapse. In 1997, the Polish successor party was voted out of office – this time to a revived Solidarity, the same movement that had originally brought down the communist regime. In the East European countries where market economies became entrenched, and the living standards of the majority began to improve, the desire for a return to 'the good old days' weakened, especially among younger generations. Certainly, the traditional form of totalitarian communist rule has gone, born and died in the twentieth century.

Key reading

> **Next step:** *Mair (1990) is a helpful collection of classic articles.*

The literature on parties is outstanding, especially for West Europe. Standard works include Lipset and Rokkan (1967) on the social base of parties, Sartori (1976) on party systems, Kircheimer (1966) on catch-all parties and Bartolini and Mair (1990) on the stabilization of European electorates. Von Beyme (1985) is a fund of information, particularly on party ideologies. Two useful comparative collections, both influenced by Panebianco (1988), are Lawson (1994) and Katz and Mair (1994). Wolinetz (1997) gathers over 20 articles. For a critique of Downs's 'rational choice' approach, see Mavrogordatos (1987). Lewis (2000) and Kitschelt *et al.* (1999) cover postcommunist parties, while Brooker (2000) offers a clear survey of parties in non-democratic regimes, both authoritarian and totalitarian.

PART 4

THE STRUCTURES OF GOVERNMENT

We examine here the key institutions of national government: legislatures, the executive and the bureaucracy. In nearly all political systems, these are the core structures through which policy is shaped and power is exercised. We also analyse territorial politics, reviewing the relationships between central, provincial and local levels of government. But we begin this part with a chapter on constitutions and the legal framework. An essential underpinning of established democracies, constitutions and the judiciary are growing in political significance as more governments come to operate within the rule of law.

Constitutions and the legal framework

Law and politics are closely linked. The development of liberal democracy has been an attempt to ensnare absolute rulers in the threads of legal restraint. In the words of A. V. Dicey, the nineteenth-century British jurist, the object was to substitute 'a government of laws' for a 'government of men'. A constitutional order, affording both protection for individual rights against arbitrary power and a means of resolving disputes between citizens and state, is the major accomplishment of liberal politics. From this perspective, law is not so much separate from politics as an achievement of it.

For four main reasons, academic interest in the study of constitutions and law has resurfaced in recent decades. First, the 1980s and 1990s witnessed an explosion of constitution-making among post-authoritarian states in Europe and Latin America. Second, several consolidated democracies – including Belgium, Canada, the Netherlands, and Sweden – also adopted new constitutions in the final portion of the twentieth century. Third, throughout the Western world, judges have become more willing to step into the political arena; judicial activism is no longer primarily an American phenomenon. Fourth, the 'legalization' of international politics increasingly impinges on domestic politics, with judges called on to arbitrate between the conflicting claims of supranational and national law, notably within the European Union. The academic study of politics began as a branch of law and belatedly these old friends are now renewing their acquaintance.

Constitutional rule

To understand the political role of constitutions we must first examine the idea of constitutional rule (also called constitutionalism). This refers to the rule of law. The British jurist A. V. Dicey defined this important if imprecise term as

> the absolute supremacy or predominance of regular law as opposed to the influence of arbitrary power . . . it means, again, equality before the law, or the equal subjection of all classes to the ordinary law of the land. (Dicey, 1959, first pub. 1885)

Constitutional rule forms the cornerstone of liberal democracy. It is the ingredient that blends the contrasting ideas of 'liberalism' and 'democracy' into a coherent whole. The rule of law entitles those citizens affected by a government action to challenge that act in independent courts – and to expect that the executive will abide by the court's rulings. Constitutional rule is therefore a constraint on government, including democratic ones (hence the radical criticism that constitutions are nothing more than 'the rule of the dead over the living'). The constitutional order developed to restrain authoritarian rulers but it offers equal cover to minorities which are threatened in a democracy by zealous majorities.

The prime illustration of a constitutional regime is undoubtedly the United States. The country was

---

BOX 12.1
Legal distinctions

Basic and statute law
'Basic law' is entrenched in that it overrides ordinary 'statute law' passed by the legislature. Constitutions are often expressed in basic law.

Constitutional and administrative law
'Constitutional law' sets out the structure of government and the rights of citizens. 'Administrative law' covers the exercise of power by the bureaucracy, particularly in relation to citizens.

Roman and common law
'Roman law' is an extensive system of codified law which is prevalent in continental Europe. It dates back to Justinian,

Roman Emperor between 527 and 565. European Union law, as expressed in the founding treatises, is influenced by the Justinian codes. The more flexible 'common law', used mainly in Britain and the USA, evolves from judges' decisions in particular cases. Because these judgments create precedents, they develop into a predictable legal environment.

Flexible and rigid constitutions
'Flexible' constitutions have the same status as statute laws. They can be amended in the same way or even (as in Britain) by the evolution of conventions. 'Rigid' constitutions are entrenched; they can only be amended through special procedures beyond those required for ordinary laws.

---

built on the foundations laid down by the Founding Fathers in Philadelphia in 1787. The constitution produced there, the world's first explicit written constitution, became America's political bible. Its central ideas – limited government and a dispersal of power – are etched into America's culture, creating not so much principles to be debated as a framework within which political debate takes place. Further, the Supreme Court has become the most influential judicial institution on earth since it secured (some time after its inception) the role of settling constitutional disputes. Constitutionalism suffuses the daily operation of American politics.

Britain, by contrast, is an example of a democracy in which constitutional government has traditionally been less secure. Britain's constitution is neither codified in a single document nor entrenched in basic law. Rather it is a flexible constitution with conventions which are, in Marshall's metaphor (1984), 'as slippery as procreating eels' (Box 12.1). More important, the traditions of monarchy still inhibit the development of the British constitution (Prosser, 1996). The eighteenth-century English jurist William Blackstone claimed, 'that the King can do no wrong is a necessary and fundamental principle of the English constitution.' Although the monarchy now has little if any direct political power, Blackstone's baleful nostrum has delayed the development of clear rights for citizens. However the Labour government elected in 1997 did remedy some of these 'weaknesses' by, for example, incorporating the European Convention on Human Rights

(1950) into domestic law. Thus the sharp contrast between American reliance on the constitution and British faith in conventions is beginning to fade.

Definition
Constitutional rule is government by law. It places limits on the scope of government, sets out individual rights and creates opportunities for redress should the government exceed its authority. Constitutional rule is a defining feature of liberal thinking which predominates in established democracies and especially in the United States.

Constitutions

We can look at constitutions in two ways. The first reflects their historic role of regulating the state's power over its citizens. For the Austrian liberal Friedrich Hayek (1960), a constitution was nothing but a device for limiting the power of government. In similar vein, Friedrich (1937) defined a constitution as 'a system of effective, regularized restraints upon government action'. From this perspective, the key feature of a constitution is its statement of individual rights. And certainly a Bill of Rights now forms part of nearly all written constitutions (Box 12.2). The first Bill of Rights comprises the 10 amendments appended to the American constitution in 1791; it covers such liberties as freedom of religion, speech, the press, assembly and (more ominously) the 'right of the people to keep and bear arms'. Recent constitutions tend to be more ambitious in their statements of rights, imposing duties on rulers such as fulfilling citizens' 'rights' to work and to medical care. An extreme case is the Brazilian constitution of 1988, a lengthy document replete with so many promises that it soon had to be revised to tone down its more extravagant commitments. More often, grand pledges made in a flourish of constitution-making are just ignored when it comes to working out who should pay.

Definition

A **constitution** sets out the formal structure of the state, specifying the powers and institutions of central government, and its balance with central authority. In addition, constitutions list the rights of citizens and in so doing create limits on and duties for the government.

The second and surprisingly neglected role of constitutions is to set out the structure of government. Described by Duchacek (1973) as power maps, constitutions prescribe the formal distribution of authority within the state. Constitutions set out the pathways of power, showing the procedures for making laws and reaching decisions. Sartori (1994, p. 198) argues that the defining feature of a constitution is this provision of a frame of government. As he says, a constitution without a declaration of rights is still a constitution, whereas a constitution whose centrepiece is not a frame of government is not a constitution. A constitution is therefore a form of political engineering, to be judged like any other construction by how well it stands the test of time. From this perspective, the American constitution, deeply embedded after more than 200 years, must be judged a triumph.

A traditional distinction contrasts written and unwritten constitutions. Yet no constitution is wholly unwritten; even the 'unwritten' British and New Zealand constitutions contain much statute and common law. A contrast between codified and uncodified systems is more useful. Most constitutions are codified – that is, they are set out in detail within a single document. The constitution of Germany, for instance, is laid down in the Basic Law ratified in 1949. The constitutions of Britain and New Zealand are unusual in that they are not formalized in this way.

Procedures for amendment are also important. Most constitutions are rigid; this makes them more acceptable to the various interests involved in their construction. Typically, amendment requires both a two thirds majority in each house of parliament and additional endorsement by the states (in federal systems) or through a referendum (in unitary countries) (Box 12.3). A rigid framework limits the damage should political opponents obtain power, for they too must abide by the values embedded in the constitutional settlement. A rigid constitution also offers the general benefit, much prized by liberals, of predictability to those subject to it. However, an entrenched constitution is necessarily difficult to modify. In Australia, for example, amendments must be endorsed not just by the national legislature but also by a referendum achieving a double majority – in most states and also in the country as a whole So far, only eight of 42 questions put to the voters have passed this test.

By contrast, the main benefit of a flexible constitution is its ready adaptability. In New Zealand, this flexibility permitted a recasting of the country's electoral system and government administration in the 1980s and 1990s. In most other countries such radical changes would have required constitutional amendment. In practice, though, many 'rigid' constitutions are more adaptable than they seem, with changing judicial interpretation providing the evolutionary key. The American Supreme Court, for

---

BOX 12.2
The structure of constitutional documents

A typical constitution contains four parts:

1. A *preamble* seeks popular support for the document with a stirring declaration of principle.

2. An *organizational section* then sets out the powers of the various institutions of government.

3. A *bill of rights* covers individual and perhaps group rights, including access to legal redress, and thereby sets limits on government.

4. Finally, *procedures for amendment* define the rules for revising the constitution.

Further reading: Duchacek (1991), Maddex (1997).

BOX 12.3

Entrenching the constitution: some examples

Country	Amendments require the approval of
Australia	both houses of parliament, then a referendum achieving majority support (a) overall and (b) in a majority of states.
Canada	both houses of parliament and two-thirds of the states containing at least half the population.
France	either (a) both houses of parliament, then a referendum, or (b) a three-fifths majority in a joint meeting of both houses.
Germany	a two-thirds majority in both houses of parliament. (1)
Japan	a two-thirds majority in both houses of parliament, then majority support in a referendum.
Spain	a two-thirds majority in both houses of parliament and, if demanded by a tenth of either house, a referendum achieving majority support. (2)
USA	a two-thirds majority in both houses of Congress and approval by three quarters of the states. (3)

Notes:
(1) The federal, social and democratic character of the German state, and the rights of individuals within it, cannot be amended.
(2) 'Fundamental' amendments to the Spanish constitution must be followed by an election, ratification by the new parliament and a referendum.
(3) An alternative method, based on a special convention called by the states and by Congress, has not been used.

live? Most often, new constitutions form part of a fresh start after a period of disruption. Such circumstances include regime change (for example the collapse of communism), reconstruction after defeat in war (for example Japan after 1945), external imposition (for example the influence of the Soviet Union on East Europe after 1945) and achieving independence (for example much of Africa in the 1950s and 1960s). The 1980s and 1990s were busy times for constitution-makers: 17 new ones were introduced in East Europe between 1991 and 1995, and over 30 in Africa during the 1990s (Vereshchetin, 1996).

Constitutions, then, are documents intended to create and mark a new regime yet they are rarely born of celebration. Mostly they are products of crisis; who would favour a new constitution if everything were going well? Usually, constitutions are compromises hammered out between political actors who may recently have been in conflict and who continue to distrust each other. An example of such negotiated settlements is South Africa's post-apartheid constitution of 1996, a compromise reached by leaders of the white and black communities against an unpromising background of near slavery. As vehicles of compromise, most constitutions are vague, contradictory and ambiguous. They are fudges and truces, wrapped in fine words (Weaver and Rockman, 1993). As a rule, drafters are more concerned with a short-term political fix than with establishing a structure that will last forever. In principle, everyone agrees constitutions should be short and clear; in practice, they serve to paper over the cracks. Even the American constitution of 1787 has been described by Finer (1997, p. 1495) as

a thing of wrangles and compromises. In its completed state, it was a set of incongruous proposals cobbled together. And furthermore, that is what many of its framers thought.

Conceived in crisis and delivered by compromise, the danger is that a new constitution will not grant the new rulers the authority needed for effective governance. The American constitution, for instance, divides power to the point where its critics allege that the 'government', and specifically the president, is virtually incapable of governing (Cutler, 1980). Far from providing a settled formula for rule, some

example, has become skilled at adapting an old document to new times. Thus one contrast between rigid and flexible constitutions is that in the former the judiciary manages evolution while in the latter politicians take the lead.

Constitutions are a deliberate creation. As the English political theorist John Stuart Mill (1991, first pub. 1861) wrote, constitutions 'are the work of men . . . Men did not wake up on a summer morning and find them sprung up'. How then do constitutions come into being? What are the circumstances that lead men – and women – to construct or revise the political order under which they

Country profile **SOUTH AFRICA**

Population: 43m
Gross domestic product per head: $3167
Composition:

Black 77%
Indian 3%
Coloured 9%
White 11%

Form of government: a democracy with an executive president and entrenched provinces.
Legislature: the National Assembly, the lower house, consists of 400 members elected for a five-year term. The president cannot dissolve the

assembly. The weaker upper house, the National Council of Provinces, contains 10 delegates from each of the nine provinces.
Executive: a president heads both the state and the government, ruling with a cabinet. The National Assembly elects the president after each general election. The president cannot normally be removed while in office.
Judiciary: the 11-member Constitutional Court decides constitutional matters and can strike down legislation. Power of appointment rests jointly with the president and a special commission. The Supreme

Court of Appeal is the highest court on nonconstitutional matters.
Electoral system: the National Assembly is elected by proportional representation. Provincial legislatures appoint members of the National Council.
Party system: the African National Congress (ANC, 266 seats and 66% of the vote in 1999) has dominated the post-apartheid republic. It governs in coalition with the mainly Zulu Inkatha Freedom Party (34 seats). The more liberal Democratic Party (38 seats) forms the official opposition.

South Africa's transformation from a militarized state based on apartheid to a more constitutional order based on democracy was one of the most remarkable political transitions of the late twentieth century. The fact that the transition was largely peaceful, defying all predictions of an 'inevitable' bloodbath, was the most astonishing fact of all.

Since white settlers came to South Africa in 1652, the country had been run by whites on the basis of exploiting black labour. After 1945, the system of apartheid (apartness) institutionalized these racial divisions. Apartheid defined the three races of white, coloured and black and outlawed marriage between them. Apartheid's survival into the 1990s showed that governments based on brute power can last a long time. Yet change was eventually induced by three factors: first, the collapse of communism which destroyed the regime's bogeyman; second, the imposition of sanctions by the EU and the United States; and third, black opposition to apartheid which began to encompass armed, and not merely nonviolent, resistance.

As so often, modest initial changes merely stimulated demands for more and faster reform. In 1990, ANC leader Nelson Mandela was released from prison after 26 years, symbolizing recognition by the white rulers that the time had come to negotiate their own downfall. Four years later, Mandela became President of a government of national unity, including the

white-led National Party (NP), after the ANC won the first multiracial elections.

In 1996, agreement was reached on a new constitution that took full effect in 1999. The constitution had taken two years to negotiate, reflecting hard bargaining between the ANC and the NP. The final 109-page document inevitably reflected the interests of the dominant ANC. It included a bill of rights covering education, housing, water, food, security and human dignity. The NP expressed its general support despite reservations that led to its withdrawal from government.

It remains to be seen whether South Africa's rainbow nation will be able to reconcile constitutional liberal democracy with the political dominance of the ANC. The ANC's strength in parliament is such that it could by itself virtually achieve the two-thirds majority required to amend the constitution, providing an exception to the generalization that fresh constitutions normally deny sufficient authority to a new government. Further, South Africa remains a minefield of unresolved social problems: crime, inequality, poverty, unemployment and Aids. Yet the country's politics, more than most, should be judged by what preceded it. By that test the achievements of the new South Africa are remarkable indeed.

Further reading: Deegan (2001), Johnson and Schlemmer (1996), Rich (1994).

constitutions do no more than pass the parcel of unresolved political problems to later generations. Too often political distrust means the new government is hemmed in with restrictions, limiting its effectiveness. The Italian constitution of 1948 illustrates the point. The hallmark of the Italian constitution is *garantismo*, meaning that all political forces are guaranteed a stake in the political system. Thus the document establishes a strong bicameral assembly and extensive regional autonomy. These checks on power were intended to prevent the prewar dictatorship from recurring. In practice, *garantismo* contributed to ineffective government and ultimately to the collapse of the 'First Republic' between 1992 and 1994.

Judicial review and constitutional courts

Constitutions are no more self-implementing than they are self-made. Some institution must be found to enforce the constitution, striking down laws and practices that offend its principles. This review power has fallen to the judiciary. Such judicial authority arises naturally in federations where the courts are needed to resolve inevitable disputes between national and state governments. But even in many unitary states, the judiciary has now taken on the position of constitutional guardian. For better or worse, judicial review gives unelected judges a unique position both in and above politics – the judiciary can override the decisions and laws produced by democratic governments. Indeed, India's Supreme Court can even override amendments to the constitution itself. Judicial power, furthermore, is only partly limited by the constitution itself, for interpretation inevitably varies with the temper of the times. As the American Chief Justice Hughes once remarked, 'we live under a constitution. But the constitution is what the judges say it is'. Basking in their privileged position, constitutional courts express a liberal conception of politics, restricting the power not just of rulers but also of the elections which generate them. In this way, judicial review both stabilizes and limits democracy.

In reality, judicial power is far from unqualified. For one thing, constitutions themselves do restrict what judges can plausibly say about them. Justices

are only 'unfree masters' of the document whose values they defend (Rousseau, 1994, p. 261). More important, the impact of a court's judgments depends on its status among those who carry out its decisions. After all, a court's only power is its words; the purse and sword belong elsewhere. So courts must consider the broad climate of opinion within which they operate. Thus, as O'Brien (1993, p. 16) concludes of the American Supreme Court,

> the Court's influence on American life is at once both anti-democratic and counter-majoritarian. Yet that power, which flows from giving meaning to the constitution, truly rests, in Chief Justice White's words, 'solely upon the approval of a free people'.

> **Definition**
> Smith (1989) defines **judicial review** as 'the power of ordinary or special courts to give authoritative interpretation of the constitution which is binding on all the parties concerned'. This covers three main areas: first, ruling on whether specific laws are constitutional; second, resolving conflict between the state and citizens over basic liberties; and third, resolving conflicts between different institutions or levels of government.

The function of judicial review can be allocated in two ways (Box 12.4). The first, more traditional method is for the highest court in the ordinary judicial system, typically called the 'supreme court', to take on the task of ensuring the constitution is protected. Australia, Canada, India and the USA are examples of this approach. Because a supreme court is part of the judicial process, its currency is legal cases which bubble up from lower courts. However, a second and more recent method, much favoured in continental Europe, is to create a special 'constitutional court' which is separate from the ordinary judicial system. Spain, for example, has both a Constitutional Tribunal to arbitrate on constitutional matters and a separate Supreme Court to oversee national criminal law. In constitutional courts, proceedings are more political and less legal: such courts can typically judge the constitutionality of a law, or even issue an advisory judgment on a proposal, without the stimulus of a specific legal case.

BOX 12.4

Institutions for judicial review: supreme courts vs. constitutional courts

Supreme court	Constitutional court
Relationship to other courts	
Highest court of appeal	A separate body dealing other courts of appeal with constitutional issues only
Style	
More judicial (decides cases)	More political (issues judgments)
Recruitment	
Legal expertise plus political approval	Political criteria more important
Normal tenure	
Until retirement	Typically one non-renewable term at six to nine years
Examples	
Australia, United States	Germany, Spain

We will first examine the supreme court approach, using the United States – the original and most renowned example of judicial review – as a case study. America's constitution vests judicial power 'in one Supreme Court, and in such inferior Courts as the Congress may from time to time ordain'. Constitutional issues can be raised at any point in the ordinary judicial system, with the Supreme Court selecting for arbitration those cases that it regards as having broad significance. However, it is important to note the constitution itself does not specify the Court's role in adjudicating constitutional disputes. Rather, this function was gradually acquired by the justices themselves, with *Marbury* v. *Madison* (1803) proving decisive.

Although the Supreme Court favours the doctrine of *stare decisis* (stand by decisions made – that is, stick to precedent), it does sometimes boldly overturn its own legal precedents. This 'inconsistency' has proved to be a source of strength, enabling the Court to adapt the constitution to changes in national mood. For example, after its rearguard struggle against the New Deal, the Court conceded the right of the national government to regulate the economy. At other times the Court has sought to lead rather than follow. The most important of these initiatives, under the leadership of Chief Justice Warren in the 1950s and 1960s, concerned black civil rights. In its major and unanimous decision in *Brown* v. *Topeka* (1954), the Court outlawed racial segregation in schools, dramatically reversing its previous policy that 'separate but equal' facilities for blacks fell within the constitution.

By contrast, continental Europe (both East and West) favours special constitutional courts, separate from the ordinary judicial system, as the mechanism for judicial review. Constitutional courts are a recent but, it seems, a successful innovation. In West Europe, they were adopted after 1945 in, for instance, West Germany, Austria, Greece and France. They represented a conscious attempt to prevent a revival of dictatorship, whether of the left or the right.

If the USA illustrates the supreme court approach, Germany is a clear example of an established constitutional court. The Federal Constitutional Court is both activist and influential. With political power still under a cloud after the war, the decisions of the Court have impinged on several areas, including abortion, university reform, funding political parties and banning extremist parties. Between 1951 and 1990, the Court judged 198 federal laws (nearly 5 per cent of the total) to contravene the Basic Law (Keating, 1993, p. 276). In framing new bills, German policy-makers anticipate the likely reaction of the Court; partly for this reason, Kommers (1994) argues that the German Court's political influence is fully the equal of America's Supreme Court. Above all, the Court has vigorously nurtured Germany's postwar democratic republic. As Conradt (2001, p.245) writes,

> More than any other postwar institution, the Constitutional Court has enunciated the view that the Federal Republic is a militant democracy whose democratic political parties are the chief instrument for the translation of public opinion into public policy. The controversial banning of the Communist and neo-Nazi Sozialistische Reichspartei in the 1950s was an expression of this philosophy.

We must conclude this section by considering the European Court of Justice (ECJ), a leading example of an international judicial body. Building on the continental tradition of constitutional courts, the ECJ played a central role in expanding the legal order of the European Union from the 1960s to the 1980s. The cumulative impact of its decisions amounted to what Weiler (1994) terms a 'quiet revolution' in converting the Treaty of Rome into a constitution for Europe. Set up in 1952, the Court's purpose is 'to settle conflicts between the states, between the organs of the Community, and between the states and the organs' (Nugent, 1999, p.41). It consists of one judge appointed from each member state for a renewable six-year term, with broad experience more important than judicial expertise. The Court's impact arose partly from its view that European law (a) applies directly to individuals, (b) takes precedence over national courts and (c) must be enforced by these courts. Like the American Supreme Court in its early decades, the Court's decisions consistently strengthened the authority of central institutions. Even though several governments began in the 1990s to question both the Court's procedures and further expansion of its authority, the ECJ remains a major example of judicial influence in modern politics (Dehousse, 1998).

Judicial activism, independence and recruitment

Throughout the Western world, judicial intervention in public policy has grown, marking the shift from government to governance (Tate and Vallinder, 1995). Judges have become more willing to enter political arenas that would have once been left to elected politicians and national parliaments. For instance, the Australian High Court under Sir Anthony Mason (Chief Justice 1987–95) boldly uncovered 'implied rights' in the constitution which had gone undetected by its timid predecessors. The Dutch Supreme Court has produced important case law on issues where parliament seemed unable to legislate, such as abortion, strikes and euthanasia. The Israeli Supreme Court has been dismissed by ultra-Orthodox Jewish parties as a 'judicial dictatorship' for issuing secular rulings such as its decision to permit shopping in kibbutzim on the Sabbath.

What explains this judicialization of politics? A central factor seems to be the increasing reliance on

regulation as a mode of governing. A regulating state is open to judicial challenge in a way that a taxing, spending and war-making government is not. Indeed, Majone (1996, p. 290) argues that 'the progressive judicialization of regulatory proceedings' is how regulation gains legitimacy in the absence of mechanisms of democratic control. Thus it is the changing nature of politics, rather than developments within the judiciary itself, which are key. For instance, the trust of the Israeli public in political parties has declined but confidence in the judiciary remains high (Edelman, 1995, p. 408). The decay of left-wing ideology has also allowed more judicial scope. Socialists were always suspicious of judges, believing them to be unelected defenders of the status quo generally and of property specifically. So in Sweden, for instance, the declining strength of social democracy has given more room to a traditionally restrained judiciary (Holmstrom, 1995). In Britain, another country with an historically timid judiciary, limiting the royal prerogative has also given more opportunities to judges. No longer can the state invoke the monarchical claim to be above the law. Throughout the democratic world, interest groups, parties and rights-conscious citizens have become more willing to continue their struggles in the judicial arena.

Finally, international conventions have given judges an extra lever they can use to break away from judicial restraint. Documents such as the United Nations Universal Declaration of Human Rights (1948) and the European Convention of Human Rights (1950) have given judges a quasi-judicial foundation on which to construct what would once have been viewed as excessively political statements.

Definition

Judicial activism refers to the willingness of judges to venture beyond narrow legal decisions so as to influence public policy. It is the opposite of **judicial restraint**, a more conservative philosophy which maintains that judges should simply apply the law (including the constitution), irrespective of policy implications and the judge's own values. The two terms developed in connection with the American Supreme Court but they have wider applicability in an era of judicial politics.

MOST ACTIVE

United States
Canada
Australia
Germany
Italy
Israel
Japan
France
United Kingdom
Sweden

LEAST ACTIVE

Source: Adapted from Holland (1991, p. 2).

Figure 12.1 Levels of judicial activism in selected democracies

Of course, judicial activism has proceeded further in some democracies than in others. In comparative rankings of judicial activism, the United States always comes top (Figure 12.1). The USA exhibits all the features which contribute to judicial activism. These include: a written constitution, federalism, judicial independence, no separate administrative courts, easy access to the courts, a common law tradition, high esteem for judges and limited government (Holland, 1991, p. 7). The United States is founded on a constitutional contract and an army of lawyers will forever quibble over the terms.

Fewer of these conditions were met in Britain, a country that is one of the few democracies to operate without judicial review. A unitary state, an unwritten constitution, strong parties and above all the concept of parliamentary sovereignty combined to keep the judiciary away from the political heartland. However, even in Britain judicial activism has increased, largely reflecting European influence, and British judges proved to be willing accomplices of the European court as it sought to establish a legal order applicable to all member states. In addition, the national judiciary grew in confidence as it witnessed the government losing cases in the European Court (Woodhouse, 1996, p. 439). The emergence of a younger generation of more activist judges, and Britain's adoption of the European Convention of Human Rights, also encouraged the country's judges to become more assertive. Devolution to Scotland and Wales will inevitably lead to conflicts with London, adding to the judiciary's growing workload.

Other democracies with a tradition of judicial restraint have also begun to move in an activist direction. Consider Canada and New Zealand. In Canada a Charter of Rights and Freedoms was appended to the constitution in 1982, which gave judges a more prominent role in defending individual rights. In the ten years after the Charter was introduced, the Supreme Court nullified 41 statutes, showing a particular interest in protecting the rights of those accused of crimes (Morton, 1995, p. 58). New Zealand introduced its Bill of Rights in 1990, protecting 'the life and security of the person' and also establishing traditional democratic and civil rights (for example the right to vote and freedom of belief, association and movement).

Where traditions of parliamentary authority are still strong, as in New Zealand and the UK, ingenuity is needed to integrate a bill of rights with the supposed sovereignty of the legislature. How can the much-vaunted principle of legislative supremacy be reconciled with judicial assertiveness? The New Zealand compromise is that the Attorney-General (a Cabinet minister who bridges the political and judicial worlds) advises MPs on whether legislative proposals are consistent with basic rights. Technically, at least, parliament retains sole responsibility for adjusting its bills accordingly (Mulgan, 1997, p. 178). Britain has adopted a similar halfway house in incorporating the European Convention of Human Rights into its law. In theory, the legislature remains supreme but in practice MPs are unlikely to override judicial opinion that a bill contradicts protected rights.

Given the growing political authority of the judiciary, the question of maintaining its independence gains in importance. Liberal democracies accept judicial independence as fundamental to the rule of law. To achieve this end, judges' security of tenure is protected. In Britain and the American federal judiciary, judges hold office for life during 'good behaviour'. Throughout continental Europe the judiciary is more closely controlled by the state than in Britain or the USA, reflecting a philosophy that views the judges as an agent of the state even if operating autonomously from it. Even so, judges still remain secure in their tenure.

FOR OR AGAINST

A POLITICAL ROLE FOR THE JUDICIARY

More than ever before, judges participate in politics, striking down policies, bills and laws deemed to be contravening the constitution. But why should the judiciary be permitted to encroach on the authority traditionally accorded to the elected branches of government? Whatever became of democracy – that is, rule by the people?

The case for

The fundamental argument for judicial authority is a liberal one: that tyranny of the majority is tyranny nonetheless. Subjecting government to the rule of law is the key achievement of Western politics, an accomplishment to be cherished rather than criticized. Dividing power between the legislature, the executive and the judiciary is in practice the only way of containing it. Of course, interpreting the constitution is bound to cause controversy but an independent judiciary is well-suited to the job of arbiter. Judicial interpretation is likely to be more stable and disinterested than that offered by elected politicians, thus providing more continuity to citizens and business alike. In any case, judicial authority is often exaggerated. Judges review after the event; political initiative remains with the executive. And an independent judiciary is never beyond political influence: politicians have a say in the appointment of senior justices, the government can always seek to change the constitution if it disagrees with judicial interpretation and in practice the executive retains ultimate responsibility for resolving crises.

The case against

In a democracy, the people must be sovereign. If a government behaves poorly, the solution lies in the polling booth, not the courtroom. Historically, judicial authority developed as a device enabling the wealthy to protect their property into a democratic era and even today the judiciary shows a built-in bias towards protecting established interests. This conservative disposition is strengthened by the extremely narrow social profile of judges, most of whom are middle-aged to elderly middle-class white men. Any radical government committed to a programme of social change can expect resistance from the judiciary, with its professional commitment to stability, precedent and the status quo. Judges may limit executive power but no mechanism exists to contain the escalation of their own authority. Even if a mechanism of constitutional arbitration is needed (and Britain has got by well enough by relying on informal conventions), why should judges, with their narrow legal training, be given the job? Why not call upon an upper chamber or that oldest of political institutions – a council of elders – to perform the task?

Assessment

The debate would benefit from fuller appreciation of the constitutional courts that have emerged in many European countries. In the political basis of their appointments, relatively rapid turnover of members and reliance on a political style of operation, constitutional courts operate very differently from traditional supreme courts. To a degree, constitutional courts have already become the 'third chamber' of politics. Indeed, Shapiro and Stone (1994, p. 405) suggest that 'in the context of executive-dominated legislative processes, the impact of constitutional courts may at times overshadow that of parliaments'. Those who want the judiciary to be kept out of politics are fighting not a losing battle but one that is already lost.

Further reading: Griffith (1997), Tate and Vallinder (1995).

Judicial independence raises the problem of how to choose and promote judges. The problem here is simple: if judges are chosen or promoted by government, they may become too political in their judgments. Alternatively, if they are left to select their own successors, they may become a self-perpetuating caste, out-of-touch with social change. Box 12.5 shows the four main solutions. Co-option by other judges is the surest guarantee of independence, but democratic election, as practised in some American states, offers more (even excessive?) responsiveness to popular concerns. Which format is preferred depends on the weight given to judicial independence, on the one hand, and responsiveness to public opinion or party balance, on the other. In practice, judges are often selected from a pool of candidates initially defined by technical qualifications, such as passing examinations and/or recommendation by a professional body. In South Africa, for instance, the President of the Republic appoints senior judges after consulting a Judicial Services Commission which includes representatives from the legal profession as well as the legislature.

For courts charged with judicial review, selection normally involves a clear political dimension. In the USA, the Supreme Court is so important that appointments to it (nominated by the president but subject to Senate approval) are key decisions. Senate ratification now often involves a set-piece battle between presidential friends and foes. Here, the judicial experience and legal ability of the nominee may matter less than ideology, partisanship and a clean personal history. Even so, Walter Dellinger, former acting US Solictior General, argues that 'the political appointment of judges is an appropriate "democratic moment" before the independence of life tenure sets in'. In European states, members of constitutional courts are usually selected by the assembly, though in Romania and Bulgaria the president also selects some members. Thus political factors influence court appointments, precluding a sharp distinction between the legal and the political.

Once appointed, judges continue to develop their approach. This means the tenor of their decisions cannot always be predicted on appointment. The classic example is Earl Warren: he became Chief Justice of the American Supreme Court in 1953 but dismayed President Eisenhower with his liberal rulings. Eisenhower later described Warren's appointment as 'the biggest damn fool mistake I ever made'. The crucial point here is tenure. While American justices hold office for life, subject to 'good behaviour', the constitutional courts of Europe usually limit their judges to one term of seven to nine years. This reflects the more political environment of an exclusively constitutional court and limits the impact of a single justice.

Constitutions and the judiciary in authoritarian states

Necessarily, constitutions are feeble documents in authoritarian regimes. The nature of such states is that any restraints on rule go unacknowledged; power, not law, is the political currency. It follows

---

BOX 12.5
Methods of selecting judges

Method	Example	Comment
Popular election	Some states in the USA	Produces responsiveness to public opinion but at what price in impartiality and competence? May be accompanied by recall procedures.
Election by the assembly	Some states in the USA, some Latin American countries	This method was also formally used for senior judges in communist states but in practice the party picked suitable candidates
Appointment by the executive	Britain, Supreme Court judges in the USA (subject to Senate approval)	'Danger' of political appointments though most judges will be appointed by an earlier administration
Co-option by the judiciary	Italy, Turkey	Produces an independent but sometimes unresponsive judiciary

that the status of the judiciary, as guardians of law, is similarly diminished. In authoritarian regimes, rulers keep the judiciary on a tight leash, particularly on cases with political overtones. In Indonesia, General Suharto (President 1968–1998) was effectively above the law. The Ministry of Justice still administers the courts and pays judges' salaries; the justices understand the implications. Many nondemocratic regimes make extensive use of Declarations of Emergency which are exempt from judicial scrutiny. Once introduced, such 'emergencies' drag on for years, even decades. A common tactic is to make use of special courts which do the regime's bidding without much pretence of judicial independence. Like many authoritarian rulers, President Fujimori of Peru found military courts useful for this purpose. He was also inclined to sack 'unsatisfactory' judges, a policy taken to extremes by Egypt's President Nasser in 1969. He got rid of 200 in one go: the 'massacre of the judges'.

This general pattern of judicial subordination to authoritarian executives becomes even more marked under military rule. The Argentine Supreme Court, for instance, routinely accepted rulings made by technically illegal military governments. The generals controlled the means of coercion and the judges adjusted their decisions to suit. In Uganda, an extreme case, President Amin had his Chief Justice shot dead. Authoritarianism and the rule of law are incompatible; black robes are poor protection against a drawn sword. Yet the willingness of judges to raise their heads above the parapet is often an early sign of the liberalization which precedes the final collapse of arbitrary power.

Communist states offered a more sophisticated rationale for downgrading constitutions and the judiciary. Communist theory explicitly rejected the Western idea of constitutional rule with its emphasis on limited government, individual rights and private property. What does the Western tradition amount to, asked the communists, other than an affirmation of the status quo? In communist states, legal documents were of little moment – nothing could hinder the party's task of building socialism and the party's mission was too important to be subject to formal limits. So communist regimes were party-led rather than legally constrained, a point confirmed by the reference in the constitutions themselves to the 'leading role' of the party. In the early decades of the People's Republic of China, legal perspectives were dismissed as 'bourgeois rightist' thinking. The Chinese constitution now grants specific rights to all but even today adds that these freedoms are conditional on supporting socialist principles, including the dictatorship of the proletariat. Communist constitutions also stressed social and economic rights such as the right to work, again in contrast to the Western emphasis on more political rights such as freedom of speech.

Just as communist states rejected the idea of a neutral constitution, so too did they dismiss the concept of judicial independence. The judges, too, must contribute to building socialism – and protecting the party's position. Throughout the communist world, judges were selected for their 'party-mindedness' and were expected to put this 'virtue' to good effect in court. Yet as with many other aspects of communist politics, this situation was often beginning to alter before the 1989 revolutions. Even authoritarian regimes can discover the advantage of applying the rules consistently. When one citizen sued another, or even when one enterprise sued another, the interests of the communist party were best served by resolving the issue through law. The courts therefore observed a measure of 'socialist legality'.

In China, too, laws became more precise after the hiatus of the Cultural Revolution. In 1979, the country passed its first criminal laws; later revisions abolished the vague crime of 'counter-revolution' and established the right of defendants to seek counsel. Law could prevail to the benefit of economic development – as long as the party was not threatened by the outcome. In practice, party officials still occupy a protected position above the law, a fact that demonstrates the authoritarian nature of the regime. However as the rule of law expands, so party privileges will become harder to defend and people will be less willing to join the party club. Creeping legalization will restrict the dominance of the party.

Constitutions and the judiciary in new democracies

New democracies are political construction sites, in which constitutional engineers seek to build a new framework of rule and enhanced respect for the judiciary (Kolstø, 2000). Establishing a state based on law in a country where brute power has previously ruled the roost is a task that is both important and arduous. Agreeing the new constitution is merely the beginning. The longer-term assignment is to ensure that an independent judiciary is available to enforce the new order and that all political actors abide by the court's decisions. The status of the judiciary needs to increase from its lowly position in the previous regime. The powerful must recognize new limits to their behaviour and the less powerful must learn to treat the courts as a realistic form of redress. As a discussion of the contrasting experience of Spain and Latin America will reveal, the successful consolidation of a new democracy turns on its ability to entrench the constitution and the autonomy of its judiciary

Spain is an instance of a deliberate and ultimately successful attempt to build the rule of law into the country's new democratic architecture. As Heywood (1995, p. 103) writes,

After nearly four decades of dictatorship under General Franco, it was to be expected that the 1978 constitution should place particular emphasis on legal accountability. A central concern of the new democracy was that it should be established as a 'state of law' in the sense of its constitutional arrangements being both legally accountable and enforceable.

Spain's constitution-makers established a new 12-member Constitutional Tribunal located not just above the executive and legislature but also above the judicial branch. To ensure its independence, members are debarred from holding any other public office or from playing a leading role in a political party or trade union. Even so, suspicions remained that Tribunal appointments, most of which are made by the legislature, reflected party patronage. Although Spain's new order rapidly consolidated into a secure liberal democracy, the judiciary initially retained its pre-democratic image as remote, inefficient and conservative. It was not until judges began investigating allegations of corruption against leading politicians in the early 1990s – thus demonstrating their practical as well as their constitutional autonomy – that their reputation began to improve.

The 'state of law' sought and found in Spain has proved more elusive in many post-military democracies in Latin America. Elected presidents in South American countries may be less cavalier with the constitution than their strong-armed predecessors but even so several have treated the constitution as a flexible document to be adapted to suit their own political requirements. For example, some have sought to abolish term limits so that they can stand for re-election. Other South American constitutions have retained privileges for departing generals, thus perpetuating a sense of an institution remaining above the law. For instance, Chile's armed forces were initially exempted from prosecution in civilian courts, a tactic that effectively enabled former generals to escape justice for politically motivated murders committed during their tenure.

In addition to the difficulties of rendering the constitution an effective framework of rule, the rule of law is held back through most of Latin America by the low standing and standards of the judiciary. Holston and Caldiera (1998, p. 263) refer to Brazil as an 'uncivil democracy' in which 'violence, injustice and impunity are norms. As a result, the institutions of law and justice lose legitimacy, the principle of legality is obstructed and the realization of democratic citizenship remains limited.' In some South American countries, the police probably commit almost as many crimes, including murder, as they solve. Coordination between the police and the courts is so poor that criminals are often left untried even when charged. Many judges are poorly trained and open to bribes. In shanty towns, the police sometimes follow a 'shoot to kill' policy while the community resorts to lynching as a form of social control, bringing about a further devaluation of official justice. Although moves to reform the judiciary are now afoot in several South American countries, the task is inevitably long-term. One legal expert estimated that reform of Chile's criminal justice system would take at least 15 years (Frühling, 1998, p. 252). The Latin American experience suggests that the rule of law should be a long-term aspiration for, rather than an immediate achievement of, new democracies.

As with other aspects of democratic consolidation, postcommunist countries vary greatly in the extent to which they have established constitutional authority and the rule of law. In the more European and parliamentary systems such as Hungary and Poland, the new constitutional order has substantially consolidated. In particular, constitutional courts have now been introduced to most post-communist regimes, usually with considerable success. For example:

- The Hungarian Court has made significant judgments on such topics as capital punishment, abortion, private property and the electoral system.
- The Polish Court (established in 1986, before communism fell) 'has become in a short time an important part of the governmental system', issuing 34 judgments on the constitutionality of laws in 1993 alone (Fitzmaurice, 1998, p. 96).
- The Czech Court is authorized to oversee the implementation within the Republic of international laws to which the country subscribes; for example, rulings of the International Court of Justice.

By contrast, many successor states to the Soviet Union have simply swapped one non-constitutional order for another. In several Central Asian republics, presidents still seem to rule in the imperious style of King Louis XIV of France: 'it is legal because I wish it.' Even in Russia, 'there has been and remains a considerable gap between individual rights on paper and their realization in practice. The further one goes beyond Moscow and St Petersburg into the provinces, the enforcement gap tends to grow greater' (Sharlet, 1997, p.134). But we should beware of judging the constitutional quality of post-communist regimes against contemporary Western standards. As Sharlet (1997, p. 134) reminds us,

While the Founding Fathers of the American republic quickly added the Bill of Rights to their newly ratified Constitution in the late eighteenth century, a number of these rights remained essentially 'parchment rights' and did not garner nationwide respect and judicial enforcement until well into the twentieth century. Is it surprising that Russia with its thousand-year authoritarian past and long tradition of legal nihilism should be proceeding slowly in Rule of Law development? Surely it is more remarkable that Russia, with the Soviet Union gone a mere half dozen years, has made the progress it has, including in the uncharted territory of civil rights.

Administrative law

Where constitutional law sets out the fundamental principles governing the relationship between citizen and state, the separate field of administrative law covers the rules governing this interaction in detailed settings. If a citizen is in dispute with an agency of government over detailed issues such as pensions entitlements, student loans or redundancy payments, the conflict is far more likely to be resolved in an administrative court or tribunal than in the regular law courts. Administrative tribunals lack the high-profile political activity of constitutional courts but by subjecting the work of public servants to clear rules they perform a function that is essential in a liberal society. The increase of government activity in the twentieth century has led to a large expansion of administrative law. Typical questions asked in administrative law are: Was an official empowered to make a particular decision (that is, competence)? Was a decision made in the correct way (for example with adequate consultation)? What should be done if a decision was incorrectly made or had undesirable results (that is, liability)? Just as the central issue of courts charged with judicial review is to apply the constitution, so the task confronting administrative law is regulation of the bureaucracy.

Definition
Administrative law sets out the specific principles that govern the making of decisions by public sector bodies, principally the bureaucracy. For instance, the decisions of British civil servants (a) must be within their authority, (b) must be made by a fair procedure, and (c) must accord with natural justice. Administrative law also sets out the remedies for a breach of such principles.

The flavour of administrative law is conveyed by its content, covering such areas as immigration disputes, planning applications, tax matters, public employment and social security. It is in these concrete areas that the citizen is most likely to experience bureaucratic high-handedness. Such topics have no direct analogy in private or commercial law and usually need to be covered by distinct rules, separate tribunals or both.

There are three broad ways of handling the problem of regulating the administration (Box 12.6). The first, found in continental Europe, is to establish a separate system of administrative courts. France is the most influential example of this *separatist* approach. The Conseil d'Etat (Council of State) stands at the apex of an elaborate system of administrative courts. All administrative decisions taken by ministers and their officials are subject to review by the Council, a wide remit which can lead to slow decision-making. Nonetheless, from its own case law the Council has developed general principles regulating administrative power. The government consults the Council on all proposed legislation. The prestige of the Council and the publicity given to its rulings enable it to check executive power even in a country with a strong state tradition (Dreyfus, 1990, pp. 142–3). The separatist approach does however run the risk of boundary disputes over whether a case should be processed through administrative or ordinary courts.

The second solution, favoured in Anglo-American countries with a common law tradition, seeks to deny the distinction between public and private law. The idea here, rarely fulfilled in practice, is that one general system of law should apply to both public and private transactions. For instance, employment in the public sector should be regulated by exactly the same laws as apply to the private sector; no special codes are needed. Just as a supreme court serves both as constitutional guardian and as a court of appeal, so too should ordinary courts be able to arbitrate disputes involving the state. A strength of this *integrationist* philosophy is that it avoids boundary disputes between ordinary and administrative courts; indeed, it eliminates the need for two sets of courts in the first place. Above all, the integrationist philosophy reflects and affirms a modest conception of the public sphere; the state must abide by the same laws as its citizens. However, in reality, special courts are rarely avoided entirely. Thus even the United States has administrative courts dedicated to tax, military and patent issues. And if there are no special courts, more informal administrative tribunals develop in their stead, dealing for instance with appeals involving employment law or social

---

BOX 12.6
Methods for judicial regulation of the bureaucracy

Method	Definition	Example
Separatist	Special codes and courts	France
Integrationist	Rely on ordinary law and courts	Anglo-American countries
Supervision	A procurator assesses the legality of administrative acts	Russia

Source: Bell (1991).

---

security regulations. They are quicker, cheaper and more flexible (though often more secretive) than the law courts. In Britain, tribunals rather than courts resolve most administrative cases. The emergence of tribunals suggests that it is not feasible in practice to resolve all administrative problems through ordinary courts.

The third approach to formal regulation of the bureaucracy is through *administrative supervision*. Peter the Great introduced this device in Russia in 1722; it is now used throughout East Europe. An officer known as the procurator supervises the legality of administrative acts and can suspend decisions pending judicial or other resolution. Russia revived the role of procurator in 1992. We should distinguish here between the procurator and the ombudsman. The ombudsman is a Western invention whose function is not to make administrative law but to investigate allegations of maladministration in individual cases. The procurator's role is broader, encompassing principles as well as cases.

Whichever approach countries adopt to the regulation of their public bureaucracy, there can be no doubting the importance of the task. The twentieth-century expansion of government created not only new rights for citizens but also fresh opportunities for public agencies to deny those rights. In many authoritarian regimes, bureaucrats continue to exploit citizens, confident that the ordinary person lacks effective redress. In a liberal state, administrative courts – even if slow, unwieldy and remote from the ordinary person – make by their mere existence a powerful statement that civil 'servants' are indeed expected to behave fairly to those they serve.

International law

International law is often dismissed as irrelevant to the real world of politics. The argument is that without a sovereign power to enforce it, international law is nothing more than moral persuasion. 'Where there is no common power, there is no law', wrote the English philosopher Thomas Hobbes (1588–1679). Yet just as we concluded that inter-governmental organizations exert some influence on states, so too must we acknowledge the role now played by international law. Its sheer density is shown by the 10 000 or so agreements registered at the United Nations. These cover such areas as international trade, the environment and human rights. In general, states obey this intricate cobweb of rules. As Henkin (1968, p. 47) writes, 'almost all nations observe almost all international law and almost all of their obligations almost all of the time'. So the lack of Hobbes's sovereign has not prevented the emergence of a law-governed international society (Bull, 1977).

Definition

International law is the system of rules which states (and other actors) regard as binding in their mutual relations. It derives from treaties, custom, accepted principles and the views of legal authorities. The term 'international law' was coined by the English philosopher Jeremy Bentham (1748–1832).

For three reasons, international law must receive attention from students of comparative politics:

- International law helped to define the division of the world into the states which structure the modern world. States were the only, and remain the major, units of international law. Through international law, states reinforced their dominant political position and it is through participation in an international legal community that 'statehood' is formally acquired.
- International law forms part of national law, often without any special mechanism of incorporation. Many constitutions are explicit on this point. The German constitution, for instance, states that

> the general rules of public international law are an integral part of federal law. They shall take precedence over the laws and shall create rights and duties for the inhabitants of the federal territory.

- International laws can apply directly to individuals and their rulers. The famous example here is the Nuremberg War Crimes Tribunal in 1946. This tribunal declined to accept the defence that individuals who committed crimes against humanity could defend themselves on the grounds that they were just obeying state orders. With the end of the Cold War, the Nuremberg principle is being rediscovered. In 1998, Britain's Law Lords ruled that General Pinochet could be extradited to Spain to face prosecution for torture committed when he was President of Chile in the 1970s and 1980s (however, the general was eventually allowed to return to Chile on grounds of ill health). The following year, a female ex-minister from Rwanda was indicted for rape by the International Criminal Tribunal on Rwanda for sexual assaults she condoned during the 1994 genocide.

International agreements constrain national policy-makers. These accords set out objectives (for example reducing carbon dioxide emissions) which national governments must – or at least should – put into effect. When states fail to abide by conventions they themselves have signed, for example in the area of human rights, individuals can in principle seek remedy through the courts, both national and international. An example from Australia illustrates this point and also draws out some broader domestic implications of international law. When Australia ratified a protocol to the International Covenant on Civil and Political Rights in 1991, Nick Toonen, a gay rights activist, lodged a complaint against Tasmania's prohibition of sexual behaviour between males. Tasmania remained resolute but the federal government in Canberra passed a liberalizing law, overriding provincial legislation. This shows how international agreements can impinge not just on the relationship between governors and governed but also on the balance between different levels of government. Indeed, critics allege that Australia's federal government could in theory use its expanding treaty commitments to interfere in virtually any area of activity which, under the national constitution, is supposedly reserved to the states (Scott, 1997). International law provides an indirect route through which one level of government can seek to influence another within its boundaries.

Key reading

Next step: *the special issue of Political Studies (1996) is an excellent survey of constitutionalism.*

Alexander (1998) and Rosenfeld (1994) are alternative sources on constitutionalism; Greenberg *et al.* (1993) examine the links with democratic transitions. Bogdanor (1988) remains a useful source on constitutions generally while Maddex (2000) surveys 100 constitutions. Howard (1993) covers constitution-making in East Europe. On the judiciary, Tate and Vallinder (1995) and Jacob et al. (1996) are cross-national studies. Hodder-Williams (1996) is a useful comparative essay, focused on the USA and the UK. O'Brien (1993) and Shapiro (1990) concentrate on the American Supreme Court while Solomon and Foglesong (2000) examine judicial reform in postcommunist Russia and Prillaman (2000) discusses the weakness of the judiciary in Latin America. On international law, Bull (1977) is a good starting point.

Federal, unitary and local government

Governing always has a territorial dimension. Rulers need to extract resources from their territory while also retaining the willingness of the population to remain within the orbit of the state. To achieve these ends, the modern state consists of an intricate network of organizations including (1) the central government, (2) its field offices in cities, towns and villages, and (3) subnational governments such as elected regional and local authorities. These bodies engage in a continuous effort to extract resources from, provide services to, and maintain the support of the population they both serve and control. In this chapter, we begin by examining the two basic solutions to the territorial organization of power – federal and unitary government. We then consider local government, the lowest level of authority within the state, before turning to the patterns of subnational government found in non-democratic states and in new democracies.

Federalism: characteristics and origins

The distinctive feature of federalism is that legal sovereignty is shared between the federal government and the constituent 'states' (the name given to provinces in a federation). A federal constitution creates two layers of government, with specific functions allocated to each. The centre takes charge of external relations – defence, foreign affairs and immigration – and some common domestic functions such as the currency. The functions of the states vary but typically include education and law enforcement. Residual powers may also lie with the states, not the centre (Box 13.1).

Definition
Federalism is the principle of sharing sovereignty between central and state (or provincial) governments; a **federation** is any political system that puts this idea into practice. A **confederation** is a looser link between participating countries which retain their separate statehood. In a confederation, the decisions of the central authority apply to the component states, rather than directly to the citizens, and unanimity may be a condition of collective action (Lister, 1996).

In a federation, the existence and functions of the states are entrenched; they can only be modified by amending the constitution. It is this protected position of the states, not the extent of their powers, which distinguishes federations (such as the USA and Canada) from unitary governments (such as the UK and France). Multiple levels of governance are integral to a federation whereas in a unitary system sovereignty resides solely with the centre and, no matter what the extent of decentralization in practice, lower levels exist at the pleasure of the centre. Further, in nearly all federations the states have a guaranteed voice in national policy-making through an upper chamber of the assembly, in which each state normally receives equal representation. In most unitary states, by contrast, the legislature consists of only one chamber.

The natural federal structure is for all the states within the union to possess identical powers under the constitution. However, asymmetric federalism arises when some states within a federation are given more autonomy than others. In post-Franco Spain, for instance, Catalonia, the Basque Country and Galicia were regarded as 'historic communites' which entitled them to an earlier and wider grant of autonomy than was awarded to other regions. In postcommunist Russia, 21 of 89 territorial units are 'republics' authorized to adopt their own constitutions, elect their own presidents and maintain law-making assemblies. In Canada, Quebec nationalists have long argued for special recognitions for their French-speaking province. Asymmetric federalism is a natural response to differences in power between regions within a federation but runs the risk of creating a spiral of instability as less favoured states seek the privileges accorded to the more autonomous provinces.

Federations must be distinguished not just from unitary states but also from confederations. In the latter, the central authority remains the junior partner and is dominated by the component states. The classic instance of a confederation is the short-lived system adopted in 1781 in what is now the United States. The weak centre, embodied in the Continental Congress, could neither tax nor regulate commerce. It also lacked direct authority over the people. It was the weakness of the Articles of Confederation that led to the drafting of a federal constitution, and to the creation of the United States proper, in 1787. A modern example of a toothless confederation is the Commonwealth of Independent States (CIS), set up in 1991 by former republics of the Soviet Union. Azerbaijan's president dismissed the CIS as 'a mere soap bubble – pretty on the surface but empty inside' (Elazar, 1998). In federations, the central government is far from toothless; indeed, today it is usually the leading political force.

Federalism is a far from uncommon solution to the problem of arranging the territorial distribution of power (Table 13.1). Elazar (1996, p. 426) counts 22 federations in existence today; these contain some two billion people or 40 per cent of the world's population. Federalism is particularly common in large countries, whether size is measured by area or population. Four of the world's largest states by area are federal: Australia, Brazil, Canada and the United States. In India, 10 of 25 provinces each contain more than 40 million people, providing a realistic framework for holding together a large and diverse country. Germany, the largest European country by population, is the main instance of federation on that continent.

Unlike some unitary states, federations are necessarily conscious creations, emerging from a deliberate constitutional settlement. The United States, for instance, emerged from a meeting of representatives of 13 American states in Philadelphia in 1787. This convention resulted in the world's first and most important federation. Similar conventions, strongly influenced by the American experience, took place in Switzerland in 1848, Canada in 1867 and Australia in 1897/98. While federalism is usually a compact between separate units pursuing a common

---

BOX 13.1
Federalism: who gets to do what?

Allocation of functions	Definition	Example
Exclusive jurisdiction	Functions allocated entirely to one level of government	Canadian provinces have exclusive jurisdiction over education
Concurrent jurisdiction	Functions shared between levels of government	In Canada, both the national and provincial governments can pass laws dealing with agriculture
Residual powers	The level of government which, by default, controls functions not specifically mentioned in the constitution	The 10th amendment to the United States constitution states, 'the powers not delegated to the United States by the constitution, nor prohibited by it to the States, are reserved to the states respectively, or to the people'.

Table 13.1 Some federations in established democracies

	Year established as a federation	Area (sq. km, thousands)	Population (million, 1999)	Number of states within the federation
United States*	1776	9373	272.6	50
Canada*	1867	9976	31.0	10
Switzerland	1874	41	7.3	26
Australia	1901	7687	18.8	6
Germany*	1949	357	82.1	16
India	1950	3288	1000.8	25
Belgium	1983	30	10.1	3

* For profiles, see p. 132 (USA), p. 205 (Canada) and p. 90 (Germany).

interest, it is possible for a unitary state to restructure as a federation. In practice, this remains a rare occurrence; to date, Belgium is the main example (Fitzmaurice, 1996). First established in 1830, Belgium has been beset by divisions between French- and Dutch-speaking regions. Constitutional revisions in 1970 and 1980 devolved more power to these groups and in 1983 Belgium finally proclaimed itself a federation. So theoretically there are two routes to a federation: either by creating a new central authority (e.g. the United States) or by transferring sovereignty from an existing national government (Belgium).

What, then, provokes people to set out on the hard road of creating a federation? Motives are more often negative than positive: fear of the consequences of failing to join together must overcome the natural desire to retain sovereignty. The most common motive, by far, is the ambition to secure the military and economic bonus accruing to large countries. Riker (1975, 1996) emphasizes the first military factor. He argues that federations emerge when there is an external threat. The American states, for instance, joined together in 1789 partly because they felt themselves to be vulnerable in a predatory world. When large beasts lurk in the jungle, smaller creatures gather for safety. The American statesman Benjamin Franklin (1706–90) put this point well when he said, 'we must all hang together or most assuredly we shall all hang separately'. Alternatively, the partners may believe that a

federation will itself be able to behave aggressively in the international arena. In Canada, for example, the framers wanted to expand their political and economic influence to the northwest in response to American expansion up the Pacific coast.

But it would be wrong to regard military motives as the sole or even the main reason for forming federations. The federal bargain has often been based on economic rather than military reasoning. Even the Australian and American federalists felt that a common market would promote economic expansion as well as military security. Although the federal status of the European Union is open to question, its development certainly owed much to the desire for a large internal market. Indeed, the Union was originally called the European Economic Community or, in popular parlance, 'the common market'.

Fear can also come from within. Federations are useful for bridging ethnic diversity within a society; they are a device for incorporating such differences within a single political community. People who differ by descent, language and culture can nevertheless seek the advantages of membership in a shared enterprise (Forsyth, 1989, p. 4). The Indian federation, for instance, has accommodated growing religious tensions between Hindus, Muslims, Sikhs and Christians. Linguistic diversity also explains the anomaly of the two countries in Table 13.1 that have adopted a federal solution despite their small area: Switzerland and Belgium. In Switzerland, federalism integrates 23 cantons, two and a half languages

Country profile **CANADA**

Population: 31m.
Gross domestic product per head:
$22 400.
Composition:

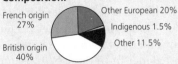

French origin 27%
British origin 40%
Other European 20%
Indigenous 1.5%
Other 11.5%

Form of government: a federal parlia-mentary democracy, with 10 provinces. Most Canadians live in Ontario or Quebec.
Legislature: the 301-seat House of Commons is the lower chamber. Most unusually for a federation, the 104 members of the Senate, the upper chamber, are appointed by the Prime Minister, not selected by the provinces.
Executive: the Prime Minister leads a Cabinet, selecting ministers with due regard for provincial representation. A Governor General serves as cere-monial figurehead.
Judiciary: Canada employs a dual (federal and provincial) court system, headed by a restrained Supreme Court. In 1982 the country intro-duced the Canadian Charter of Rights and Freedoms.
Electoral system: a plurality system with single member districts. This produces massive swings and distor-tions in representation in the Commons yet electoral reform is rarely considered.
Party system: the party system is strongly regional, with the governing Liberals dominating the key province of Ontario. Currently, the main oppo-sition parties are the Bloc Québécois and the Western-based Alliance. The once-powerful Conservatives and the left-wing New Democratic Party are smaller opposition parties.

Canada is a large country with a relatively small pop-ulation. Its land-mass is the second largest in the world but its population is little more than a tenth of its powerful American neighbour. Most Canadians live in urban settlements in a 100-mile strip border-ing the United States. Canada's economy depends heavily on the USA, a relationship reinforced by the formation of the North American Free Trade Association in 1994.

Reflecting British influence, Canada's constitution, originally set out in the British North America Act of 1867, established parliamentary government in a centralized federation. Since then, 'Canada has moved from a highly centralized political situation to one of the most decentralized federal systems in the world' (Landes, 1995, p. 101). This reflects the central issue of Canadian politics: the place within it of French-speaking Quebec. The origins of this problem go back to the founding of the country. From the sixteenth century, first France and then Britain colonized the territories of Canada, then inhabited by around ten million indigenous people. Britain finally defeated the French in 1759.

For many Francophones, Canada consists of two founding peoples – the British and French – whose status should be equal. This is taken to imply that Quebec should be more than just one among the 10 provinces of the federation. Since the 1960s a revived nationalist party in Quebec has sought to implement this vision. However the federal response has been to decentralize power to all 10 provinces, not just Quebec. This is an understandable response – the danger of 'asymmetric federalism' (in which a few strong provinces receive special treatment) is that it breeds resentment elsewhere. For example the Lake Meech Accord of 1987, which proposed consti-tutional recognition of Quebec's special status, fell because two provinces refused to endorse it.

In Quebec itself, the Parti Québécois, elected to power in 1994, held a provincial referendum in 1995 on 'sovereignty association' for Quebec. This would have combined political sovereignty for Quebec with continued economic association with Canada. The proposal lost but by the narrowest of margins. Subsequently, the issue of constitutional reform declined in intensity as Quebec focused, with some success, on improving its economy.

Yet as Williams (1995, p. 69) writes,

> despite all Canada's domestic turmoil, it is endowed with a responsive federal system. Over time this has created a good safe place to raise a family and earn a crust, the ultimate test of a state's obligations to its citizens.

The UN's Human Development Index, an overall ranking of the world's countries by life expectancy, education and income, confirms Williams's point. Since 1994 Canada has topped the table.

Further reading: Watts (1996), Williams (1995).

(German and French, plus Italian) and two religions (Catholic and Protestant). Belgium is another instance of ethnic federalism. Its rebirth in 1983 as a federal state reflected a desire to give more self-government to French- and Dutch-speaking cultures in a linguistically divided country.

In the relatively peaceful environment of the twenty-first century, there are currently few military reasons for forming new federations. Even when a common threat does exist, a traditional alliance between independent states might serve the purpose more readily than sharing sovereignty through a federation. Similarly, the economic case for federations currently looks rather weak. States are increasingly finding that advantages of scale can be obtained by creating a free trade area, such as the North American Free Trade Association, again without compromising political sovereignty. Ethnic federalism, however, is attracting some attention from countries seeking to maintain the unity of the state in multinational societies (G. Smith, 1995). Its advocates claim that federalism permits diversity within unity and is thus an important model for situations of conflicting identities – as found, for instance, in the Balkans or Northern Ireland.

Federal–state relations

The relations between federal and state governments are the crux of federalism. A federal framework creates an inherent conflict between the two levels and indeed between the states themselves. Federalism creates both competition and the need for its containment through compromise. It is helpful here to distinguish two approaches. The original federal principle, as understood by the Founding Fathers in the United States, was that the national and state governments would operate independently, each tier acting autonomously in its own constitutional sphere. In particular, the federal government was required to confine its activities to functions explicitly allocated to it, such as the power 'to lay and collect taxes, to pay the debts and provide for the common defence and welfare of the United States'. In the circumstances of eighteenth-century America, extensive coordination between federal and state administrations was considered neither necessary nor feasible. This model of separated gov-

ernments, linked only through a constitutional contract, is known as *dual federalism*. Perhaps always a myth, dual federalism has long since disappeared, overwhelmed by the demands of an integrated economy and society. Even so, it expresses the essential spirit of federalism.

While the USA is the exemplar of federalism, we should recognize that European federalism, as found in Austria, Germany and Switzerland, has contrasting origins. While federalism in the USA was and remains a contract in which the states join together to form a central government with limited functions, European federalism (particularly in Germany) rests on the idea of cooperation between levels of government. Such solidarity expresses a shared commitment to a united society; federalism displays organic links that bind the participants together. The moral norm is solidarity but the operating principle is subsidiarity – the idea that decisions should be taken at the lowest level possible. The central government offers overall leadership but leaves implementation to lower levels – a division rather than a separation of tasks. This model is sometimes termed *cooperative federalism*; it lacks the simplicity of the dual model but, as a more recent variation, offers a more realistic account of how federal governance proceeds in practice.

Definition
Dual federalism, as originally envisaged in the USA, meant that the national and state governments in a federation retained separate spheres of action. Each level independently performed the tasks allocated to it by the constitution. In reality, the main feature of contemporary federations is interdependence rather than independence of levels. **Cooperative federalism**, as practised in Germany, is explicitly based on the principles of cooperation and interdependence between levels. National and state governments are expected to collaborate in pursuit of the interests of the whole, a philosophy at odds with the contractual foundations of dual federalism.

Consider German cooperative federalism in more detail. Unlike the United States, German federalism from its inception stressed interdependence, not independence, between the two levels. Imposed by the allies in 1949 as a barrier against dictatorship, federalism built on regional traditions to become an accepted part of the country's political order. In Germany, all the Länder (states) are expected to contribute to the success of the whole; in exchange, they are treated with respect by the centre. This collaborative spirit is encouraged both by the device of 'framework legislation' – laws passed by the centre which are then fleshed out in land legislation – and by the powerful Constitutional Court, which has expected the participants to show due sensitivities to the interests of other actors in the federal system. Although German federalism remains far more organic than its American equivalent, its cooperative ethos has come under some pressure. Growing economic inequalities have led the richer Länder, notably Bavaria, to complain about the use of equalization grants to help poorer provinces like Saarland. Representation of the Länder in the upper chamber of the federal parliament gives them a platform from which to voice their concerns and, if necessary, oppose the federal government's proposals (Gunlicks, 1999). The political reality is that 'cooperative federalism' coexists with significant competition between the players.

Whatever their origins or philosophy, most federations have witnessed growing interdependence between the two tiers. Today, federations are characterized by extensive 'intergovernmental relations' in which federal, state (and local) governments work together, seeking to identify policies on which all participants can agree. In such areas as education,

transport and the environment, policy is made, funded and applied at all levels of government. In Canada, this mingling is called 'executive federalism'.

Equally important, in most federations the central government tended to gain influence until the final decades of the twentieth century. Partly, this reflected the centre's financial muscle (Box 13.2). The flow of money became more favourable to the centre as income tax revenues grew with the expansion of the workforce and rising living standards. Income is invariably taxed mainly at national level because otherwise there would be too many opportunities for people and corporations to move to low-tax states. By contrast, the states must depend for their own independently raised revenue on sales and property taxes, sources that have generally grown more slowly than income tax. This shift in financial strength is seen in Australia, where about 60 per cent of the states' total revenue now comes from the federal government.

The enhanced authority of the centre in federal systems has been more than a financial matter. More than anything, it reflects the emergence of a national economy demanding overall planning and regulation. To take just one example, when California experienced an electricity shortage in 2000, the federal government inevitably became involved as California began to suck in power from surrounding states. Similarly, the task of developing a national transport system invariably requires central coordination. The wars and depressions of the last century invariably empowered the central authority; such additional powers, once acquired, tend to be retained. And the postwar drive to complete a welfare state offering equal rights to all citizens also strengthened national government.

By the end of the 1980s, however, budget deficits at national level combined with resistance to income tax increases forced central governments to become less generous in their support of the provinces. As an American Treasury Secretary said, revenue-sharing ended 'because there was no revenue left to share'. As American states were forced to rely on their own sources of income, so they rediscovered their autonomy. State policies became more creative. Innovations extended to important social issues such as welfare reform and education. Walker (1991, p. 130) referred to 'the renaissance of the states' as they again became 'laboratories of democracy'. This

---

BOX 13.2

Financial transfers from the federal government to states

Form of transfer	Definition
Categorical grants	For specific projects (e.g. a new hospital)
Block grants	For particular programmes (e.g. for medical care)
Revenue-sharing	General funding which places few limits on the recipient's use of funds
Equalization grants	Used in some federations (e.g. Germany) in an effort to equalize financial conditions between the states. Can create resentment in the wealthier states.

caused some irritation at the centre, as when Massachusetts launched a boycott in 1996 of firms trading with military-led Burma. Critics felt the state's action had compromised both America's internal market and Washington's control of foreign policy, two traditional functions of the national government.

Constitutional courts have generally acceded to central initiatives, particularly when justified on grounds of national emergency. In the rulings of the US Supreme Court, federal law prevailed over state law for most of the twentieth century. For instance, in *Garcia* v. *San Antonio Metropolitan Transit Authority* (1984) the Court declared that the federal government could require local authorities to set minimum wage levels. In this case, the Court ruled that restrictions on federal intervention were a matter for the political rather than the judicial process. In Australia, decisions of the High Court have favoured the centre to the point where some commentators regard federalism as sustained more by political tradition than by the constitution. Of the major Western federations, only Canada has seen a long-term drift away from the centre. However, by the 1990s there were signs that courts in a number of federal systems were seeking to restore at least some autonomy to the states. In the USA a more conservative Supreme Court has favoured lower tiers of government, contributing to the resurgence of the states. Just as the financial balance has moved back in favour of the states, so too has ideological fashion – indeed, the latter trend surely flows from the former.

There remains the awkward case of the European Union (EU). How should this body be located within the federal/unitary classification? A case can certainly be made for regarding the EU as a true federation. Its well-developed institutions include a powerful Commission, an influential Court and a parliament that is directly elected by the citizens of member states. EU decisions must be implemented by member states and these decisions apply directly to citizens. There is no provision for member states to withdraw from the Union. Yet the EU also lacks the institutional architecture of an orthodox federal state. As Scharpf (1996) argues, a fully federal Europe would require the Commission (as the executive) to become accountable to the parliament. It would also need the Council of Ministers (repre-

senting the member states) to become a second chamber, like the American Senate. Although federal Germany supports such developments, public scepticism is currently holding back further moves in a federal direction. The EU continues to involve a strong element of intergovernmental decision-making. It remains a unique hybrid, more than a confederation but less than a true federation (Siedentop, 2000).

Unitary government

Most contemporary states are unitary, which means that sovereignty lies exclusively with the central government. Subnational authorities, whether regional or local, may make policy as well as implement it but they do so by permission of the centre. In theory, the national government could abolish lower levels if it wished. Unitary states emerge naturally in societies with a history of rule by sovereign emperors and monarchs, such as Britain, France and Japan. Unitary structures are also the norm in smaller democracies, particularly those without strong ethnic divisions, for example Scandinavia. In Latin America, with its history of centralized presidential rule, nearly all the smaller countries are unitary. In most unitary states, the legislature has only one chamber since there is no need for an upper or states' house. After the complexities of federalism, a unitary structure may seem straight-forward and efficient. However, the location of sovereignty is rarely an adequate guide to political realities and unitary government is not necessarily centralized in its operation. Indeed in the 1990s many unitary states attempted to push responsibility for more functions (including raising money from the tax-payer) on to lower levels. In practice, unitary states, just like federations, involve constant bargaining between levels of government. In West Europe, of course, these multi-level games extend beyond the state to include the European Union.

We can distinguish three broad ways in which unitary states can disperse power from the centre (Box 13.3). The first, and least significant, is *deconcentration*. This is purely a matter of administrative organization; it refers to the location of central government employees away from the capital. The case for a deconcentrated structure is that it spreads the

FOR OR AGAINST

FEDERALISM

What assessment can we give of the federal experiment? With two hundred years of experience in the USA, and the more recent history of other federations, political science should be able to provide a balanced judgment of the pros and cons of federalism. Such an assessment is particularly relevant today as governments seek a way of enabling different ethnic groups to live together in the same country.

The case for

Federalism is a natural and practical arrangement for large states. It provides checks and balances on a territorial basis, keeping some government functions closer to the people and allowing for the representation of ethnic differences. Federalism reduces overload at the centre. The existence of several states produces healthy competition and opportunities for experiment. Citizens and firms also have the luxury of choice: if they dislike governance in one state, they can always move to another. The central–local balance can evolve in response to changing conditions, producing flexible governance. Above all, federalism reconciles two modern imperatives too often viewed as incompatible: it secures the economic and military advantages of scale while retaining, indeed encouraging, cultural diversity. For such reasons, federation should be considered a historically proven way forward for countries (such as the member states of the EU) seeking to respond to a world which combines growing interdependence between countries with increasing diversity within them.

The case against

Federalism is ineffective, inefficient and complex. Decisions are too slow to emerge, requiring successful negotiation between central and provincial levels. When a gunman ran amok in Tasmania in 1996, killing 35 people, federal Australia experienced some political problems before it tightened gun control uniformly across the country. By contrast, unitary Britain acted quickly when a comparable incident occurred at Dunblane primary school in Scotland. Similarly, federalism in Germany enables the Länder to hold the central authority hostage, producing *reformstau* (reform blockage). Further, federalism complicates accountability, with opportunities for politicians to pass the buck to the other level. An additional weakness is that federalism distributes power by territory when the key conflicts in society are social (e.g. race and gender) rather than geographical. Despite their claim to represent social diversity, federal states do not formally incorporate 'minority' groups such as women and indigenous peoples into the federal framework. Today, free trade areas are a simpler method of securing the economic advantages of scale. In short, federalism is an eighteenth-century leftover, a legacy to be tolerated rather than a model to be emulated.

Assessment

As with other political institutions, evaluations of federalism depend on taking a view of the proper balance between the concentration and diffusion of political power. Should power rest with one body to allow decisive action? If so, federalism is likely to be seen as an obstacle and impediment – as an anti-majoritarian and therefore an anti-democratic device. Alternatively, should power be dispersed among a range of actors so as to reduce the danger of tyranny, including majority dictatorship? Through this lens, federalism will appear as an indispensable technique for protecting the liberty of the people.

Further reading: Elazar (1996), Smith (1996), Wheare (1963).

BOX 13.3

Methods for distributing power away from the centre

Method	Definition	Illustration
Deconcentration	Central government functions are executed by staff 'in the field'	Almost 90 per cent of US federal civilian employees work away from Washington, D.C.
Decentralization	Central government functions are executed by subnational authorities	Local governments administer national welfare programmes in Scandinavia
Devolution	Central government grants some decision-making autonomy to new lower levels	Regional governments in France, Italy and Spain

Note: Deconcentration and decentralization occur in federal as well as unitary states.

---

work around, enabling field offices to benefit from local knowledge and freeing central departments to focus on policy-making. As a French decree of 1852 put it, 'one can govern from afar but must be close to administer.'

The second, and politically more significant way of dispersing power is through *decentralization*. This means delegating policy execution to subnational bodies, traditionally local authorities but also (and increasingly) a range of other agencies. In Scandinavia, for instance, local governments have put into effect many welfare programmes agreed at national level. In the UK, too, local government has proved to be the workhorse of central authority.

The third and most radical form of power dispersal is *devolution*. This occurs when the centre grants decision-making autonomy (including some legislative powers) to lower levels. In the United Kingdom, for instance, devolved assemblies have been set up in Scotland and Wales and a similar body reintroduced to Northern Ireland. In theory, Britain will remain a unitary state because control over the constitution will continue to be exercised from Westminister; as the English politician Enoch Powell said, 'power devolved is power retained'. Yet Powell was perhaps relying too heavily on theory. In practice, the newly-devolved British state may be no more centralized than some federations.

Developments in unitary Spain offer a further test of the boundary with federations. Spanish regions were created rapidly in the transition to democracy following General Franco's death in 1975. Seeking to integrate a centralist tradition with strong regional identities, Spain's constitution-makers created a system in which the country's 'autonomous communities' (that is, regions) could decide their own level of autonomy. The 'historic communities' of the Basque Country and Catalonia, quickly followed by Galicia, were the first to receive their 'Statutes of Autonomy'. Spain's compromise delivered near-federalism within the frame of a unitary state. This was a messy but politically effective solution for a country that has always needed to reconcile a strong centre with some assertive regions.

A distinctive trend within unitary states has been the development of at least one level of government which stands between central and local authorities. France, Italy and Spain have introduced elected regional governments. The smaller Scandinavian countries took a different route, strengthening and refurbishing their traditional counties. Even a small country like New Zealand has developed 12 elected regional councils. In unitary states, the standard pattern now is to have three levels of subnational government – regional, provincial and local – as in France and Italy (Table 13.2). Regional and provincial governments are intermediate levels which form the 'expanded middle' of modern states. The result is a multi-level system that is even more intricate than the two levels of subnational authority – state and local – in a federation. Whether federal or unitary, never-ending negotiation between levels of government has become a permanent feature of territorial governance in every established democracy.

In Europe, the revival of regional ethnic nationalism, as with the Basques in Spain, has undoubtedly played a part in the move to establish regional governments. But the European Union has also contributed. The EU has stimulated regions within

Table 13.2 Subnational government in some unitary states

	France	Italy	Japan	Norway
Regional level	22 regions	20 regions	–	–
Provincial level	96 departments	94 provinces	47 prefectures	19 counties
Local level	36 673 communes	8 074 communes	3 200 municipalities	448 municipalities

Note: Figures are from about 1997.

member states to lobby for aid through the European Regional Development Fund (ERDF). The EU's policy of distributing aid directly to regions, rather than through member states, has offered further encouragement. Scenting money, regions have sought direct representation in Brussels; by 1999, more than 150 were represented there, compared to just six in 1985. This squeeze on central governments has encouraged regional nationalists to postulate a 'Europe of the Regions' in which the EU and revived regions exert a pincer movement on national power. The notion, perhaps exaggerated but still significant in itself, is that the European Union and the regions gradually become the leading policy-makers, outflanking central governments which are left with less to do. The EU encouraged such aspirations by introducing a Committee of the Regions and Local Communities, a body composed of subnational authorities, in 1988. Although this committee is only consultative, its mere existence indicates the growing pressures facing unitary European states in maintaining claims to exclusive sovereignty over 'their' territory (Jones and Keating, 1995).

Although regional governments can pass laws in their designated areas of competence, their main contribution has been in economic planning and infrastructure development. In the Spanish region of Valencia, for example, the authority has sought to improve telecommunications, roads, railways, ports and airports. Such tasks are beyond the scope of small local authorities but beneath the national vision of the central government. Using regional taxes, loans and central grants, French regions in particular have exerted leverage over lower-level departments, even though regions remain the poor relation in financial terms (Loughlin and Mazey, 1995). In Italy, too, regional authorities outside the South have made a notable contribution, with some

left-wing parties determined to display their competence through showpiece governance. Thus, the evolution of regional government suggests a move away from the original demand for greater self-government toward a more administrative role as an intermediary between other levels of government. As Balme (1998, p. 182) concludes of France, regional governments are becoming arenas in which policies are formed, even if they seem unlikely to become decisive actors, given the strong unitary tradition in Europe.

Local government

Local government is universal, found in federal and unitary states alike. It is the lowest level of elected territorial organization within the state. Variously called communes, municipalities or parishes, local government is constitutionally subordinate to provincial authority (in federations) or to national government (in unitary states). Even so, as Teune (1995b, p, 16) says, 'it is where the day-to-day activity of politics and government gets done'.

The status of local government differs sharply between the new world (for instance, the USA, Canada, Australia and New Zealand) and the old world of Europe. In the new world, local government has a pragmatic, utilitarian character. Local authorities were set up as needed to deal with 'roads, rates and rubbish'. Special boards (appointed or elected) were added to deal with specific problems from mosquito control to licensing, harbours and land drainage. The policy style was apolitical: 'there is no Democratic or Republican way to collect garbage'. Indeed special boards were often set up precisely to be independent of party politics. The consequence is diversity in organization. For instance, the USA is governed at local level by a smorgasbord of over 80 000 cities, counties, school districts, townships and special districts.

On the European continent, local government has higher status and a more coherent character than in the new world. In part, this position reflects the unitary nature of most European states, allowing direct links between local administrations (especially large cities) and the centre. In addition, local governments represent historic communities that pre-date the emergence of strong national governments. Reflecting this status, national constitutions normally mandate some form of local self-government. Sweden's 'Instrument of Government' is an example. It roundly declares that Swedish democracy 'shall be realized through a representative and parliamentary polity and through local self-government'. In addition, local authorities in continental Europe normally enjoy 'general competence': that is, the authority to make regulations in any matter of concern to the area. Germany's Basic Law, for instance, gives the *gemeinden* (municipalities) 'the right to regulate under their own responsibility and within the limits of the law all the affairs of the local community'.

Definition

General competence is the authority of local governments to make regulations in any matter of concern to the area. These regulations must be consistent with national law. The power of general competence signals the status of local government within the political system; where local government can only perform those functions explicitly granted to it by the centre, as in England, its status is weak.

In the next sections, we will discuss three aspects of local government: (a) its relationship with the centre, (b) its functions and structure, (c) its difficulty in reconciling its small scale with efficient operation.

Relationship with the centre

The pattern here is usually based on one of two models: dual or fused. The test is whether local governments is seen as an organization separate from the centre (a dual system) or as part of a single state system (a fused system). The distinction is significant in that it expresses contrasting notions of public authority as a whole.

Under a *dual* system, local governments retain freestanding status, setting their own internal organization and employing staff on their own conditions of service. Staff tend to move horizontally – from one local authority to another – rather than vertically, between central and local government. Ultimate authority rests with the centre but local government employees do not regard themselves as working for the same employer as civil servants based at the centre. Traditionally, Britain was regarded as an example of a dual system. Despite operating under London's long shadow, many local authorities drew on their own history to develop pride in their own professional standards. In a dual system, public authority is seen as separated rather than integrated; the spirit is federalist even if the constitution is not. However, severe centralization under Conservative administrations in the 1980s reduced the status of local authorities to virtual servants of central government.

Definition

A **dual** system of local government (as in Britain) maintains a formal separation of central and local government. Although the centre is sovereign, local authorities are not seen as part of a single state structure. In a **fused** system, characteristic of strong states such as France, a centrally appointed prefect supervises local authorities. The localities, although possessing considerable autonomy in practice, form part of a uniform system of administration applying across the country.

Under a *fused* system, by contrast, central and local government combine to form a single sphere of public authority. Both levels express the leading authority of the state. The two levels are normally joined in the office of the prefect, a central appointee who oversees the administration of a particular community and reports to the Ministry of the Interior in the capital. In theory, a prefectoral system signals central dominance by establishing a clear unitary hierarchy running from national government through the prefect to local authorities. France is the classic example of this fused approach. Established by Napoleon early in the nineteenth century, the system consists of 96 departments, each with its own prefect and elected assembly. The framework is uniform and rational but in practice the prefect must cooperate with local councils rather than simply oversee them. The prefect is now as much an agent of the department as of the centre, representing views upwards as well as transmitting orders downwards. Although the powers of the prefect have declined, the French model remains influential. Many other countries have adopted it, including all France's ex-colonies and several postcommunist states.

One effect of a fused system is the ease with which politicians can move between, or even straddle, the national and the local. France is again an interesting case. National politicians often become or remain mayor of their home town, a feature called the *cumul des mandats* (accumulation of offices). Although the *cumul* came under attack from Lionel Jospin when he became Prime Minister in 1997, defenders argue that the system helps the locality to protect its interests at national level. The technique also provides a way of sidestepping unhelpful prefects. In countries with a dual system, such as Britain, politicians rarely straddle the two worlds though local government can still be a launching pad for a separate national political career.

Functions and structure

What do local governments do? Broadly, their tasks are two-fold: to provide local public services (such as refuse collection) and to implement national welfare policies (Box 13.4). However, a static description of functions fails to reveal how the role of local government evolved in the 1990s. The major trend has been for municipal authorities to reduce their direct provision of services by delegating tasks to private organizations, both profit-making and voluntary. In Denmark, for example, many local governments have set up 'user boards' in primary schools. These boards are given block budgets and the authority to hire and fire staff (Bogason, 1996). In some American cities, private firms located in an area have taken over much of the responsibility for funding and even organizing improvements to local services such as street-cleaning.

In this way the local authority's role is changing from a provider to an enabler. The council does not so much provide services as ensure that they are supplied. This enables the authority to become a smaller, coordinating body, more concerned with

governance than government. More organizations become involved in local policy-making, many of them functional (for example school boards) rather than territorial (for example county councils). Reflecting this trend, the role of citizen in local government may be evolving from *voter* at elections to a *customer* for specific services (for example care for the elderly). This shift represents an important transition in conceptions of how local governments should go about their task of serving their communities.

> **Definition**
> The **enabling authority** is a term used to summarize one vision of local government. Such an authority is concerned with coordinating the provision of services and representing the community both within and beyond its territory. Its role is strategic, with specific services contracted out to private agencies, whether voluntary or profit-making.

In structuring local government, a significant issue is the balance between the council and the mayor. In some countries, including Britain and parts of the United States, the mayor is a ceremonial post, usually a reward offered by the other councillors to a colleague with long service. Real power rests with the elected council, often operating through powerful committees in which professional appointees (such as architects and accountants) play a significant role. However, one weakness of this format is its lack of visibility to the electorate. Under the increasingly popular 'strong mayor' system, the mayor acts as a directly elected chief executive, pro-

> **BOX 13.4**
> ## *Typical powers of local authorities*
>
> | | |
> |---|---|
> | Cemeteries | Recreation |
> | Economic development | Refuse disposal |
> | Environmental protection | Roads |
> | Fire service | Social assistance |
> | Homes for the elderly | Social housing |
> | Libraries | Tourism |
> | Local planning | Water supply |
> | Primary education | |
>
> *Source:* Norton (1991, table 2.2).

viding a focal point for local government and stimulating public interest in its activities. This system first emerged in American cities from the 1880s in reaction to a 'weak mayor' system based on a separation of powers between the mayor and a legislative council. Recently, the perceived success of strong American mayors such as New York's Rudy Giuliani encouraged Britain to consider introducing elected mayors as a way of reviving a demoralized local government sector. London led the way, with the former Labour activist Ken Livingstone elected as an independent in 2000. As the London example shows, the focus of a strong-mayor system on individuals tends to weaken the grip of established parties on local power structures. Italy introduced such a mayoral system somewhat earlier, in 1993.

Scale and efficiency

Local governments express both the virtues and the vices of their limited scale. At their best, local governments represent natural communities, remain accessible to their citizens, reinforce local identities, act as a political recruiting ground, serve as a first port of call for citizens with a problem and distribute resources in the light of local knowledge and needs. Yet local governments also have characteristic weaknesses. They are often too small to deliver local services efficiently, they lack financial autonomy and they are easily dominated by local élites. Thus the perpetual 'problem' of local government: how to marry local representation with efficient delivery of services. As Teune (1995a, p. 8) notes,

> there never has been a sound theoretical resolution [at local level] to the question of democracy and its necessity for familiarity, on the one hand, with the size and diversity required for prosperity, on the other.

Various schemes have been adopted to counter the inefficiencies of small scale (Box 13.5). First, local governments can collaborate with their neighbours. For instance by 1994 the 36 000 communes in France had arranged themselves into 18 000 consortia for such purposes as supplying water and electricity. Second, special-purpose authorities, often formally separate from the system of territorial government, can be set up to serve larger areas.

BOX 13.5

Balancing local government with economies of scale

Solution	Example
Establish consortia of local councils to provide specific services	French communes jointly supplying electricity
Set up separate boards to provide specific services	School boards in the USA
Merge local government units	Sweden and especially England
Restrict local councils to a lobbying role	Many French communes

---

Examples include elected school boards in the United States and the old road boards in New Zealand. Third, local governments can be combined to increase the population served. Sweden, for example, had 2500 communes in 1952; by 1969 the number had fallen to just 278, with an average population of 30 000 (Table 13.3). Fourth, local gov-

Table 13.3 Average population of elected local authorities in selected European democracies

Country	Average population of local authorities (lowest level)
England	127 000
Scotland	91 620
Ireland	41 910
Sweden	30 000
Netherlands	17 860
Belgium	16 740
Finland	10 646
Norway	9 145
Germany	7 240
Italy	6 800
Spain	4 700
France	1 500

Source: Norton (1991, table 2.2).

ernment can cease to deliver services altogether, becoming instead an interest group for voicing community needs at higher level. This has been the inevitable fate of many French communes, most of which still have under 500 inhabitants.

Subnational government in authoritarian states

In authoritarian and totalitarian regimes, a crucial distinction is between between local government and local power. The former is weak: authority flows from the top down and so bottom-up institutions of local representation are inherently subordinate. Local government becomes local administration: a branch of the centre rather than an affirmation of local autonomy. Where national power is exercised by the military or a ruling party, these institutions typically establish a parallel presence in the provinces, where their authority overrides local government officials. For a humble mayor in such a situation, the main skill required is to avoid making initiatives.

But it would be wrong to conclude that authoritarian regimes are highly centralized. Rather, central rulers – just like medieval monarchs – often depend on provincial 'nobles' to sustain their own, sometimes tenuous, grip on power. Central–local relations therefore tend to be more personal and less structured than in an established democracy. The hold of regional strong-men on power is not embedded in local institutions and such rulers command their fiefdoms, replicating the authoritarian pattern found at national level. Central and local rulers are integrated by patronage: the national ruler effectively buys the support of local big-wigs who in turn maintain their position by selectively passing over resources to their own supporters. Patronage, not institutions, binds centre and periphery.

As always, totalitarian regimes offered more sophisticated excuses for a centralized order. Fascism, for example, sought unqualified obedience to the state and its supreme leader. Unity in the state meant a unitary state; dividing power between multiple levels of government was dismissed as liberal folly. In Italy, Mussolini relied on centrally appointed prefects to run local areas, decreeing that the prefect represented the 'entire, undiminished

power of the state'. Spain under Franco proceeded similarly, with a Civil Governor in each province overseeing an elaborate structure of central government outposts. Given that the supreme leader could not in fact take all decisions, in practice the local representatives of the state exerted considerable influence over their own areas. They sought to become their own little dictators and they often succeeded.

It was perhaps only some communist regimes, notably the Soviet Union, which achieved real political centralization. In communist states, the leading role of the party in constructing a socialist utopia always took precedence over local concerns. As long as the party itself remained highly centralized, national leaders could command the regions. In the Soviet Union, the ability of communist leaders to command the vast territory of the country through the device of the party was an unparalleled organizational achievement. Technically, the 'Union of Soviet Socialist Republics' was a federation but in reality any attempt by a republic to exercise its constitutional right to 'freely secede from the USSR' would have been crushed by force. Centralized control exercised through the party overwhelmed federalist fiction. Thus it is customary, and indeed largely correct, to dismiss Soviet federalism as 'false', 'façade' or at best 'incomplete' federalism, a cover for what amounted to a Russian empire.

Even in the Soviet Union, however, a measure of decentralization was introduced from the 1960s and the situation was always complicated by Soviet nationalities policy. Political centralization was combined with active encouragement of national cultural diversity, at least for the first generation of communist rulers. As Ulam (1974, p. 70) writes, 'the theory of Soviet federalism was militantly nationalistic insofar as the cultural rights of each, even the tiniest, nationality was concerned. If socialism was eventually to unite all nations of the world in one great union, why be afraid of Ukrainian, Armenian or Kazak nationalism?' Thus, the USSR's promotion of national diversity amid the creation of a uniquely centralized political and economic order provides a complex legacy for Russia's postcommunist rulers. Even though many of the USSR's constituent republics became independent states in the break-up of the Soviet Union in 1991, Russia itself remains a country in which multiple nationalities continue to jostle – as seen in Chechnya's failed war of independence, savagely repressed by a Russian élite (and public) determined to protect its own pre-eminence in what is now, more than ever, a multi-national state.

Subnational government in new democracies

When authoritarian rule gives way to democracy, local government is usually in an under-nourished condition. Under the pre-democratic regime, institutions of local and regional governance withered if indeed they existed at all. Authoritarian rulers viewed the provinces defensively, as a threat to their own power. One index of a consolidated democracy is precisely the development of subnational institutions with a stable and regulated relationship to the national government. In the actual transition to democracy, however, little attention is paid to regional and local levels. An outburst of local participation may herald the new order but the new activists are often inexperienced, launching initiatives which breach national guidelines (Fitzmaurice, 1998). The real action is in the capital where the priority is to establish a new order of national power. Only when this primary goal is achieved can the focus turn to lower levels of governance. Establishing a uniform set of institutions beneath the national level, with clear functions, sound financing and competitive elections, tends to be an outcome as well as a dimension of democratic consolidation.

For instance, the struggles of local government to become established in postcommunist states exemplify the problems of institutional development amid the difficult inheritance of a collapsed dictatorship. Under communism, local government was functionless and spineless – and often deliberately kept so by frequent reorganization. Regional party bosses, not elected councillors, wielded the real power. In the former Soviet republics (and to a lesser extent in Eastern Europe) local government was massively unprepared for the postcommunist era. 'We are starting from less than zero', complained a city official in Kiev, the capital of Ukraine, after the collapse of communist party rule. Local authorities had little revenue and the central government, preoccupied with its own survival, had no money to

spare. Often local government officers worked from buildings that were still technically owned by their former master, the communist party. Despite chronic under-resourcing, local officials had to pick up the enormous welfare problems created by industrial collapse. They sought to resolve these difficulties in the context of societies which had gone without authentic local social organization for at least a generation. Futher, intermediate levels of government between the centre and the localities were still being created; local government initially had no regional bodies to provide support.

In countries with a pluralist tradition and a less severe history of communism (notably Hungary, Poland and the Czech Republic), subnational government has certainly begun to take root, usually drawing on the precommunist heritage. Take Poland as an illustration. In 1999 – a full ten years after the collapse of communism – Poland reintroduced its precommunist subnational structure, with 16 *voivodships* (regions) given responsibility for economic development within their territory. The leader of each *voivodship* was no longer appointed by the centre but was drawn from an elected council. As with other East European countries, Poland's focus on the regional level was stimulated by the desire to join, and extract resources from, the European Union. Beneath the regions in Poland stand two smaller levels: districts of about 80 000 people and local community councils. So Poland has finally moved to the three-level subnational structure familiar in the West. However, many other post-communist countries – especially those remote from the EU – are still administered in a highly centralized and authoritarian fashion which leaves little scope for coherent government at local level.

Some of the difficulties experienced in breathing life into subnational government in postcommunist states find echoes in postmilitary Latin America. There, a tradition of centralized personal power persists into the democratic era, holding back efforts to raise the status of elected local officials. Mexico, for instance, is a federal and substantially democratic state at national level but the political legacy of centralized control by the PRI, and the traditional sway of rural landowners, still prevents any sensible comparison with the federal character of its North American neighbours. Even where federalism is more authentic, as in Brazil, excessive spending by some states has caused considerable difficulties for the national government in maintaining its credibility with the international financial community. Where fundamental problems arising from economic mismanagement still need to be resolved, there is a case for retaining the levers of power at national level. For such reasons, Domínguez and Giraldo (1996, p. 27) question the desirability of decentralization in contemporary Latin America:

> Subnational governments can undermine the efforts of national governments to carry out economic reforms. Decentralization can also undermine democratization by reinforcing the power of local élites, their practices of clientelism and the power of their military or paramilitary allies. Decentralization may some day empower ordinary citizens to take better charge of their government, and permit a wider range of innovation at the local level, but there is still a long way to go before these promises are realized.

Key reading

Next step: *G. Smith (1995) is a thoughtful collection assessing the contribution which federalism can make to a world of growing ethnic conflict.*

On federalism, useful comparative collections are Burgess and Gagnon (1993), and, from a European perspective, Hesse and Wright (1996). Elazar (1996) provides an enthusiast's overview while Wachendorfer-Schmidt (2000) compares the performance of federal and unitary states. Of the older works, Riker (1975) and Wheare (1963) remain excellent starting points. For Canada specifically, see Taylor (1993) or Rocher and Smith (1995). Le Galès and Lequesne (1998) is a standard source on regional government in Europe, best supplemented by Jones and Keating (1995) or Gidlund and Jerneck (2000) on regions in the context of the EU. Collections on local government include Teune (1995a), a special issue of the *International Political Science Review* (1998) and Chandler (1993). Norton (1994) examines local government in nine countries. Two edited collections on local government in postcommunist states are Coulson (1995) and Gibson and Hanson (1996).

CHAPTER **14** | # Legislatures

Legislatures are symbols of popular representation. They are not governing bodies, they do not take major decisions and usually they do not even initiate proposals for laws. Yet they are still the foundation of both liberal and democratic politics. How then does this significance arise? The importance of legislatures rests on what they stand for rather than what they do. As Olson (1994, p. 1) writes,

> legislatures join society to the legal structure of authority in the state. Legislatures are representative bodies: they reflect the sentiments and opinions of the citizens.

Legislatures are, in potential and often in reality, the authentic representative of the people's will. For this reason they help to 'mobilize consent' for the system of rule (Beer, 1982). As representative democracy spreads throughout the world, so more legislatures are gaining the political weight which comes from standing for the people.

To appreciate the representative role of assemblies (and we will use the words 'legislature', 'assembly' and 'parliament' interchangeably), it is helpful to consider their origins in medieval Europe. Their purpose then was to represent the various estates – the clergy, the nobility and the towns – into which society was divided. As these orders became more important in the thirteenth and fourteenth centuries, so kings began to consult estate leaders on issues of war, administration, commerce and

taxation. Myers (1975, p. 23) describes how these early assemblies developed:

> the leading members [of estates] might appear in the assemblies either by virtue of their office or status, or because of election. At first the composition and functions of such assemblies were very ill defined and fluid, but gradually they solidified into increasingly definite forms which, in a traditionally-minded society, came to be regarded as customary and therefore respected.

So European assemblies were representative bodies long before they became legislatures with the sovereign right to pass laws. By contrast, in new republics such as the United States, Congress was given the right to legislate from the start. The first section of the first article of the American constitution states: 'All legislative powers herein granted shall be vested in a Congress of the United States.' James Madison, an architect of the American constitution (and of modern political thought) declared that 'in republican government, the legislative power necessarily predominates'. And so, in the United States, it did. A leading role for the legislature was judged an essential defence against tyranny; today, Congress remains the most influential legislature in the world.

Definition

A **legislature** is a multimember representative body which considers public issues. Its main function is to 'give assent, on behalf of a political community that extends beyond the executive authority, to binding measures of public policy' (Norton, 1990a, p. 1). The words used to denote these bodies reflect different aspects of their representative role: 'assemblies' meet, 'parliaments' talk and 'legislatures' pass laws.

Structure

Only two things, claims Blondel (1973), can be said with certainty about every assembly in the world: how many members and chambers it has. Both are important aspects of parliamentary structure. But a third factor, the committee system, is perhaps the most important influence on how modern parliaments work. In this section, we examine all three features of assembly structure.

Assembly size

A large population generally means a large assembly (Figure 14.1). The National Peoples' Congress in China (population 1247m) has almost 3000 members. By contrast, the smallest assembly in the world, with a mere 12 members, is in the South Pacific island of Tuvalu (population 8624). But with

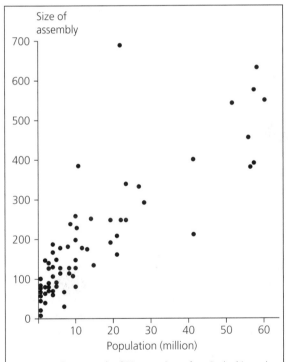

Note: Based on a sample of 70 states drawn from Derbyshire and Derbyshire (1996). Some large countries not shown include: Brazil (population 172m, assembly size 517), China (1247m, 2970), India (1001m, 545), Indonesia (216m, 500), Japan (126m, 511) and the United States (273m, 435). Size of assembly is measured by the lower chamber for bicameral assemblies.

Figure 14.1 Population and assembly size

parliaments size does not equal power. Indeed, a very large chamber – say, more than the 500–600 characteristic of the larger European democracies – will be unable to act as a cohesive collective body. It will be in constant danger of being taken over by more coherent actors such as parties or even by its own committees. By contrast, a very small chamber – say, under 100 – offers opportunities for all deputies to have their say in a collegial environment. A small chamber may be entirely appropriate for the small island communities in the Pacific and the Caribbean where such legislatures abound.

Where legislatures consist of two chambers the upper house is normally the smaller, thus gaining the advantage of intimacy. Indeed, the 'nexus clause' of the Australian constitution requires the upper house to be half the size of the lower chamber. In federations, the upper chamber normally contains a set number of members per state, placing a natural limit on size. Thus, the American Senate contains two members for each of 50 states, compared to the 435 members of the much larger and more impersonal House of Representatives.

In 2000, 112 of the world's 178 parliaments (63 per cent) had only one chamber. This proportion has risen since the war as several established democracies have abolished their second chamber, notably New Zealand (1950), Denmark (1954) and Sweden (1971). However, the main factor predisposing to unicameralism is small size; at 24 million, the average population of unicameral states is barely half that of bicameral countries (Russell, 2000b, p. 131). Unicameral assemblies are also common among new, unitary and postcommunist states.

> *Definition*
> Although some European assemblies originally contained multiple chambers, one for each of the various feudal estates, most parliaments today are either **unicameral** (one chamber) or **bicameral** (two chambers). A bicameral legislature consists of a lower chamber (the first chamber, often called the House) and an upper chamber (the second chamber, often called the Senate).

The choice between one and two chambers is not just a technical matter of institutional design. Fundamentally, the decision reflects contrasting visions of democracy. Unicameral parliaments are justified by an appeal to a majoritarian reading of popular control. According to this view, an assembly based on direct popular election reflects the popular will and should not be obstructed by a second chamber. The radical French cleric Abbé Sièyes (1748–1836) put the point well: 'if the second chamber agrees with the first, it is useless; and if it disagrees, it is dangerous'. In addition to this traditional argument, modern analysts argue that a single chamber precludes the petty politicking and point-scoring which become possible as soon as two houses exist (Tsebelis and Money, 1997).

The defenders of bicameral parliaments reject Sièyes's majoritarian logic. They stress the liberal element of democracy, arguing that the upper chamber provides checks and balances. It can defend individual, group and regional interests against a potentially oppressive majority in the lower house. An upper chamber helps to keep the lower house honest as well as providing a modern approximation to the traditional idea of a council of elders. The nineteenth-century British Prime Minister Lord Salisbury claimed that the House of Lords, the upper chamber, 'represents the permanent, as opposed to the passing, feelings of the nation'. Certainly the second house can play a restraining and revising role, providing an opportunity for sober second thoughts. Specifically, it can make useful revisions to bills, delay intemperate legislation, adopt a broad view of national problems and share the workload of the lower chamber.

Above all, a second chamber can guarantee a voice in parliament for distinct territories within the state. Thus most major federations provide for an upper chamber or 'states' house' to represent the component provinces. This device provides particular reassurance for small provinces which otherwise fear their voice might be overwhelmed by the lower chamber, where representation is based on population. So each state in the USA has two senators irrespective of population; Alaska with about 500 000 inhabitants has the same representation as California with a population exceeding 25 million. Australia, a federal system with just six states, grants 12 senators to each (plus two each to the Northern and Capital Territories). The German Bundesrat offers three to six seats to each land, according to population. Membership is still weighted towards the smaller states but not to the same extent as in Australia.

Whether federal or unitary, a bicameral structure raises the question of how the membership of each chamber should be chosen; some divergence in selection procedure is needed if one chamber is not simply to mirror the other. Generally, the members of the upper house are given longer tenure – typically, six years compared to between three and five in the lower chamber. In the United States, the Founding Fathers gave senators a six-year term, expecting that they would exhibit, in James Madison's words, 'superior coolness ... and wisdom' compared to their colleagues in the House. By and large they have done just that. Further, continuity of membership is often ensured by phasing elections to the upper chamber. Thus, elections to the American Senate are held every two years, with only a third of the 100 seats up for election at any one time. In contrast, the entire membership of the House of Representatives must stand for re-election on a demanding two-year cycle (King, 1997).

The three main principles of selection to the upper house are, in order of frequency, direct election (used by 27 of 66 upper houses), indirect election through regional or local governments (used by 21), and some form of appointment, usually by the government (16 countries). Even when election is the dominant principle, room is sometimes still found for some appointed members, as for instance in Italy and India (Table 14.1). As the method of appointment moves away from election, so in a democratic age the danger grows that the upper house will lose authority. In Canada, despite its federal structure, senators are appointed for life by the Prime Minister; as a result, the institution has been condemned as a dumping-ground for old politicians.

As a footnote to history, we should also mention a fourth method of appointment to the upper chamber: heredity. Selection through inheritance was employed by Britain's House of Lords until this quaint device was abolished in 1999 by a modernizing Labour administration. However, an earlier reform in 1958 allowed for the appointment by government of life peers (including women) who sat alongside the lords by inheritance; the life peers proved to be the more active group.

In most bicameral legislatures, the lower chamber predominates. This is especially so under parliamentary government, where the government's survival depends on maintaining the assembly's

Table 14.1 Selection to the second chamber in some established democracies

Country	Chamber	Members	Term (years)*	Method of selection
Australia	Senate	76	6	Direct election by PR in each state
Canada	Senate	104	–	Appointed by the Prime Minister
France	Senate	321	9	Indirect election via *départements*#
Germany	Bundesrat	69	–	Appointed by state governments
India	Council of States	245	6	Indirect election via state assemblies+
Japan	House of Councillors	252	6	Direct election by a mixed member system
USA	Senate	100	6	Direct election by plurality voting in each state

Notes:
* where elected.
# units of local government (100 in total, including 4 overseas territories).
+ except for 12 presidential nominees.

support. As Wheare (1968) points out, in such conditions 'a cabinet, it would seem, must be responsible to one chamber. It cannot be responsible to two.' If a government were equally accountable to two chambers, it might be caught in the grip of contradictory pressures, unable to command the confidence of one or other chamber. To forestall such crises, one chamber, normally the lower house with its popular mandate and control over the budget, emerges as the focus of government accountability. Britain is an example. The House of Commons is the dominant partner: ministers and governments emerge from the lower chamber and remain accountable to it. Further, the Commons – like most lower chambers – dominates consideration of financial bills. However, their lordships are not entirely toothless; they can currently delay non-financial legislation for a year.

Nearly all strong upper houses are found in federations: for example, Australia, Germany, Switzerland and the United States (Italy is a rare example of strong bicameralism in a unitary setting). In a federation, the democratic principle expressed in the lower house is qualified by territorial representation through the upper chamber. The American Congress is the best illustration. The Senate plays a full part in the country's legislative and budget-making process, with most bills ending up in a joint committee of both houses. Conflict and even deadlock between the two chambers is a real possibility. Since the president is directly elected, his continuation in office does not depend on Congress, thus forestalling any requirement for accountability to focus on a single chamber.

Committees

Given the complexity of many modern issues, a powerful assembly needs a well-developed committee structure if it is to exert real influence. Committees are small workgroups of members, created to cope with the volume of business in the house. Their functions are threefold:

• to consider bills and financial proposals
• to scrutinize government administration and past expenditure
• to investigate general matters of public concern.

A strong committee system largely defines a 'working' (committee-oriented) as opposed to a 'talking' (chamber-oriented) assembly.

Definition
In a **talking assembly,** such as the British House of Commons, floor debate is the central activity; it is in the main chamber that major issues are addressed and reputations are gained and lost. In a **working assembly,** such as the American Congress, the core activity takes place in committee rooms. There, legislators shape bills, authorize expenditure and scrutinize the executive.

The American Congress is unique in the impact of its committees. Although unmentioned in the constitution, committees rapidly became vital to Congress's work: 'Congress in its committee rooms is Congress at work', wrote Woodrow Wilson over a century ago. James Bryce, a nineteenth-century British observer of American politics, described the House of Representatives as 'a huge panel from which committees are selected'; his comment still applies and to both chambers. In 1994 the Senate alone had 20 permanent standing committees plus 87 subcommittees. In both chambers committees are uniquely well-supported, employing over 3500 policy specialists. In the absence of dominant parties, committees decide the fate and shape of most legislation. So autonomous did these 'little legislatures' become that they reduced the overall coherence of Congress. Their chairs became Congressional lions, powerful and protective of their own territory. By the early 1990s, party leaders sought to rein in the committees, settling issues outside the committee structure and developing 'megabills' which were impossible for any one committee to digest. But even now, the American Congress remains an institution defined by its numerous, open and specialized committees.

Committees have less influence on legislation in party-dominated legislatures. In the British House of Commons, for instance, government bills are examined by *standing* committees which largely replicate party combat on the floor of the chamber (Box 14.1). These committees, unlike those of Congress, do not challenge executive dominance in framing legislation. They are unpopular, unspecialized and under-resourced. However, like many other legislatures the Commons has expanded its system of *select* committees of scrutiny. These bodies now shadow all the main government departments, probing government policy and monitoring its implementation. The members of a select committee can develop a shared outlook which at least moderates the war of the parties still waged on the floor of the House. In the context of a parliament which remains under firm executive control, Norton (1997, p. 166) suggests Britain's select committees 'mark a remarkable advance in terms of parliamentary scrutiny'.

When the political style is less adversarial and policy emerges through agreement, influential com-

BOX 14.1
Types of parliamentary committee

Type	Function
Standing committee	Detailed consideration of bills
Select committee	To scrutinize the executive and conduct special investigations. (often one committee for each main government department)
Joint or conference committees	To iron out differences between the bills passed by the two chambers (bicameral legislatures only)

mittees can coexist with strong parties. In the German Bundestag (lower house), party discipline is firm but the committee members have more regard for objectivity than point-scoring. Scandinavian politics, also characterized by coalition governments, is similar. Its governing style is 'committee parliamentarianism', which means that influential standing committees negotiate the policies and bills on which the whole parliament later votes. In Sweden, for instance, committees modify about one in three government proposals and nearly half these changes are substantial. The figures for Norway and Finland are comparable (Sjolin, 1993, p. 174). Legislative committees are the vehicle for the extensive consultation which underlies policy-making in Scandinavia.

Apart from the party system, the key to the influence of committees lies in their expertise. This is itself a product of four factors: specialization, permanence, intimacy and support. Committees with *specialized responsibilities* and a clear field of operation are most likely to develop the expertise needed to challenge government proposals. Similarly, permanent committees with *continuity of membership* will develop a fund of knowledge which is impossible for committees created anew each session. *Intimacy* emerges from small size. Particularly when meetings take place in private, a small group setting can encourage cooperation and consensus. *Support*, finally, refers to the use of qualified staff to advise committees. Significantly, all four of these factors are present in the American Congress.

Functions

The key functions of modern legislatures are representation, deliberation and legislation. Other functions, crucial to some but not all parliaments, are: making governments (in parliamentary systems only), authorizing expenditure and scrutinizing the executive. We examine each of these functions in turn.

Representation

We have suggested that the essence of assemblies is that they 'represent' the wider society to the government. But how can we judge whether, and how well, that function is fulfilled? What features would a fully 'representative' assembly exhibit? One interpretation, plausible at first sight, is that a representative assembly should be a *microcosm* of society. The idea here is that a legislature should be society in miniature, literally 're-presenting' society in all its diversity. Such a parliament would balance men and women, rich and poor, black and white, even educated and uneducated, in the same mix as in society. Yet, ironically, achieving such a mirror of society would require interfering with the normal process of election. A microcosm could only be achieved by quota, not election. Communist states, for instance, successfully ensured high levels of representation of peasants, workers and women. But this was at the price of noncompetitive elections. Indeed, a true microcosm is best obtained by random selection, dispensing with elections altogether (as with juries). Also to prevent representatives becoming untypical of society, they would need to be replaced regularly. In truth, the assembly as microcosm is an impractical ideal – if it is an 'ideal' at all.

Today representation in most assemblies operates through *party*. That is, victorious candidates owe their election primarily to their party and they vote in parliament largely according to their party's dictates. In many countries employing proportional representation, electors vote for a party list and may neither know nor care which candidates are on it. Further, in parliamentary regimes it is the party balance in the lower house which decides the composition of government. Party discipline is also entrenched in Britain and many of its ex-colonies.

In New Zealand, Labour members must sign a pledge committing them to abide by the decisions of the party caucus. In India, an extreme case, members lose their seat if they vote against their party, the theory being that they are deceiving the voters if they cease to march behind the party under whose banner they were elected. MPs are slowly becoming less reliable lobby fodder but they are still defined, first and foremost, by their party label.

Elsewhere, party discipline is combined with at least some independence for members. In France and Germany, for instance, party obligations must be reconciled with the constitutional requirement that members of the legislature owe allegiance to the nation and not to any group within it. In practice, members of the legislature in parliamentary systems must form their own interpretation of representation, balancing the demands of country, party, constituency – and conscience.

Deliberation

An important function of all legislature, is to serve as a *deliberative* assembly, debating public matters of moment. In the eighteenth and nineteenth centuries, before the rise of disciplined parties, representation was often equated with deliberation. The theory was that politicians should serve primarily as trustees of the nation, not as constituency delegates or party mouthpieces. A deliberative legislature should represent the interests of the whole nation and the representatives themselves were expected to apply exceptional knowledge and intelligence to public problems. The British conservative Edmund Burke (1729–97) gave the classic exposition of the representative's deliberative role. Elected member of parliament for Bristol in 1774, Burke admitted in his victory speech that he knew nothing about the constituency and had played little part in the campaign. But, he continued,

> Parliament is not a congress of ambassadors from different and hostile interests; which interests each must maintain, as an agent and advocate against other agents and advocates; but Parliament is a deliberative assembly of one nation, with one interest, that of the whole; where, not local purposes, not local prejudices, ought to guide, but the general good, resulting from the general reason

of the whole. You choose a member indeed; but when you have chosen him, he is not a member for Bristol, but he is a member of Parliament.

Deliberation of course continues today even if its status is no longer as exalted as in Burke's time. However, the deliberative style varies across countries and two approaches can be contrasted. In 'talking assemblies' such as Britain's and New Zealand's, deliberation takes the form of debate in the chamber. In Britain, most issues of moment eventually make their way to the floor of the House of Commons. Questions of war and peace, of the rise and fall of governments, of turning points in national affairs, are debated there with passion and sometimes with flair. Floor debate sets the tone for national political discussion, forming part of a continuous election campaign. In 'Considerations on Representative Government' (first pub. 1861), the English political philosopher John Stuart Mill (1806–73) makes the case for such a talking assembly:

> I know not how a representative assembly can more usefully employ itself than in talk, when the subject of talk is the great public interests of the country, and every sentence of it represents the opinion either of some important body of persons in the nation, or of an individual in whom such body have reposed their confidence.

By contrast, in 'working assemblies' such as the American Congress and the Scandinavian parliaments, deliberation is less theatrical. It takes the form of policy debate in the committee room. The style here is more careful and detailed – deliberative in the literal sense.

Legislation

Most constitutions explicitly assert the legislative function of parliaments. The end of absolute executive power is affirmed by giving to parliament, and it alone, the right to make laws. Arbitrary government is replaced by a formal procedure for lawmaking in a representative assembly . The very complexity of the legislative process, usually involving several 'readings' (debates), signals the symbolic importance attached to law assembly (Figure 14.2).

Although it would be a strange 'legislature' which could not pass laws, paradoxically legislation is rarely the function where assemblies exert most influence. In executive- and party-dominated parliaments, bills (proposed laws) pass through the assembly without being initiated or even transformed by it. In Australia, the government treats the legislative

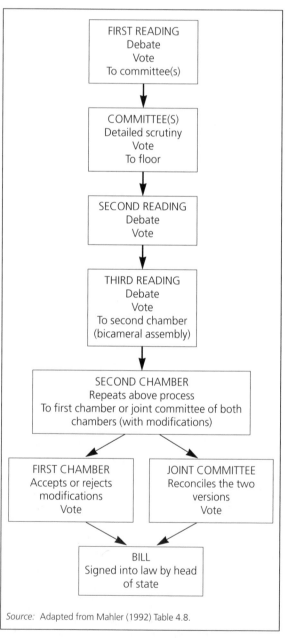

Source: Adapted from Mahler (1992) Table 4.8.

Figure 14.2 Typical steps in making a law

function of parliament with virtual contempt. For example, on a single night in 1991 it aimed to put 26 bills through the Senate between midnight and 3.00 a.m. A New Zealand Prime Minister once boasted that an idea he had while shaving could be on the statute book by the evening, truly a case of slot-machine law. In Britain, 97 per cent of bills proposed by government between 1945 and 1987 became law. As Rose (1989, p. 173) says of Britain, 'laws are described as acts of Parliament but it would be more accurate if they were stamped "Made in Whitehall"'. In the party-dominated parliaments of Britain and its ex-colonies, the legislative function reduces to quality control: patching up errors in bills prepared in haste by ministers and civil servants. Parliament is reactive rather than active.

By contrast, in the parliamentary systems of continental Europe, many legislatures do help to shape laws. Typically, the assembly works with the government in initiating and discussing bills, a cooperative pattern which is especially common in smaller European democracies. In Switzerland, a bill may originate in either house of the federal assembly on the initiative of any member, or it may be proposed by the federal council or requested by a canton. Another example of a country where members of parliament stand a realistic chance of initiating legislation is Israel, a rare case of a parliamentary system where the executive is the source of only a minority of the laws passed by the assembly (Hazan, 1997b). With parties still developing in Eastern Europe, individual deputies there also stand a fair chance of seeing their proposals or at least their amendments pass into law. A weak party system permits both legislators and the legislature more autonomy in the business of lawmaking.

But it is in some presidential systems, notably the United States, that the assembly achieves maximum autonomy in the legislative process. In the USA, the separation of powers limits executive influence in Congress, a constitutional fact which is often reinforced by 'divided government'. This means that one party controls the White House while the other has a majority in either or both houses of Congress. Even in the United States, it should be noted, most serious bills originate in the executive. However, they are then transformed in Congress if indeed they do not expire in its maze of committees. 'You supply the bills and we work them over', a member of Congress

said to an administration official. America's uniquely pluralistic lawmaking process means that, crises apart, a bill will only prosper if it does not cause offence to powerful interests. Inevitably, this reduces the coherence of the legislative programme. As President Kennedy said, 'It is very easy to defeat a bill in Congress. It is much more difficult to pass one.' Or as Davy Crockett wrote much earlier, 'Woe betide a bill that is opposed. It is laid aside for further time, and that never comes.' Because legislation is still difficult to pass even when the need for change is widely recognized, the American experience suggests that an assembly which really does control the legislative process is more of a mixed blessing than might be imagined.

> **Definition**
> The **90 per cent rule** is a summary description of the legislative process which approximates the situation in many parliamentary systems. The rule maintains that about 90 per cent of bills come from the executive, and that around 90 per cent of its bills become law. Presidential systems, especially the USA, are exceptions to the 90 per cent rule and to the executive dominance of the legislative process which underpins it.

Authorizing expenditure

This is one of the oldest functions of parliament and of the lower house in particular. The origin of European parliaments lay in the monarch's requirement for money. This need gave assemblies leverage to establish the right to raise grievances before granting supply (revenue) to the rulers. In Britain, this tradition continued until recently with 'supply days' during which the opposition could raise any issues it wanted.

The power to authorize spending may be one of parliament's oldest functions but in many democracies it has become purely nominal. Like the legislative role, it forms part of the myth rather than the reality of parliamentary power. Indeed lack of real financial control is a major weakness of the modern assembly: the executive prepares the budget which is then reported to parliament but rarely modified there.

In many countries (including Britain and New Zealand) parliament cannot initiate its own expenditure proposals; it can only approve or reject spending proposed by the government. Parliamentary approval is largely after the fact, serving to confirm complicated budget compromises worked out between government departments. Since governments cannot run without money, the parliament is always under pressure to approve a budget. For instance, if the legislature in Israel does not pass a budget within 90 days it is dissolved and new elections are held. In most democracies, once the budget reaches the assembly (or, more often, special committees thereof), it is usually a done deal. If the assembly began to unpick any part of the budget, the whole package would fall apart. Australia is an extreme case of government control over the budget. Emy and Hughes (1991, p. 361) describe the political realities:

> there is no suggestion of the House of Representatives ever 'refusing supply' since control over the whole process of financial appropriations is firmly in the hands of the executive. Only they may propose to spend money ... Moreover, it seems members of the House themselves lack both the knowledge of, and an interest in, the financial procedures which are, ultimately, crucial to the concept of parliamentary control.

The United States presidential system is, yet again, exceptional. Congress remains central to the confused tangle of American budget-making. The constitution places the power of taxation with Congress and the House specifically: 'All bills for raising revenue shall originate in the House of Representatives.' Similarly, all money spent by executive departments must, under the constitution, be allocated under specific spending headings approved by members of Congress. No 'appropriations' by Congress means no government programme. As Flammang *et al.* (1990, p.422) write, 'without the agreement of members of Congress, no money can be doled out for foreign aid, salaries for army generals or paper clips for bureaucrats'. Given the separation of powers, the executive cannot assume that such agreement will be forthcoming. The overall federal budget which the president is required by law to present to Congress each year, as well as its component parts, is also subject to congressional review. And Congress can now deploy

exceptional financial expertise in analysing the president's proposals; in the 1970s it created a Congressional Budget Office in an effort to match the skills available on the executive side.

The result is that the annual American budget has become an elaborate game of chicken. The executive and the legislature hope the other side will accede to its own proposals before the money runs out and federal employees have to be sent home without pay (this does happen). This is a rather alarming method of budget-making and evidence for the proposition that financing the modern state, like the law-making function, is too important to be left to the assembly's many hands.

Making governments

The role of parliaments in making and breaking governments is easily over-estimated. It is confined to parliamentary systems, since in presidential systems the chief executive is by definition directly elected by the people and cannot normally be removed by the legislature. Thus in the United States the president can only be removed by Congress for 'high crimes and misdemeanours'. Here, then, is one legislative function where the normally influential Congress has no role at all. By contrast, the basis of parliamentary systems is the supremacy of the legislature. The executive governs only while it retains the confidence of the assembly and must resign if it loses parliament's confidence. However, the theoretical sovereignty of the assembly in a parliamentary system does not mean that in reality it dominates government-making. In the few countries using the plurality electoral system, notably Britain and Canada, one party normally achieves a clear majority in the legislature; this party then automatically forms the government and from then on needs only the continued support of its own backbenchers to remain in office. Given that the ruling party maintains a grip on its members of the legislature, the political reality is that government is selected *through* parliament rather than *by* it.

However, in the more common situation of a parliamentary system employing proportional representation (PR), a different political logic applies. PR rarely delivers a parliamentary majority for a single party so some parties must join together to make a coalition acceptable to the legislature. In this situation the assembly does become a crucial political arena in which governments are made and in turn brought down. After an election, parliament – more specifically, the lower house in bicameral assemblies – provides the context for complex and protracted bargaining between the parties. Clearly, the initiative after an election lies with the party with most seats. However, small swing parties (so-called because they can form a majority government in combination with any of several larger parties) can also strike a hard bargain. In the end a coalition will emerge, most often containing the minimum number of parties needed to make a viable government. Sometimes the government that emerges will not even have a majority in the assembly; minority cabinets account for about one in three postwar governments in parliamentary systems (Strom, 1990, p. 8). They are usually viable as long as a majority cannot be mustered to vote them out of office through a no-confidence vote.

Definition

A **minimum winning coalition** (MWC) is a phrase used in analysing how coalition governments form. The term describes the smallest number of parties that can together command a bare majority in the assembly and therefore form a government. Theory suggests that coalitions should be MWCs, since including additional parties in a coalition would simply dilute the number of government posts each of the participating parties obtains. In practice, though, many coalitions are **oversize**: they contain more parties than are needed for a MWC (Riker, 1962). One rather unusual form of oversize coalition is a **grand coalition** of leading parties which together dominate the assembly; an example is the 'black–red' coalition between the People's and Socialist parties which ruled Austria from 1947 to 1966.

Once a coalition has formed, the ruling parties must treat backbenchers with respect lest they lose the support of members on whom their government depends. When a coalition government does fall through a vote of no confidence, the focus moves back to the assembly. A new coalition composed of a fresh combination of parties often emerges without another election. This explains why some European countries have had more governments than elections

since the war: these cases include Belgium, Denmark and Italy. Even where government is by coalition, the assembly does not itself govern but it does provide the forum for government-making (for more on coalitions in parliamentary systems, see p. 240).

Scrutiny

The final function of legislatures is scrutiny (or oversight) of the executive. This is one of the most useful contributions of the modern assembly and its growing significance gives the lie to unqualified assertions of legislative decline. Scrutiny enables parliament to monitor the activities of the government, checking the quality of governance. To emphasize the scrutiny function is to accept that the executive, not the legislature, must govern. However the assembly can restate its key role as representative of the people by acting as a watchdog over the administration. To an extent, effective scrutiny can compensate for the downgrading of the assembly's legislative and expenditure functions.

A modern assembly possesses a range of instruments with which to scrutinize the government. The three main ones are (1) questions and interpellations, (2) emergency debates and (3) committee investigations. Questions and interpellations refer to direct queries of ministers. In talking assemblies, oral and written questions are mainstays of oversight. In Britain, for example, members of the House of Commons ask a total of over 70 000 questions a year. All ministers must face the Commons from time to time; prime minister's Question Time occurs once a week and is a theatrical if not always revealing opportunity for jousting between the PM and the leader of the opposition. In other countries, questions have lower status. French ministries often fail to answer questions at all, and in the Australian House of Representatives ministers give long prepared answers to questions from their own side precisely so less time is left for opponents' queries. An interpellation is simply a substantial form of question followed by a vote on the assembly's satisfaction with the answer given. This technique is favoured in several European parliaments, including Finland, France and Germany.

Emergency debates are a second and higher-profile way of calling the government to account. Normally a minimum number of members, and the Presiding Officer (Speaker), must approve a proposal for an emergency debate. Although the event normally ends with a vote – and a government win – the significance lies in the debate itself, and the fact of its calling, rather than the outcome. An emergency debate creates publicity and requires a careful response from the government.

> **Definition**
> An **interpellation** is an enquiry of the government, initiated by the opposition, which is followed by a debate and usually a snap vote on the assembly's satisfaction with the answers given. This technique, often linked to a vote of no confidence, brought down several governments in the French Third and Fourth Republics.

Committee investigations are the third and most important form of detailed oversight. The American Congress is the exemplar here. Congress delegates many functions allocated to it under the constitution to the bureaucracy, a fact that gives Congress exceptional powers of supervision. The sheer extent of committee oversight is remarkable. On defence issues alone, 14 committees and 43 subcommittees of Congress held hearings in 1988, creating a large and possibly excessive burden on the Pentagon (Laffin, 1994, p. 184). With more than 3000 committee staffers offering support, Congress achieves a unique level of scrutiny. However even in the USA, oversight by committee is limited. It can only cast light on a few corners of a vast bureaucracy; Congress often micro-manages departments rather than setting broad targets; and committees must concern themselves with finance and legislation as well as scrutiny. But even the possibility of a Congressional investigation influences the behaviour of public officials; scrutiny is an important feature of the elaborate game that is Washington politics.

Recruitment

In a democracy, by definition, virtually the entire adult population can stand for election. Legislative recruitment is the process by which this huge pool of potential members of parliament is reduced to the small number who achieve election. In any political system, the key test for the recruitment process is its ability to deliver politicians who can contribute to their country's governance. In parliamentary systems, especially, government ministers are usually selected from the assembly so the legislature becomes the key channel of recruitment to political office. In these circumstances, legislative recruitment is a crucial political process.

Table 14.2 outlines a four-stage model of political recruitment, based on legal, social, party and electoral filters. At the first stage, legal considerations reduce the entire population to those who are technically eligible to stand as parliamentary candidates. For example, many countries apply more stringent age limits for candidates than for voters; thus, the minimum age is 25 in Italy, Japan and the USA and 21 in Ireland, Israel, the Netherlands and the UK, compared to a voting age of 18 (Norris, 1996). At the second stage, a significant social filter reduces those who are eligible to stand to those with the ambition to do so. Here, social influences on political interest and confidence, such as being brought up in a political family, are critical. At the third stage, a party filter reduces the aspirants to the small subset of those who succeed in convincing the gatekeepers that they should be nominated. Here, rules such as gender quotas are important as is the ability to present oneself well to the selectors. And the fourth

Table 14.2 Stages of recruitment to the legislature

Segment of the population	Main influence	Example
Population ↓	Legal rules	Age and residence requirements
Eligibles ↓	Socialization	Growing up in a political family
Aspirants ↓	Party gatekeepers	Quotas by gender
Candidates ↓	Elections	Popularity of government
Members of the legislature		

Source: Adapted from Norris (1996), fig. 7.1, p. 196.

Country profile **UNITED KINGDOM**

Population: 58.5m.

GDP per head: $19 500.

Form of government: a parliamentary democracy, with a hereditary monarch playing a largely ceremonial role.

Legislature: the House of Commons (659 members) is the dominant chamber. The House of Lords (the composition and powers of which are currently under review) acts in a revising and restraining capacity.

Executive: the Cabinet is the top decision-ratifying body; the Prime Minister selects and dismisses Cabinet members. Most policy is formed outside the full Cabinet, either in Cabinet committees and surrounding discussions or in informal groups led by the Prime Minister.

Judiciary: based on the common law tradition. Britain's membership of the European Union and devolution to Scotland and Wales have given more scope to a traditionally restrained judiciary.

Electoral systems: national and local elections still use the plurality system. The new Scottish and Welsh parliaments were elected in 1999 using an additional member system. The 1999 election to the European parliament used party list PR.

Britain is an established democracy whose political system has nonetheless been in transition. Traditional models portrayed Britain as a centralized, unitary state; as a two-party system, as an exemplar of parliamentary sovereignty in which ministers were held to account by the assembly; and as a political system whose uncodified constitution offered little formal protection of individual rights. Yet the accuracy of all these images has come under review, only partly as a result of the election in 1997 of a modernizing Labour administration.

The centralized and even the unitary character of the United Kingdom has been put in question by creating elected assemblies for Scotland and Wales. The two-party system has been challenged by the rise of the centre-left Liberal Democrats. Parliamentary sovereignty has been dented by British membership of the European Union and a more assertive judiciary. Ministerial accountability has been complicated by the delegation of government tasks to semi-independent agencies. And individual rights now receive clearer protection from the incorporation into British law of the European Convention of Human Rights.

The new era of transition in British politics is certain to impinge on its assembly. Traditionally, Britain's parliament (the oldest in the world) mixed omnipotence and impotence in a seemingly impossible combination. Omnipotence, because parliamentary sovereignty, allied to an uncodified constitution, meant there could be no higher authority in the land. Impotence, because the governing party exercised tight control over its own backbenchers, turning parliament into an instrument rather than the wielder of power.

Today, parliament's position has become less certain. The tired rituals of adversary politics in the Commons have become less convincing, not least for the 260 new MPs elected in 1997. The notion that parliament still possesses some abstract quality called 'sovereignty' continues to carry weight but, like many assemblies, Britain's legislature runs the risk of being left behind by the pace of political change. But not all developments are negative. MPs themselves have become more professional and committed. The era of the amateur MP is over. And new select committees have begun to enter the debate over policy.

To strengthen its position in an evolving political system, parliament will need to step further down the road of reform. Besides its traditional function as a talking assembly, the legislature will need to become a more effective working body. To influence a more complex decision-making process, committee reports must offer well-researched recommendations. Yet even as the British parliament tries to broaden its repertoire, it will surely continue to do what it has always done best: acting as an arena for debating issues of central significance to the nation, its government and its leaders.

Further reading: Cowley (2000), Norton (1993), Searing (1994).

and final electoral filter reduces those who stand as candidates to those who win the contest and finally realize their ambition of joining the national parliament. This model reveals that political recruitment is a far broader process than election; indeed, the voters join the game only at the end, when most winnowing out has already taken place.

Presidential systems operate rather differently. There, the separation of powers means that the legislature is less crucial as a recruiting agent to high office. In the USA, of course, recent presidents have tended to be drawn from state governments rather than Congress. However, Congress's scope is so wide that a career there remains attractive; the difficulty is not so much attracting qualified aspirants as ensuring that current members do not outlast their usefulness. In other presidential systems with a less powerful legislature, the danger is that is that the assembly fills up with inconsequential yes-men, as was traditionally the case in many presidential systems in Latin America. This problem is particularly acute when legislators are limited by the constitution to one or two terms of office.

Although the details of legislative recruitment vary from one democracy to another, one consistent finding stands out: in every country, the profile of parliamentarians is statistically unrepresentative of the wider society. No democratic legislature is a microcosm of society. Reflecting wider patterns of political participation, democratic assemblies remain dominated by well-educated, middle-aged white men. As Berrington (1995, p. 429) says,

almost every study of legislators in Western democracies shows that they come from more well-to-do backgrounds, are drawn from more prestigious and intellectually satisfying backgrounds and are much better educated than their electors.

Generally, representatives of right-wing parties come from business, especially finance, while education provides a fruitful recruiting ground for parties of the left. In the United States, law is the most common professional background (Table 14.3). Throughout the world, a surprising number of representatives are drawn from highly political families, suggesting that politics is in danger of becoming, to some extent, an occupational caste.

An important theme in the recruitment of legislators is the rise of the career politician. Increasingly, the professional politician, often with no background in any work other than politics, is coming to dominate democratic parliaments. The local farmer, the loyal trade unionist, the prominent business executive who takes up politics for a few years – all are losing ground to the professional politician for

Table 14.3 Occupational backgrounds of members of the lower house, 1990–92 (per cent)

	Australia	Canada	France	New Zealand	USA	UK
Law	11	19	6	14	35	13
Administration	8	10	20	–	–	11
Politics	11	1	–	–	11	7
Business	22	25	6	26	10	26
Education	18	15	26	12	11	16
Journalism	2	5	3	–	5	7
Medicine	4	4	12	3	1	1
Agriculture	–	5	3	15	4	2
Manual	10	–	3	5	1	10
Not available/other	14	16	21	25	22	7
Tota	100	100	100	100	100	100

Source: Norris (1995, table 1).

whom politics is a sole and full-time career. For the modern career politician, a typical recruitment trajectory begins as a legislator's research assistant, moves on to local politics and culminates in a prized seat in the national parliament.

What are the consequences of the rise of the career legislator? On the one hand, such members are assiduous, hardworking and ambitious. They burrow away in committees, serve their constituents and influence public policy. They are sensitive to the demands of their party and understand how to develop their own career within it (Müller and Saalfeld, 1997). On the other hand, as Berrington (1995, p. 446) comments, 'the career politician does not know when to leave alone'. An assembly peopled by career politicians is a 'restless, assertive institution' (King, 1981). It lacks both the ballast of people for whom politics is not all-consuming and the judgment of those with work experience beyond politics. A case can certainly be made that politics is not inherently a technical profession and that assemblies benefit from a few colourful amateurs to offset the dark suits of the career politician.

Definition

Career politicians are described by King (1981, p. 255) as:

people committed to politics. They regard politics as their vocation, they seek fulfillment in politics, they see their future in politics, they would be deeply upset if circumstances forced them to retire from politics. In short, they are hooked.

Of course, career politicians can only flourish in parliament when re-election prospects are good; if members are turfed out after each election, no parliamentary career is possible. This does happen. In Mexico, for instance, legislators cannot be re-elected once their six-year term is complete. In Canada's House of Commons, re-election is permitted but large electoral swings condemn many MPs to defeat. Three-quarters of Canadian MPs serve less than eight years and most members are political tourists, on vacation from other more satisfying careers (Laponce, 1994). The esteem of the institution inevitably suffers.

But such cases are exceptional. In most parliaments, re-election rates are high. The success rate of

Table 14.4 Average length of service in national parliaments

	Years
United Kingdom	20
Japan	15
New Zealand	12
United States (House)	12
United States (Senate)	11
Israel	11
Germany	8
Denmark	8
France	7
Canada	6

Source: Somit (1994, p 13). Except where indicated, the figure for bicameral assemblies refers to the lower house.

incumbents in winning re-election is over 85 per cent in Denmark, Germany, Japan, New Zealand and the USA. It is around 60 per cent in France, Great Britain and Israel. Average length of service reaches 20 years in the UK and 15 years in Japan (Table 14.4), which is certainly sufficient time to develop a parliamentary career. Indeed, the question is whether the incumbency effect (the electoral bonus to sitting members arising from their visibility and access to resources) damages legislatures. In the United States, for instance, members spend so much time 'bringing home the pork' for their districts that they can lose sight of national problems. One danger of virtually automatic re-election is that parliaments become inward-looking, lacking the new ideas which fresh blood can provide.

Legislatures in authoritarian states

Since assemblies are symbols of popular representation in politics, their significance is naturally limited in authoritarian regimes. The representative role shrinks and the assembly's importance declines. Yet although a few non-democratic rulers dispense with parliaments altogether, legislatures are difficult to extinguish completely; they are resilient institutions. In 1990 only 14 out of 164 independent states had

FOR OR AGAINST

THE DECLINE OF LEGISLATURES?

The decline of parliament thesis is that legislatures in established democracies are losing, or have lost, power to the executive. The argument is commonly encountered. As Petersson (1989, p. 96) notes, 'every description of the form of government of the modern state seems to end up with a discouraging conclusion about the actual role of parliament'. Since parliaments express popular sovereignty, the implication of the decline thesis is that democracy itself is in retreat. But is the assertion of a general loss of parliamentary authority correct?

The case for

Assemblies have lost control of the legislative process. Bills pass through the assembly on their way to the statute book but their origins lie elsewhere: in the executive, the bureaucracy and interest groups. As early as 1921, the British historian Lord Bryce (p. 370) noted that 'general causes ... have been tending to reduce the prestige and authority of legislative bodies'. He referred specifically to the growth of disciplined parties and the increased complexity of policymaking, both of which strengthen the executive. Since then, growing interdependence between countries has posed insuperable problems for assemblies. Parliaments are creatures of the state; they are poorly adapted to a global era. How can national parliaments grapple with a world of international trade, intergovernmental deals, complex treaties, intricate diplomacy and war? To be sure, a European Parliament now exists but it remains the runt in the litter of EU institutions, lacking the normal powers of a legislature. In today's conditions, the executive is where the action is; parliaments have become political museum-pieces.

The case against

To speak of the decline of legislatures in a global era is too simple. First, even if parliaments no longer initiate many bills, they continue to perform such functions as representation, scrutiny and in parliamentary systems recruitment to government office.

Second, the alleged 'golden age' of parliaments was as long ago as the mid nineteenth century; there is little evidence demonstrating that parliaments have lost further ground since 1945. Third, in some ways assemblies are growing in importance. Parliaments are becoming more significant as arenas of debate, as intermediaries in transitions from one political order to another, as raisers of grievances and especially as agencies of oversight. Televising proceedings has raised the profile of assemblies among voters. Moreover, where the American Congress led the way in equipping assembly members with the resources to do their jobs professionally, other legislatures are following suit. Throughout the democratic world, backbench members have become more assertive: party leaders can no longer expect career politicians to be totally deferential. Specialized committees, and members with a driving interest in policy, are increasingly successful in contributing to political debate. And the American Congress is still heavily involved in international trade and foreign policy, in effect functioning as legislature for the world. Anyone who claims legislatures are everywhere in retreat should visit Washington, D.C.

Assessment

The role of parliaments is changing rather than (as well as?) declining. The reality is that legislatures do not initiate many laws but this fact need not be mourned. Indeed, why should the main responsibility for initiating legislation rest in the assembly; what could be more odd, asked the nineteenth-century English writer, Walter Bagehot, than government by public meeting? What modern assemblies can do, and what many are now more equipped to do, is to oversee the executive. Legislatures possess a unique authority to force politicians and civil servants to account for their actions before a body which still represents the nation.

Further reading: Norton (1998), Sjolin (1993).

no assembly. Of those 14, only five (traditional dynastic states in the Arabian Gulf) had no experience of assemblies at all. But assemblies in non-democracies generally function only as shadow institutions; sessions are often kept short and some members are simply appointed by the government. In Mezey's (1979) influential classification, assemblies in non-democratic systems play only a marginal or a minimal role in policy-making (Table 14.5). Members concentrate on raising grievances, pressing constituency interests and sometimes lining their own pockets – all of which are regarded as non-threatening activities by the real rulers. The real issues of national politics are left untouched.

The value of marginal or minimal legislatures to authoritarian rulers is three-fold. First, a parliament provides a fig-leaf of legitimacy for the regime. Authoritarian rulers value the appearance of public consent which even the tamest legislature provides. Second, raising constituents' grievances and lobbying for local interests provides a measure of integration between centre and periphery, state and society. Such activity oils the political wheels without threatening the drivers. Third, even marginal or minimal assemblies provide a useful pool of potential recruits to the political élite.

In totalitarian systems, assemblies were even more marginal than in authoritarian regimes. Fascist states, in particular, had no time for parliamentary debate – or indeed for parliaments. Fascism was state-centred and opposed to parliamentary government. It glorified decisive action, not weak debates. It favoured the concentration of power in a single leader, not its dilution through a separation of powers. Parliament was seen as divisive, pitting party against party and constituency against constituency. Fascists condemned sovereign legislatures as the institutional expression of liberalism. For such reasons, Mussolini abolished the remnants of the Italian parliament in 1938 and introduced a new if equally minimal corporate institution in its place (p. 164).

In communist states, legislatures were not treated with quite the same contempt. Indeed, communist regimes often produced statistically representative assemblies, with substantial representation for women and favoured groups such as industrial workers. However, this feature reflected tight party control of the nomination process and the limited political significance of the legislature. In practice, a socially representative assembly has been a sign of an impotent institution; this is one reason why female representation has actually fallen in postcommunist parliaments compared to the communist era. The short sessions of communist assemblies (typically around ten days a year) were dominated by the party, which used them to outline past successes and future targets. Standing ovations were part of the script; free debate was not.

As communist regimes became somewhat more pluralistic in their later decades, so legislatures acquired a measure of autonomy. China is the notable case today. In the twelve years before Mao Zedong's death in 1976, the National People's Congress (NPC) did not even meet. However in the subsequent era of economic reform, the NPC flourished. A growing emphasis on the rule of law raised the status of the legislature. Senior figures drafted

---

Table 14.5 A policy classification of assemblies

Type	Definition	Example
Active	Assembly makes policy autonomously	US Congress
Reactive	Assembly reacts to but can influence government policy	UK House of Commons
Marginal	Assembly is a minor partner in policy-making	Many legislatures in communist states
Minimal	Assembly is a rubber-stamp under executive domination	Many African states in the era of one-party rule

Source: Mezey (1979).

into the assembly skilfully strengthened the NPC's position in Chinese politics, not by confrontation with the ruling party but by assisting the transition to a market economy and by making efforts to encourage national integration through links with sub-national congresses. However the NPC, the world's largest legislature, remains strongly hierarchical in its internal functioning. Plenary sessions remain formal and, more than in any democracy, legislative influence operates through small subgroups of senior figures (Xia, 1999). As with Chniese politics generally, authority is focused on a few senior figures, not on the institution as a whole. In short, the NPC has become part of the Chinese power network but even today its position cannot be understood through Western notions of the separation of powers and the representative function of parliaments.

Legislatures in new democracies

The transition to democracy provides opportunities for legislatures to assert themselves. Since parliaments embody the idea of representation, we should expect their stature to grow in newly-minted democracies. And the status of legislatures has undoubtedly risen in almost all new democracies, at least compared to their enfeebled position under the preceding authoritarian regime. However, parliaments remain weaker and less insitutionalized in new democracies than in consolidated democracies. Most rulers remain reluctant to grant rights of investigation to the legislature; scrutiny of the executive remains a contested function which most assemblies are still struggling to develop, not least because many new parliaments have yet to develop effective committees. The political experience of new legislators drawn into the assembly by democratization is often limited and remains so where term limits apply, as in much of Latin America (Carey, 1998). This combination of limited powers, resources and experience limits the standing of parliaments in new democracies. The revival of assemblies in post-authoritarian settings is proving to be a long-term task, a theme we can develop by reviewing the assembly's role in transitions in Southern Europe, Latin America and Eastern Europe.

Southern Europe

In Greece, Italy, Portugal and Spain, parliaments had to recover from highly subordinate positions under right-wing dictatorships. In the Spanish transition to democracy, parliament did play a key role in developing the new democratic system because it 'was the only meeting place for the democratically-minded. At the outset of democracy, it was the place where all the advocates of renewal met' (Giol, 1990, p. 96). Yet once the new democracy consolidated, the esteem of parliament soon declined as it became dominated by disciplined parties and strong leaders. Parliaments played a less crucial role in the other Southern European transitions and they remain weaker institutions than in Northern Europe. Pridham (1990, p. 246) notes that one feature of the new party-dominated democracies of Southern Europe is the limited expectations held of their parliaments.

Latin America

The position of legislatures in Latin America has undoubtedly strengthened in the postmilitary era. However, parliaments have rarely achieved more than marginal status and institutionalization remains limited; overall, their position is even weaker than in Southern Europe. In part this reflects the strong-man tradition of political leadership; the president crowds out the legislature. A common tactic has been to deny deputies even the most basic facilities. In Nicaragua, for instance, the National Assembly contains no rooms for committee meetings and at one time *los diputados* had to hold committee meetings in the open air. Reflecting these constraints, many legislators are of low calibre, a weakness reinforced by the tradition and sometimes the stipulation of rapid turnover. Many deputies remain more concerned with gaining patronage, for themselves and their district, than with shaping policy. When Nicaragua received overseas aid to improve its parliamentary facilities, the grant 'disappeared', benefiting the deputies but not the assembly. Even in a more democratic era, the realistic goal facing Latin American legislatures is not to gain sovereignty but rather to find some ways of 'restraining the prince and disciplining the powerful' (Chalmers, 1990).

Eastern Europe

In a few Eastern European countries, such as Poland and Hungary, legislatures were beginning to achieve modest grievance-raising and policy-influencing powers even before the collapse of communist rule. This experience undoubtedly helped to prepare such legislatures for the postcommunist era. In several ways, postcommunist parliaments are in a favourable position to influence legislation and policy. Unlike Southern Europe, political parties and interest groups remain weak, giving legislators exceptional autonomy in their work. Yet this potential is only partly realized. High turnover, limited calibre, poor support and weak internal procedures limit the assembly's ability to confront assertive executives (Ägh, 1996). As in Southern Europe, the general esteem of East European parliaments declined sharply once the immediate crisis of transition was over. And as in Latin America, presidents are no friends of parliaments. In Russia, President Yeltsin often disregarded the Duma; at one point, he even denied the legislature the funds needed to buy paper on which to print its laws. In a semi-democracy such as Russia's, the standing of parliament – as a body representing society and even the people – remains inherently uncertain.

Key reading

Next step: *Norton (1990a) is a helpful volume, drawing together the most influential writings on legislatures.*

Olson (1994) and Mezey (1979) offer comparative treatments of parliaments. For studies of parliaments in specific regions see Norton (1998) on Western Europe, Damgaard (1993) on Scandinavia, Close (1995b) on Latin America, Baaklini, Denoeux and Springborg (1999) on the Arab world and Norton and Ahmed (1999) on Asia. Searing (1994) is an impressive analysis of the roles adopted by British MPs. On the European Parliament, see Jacobs and Corbett (1992). The most intensively studied legislature is the American Congress; Davidson and Oleszek (1999) is a standard text, while King (1997) skilfully argues the thesis that American politics requires members of Congress to pay excessive attention to their own re-election. Committees are examined comparatively in Longley and Davidson (1998). On bicameralism, a demanding source is Tsebelis and Money (1997); Patterson and Mughan (1999) and Russell (2000a) are straightforward surveys of upper chambers. For comparative studies of assemblies in democratic transitions see Liebert and Cotta (1990) on Southern Europe and Olson and Norton (1997) on East Europe.

The political executive

The political executive is the core of government. Governing without an assembly or judiciary is perfectly possible but ruling without an executive is impossible. The 'political executive' refers to the political leaders who form the top slice of government: presidents and ministers, prime ministers and cabinets. The executive is the regime's energizing force, setting priorities, making decisions and supervising how they are carried out. Hence the executive, which makes policy, must be distinguished from the bureaucracy, which puts policy into effect. Unlike appointed officials, the members of the executive are chosen by political means, most often by election, and can be removed by the same method. The executive is accountable for the activities of government; it is where the buck stops.

Definition

The **executive** is the political tier at the apex of government. It is charged with directing the nation's affairs, supervising how policy is carried out, mobilizing support for its goals and providing crisis leadership. In democracies, the executive takes a presidential, parliamentary or semi-presidential form.

The categories of democracy and authoritarian rule are defined by how the executive operates. Liberal democracies have succeeded in the delicate task of subjecting executive power to constitutional limits. These restrain the exercise of power and set out rules of succession to executive office. Both in theory and in practice, political leaders in liberal democracies are accountable for their conduct. In an authoritarian executive, by contrast, constitutional and electoral controls are either unacknowledged or ineffective. Power may be far from total but the scope of rule is limited only by political realities, not by the constitution.

In liberal democracies, executives fall into three groups: presidential, parliamentary and semi-presidential. In *presidential government*, of which the USA is the leading example, the chief executive is elected independently of the assembly and for a fixed tenure. Presidents are elected by, and remain responsible to, the electorate. In *parliamentary government*, found in most of Europe as well as many other democracies, the head of government leads a council of ministers which emerges from the assembly and continues in office just so long as it retains the support of the legislature. An elected president or hereditary monarch serves as ceremonial head of state. *Semi-presidential government* (sometimes known as the 'dual executive') mixes the two pure types. Here, a powerful elected president coexists with a prime minister accountable to the assembly. This semi-presidential executive is exemplified by the Fifth French Republic. We will examine each of these three forms of constitutional rule in established democracies before turning to the executive in authoritarian and totalitarian states. We conclude with a discussion of executive patterns in new democracies.

Presidential government

The world contains many presidents but few examples of presidential government. All tin-pot dictators can style themselves 'president' and many do so. However, the existence of a self-styled president is far from a sure sign of presidential government. Presidentialism proper is a form of constitutional rule in which the chief executive governs using the authority derived from direct election, with an independent legislature (Figure 15.1). Presidential government is rare, confined largely to the United States where the system began, and Latin American countries influenced by the USA. Just as Europe is the fount of parliamentary government, so the home of presidentialism is the Americas. To understand presidentialism, therefore, we must pay careful attention to the American experience.

For the framers of the American constitution meeting at Philadelphia in 1787, the issue of the executive posed a dilemma. They wanted to avoid anything that might prove to be a 'foetus of monarchy'. After all, the American revolution had just rid the new nation of England's George III. But parliamentary government, in which a prime minister and cabinet are accountable to the legislature, was not yet established, even in Britain. Had it been so, the Philadelphia convention might well have adopted a parliamentary form for its new republic (Dahl, 1998, p.122). But in fact the delegates took it for granted that a single executive was

needed for 'decision, activity, secrecy and despatch'. The founders' creative solution was the presidency, an office that would offer energy to government in a republic in which Congress was nonetheless expected to play the leading role.

The United States constitution tersely states that 'the Executive Power shall be vested in a President of the United States'. He (and all have been men) is chosen by popular election, operating through what has become a nominal electoral college, for a four-year term. Under a constitutional amendment of 1951, presidents are limited to two terms of office. During his tenure, the president can only be dismissed through impeachment by Congress for 'high crimes and misdemeanours'. Just as Congress cannot normally remove the president, neither can the president dissolve Congress and call new elections. This separation of executive and legislative institutions is the hallmark of the presidential system.

> *Definition*
> **Presidential government** consists of three features:
> - Popular election of the president who directs the government and makes appointments to it
> - Fixed terms of offices for the president and the assembly, neither of which can be brought down by the other (to forestall arbitrary use of power)
> - No overlap in membership between the executive and the legislature
>
> *See* Shugart and Carey (1992); von Mettenheim and Rockman (1997).

Although the American presidency is often seen as a symbol of power, the institution was designed as part of a concerted attempt to control executive pretension. The smallprint of the constitution hems in the office with restrictions. The president is commander in chief but Congress retains the power to declare war. He makes government appointments but only with Senate approval. He 'recommends to Congress such measures as he shall judge necessary and expedient' but is offered no means to ensure his proposals are accepted. He can veto legislation but Congress can in turn override his objections. Congress, not the president, controls the purse strings. President Kennedy summarized the peculiar ambivalence of the office:

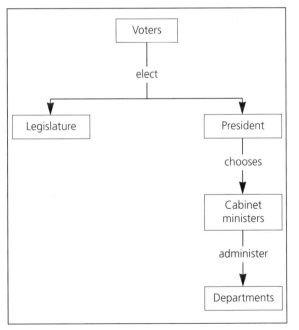

Figure 15.1 Presidential government

The president is rightly described as a man of extraordinary powers. Yet it is also true that he must wield those powers under extraordinary limitations.

Two points flow from the president's constitutional position. First, to describe the relationship between the president and Congress as a 'separation of powers' is misleading. In reality there is a separation of institutions rather than of legislative and executive powers. President and Congress share the powers of government: each seeks to influence the other but neither is in any position to dictate. This separated system, as C. Jones (1994) calls it, is subtle, intricate and balanced. It reflects a successful attempt by the founders to build checks and balances into American government.

Second, in a system of shared control presidential power becomes the power to persuade (Neustadt, 1991). As President Truman said, 'the principal power that the president has is to bring people in and try to persuade them to do what they ought to do without persuasion'. In this task of persuasion, the president has three options: going Washington; going public; and going international (Rose, 2000):

- 'Going Washington' involves the president in wheeling and dealing with Congress and its members, assembling majorities for his legislative proposals.
- 'Going public' means the president uses his unrivalled access to the mass media to influence public opinion and persuade Washington indirectly; Ronald Reagan was a master of this strategy.
- 'Going international', finally, reflects American involvement in world affairs. Every president now spends most time on foreign relations and national security issues, partly as an escape from the uncertainties of Washington politics but partly because a triumph on the world stage can pay political dividends back home.

The paradox of the American presidency – political weakness amid the trappings of omnipotence – is reflected in the president's support network. To meet presidential needs for information and advice, a conglomeration of supporting bodies has evolved. Collectively known as the Executive Office of the President, these bodies provide far more direct support than is available to the chief executive in parliamentary systems. Yet this apparatus of advice has often proved to be a weakness. Many advisers are political outsiders, appointed by the president at the start of his tenure before his eye for Washington's politics is in. Far from helping the president, advisers sometimes end up undermining his position. The Watergate scandal in the 1970s destroyed the presidency of Richard Nixon; the Iran–Contra scandal in the 1980s undermined the reputation of Ronald Reagan. One problem is that the presidential system lacks a strong Cabinet to offer a counterbalance to personal advisers. In the USA, Cabinet meetings are little more than a presidential photo-opportunity. Department heads follow their own agenda, not the president's. This is in sharp contrast to the parliamentary executive in which the cabinet forms the collective apex of the decision-making process.

The experience of Latin America democracies such as Chile, Venezuela and Costa Rica strengthens the conclusion that presidents are in a weak position unless they can succeed in mobilizing support from other branches of government. As in the United States, democratically elected presidents in Latin America have experienced difficulty in passing legislation through hostile assemblies. Indeed, as the status of legislatures has risen with democratization, so presidents have found the problems of effective governance increasing. Mainwaring's conclusion (1992, p. 113) is sobering for those who equate presidential rule with strong government: 'effective executive power is almost indispensable if democracy is to thrive, yet the history of presidential democracies in Latin America has often been one of immobilized executives'. Many strong men have ended their careers as weak presidents (see p. 252).

Parliamentary government

Where the presidential executive is separate from the assembly and independently elected, the parliamentary executive is organically linked to the legislature (Figure 15.2, p. 240). The government emerges from the assembly and can be brought down by a vote of no confidence. By the same token the government can, in most cases, dissolve parliament and call fresh elections. If the paradox of presidentialism is executive weakness amid the appearance of strength, the puzzle of parliamentary government is to explain why effective government can still emerge from this mutual vulnerability of the assembly and the executive.

Definition

Parliamentary government has three main features:

- The governing parties emerge from the assembly. Government ministers are usually drawn from, and remain members of, the legislature.
- The head of the government (called prime minister, premier or chancellor) and the council of ministers (called the cabinet) can be dismissed from office through a vote of no confidence by parliament. The post of prime minister is usually separate from that of head of state.
- The executive is collegial, taking the form of a cabinet in which the prime minister was traditionally just first among equals. This plural executive contrasts with the focus in presidential government on a single chief executive.

Source: Lijphart (1992).

If the United States is the classic instance of presidentialism, Europe is the homeland of parliamentary government. Within Europe, Britain offers a distinctive illustration. After an election the party which wins a majority of seats in the House of Commons forms the government; the leader of the winning party becomes Prime Minister (PM) and selects 20 or so parliamentary colleagues to form the cabinet. The cabinet is the formal lynchpin of the system; it is the focus of accountability to parliament and even the strongest PM cannot govern without its support. The cabinet meets weekly, chaired by the PM. Government accountability to the assembly is tight. All ministers, including the PM, must regularly defend their policies 'in the house'; the opposition will demand a vote of no confidence whenever it senses an advantage from launching an attack. However the government's majority normally offers in-built protection against such assaults. The monarch sits above the entire political process, meeting regularly with the PM but rarely if ever intervening in political decisions.

The party system and parliamentary government

The crucial influence on the operation of parliamentary government is the party system. Where a single party holds a majority in the assembly (as in Britain), government is stable and decisive, perhaps even excessively so. But the British model of single–party government, though influential, is exceptional. In most European countries, no single party wins a majority in the legislature, leading to coalition governments which are slower to form and quicker to fall. So, in effect, parliamentary government has two variants, depending on the party system. Single-party and coalition government are cousins within the family of parliamentary government; any comparison of presidential and parliamentary government will mislead unless this diversity within the parliamentary category is taken into account.

Single party government

In Britain, the governing party bridges cabinet and assembly. Through party discipline, the executive dominates the assembly, controlling its agenda and timetable. The cabinet is officially the top committee of state but it is also an unofficial meeting of the party's leaders. As long as the senior party figures represented in the cabinet remain sensitive to the views of their backbenchers (and often even if they do not), they can control the Commons. Each party has a Whip's Office to ensure backbenchers (ordinary MPs) vote as the party's leaders require. Even without the attentions of the whips, MPs will generally toe the party line if they want to become ministers themselves. In a strong party system such as Britain's, showing too much independence is an unwise career move. MPs who are thrown out of their party are unlikely to win re-election from constituents for whom a party label is still crucial.

The importance of party to the effective operation of parliamentary government is seen even more clearly in other British-style 'Westminster' systems. In Canada, 'party discipline is conformed to even more rigidly than in the UK' (Brooks, 1996, p.100). In Australia, a cabinet is more a meeting of the ruling party than of the government; cabinet is captured by party. So where the executive can count upon disciplined majority support in the assembly,

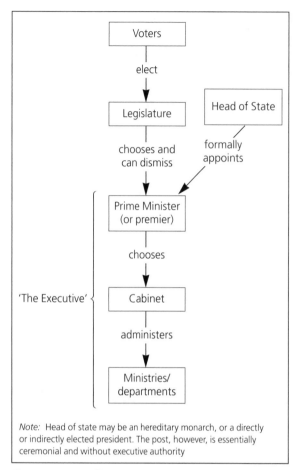

Note: Head of state may be an hereditary monarch, or a directly or indirectly elected president. The post, however, is essentially ceremonial and without executive authority

Figure 15.2 Parliamentary government

Table 15.1 Government duration in Western European parliamentary systems

Country	Period	Mean duration (months)
France (Fourth republic)	1945–58	4.7
Italy	1948–89	8.3
Portugal	1976–89	10.3
Finland	1947–89	10.5
Belgium	1946–89	14.8
Denmark	1945–89	19.0
Netherlands	1946–89	21.4
West Germany	1948–89	22.1
Sweden	1948–89	24.5
Norway	1945–89	24.8
Austria	1945–89	26.3
United Kingdom	1945–89	28.0
Spain	1979–89	30.4
Ireland	1948–89	30.7

Source: Warwick (1994), table 1.1.

as in these Westminster systems, government can be decisive.

Coalition government

Throughout continental Europe (and since 1996 in New Zealand), proportional electoral systems enable a range of parties to secure seats in the assembly; a majority party is unusual if not unknown. The result is government by coalition, a form of rule that contrasts sharply with single-party government Westminster-style. In the complex situation of a fragmented legislature, the formation and operation of government becomes cautious and consensual. After an election, the outgoing government remains as a caretaker administration until a new coalition emerges, a process which can take several months of hard bargaining. Typically, the head of state appoints

the leader of the largest party as *formateur*, to form an administration through negotiation with other parties (Figure 15.3). Once a coalition has been agreed, some countries demand a formal vote of investiture from the legislature demonstrating majority support for the new government: for instance, Belgium, Italy and Sweden. Similarly, when a government loses a vote of confidence mid-session and resigns, normally as a result of a defection of one of the coalition partners, the same procedure is followed to form a new administration, unless another election is deemed necessary.

Coalition government can be unstable but the danger is often exaggerated. Certainly, in extreme cases such as Italy's First Republic and France's Fourth, government duration was measured in months rather than years (Table 15.1). But coalitions can also be long-lasting. In Germany coalition government has proved fairly durable, helped by the constructive vote of no confidence, now also adopted in Hungary. In Ireland, coalitions have been sustained by the exceptional party loyalty of MPs and by the single-minded commitment of governing parties to their own survival in office. As a rule, coalition governments last longer when:

- the participating parties have a parliamentary majority and a compatible ideology
- the coalition is based on a small number of parties
- the economy is strong
- the government remains popular in the country (Warwick, 1994, p. 9).

> **Definition**
>
> **The constructive vote of no confidence** requires an assembly to select a new prime minister before it can dispose of the incumbent. The purpose of this rule is to prevent legislatures from acting destructively by bringing down one government without any thought to its successor. The device comes from Germany, where only one Chancellor (Helmut Schmidt in 1982) has been ousted by this method since the founding of the Federal Republic in 1949.

In any case, a slight modification of the parties in government does not constitute a political earthquake in European countries accustomed to coalitions. In due course many of the same characters return, often to the same ministries, so that continuity of personnel and policy is maintained. Indeed, in Italy one government was defeated only for the exact same parties to resume office when no other combination proved to be feasible. For this reason, Mershon (1996, p. 549) describes Italy as a case of 'transitory cabinets staffed by permanent incumbents'. Observers accustomed to single-party government often exaggerate the instability associated with minor changes to a multi-party coalition.

Heads of state and parliamentary government

One of the hallmarks of a parliamentary system is, in Bagehot's classic analysis, the distinction between the 'efficient' and 'dignified' aspects of government (Bagehot, 1963, first pub. 1867). Where presidential systems combine the head of state and the head of government in the one post, parliamentary rule separates the two roles. As we have seen, efficient leadership rests with the cabinet, premier and min-

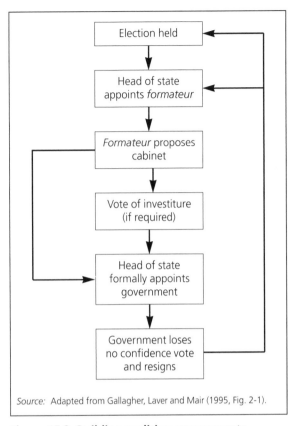

Source: Adapted from Gallagher, Laver and Mair (1995, Fig. 2-1).

Figure 15.3 Building coalition governments

isters. But dignified or ceremonial leadership is the responsibility of the head of state, a position which despite its formal location above politics still merits some attention. So how are heads of state selected? And what do they do?

The position of head of state is either inherited (a monarchy) or elected (a president). At least in Europe and Asia, royal heads of state remain surprisingly numerous (Box 15.1). Half the countries of West Europe are constitutional monarchies, including Belgium, Denmark, the Netherlands, Spain and the United Kingdom. In some former British colonies such as Canada, a governor-general acts as a stand-in for the monarch. Certainly, the duties of most modern monarchs (or substitutes) are ceremonial: banquets without end. Such worthy activity does take some pressure off prime ministers, creating more time for them to concentrate on the political aspects of their job.

Yet royal influence can occasionally be significant,

BOX 15.1

Selecting the head of state in some parliamentary democracies

Country	Head of state	Method of selection	Tenure
Austria	President	Direct popular election	6 years
Belgium	Monarch	Heredity	Life[#]
Canada	British monarch*	Heredity	Life[#]
Germany	President	Election by a joint Bundestag and Land convention	5 years
India	President	Election by a college of federal and state assemblies	5 years
Ireland	President	Direct popular election	7 years
Israel	President	Election by the Knesset	5 years
Italy	President	Election by a college containing regional representatives and both chambers of the assembly	7 years
Sweden	Monarch	Heredity	Life[#]
United Kingdom	Monarch	Heredity	Life[#]

[#] Or until abdication.

* Represented in Canada by a Governor General appointed for five years by the monarch on a recommendation from Canada's Prime Minister.

---

especially in fragmented political systems undergoing change. In the 1970s, King Juan Carlos helped to steer Spain's transition to democracy. More recently, the King of Belgium played a conciliatory role in his country's long march to federal status, leading Senelle (1996, p. 281) to claim that

> were it not for the monarchy as symbol of the cohesion of the kingdom and therefore the visible incarnation of federal loyalty, the Belgian experiment would be doomed to failure.

How are presidents appointed where parliamentary government takes a republican form? In most cases, election is employed though not always in a direct way. Sometimes the president is directly elected (e.g. Ireland); in other cases the occupant is elected by parliament (e.g. Israel) or by an electoral college usually comprising the national legislature plus representatives of regional or local government (e.g. Germany).

But whether presidents in a parliamentary system are appointed or elected, their duties are – like those of monarchs – mostly honorific. Presidents use their public position only occasionally to nudge the political agenda towards problems receiving inadequate attention from the politicians. Even directly elected presidents in parliamentary systems are expected to speak for the nation as a whole, leaving the detailed politics to parliament. One reason for the success of

Mary Robinson (President of Ireland, 1990–97) was precisely her ability to capture a *national* mood of a modernizing country.

Who governs: prime minister, cabinet or ministers?

Parliamentary government lacks the clear focus of the presidential system on a single chief executive. Rather, it involves a subtle, variable and evolving relationship between the prime minister and a ministerial college, between hierarchy and collegiality. This relationship is one of the key features of the parliamentary system. We can distinguish three broad patterns: (1) cabinet government, in which the cabinet determines overall policy through discussion, (2) prime ministerial government, in which the PM is the dominant figure, dealing directly with individual ministers and (3) ministerial government, largely a default form arising when neither the prime minister nor the cabinet offers coherent direction to inidividual ministers.

Finland provides an exceptionally clear case of *cabinet* government. By law, the Finnish State Council is granted extensive decision-making authority and in 1988, for example, it handled 4472 agenda items in 81 formal sessions (Nousiainen, 1994, p. 91). Both the Prime Minister and individual ministers are subject to constraints arising from Finland's complex multiparty coalitions. Prime

---

BOX 15.2
Chancellors of the Federal Republic of Germany

Dates	Chancellor	Party	Age at 1945	Principal achievement
1949–63	Konrad Adenauer	CDU	69	Political stability and economic recovery
1963–66	Ludwig Erhard	CDU	48	–
1966–69	Kurt-Georg Kiesinger	CDU	41	Managed CDU/SPD Grand Coalition
1969–74	Willy Brandt	SPD	32	Reconciliation with the Soviet Union (Nobel Peace Prize, 1971)
1974–82	Helmut Schmidt	SPD	27	Effective stewardship of the economy
1982–98	Helmut Kohl	CDU	15	Reunification
1998–	Gerhard Schröder	SPD	1	

Note:
CDU, Christian Democratic Union (Centre-right)
SPD, Social Democratic Party (Left of centre)

Ministers (who last only two years on average) are little more than chairs of council meetings; they find their authority further squeezed by an influential elected president. Individual ministers also find their hands tied by their party and its coalition agreements.

At the other extreme, Germany is an example of *prime ministerial* government, called chancellor democracy in Germany. The guiding principle here is hierarchy rather than collegiality. Accountability to the Bundestag (lower house) is mainly channelled through the chancellor. He answers to parliament; ministers answer to him. The strong position of Germany's chief executive derives from the Basic Law of the Federal Republic. This states that the 'chancellor shall determine, and be responsible for, the general policy guidelines'. The powerful Chancellor's Office has a large staff of about 500. The status of the job has been further enhanced by a series of long-lasting incumbents. Just seven chancellors have held office since the Federal Republic was established in 1949 (Box 15.2). The strength of the chancellor diminishes the role of the cabinet, where many matters are despatched without discussion. For instance, the key decisions about German reunification were made by Chancellor Kohl and simply reported to the cabinet. Germany's chancellor democracy, with its emphasis on clear leadership in a parliamentary framework, attracted interest from Central European states as they designed their executives for the postcommunist era.

In parliamentary as well as presidential systems, authority can drift away from the formal leaders – whether prime minister, cabinet or president – to individual ministers and departments. Without coherent leadership, the executive is always prone to fragmentation. Indeed, the debate over whether the prime minister or the cabinet holds the upper hand ignores the question of whether either does so. When central leadership falters, the result is *ministerial* government. For instance, the Italian constitution enjoins collective responsibility of the Council of Ministers to parliament but this has been notably lacking. Especially in the First Republic (1948–94), interdepartmental coordination of policy was notoriously weak and conflict became endemic. The underlying problem was that the parties composing the governing coalition were themselves extremely factionalized. These factions tended to colonize different ministries, which were thus at odds with departments belonging to other factions. Prime ministers were in no position to impose coherence on this fragmented executive; they were often anonymous figures whose main virtue was their acceptability to all the parties in the coalition. Their fleeting presence contrasts sharply with the long tenure and powerful impact of German chancellors. though even in Germany Chancellors are expected to respect the specialist authority of their ministers.

In accounting for the strength of the prime minister in parliamentary government, a crucial issue is the premier's ability to exercise 'hire and fire' control of cabinet appointments. Again, this power varies across countries. British prime ministers have exceptional room for manoeuvre: subject to some constraints of party balance they form a government of their choosing from the talent available in the parliamentary party. Only a handful of senior figures possess such stature or experience as to be too important – or too dangerous – to be excluded. Moreover, what prime ministers give they may also take away; cabinet reshuffles are frequent. Further, British prime ministers, unlike many others, can restructure government so as to vary the number of ministries. But where coalition government is the norm, the autonomy of the prime minister is reduced. In many continental countries the distribution of ministerial posts is the result of bargaining between the coalition partners, with each party filling its share from its own nominees. In Japan under LDP rule the same principle applies, but operating within the party's factions. In these conditions the premier's role is diminished, with ministers owing more loyalty to their party than to the prime minister. The chief executive is neither a chief nor an executive but a skilled negotiator and conciliator.

The final issue to address here is trends in the balance between prime minister and cabinet. The main point to note here is the flexibility of the parliamentary system: in particular, the balance changes over time with the political strength of the individual occupying the office. In Britain, for instance, Margaret Thatcher was for a long period in a stronger political position than her successor, John Major, though eventually even Mrs Thatcher was forced into resignation. Undoubtedly, the comparative trend is for prime ministers to acquire more weight in relation to the cabinet, reflecting three factors:

- Increasing media focus on the premier
- The international role of the chief executive in a global era
- The growing need for coordination of policy as governance becomes more complex (King, 1994a).

Less publicized but equally significant changes have taken place in the operation of the cabinet system. Whether or not the role of cabinet is declining, it is certainly evolving. One theme here is the growth of government and hence of cabinets. In Canada, the cabinet reached the unwieldy size of 40 by 1987, reflecting the representation principle which requires the various provinces and linguistic groups to be included in a strongly federal cabinet. Elsewhere cabinets have been kept to a more manageable size, usually around two dozen, by excluding some ministers from cabinet. This creates an outer ministry alongside the inner ministry of cabinet members. To belong to 'the ministry', to use a New Zealand phrase, does not guarantee a seat round the cabinet table. Canada has now introduced the device of non-cabinet ministers to pare the size of its cabinet.

However, the crucial development in the operation of cabinets has been the emergence of cabinet committees as key decision sites. In many countries, committees developed during and after wars, reflecting the volume and urgency of business. They then obtained more formal status in peace-time. In most parliamentary systems, full cabinet now acts mainly as a ratifying body – an umpire rather than a decision-taker. In Blair's Britain, for example, cabinet meetings rarely last more than an hour; some are over in 30 minutes (Holliday, 2000, p. 89). Decisions made by Australia's nine cabinet committees can only be reopened in full cabinet with the approval of the Prime Minister. New Zealand has around 12 committees, including an influential one that addresses overall strategy. So cabinet government, to the extent that it still exists, has become government by the cabinet *system*, with the real decisions made in cabinet committees. Indeed, even these committees now largely ratify decisions fixed up informally before the committee meets. The implication is that the strength of prime ministers now depends on their capacity to manipulate the entire network of cabinet committees, not simply the increasingly formal meetings of the full cabinet.

Semi-presidential government

Presidential and parliamentary government are pure models of the political executive. With semi-presidential (or dual) government we enter more complex and varied territory. The semi-presidential executive draws on both formats, combining an elected president with a prime minister and cabinet accountable to parliament. The classic definition of semi-presidential government comes from Duverger (1980):

> A political regime is considered semi-presidential if the constitution which established it combines three elements: (1) the president of the republic is elected by universal suffrage; (2) he possesses quite considerable powers; (3) he has opposite him, however, a prime minister and ministers who possess executive and governmental power and can stay in office only if the parliament does not show its opposition to them.

The semi-presidential executive is a hybrid, seeking to marry within the executive the national focus of an elected president with a prime minister who responds to the specific interests represented in the assembly (Figure 15.4). The president in such a system usually has special responsibility for foreign affairs and can also appoint ministers (including the prime minister), initiate referendums, veto legislation and dissolve the assembly. A president can offer consistent leadership on foreign affairs while parliament, and the government accountable to it, addresses the intricacies of domestic politics. Whatever the specific powers, the president in a semi-presidential executive is *in* rather than *above* politics. This feature distinguishes the semi-presidential executive from a parliamentary system in which an elected president plays a ceremonial role. As a two-headed system, the semi-presidential executive creates a division of authority within the executive and, for that reason, an invitation to struggle between president and prime minister.

Semi-presidential government held particular appeal to European countries facing international difficulties. France adopted a semi-presidential solution in 1958 at a time of serious unrest in its Algerian colony. Finland found a semi-presidential system helpful in managing its sensitive relationship with its large Russian neighbour. And a dual executive also proved attractive to Central European states seeking a stable relationship with the European Union after communism's fall. As international pressures recede, however, so the president's star tends to wane. France is considering reducing the president's tenure from seven years to five, Finland modified its

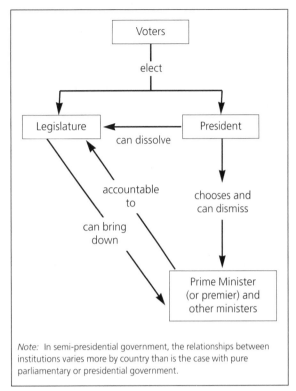

Note: In semi-presidential government, the relationships between institutions varies more by country than is the case with pure parliamentary or presidential government.

Figure 15.4 Semi-presidential government

constitution in 2000 to 'strengthen the parliamentary features of the governmental system' and some postcommunist countries, notably Hungary, are now strongly parliamentary rather than semi-presidential. While it would be wrong to dismiss the dual executive as purely a transitional device, the system has not mounted a long-term challenge to parliamentary government in Europe. Even so, the French experiment is worth closer consideration.

Definition

Semi-presidential government combines an elected president performing political tasks with a prime minister who heads a cabinet accountable to parliament. The prime minister, usually appointed by the president, is responsible for day-to-day domestic government (including relations with the assembly) but the president retains an oversight role, responsibility for foreign affairs, and can usually take emergency powers. The best-established examples are France and Finland.

France

If the United States exemplifies the presidential system, the French Fifth Republic provides the model for the semi-presidential executive. The system formed part of the new constitution of 1958, introduced to overcome ineffective governance amid fears of political instability. At the time, a war in Algeria seemed to threaten violent conflict in France itself while the preceding parliamentary Fourth Republic was widely condemned for rendering governments vulnerable to an unruly assembly. In reaction, a guiding principle of the new constitution was to free the executive from its dependence on the legislature. In particular, the constitution created a presidency fit for the dominating presence of its first occupant, General Charles de Gaulle. Regarding himself as national saviour, De Gaulle argued that 'power emanates directly from the people, which implies that the head of state, elected by the nation, is the source and holder of that power'. In office, De Gaulle's imperious style developed the office to – and perhaps even beyond – its constitutional limits. Indeed, the Fifth Republic has often been called a 'republican monarchy', a phrase reflecting the paradox of a majestic presidency in a country where the concept of popular sovereignty remains embedded.

France's president is certainly granted extensive powers. Directly elected since 1962, he serves for the unusually long and renewable period of seven years (now under review). He appoints the Prime Minister, presides over the Council of Ministers, signs decrees, appoints top civil servants and three members of the Constitutional Council, is commander in chief, can call referendums, dissolve the assembly, exercise emergency powers and has special responsibility for foreign affairs (Meny and Knapp, 1998, p. 223). In pursuing these roles, the president is supported by an influential personal staff in the Élysée Palace. So far, all five Presidents have sought to govern in expansive style (Box 15.3). Following de Gaulle, they have sought to pilot the ship of state and not simply to act as an arbiter of conflicts emerging from below.

What of the prime minister in France's semi-presidential executive? Appointed by the president but accountable to parliament, the prime minister's task is never easy. He or she (Edith Cresson was PM 1991–92) directs the day-to-day work of the government, operating within the style and tone set by the President. Since the government remains accountable to parliament, much of the prime minister's work focuses on managing the National Assembly. The ability of the assembly to force the prime minister and the Council of Ministers to resign after a vote of censure provides the parliamentary component of the semi-presidential executive.

Definition

Cohabitation occurs in a semi-presidential executive when the president's party is opposed by a majority in the assembly. This situation, which has occurred three times in the French Fifth Republic, intensifies competition between president and prime minister. In particular, the president is placed in the awkward position of becoming unofficial leader of the opposition while remaining under an obligation to represent the national interest.

The crucial relationship in the semi-presidential executive is between the president on the one hand, and prime minister and assembly on the other. While the constitution may give control of foreign affairs to the president and reserve domestic policy to the prime minister, an interdependent world does not permit such pigeon-holing. France's relationship with the EU, for instance, encompasses both foreign and domestic affairs, complicating the decision-making process. Before one EU summit, Germany's Chancellor insisted on meeting the French president and prime minister together, to speed negotiations. Presidents and prime ministers therefore need to work in harmony, a task made easier when the party in the Élysée Palace also has a majority in the assembly. This was the case from 1962 to 1986 and in these circumstances presidential power tended to flourish; incumbents enjoyed exercising their luxurious constitutional powers.

However, between 1986 and 1988 and again from 1993 to 1995, socialist President Mitterrand confronted a conservative assembly. After the 1997 parliamentary election the situation was reversed: a Gaullist President, Jacques Chirac, had to work alongside a left-of-centre Prime Minister, Lionel Jospin. In such periods of cohabitation, presidential power tends to shrink as prime ministers assert their constitutional duty to 'determine and direct the

---

BOX 15.3
Presidents of the Fifth French Republic

Dates	President	Party	Political orientation
1959–69	Charles de Gaulle	Union for a New Republic (UNR)	Gaullist
1969–74	Georges Pompidou	Union of Democrats for the Republic (UDR)	Neo-Gaullist
1974–81	Valéry Giscard d'Estaing	Republican party/Union for French Democracy (UDF)	Centre-right
1981–95	François Mitterrand	Socialist Party	Left
1995–	Jacques Chirac	Rally for the Republic (RPR)	Neo-Gaullist

Note: 'Gaullism' stood for the unity, stability, international standing and independence of France.

---

policy of the nation'. Supporters of the current proposal to reduce the president's term from seven years to five claim that the *quinquennat* (five-year tenure) would reduce the chance of cohabitation because presidential contests would be more likely to coincide with parliamentary elections; the assembly's maximum (but not fixed) term is itself five years.

Crucially, though, cohabitation has not led to a crisis of the regime. The Fifth Republic has delivered the stability that its architects intended. Just as the United States copes with power divided between the White House and Congress, so the French experience confirms that the semi-presidential executive can provide stable government even when president and prime minister belong to different parties.

The executive in authoritarian states

In authoritarian states, formal executive structures – the executive, legislature and the judiciary – are less well-developed than in democracies. The object is to focus power on the leader and his supporters, not to distribute it among competing institutions. The top office may consist of a presidency (as in many civilian regimes) or a ruling council (as in many military regimes) but the central feature of the non-democratic executive is its relative lack of institutionalization. Jackson and Rosberg's concept of 'personal rule' (1982), although developed in the context of African politics, travels well throughout the non-democratic world. Politics takes precedence

over government and personalities typically matter more than the top tier of institutions – a case of presidents rather than presidencies. Further, non-democratic rulers rely more heavily on the controlling and repressive apparatus of the state: the bureaucracy, the police and the security services, the latter often reporting directly to the governing élite.

> **Definition**
> **Personal rule** is defined by Jackson and Rosberg (1982, p. 19) as 'a system of relations linking rulers not with the "public" or even with the ruled but with patrons, associates, clients, supporters and rivals who constitute the "system". The system is "structured" not by institutions but by the politicians themselves. The fact that it is ultimately dependent upon persons rather than institutions is its essential vulnerability.'

Weak institutionalization creates characteristic difficulties: struggles over succession, insufficient emphasis on policy, poor governance and even the danger of regime collapse. The lack of a succession procedure (except for hereditary monarchies) is a particular weakness, producing a conflict among potential successors not just after the leader's exit but also in the run-up to it. As a result, many leaders of non-democratic states find themselves preoccupied with politics rather than policies. Authoritarian leaders keep their job for just as long as they can ward off rivals. Thus they must mount a constant watch for threats from competitors and be prepared to neuter those who are becoming too strong. Further, the price of defeat is high; politics can be a matter of life and death. When an American presi-

Country profile FRANCE

Population: 59m.

Gross domestic product per head: $22 600.

Form of government: a unitary democratic republic, headed by an elected president. The current Fifth Republic was established in 1958.

Legislature: the lower chamber, the National Assembly, contains 577 directly elected members. The 321 members of the Senate are indirectly elected, a third at a time, through local government for a long nine-year term. The legislature is weaker than in many democracies.

Executive: France's distinctive semi-presidential executive combines a strong president, directly elected for seven years, with a prime minister who leads a Council of Ministers accountable to the assembly.

Judiciary: French law is still based on the Napoleonic Codes (1804–11). The Constitutional Court has grown in significance during the Fifth Republic.

Electoral system: a two-ballot system is used for both presidential and assembly elections, with a majority needed to win on the first round. The last experiment with PR was in 1986 for the National Assembly.

Party system: left–right conflict remains central to French politics, though parties have been less stable. The system has become largely bipolar, with coalitions of the left and right contesting the second ballot. Jacques Chirac won the presidency for the Gaullist RPR (Rally for the Republic) in 1995. The Socialist Party under Lionel Jospin was the dominant partner in the left's victory in assembly elections in 1997.

Just how different is modern France? The case for French exceptionalism can be stated in three words: the French revolution. Of course, the shock-waves of the revolution of 1789 reverberated throughout Europe as the destruction of absolute monarchy laid the groundwork for the emergence of modern, secular nation-states. But the revolution created a distinctive ethos within France itself. Like other states built on revolution, notably the United States, France is an idea as well as a country. But in France the myths remain contested.

The legacy of the revolution is not just a disputed creed of liberty, equality and fraternity. It is also a widespread belief in the ability of the state to implement its ideas rationally, even against opposition from a diverse and sometimes hostile society. The result, it is claimed, is a strong but unstable political system characterized by haughty bureaucrats, extensive regulation, limited pluralism and a mass political culture which combines dependence on, with hostility towards, the state.

Yet French uniqueness certainly declined, and possibly disappeared, in the second half of the twentieth century. Rapid modernization, urbanization and industrialization created a more conventional and consolidated democracy. The retreat from empire left France, like Britain, as a middle-ranking European power. Membership of the European Union encouraged the French political class to negotiate and compromise with its new partners.

France's governing architecture of a semi-presidential executive remains distinctive but it works: policies are formed, decisions are reached. The party system has settled and even the judiciary has acquired some weight. 'The revolutionary impulse is exhausted', concludes Hayward (1994, p. 32). France today seems to be a normal country, preoccupied with the workaday question of maintaining economic growth and full employment.

So contemporary France is certainly no longer a revolutionary society. But to portray France as just another democracy is to go too far. Inherited traditions still condition the way France approaches its typically European combination of a cossetted workforce amid considerable affluence. Public discourse still tends to assume that the state must be capable of both creating new jobs and protecting the rights of existing workers. *Dirigisme* (state direction), suggests Wright (1997), has evolved rather than disappeared. Sovereignty is still presented as a cardinal virtue, with the result that globalization is seen as much as a threat as an opportunity. American influences, in particular, are strongly resisted. Even if *l'exception française* is a myth, it is a legend which remains important to the French way of politics.

Further reading: Morris (1994), Stevens (1996), Wright (1989, 1997).

dent leaves office, he can retire to his library to write his memoirs; ousted dictators risk a harsher fate. By necessity, then, the governing style is prone to be ruthless. The ruler needs allies but must also prevent them from becoming a threat. So favourites come and go and political management, rather than policy leadership, is the core task. We will use post-colonial Africa, the Middle East and some postcommunist countries to illustrate these themes.

Before the current era of democratization, post-colonial Africa illustrates both the weaknesses of governing institutions and the importance of personal leadership in authoritarian regimes. As Jackson and Rosberg (1982, p.1) write,

> African politics are most often a personal or factional struggle to control the national government or to influence it: a struggle that is restrained by private and tacit agreements, prudential concerns, and personal ties and dependencies rather than by public rules and institutions.

Leaders emerged who were adept at using the coercive and financial resources of the regime to reward friends and punish enemies. Other government institutions lacked the weight to provide a check on the personal rule of presidents. The incentives of patronage and the risks of non-cooperation with the government ensured that assemblies were docile, elections were uncompetitive and the courts unassertive. Such conditions favoured personal rather than institutional rule. However, like most authoritarian executives, personal rule in Africa was far from absolute. Inadequately accountable in a constitutional sense, these personal rulers were highly constrained by other political actors such as the military, leaders of ethnic groups, landowners, the business class, the bureaucracy, multinational companies and even factions in the leader's own court. To survive, leaders had to distribute the perks of office so as to maintain a viable coalition of support, a challenge that left little room for concern over broader issues of national development.

In the Middle East, personal rule remains central to authoritarian rule, for example in Saudi Arabia (Bill and Springborg, 2000). In these oil-rich states, shahs, sheikhs and sultans continue to rule in traditional patriarchal fashion. 'Ruling' rather than 'governing' is the appropriate term. Advancement within the ruler's circle depends not on merit but on closeness to the sovereign and his network of advisors, relatives, friends, flatterers and guards. Public and private are not sharply distinguished; each forms part of the ruler's sphere. Government posts are not secure but are occupied on good behaviour, demonstrated through unquestioned loyalty to the ruler's interests. Such systems of personal rule have survived for centuries, limiting the development of strong government institutions. In the Middle East, the paradox is that personal rule itself constitutes a stable system, providing an exception to the general theme of political instability in the authoritarian executive.

Personal rule also characterizes the more authoritarian postcommunist states. While central Europe has moved in a democratic direction, the more eastern postcommunist countries (including the successor republics to the Soviet Union) have seen the rise of authoritarian regimes with strong, personalized and barely accountable presidents. In the impoverished republics of central Asia, where invasions have been commonplace and democracy has never flourished, rulers are concerned with power and voters with their daily struggle; neither group cares greatly for government structures. In 1999 Western observers even declined to monitor the presidential election in Kazakhstan on the grounds that the incumbent president had manipulated the build-up in his favour. In Belarus the president initiated a referendum in 1996 to extend his term of office and to acquire greater powers over both the assembly and the constitutional court. In the central Asian republic of Uzbekistan, the presidency is even more personalized:

> power resides as much in the person of the president as in the office. The Uzbek presidency is not just a formal power position; it is also the center of an extensive informal network of regionally-based, patron-client ties. The president is, in effect, the chief patron. (Easter, 1997)

We might expect executive institutions to have played a more central role in the totalitarian systems of fascism and communism. After all, these were regimes that were politically driven. But in fascist states, at least, the institutions of government were secondary. The driving force was the personal authority of the ruler rather than the institutions of state. The state was idolized more than institutionalized. Both Hitler and Mussolini relied on the fascist party as a device for obtaining power. Once this goal was achieved, state and party merged as vehicles of the supreme ruler. The leader defined the interests of the regime and duties owed to the dictator took priority over any obligations to state or party. In Nazi Germany, for example, the notorious SS (*Schutzstaffel* or protection units) began as a party security force but underwent a huge expansion after Hitler came to power, becoming the personal instrument of the Führer (Brooker, 2000, p.136). Nazi Germany, less so Mussolini's Italy, was a political, or even a revolutionary, regime in which power bases were established informally with Hitler acting as an arbiter of conflict among the barons beneath. Power was neither contained in institutions nor exercised through bureaucratic rules; had it been, the Führer's personal ascendancy would have been threatened.

The situation differed again in communist states. Here, power was often more regularized than in fascist regimes but the driving force was the party rather than the state, at least in early decades. Of course, most communist states did have a clear structure of government (Figure 15.5). At the top, the governing executive consisted of a presidium (council) headed by a chairperson who was, in effect, prime minister, leading the communist equivalent of a cabinet. The presidium was, in turn, an inner steering body of a larger Council of Ministers which was itself formally 'elected' by the parliament. So the formal structure was parliamentary in character

though – as in many Western democracies – an honorific post of state president also existed. But in practice the ruling communist party dominated the formal institutions of the state; the key post was general secretary of the party, not chairman of the presidium. The party secretary might confirm his supremacy by taking the post of either prime minister or president but, were he to lose his party position, his power would also have gone. In China, where politics has always been more fluid and personalized than in other communist states, some top leaders have not occupied any formal positions at all, whether in the party or the government. Indeed, the Chinese case confirms that even communist rule can become highly personal in character.

Given the personal basis of rule in many non-democratic regimes, a key issue is whether such states always risk degenerating into despotism and even barbarism (Brooker, 2000, p. 129). Certainly, some communist states fell victim to brutal tyrants, despite the strong organization provided by the communist party. The Soviet Union under Joseph Stalin was an extreme but important example. After Lenin's death in 1924, Stalin slowly acquired ascendancy over the party. He methodically picked off the other party leaders, becoming undisputed ruler of the Soviet Union by 1929 and remaining so until his death in 1953. Having risen to power through the party, he eventually reshaped it into one of his personal instruments, alongside the political police and the state bureaucracy. Stalin's methods were fierce:

> In the Great Terror of 1937–38, the political police arrested some five million people, executed over 800 000 of them and incarcerated most of the remainder in prisons or labour camps. Among the victims were a large majority of the party's Central Committee and more than half the delegates to the most recent Party Congress. The Terror destroyed the party as an independent political entity; it was now officially described as a party of Lenin–Stalin followers. (Brooker, 2000, p.138)

The question remains of how far such excesses are an inevitable risk of a non-democratic executive. Certainly, one-man rule and extreme leadership cults were features of many other communist states:

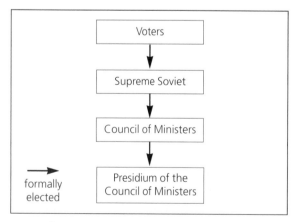

Figure 15.5 Typical executive structure in communist states

Voters

Supreme Soviet

Council of Ministers

Presidium of the Council of Ministers

formally elected

for instance, Mao Zedong in China, Castro in Cuba, Ho Chi Minh in Vietnam, Tito in Yugoslavia, Ceauçescu in Romania and Kim Il Sung in North Korea. Such cults of personality were often linked with extreme brutality, albeit rarely on the scale of Stalin's Russia. But not all totalitarian, and still less all authoritarian, regimes descended into barbarity. After all, Stalin drew not just on communist ideology and party organization but also on Russia's highly autocratic traditions. Elsewhere, communist rule was less severe. The case of Janos Kadar, the harmless Hungarian party leader (1958–88) who rode the tramcar each day to work unrecognized by his people, is too easily forgotten. In any case, many non-communist authoritarian rulers have lacked the means of social control needed to indulge in Stalinist terror. The experience of black Africa and the Middle East is that personal rule is far from despotic; it can be a balanced and stable, if rarely progressive, form of governance.

The executive in new democracies

'There is no getting away from context', comments Sartori (1994, p.135) in his discussion of constitutional engineering. By this he means, 'that political form is best that applies best'. And certainly the new democracies established in the final decades of the twentieth century are by no means uniform in their choice of executive structure. In general, post-military Latin America has retained presidential systems despite some serious academic prodding in the direction of parliamentary government (Linz, 1990). The continent's continuing bias to presiden-

tial government reflects the fear of social instability, and even violence, in the absence of strong political authority. Presidential rule may or may not help to resolve the underlying tensions of unequal societies but, given the continent's strong-man traditions, the presidential option is considered the safer choice. By contrast, postcommunist democratic states in Europe have adopted parliamentary or at most semi-presidential systems. They have sought to contain rather than concentrate political power. Their aim has been to reflect social and political divisions within parliament and to create a balance within the executive between president and prime minister. Reflecting the communist legacy, government itself, rather than the society it seeks to control, is deemed to be the danger.

The evolution of the executive in the postcommunist democracies has been particularly interesting. Eastern European countries have adopted a form of government that combines a president with a prime minister accountable to parliament. Initially, presidential authority was considerable, particularly where the initial incumbents were endowed with the moral authority resulting from leading the revolt against communism, as with Lech Walesa in Poland and Vaclav Havel in Hungary. As Fitzmaurice (1998, p. 65) writes,

There was a need for a presidency that could, in this extraordinary period of political turbulence, represent a centre of stability in shifting and often unstable parliamentary situations. There was also a need for a moral symbol in difficult times and for a respected national representative towards the outside world who could be an asset on the

---

BOX 15.4
Presidential powers in some East European democracies

	Directly elected?	Nominate PM and dissolve assembly?	Emergency powers?	Authority over foreign and defence policy?	Introduce bills?
Czech Republic	No	Yes	No	No	No
Hungary	No	Yes	Yes	Yes	Yes
Poland	Yes	Yes	No	Yes	Yes
Slovakia	No	Yes	No	No	Yes

Source: Baylis (1996). See also Taras (1998) and Fitzmaurice (1998).

PRESIDENTIAL GOVERNMENT FOR A NEW DEMOCRACY

In the final decades of the twentieth century, many countries emerged from military or communist rule to embrace democracy. In these new regimes, constitution-writers faced the question of whether to adopt a presidential or parliamentary form of government for the new democratic order. Even though they were working under time pressure, those drafting the new constitution often sought advice from political scientists in established democracies. Had we been asked, should we have argued for or against presidential government for a new democracy?

The case for

A presidential system offers the stability which is the first requirement for a new regime. The president's fixed term provides continuity in the executive, avoiding the frequent collapse of governing coalitions to which parliamentary governments are prone. Winning a presidential election requires candidates to develop broad support across the country. Elected by the country at large, the president can then take a national view, rising above the squabbles between minority parties in the assembly. A president provides a natural symbol for a new regime, offering a familiar face for domestic and international audiences alike. The leader can pursue a steady course in foreign policy, free from the volatility which would arise if the executive were directly accountable to a fractious parliament. Since a presidential system necessarily involves a separation of powers, it should also encourage limited government and thereby protect liberty. Remember, finally, that the USA is the world's dominant power and has sustained presidential government for over 200 years; there is surely pragmatic good sense in following No.1.

The case against

Presidential government is inappropriate for a new democracy. The problem is that only one party can win the presidency; everyone else loses. All-or-nothing politics is unsuited to a new regime where political trust has still to develop. In addition, fixed terms of office are too inelastic, 'everything is rigid, specified, dated', wrote Bagehot. The risk of deadlock when executive and legislature disagree means that the new political system may be unable to address pressing problems. There is a danger, too, that presidents will grow too big for their boots: Latin American experience shows that, not infrequently, they seek to amend the constitution so as to continue in office beyond their one- or two-term limit. In particular, a frustrated or ambitious president may turn into a dictator; presidential democracies are more likely to collapse than are parliamentary democracies. The USA is an exception to be admired but not a system to copy; it remains the world's only case of stable presidential government over the long term (Stepan and Skach, 1993). In presidential government, too much depends on one person. Prudence suggests a parliamentary system in which a range of interests and parties are represented not just in the assembly but also in the executive coalition.

Assessment

In practice, the choices made by new democracies seem to reflect history and geography more than the advice of politics professors. Central European countries such as the Czech Republic and Hungary have adopted the parliamentary form which dominates West Europe, mindful no doubt of the prospect of joining the European Union. By contrast, post-military regimes in Latin American countries have drawn on their own political histories, and the presence of the USA to the north, to embrace presidential government. The ambition of Latin America's democrats is to replace the authoritarian presidents of yesteryear with accountable presidential systems. If that experiment succeeds, the stock of presidential government will deservedly rise.

Further reading: Linz (1990), Mainwaring and Shugart (1997a), Manuel and Cammisa (1999).

European and world stage, especially in the battle for membership of the IMF, Council of Europe, NATO and the EU.

But as these new democracies have stabilized, so the parliamentary dimension has gained ground. Taras (1998, p.113) judges the formal powers of presidents in the Czech Republic, Hungary, Poland and Slovakia now to be 'weak'. Indeed, the president is denied the legitimacy of direct election in all these countries except Poland (Box 15.4). In practice, presidents retain a role of arbiter which goes beyond the ceremonial duties of presidents in West European parliamentary systems but, particularly in the Czech Republic and Hungary, executive authority now rests with the prime minister and cabinet, not the president. The experience of postcommunist democracy confirms that the dividing line between semi-presidential and parliamentary government is not always clear-cut and that parliamentary government remains Europe's natural democratic form.

Key reading

Next step: *Lijphart (1992) is an excellent collection on parliamentary and presidential government.*

Linz and Valenzuela (1994) and Mainwaring and Shugart (1997b) are rewarding analyses of the political executive. Elgie (1995) covers a range of democracies in his account of political leadership. On the American presidency, see Rose (1991), C. Jones (1994) and the classic by Neustadt (1991). Mainwaring (1992) covers presidencies in Latin America. Comparative studies of parliamentary government include Laver and Shepsle (1994) and on Western Europe, Heywood and Wright (1997). For cross-national comparisons of prime ministers see Wright, Guy Peters and Rhodes (2000) and Jones (1991); Rose (2001) examines the British prime minister in an interdependent world. On the semi-presidential executive, the original source is Duverger (1980); see Elgie (1999) for a more recent perspective. On personal rule, Jackson and Rosberg (1982) consider Africa, Bill and Springborg (2000) examine the Middle East, and Clapham (1985, ch. 4) offers a general account. Finally, Brooker (1995) assesses twentieth-century dictatorships.

The bureaucracy

The bureaucracy is the state's engine room. It consists of permanent salaried officials employed by the state to advise on, and carry out, the policies of the political executive. The bureaucracy is indispensable to modern government yet, lacking the legitimacy of election, it has always aroused controversy. The central strands of this debate are responsiveness and efficiency. On responsiveness, the question is how can civil servants be made accountable to the politicians they notionally serve? And on effectiveness, the issue is how in the absence of a competitive market can we ensure that the bureaucracy does its job with efficiency and economy? This theme of value for money became particularly prominent in the era of lean government in the 1990s.

Delimiting the bureaucracy raises tricky issues of definition. Reflecting the complexity of modern government, public employees have a range of employment relationships with the state (Figure 16.1). The broadest term is the *public sector*, also called the public service or public administration. This covers all employees whose salary comes directly or indirectly from the public purse. However, the public sector includes several areas not normally counted as part of the civil service, such as teachers and the armed forces. *Civil servants* proper are usually defined as employees who are

- Paid directly by the national exchequer.
- Subject to the state's conditions of service (including access to its pension scheme).
- Engaged in shaping or more commonly implementing government decisions.

Just to complicate matters, a few countries such as Germany do extend civil service status to teachers, even though this group works at one remove from the government.

Definition
Bureaucracy is, literally, rule by officials. The word 'bureau' comes from the Old French term, *burel*, meaning the cloth used to cover a writing desk or bureau. The second half of the word comes from the Greek *kratos*, meaning rule, just as in demo*cracy*. Today, the bureaucracy refers to the salaried officials who conduct the detailed business of government, advising on and applying policy decisions.

The number of civil servants with a direct *policy-advising* role, the group of special political interest, is no more than a few thousand. Most civil servants work in the field, applying policy away from the decision-making centre. Traditionally, the 'mandarins' (to use the old Chinese term for high-level bureaucrats) formed a special grade in the civil service, often filled by able graduates recruited straight from university. However, some countries have now introduced more flexible practices at this highest level, making more use of short-term contracts and open recruitment. Examples include the Senior Executive Services established in the United States (1978), Australia (1984) and New Zealand (1988).

While the word 'bureaucracy' is often used descriptively as a synonym for the civil service, it is also employed in a more abstract way as a model for organizing public administration. The analysis of bureaucracy presented by the German sociologist Max Weber (1864–1920) is pre-eminent here. Weber conceived of bureaucracy as a structured hierarchy in which salaried officials reached rational decisions by applying explicit rules to the facts before them. Specifically, Weber's model contains the following features:

- Bureaucracy involves a carefully defined division of tasks.
- Authority is impersonal, vested in the rules that govern official business. Decisions are reached by methodically applying rules to particular cases; private motives are irrelevant.
- People are recruited to serve in the bureaucracy based on proven or at least potential competence.
- Officials who perform their duties competently have secure jobs and salaries. Competent officials can expect promotion according to seniority or merit.
- The bureaucracy is a disciplined hierarchy in which officials are subject to the authority of their superior.

Weber's central claim was that bureaucracy made administration more efficient and rational; he believed that it was the means by which modern industrial efficiency could be brought to bear on civil affairs. To quote Weber himself:

the fully developed bureaucratic apparatus compares with other organizations exactly as does the machine with non-mechanical modes of production. Precision, speed, clarity, knowledge of files, continuity, discretion, unity, strict subordination, reduction of friction and of material and personal costs – these are raised to the optimum in the strictly bureaucratic administration. (Gerth and Mills, 1948)

For Weber, the ideal bureaucracy was a fine piece of administrative machinery. But like many modern devices, bureaucracy brought the risk of dominating its supposed masters. Weber's contribution was therefore to pose the question of the relationship between bureaucracy and democracy, a concern that inspired much discussion of the bureaucracy in the twentieth century.

Evolution

To appreciate why Weber considered modern bureaucracy so efficient, we must consider what preceded it. The precursors varied between Europe and the new world. In Europe, clerical servants were originally agents of the royal household, serving under the personal instruction of the ruling monarch (Raadschelders and Rutgers, 1996). Many features of modern bureaucracies – regular salaries, pensions, open recruitment – arose from a successful attempt to overcome this idea of public employment as personal service to the monarch. Indeed, the evolution of royal households into twentieth-century Weberian bureaucracies was a massive transformation, intimately linked to the rise of the modern state itself. It was a transition from patriarchy to bureaucracy, a story of the depersonalization of administration as the royal household was slowly converted into public service (Hyden, 1997, p. 243). Today, we take the features of bureaucratic organization for granted but for Weber the form was strikingly new, a modern phenomenon to be both admired and feared.

In the new world, however, civil service development was more pragmatic. Lacking the long state tradition of West Europe, public administration was initially considered a routine application of political directives. In the United States, the original philosophy was that almost every citizen was qualified for almost every public job; indeed, a professional civil service was considered somewhat undemocratic (Christensen and Guy Peters, 1999, p. 100). This populist theory conveniently underpinned the spoils system, a term deriving from the phrase 'to the

Figure 16.1 Delimiting the bureaucracy

victor, the spoils'. Spoils meant that successful candidates, including newly-elected presidents, were expected to distribute government jobs to those who had taken the trouble to support their campaign. The spoils system continued at least until 1883 when the Pendleton Act created a Civil Service Commission to recruit and regulate federal employees. So where a merit-based bureaucracy had emerged in Europe in reaction to monarchy, in the USA a professional administration supplanted spoils.

In the twentieth century, bureaucracies reached their zenith. The depression and two world wars vastly increased government intervention in society. The welfare state, completed in Europe in the decades following the Second World War, required a massive Weberian bureaucracy to distribute grants, allowances and pensions in accordance with complex eligibility conditions set by politicians. By 1980, public employment accounted for almost a third of the total in Britain and Scandinavia, though much of the expansion had occurred at local level.

However, the final quarter of the twentieth century witnessed declining faith in government and, more to the point, deteriorating public finances. Seizing on this fiscal crisis, right-wing politicians such as Ronald Reagan and Margaret Thatcher called for, and to an extent delivered, not just a reduced role for the state but also a changing style of bureaucratic operation away from strict Weberian guidelines. As a result, the contemporary emphasis is on management, results and efficiency. At the start of the twenty-first century, modern civil servants therefore face conflicting expectations. At one and the same time, they are expected to show flexibility but also to abide by rules; to deliver results but also to work within set procedures; and to act decisively while also consulting widely.

Recruitment

Recruitment to bureaucracies has evolved in tandem with the development of the civil service itself. The shift from patrimonial to Weberian bureaucracies was a transition from recruitment by personal links with the ruler to open selection on merit. Jobs became available, at least in theory, to the whole population. Even though these reforms occurred in

most democracies as long ago as the late nineteenth century, recruitment to the civil service remains an important theme. Selection methods and employee profiles are scrutinized more carefully than in the private sector. Further, what counts as 'merit' still varies between countries, revealing subtle contrasts in conceptions of a civil servant's role.

> **Definition**
> In a **unified** (or **generalist**) bureaucracy, recruitment is to the civil service as a whole, not to a specific job within it. Administrative work is conceived as requiring intelligence, education and appropriate personal skills but not technical knowledge. By contrast, a **departmental** (or **specialist**) approach recruits people with specialist backgrounds to a specific department or job. Unified bureaucracies are career-based while departmental civil services are job-based.

Britain exemplifies the unified (or generalist) tradition, pushing the cult of the amateur to extremes. Administration is seen as the art of judgment, born of intelligence and honed by experience. Specialist knowledge should be sought by bureaucrats but then treated with scepticism; experts should be on tap but not on top. Recruiters look for general ability, not technical expertise. All-round ability should enable successful candidates to acquire or at least interpret whatever technical knowledge is needed; the key requirement is not knowledge but the ability to learn. For the same reason, a good administrator should be able to serve in a variety of departments and will be more rounded for doing so.

An alternative method of pursuing the unified approach is to recruit to a *corps* (body) of civil servants rather than to a specific job in a ministry. The French civil service, for example, recruits civil service through competitive examinations to such bodies as the Diplomatic Corps or the Finance Inspectorate. Certainly, these *corps* offer their own specialized post-entry training but the seemingly technical basis of this training is rather misleading. Although civil service recruitment is in theory to a specific *corps*, it is in reality as much to an élite which encompasses both public and private realms. Even within the civil service over a third of *corps* members are working away from their home *corps* at any one time. At its highest levels, the French bureaucracy is clearly generalist albeit with *corps* that provide more of a bow to specialized training than is offered in Britain.

> **Definition**
> The theory of **representative bureaucracy** claims that a civil service recruited from all sections of society will produce policies that are responsive to the public and, in that sense, democratic (Meier, 1993, p. 1). **Passive representation** exists when the demographic profile of the bureaucracy matches that of the population. **Active representation** occurs when civil servants take the same decisions as would be made by the represented – that is, the public.

Some unified civil services stress one particular form of technical expertise: law. In many European countries with a codified law tradition, a legal training is common among higher bureaucrats. Germany is a good illustration. Over 60 per cent of top German civil servants are lawyers, compared to just 20 per cent in the United States. The German model has influenced other countries, notably Japan, where the recruitment base is narrower still. Most of those who pass through the 'dragon gate' examination for recruitment to high-level positions in the Japanese civil service are graduates of just one department: Tokyo University's law school. Where law is less central to politics, however, the dominance of legal training has declined as other degrees, such as economics, have achieved recognition. For instance since 1945, the percentage of law graduates among civil servants working in Norway's central ministries has fallen from a half to a fifth (Christensen and Egeberg, 1997).

In a departmental (specialist) system, recruiters follow a different philosophy from the generalist approach of, say, Britain. They look for specialist experts for individual departments, with more movement in and out of the civil service at a variety of levels. The Finance Ministry will recruit economists and the Department of Health will employ staff with medical training. Recruitment is to particular posts, not to an élite group or corps. This model is common in countries with a weak state in which the administration lacks the status produced by centuries of service to pre-democratic rulers. The United States, New Zealand and the Netherlands are examples. In the Netherlands, each department sets its own recruitment standards, normally requiring

training or expertise in its own area. Once appointed, mobility within the civil service is limited; staff who remain in public service usually stay in the one department for their entire career (Andeweg and Irwin, 1993, p. 176). The notion of recruiting talented young graduates to an élite, unified civil service is weak or non-existent.

Organization

Here we examine the detailed organization of central government activity, looking at how the cogs of the administrative machine are arranged. Although structures – and labels – vary by country, we can distinguish three kinds of organization (Box 16.1). The first and most important unit is the department (sometimes called ministry) where policy is made. In nearly all countries, a dozen or so established departments form the stable core of central government. A second unit comprises the divisions, sections or bureaus into which departments are divided. These are the operating units of government – the powerhouses where expertise resides and in which detailed policy is both formed and applied (to complicate matters, these divisions are sometimes called 'depart-

> **BOX 16.1**
> *The organization of government: departments, divisions and agencies*
>
> **Government department or ministry**
> An administrative unit over which a minister exercises direct management control. Usually structured as a formal hierarchy and often established by statute.
>
> **Division, section or bureau**
> An operating unit of a department, responsible to the minister but often with considerable independence in practice (especially in the USA, where many such divisions are called 'agencies').
>
> **Non-departmental public body**
> Operates at one or more removes from the government, in an attempt to provide management flexibility and political independence. Sometimes called 'quangos', a term of American origin that originally meant 'a quasi non-governmental organization' but which is often now taken to mean a 'quasi-governmental organization'.

FOR OR AGAINST

A REPRESENTATIVE BUREAUCRACY?

The social background of senior civil servants is invariably unrepresentative of the general population. In the Western world, the typical high-level civil servant is a male graduate, from an urban background and from a middle or upper-class family that was itself active in public affairs (Aberbach *et al.*, 1981, p. 80). These findings have disturbed advocates of a 'representative bureaucracy'. This term was introduced by Kingsley (1944), an American scholar who claimed that the middle-class composition of Britain's civil service exploded the myth of its supposedly neutral bureaucracy. By implication, the same argument could be applied to other countries. But should we concerned about the social skew of public servants? And, if so, should recruitment on merit be modified by positive discrimination in favour of under-represented groups such as ethnic minorities and women?

The case for

Three arguments support the thesis that a bureaucracy should reflect the social profile of the population:

- Civil servants whose work involves direct contact with specific groups will be better at the job if they also belong to that category. A shared language is the most obvious example but the point can perhaps be extended to ethnicity and gender.
- A civil service balanced between particular groups, such as religions or regions, may encourage stability in divided societies such as Northern Ireland.
- Democracy is said to involve government by, and not just for, the people. A representative civil service, involving participation by all major groups in society, will enhance the acceptability of decisions. Positive discrimination in favour of under-represented groups is the only effective solution to the problem. But it will only be needed for a short period because, once a representative bureaucracy is established, it will maintain itself naturally as minorities notice the role models in post and become more likely to apply for jobs themselves.

The case against

The principle of recruitment on merit is fundamental to public administration and should not be abandoned in favour of social engineering. The public interest is best served by selecting the best people for the job, irrespective of their background. The correct solution to under-representation is not positive discrimination but improving the qualifications of the excluded minorities. In any case, positive discrimination creates two problems of its own. First, those denied jobs because they belong to the 'wrong' social category are naturally resentful. Secondly, those who are accepted just because they come from the 'right' social background are placed in an awkward position. In any case, it is far from clear that the narrow social background of senior civil servants does produce the prejudice against the left that Kingsley claimed to detect. Norwegian studies show that the attitudes of civil servants depend more on their post, level and department than on their social or educational background: 'where you stand depends on where you sit' (Laegreid and Olsen, 1978). And where civil servants are allowed to pursue political careers, they frequently join parties of the left. In France, a third of the senior public servants elected to the French National Assembly in 1978 were members of the Socialist Party. Generally, the dominant ideology among top bureaucrats seems to be centrist, not conservative (Aberbach *et al.*, 1981). Broadening the social base of recruits would not, in practice, change bureaucratic decisions.

Assessment

The arguments for a representative public service did lead to affirmative action programmes in some countries, notably the United States, in the 1970s and 1980s. Considerable efforts were made to ensure that the staff profile matched that of the wider population. Canadian governments, concerned since the 1960s to improve recruitment from French-speakers, also extended their recruitment efforts. However, such schemes never achieved the same popularity in Europe, perhaps because they would have involved accepting the inadequacy of the constitutional requirement of neutrality imposed on some civil services there. Even in North America, attitudes were ambivalent, reflecting a tension between social engineering and merit-based recruitment. In any event, affirmative action schemes lost momentum in the more conservative 1990s.

Further reading: Birch (1972), Kingsley (1944), Meier (1993), van der Meer and Roborgh (1996).

ments' in countries where the larger unit is termed a 'ministry'). And the third unit is the non-departmental body operating at one or more removes from ministries. These semi-detached organizations combine public funding with operational autonomy; they are growing in number and significance.

Departments and divisions

Government departments (or ministries) form the centrepiece of modern bureaucracies. Here we find the bodies pursuing the traditional tasks of government: for example, finance, defence and foreign affairs. The United States has 14 departments, each headed by a Secretary of State appointed by the President. The Netherlands has 13; Canada, always prone to political inflation, has over 20. New Zealand leads the field with around 40 departments, though a single minister may take charge of several departments.

Most countries follow a similar sequence in introducing departments. The first to be established are those performing the core functions of the state: finance, law and order, defence and foreign affairs. These ministries are often as ancient as the state itself. In the United States, for instance, the Departments of State, Defense, Justice and the Treasury each date from 1789. At a later stage countries add extra ministries to deal with new functions. Initially these are usually agriculture (1889 in the USA) and commerce (1913), followed later in the twentieth century by welfare departments dealing with social security, education, health and housing.

Reflecting Weber's principles, departments are usually organized in a clear hierarchy. A single minister sits at the pinnacle of the organization albeit often supported in large departments by junior ministers with responsibilities for specific divisions. A senior civil servant, often called the Secretary, is responsible for administration and for forming the crucial bridge between political and bureaucratic levels (in Japan this person is called the vice-minister, reflecting the high status of top bureaucrats there). Table 16.1 shows the elaborate structure of the German Economics Ministry, a fine illustration of Weber's quasi-military chain of command.

Departments are typically arranged into several

Table 16.1 The structure of Germany's Ministry of Economics

Position	Number of positions	Service level
The minister	1	–
State secretaries	2	Political officials
Department heads	8	Political officials
Subdepartment heads	34	Higher service
Section heads	175	Higher service
Section assistants	460	Higher service
Caseworkers	615	Elevated service
Clerical/secretarial	822	Intermediate service
Messengers etc.	288	Lower-level service

Note: In Germany, 'political officials' are tenured civil servants who must be transferred to another job of suitable status if not retained by their minister.

Source: Conradt (2001) table 8 1.

divisions, each responsible for an aspect of the organization's work. Thus an Education Department might have separate divisions for primary, secondary and higher education – and, in practice, for many other aspects of its work. Divisions are the operating units of departments, the sections within which the work gets done. They are the work-horses of government, the store of its experience and, in practice, the site where many important decisions are reached. In short, divisions within ministries are the engine-rooms of government.

In many democracies, such divisions or bureaus acquire added importance because they are partially autonomous from their parent department. The extreme example is the USA, whose bureaucracy is the great exception to the principle of hierarchy in departments. Even in their formal structure, American departments are more like multinational corporations, containing many divisions jostling within a single shell. The departments are merely the wrapping round a collection of disparate divisions and it is these bureaus which form the main operating units of the federal government. For example, within the Department of Health and Human

Services it is divisions such as the Social Security Administration and the Family Support Administration which administer specific federal welfare schemes. Reporting formally to the President, bureau chiefs spend much of their time ensuring their operational independence from the White House. Congress, not the president, creates and funds bureaus. And what Congress gives it can (and occasionally does) take away. The autonomy of bureaus within American departments is a major and often under-estimated reason why American presidents experience such difficulty in imposing their will on Washington's complex political process.

The contrast between America's fragmented bureaucracy and the German system of hierarchical departments could hardly be more extreme. Even in Germany, however, it would be wrong to suppose that working practices correspond exactly to the organization chart implied in Table 16.1, with its reassuring impression of information moving smoothly up and down the administrative pyramid. In practice, the 2000 divisions ('sections') of the German federal ministries possess a concentration of expertise that enables them to block or at least circumvent changes proposed from on high. In most other democracies, too, divisions within departments possess their own ethos derived from long experience with their area. This 'house view' can breed a natural cynicism towards the latest political initiative and the top minister may need to circumvent divisional resistance by seeking advice from political advisers.

Non-departmental public bodies

The defining feature of non-departmental public bodies is that in theory they operate at one remove from government departments, with a formal relationship of at least semi-independence. Such institutions occupy an ambivalent position, created and funded by the government but in contrast to divisions within a department they are free from day-to-day ministerial control. Once appointed by the government, the members of such bodies are expected to operate with considerable autonomy. In the United States, where such agencies are prominent, leading examples include the Central Intelligence Agency (CIA), the Environmental Protection Agency (EPA) and the National Aeronautics and Space Administration (NASA).

Scandinavian countries, notably Sweden, have also long relied on non-departmental bodies to implement policy set by the ministry.

In Sweden, government departments are small and ministers exercise no authority over the implementation of policy. Rather, a network of independent and relatively autonomous central boards and agencies – the Social Welfare Board, the National Labour Market Board, the National Pensions Board, etc. – oversee policy directives (Arter, 1999, p. 154).

Non-departmental public bodies are established for a range of reasons. These include: to provide protection from political influence, to operate with more flexibility than would be acceptable for a division of a ministry, to acknowledge the professional status of staff employed in them or simply as a response to short-term pressure to 'do something' about a problem. Throughout the democratic world, non-departmental bodies are growing in number, complicating not just the academic task of mapping government but also the practical job of ensuring that the government as a whole acts in a coherent manner. Indeed, modern governance cannot be understood without delving deeper into the undergrowth of these organizations.

A traditional and distinctive form of non-departmental public body was the government corporation, a state-owned enterprise (SOE) established by law to sell goods and services, with no private shareholders. Examples include Canada's Crown Corporations, the US Postal Service and Britain's nationalized industries. Although such bodies were supposed to operate at arm's-length from government, political interference often led to overstaffing and under-investment. In Britain, most government corporations were sold back to the private sector during Conservative rule between 1979 and 1997, a policy that has now been copied by other countries. Indeed, the SOEs that remain in public hands in Britain, such as the Post Office, face growing competition in international markets from private companies advantaged by their freedom to raise money from the market for investment.

Yet far from the privatization earthquake destroying the role of the state in the economy, it has simply reshaped the landscape of regulation. Ownership and control have given way to supervision. Today, the most important non-departmental public bodies are not government corporations but regulatory agencies. These are organizations charged (normally by statute) with regulating not just newly-privatized sectors but also any aspect of social life where a public interest is held to be at stake – such as natural monopolies (e.g. water supply), adoption, broadcasting, medical research and nuclear energy. Britain now has well over 100 regulatory bodies, employing over 20 000 people and costing around £1 billion ($1.5 billion) per year. The media entrepreneur Rupert Murdoch even claims that regulation represents socialism's comeback trail; his view is that 'socialism is alive and well, and living in regulatory agencies' (see also p. 281).

Certainly, newly-privatized companies are subject to detailed regulation, especially when – as with telecommunications corporations – they inherit a dominant market share. The hope, at least partly reflected in reality, is that regulatory agencies will act as a buffer between the government and the regulated bodies, reducing the excessive intervention which held back many government corporations. However, the danger is that such agencies will come to serve the interests of those they supervise. This phenomenon is called 'regulatory capture' and has been widely observed, not least with state utility commissions in the United States (Wilson, 1989). Even if regulators avoid capture, they will still want to perpetuate their own existence, a bias which leads them to over-value the need for public regulation in sectors that may have become at least as competitive as those which have no such supervision at all.

Reflecting their importance, government corporations and regulatory agencies are usually established by a specific statute (i.e. law). However, ministers also set up non-statutory organizations to offer advice or provide an executive function in specialized areas of activity. Whether a particular function is handled by a statutory or non-statutory body varies by country but non-statutory examples might include scientific advisory panels, research funding committees, arts councils and training boards. Although much of their work is routine, non-statutory bodies still attract recurring if sometimes unjust criticism. In contrast to bodies established under law, they usually report to the sponsoring minister, not to the assembly. Membership tends to be seen as political patronage and accountability is regarded as

opaque and intermittent. Criticism is especially sharp in countries such as Britain where the myth of parliamentary sovereignty still conditions political discourse. But even in Britain many non-statutory bodies survived a crusading cull launched by Mrs Thatcher in the 1980s. Indeed, the subsequent Labour administration was inclined to create more new ones. Even if many non-statutory bodies do outlast their usefulness, the device seems to be indispensable in providing ministers with a flow of information and advice on specialized topics.

Accountability

How should civil servants be accountable for their actions? Given its detailed knowledge, its permanence, its scale and its control of policy implementation, the bureaucracy is bound to be more than a mechanical conduit for political directives. Senior public employees – department secretaries, heads of divisions, chairs of non-departmental public bodies – are invariably in a position to influence policy. The 'problem' of controlling bureaucratic 'power' in a democracy was a particular concern of Weber's (Gerth and Mills, 1948, pp. 232–5). He identified the danger of public 'servants' coming to dominate their elected 'masters'. Indeed, Weber argued that

under normal conditions, the power position of a fully developed bureaucracy is always overwhelming. The 'political master' finds himself in the position of the 'dilettante' who stands opposite the 'expert,' facing the trained official who stands within the management of administration.

As Weber himself realized, his model of civil servants reporting to a single minister in a self-contained department provided inadequate accountability in practice. Today, more emphasis is placed on a looser but also more flexible view of accountability. High-level civil servants are increasingly subject to 'multiple accountabilities' – for example, to the prime minister, the finance ministry and to agreements with other organizations (international and domestic) as well as to the ministers in their own department. Polidano (1998, p. 3) argues that in a complex environment, where most policy-making involves coordination between several organizations, 'bureaucrats can be prevented from complying with ministerial directions, however legitimate those directions may be. Multiple accountabilities are an inescapable part of the reality of government' (Polidano, 1998, p. 35). For such reasons, many analysts now accept that senior administrators should learn and indeed be taught 'political craft' – the ability to see policy options in their political context (Goetz, 1997).

So the issue today is not so much preventing the bureaucrats from influencing policy as ensuring some measure of accountability for the decisions which public servants help to shape. Box 16.2 distinguishes two main forms of accountability: internal controls within the civil service (including here direction by the minister) and the increasing range of accountabilities to external bodies such as the legislature and the judiciary. We discuss each type separately.

Internal controls

The traditional form of bureaucratic accountability is, of course, to the minister in charge of the department. Ministers direct; public servants execute. Although no longer sufficient, hierarchical control by a minister remains an essential part of bureaucratic accountability. However, in practice, the capacity of ministers to exert such control is conditioned by two other factors: the reach of political appointments into the bureaucracy and the use ministers make of personal advisers.

In theory, the greater the number of political appointments to a department, the easier it is to ensure political accountability. Recognizing that senior bureaucrats must inevitably set their work in a political context, many established democracies now tend to staff important ministries with politically loyal and sympathetic civil servants. This practice, long familiar in Germany and Finland, is spreading to other Western democracies. Increasingly, politicians want civil servants who are, in Mrs Thatcher's famous phrase, 'one of us.' As Page and Wright (1999, p. 278) write,

> there is a common trend among administrative systems which stress the norm of civil service neutrality to appoint, either as civil servants or advisers, people in whom one has trust. Increasing

---

BOX 16.2
Forms of bureaucratic accountability

Internal controls

Ministerial direction
Formal regulation
Competition between departments
Professional standards

External scrutiny by

Legislature and judiciary
Ombudsmen
Interest groups and the mass media

Sources: Polidano (1998), Stone (1995).

---

political influence in senior appointments suggests the possibility that membership of a 'neutral' civil service is decreasing as a guide to trust among political élites.

Yet it is far from clear that in practice ministerial control does increase with the number of political appointments. In the United States, an incoming president appoints around 3000 people, a task which itself becomes an administrative distraction for a new president. Ministers who want to get things done might be well-advised to trust their civil servants more and not seek ever-closer political control.

Political accountability of the bureaucracy can also be aided by providing ministers with personal advisory staff. Because such gurus are not part of the department's permanent staff, they can act as their minister's eyes and ears, reporting back on issues which might otherwise be lost in the official hierarchy. The Executive Office of the President and the White House Office of the American presidency are the fullest expression of this approach. These offices form a counter-bureaucracy within the political system and one that is more likely to be ideologically or politically driven than the formal bureaucracy. Again, however, this sword has two edges. Political advisers may help to assert political control but they create their own problems of accountability. Advisers are neither elected nor vetted by Congress. The danger is that they are too dependent on their patron, preferring to offer blandishments and flattery rather than home truths.

A preferable system, perhaps, is the French *cabinet* (not to be confused with the cabinets which form the apex of the government in parliamentary systems). A French *cabinet* is a group of about 15 to 20 people who form the minister's personal advisory staff and work directly under his or her control. *Cabinets* provide the minister with ideas and help in liaising with the department, other ministries, the party and the constituency. However, most *cabinet* members come from the civil service and return to it after a few years with their minister. Thus the French system offers a method of securing political advisers who are more than mere yes-men.

In addition to formal control by their minister, public officials are subject to increasing scrutiny by an army of regulators within government: the 'waste watchers, quality police and sleaze busters' as Hood *et al.* (1999) term them. Auditors inspect the books, standard-setters check performance, funders assess the outcomes achieved and assorted inspectors monitor everything from employment trends to recycling rates. Contemporary ideology may preach a bonfire of regulations but modern practice is an overdose of inspection, sometimes breeding cynicism among officials and occasionally distracting from the main business at hand. To illustrate the growth of oversight, Hood *et al.* (1999, p. 42) project 10 regulating bodies for each UK government department by the end of the twenty-first century should the rate of regulatory expansion observed in the final quarter of the twentieth century continue unchecked.

A more informal, but no less effective, internal device for regulating the bureaucracy is competition between departments. Spending ministries must compete against each other for money, with the finance ministry acting as umpire and cashier. In addition, established democracies rely on the professional standards of civil servants, particularly in bureaucracies with a strong technical emphasis. In Norway and Sweden, for instance, many civil servants work in specialist directorates covering areas such as engineering, medicine and railways. These directorates give expression to professional expertise and are at least partially independent of ministries. In these small and homogenous Scandinavian countries, trust between politicians and bureaucrats remains high and the system usually functions smoothly. In the main, senior civil servants respond to political signals without explicit direction (Christensen and Peters, 1999).

External scrutiny

External scrutiny is an expanding form of accountability for public servants. Traditionally, bureaucrats could easily escape both political and public scrutiny when, as in Britain, ministers alone were considered responsible to parliament for the actions of their officials. Civil servants could and did hide under their minister's skirts. Fortunately, perhaps, the British stress on the anonymity of higher civil servants was never matched in other liberal democracies. In the United States, bureaucrats are more forthcoming in their congressional appearances. But even in secretive Britain the rise of legislative committees of scrutiny has added a new dimension to bureaucratic accountability. Slowly and shyly, public officials are becoming willing to account in public for their work.

> **Definition**
> An **ombudsman** is a public official who investigates allegations of maladministration in the public sector. These watchdogs originated in Scandinavia but they have been emulated elsewhere though often with more restricted jurisdiction and resources.

As with other areas of politics, the judiciary is also growing in importance as an arena in which the bureaucracy can be called to account. Judges are increasingly willing to use administrative law as a device for influencing bureaucratic procedures (p. 198). A more recent addition to the mechanisms of external scrutiny is the Ombudsman. This watchdog was first introduced in Sweden and then emulated in New Zealand, followed later by other European countries. Assigned to investigate complaints of maladministration, ombudsmen must have strong powers of investigation if they are to succeed. So far, governments outside Scandinavia have proved reluctant to grant this facility. Finally, interest groups and the mass media also provide increasing external checks on bureaucratic bungling. A vigorous mass media can also act as a selective check on the bureaucracy: regular television programmes, for example, now specialize in exposing public scandal and bureaucratic ineptitude. However, oversight tends to be selective and, in the case of the media, short-term. Exposés rarely lead to structural reform; the specific case may be resolved but the complacency of the bureaucracy often continues.

New public management

'Government is not the solution to the problem; government is the problem.' This famous declaration by Ronald Reagan is one inspiration behind the new public management (NPM), a creed which swept through the Anglo-American world of public administration in the final decades of the twentieth century. NPM represents a powerful critique of Weber's ideas about bureaucracy. It has attracted many specialists who do not share the ideological perspective of Ronald Reagan, it is spoken of warmly by international bodies such as the OECD and it has led to radical change in the public sectors of Australia, Canada, the United Kingdom and especially New Zealand.

The best way to approach NPM is to consider Osborne and Gaebler's *Reinventing Government* (1992), an exuberant statement of the new approach. Subtitled 'how the entrepreneurial spirit is transforming the public sector', this American best-seller outlined ten principles which government agencies should adopt to enhance their effectiveness (Box 16.3). Where Weber's model of bureaucracy was based on ideas of efficiency drawn from the Prussian army, Osborne and Gaebler are inspired by the freewheeling world of American business.

The authors cite with enthusiasm several examples of public sector organizations which have followed their tips. One is the California parks department that allowed managers to spend their budget on whatever they needed, without seeking approval for individual items of expenditure. Another is the public convention centre which formed a joint venture with private firms to bring in well-known entertainment acts, with each side sharing both the risk and the profit. The underlying theme in such anecdotes is the gains achievable by giving public servants the flexibility to manage by results (that is, 'managerialism'). And the significance of this, in turn, is the break it represents with Weber's view that

---

BOX 16.3

Steer, don't row! Osborne and Gaebler's 10 principles for improving the effectiveness of government agencies

- Promote competition between service providers.
- Empower citizens by pushing control out of the bureaucracy into the community.
- Measure performance, focusing not on inputs but on outcomes.
- Be driven by goals, not rules and regulations.
- Redefine clients as customers and offer them choices – between schools, between training programmes, between housing options.
- Prevent problems before they emerge, rather than offering services afterwards.
- Earn money rather than simply spend it.
- Decentralize authority and embrace participatory management.
- Prefer market mechanisms to bureaucratic ones.
- Catalyze all sectors – public, private and voluntary – into solving community problems.

Source: Osborne and Gaebler (1992).

---

the job of a bureaucrat is to apply fixed rules to cases. For its supporters, NPM is public administration for the twenty-first century; Weber's model is dismissed as history. Public administration has been displaced by public management.

While Osborne and Gaebler provide a convert's handbook, Hood (1996, p. 271) offers a more dispassionate and comparative perspective (Box 16.4). Hood shows that NPM has penetrated furthest in Anglo-American countries and Scandinavia, where the public sector is most amenable to political control. By contrast, countries with a strong state and high-prestige bureaucracy, for example Germany, Japan and Spain, have made little progress in implementing the new philosophy. In these countries, senior civil servants continue to guard the public interest; their task is to apply codified law to specific cases. Given such traditions, the managerial ethos of economy, efficiency and effectiveness will not easily prosper. A particular problem is that the status and duties of civil servants are entrenched in extensive legal codes, making radical change impossible without legislation.

Within the Anglo-American countries, New

Zealand proved to be testing-ground for NPM. In the 1980s and 1990s, successive governments – first Labour and then National – revolutionized the structure, management and role of the public sector. A remarkable coalition (perhaps even conspiracy) of economic theorists in the Treasury, senior politicians from both major parties and business leaders came together to ram through unpopular but far from ineffective reforms. One particular feature of the 'New Zealand model' is its massive use of contracts (Boston, 1995b). This goes far beyond the standard fare of using private firms to supply local services such as garbage collection. It extends to engaging private suppliers in sensitive areas such as debt collection. By such means, the Department of Transport reduced its direct employees from around 5000 staff in 1986 to less than 50 in the mid-1990s, an astonishing transformation. In addition, contracts are widely used *within* New Zealand's public sector to govern the relationships between purchasers (for example the Transport Department) and providers (for example Transit New Zealand, responsible for roading, and the Civil Aviation Authority, charged with air safety and security). 'Contractualism' within the public sector is an additional step, and a more direct challenge to Weber's model, than simply contracting out services to the private sector.

What lessons can be learned from New Zealand's ambitious innovations in public administration? Mulgan (1997, p. 146) offers a balanced assessment. He concludes that

> the recent reorganization of the public service has led to greater clarity of government functions and to increased efficiencies in the provision of certain services to the public. At the same time, it has been expensive in the amount of resources consumed by the reform process itself and also in the added problems of coordination caused by the greatly increased number of individual public agencies.

The rise of NPM and the contract culture is one reason why the accountability of public officials has become more complex. When something goes wrong with a service provided by an agency operating under contract to government, who should take the blame: the supplier or the department? In Britain, parliament has traditionally held ministers

---

BOX 16.4

Components of new public management

- Managers are given more discretion but are held responsible for results.
- Explicit targets are set and used to assess results.
- Resources are allocated according to results.
- Departments are 'unbundled' into more independent operating units.
- More work is contracted out to the private sector.
- More flexibility is allowed in recruiting and retaining staff.
- Costs are cut in an effort to achieve more with less.

Source: Hood (1996)

---

to account for all the actions carried out in their name. As *The Times* wrote in 1977, 'the constitutional position is both crystal clear and entirely sufficient. Officials propose. Ministers dispose. Officials execute.' Yet by 1994 most British civil servants were working in one of about 100 semi-independent agencies (O'Toole and Chapman, 1995). In theory, the minister sets the policy and the agency carries it out. But when a political storm blows up – when convicts escape from prison or the child support agency pursues absent fathers too zealously – it is still ministers who are hauled before parliament. Knowing this, ministers are inclined to interfere with operational matters, thus contradicting the original purpose of the reform. Agency managers discover that they are not free to manage after all, with damage to morale.

The complexities of accountability in a reformed civil service lead some critics to suggest that 'a huge hole now exists in the operation of British democracy' (Campbell and Wilson, 1995, p. 287). Public servants are becoming more responsive downwards, to their users, and also more open to scrutiny from alternative political authorities, such as parliamentary committees. Probably, these developments represent a change in accountability rather than a decline. Control is melting away from the minister's office to a diffuse set of agencies and their clients. Weber's hierarchy of control based on direct provision by departments is giving way to a looser network based on persuasion rather than order-giving. Governance is replacing government. For previously centralized countries, notably Britain and New Zealand, the political implications of NPM are profound. Members of parliament wedded to the idea of ministerial accountability to the assembly are not pleased to discover that their cherished myth of sovereignty has shrivelled under pressure from the complex realities of modern policy-making.

Bureaucracy in authoritarian states

The bureaucracy, like the military, is usually a more powerful force in non-democratic regimes than it is in democracies. By definition, institutions of representation – elections, competitive parties and freely organized interest groups – are weak in authoritarian regimes, leaving more room for agencies of the state to prosper. A dictator can dispense with elections or even with legislatures but he cannot rule without bureaucrats to implement his will. But the bureaucracy can be more than a dictator's service agency, not least in developing countries. Often in conjunction with the military, it can itself become a leading political force, claiming that its technical expertise and ability to resist popular pressures is the only route to long-term economic development. This claim may have initial merit but eventually, bureaucracies in non-democratic regimes are prone to becoming bloated, over-politicized and inefficient, acting as a drag on rather than a stimulus to further progress. In the long run, bureaucratic regimes, like military governments, become part of the problem rather than the solution.

The bureaucracy has undoubtedly played a positive role in most authoritarian regimes that have experienced rapid economic growth. In the 1950s and 1960s, for instance, the bureaucracy helped to foster economic modernization in several Middle East regimes. In conjunction with the military and a strong national leader such as Abdul Nasser (President of Egypt, 1956–70), modernizing bureaucracies were able to initiate state-sponsored development even against the opposition of conservative landowners. In similar vein, O'Donnell (1973) coined the term 'bureaucratic authoritarianism' to describe Latin American countries such as Brazil and Argentine in which bureaucratic technocrats, protected by a repressive military govern-

ment, imposed a more modern economy against opposition from some social groups. Many of the high-performing economies of East Asia provide more recent examples of the contribution the bureaucracy can make to development in authoritarian settings. In countries such as Indonesia and Malaysia, a powerful bureaucracy was able to ensure that long-term investment occurred, with strong political leaders able to resist pressures for short-term improvements for ordinary people.

But instances of the bureaucracy instigating successful modernization are the exception rather than the rule. More often, the bureaucracy has tended to inhibit rather than encourage economic development. The experience of sub-Saharan Africa following independence provides a more sobering and representative assessment of the role of bureaucracy in non-democratic regimes. After colonial rulers departed, authoritarian leaders used their control over public appointments as a political reward, overwhelming the delicate distinction between politics and administration. Their cavalier approach to public appointments was compounded by chronic unemployment which led to excess labour, especially among the newly-educated, being absorbed into the administration as a way of buying off trouble. The result was uncontrolled expansion of the civil service; by the early 1990s, public employment accounted for most non-agricultural employment in Africa (Smith, 1996, p.221). Once appointed, public employees found that ties of kinship meant that they were duty-bound to use their privileged positions to reward their families and ethnic group, producing further expansion of the civil service. The result was a fat bureaucracy incapable of acting as an effective instrument for development. Rather, the expanding administrative 'class' extracted resources from society for its own benefit, in that sense continuing rather than replacing the colonial model. Only towards the end of the twentieth century, under pressure from international agencies, were attempts made to rein in the public sector through an emphasis on building 'administrative capacity' – that is, developing the bureaucracy's ability to address social problems through effective management and implementation (Turner and Hulme, 1997, p. 90).

Even where bureaucratic-led development has succeeded, the formula often outlasts its usefulness. As several East Asian states began to discover at the end of the twentieth century, public administrators are more effective at building an industrial economy than at continuing to manage it once it becomes mature and open to international competition. In Indonesia, for example, the Asian financial crisis of the late 1990s exposed the extent to which investment patterns had been distorted by 'crony capitalism', with access to capital depending on official contacts rather than the anticipated rate of return.

The position of the bureaucracy in totalitarian systems in some ways echoes its role in authoritarian regimes. But one key difference marks out administration in the communist world in particular: its sheer scale. The size of the bureaucracy under communism flowed from the totalitarian character of its guiding ideology. To achieve its theoretical mission of building a new society, the party had to control all aspects of development, both economic and social, through the state. Most obviously, the private sector disappeared and the economy became an aspect of state administration. In the extreme case of the Soviet Union virtually every farm, factory and shop formed part of the bureaucracy. The shop assistant, the butcher, the electrician – all were employees of the Union of Soviet Socialist Republics. This required one army of administrators to do the work and another to provide coordination. The Soviet Union became the most bureaucratic state the world had ever seen.

In addition, communist bureaucracies were intensely politicized, with the ruling party penetrating deeply into the administration. Indeed, the essence of communist rule lay in combining bureaucratic and political rule in one gigantic system. The party regarded the bureaucracy as both indispensable and potentially unreliable – as a force which through its control of implementation might one day dominate its political masters (Lewin, 1997). Hence, the party sought to dominate the bureaucracy in the same way that it controlled the armed forces: by controlling all major appointments. It achieved this goal through the *nomenklatura*, a Russian term meaning 'list of names'. The *nomenklatura* was a list of those people approved by the party for appointment to significant posts in the bureaucracy; its existence provided a powerful incentive for the ambitious to gain and retain a sound reputation within the party. The *nomenklatura* system continues to this day in China, where the list is now said to contain over eight million names (Manion, 2000, p 434).

Fascist regimes provide both similarities and contrasts with the communist approach to bureaucracy. Like communist states, fascism was an ideology of mobilization, seeking to place the entire resources of the society at the service of an expansionist state. Although in Germany Hitler sought 'war in peacetime', unlike communist leaders Hitler was not interested in how the administration should achieve his demanding objectives. Instead, the 'leadership of men' was regarded as superior to sterile rules and bureaucratic procedures. Hitler applauded the personal form of rule practised in Germany's annexed territories, where local commanders wielded complete power. The Führer himself was a poor administrator, preferring highly informal decision-making when indeed he could be persuaded to take decisions at all. As Mommsen (1997, p. 75) writes, 'the Nazi dictatorship did not so much expand governmental prerogatives through bureaucratic means as progressively undermine hitherto effective public institutions through arbitrary use of power'. Caplan (1988, pp. 322–3) argues that under Hitler the 'subversion of the civil service was piecemeal and *ad hoc*, the effect of incompetence, impatience and neglect rather than the pursuit of a clear alternative'. The profoundly non-bureaucratic character of Nazi rule – described by Caplan as 'government without administration' – contrasts deeply with communist practice.

Bureaucracy in new democracies

A common legacy of an authoritarian regime is an over-powerful, unaccountable and corrupt bureaucracy. Overcoming this difficult inheritance by establishing the supremacy of elected over bureaucratic authority is an important component of democratic consolidation. In particular, the task is to move the bureaucracy away from the highly political mode of operation under the old order toward a more professional Weberian model, where appointments are based on merit and corruption is contained. Only when these challenging long-term goals have been achieved does it make sense to contemplate applying the fads and fashions of new public management to the public sector. A bureaucracy based on 'old fashioned' Weberian ideas

Country profile JAPAN

Population: 126m.

Gross domestic product per head: $23 100.

Form of government: unitary parliamentary state with a ceremonial Emperor.

Legislature ('Diet'): the 480 members of the House of Representatives are elected for a four-year term. The smaller upper house, the House of Councillors, is less significant.

Executive: an orthodox parliamentary executive, with a cabinet and prime minister accountable to the Diet.

Senior bureaucrats play a major role in policy-making.

Judiciary: the 15-member Supreme Court possesses the power of judicial review under the 1946 constitution but has proved to be unassertive.

Electoral system: under the additional member system introduced in 1996, 300 members of the lower house are elected in single-member constituencies while the other 200 are elected by proportional representation. Although the new system was designed to reduce corruption and increase policy debate, turnout in 1996 fell seven points to 60 per cent.

Party system: postwar Japanese politics has been dominated by the conservative Liberal Democratic Party (LDP). It monopolized power from its formation in 1955 until 1993 and has participated in coalition rule since 1994. In 2000, the LDP won 232 seats, with the main opposition coming from the reformist Democratic Party of Japan.

Contained in a series of islands the size of Montana, and lacking all major natural resources, Japan's 126m people have built the second largest economy in the world. From the ashes of defeat in the Second World War, Japan by the early 1990s had become the world's largest creditor nation and donor of economic aid. How was this transformation achieved?

Specific historical factors were part of the answer. After the war, American aid, an undervalued yen, cheap oil and the procurement boom caused by the Korean War all contributed to economic recovery. Yet Japan took remarkable advantage of these favourable circumstances, focusing its initial efforts on heavy industry but eventually becoming the world's leading producer and exporter of sophisticated industrial and consumer goods.

'Japan, Inc.' was a popular (and populist) explanation of the country's success. According to this interpretation, the ethnically homogenous Japanese were driven not just by memories of wartime hunger but also by a shared desire to catch up with the West. A more sophisticated explanation was institutional. Although the country's post-war constitution was an American-imposed liberal democracy, in practice the political system was dominated by business. This enabled long-term investment to proceed by repressing any popular demands for rapid increases in domestic consumption, creating the Japanese paradox of 'a rich country with poor people'.

The Japanese civil service is accorded high status, attracts able recruits through open competition and motivates them with the thought of plum post-retirement jobs in the private sector. As Johnson (1987, p. 68) writes, senior bureaucrats form part of 'the economic general staff, which is itself legitimated by its meritocratic character'. The bureaucracy certainly played a major role in postwar reconstruction. It was intertwined with the dominant Liberal Democratic Party (conservative in all but name) and big business. These groups formed a ruling élite though one that is now declining in coherence.

The professional economic bureaucracy, and in particular the Ministry of International Trade and Industry (MITI), was a key force behind Japan's success. As postwar reconstruction began, MITI targeted specific growth industries such as cameras which were shielded from overseas competition until they became competitive. MITI operated mainly through persuasion, thus reducing the risk of major mistakes.

In the 1990s, Japan's economy suffered prolonged asset deflation and even the once-dominant LDP was forced into coalition. State-led deflation painted the bureaucracy in a harsher light than did state-led growth. Corruption scandals made large companies wary of hiring retired bureaucrats. But in the earlier postwar decades, Japan was a pre-eminent example of how a small, meritocratic bureaucracy, operating largely on the basis of persuasion, can guide economic development within a predominantly market economy.

Further reading: Johnson (1987), Koh (1989), Rosenbluth and Thies (2000).

remains a sensible and even demanding aspiration for a new democracy even as it comes to be seen as inadequate for a consolidated democracy (Verheijen, 1998).

Spain's transition to democracy illustrates the difficulties of bringing a post-authoritarian bureaucracy to heel. Under the old regime dominated by General Franco, 'the bureaucracy had been a central linchpin of the highly centralized, backward-looking dictatorship and was accordingly well-represented within the power élite' (Heywood, 1995, p. 130). Especially in the dictatorship's early years, the dominant test of appointment as a public official was loyalty to the regime. In operation the bureaucracy remained overstaffed and corrupt – albeit with some modernization as Franco's rule began to soften before the General's death in 1975. Even after the old order collapsed, administrative restructuring remained a low priority amid the drama of democratic transition. It was not until the crushing electoral victory of the Socialists in 1982 that major reforms of a now-demoralized service were attempted. The Socialists initiated such obvious changes as preventing the same person from occupying more than one public post; they sought also to reduce the significance of *cuerpos* (corps of officials) by focusing recruitment on specific jobs in particular ministries. But these changes met with only partial success. They were followed by further reforms later in the 1980s aimed at inducing a more managerial and less legalistic outlook among public servants. Yet again the outcome was mixed. As late as 1992, Socialist Prime Minister Felipe Gonzalez could describe the continuing inertia of the public service as the greatest frustration of his premiership. Continuing public distrust of state offices is one of the few weaknesses in Spain's generally successful transition to democracy. The Spanish experience reveals in particular that adapting an authoritarian bureaucracy to a democratic environment is a long-term task.

The difficulties of establishing an efficient public administration are even greater in postcommunist countries. After all, the collapse of communism was not just the end of a dictatorship; it was also the disintegration of an all-pervasive, over-extended and over-politicized bureaucracy. Initially, regime change led to administrative chaos. For example, many civil servants only received their salary on an irregular basis, forcing them to find ways of supplementing their income. A common response was to exploit the massive bank of formal regulations inherited from the communist era. An official stamp, for example to authorize a new business, remained a valuable commodity. One result of postcommunism, suggests Crawford (1996, p. 105), was simply that the price of bribes went up. And a distinctive feature of postcommunist societies was, of course, the vast inheritance of public ownership. Bureaucrats found that they could manipulate privatization or exploit the monopoly position of newly-privatized companies for their own benefit. So *post*communist bureaucracies remained in a *pre*Weberian stage – they did not operate by the consistent application of formal regulations. The bureaucracy was extensive but weakly controlled, allowing its employees to continue extracting resources from society in an arbitrary and unaccountable fashion. As with the royal households of premodern Europe, a public job was valued as an opportunity to tax as much as a source of a regular salary. Ironically, public officials found themselves perfectly positioned to exploit the transition to a 'market economy'.

Some postcommunist states, particularly the Czech Republic, Hungary, Poland and Slovenia, have now made considerable progress in overcoming these problems. In 1992, for instance, Hungary became the first country in Central and Eastern Europe to introduce a Civil Service Act, specifying procedures for recruiting, training, promoting, paying and dismissing bureaucrats (Baka, 1998). Such legislation is a sensitive issue throughout the postcommunist world because it breaks with the communist practice of political control of appointments. Civil service laws are part of an attempt to strengthen the distinction between political and administrative roles, pushing the bureaucracy in a Weberian direction. However, in the least democratic postcommunist countries, such battles have often been lost. In Bulgaria, for instance, 'the civil service has traditionally been considered to be a tool of a particular political party rather than a servant of society as a whole. The civil service is perceived not only as a tool to govern but also as a weapon against the political opponent' (Nikolova, 1998). Only a dreamer, suggests Stainov (1993), could imagine 'a picture where, when a government [in Bulgaria] is changed, the civil servant remains firmly in his place without caring too much about the political subject in power.'

Key reading

> **Next step:** *Guy Peters (2000) is a clear and comparative introduction to bureaucracy.*

Heady (1996) is an alternative to Peters, while Page (1992) is a comparative study adopting a Weberian approach. Bekke, Perry and Toonen (1996) is a lively edited collection. Osborne and Gaebler (1993) is an enthusiast's account of new public management. Verheijen and Coombes (1998) assess NPM's impact in Europe, both East and West, while Minogue, Polidano and Hulne (1999) focus more on developing countries. For bureaucracy in particular countries and regions, see Chandler (2000) for a range of consolidated democracies, Fesler and Kettl (1996) for the United States, Campbell and Wilson (1995) for Britain viewed comparatively, Boston (1995) for New Zealand and Page and Wright (1999) for Europe. For Japan, Johnson (1987) is an influential interpretation. Kershaw and Lewin (1997) contains useful chapters on bureaucracy in the contrasting dictatorships of Stalin and Hitler. With an emphasis on the relationship between administration and development, Turner and Hulme (1997) portray the role of bureaucracy in authoritarian regimes.

PART 5

PUBLIC POLICY

Politics matters. In one country, government actions may be the principal cause of human misery. In another, public policies may help to create the conditions under which people can fulfil their potential. In this final chapter, therefore, our focus shifts from the structures and processes of government to the policies that governments pursue. We explore the concepts used in policy analysis and the changing agendas confronting rulers.

CHAPTER **17** | # The policy process

The task of policy analysis is to understand what governments do, how they do it and what difference it makes (Dye, 1997). Where orthodox political science examines the political factory, policy analysis examines the products emerging from it. So the focus is on the content, instruments, impact and evaluation of policy. The prime emphasis is downstream, on the implementation and results of policy, rather than upstream, on the origins of policy in its institutional source. Thus policy analysis expresses a more practical spirit than other aspects of comparative politics. The profession of policy analysis, suggest Hogwood and Peters (1985, pp. 3–4), is to social science what medicine is to biology: it applies a general body of knowledge to specific cases.

> *Definition*
> A **policy** is a more general notion than a decision. A policy covers a bundle of decisions, and it involves a predisposition to respond in a specific way. When a government says, 'our policy favours public transport', it is merely stating an intention to make specific decisions with this attitude in mind. In fact, the practical 'decisions' may never arrive; some policies are just window-dressing.

Stages of the policy process

In approaching the study of public policy, it is helpful to distinguish the five stages of the policy process shown in Figure 17.1. These divisions are more analytical than chronological, meaning that in real policy-making they often overlap. Even so, a brief review of these phases helps to clarify the distinctiveness of the policy approach:

- *Initiation* – the decision to make a decision in a particular area; also called agenda-setting.
- *Formulation* – the detailed development of a policy into concrete proposals.
- *Implementation* – putting the policy into practice.
- *Evaluation* – appraising the effects and success of the policy.
- *Review* – continuate, revise or terminate?

Initiation

Why did governments expand welfare policy for the first three decades after 1945 and then reduce it thereafter? Why did many Western governments take companies into public ownership after the war and then start selling them back to the private sector in the 1980s and 1990s? These are questions about policy initiation – about the decision to make (or, just as important, not to make) policy in a particular area. Initiation emerges from the political agenda. In an established democracy, the agenda cannot be controlled by a single group; it is the product of debate between a variety of competing though often unequal forces. Clearly, the governing party exerts a large and proximate influence on the agenda; this is especially so in countries such as the United Kingdom, where party manifestos are examined intensively during an election campaign and the single winning party is given the tools to put its proposals into effect. Elsewhere in the democratic world, however, coalition bargaining and a tradition of consensus politics conspire to ensure that the connection between election outcomes and policy initiation is more opaque. Indeed, even in the United Kingdom, ministers find their time increasingly occupied by pressing tasks unrelated to manifesto promises (Rose, 1976). Policy agendas are fluid and fast-flowing because they are made as much by events as by politicians. Hence 'policy initiation' is too rational a word for the mysterious process by which issues first float to the top of the agenda and then sink back into the murky bog of non-issues.

Beyond the political process itself, we can identify three general influences on policy initiation: science, technology and the media. *Science* is clearly one driver of policy agendas. The current concern with global warming, for instance, rests primarily on scientific assessments of its future implications. The science forewarned us that a problem was on its way. However, we should note that governments commission as well as consume science; ministers' power over the production of knowledge can help them to keep uncomfortable issues off the policy agenda. The British government, for instance, was unduly slow in commissioning research into mad-cow disease which swept through the country's herds (and into the brains of an unknown number of its people) in the 1990s. In this case, manipulation of the research process proved fatal. Thus scientific research cannot be seen as wholly external to politics.

Second, applications of science – that is, *technology* – also influence policy initiation. Governments have an incentive to encourage new technology; it stimulates economic competitiveness and prompt introduction allows a country to steal a march on other states. But many new technologies involve regulation. Designs for nuclear power stations must be assessed for safety; frequencies for mobile telephones must be allocated; new drugs must be examined for side-effects; and the effects of allowing genetically altered plants, fish and animals into the environment must be considered. In all these cases technological innovation forces policy initiation from government. Again, the danger is that governments will approve those 'advances' which offer clear short-term gain at the cost of intangible, long-term risk. Nuclear energy is arguably an example.

Third, the ability of the *media* to highlight issues means they are also a significant, if sometimes overstated, influence on policy initiation. A single and perhaps unusual incident is often taken up by one outlet and then, through pack journalism, amplified by other media until politicians are forced to respond to what has suddenly become a serious social problem. Common topics of such media-induced moral panics include food scares, teenage hooligans, gang wars, welfare scroungers, mad dogs, infectious diseases, drug crazes and crime waves (Henshel, 1990). These balloons of concern often collapse as quickly as they are inflated; in only a few cases are the media turning their searchlight on a problem where public policy does indeed need to be initiated.

Formulation

Once a decision has been taken to address a specific problem, policy must be formulated, and translating a feeling that something should be done into precise legislation or administrative proposals is a core political craft. In analysing policy formulation, analysts have developed two models – the rational or synoptic model associated with Simon (1983) and the incremental model associated with Lindblom (1979). Since these accounts form part of the policy analysis tradition, we must consider them in more detail. The key difference between the two models is this: the rational model views policy as emerging from a systematic search for the most efficient means

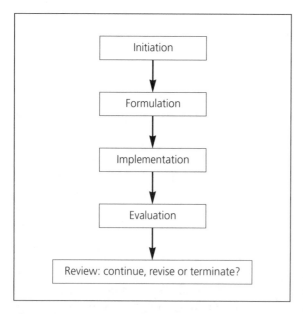

Figure 17.1 Stages of the policy process

of achieving defined goals; while by contrast, the incremental model sees policy as resulting from a compromise between actors who have ill-defined, or even contradictory, goals (Box 17.1).

An example will clarify the contrast. Suppose we were in charge of education policy. If we adopted a rational approach we would first specify the outcomes sought, such as the number and level of student qualifications. Then we would consider the most efficient means of maximizing that goal; should we invest in new schools, more teachers or some combination of the two? An incremental approach, however, starts at a different point. Here we would begin (and end) with regular consultation with all the organized interests: teacher unions, parents' associations, educational researchers. We would hope that from these discussions a consensus would slowly emerge on how best to spend extra resources. The long-term goals of this expenditure might not be measured or even specified but we would assume that a policy acceptable to all is unlikely to be disastrous. Such an approach is policy-making by evolution, not revolution; hence the word 'incremental' (small steps).

Certainly, the incremental approach is less demanding than the rational model. According to the rational model, policy-makers must rank all their values, formulate clear options, calculate all the results of choosing each option and select the alternative that achieves most values. This is an unrealistic counsel of perfection. It requires policy-makers to foresee the unforeseeable and measure the unmeasurable. Even so, several techniques have been developed in an attempt to implement aspects of the rational model (Carley, 1980; Nigro, 1984).

Cost–benefit analysis (CBA), for example, involves giving a monetary value (positive or negative) to every consequence of choosing each option and then selecting the option with the highest net benefit. Thus, the efficiency gain from adding a new runway to an airport can be netted off against the additional noise pollution for local residents. Or the environmental return from building houses with solar heating can be compared with that from wind farms, thus ensuring that the limited budget for reducing carbon dioxide emissions (and all budgets are limited) is used to maximum effect.

CBA, and with it the rational model, does have

***

BOX 17.1

Rational and incremental models of policy-making

Rational model	Incremental model
Goals are set before means are considered	Goals and means are considered together
A 'good' policy is the most appropriate for the desired ends	A 'good' policy is one on which all main actors can agree
Analysis is comprehensive; all effects of all options are addressed	Analysis is selective; the object is good policy, not the best policy
Theory is heavily used	Comparison with similar problems is heavily used

Sources: Modified from Lindblom (1959, p. 81) and Parsons (1995, p. 285)

***

strengths. It brings submerged assumptions to the surface and can benefit those interests which would otherwise lack political clout. It contributes to transparent policy-making by forcing decision-makers to account for policies where costs exceed benefits. In other words CBA can help to keep policy-makers honest. For such reasons, CBA is now applied to any regulatory proposal in the USA expected to have an impact on the economy exceeding $100m. However CBA also has weaknesses. It underplays 'soft' factors such as fairness and the quality of life. It is also cumbersome and expensive and in the real political world its conclusions are often side-stepped. Thus a CBA of CBA might yield negative results.

The incremental model was developed by Lindblom (1959) as part of a reaction against the rational model. Lindblom's starting point is that policy is continually remade in a series of minor adjustments, rather than as a result of a single, comprehensive plan. Incrementalism represents what Lindblom calls the 'science of muddling through'. This approach may not lead to achieving grand objectives but it does at least avoid making huge mistakes. In incremental policy-making, what matters is not that those involved should agree on objectives but that agreement should be reached on the desirability of following a particular policy, even when objectives differ. Hence policy emerges from, rather than precedes, negotiation with interested groups.

As Lindblom (1977, 1990) himself came to recognize, incremental policy-formulation deals with existing problems rather than with avoiding future ones. It is politically safe but unadventurous; public policy becomes remedial rather than innovative. But the threat of ecological disaster, for instance, has arisen precisely from human failure to consider the long-term, cumulative impact of industry upon the environment. So incrementalism is an inadequate response to complex global issues. The trick is to find ways of dealing with such problems which do not fall victim to the shortcoming of the rational model, namely demanding more of policy-makers than they can possibly deliver.

Implementation

Probably the main achievement of policy analysis has been to direct attention to problems of implementation. Traditional political science stopped at the point where government took a decision and even today putting the policy into practice is sometimes still regarded as a technical matter of administration. However that assumption is far too simple. The British government's failure to prevent mad-cow disease from crossing the species barrier to humans in the late 1980s is a classic instance of implementation failure. Official committees instructed abattoirs to remove infective material (such as the spinal cord) from slaughtered cows but initially took no special steps to ensure these regulations were carried out carefully. As a result of incompetence in slaughterhouses, the disease agent continued to enter the food chain.

Again reflecting the standard conventions of political science, the traditional view of implementation adopted a top-down approach (Hogwood and Gunn, 1984). The question posed was the classical problem of bureaucracy: how to ensure political direction of unruly public 'servants'. Elected ministers had to be able to secure compliance from departments and agencies already committed to pet projects of their own. From a policy perspective, though, implementation is often viewed, and is perhaps better viewed, from a bottom-up perspective. Writers in this tradition ask: what if circumstances have changed since the policy was formu-

lated? And what if the policy itself is poorly designed? (Barrett and Fudge, 1981). Policy analysts suggest that objectives are more likely to be met if those who execute policy are given flexibility over its application and therefore its content. At street level (the point where the policy is put into effect), policy emerges from interaction between local bureaucrats and affected groups. Here at the sharp end, goals can often be best achieved by adapting them to local conditions. For example, education, health care and policing must surely differ between the rural countryside and multicultural areas in the inner city. Further, local implementers are more likely to be aware of how policies interact, and sometimes contradict, each other. So a bottom-up approach reflects an incremental view of policy-making in which implementation is seen as policy-making by other means; it is more in tune with the contemporary emphasis on governance.

Definition

A **top-down** approach conceives the task of policy implementation as ensuring that policy execution delivers the outputs and outcomes as specified by the policy-makers. By contrast, a **bottom-up** approach considers that the role of those who execute policy in reshaping broad objectives to fit local and changing circumstances should be both recognized and welcomed. The bottom-up approach reflects the contemporary emphasis on governance, with its stress on the multiple actors involved in the policy process.

Evaluation

The job of policy evaluation is to work out whether a policy has achieved its goals. Like the famous recipe for rabbit stew which begins 'first catch your rabbit', this neatly sidesteps initial difficulties. The motives behind a policy are often multiple, unclear and even contradictory. This 'mushiness of goals', to use Fesler and Kettl's phrase (1996, p. 287), means that policy-makers' intent is often a poor benchmark for evaluation. Working out the objectives of policy is no easy task.

As with implementation, so with evaluation: the problem was largely ignored not just in traditional political analysis but also by governments themselves. Sweden is a typical example. In the postwar decades a succession of Social Democratic governments concentrated on building a universal welfare state without even conceiving of a need to evaluate the effectiveness with which services were delivered by an expanding bureaucracy. Yet without some evaluation of policy, governments will fail to learn the lessons of experience. In the United States, Jimmy Carter (President, 1977–81) did insist that at least one per cent of the funds allocated to any project should be devoted to evaluation. The vast number of reports required meant a bonanza for photocopier makers but did not noticeably improve the policy effectiveness. It was not until a wave of public sector reform in the 1990s that evaluation began to return to the fore. To take the USA again, the Government Performance and Results Act (1993) requires each agency to perform an annual programme evaluation which is then intended to be used by the government to revise plans and budgets. Throughout the Western world, public officials are beginning to think, often for the first time, of the outcomes their policies are supposed to achieve.

Definition
Policy outputs are what government does; **policy outcomes** are what government achieves. Outcomes are the activity; outcomes are the effects, both intended and unforeseen. Outputs are measured easily enough: for instance, so many new prisons built or a specified increase in the state pension. Outcomes are harder to ascertain: for instance, a reduction in recidivism or in the number of elderly people living in poverty.

Policy evaluation requires outcomes (what government achieves, including unintended consequences) to be distinguished from outputs (what government does). The link between the two is often tenuous. In 1966, for example, the US government published the results of the Coleman report, a massive sociological study of American secondary schools. This study found that outputs such as teachers' salaries and educational expenditure had little effect on the ultimate outcome of education: children's learning. The main influence on outcomes (that is, children's educational success) was the family background of the child and its peers. Children from a lower-class background were likely to underperform even if they were placed in a well-

resourced school. The Coleman report illustrates a point familiar to policy-makers in most sectors: outcomes resist change, even when resources are devoted to altering them.

Just as policy-implementation in accordance with the top-down model is an unrealistic goal, so judging policy effectiveness against precise objectives is an implausibly scientific approach to evaluation. A more bottom-up, incremental view is that evaluation should simply gather in the opinions of all the stakeholders affected by the policy. As Parsons (1995, p. 567) describes this approach,

> evaluation has to be predicated on wide and full collaboration of all programme stakeholders: agents (funders, implementers); beneficiaries (target groups, potential adopters); and those who are excluded ('victims').

In such a naturalistic evaluation, the varying objectives of different interests are welcomed rather than dismissed as a barrier to objective scrutiny of policy. This is a more bottom-up – indeed incremental – approach because the stakeholders might agree on the success of a policy even though they judge it against different standards.

Review

Once a policy has been evaluated, or even if it has not, the three possibilities are: to continue, to revise or to terminate. Most policies, along with the agencies set up to carry them out, continue with only minor revisions. Organizations rarely fold up when their job is done. In 1996, 27 years after Neil Armstrong stepped onto the moon, the space agency Nasa seized on dubious reports that life may once have existed on Mars as a source of new goals to justify its continued existence. There is, it has been said, nothing so permanent as a temporary government organization. The intriguing question is: why is policy termination so rare? Bardach (1976) suggests five reasons:

- Policies are designed to last a long time
- Termination brings conflicts which leave too much blood on the floor
- No one wants to admit the policy was a bad idea
- Termination may affect other programmes

- Politics rewards innovation rather than tidy house-keeping.

The conclusion here is that introducing new policies is simplicity itself compared to ending old ones.

Public policy in established democracies

Our purpose here is to chart the major shifts in the policy agenda of Westerns states, transformations which reflect evolving conceptions of the state itself but which remain understated in traditional analysis of government institutions. Broadly, we can divide the history of public policy in what are now the consolidated democracies into three phases: the night watchman or liberal state of the nineteenth century and earlier, the welfare state of the later twentieth century and the emerging regulatory state of the twenty-first century (Box 17.2). Such a scheme fits the experience of North European states, including the UK, with fair accuracy. However, the history of the USA, which never developed a welfare state but which was one of the first democracies to introduce independent regulatory agencies, is exceptional.

The *night-watchman state* was a minimal operation, concentrating on maintaining law and order, protecting private property and extracting sufficient resources to allow rulers to pursue their foreign policy. The state apparatus remained poorly devel-

oped, with a limited bureaucracy and local administration largely the responsibility of provincial notables. The night-watchman role was an early form taken by the post-feudal but pre-democratic state in much of Europe, notably the United Kingdom; it reflected a liberal philosophy of non-intervention. The night-watchman metaphor comes from John Locke (1632–1704), an English philosopher who laid the early foundations of liberal thinking. Locke considered the sole function of government to be that of protecting natural, God-given rights to life, liberty and property; citizens should merely be provided with order, protection and the means of enforcing contracts. In the United States, a country built to a liberal design, Thomas Jefferson (1743–1826) expressed the night-watchman conception when he wrote: 'that government is best which governs least.' The night-watchman state had no interest in public welfare: 'the drunkard in the gutter is just where he ought to be', commented the American sociologist William Sumner (1840–1910). This liberal philosophy of clear but limited individual rights originally emerged from the battle for religious toleration but limiting the state to a night-watchman role also proved highly congenial to the emerging business class. Indeed, the free-market doctrine of *laissez faire* ('to leave to be') was perhaps the most significant element in the night-watchman construct. As Opello and Rosow (1999, p. 97) comment,

> The liberal state, then, is in one respect a minimal state; that is, it is deliberately structured not to be itself a threat to the 'natural right' of property ownership, which is the ultimate justification for the dominant position of the bourgeoisie within the state.

The *welfare state*, which reached its zenith in West and especially North Europe in the 1960s and 1970s, was clearly based on a more expansive and positive view of the state's role in protecting its citizens' welfare. However, the culmination of the welfare state in the post-war decades reflected a long evolution. Even as industrialization proceeded in the nineteenth century, the night-watchman state was drawn into a measure of economic regulation. Unhealthy working conditions in industrial factories and the use of child labour led to factory legislation

---

BOX 17.2

The changing agenda of the Western state

Type	Domestic agenda	Period
Night-watchman state	Maintains law and order and protects private property	Nineteenth century and earlier
Welfare state	Provides minimum welfare to all citizens	Second half of twentieth century
Regulatory state	Sets rules and standards	Final decades of the twentieth century and later

while the American depression of the 1930s also increased government responsibilities for both the economy and welfare through the New Deal. However, the real origins of collective welfare provision lay in Germany before the First World War. Under Bismarck, Germany had pioneered social insurance schemes which shared risks such as accident and illness, at least for industrial workers. Building on the German model, the period from the 1920s saw the gradual extension of collective welfare in most democracies to more areas of life (e.g. pensions and family allowances) and to more groups in the population (e.g. rural people and dependents of industrial workers). By the 1970s, virtually the entire population was covered in most democracies for the main aspects of welfare (Table 17.1).

By then, European democracies had become 'welfare states' in a triple sense. First, the state took a prime role in ensuring the provision of a minimum standard of welfare to all its citizens, supplanting the *ad hoc* provision through churches and charities in the night watchman state. Second, providing welfare became the main function of public administration, consuming the lion's share of both tax-payers' revenue and officials' time. Third, welfare rights

became an expression of 'social citizenship', a notion which sought to extend the scope of democracy itself. In an influential account, the British sociologist T. H. Marshall (1893–1981) defined social citizenship as covering 'the whole range from the right to a modicum of economic welfare and security to the right to share to the full in the social heritage and to live the life of a civilized being according to the standards prevailing in society' (1950, pp. 16–19). Several democracies – for instance, France – embedded a statement of welfare rights in their constitution. This development of social citizenship contrasts sharply with the night-watchman state in which those who received public welfare through the poor laws were denied the vote. Where the night-watchman state gave priority to liberty, the welfare state was premised on equality (Lane and Ersson, 1999, pp. 8–12).

Of course, democracies continued to vary both in their levels of welfare support and in the ideological support offered. The proportion of gross national product spent by a country on welfare depended first and foremost on its level of affluence; richer countries spent a higher proportion of national income, and not just a higher amount, on welfare

Table 17.1 Introduction of social insurance, selected countries

	Industrial accident	Health	Pensions	Unemployment benefit	Family allowances
Australia	1902	1945	1909	1945	1941
Austria	1887	1888	1927	1920	1921*
Canada	1930	1971	1927	1940	1944
Denmark	1898	1892	1891	1907	1952
Finland	1895	1963	1937	1917	1948
France	1898	1898	1895	1905*	1932
Germany	1871*	1883*	1889*	1927	1954
Italy	1898	1886	1898	1919	1936
Netherlands	1901	1929	1913	1916	1940
New Zealand	1900	1938	1898	1938	1926
Norway	1894	1909	1936	1906	1946
Sweden	1901	1891	1913	1934	1947

* innovator

Source: Pierson (1998, table 4.1).

(Wilensky, 1984). In addition, centralized states (such as Britain) and those where parties of the left predominated (such as Sweden) tended to be high spenders as did countries (such as Austria) in which Catholic parties were a major governing force. By contrast, low spenders included several federal states (such as the USA) and those where the right had been more influential (such as Italy). Spending remained particularly low in countries where collective provision was still seen as 'state welfare' rather than a 'welfare state'. The main examples of these 'residual' or 'liberal' welfare states were the USA, Canada and Australia (Esping-Andersen, 1990).

Definition

In a public **pay-as-you-go** pension scheme, the pensions of retirees are paid directly by contributions from current workers. This system, which forms an important plank of pensions provision in much of continental Europe, can become unsustainable as the population ages and the **dependency ratio** (the number of pensioners divided by the number of contributors) deteriorates. The state is required to take corrective action. By contrast, in a **funded pension** system, usually operated through private pension providers, individual contributions are invested for that person so that a pot of capital accumulates over time from which the individual draws an income in retirement. Provided the invested contributions show a fair return, there should be little call on the public purse. Funded pensions predominate in, for example, the Netherlands, the United Kingdom and the USA.

The 1980s witnessed the first real setbacks for the welfare state. The underlying problem was financial: as the average age of the population increased, so the total cost of pensions, medical care and support services went up – and was projected to continue growing well into the twenty-first century. At the same time the working population, which shoulders the burden, declines in number. Financial projections looked particularly bleak in those countries such as Germany where employees' pension contributions were not invested but instead were used directly to pay the pensions of the retired population – the pay-as-you-go system. International economic pressures also mattered. If the cost of one country's welfare system was higher than all the rest, the international competitiveness of its economy might be

endangered. Pierson (1998) suggests that the move to a more open international economy 'curtailed opportunities for the further development of national welfare states.' Certainly the oil crises of the 1970s, marking a transition to slower growth in the established democracies, were a catalyst to rethinking first the feasibility and then the desirability of welfare from cradle to grave. The oil crises dealt a fatal blow to easy assumptions that the long post-war economic boom could continued unabated and untended.

Such problems led to some retrenchment of the welfare state in the 1980s and 1990s. Benefits were marginally reduced, eligibility rules were tightened, charges were introduced for services such as medical treatment, few new commitments were taken on and the state made an effort to revive the old caring agencies, such as charities and the church. But the welfare state experienced a correction rather than a crisis. On the whole, tax-payers' revolts did not materialize; the basic structures of the welfare state remained in place. In Scandinavia, public support for the welfare state increased again after the 1970s (Alber, 1988). Marshall's notion of social citizenship is touted less often in the twenty-first century but both its cash value and its public popularity remain substantial.

Although the 'crisis' of the welfare state may have been overplayed, the final decades of the twentieth century did witness a fundamental shift in the agenda and focus of public policy in many established democracies, especially in Europe. In social welfare, service delivery was increasingly contracted out to private agencies or at least to lower tiers of government. Generally, governments sought to reduce their direct provision of goods and services; in the economy, for instance, public industries were privatized. Since one motive here was to render economies more competitive, this transition is sometimes discussed as a move from a welfare state to a competition state (Cerny, 1990). But it is not clear that the frontiers of the state have been decisively modified; indeed, newly-privatized monopolies must be regulated and public oversight has become more intense in such sectors as education, the environment, employment, scientific research and consumer protection. Indeed, it would probably be wrong to conceive of public regulation as simply a burden on competitiveness. Smart regulation –

allocating radio frequencies to mobile telephony, encouraging internet use, developing digital television – can enhance growth in advanced economies. For want of a happier term we will describe the shift in the policy approach from provision to regulation as a transition to a *regulatory state*. A regulatory state uses rules, standards, and other public statements as major policy instruments, rather than relying on direct provision of goods and services. More than in most democracies, regulation has always been a leading mode of governance in the USA; the notion of a regulatory state suggests that American practice is now diffusing to other established democracies in Europe and elsewhere.

The most striking evidence for the retreat of the state from direct provision comes from the influential policy of privatization followed by Britain's

Table 17.2 Case-by-case privatization in the United Kingdom, 1980s		
Year	Company	Proceeds (£ million)
1981	British Aerospace	149
1981	Cable & Wireless*	224
1982	Britoil	549
1983	BP*	565
1984	Enterprise Oil	392
1984	Jaguar Cars	294
1984	British Telecom*	3916
1985	British Aerospace	551
1986	British Gas	5434
1987	British Airways	900
1987	Rolls Royce	1362
1987	British Airports Authority	1281
1988	British Steel Corporation	2482
1989	Water Authorities	5240

* Privatized in stages; only the first tranche is shown.

Note: Only privatizations yielding over £100m are shown. Electricity was privatized in 1990 (distribution; £5200m) and 1991 (generation, £2200m). Case-by-case (one at a time) privatization contrasts with the mass or simultaneous privatization attempted in many postcommunist countries.

Source: Adapted from Prosser and Moran (1994, table 3.2).

Conservative government under Mrs Thatcher in the 1980s. The speed and thoroughness with which the government 'sold off the family silver' (to quote the disapproving phrase used by former Conservative prime minister Harold Macmillan) attracted international interest (Table 17.2). Just as nationalization had been seen by the postwar Labour government as a way of introducing public control and rational planning to key industrial sectors, so privatization reflected an ideologically charged desire to 'roll back the frontiers of the state'. The key point, though, was that creating private monopolies – as with telephones, gas and electricity – required the creation of new offices of regulation at least until competition became established. As Majone (1996, p.2) notes, 'in Britain and elsewhere, the privatization of the public utilities has been followed by price regulation … the last fifteen years have been a period less of deregulation than of intense regulatory reform'. The outcome is more a regulatory state than a rolled-back state.

Analysing the rise of the regulatory state in Britain, Moran (2001) identifies its three major dimensions:

- regulation of privatized industries
- external supervision of previously self-regulating institutions such as universities and financial markets
- social regulation in such areas as equal opportunities, health and safety and food standards.

A new style of governance does however bring forth new problems. Again, Moran identifies three in particular: the costs of compliance, the legitimacy of regulation in a country which has traditionally placed greater store on majoritarian decision-making and parliamentary sovereignty, and the problem of regulatory capture. Underlying such seemingly technical issues is the more fundamental question of ensuring at least an efficient compromise, and preferably a positive relationship, between public regulation and economic competitiveness. This agenda is likely to become more prominent as the regulatory state matures.

Interestingly, the new agenda of the regulatory state did bring forth institutional change and not just in the UK. Most new regulatory bodies operate not as divisions of ministries but as agencies operating at one remove from the centres of political – and therefore democratic – power. Similar attempts to depoliticize regulation can be observed in the independence given to central banks to set interest rates, as now applies in both Britain and the European Union. Majone (1996) suggests that this trend can be defended even though it runs counter to orthodox democractic thinking. Autonomous agencies can adopt more consistent, credible and long-term policies than is feasible for elected politicians who remain subject to short-term pressures from the electorate, party competition and the legislature. In addition, delegating political authority to specialized professional regulators is more appropriate where the issues are technical (e.g. telecommunications standards) rather than redistributive (e.g. taxation). In any event, the effect has been to export the established American model of independent regulatory agencies to many other consolidated democracies. However, the question of the legitimacy of the regulatory state, an issue never entirely resolved in the USA, remains to be settled elsewhere – and notably in the European Union, where the capacity of the unelected Commission to issue enforceable regulations represents its major lever of influence. Thus the seemingly technical issue of regulation is raising a major issue about the thinning of democracy in contemporary Western states.

Public policy in authoritarian regimes

Studying public policy in non-democratic regimes confirms the importance of distinguishing between forms of authoritarianism. At one extreme, many communist states attempted a type of planning virtually without precedent in history; every communist state formulated clearer national goals and targets than any democracy. The result was an often decisive and generally ruthless commitment to a single goal, notably industrialization. At the other extreme, many military and personal rulers show immense concern about their own prosperity but none at all for their country's, leading to a policy shortage. If there is a general theme to the policy process in non-democracies (including even communist states), it is this subservience of policy to politics. In the more competitive world in which

authoritarian rulers now find themselves, such weaknesses are increasingly exposed, adding to pressures for democratic reform. In this section, we will review the communist experience before turning to the policy process in contemporary authoritarian regimes.

Communist states differed enormously from established democracies in their policy goals and means. For one thing, the ruling party articulated clear objectives for society; for another, the state sought to implement these goals though detailed planning. Yet planning eventually yielded economic stagnation and thus contributed to the collapse of communism in East Europe and the Soviet Union. But why did planning fail? To answer these questions, we must first look at how planning worked. The Soviet Union is the clearest example because it ran the most planned economy on earth. The Soviet Union was the land of The Plan. Gosplan, the State Planning Committee, drew up annual five-year plans which were given the status of law once they had received political approval. Implementation was the responsibility of ministries which controlled individual enterprises through a complex administrative network. Detailed planning was forced by a command economy. A factory could not buy its components on the market when there was no market. Instead arrangements had to be made for another factory to manufacture the parts and deliver them on time – and that factory in turn had to be supplied with raw materials.

The flaw was obvious. For anything to go right everything had to go right – so inevitably something went wrong! Because the right components did not arrive at the right time, all sorts of informal and often illegal deals had to be fixed up to ensure that the (often arbitrary) production quota was met. Further, the system was dominated by planners and producers, rather than customers. Targets were based on quantity, not quality. As a result, goods were shoddy when they were produced at all. Local managers had no room for initiative, even though they were well aware of what needed to be done. Endemic shortages led to corrupt swaps among individuals with access to resources: good cuts of meat in exchange for cigarettes, train tickets for university places. Those with little to offer, notably old people, just waited in line – for an average of three hours a day in the Soviet Union.

So was the planned economy an unmitigated disaster? Notably in the USSR, it did prove successful at building the foundations of industrial development, albeit at a horrifying human price. Heavy industry was the great success of the planned economy, both in communist states which were undergoing industrialization for the first time and in those which were rebuilding after the Second World War. This success derived from the policy of the 'big push'. Communist leaders gave high priority to specific objectives, sometimes extending beyond the economy: for example, adequate housing and improved life expectancy. They then allocated the resources needed to meet the goal. A single end took priority and other consequences (including a degraded environment in the case of industrialization) were ignored. Objectives determined budgets rather than vice versa. The big push was a deliberately blinkered approach which ignored the overall view but often succeeded its achieving its specific targets. For instance, Stalin's drive to industrialize Russia transformed a society of peasants into a world industrial power within a generation. Later, China and Cuba applied the big push to their own societies, again with spectacular results.

Where, then, does the collapse of state planning leave the remaining 'communist' states, notably China? The PRC's rulers have certainly reduced the importance of central planning yet they can hardly be said to have created the conditions for a market economy. Massive, and massively inefficient, state-owned enterprises still pervade the economy, soaking up labour and serving as an indirect welfare state. The expansion of the 'non-state' sector has stimulated continued growth but party contacts still determine access to economic opportunities. To Western eyes, the system is inherently corrupt; it is certainly technically inefficient in that political criteria distort economic decisions, leading to huge misallocations of capital. Yet this idiosyncratic model is still delivering growth in what is still a poor country. As long as economic growth continues, China's nominally communist rulers may succeed in resolving the political tensions induced by corruption and increasing inequality. Yet judging by the experience of communism in East Europe and the Soviet Union, that same growth will eventually deliver a demand for more fundamental political reform.

While some non-communist rulers have also delivered economic development, policy stagnation is a more familiar pattern in other authoritarian states. Policy inertia often results from a lack of motivation among the ruling élite. Often, the key task for non-elected rulers is to play off domestic political forces against each other so as to ensure the ruler's own continuation in office, an art particularly well understood by the ruling families of the Middle East. Or the ruler may want to enrich himself, his family and his ethnic group, a task hardly conducive to orderly policy development. More commonly, patronage is the main political currency; the age-old game of building up and paying down political debts again works against coherent policy, transparently applied. As Chazan *et al.* (1999, p. 171) note in their discussion of Africa:

> Patriarchal rule has tended to be conservative: it propped up the existing order and did little to promote change. It required the exertion of a great deal of energy just to maintain control.

Finally, rulers may simply lack the ability to make coherent policy. This weakness was common enough among military governments. The generals may seize power in an honest attempt to eliminate corruption and improve policy-making but they soon discover that governance is more complicated than they had imagined. Often, they slink back to their barracks in due course, with little achieved.

Public policy in new democracies

'Rebuilding the ship at sea' is an apt metaphor for the problems confronting new, and particularly post communist democracies (Elster, Offe and Preuss,1998). A key point here is that the familiar distinction between institutions and policies – between who governs and what governments do – breaks down in the case of new democracies. The policy challenge is precisely to design new institutions that restructure the role of the state in society. In established democracies, existing institutions process new policies; in new democracies, the policy is to develop new institutions. On the one hand, the state must reduce its involvement in some sectors, notably the economy, to allow room for a more competitive private sector to develop. On the other hand, the state must simultaneously develop new modes of regulation: for example, overseeing the functioning of markets, giving independent authority to the judiciary and creating an efficient and professional bureaucracy. Thus the state in a new democracy must alter its entire shape, thinning out in some areas but building up in others. The scope of the policy changes needed to consolidate a new democracy is far greater than that involved in the transition from welfare to regulatory states in established democracies. Further, the difficulties are increased by the politically threatening combination of unrealistic expectations and economic decline which often occurs in the aftermath of transition. If there is one lesson to learn from the policy experience of third-wave democracies, it is that freshly elected governments – and especially their army of Western advisers – vastly understated the size, complexity and likely duration of the task of reshaping their relationship with society, to the detriment of the new democracies themselves.

Postcommunist states provide the most dramatic examples of the policy transformation required of new democracies. When the communist order collapsed, an entire method of organizing society went with it; far from springing a leak, the ship sank. The task facing new leaders was to transform societies fuelled by power into societies based on rules, a project that still continues. Take the economy as an example. Under communism, the state owned most major enterprises, with a central plan to provide coordination. Large enterprises also served as welfare providers, producing what Elster, Offe and Preuss (1998, p. 204) describe as a 'tight coupling' between production and social policy:

> Firms provided crèches, holiday homes, housing, health services, training and other welfare facilities for their staff. Continuous and lifelong participation in the production process was the proviso of collectivist protection.

This elaborate, inefficient but functioning network could not be quickly replaced by market mechanisms. Partly as a result of the postcommunist experience, it is now clear that a successful *private* economy, as in the established democracies, is an intricate *public* and even political achievement. It requires entrepreneurs to show initiative, capital markets to provide resources for investment, consumers to spend money, courts to resolve disputes, bureaucrats to keep their fingers out of the pie and a government to act as an umpire rather than a player.

Initially, few of these conditions were met in any postcommunist state. The legal challenge of establishing property rights (not to mention tax, competition and bankruptcy laws) was considerable in itself. In addition, state-owned enterprises had no experience of marketing their products. To understand the transformation required, Schmieding (1993, p. 236) invites us to imagine

> the problems that would befall a Western market economy if all firms discovered one morning that their entire staff for sales, advertising, finance and legal matters had gone off on a three-year holiday to Mars – together with all the lawyers, judges, bankers and public administrators.

A comparison of privatization policy with the established democracies demonstrates the difficulties confronting postcommunist states. In Britain, privatization proceeded on a case-by-case basis, with a sophisticated financial sector available to underwrite the issue (that is, to buy any shares left unsold) and to offer advice on pricing and marketing. State-owned companies were sold into an established private sector, with sweeteners offered to small investors who were pleased to take an easy profit. By contrast, in postcommunist states, the object was not to sell into the private sector but to create a private sector by, in effect, disposing of an entire economy. Further, individual enterprises were often in poor condition and any commercial banks lacked both the sophistication and the access to capital available in London's financial district. Difficulties abounded. What if the original owners of the enterprise, whose property had been taken over by the communists, demanded restitution? What about the enterprises' welfare obligations? Why should investors trust governments to deliver on their promises? And, most important, who had money to buy?

In practice, postcommunist states adopted a range of strategies in restructuring their economies. Several East European countries such as Hungary and Czechoslovakia could draw on economic liberalization which had preceded communism's fall. Throughout the postcommunist world, many enterprises were acquired by existing managers ('spontaneous privatization'), whether by design, default or theft. Occasionally, organizations were sold to overseas companies, a method of bringing in foreign expertise and capital which nonetheless risked political unpopularity at home. Or, in many cases, strategic parts of the economy were simply left in public hands with the expectation that performance would improve as market disciplines emerged, permitting a case-by-case solution later, if at all.

Definition
Mass privatization refers to attempts by post communist governments to sell off many state-owned enterprises at the same time, often by providing the public with low cost vouchers exchangable for shares. By contrast, established democracies (notably Britain) practised **case-by-case privatization** in which public corporations were sold one at a time.

Interestingly, many postcommunist countries (excluding Hungary) also attempted mass or voucher privatization at the early stage. Here, coupons were offered to the public at little or no cost. These coupons could then be exchanged for shares in newly privatized enterprises, with the exchange rate between vouchers and shares determined by an auction. Alternatively, vouchers could be placed with investment companies that stood between the investing citizen and the enterprise. Mass privatization succeeded in disposing of many enterprises at once, using a standard charter for each enterprise, and contributed to public education about investment; it achieved far more – and far faster – than the better-known case-by-case method pioneered in Britain. Given the turbulence of early postcommunism, mass privatization can be viewed as a significant policy achievement. But mass privatization created excessive expectations since many of the enterprises turned out to be worthless; the citizens of East Europe gained fewer rewards than did Mrs Thatcher's army of small shareholders in the UK. Also, vouchers tended to fragment control over enterprises at a time when a few powerful shareholders might have been able to force through much-needed restructuring; Hungary's emphasis on 'real owners' rather than voucher ownership was

understandable. In retrospect, the voucher method was simply one step along a winding road to a functioning market economy. Lieberman, Nestor and Desai (1996, p. 9) offer an overall assessment:

> Mass privatization achieved a great deal by creating a critical mass of private companies on which other reforms can build. But considerable effort will be needed to complete the privatization process, largely through case-by-case privatization of large strategic enterprises. Moreover, governments need to move from active intervention in the economy to facilitation and regulation as required.

Although postcommunist states require most rebuilding, the nature of the task is fundamentally similar in other new democracies with a strong state tradition. In authoritarian Latin America, for example, the state had not replaced the capitalist sector but had protected and nurtured powerful corporations (and industrialists) within it, producing a requirement for privatization, deregulation and an opening up to both domestic and international competition. Thus Lijphart and Waisman (1996a) note three common features linking privatization in East Europe and Latin America:

- In both regions, the transition occurred as a result of an economic as well as political crisis of the old regime, including in the case of Argentina, hyperinflation and massive capital flight
- In both regions, the transition was carried out by the state itself, allowing the old élite to recycle itself as the new bourgeoisie
- In both regions, privatization was contested, with opposition centred on those whose wealth was threatened by liberalization.

When we turn to new democracies in the smaller states of Africa and Latin America, we find that the problems of institution-building are even greater. The policy agenda here is about strengthening the capacity of *both* the public sector and the private sectors; the emphasis in established democracies on rebalancing the relationship between the two is a dubious prescription for new democracies in poor countries. It is certainly true that the state has been a dominant economic and political force, perhaps crowding out the private sector. But the solution is not so much less government but a different kind of government: one embedded in rule-following institutions rather than personal rule. Similarly, there is little point in adopting or even adapting Western ideas of new public management within the bureaucracy; rather, the purpose is to build up an orthodox civil service that applies rules consistently and economically. Developing the market also requires enhancing the public infrastructure of transport, communication and education.

In Africa, however, fragmentary attempts at capacity-building have so far produced only meagre results. Governments often lack the ability to implement their policies throughout the territory. They lack numbers on the ground and must often rely on traditional local leaders who are therefore able to veto the implementation of the reform agenda. A state that barely exists cannot be expected to engage in serious and effective policy-making and implementation. It is of course true, as Chazan *et al.* note (1999, p. 344), that the underlying problems of the continent extend well beyond politics; the difficulties include poor soil, an arid climate, tropical diseases and a labour surplus. As a result, even in a world that is more democratic than ever before,

millions of people continue to live lives of extreme poverty and degradation. If solutions are to be had, the comparative study of politics should help to find them.

Key reading

Next step: *Parsons (1995) is a comprehensive introduction to policy analysis.*

Dunn (1994) or Anderson (1984) are alternatives to Parsons. Hogwood and Gunn (1984) or Bobrow and Dryzek (1987) remain excellent discussions of the concepts used in the field. The starting-point on implementation is the classic American study by Pressman and Wildavsky (1973). Barrett and Fudge (1981) is an influential British work. Mazmanian and Sabatier (1989) offer an overall perspective on implementation. Rose (1993) is a comparative study of lesson-drawing in public policy. Pierson (1998, 2000) are excellent sources on the welfare state, while Majone (1996) is outstanding on regulation. Elster, Offe and Preuss (1998) cover institutional design in postcommunist societies, while Lijphart and Waisman (1996b) draw comparisons with Latin America. On privatization, see Wright (1994) for West Europe and Lieberman, Nestor and Desai (1997) for East Europe.

References

Abbink, J. and Hesseling, G. (eds) (1999) *Election Observation and Democratization in Africa* (London: Macmillan).

Aberbach, J. et al. (1981) *Bureaucrats and Politicians* (Cambridge, Mass.: Harvard University Press).

Abramson, P. and Inglehart, R. (1992) 'Generational Replacement and Value Change in Eight Western Societies', *British Journal of Political Science* (22) 183–228.

Ägh, A. (1996) 'Democratic Parliamentarism in Hungary: The First Parliament (1990–94) and the Entry of the Second Parliament', in *The New Parliaments of Central and Eastern Europe,* ed. D. Olson and P. Norton (London: Frank Cass) pp. 16–39.

Ägh, A. (1998) *The Politics of Central Europe* (London and Thousand Oaks, Calif.: Sage).

Agüero, F. and Stark, J. (eds) (1998) *Fault Lines of Democracy in Post-Transition Latin America* (Coral Gables, Fla.: University of Miami).

Ahmed, N. and Norton, P. (eds) (1999) *Parliaments in Asia* (London: Frank Cass).

Alber, J. (1988) ' Is There a Crisis of the Welfare State? Cross-National Evidence from Europe, North America and Japan', *European Sociological Review* (4) 181–207.

Alesina, A., Spolaore, E. and Wacziarg, R. (1997) *Economic Integration and Political Disintegration* (Working Paper 6163) (Chicago, Ill.: National Bureau of Economic Research).

Alexander, L. (ed.) (1998) *Constitutionalism: Philosophical Foundations* (Cambridge and N.Y.: Cambridge University Press).

Allison, L. (1996) 'Politics', in *The Concise Oxford Dictionary of Politics,* ed. I. McLean (Oxford and N.Y.: Oxford University Press) pp. 388–9.

Almond, G. and Verba, S. (1963) *The Civic Culture* (Princeton, N.J.: Princeton University Press).

Almond, G. and Verba, S. (eds) (1980) *The Civic Culture Revisited* (Princeton, N.J.: Princeton University Press).

Almond, G. and Bingham Powell, G. (1996) *Comparative Politics Today: A World View,* 6th edn (N.Y.: HarperCollins).

Almond, G. and Bingham Powell, G. (2000) *Comparative Politics Today: A World View,* 7th edn (N.Y.: Harper-Collins).

Anderson, C. and Ward, D. (1996) 'Barometer Elections in Comparative Perspective', *European Journal of Political Research* (15) 447–60.

Anderson, J. (1984) *Public Policy-Making* (Orlando, Fla.: Holt, Rinehart & Winston).

Andeweg, R. (1991) 'The Dutch Prime Minister: Not Just a Chairman, Not Yet a Chief?', *West European Politics* (14) 116–32.

Andeweg, R. (1997) 'Collegiality and Collectivity: Cabinets, Cabinet Committees and Cabinet Ministers', in *The Hollow Crown: Countervailing Trends in Core Executives,* ed. P. Weller, H. Bakvis and R. Rhodes (Basingstoke: Macmillan, and N.Y.: St. Martin's Press) pp. 58–83.

Andeweg, R. and Irwin, G. (1993) *Dutch Government and Politics* (Basingstoke: Macmillan).

Anton, T. (1969) 'Policy-Making and Political Culture in Sweden', *Scandinavian Political Studies* (19) 167–77.

Arblaster, A. (1994) *Democracy,* 2nd edn (Milton Keynes: Open University Press, and Minneapolis: University of Minnesota Press).

Arendt, H. (1958) *The Human Condition* (Chicago: University of Chicago Press).

Arendt, H. (1966) *The Origins of Totalitarianism* (N.Y.: Harcourt Brace). First pub. 1951.

Arendt, H. (1970) *On Violence* (London: Penguin).

Aristotle (1962 edn) *The Politics* (Harmondsworth: Penguin).

Arter, D. (1999) *Scandinavian Politics Today* (Manchester: Manchester University Press, and N.Y.: St. Martin's Press).

Asher, H. (1988a) *Presidential Elections and American Politics,* 4th edn (Pacific Grove, Calif.: Brooks/Cole).

Asher, H. (1988b) *Polling and the Public: What Every Citizen Should Know* (Washington, D.C.: Congressional Quarterly, Inc.).

Astin, A. (1977) *Four Critical Years: Effects of College on Beliefs, Attitudes and Knowledge* (San Francisco, Calif.: Jossey-Bass).

Baaklini, A., Denoeux, G. and Springborg, R. (1999) *Legislative Politics in the Arab World: The Resurgence of Democratic Institutions* (Boulder, Colo. and London: Lynne Rienner).

Baer, M. (1993) 'Mexico's Second Revolution: Pathways to Liberalization', in *Political and Economic Liberalization in Mexico: At a Critical Juncture?,* ed. R. Roett (Boulder, Colo. and London: Lynne Rienner) pp. 51–68.

Bagehot, W. (1963 edn) *The English Constitution* (London: Fontana). First pub. 1867.

Baka, A. (1998) 'The Framework for Public Management in Hungary', in *Innovations in Public Management: Perspectives from East and West Europe,* ed. T. Verheijen and D. Coombes (Cheltenham and Northampton, Mass.: Edward Elgar) pp. 128–42.

Ball, T. and Dagger, R. (1995) *Political Ideologies and the Democratic Ideal,* 2nd edn (N.Y.: HarperCollins).

Balme, R. (1998) 'The French Region as a Space for Public

Policy', in *Regions in Europe,* ed. P. Le Galès and C. Lequesne (London and N.Y.: Routledge) pp. 181–98.

Barber, J. (1992) *The Pulse of Politics: Electing Presidents in the Media Age* (New Brunswick, N.Y. and London: Transaction Books).

Bardach, E. (1976) 'Policy Termination as a Political Process', *Policy Sciences* (7) 123–31.

Barnes, S. and Kaase, M. (1979) *Political Action: Mass Participation in Five Western Democracies* (Thousand Oaks, Calif. and London: Sage).

Barrett, S. and Fudge, C. (1981) *Policy and Action* (London: Methuen).

Barry, B. (1988) *Sociologists, Economists, and Democracy* (Chicago: University of Chicago Press).

Bartle, J. and Griffiths, D. (eds) (2001) *Political Communications Transformed: From Morrison to Mandelson* (Basingstoke: Palgrave).

Bartolini, S. and Mair, P. (1990) *Identity, Competition and Electoral Availability: The Stabilization of European Electorates 1885–1985* (Cambridge and N.Y.: Cambridge University Press).

Batley, R. and Stoker, G. (eds) (1991) *Local Government in Europe: Trends and Developments* (Basingstoke: Macmillan).

Bayart, J.-F. (1993) *The State in Africa: the Politics of the Belly* (Harlow and N.Y.: Longman).

Baylis, T. (1996) 'Presidents Versus Prime Ministers: Shaping Executive Authority in Eastern Europe', *World Politics* (48) 297–322.

Bayne, N. (1997) 'What Governments Want from International Economic Institutions', *Government and Opposition* (32) 361–79.

Beer, S. (1982) *Britain against Itself* (London: Faber & Faber).

Bekke, H., Perry, J. and Toonen, T. (1996) *Civil Service Systems in Comparative Perspective* (Bloomington, Ind.: Indiana University Press).

Bell, D. *et al.* (ed.) (1995) *Towards Illiberal Democracy in Pacific Asia* (London: Macmillan).

Bell, J. (1991) 'Administrative Law' in *The Blackwell Encyclopaedia of Political Science,* ed. V. Bogdanor (Oxford and Cambridge, Mass.: Blackwell) pp. 9–12.

Bentley, A. (1908) *The Process of Government* (Chicago, Ill.: University of Chicago Press).

Bentley T., Jupp B. and Stedman Jones D. (2000) *Getting to Grips with Depoliticization* (London: Demos) at http://www.demos.co.uk.

Berglund, S. (1990) 'Finland in a Comparative Perspective', in *Finnish Democracy,* ed. J. Sunberg and S. Berglund (Jyväskylä: Finnish Political Science Association) pp. 11–25.

Berrington, H. (1995) 'Political Ethics: The Nolan Report', *Government and Opposition* (30) 429–51.

Bill, J. and Leiden, C. (1984) *Politics in the Middle East* (Boston: Little, Brown).

Bill, J. and Springborg, R. (2000) *Politics in the Middle East*, 4th edn (N.Y.: Longman).

Birch, A. (1972) *Representation* (London: Pall Mall).

Blais, A. and Massicote, L. (1996) 'Electoral Systems', in *Comparing Democracies: Elections and Voting in Global Perspective,* ed. L. LeDuc, R. Niemi, and P. Norris (Thousand Oaks, Calif. and London: Sage) pp. 49–82.

Blais, A., Massicotte, L. and Dobrzynska, A. (1997) 'Direct Presidential Elections: A World Summary', *Electoral Studies* (16) 441–55.

Blake, D. and Walters, R. (2001) *The Politics of Global Economic Relations,* 5th edn (Englewood Cliffs, N.J.: Prentice Hall).

Block, F. (1977) 'The Ruling Class Does Not Rule', *Socialist Revolution* (3) 6–28.

Blondel, J. (1973) *Comparative Legislatures* (Englewood Cliffs, N.J.: Prentice Hall).

Blondel, J. (1993) 'Consensus Politics and Multiparty Systems', Paper presented at the Conference on Consensual Policymaking and Multiparty Politics, Australian National University, 1993.

Bobrow, D. and Dryzek, J. (1987) *Policy Analysis by Design* (Pittsburgh, Pa.: Pittsburgh University Press).

Bogason, P. (1996) 'The Fragmentation of Local Government in Scandinavia', *European Journal of Political Research* (30) 65–86.

Bogdanor, V. (1988) 'Introduction', in *Constitutions in Democratic Politics,* ed. V. Bogdanor (Aldershot: Gower) pp. 1–13.

Bogdanor, V. (1990) 'Founding Elections and Regime Change', *Electoral Studies* (9) 295–302.

Bogdanor, V. (ed.) (1991) *The Blackwell Encyclopaedia of Political Science* (Oxford and Cambridge, Mass.: Blackwell).

Bohman, J. and Rehg, W. (eds) (1997) *Deliberative Democracy. Essays on Reason and Politics* (Cambridge, Mass. and London: MIT Press).

Boli, J. and Thomas, G. (eds) (1999) *Constructing World Culture: International Non-Governmental Organizations since 1875* (Stanford, Calif.: Stanford University Press).

Borón, A. (1998) 'Faulty Democracies? A Reflection on the Capitalist "Fault Lines"', in *Fault Lines of Democracy in Post-Transition Latin America,* ed. F. Agüero and J. Stark (Coral Gables, Fla.: University of Miami) pp. 41–66.

Boston, J. (1995a) 'Inherently Governmental Functions and the Limits to Contracting Out', in *The State Under Contract,* ed. J. Boston (Wellington: Bridget Williams) pp. 78–111.

Boston, J. (ed.) (1995b) *The State Under Contract* (Wellington: Bridget Williams).

Boulding, K. (1989) *Three Faces of Power* (Thousand Oaks, Calif. and London: Sage).

Bourgault, L. (1995) *Mass Media in Sub-Saharan Africa* (Bloomington, Ind.: Indiana University Press).

Bovens, M. and Hart, P. (1996) *Understanding Policy Fiascos* (New Brunswick, N.J. and London: Transaction Publishers).

Bowen, S. (2000) 'Gap Narrows in Peru's Presidential Race', *Financial Times,* April 7 2000, p. 13.

Bowler, S. and Farrell, D. (eds) (1992) *Electoral Strategies and Political Marketing* (London: Macmillan).

Bratton, M. (1997) 'Deciphering Africa's Divergent Transitions', *Political Science Quarterly* (112) 67–93.

Bratton, M. (1998) 'Second Elections in Africa', *Journal of Democracy* (9) 51–66.

Bratton, M. and van de Walle, N. (1997) *Democratic Experiments in Africa: Regime Transitions in Comparative Perspective* (Cambridge and N.Y.: Cambridge University Press).

Breuilly, J. (1993) *Nationalism and the State*, 2nd edn (N.Y.: St. Martin's Press).

Brooker, P. (1995) *Twentieth-Century Dictatorships: The Ideological One-Party States* (Basingstoke: Macmillan).

Brooker, P. (2000) *Non-Democratic Regimes: Theory, Government and Politics* (Basingstoke: Macmillan, and N.Y.: St. Martin's Press).

Brooks, S. (1996) *Canadian Democracy: An Introduction*, 2nd edn (Toronto and Oxford: Oxford University Press).

Broughton, D. (1995) *Public Opinion Polling and Politics in Britain* (Hemel Hempstead: Harvester Wheatsheaf).

Bryce, J. (1921) *Modern Democracies* (Vol. 2) (N.Y.: Macmillan).

Brzezinski, Z. (1976) 'Soviet Politics: From the Future to the Past', in *The Dynamics of Soviet Politics,* ed. P. Cocks, R. Daniels and N. Heer (Cambridge, Mass.: Harvard University Press).

Brzezinski, Z. (1997) 'The New Challenge to Human Rights', *Journal of Democracy* (8) 3–8.

Bull, H. (1977) *The Anarchical Society: A Study of Order in World Politics* (Basingstoke: Macmillan).

Bullock, A. (1990) *Hitler: a Study in Tyranny* (London: Penguin Books).

Bunce, V. (1997) 'Presidents and the Transition in Eastern Europe', in *Presidential Institutions and Democratic Politics: Comparing Regional and National Contexts,* ed. K. von Mettenheim (Baltimore, Md. and London: Johns Hopkins University Press) pp. 161–76.

Burgess, M. and Gagnon, A. (eds) (1993) *Comparative Federalism and Federation: Competing Traditions and Future Directions* (Hemel Hempstead: Harvester Wheatsheaf).

Butler, D. (1989) *British General Elections Since 1945* (Oxford and Cambridge, Mass.: Blackwell).

Butler, D. (1996) 'Polls and Elections', in *Elections and Voting in Global Perspective,* ed. L. LeDuc, R. Niemi and P. Norris (Thousand Oaks, Calif. and London: Sage) pp. 236–53.

Butler, D. and Ranney, A. (eds) (1994) *Referendums Around the World: The Growing Use of Direct Democracy* (Washington, D.C.: American Enterprise Institute, and Basingstoke: Macmillan).

Camp, R. (ed.) (1999) *Politics in Mexico: The Decline of Authoritarianism*, 3rd edn (Oxford and N.Y: Oxford University Press).

Campbell, A. (1996) 'City Government in Russia', in *Transformation from Below: Local Power and the Political Economy of Postcommunist Transitions,* ed. J. Gibson and P. Hanson (Aldershot and Brookfield, Vt.: Edward Elgar) pp. 37–56.

Campbell, A., Converse, P., Miller, A. *et al.* (1960) *The American Voter* (N.Y.: Wiley).

Campbell, C. and Wilson, G. (1995) *The End of Whitehall: Death of a Paradigm?* (Oxford and Cambridge, Mass.: Blackwell).

Canel, E. (1992) 'Democratization and the Decline of Urban Social Movements in Uruguay: A Political Institutional Account', in *The Making of Social Movements in Latin America: Identity, Strategy and Democracy,* ed. A. Escobar and S. Alvarez (Boulder, Colo. and Oxford: Westview) pp. 276–90.

Caplan, J. (1988) *Government Without Administration: State and Civil Service in Weimar and Nazi Germany* (Oxford: Clarendon Press).

Carey, J. (1998) *Term Limits and Legislative Representation* (Cambridge and N.Y.: Cambridge University Press).

Carley, M. (1980) *Rational Techniques in Policy Analysis* (London: Heinemann).

Case, W. (1996) 'Can the "Halfway House" Stand? Semidemocracy and Elite Theory in Three Southeast Asian Countries', *Comparative Politics* (28) 437–64.

Centeno, M. and Silva, P. (1998) 'Introduction', in *The Politics of Expertise in Latin America,* ed. M. Centeno and P. Silva (Basingstoke: Macmillan, and N.Y.: St. Martin's Press) pp. 1–12.

Cerny, P. (1990) *The Changing Architecture of Politics* (Thousand Oaks, Calif. and London: Sage).

Chalmers, D. (1990) *Dilemmas of Latin American Democratization: Dealing with International Forces* (Papers on Latin America No.18) (N.Y.: Columbia University Institute of Latin American and Iberian Studies).

Chandler, J. (1993) *Local Government in Liberal Democracies: An Introductory Survey* (London and N.Y.: Routledge).

Chandler, J. (ed.) (2000) *Comparative Public Administration* (London and N.Y.: Routledge).

Chazan, N. *et al.* (1999) *Politics and Society in Contemporary Africa*, 3rd edn (Boulder, Colo.: Lynne Rienner).

Chebabi, H. and Linz, J. (eds) (1998) *Sultanistic Regimes* (Baltimore, Md. and London: Johns Hopkins University Press).

Christensen, T. and Egeberg, M. (eds) (1997) *Forvaltnings-kunnskap* (Oslo: Aschehoug Tano).

Christensen, T. and Guy Peters, B. (1999) *Structure, Culture and Governance: A Comparison of Norway and the United States* (Lanham, Md. and Oxford: Rowman & Littlefield).

CIA (1994) *Handbook of International Economic Statistics* (Washington, D.C.: CIA).

CIA (1997) *Handbook of the Nations* (Washington, D.C.: Gale) at http://www.cia.org.

Cigler, C. and Loomis, B. (eds) (1998) *Interest Group Politics*, 5th edn (Washington, D.C.: Congressional Quarterly Press).

Clapham, C. (1982) *Private Patronage and Public Power: Political Clientelism in the Modern State* (London: Pinter).

Clapham, C. (1985) *Third World Politics: An Introduction* (Beckenham: Croom Helm).

Close, D. (ed.) (1995) *Legislatures and the New Democracies in Latin America* (Boulder, Colo. and London: Lynne Rienner).

Collier, D. (1991) 'The Comaparative Method: Two Decades of Change', in *Comparative Dynamics: Global Research Perspectives*, ed. D. Rustow and K. Erickson (N.Y.: HarperCollins) pp. 7–31.

Comstock, W. *et al.* (1971) *Religion and Man: An Introduction* (N.Y.: Harper & Row).

Conaghan, C. (1995) 'Politicians against Parties: Discord and Disconnection in Ecuador's Party System', in *Building Democratic Institutions: Party Systems in Latin America,* ed. S. Mainwaring and T. Scully (Stanford, Calif.: Stanford University Press) .

Conover, P. and Searing, D. (1994) 'Democratic Citizenship and the Study of Political Socialization', in *Developing*

Democracy: Essays in Honour of J. F. P .Blondel, ed. I. Budge and D. McKay (Thousand Oaks, Calif. and London: Sage) pp. 24–55.

Conradt, D. (2001) *The German Polity,* 7th edn (N.Y.: Longman).

Cornelius, W. (2000) 'Politics in Mexico' in *Comparative Politics Today: A World View,* ed. G. Almond and G. Bingham-Powell, 7th edn (N.Y.: HarperCollins) pp. 463–514.

Coulson, A. (ed.) (1995) *Local Government in Eastern Europe,* 4th edn (Cheltenham and Brookfield, Vt.: Edward Elgar).

Cowley, P. (2000) 'Legislatures and Assemblies', in *Developments in British Politics 6,* ed. P. Dunleavy *et al.* (Basingstoke: Macmillan, and N.Y.: St. Martin's Press) pp. 108–26.

Cox, T. (1993) 'Democratization and the Growth of Pressure Groups in Soviet and Post-Soviet Politics' in *Pressure Groups,* ed. J. Richardson (Oxford and N.Y.: Oxford University Press) pp. 71–85.

Crawford, K. (1996) *East Central European Politics Today* (Manchester: Manchester University Press, and N.Y.: St. Martin's Press).

Crick, B. (2000) *In Defence of Politics,* 5th edn (Harmondsworth: Penguin) First pub. 1962.

Cronin, T. (1989) *Direct Democracy: The Politics of Initiative, Referendum and Recall* (Cambridge, Mass. and London: Harvard University Press).

Crouch, H. (1996) *Government and Society in Malaysia* (Cornell, N.Y.: Cornell University Press).

Cutler, L. (1980) 'To Form a Government', *Foreign Affairs* (59) 126–43.

Dahl, R. (1957) 'The Concept of Power', *Behavioral Science* (2) 201–15.

Dahl, R. (1961) *Who Governs? Democracy and Power in an American City* (New Haven, Conn. and London: Yale University Press).

Dahl, R. (1989) *Democracy and its Critics* (New Haven, Conn. and London: Yale University Press).

Dahl, R. (1991) *Modern Political Analysis,* 5th edn (Englewood Cliffs, N.J.: Prentice Hall).

Dahl, R. (1993) 'Pluralism', in *The Oxford Companion to Politics of the World,* ed. J. Krieger (N.Y. and Oxford: Oxford University Press) pp. 704–7.

Dahl, R. (1998) *On Democracy* (New Haven, Conn. and London: Yale University Press).

Dahl, R. (1999) 'Can International Organizations Be Democratic?', in *Democracy's Edges,* ed. I. Shapiro and C. Hacker-Cordón (New Haven and London: Yale University Press) pp. 19–36.

Dalton, R. (1994) *The Green Rainbow: Environmental Groups in Western Europe* (New Haven, Conn. and London: Yale University Press).

Dalton, R. (1996) 'Political Cleavages, Issues and Electoral Change', in *Elections and Voting in Global Perspective,* ed. L. LeDuc, R. Niemi and P. Norris (Thousand Oaks, Calif. and London: Sage) pp. 319–42.

Dalton, R. and Kuechler, M. (1990) *Challenging the Political Order: New Social and Political Movements in Western Democracies* (Cambridge: Polity).

Dalton, R. and Wattenberg, M. (2000) *Politics Without Partisans: Political Change in Advanced Industrial Democracies* (Oxford and N.Y.: Oxford University Press).

Damgaard, E. (ed.) (1993) *Parliamentary Change in the Nordic Countries* (Oxford and N.Y.: Oxford University Press).

Danks, C. (2001) Russian Politics and Society (Harlow and N.Y.: Longman).

Davidson, R. and Oleszek, W. (1999) *Congress and Its Members,* 7th edn (Washington, D.C.: Congressional Quarterly).

Davies, J. (1962) 'Toward a Theory of Revolution', *American Sociological Review* (27) 5–18.

Davies, N. (1996) *Europe: A History* (Oxford and N.Y.: Oxford University Press).

Dawson, R., Prewitt, K. and Dawson, K. (1977) *Political Socialization* (Boston, Mass.: Little, Brown).

de Swaan, A. (1973) *Coalition Theories and Cabinet Formation* (Amsterdam: Elsevier).

de Tocqueville, A. (1966) *Democracy in America* (N.Y.: Vintage Books). First pub. 1835.

de Tocqueville, A. (1954) *The Ancien Regime and the Revolution in France* (London: Fontana). First pub. 1856.

Deegan, H. (2001) *The Politics of the New South Africa: Apartheid and After* (Harlow and N.Y.: Longman).

Dehousse, R. (1997) 'European Integration and the Nation-State', in *Developments in West European Politics,* ed. M. Rhodes, P. Heywood and V. Wright (Basingstoke: Macmillan) pp. 37–56.

Dehousse, R. (1998) *The European Court of Justice* (London: Macmillan).

Dempsey, J. (1993) 'East European Voices', in *Developments in East European Politics,* ed. S. White, J. Batt and P. Lewis (Basingstoke: Macmillan) pp. 280–8.

Denver, D. (1994) *Elections and Voting Behaviour in Britain,* 2nd edn (Hemel Hempstead: Philip Allan).

Diamond, L. (1992) 'Economic Development and Democracy Reconsidered', in *Reexamining Democracy: Essays in Honor of Seymour Martin Lipset,* ed. G. Marks and L. Diamond (Thousand Oaks, Calif. and London: Sage) pp. 93–131.

Diamond, L. (1993) 'Introduction: Political Culture and Democracy', in *Political Culture and Democracy in Developing Countries,* ed. L. Diamond (Boulder, Colo. and London: Lynne Rienner) pp. 1–36.

Diamond, L. (1997) 'Democracy in the Americas', *Annals of the American Academy of Political and Social Sciences* (550) 12–41.

Diamond, L., Linz, J. and Lipset, S. (1995) 'Introduction: What Makes For Democracy?', in *Politics in Developing Countries: Comparing Experiences with Democracy,* ed. L. Diamond, J. Linz and S. Lipset (Boulder, Colo. and London: Lynne Rienner) pp. 1–33.

Diamond, L. and Lipset, S. (1995) 'Legitimacy', in *The Encyclopaedia of Democracy,* ed. S. Lipset (London and N.Y.: Routledge) pp. 747–51.

Diamond, L. and Plattner, M. (eds) (1996) *The Global Resurgence of Democracy,* 2nd edn (Baltimore, Md. and London: John Hopkins University Press).

Diamond, L., Kirk-Greene, A. and Oyediran, O. (eds) (1997) *Transition without End: Nigerian Politics and Civil Society under Babanginda* (Boulder, Colo. and London: Lynne Rienner).

Dicey, A. (1959) *Introduction to the Study of the Law of the Constitution*, 10th edn (London: Macmillan) First pub. 1885.

DiPalma, G. (1990) *To Craft Democracies: An Essay on Democratic Transitions* (Berkeley, Calif. and Oxford: University of California Press).

Dogan, M. and Pelassy, G. (1990) *How to Compare Nations* (Chatham, N.J.: Chatham House).

Dogan M. and Kazancigil, A. (eds) (1994) *Comparing Nations: Concepts, Strategies, Substance* (Cambridge, Mass. and Oxford: Blackwell).

Domhoff, G. (1983) *Who Rules America Now? A View for the '80s* (Englewood Cliffs, N.J.: Prentice Hall).

Domínguez, J. and Giraldo, J. (1996) 'Parties, Institutions and Market Reforms in Constructing Democracies', in *Constructing Democratic Governance: Mexico, Central America and the Caribbean in the 1990s,* ed. J. Domínguez and A. Lowenthal (Baltimore, Md. and London: Johns Hopkins) pp. 3–41.

Donovan, M. (1995) 'The Politics of Electoral Reform in Italy', *International Political Science Review* (16) 47–64.

Dowding, K. (1995) *The Civil Service* (London and N.Y.: Routledge).

Downs, A. (1957) *An Economic Theory of Democracy* (N.Y.: Harper).

Downs, G., Roche, D. and Baroom, P. (1996) 'Is the Good News about Compliance Good News about Cooperation?', *International Organization* (50) 379–406.

Dreyfus, F. (1990) 'The Conseil d'Etat', in *Developments in French Politics,* ed. P. Hall, J. Hayward and H. Machin (Basingstoke: Macmillan) pp. 133–51.

Duchacek, I. (1970) *Federalism: The Territorial Dimension of Politics* (N.Y.: Holt, Rinehart & Winston).

Duchacek, I. (1973) *Power Maps: The Comparative Politics of Constitutions* (Santa Barbara, Calif.: ABC Clio).

Duchacek, I. (1991) 'Constitutions/Constitutionalism', in *The Blackwell Encyclopaedia of Political Science,* ed. V. Bogdanor (Oxford and Cambridge, Mass.: Blackwell) pp. 142–4.

Dunleavy, P., and O'Leary, B. (1987) *Theories of the Liberal Democratic State* (London: Macmillan).

Dunn, W. (1994) *Public Policy Analysis: An Introduction*, 2nd edn (Englewood Cliffs, N.J.: Prentice Hall).

Duverger, M. (1954) *Political Parties* (London: Methuen).

Duverger, M. (1980) 'A New Political System Model: Semi-Presidential Government', *European Journal of Political Research* (8) 165–87.

Dye, T. (1997) *Understanding Public Policy*, 9th edn (Englewood Cliffs, N.J.: Prentice Hall).

Dyson, K. (1980) *State Tradition in Western Europe: A Study of an Idea and Institution* (Oxford and N.Y.: Oxford University Press).

Easter, G. (1997) 'Preference for Presidentialism: Post-communist Regime Change in Russia and the NIS', *World Politics* (49) 184–211.

Easton, D. (1965a) *A Framework for Political Analysis* (Englewood Cliffs, N. J.: Prentice Hall).

Easton, D. (1965b) *A Systems Analysis of Political Life* (N.Y.: Wiley).

Eatwell, R. (1996) *Fascism: A History* (London: Chatto & Windus).

Eatwell, R. (ed.) (1997) *European Political Cultures: Conflict or Convergence?* (London and N.Y.: Routledge).

Eberle, J. (1990) 'Understanding the Revolutions in Eastern Europe', in *Spring in Winter: The 1989 Revolutions,* ed. G. Prins (Manchester: Manchester University Press) pp. 193–209.

Eckstein, H. (1998a) 'Congruence Theory Explained', in *Can Democracy Take Root in Post-Soviet Russia? Explorations in State–Society Relations,* ed. H. Eckstein *et al.* (Lanham, Md. and Oxford: Rowman & Littlefield) pp. 3–33.

Eckstein, H. (1998b) 'Russia and the Conditions of Democracy', in *Can Democracy Take Root in Post-Soviet Russia? Explorations in State–Society Relations,* ed. H. Eckstein *et al.* (Lanham, Md. and Oxford: Rowman & Littlefield) pp. 349–81.

Eckstein, H. *et al.* (1998) *Can Democracy Take Root in Post-Soviet Russia? Explorations in State–Society Relations* (Lanham, Md. and Oxford: Rowman & Littlefield).

Edelman, M. (1964) *The Symbolic Uses of Politics* (Urbana, Ill.: University of Illinois Press).

Edelman, M. (1995) 'Israel', in *The Global Expansion of Judicial Power,* ed. C. Tate and T. Vallinder (N.Y. and London: New York University Press) pp. 403–16.

Elazar, D. (1996) 'From Statism to Federalism: A Paradigm Shift', *International Political Science Review* (17) 417–30.

Elazar, D. (1998) *Constitutionalizing Globalization: The Postmodern Revival of Confederal Arrangements* (Lanham, Md. and Oxford: Rowman & Littlefield).

Elgie, R. (1995) *Political Leadership in Liberal Democracies* (Basingstoke: Macmillan).

Elgie, R. (ed.) (1999) *Semi-Presidentialism in Europe* (Oxford and N.Y.: Oxford University Press).

Elster, J., Offe, C. and Preuss, U. (1998) *Institutional Design in Post-Communist Societies: Rebuilding the Ship at Sea* (Cambridge and N.Y.: Cambridge University Press).

Elwin, W. (1934) *Fascism at Work* (London: Hopkinson).

Emy, M. and Hughes, O. (1991) *Australian Politics: Realities in Conflict* (South Melbourne: Macmillan).

Eriksen, E. (1990) 'Towards the Post-Corporate State?', *Scandinavian Political Studies* (13) 345–64.

Escobar, A. and Alvarez, S. (eds) (1992) *The Making of Social Movements in Latin America: Identity, Strategy and Democracy* (Boulder, Colo. and Oxford: Westview).

Esping-Andersen, G. (1990) *The Three Worlds of Welfare Capitalism* (Oxford: Polity).

Esping-Andersen, G. (1996a) 'After the Golden Age? Welfare State Dilemmas in a Global Economy', in *Welfare States in Transition: National Adaptations in Global Economies,* ed. G. Esping-Andersen (Thousand Oaks, Calif. and London: Sage) pp. 1–31.

Esping-Andersen, G. (ed.) (1996b) *Welfare States in Transition: National Adaptations in Global Economies* (Thousand Oaks, Calif. and London: Sage).

Esposito, J. (1997) *Political Islam: Revolution, Radicalism or Reform?* (Boulder, Colo. and London: Lynne Rienner).

Eulau, H. (1963) *The Behavioral Persuasion in Politics* (N.Y.: Random House).

Evans, P. (1995) 'The Role of Theory in Comparative Politics', in *World Politics* (48) 2–10.

Evans, P., Rueschemeyer, D. and Skocpol, T. (eds) (1985) *Bringing The State Back In* (Cambridge and N.Y.: Cambridge University Press).

Farnen, R. and Meloen, J. (eds) (2000) *Democracy, Authoritarianism and Education* (Basingstoke: Palgrave).

Farrell, D. (1997) *Comparing Electoral Systems* (Hemel Hempstead: Prentice Hall).

Farrell, D. (2001) *Electoral Systems: A Comparative Introduction* (Palgrave: Macmillan).

Feldman, O. (1993) *Politics and the News Media in Japan* (Ann Arbor, Mich.: University of Michigan Press).

Fenno, R. (1978) *Home Style: House Members in their Districts* (Boston: Little Brown).

Fesler, J. and Kettl, D. (1996) *The Politics of the Administrative Process* (Chatham, N.J.: Chatham House).

Finer, S. (1974) *Comparative Government* (Harmondsworth: Penguin).

Finer, S. (ed.) (1975) *Adversary Politics and Electoral Reform* (London: Anthony Wigram).

Finer, S. (1988) *The Man on Horseback: The Role of the Military in Politics* (Boulder, Colo.: Westview). First pub. 1962.

Finer, S. (1997) *The History of Government from the Earliest Times* (Oxford and N.Y.: Oxford University Press, three volumes.).

Finley, M. (1985) *Democracy Ancient and Modern* (London: Hogarth Press).

Fiorina, M. (1981) *Retrospective Voting in American National Elections* (New Haven, Conn.: Yale University Press).

Fishkin, J. (1991) *Democracy and Deliberation: New Directions for Democratic Reform* (New Haven, Conn. and London: Yale University Press).

Fitzmaurice, J. (1991) *Austrian Politics and Society Today* (Basingstoke: Macmillan).

Fitzmaurice, J. (1996) *The Politics of Belgium: A Unique Federalism* (London: Hurst).

Fitzmaurice, J. (1998) *Politics and Government in the Visegrad Countries: Poland, Hungary, the Czech Republic and Slovakia* (London: Macmillan, and N.Y.: St. Martin's Press).

Flammang, J. *et al.* (1990) *American Politics in a Changing World* (Pacific Grove, Calif.: Brooks/Cole).

Foley, M. (1999) 'In Kiev They Fine a Journalist $1m and Cut Off All the Phones', *The Times,* April 2 1999, p. 45.

Forsyth, M. (1989) *Federalism and Nationalism* (Leicester: Leicester University Press).

Frank, A. (1969) *Capitalism and Underdevelopment in Latin America* (N.Y.: Monthly Review Press).

Franklin, B. (1994) *Packaging and Politics: Political Communication in Britain's Media Democracy* (London: Edward Arnold, and N.Y.: Routledge, Chapman and Hall).

Franklin, D. and Baun, M. (eds) (1995) *Political Culture and Constitutionalism: A Comparative Approach* (Armonk, N.Y. and London: M. E. Sharpe).

Franklin, M. (1992) 'The Decline of Cleavage Politics', in *Electoral Change: Responses to Evolving Social and Attitudinal Structures in Western Countries,* ed. M. Franklin, T. Mackie and H. Valen (Cambridge and N.Y.: Cambridge University Press) pp. 383–405.

Franklin, M. (1996) 'Electoral Participation', in *Elections and Voting in Global Perspective,* ed. L. LeDuc, R. Niemi and P. Norris (Thousand Oaks, Calif. and London: Sage) pp. 216–35.

Franklin, M., Mackie, T., Valen, H. *et al.*(eds) (1992) *Electoral Change: Responses to Evolving Social and Attitudinal Structures in Western Countries* (Cambridge and N.Y.: Cambridge University Press).

Fried, R. (1990) *Nightmare in Red: The McCarthy Era in Perspective* (N.Y. and Oxford: Oxford University Press).

Friedrich, C. (1937) *Constitutional Government and Politics* (N.Y.: Harper).

Friedrich, C. and Brzezinski, Z. (1965) *Totalitarian Dictatorship and Autocracy* (N.Y.: Praeger).

Frühling, H. (1998) 'Judicial Reform and Democratization in Latin America', in *Fault Lines of Democracy in Post-Transition Latin America,* ed. F. Agüero and J. Stark (Coral Gables, Fla.: University of Miami) pp. 237–62.

Fuchs, D. (1999) 'The Democratic Culture of Unified Germany', in *Critical Citizens: Global Support for Democratic Governance,* ed. P. Norris (Oxford and N.Y.: Oxford University Press) pp. 123–45.

Fukuyama, F. (1989) 'The End of History?', *National Interest* (16) 3–18.

Gallagher, M. (1997) 'Electoral Systems and Voting Behaviour', in *Developments in West European Politics,* ed. M. Rhodes, P. Heywood and V. Wright (Basingstoke: Macmillan) pp. 114–30.

Gallagher, M. and Uleri, P. (eds) (1996) *The Referendum Experience in Europe* (Basingstoke: Macmillan).

Gamble, A. and Payne, A. (eds) (1996a) *Regionalism and World Order* (Basingstoke: Macmillan).

Gamble, A. and Payne, A. (1996b) 'The New Regionalism', in *Regionalism and World Order,* ed. A. Gamble and A. Payne (Basingstoke: Macmillan) pp. 247–64.

Gardner, J. (2000) *About Common Cause.* Common Cause Home Page. Available at: http://www.commoncause.org/about/fact.htm .

Geertz, C. (1993) 'Thick Description: Toward an Interpretative Theory of Culture', in *Interpretation of Cultures,* ed. C. Geertz (London: Fontana) pp. 1–33. First pub. 1973.

Gerth, H. and Mills, C. (1948) *From Max Weber* (London: Routledge & Kegan Paul).

Gibson, J. and Hanson, P. (eds) (1996) *Transformation from Below: Local Power and the Political Economy of Postcommunist Transitions* (Aldershot and Brookfield, Vt.: Edward Elgar).

Gidlund, J. and Jerneck, M. (eds) (2000) *Local and Regional Governance in Europe* (Aldershot and Brookfield, Vt.: Edward Elgar).

Gilbert, P. (1995) *Terrorism, Security and Nationality* (London and N.Y.: Routledge).

Gill, G. (2000) *The Dynamics of Democratization: Elites, Civil Society and the Transition Process* (Basingstoke: Macmillan, and N.Y.: St. Martin's Press).

Gill, G. and Markwick, R. (2000) *Russia's Stillborn Democracy: From Gorbachev to Yeltsin* (Oxford and N.Y.: Oxford University Press).

Gills, B., Rocamora, J. and Wilson, R. (eds) (1993) *Low Intensity Democracy: Political Power in the New World Order* (Boulder, Colo. and London: Pluto).

Ginsberg, B. (1982) *The Consequences of Consent* (Reading, Mass.: Addison Wesley).

Ginsberg, B. (1986) *The Captive Public: How Mass Opinion Promotes State Power* (N.Y.: Basic Books).

Giol, J. (1990) 'By Consociationalism to a Majoritarian Parliamentary System: The Rise and Decline of the Spanish Cortes', in *Parliament and Democratic Consolidation in Southern Europe*, ed. U. Liebert and M. Cotta (London: Pinter) pp. 92–131.

Gleason, A. (1995) *Totalitarianism: The Inner History of the Cold War* (N.Y.: Oxford University Press).

Goban-Klas, G. (1997) 'Politics versus the Media in Poland: A Game without Rules', in *Postcommunism and the Media in Eastern Europe*, ed. P. O'Neill (London and Portland, Ore.: Frank Cass) pp. 24–41.

Goban-Klas, T. and Sasinka-Klas, T. (1992) 'From Closed to Open Communication Systems', in *Democracy and Civil Society in Eastern Europe*, ed. P. Lewis (London: Macmillan, and N.Y.: St. Martin's Press) pp. 76–90.

Goetz, K. (1997) 'Acquiring Political Craft: Training Grounds for Top Officials in the German Core Executive', *Public Administration* (75) 753–75.

Goldstone, J. (1991) 'An Analytical Framework', in *Revolutions of the Late Twentieth Century*, ed. J. Goldstone, T. Gurr and F. Moshiri (Boulder, Colorado and Oxford: Westview) pp. 37–51.

Gould, R. and Jackson, C. (1995) *A Guide for Election Observers* (Aldershot and Brookfield, Vt.: Dartmouth).

Graber, D. (1997) *Mass Media and American Politics*, 5th edn (Washington, D.C.: CQ Press).

Green, D. and Shapiro, I. (1994) *Pathologies of Rational Choice Theories* (New Haven, Conn. and London: Yale University Press).

Greenbaum, T. (1998) *The Handbook for Focus Group Research*, 2nd edn (Thousand Oaks, Calif. and London: Sage).

Greenberg, D. *et al.* (ed.) (1993) *Constitutionalism and Democracy: Transitions in the Contemporary World* (N.Y. and Oxford: Oxford University Press).

Griffith, J. (1997) *The Politics of the Judiciary*, 4th edn (London: Fontana).

Gundle, S. and Parker, S. (eds) (1996) *The New Italian Republic: From the Fall of the Berlin Wall to Berlusconi* (London and N.Y.: Routledge).

Gunlicks, A. (1999) 'Fifty Years of German Federalism: An Overview and Some Current Developments', in *The Federal Republic of Germany at Fifty: The End of a Century of Turmoil*, ed. P. Merkl (London: Macmillan) pp. 186–202.

Gurr, T. (1980) *Why Men Rebel* (Princeton, N.J.: Princeton University Press).

Guy Peters, B. (1993) *American Public Policy: Promise and Performance*, 3rd edn (Chatham, N.J.: Chatham House).

Guy Peters, B. (2000) *The Politics of Bureaucracy*, 5th edn (White Plains, N.Y.: Longman).

Guy Peters, B. (1999) *Institutional Theory in Political Science: The 'New Institutionalism'* (London and N.Y.: Pinter).

Habermas, J. (1978) *Knowledge and Human Interests*, 2nd edn (trans. J. Shapiro) (London: Heinemann Education).

Habermas, J. (1982) *Moral Consciousness and Communicative Action* (trans. C. Lenhardt and S. Nicholsen) (Cambridge, Mass.: MIT Press) .

Hadenius, A. (ed.) (1997) *Democracy's Victory and Crisis* (N.Y. and Cambridge: Cambridge University Press).

Hagopian, F. (1998) 'Democracy and Political Representation in Latin America in the 1990s: Pause, Reorganization or Decline?', in *Fault Lines of Democracy in Post-Transition Latin America,* ed. F. Agüero and J. Stark (Coral Gables, Fla.: University of Miami) pp. 99–144.

Hall, P. and Ikenberry, G. (1989) *The State* (Milton Keynes: Open University Press).

Halliday, F. (1999) *Revolution and World Politics: The Rise and Fall of the Sixth Great Power* (Basingstoke: Macmillan).

Handelman, H. (1997) *Mexican Politics: The Dynamics of Change* (N.Y.: St. Martin's Press).

Hansen, M. (1991) *The Athenian Democracy in the Age of Demosthenes* (Oxford and Cambridge, Mass.: Blackwell).

Hansen, T. (1993) 'Intermediate-Level Reforms and the Development of the Norwegian Welfare State', in *The Rise of Meso Government in Europe*, ed. L. Sharpe (Thousand Oaks, Calif. and London: Sage) pp. 154–82.

Harriss, J. (1995) 'A Time of Troubles: Problems of Humanitarian Intervention in the 1990s', in *The Politics of Humanitarian Intervention,* ed. J. Harriss (London and N.Y.: Pinter) pp. 1–15.

Harrop, M., and Miller, W. (1987) *Elections and Voters: A Comparative Introduction* (Basingstoke: Macmillan).

Hayek, F. (1960) *The Constitution of Liberty* (Chicago: University of Chicago Press).

Haynes, J. (1993) *Religion in Third World Politics* (Buckingham and Philadelphia, Pa.: Open University Press).

Haynes, J. (1996) *Religion and Politics in Africa* (London and Atlantic Highlands, N.J.: Zed Books).

Haynes, J. (1998) *Religion in Global Politics* (Harlow and N.Y.: Addison Wesley Longman).

Hayward, J. (1994) 'Ideological Change: The Exhaustion of the Revolutionary Impulse', in *Developments in French Politics,* ed. P. Hall, J. Hayward and H. Machin (Basingstoke: Macmillan) pp. 15–32.

Hazan, R. (1997a) 'The 1996 Election in Israel: Adopting Party Primaries', *Electoral Studies* (16) 95–102.

Hazan, R. (1997b) 'Legislative–Executive Relations in an Era of Accelerated Reform: Reshaping Government in Israel', *Legislative Studies Quarterly* (22) 329–50.

Hazan, R. and Maor, M. (2000) 'Introduction', in *Parties, Elections and Cleavages: Israel in Comparative and Theoretical Perspective,* ed. R. Hazan and M. Maor (Portland, Ore. and London: Frank Cass) pp. 1–12.

Heady, F. (1996) *Public Administration: A Comparative Perspective*, 5th edn (N.Y.: Marcel Dekker).

Hechter, M. (2000) *Containing Nationalism* (Oxford and N.Y.: Oxford University Press).

Heclo, H. (1974) *Modern Social Policies in Britain and Sweden* (New Haven, Conn. and London: Yale University Press).

Heclo, H. (1978) 'Issue Networks and the Executive Establishment', in *The New American Political System,* ed. A. King (Washington, D.C.: American Enterprise Institute) pp. 87–124.

Held, D. (1995) *Democracy and the Global Order* (Cambridge: Polity).

Held, D. (1996) *Models of Democracy*, 2nd edn (Cambridge: Polity).

Helms, D. (ed.) (2000) *Institutions and Institutional Change in the Federal Republic of Germany* (Basingstoke: Palgrave).

Henkin, L. (1968) *How Nations Behave: Law and Policy* (London: Pall Mall).

Henshel, R. (1990) *Thinking About Social Problems* (N.Y.: Harcourt Brace Jovanovich).

Herbst, S. (1998) *Reading Public Opinion: How Political Actors View The Political Process* (Chicago and London: University of Chicago Press).

Hesse, J. and Wright, V. (eds) (1996) *Federalizing Europe? The Costs, Benefits and Preconditions of Federal Political Systems* (Oxford and N.Y.: Oxford University Press).

Hettne, B. (ed.) (1999) *Globalism and the New Regionalism* (Basingstoke: Macmillan).

Heywood, A. (1998) *Political Ideologies*, 2nd edn (Basingstoke: Macmillan).

Heywood, P. (1995) *The Government and Politics of Spain* (Basingstoke: Macmillan).

Heywood, P. and Wright, V. (1997) 'Executives, Bureaucracies and Decision-Making', in *Developments in West European Politics,* ed. M. Rhodes, P. Heywood and V. Wright (Basingstoke: Macmillan) pp. 75–94.

Hirst, P. and Thompson, G. (1999) *Globalization in Question: the International Economy and the Possibilities of Governance,* 2nd edn (Oxford and Cambridge, Mass.: Blackwell).

Hitler, A. (1969) *Mein Kampf (My Struggle)* (Boston, Mass.: Houghton Mifflin). First pub. 1933.

Hobsbawm, E. (1990) *Nations and Nationalism since 1780* (Cambridge and N.Y.: Cambridge University Press).

Hobsbawm, E. (1994) *Age of Extremes: The Short Twentieth Century 1914–1991* (London: Michael Joseph).

Hodder-Williams, R. (1996) *Judges and Politics in the Contemporary Age* (London: Bowerdean).

Hoffman, S. (1995) 'The Politics and Ethics of Military Intervention', *Survival* (37) 29–51.

Hogwood, B. and Gunn, L. (1984) *Policy Analysis for the Real World* (Oxford: Oxford University Press).

Hogwood, B. and Guy Peters, B. (1985) *The Pathology of Public Policy* (Oxford: Clarendon).

Holland, K. (1991) 'Introduction', in *Judicial Activism in Comparative Perspective,* ed. K. Holland (Basingstoke: Macmillan) pp. 1–11.

Holland, R. (1988) 'Statistics and Causal Inference', *Journal of the American Statistical Association* (81) 945–60.

Holliday, I. (2000) 'Executives and Administrations', in *Developments in British Politics 6,* ed. P. Dunleavy *et al.* (Basingstoke: Macmillan, and N.Y.: St. Martin's Press) pp. 88–107.

Hollifield, J. and Jillson, C. (2000) 'The Democratic Transformation: Lessons and Prospects in Pathways to Democracy', in *The Political Economy of Democratic Transitions,* ed. J. Hollifield and C. Jillson (London and N.Y.: Routledge) pp. 3–20.

Holman, M. and Wallis, W. (2000) 'In Office But Out of Power', *Financial Times Survey of Nigeria,* 30 March, p. 1.

Holmberg, S. (1994) 'Party Identification Compared Across the Atlantic', in *Elections at Home and Abroad: Essays in Honor of Warren E. Miller,* ed. K. Jennings and T. Mann (Ann Arbor, Mich.: University of Michigan Press) pp. 93–122.

Holmes, L. (1997) *Postcommunism: An Introduction* (Cambridge: Polity).

Holmes, S. (1996) 'Cultural Legacies or State Collapse? Probing the Postcommunist Dilemma', in *Postcommunism: Four Perspectives,* ed. M. Mandelbaum (N.Y.: Council on Foreign Relations) pp. 22–76.

Holston, J. and Caldiera, T. (1998) 'Democracy, Law and Violence: Disjunctions of Brazilian Citizenship', in *Fault Lines of Democracy in Post-Transition Latin America,* ed. F. Agüero and J. Stark (Coral Gables, Fla.: University of Miami) pp. 263–98.

Holmstrom, B. (1995) 'Sweden', in *The Global Expansion of Judicial Power,* ed. C. Tate and T. Vallinder (N.Y. and London: New York University Press) pp. 345–68.

Hood, C. (1996) 'Exploring Variations in Public Management Reform in the 1990s', in *Civil Service Systems in Comparative Perspective,* ed. H. Bekke, J. Perry and T. Toonen (Bloomington, Ind.: Indiana University Press) pp. 268–87.

Hood, C. *et al.* (1999) *Regulation Inside Government: Waste-Watchers, Quality Police and Sleaze-Busters* (Oxford and N.Y.: Oxford University Press).

Howard, A. (1993a) 'How Ideas Travel: Rights at Home and Abroad', in *Constitution-Making in Eastern Europe,* ed. A. Howard (Washington, D.C.: Woodrow Wilson Center Press) pp. 9–20.

Howard, A. (ed.) (1993b) *Constitution-Making in Eastern Europe* (Washington, D.C.: Woodrow Wilson Center Press).

Howarth, D. (1995) 'Discourse Theory', in *Theory and Methods in Political Science,* ed. D. Marsh and G. Stoker (Basingstoke: Macmillan) pp. 115–33.

Hrebenar, R. and Scott, R. (1997) *Interest Group Politics in America,* 3rd edn (Englewood Cliffs, N.J.: Prentice Hall).

Huntington, S. (1991) *The Third Wave: Democratization in the Late Twentieth Century* (Norman, Okla. and London: University of Oklahoma Press).

Huntington, S. (1993) 'Clash of Civilizations', *Foreign Affairs* (72) 22–49.

Huntington, S. (1996) *The Clash of Civilizations and the Making of World Order* (N.Y.: Simon & Schuster).

Hurrell, A. (1995) 'Explaining the Resurgence of Regionalism in World Politics', *Review of International Studies* (21) 331–58.

Hyden, G. (1997) 'Democratization and Administration', in *Democracy's Victory and Crisis,* ed. A. Hadenius (Cambridge and N.Y.: Cambridge University Press) pp. 242–62.

Ignati, P. (1992) 'The Silent Counter-Revolution: Hypotheses on the Emergence of Extreme Right-Wing Parties in Europe', *European Journal of Political Research* (22) 3–35.

Illner, M. (1998) 'Local Democratization: the Czech Republic after 1989', in *Participation and Democracy: Comparisons and Interpretations,* ed. D. Rueschmeyer, M. Rueschmeyer and B. Wittrock (Armonk, N.Y. and London: M. E. Sharpe) pp. 51–82.

Inglehart, R. (1971) 'The Silent Revolution in Europe:

Intergenerational Change in Post-Industrial Societies', *American Political Science Review* (65) 991–1017.

Inglehart, R. (1988) 'The Renaissance of Political Culture', *American Political Science Review* (82) 1203–30.

Inglehart, R. (1990) *Culture Shift in Advanced Industrial Society* (Princeton, N.J.: Princeton University Press).

Inglehart, R. (1997) *Modernization and Postmodernization: Cultural, Economic and Social Change in 43 Societies* (Princeton. N.J. and London: Princeton University Press).

Inkeles, A. (1990) 'On Measuring Democracy', *Studies in Comparative International Development* (25) 3–6.

Inter Parliamentary Union (2000) *Women in National Parliaments.* IPU home page at: http://www.ipu.org/wmn-e/world.htm.

International Labour Office (1997) *Labour Report 1997* (Geneva: International Labour Organisation).

Jackson, J. (1996) 'Political Methodology: An Overview', in *A New Handbook of Political Science*, ed. R. Goodin and H. Klingemann (Oxford and N.Y.: Oxford University Press) pp. 714–48.

Jackson, J. (1998) *The World Trade Organization* (Herndon, Va. and London: Cassell).

Jackson, R. (1989) *Quasi-States: Sovereignty, International Relations and the Third World* (Cambridge and N.Y.: Cambridge University Press).

Jackson, R. and Rosberg, C. (1982) *Personal Rule in Black Africa: Prince, Autocrat, Prophet, Tyrant* (Berkeley, Calif.: University of California Press).

Jacob, H. *et al.* (1996) *Courts, Law and Politics in Comparative Perspective* (New Haven, Conn. and London: Yale University Press).

Jacobs, F., and Corbett, R. (1992) *The European Parliament*, 2nd edn (London and N.Y.: Longman).

Jacobson, H. (1985) *Networks of Interdependence: International Organizations and the Global System* (N.Y.: Alfred Knopf).

Jayanntha, D. (1991) *Electoral Allegiance in Sri Lanka* (Cambridge and N.Y.: Cambridge University Press).

Jenkinson, S. (1991) 'Church and State', in *The Blackwell Encyclopaedia of Political Thought*, ed. D. Miller *et al.* (Oxford and Cambridge, Mass.: Blackwell) pp. 67–72.

Johnson, C. (1987) *Japan: Who Governs? The Rise of the Developmental State* (N.Y. and London: Norton).

Johnson, R. and Schlemmer, L. (eds) (1996) *Launching Democracy in South Africa: The First Open Election, April 1994* (New Haven, Conn. and London: Yale University Press).

Jones, B. (1993) 'Sweden', in *Local Government in Liberal Democracies: An Introductory Survey*, ed. J. Chandler (London and N.Y.: Routledge) pp. 118–37.

Jones, B. and Keating, M. (eds) (1995) *The European Union and the Regions* (Oxford and N.Y.: Oxford University Press).

Jones, C. (1994) *The Presidency in a Separated System* (Washington, D.C.: The Brookings Institution).

Jones, G. (ed.) (1991) *West European Prime Ministers* (London: Frank Cass).

Jones, M. (1995a) 'A Guide to the Electoral Systems of the Americas', *Electoral Studies* (14) 5–21.

Jones, M. (1995b) *Electoral Laws and the Survival of Presidential Democracies* (Notre Dame, Ind.: University of Notre Dame Press).

Jones, P. (1994) *Rights* (Basingstoke: Macmillan, and N.Y.: St. Martin's Press).

Joseph, R. (ed.) (1998) *State, Conflict and Democracy in Africa* (Boulder, Colorado and London: Lynne Rienner).

Kamarck, E. and Nye, J. (1999) *Democracy.com? Governance in a Networked World* (Hollis, N.H.: Hollis).

Karsh, E, and Rautsi, I. (1991) *Saddam Hussein: A Political Biography* (London: Brassey's).

Katz, R. (1996) 'Party Organizations and Finance', in *Elections and Voting in Global Perspective*, ed. L. LeDuc, R. Niemi and P. Norris (Thousand Oaks, Calif. and London: Sage) pp. 107–33.

Katz, R. (1997) *Democracy and Elections* (Oxford and N.Y.: Oxford University Press).

Katz, R. and Mair, P. (eds) (1994) *How Parties Organise: Change and Adaptation in Party Organization in Western Democracies* (Thousand Oaks, Calif. and London: Sage).

Katz, R. and Mair, P. (1995) 'Changing Models of Party Organization and Party Democracy: The Emergence of the Cartel Party', *Party Politics* (1) 5–28.

Katzenstein, P. (1996) 'Regionalism in a Comparative Perspective', *Cooperation and Conflict* (31) 123–60.

Keating, M. (1993) *The Politics of Modern Europe* (Aldershot and Brookfield, Vt.: Edward Elgar).

Keddie, N. (1991) 'The Revolt of Islam and its Roots', in *Comparative Political Dynamics: Global Research Perspectives*, ed. D. Rustow and K. Erickson (N.Y.: HarperCollins) pp. 292–308.

Kegley, C. and Wittkopf, E. (2000) *World Politics: Trend and Transformation*, 8th edn (Basingstoke: Palgrave, and Boston, Mass.: Bedford/St. Martin's).

Keman, H. (ed.) (1993) *Comparative Politics: New Directions in Theory and Method* (Amsterdam, VU University Press).

Keohane, R. (1994) 'International Institutions: Two Approaches', in *International Organization: A Reader*, ed. F. Kratochwil and E. Mansfield (N.Y.: HarperCollins) pp. 44–60.

Kershaw, I. and Lewin, M. (eds) (1997) *Stalinism and Nazism: Dictatorships in Comparison* (Cambridge and N.Y.: Cambridge University Press).

Kettle, S. (1997) 'The Development of Czech Media Since the Fall of Communism', in *Postcommunism and the Media in Eastern Europe*, ed. P. O' Neill (London and Portland, Ore.: Frank Cass) pp. 42–60.

Khaidagala, G. (1995) 'State Collapse and Reconstruction in Uganda', in *Collapsed States: The Disintegration and Restoration of Political Authority*, ed. I. Zartman (Boulder, Colo. and London: Lynne Rienner) pp. 33–48.

Khong, Y. (1992) *Analogies at War: Korea, Munich, Dien Bien Phu and the Vietnam Decisions of 1965* (Princeton, N.J.: Princeton University Press).

King, A. (1981) 'The Rise of the Career Politician in Britain – and its Consequences', *British Journal of Political Science* (11) 249–85.

King, A. (1994a) 'Ministerial Autonomy in Britain', in *Cabinet Ministers and Parliamentary Government*, ed. M. Laver and K.

Shepsle (Cambridge and N.Y.: Cambridge University Press) pp. 203–25.

King, A. (1994b) '"Chief Executives" in Western Europe', in *Developing Democracy: Comparative Research in Honour of J. F. P. Blondel*, ed. I. Budge and D. McKay (Thousand Oaks, Calif. and London: Sage) pp. 150–64.

King, A. (1997) *Running Scared: Why American Politicians Campaign Too Much and Govern Too Little* (N.Y. and London: Free Press).

Kingdon, J. (1984) *Agendas, Alternatives and Public Policy* (Boston, Mass.: Little, Brown).

King, G., Keohane, R. and Verba S. (1994) *Designing Social Inquiry: Scientific Inference in Qualitative Research* (Princeton, N.J.: Princeton University Press).

Kingsley, J. (1944) *Representative Bureaucracy* (Yellow Springs, Ohio: Antioch).

Kingsley, J. (1964) 'Bureaucracy and Political Development, with Particular Reference to Nigeria', in *Bureaucracy and Political Development,* ed. J. LaPalombara (Princeton, N.J.: Princeton University Press) pp. 301–17.

Kircheimer, O. (1966) 'The Transformation of the Western European Party Systems', in *Political Parties and Political Development,* ed. J. LaPalombara and M. Weiner (Princeton, N.J.: Princeton University Press) pp. 177–200.

Kirkpatrick, J. (1993) 'The Modernizing Imperative', *Foreign Affairs* (72) 22–27.

Kitschelt, H. *et al.* (1999) *Postcommunist Party Systems: Competition, Representation and Inter-Party Competition* (Cambridge and N.Y.: Cambridge University Press).

Klapper, J. (1960) *The Effects of Mass Communication* (N.Y. and London: Free Press).

Knutsen, O. (1990) 'Materialist and Postmaterialist Values and Structures in the Nordic Countries', *Comparative Politics* (23) 85–101.

Kobach, K. (1997) 'Direct Democracy and Swiss Isolationism', *West European Politics* (20) 185–211.

Koh, B. (1989) *Japan's Administrative Elite* (Berkeley, Calif.: University of California Press).

Kolstø, P. (2000) *Political Construction Sites: Nation-Building in Russia and the Post-Soviet States* (Boulder, Colo.: Westview Press).

Kommers, D. (1993) 'The Federal Constitutional Court in the German Political System', *Comparative Political Studies* (26) 470–91.

Konrad, G. (1984) *Antipolitics: An Essay* (N.Y. and London: Harcourt, Brace, Jovanovich).

Kopecki, P. (1995) 'Developing Party Organizations in East-Central Europe: What Type of Party is Likely to Emerge?', *Party Politics* (1) 515–34.

Kostiner, J. and Teitelbaum, J. (2000) 'State Formation and the Saudi Monarchy', in *Middle East Monarchies: The Challenge of Modernity,* ed. J. Kostiner (Boulder, Colo. and London: Lynne Rienner) .

Kratochwil, F. and Ruggie, J. (1994) 'International Organization: A State of the Art or an Art of the State?', in *International Organization: A Reader,* ed. F. Kratochwil and E. Mansfield (N.Y.: HarperCollins) pp. 4–19.

Kratochwil, F. and Mansfield, E. (eds) (1994) *International Organization: A Reader* (N.Y.: HarperCollins).

Kudrle, R. and Marmor, T. (1981) 'The Development of Welfare States in North America' in *The Development of Welfare States in Europe and America,* ed. P. Flora and A. Heidenheimer (New Brunswick, N.J. and London: Transaction) pp. 187–236.

Kuhn, R. (1997) 'The Media and Politics', in *Developments in West European Politics,* ed. M. Rhodes, P. Heywood and V. Wright (Cambridge and N.Y.: Cambridge University Press) pp. 263–80.

Kuhn, T. (1970) *The Structure of Scientific Revolutions* (Chicago, Ill.: University of Chicago Press).

Kumar, K. (ed.) (1998) *Postconflict Elections, Democraization and International Assistance* (Boulder, Colorado and London: Lynne Rienner).

Kvavik, R. (1976) *Interest Groups in Norwegian Politics* (Oslo, Bergen and Tromsø: Universitetforlaget).

Lachmann, R. (1997) 'Agents of Revolution: Elite Conflicts and Mass Mobilization from the Medici to the Yemen', in *Theorizing Revolutions,* ed. J. Foran (London and N.Y.: Routledge) pp. 73–101.

Laegreid, P. and Olsen, J. (1978) *Byråkrati og Beslutninger* (Bergen: Norwegian University Press).

Laffan, B. (1999) 'Democracy and the European Union', in *Developments in the European Union,* ed. L. Cram, D. Dinan and N. Nugent (Basingstoke: Macmillan, and N.Y.: St. Martin's Press) pp. 330–52.

Laffin, M. (1994) 'Reinventing the Federal Government', in *Developments in American Politics 2,* ed. G. Peele *et al.* (Basingstoke: Macmillan) pp. 172–99.

Landes, R. (1995) *The Canadian Polity: A Comparative Introduction* (Scarborough, Ontario: Prentice-Hall Canada).

Lane, J.-E. and Ersson, S. (1999) *Politics and Society in Western Europe,* 4th edn (Thousand Oaks, Calif. and London: Sage).

LaPalombara, J. (1974) *Politics Within Nations* (Englewood Cliffs, N. J.: Prentice Hall).

LaPalombara, J. (1987) *Democracy Italian Style* (New Haven, Conn. and London: Yale University Press).

Laponce, J. (1994) 'Democracy and Incumbency: the Canadian Case', in *The Victorious Incumbent: A Threat to Democracy?,* ed. A. Somit *et al.* (Aldershot and Brookfield, Vt.: Dartmouth) pp. 122–49.

Lardy, N. (1998) *China's Unfinished Economic Revolution* (Washington, D.C: The Brookings Institution).

Laver, M. (1983) *Invitation to Politics* (Oxford: Martin Robertson).

Laver, M. and Shepsle, K. (eds) (1994) *Cabinet Ministers and Parliamentary Government* (Cambridge and N.Y.: Cambridge University Press).

Lawson, C. (1997) 'Mexico's New Politics: The Elections of 1997', *Journal of Democracy* (8) 13–27.

Lawson, K. (ed.) (1994) *How Political Parties Work: Perspectives from Within* (Westport, Conn. and London: Praeger).

Lazarsfeld, P. and Merton, R. (1996) 'Mass Communication, Popular Taste and Organized Social Action', in *Media Studies: A Reader,* ed. P. Marris and S. Thornham (Edinburgh: Edinburgh University Press) pp. 14–24.

Le Galès, P. and Lequesne, C. (eds) (1998) *Regions in Europe* (London and N.Y.: Routledge).

LeDuc, L., Niemi, R. and Norris, P. (eds) (1996a) *Elections and*

Voting in Global Perspective (Thousand Oaks, Calif. and London: Sage).

LeDuc, L., Niemi, R. and Norris, P. (1996b) 'Introduction', in *Elections and Voting in Global Perspective,* ed. L. LeDuc, R. Niemi and P. Norris (Thousand Oaks, Calif. and London: Sage) pp. 1–48.

Lenin, V. (1963) *What Is To Be Done?* (Oxford: Clarendon Press). First pub. 1902.

Lesch, A. (2000) 'Politics in Egypt', in *Comparative Politics Today: A World View,* 7th edn, ed. G. Almond *et al.* (N.Y.: Longman) pp. 571–629.

Levitsky, S. (2000) 'The "Normalization" of Argentine Politics', *Journal of Democracy* (11) 56–69.

Lewin, M. (1997) 'Bureaucracy and the Stalinist State', in *Stalinism and Nazism: Dictatorships in Comparison,* ed. I. Kershaw and M. Lewin (Cambridge and N.Y.: Cambridge University Press) pp. 53–74.

Lewis, P. (ed.) (1996a) *Party Structure and Organization in East-Central Europe* (Aldershot and Brookfield, Vt.: Edward Elgar).

Lewis, P. (1996b) 'Introduction and Theoretical Overview', in *Party Structure and Organization in East-Central Europe,* ed. P. Lewis (Aldershot and Brookfield, Vt.: Edward Elgar) pp. 1–19.

Lewis, P. (2000) *Political Parties in Postcommunist Eastern Europe* (London and N.Y.: Routledge).

Lewis-Beck, M. (1995) *Data Analysis: An Introduction* (Thousand Oaks, Calif. and London: Sage).

Lieberman, I., Nestor, S. and Desai, R. (eds) (1996) *Between State and Market: Mass Privatization in Transition Economies* (Washington, D.C.: The World Bank).

Liebert, U. and Cotta, M. (eds) (1990) *Parliament and Democratic Consolidation in Southern Europe* (London: Pinter).

Lieberthal, K. (1995) *Governing China: From Revolution Through Reform* (N.Y. and London: Norton).

Lijphart, A. (1971) 'Comaprative Politics and the Comparative Method', *American Political Science Review* (65) 682–93.

Lijphart, A. (1977) *Democracy in Plural Societies: A Comparative Exploration* (Berkeley, Calif.: University of California Press).

Lijphart, A. (1984) *Democracies: Patterns of Majoritarian and Consensual Government in Twenty One Countries* (New Haven, Conn. and London: Yale University Press).

Lijphart, A. (ed.) (1992) *Parliamentary versus Presidential Government* (Oxford and N.Y.: Oxford University Press).

Lijphart, A. (1994) *Electoral Systems and Party Systems* (New Haven, Conn. and London: Yale University Press).

Lijphart, A. (1997) 'Unequal Participation: Democracy's Unresolved Dilemma', *American Political Science Review* (91) 1–14.

Lijphart, A. (1999) *Patterns of Democracy: Government Forms and Performance in Thirty Six Countries* (New Haven, Conn. and London: Yale Univeristy Press).

Lijphart, A. and Crepaz, M. (1991) 'Corporatism and Consensus Democracy in Eighteen Countries: Conceptual and Empirical Linkages', *British Journal of Political Science* (21) 235–46.

Lijphart, A. and Waisman, C. (1996a) 'The Design of Democracies and Markets: Generalizing Across Regions', in *Institutional Design in New Democracies: Eastern Europe and Latin America,* ed. A. Lijphart and C. Waisman (Boulder, Colo. and Oxford: Westview) pp. 235–48.

Lijphart, A. and Waisman, C. (eds) (1996b) *Institutional Design in New Democracies: Eastern Europe and Latin America* (Boulder, Colo. and Oxford: Westview).

Lindblom, C. (1959) 'The Science of Muddling Through', *Public Administration* (19) 78–88.

Lindblom, C. (1977) *Politics and Markets* (N.Y.: Basic Books).

Lindblom, C. (1979) 'Still Muddling, Not Yet Through', *Public Administration Review* (39) 517–26.

Lindblom, C. (1990) *Inquiry and Change: The Troubled Attempt to Understand and Shape Society* (New Haven, Conn. and London: Yale University Press).

Linz, J. (1970) 'An Authoritarian Regime: The Case of Spain', in *Mass Politics: Studies in Political Sociology,* ed. E. Allard and S. Rokkan (N.Y.: Free Press and London: Collier-Macmillan) pp. 251–83.

Linz, J. (1978) 'Crisis, Breakdown and Re-equilibration', in *The Breakdown of Democratic Regimes,* ed. J. Linz and A. Stepan (Baltimore, Md. and London: Johns Hopkins University Press) pp. 1–124.

Linz, J. (1990) 'The Perils of Presidentialism', *Journal of Democracy* (1) 51–69.

Linz, J. (2000) *Totalitarian and Authoritarian Regimes* (Boulder, Colo. and London: Lynne Rienner). First pub. 1975.

Linz, J. and Stepan, A. (eds) (1978) *The Breakdown of Democratic Regimes* (Baltimore, Md. and London: Johns Hopkins University Press).

Linz, J. and Stepan, A. (1996) *Problems of Democratic Transition and Consolidation: Southern Europe, South America and Postcommunist Europe* (Baltimore, Md. and London: Johns Hopkins University Press).

Linz, J. and Valenzuela, A. (eds) (1994) *The Failure of Presidential Democracy* (Baltimore, Md.: Johns Hopkins University Press).

Lippman, W. (1922) *Public Opinion* (London: Allen & Unwin).

Lipset, S. (1983) *Political Man* (N.Y.: Basic Books). First pub. 1960.

Lipset, S. (1990) *Continental Divide: The Values and Institutions of the United States and Canada* (London and N.Y.: Routledge).

Lipset, S. (1996) *American Exceptionalism: A Double-Edged Sword* (N.Y.: Norton).

Lipset, S. and Rokkan, S. (1967) 'Cleavage Structures, Party Systems and Voter Alignments', in *Party Systems and Voter Alignments,* ed. S. Lipset and S. Rokkan (N.Y. and London: Free Press) pp. 1–65.

Lister, F. (1996) *The European Union, the United Nations and the Revival of Confederal Governance* (Westport, Conn.: Greenwood Press).

Lloyd, J. (1998) 'Low Resistance to Cultural Invasion', *Financial Times,* 28 December, p. 14.

Loader, B. (1997) *The Governance of Cyberspace* (London and N.Y.: Routledge).

Longley, L. and Davidson, R. (eds) (1998) *The New Roles of Parliamentary Committees* (London: Frank Cass).

Loughlin, J. and Mazey, S. (eds) (1995) *The End of the French Unitary State?* (London: Frank Cass).

Lowi, T. (1969) *The End of Liberalism* (N.Y.: Norton).

Luckham, L. (1996) 'Faustian Bargains: Democratic Control over Military and Security Establishments', in *Democratization in the South: The Jagged Wave,* ed. R. Luckham and G. White (Manchester and N.Y.: Manchester University Press) pp. 119–77.

Luckham, R. and White, G. (eds) (1996a) *Democratization in the South: The Jagged Wave* (Manchester and N.Y.: Manchester University Press).

Luckham, R. and White, G. (1996b) 'Democratizing the South', in *Democratization in the South: The Jagged Wave,* ed. R. Luckham and G. White (Manchester and N.Y.: Manchester University Press) pp. 1–10.

Lukes, S. (1974) *Power: A Radical View* (London: Macmillan).

Lukes, S. (ed.) (1986) *Power* (Oxford and Cambridge, Mass.: Basil Blackwell).

Machel, G. (1996) *Children and War* (N.Y.: United Nations).

Mackenzie, W. (1958) *Free Elections* (London: Allen & Unwin).

Macqueen, A. (1989) 'The Art of Shopping', in *The Soviet Union: The Challenge of Change*, ed. M. Wright (Harlow: Longman) pp. 78–85.

Maddex, R. (2000) *Constitutions of the World*, 2nd edn (Washington, D.C. and London: CQ Press).

Madeley, J. (1991) 'Church and State', in *The Blackwell Encyclopaedia of Political Science,* ed. V. Bogdanor (Oxford and Cambridge, Mass.: Blackwell) pp. 91–3.

Magleby, D. (1994) 'Direct Legislation in the American States', in *Referendums around the World: The Growing Use of Direct Democracy,* ed. D. Butler and A. Ranney (Washington, D.C.: AEI Press) pp. 213–314.

Magyar, K. (1992) 'Military Intervention and Withdrawal in Africa: Problems and Perspectives', in *From Military to Civilian Rule,* ed. C. Danopoulos (London and N.Y.: Routledge) pp. 230–48.

Mainwaring, S. (1992) 'Presidentialism in Latin America', in *Parliamentary versus Presidential Government,* ed. A. Lijphart (Oxford and N.Y.: Oxford University Press) pp. 111–17.

Mainwaring, S. and Scully, T. (eds) (1995) *Building Democratic Institutions: Party Systems in Latin America* (Stanford, Calif.: Stanford University Press).

Mainwaring, S. and Shugart, M. (1997a) 'Juan Linz, Presidentialism and Democracy: A Critical Appraisal', *Comparative Politics* (29) 449–72.

Mainwaring, S. and Shugart, M. (eds) (1997b) *Presidentialism and Democracy in Latin America* (Cambridge and N.Y.: Cambridge University Press).

Mair, P. (ed.) (1990) *The West European Party System* (Oxford and N.Y.: Oxford University Press).

Mair, P. (1994) 'Party Organizations: From Civil Society to the State', in *How Parties Organize: Change and Adaptation in Party Organizations in Western Democracies,* ed. R. Katz and P. Mair (Thousand Oaks, Calif. and London: Sage) .

Mair, P. (1996) 'Comparative Politics: An Overview', in *A New Handbook of Political Science,* ed. R. Goodin and H. Klingemann (Oxford and N.Y.: Oxford University Press) pp. 309–35.

Mair, P. (1997) 'E. E. Schattschneider's "The SemiSovereign People"', *Political Studies* (45) 947–54.

Mair, P. and van Biezen, I. (2001) 'Party Membership in Europe, 1980–2000', *Party Politics* (7) 5–22.

Majone, G. (1996) *Regulating Europe* (London and N.Y.: Routledge).

Maley, W. (1997) *Fundamentalism Reborn? Afghanistan under the Taliban* (London: Hurst).

Maltese, J. (1994) *Spin Control: The White House Office of Communications and the Management of Presidential News,* 2nd edn (Chapel Hill, N.C.: University of North Carolina Press).

Manin, B. (1997) *The Principles of Representative Government* (Cambridge and N.Y.: Cambridge University Press).

Manion, M. (2000) 'Politics in China', in *Comparative Politics Today: A World View,* 7th edn, ed. G. Almond *et al.* (N.Y.: Longman) pp. 419–62.

Mann, M. (1986) *The Sources of Social Power, Volume 1: A History of Power from the Beginning to AD 1780* (Cambridge and N.Y.: Cambridge University Press).

Mann, M. (1997) 'The Contradictions of Continuous Revolution', in *Stalinism and Nazism: Dictatorships in Comparison,* ed. I. Kershaw and M. Lewin (Cambridge and N.Y.: Cambridge University Press) pp. 135–57.

Mann, T. and Orren, G. (eds) (1992) *Media Polls in American Politics* (Washington. D.C.: The Brookings Institution).

Manuel, P. and Cammisa, A. (1999) *Checks and Balances? : How a Parliamentary System Could Change American Politics* (Boulder, Col.: Westview Press).

March, D. and Olsen, J. (1984) 'The New Institutionalism: Organizational Factors in Political Life', *American Political Science Review* (78) 778–49.

March, J. and Olsen, J. (1995) *Democratic Governance* (N.Y. and London: Free Press).

Marks, G. and Diamond, L. (eds) (1992) *Reexamining Democracy: Essays in Honour of Seymour Martin Lipset* (Thousand Oaks, Calif. and London: Sage).

Marsh, A. (1990) *Political Action in Europe* (Basingstoke: Macmillan).

Marsh, D. and Rhodes, R. (eds) (1992) *Policy Networks in British Government* (Oxford and N.Y.: Oxford University Press).

Marshall, G. (1984) *Constitutional Conventions* (Oxford and New York: Clarendon Press).

Marshall, T. (1950) *Citizenship and Social Class and Other Essays* (London: Pluto Press). 1991 edn.

Marvin, C. (1988) *When Old Technologies Were New: Thinking about Communications in the Late Nineteenth Century* (Oxford and N.Y.: Oxford University Press).

Matthews, T. (1989) 'Interest Groups', in *Politics in Australia,* ed. R. Smith and L. Watson (Sydney: Allen & Unwin) pp. 211–27.

Mavrogordatos, G. (1987) 'Downs Revisited', *International Political Science Review* (8) 333–42.

Mayall, J. (1996) *The New Interventionism, 1993–1994: United Nations Experience in Cambodia, Former Yugoslavia and Somalia* (Cambridge and N.Y.: Cambridge University Press).

Mayhew, D. (1974) *Congress: The Electoral Connection* (New Haven, Conn. and London: Yale University Press).

Mazey, S. and Richardson, J. (eds) (1993) *Lobbying in the*

European Community (Oxford and N.Y.: Oxford University Press).

Mazey, S. and Richardson, J. (eds) (1998) *Interest Intermediation in the EU* (London and N.Y.: Routledge).

Mazmanian, D. and Sabatier, P. (1989) *Implementation and Public Policy* (Lanham, Md. and London: University Press of America).

McKay, D. (1997) *American Politics and Society*, 4th edn (Oxford and Cambridge, Mass.: Blackwell).

McLean, I. (ed.) (1996) *The Concise Oxford Dictionary of Politics* (Oxford and N.Y.: Oxford University Press).

Medhurst, K. (1991) 'Politics and Religion in Latin America', in *Politics and Religion in the Modern World,* ed. G. Moyser (London and N.Y.: Routledge) pp. 189–221.

Meier, K. (1993) 'Representative Bureaucracy: A Theoretical and Empirical Exposition', *Research in Public Administration* (2) 1–35.

Mendelsohn, M. and Parkin, A. (eds) (2001) *Referendum Democracy: Citizens, Elites and Deliberation in Referendum Campaigns* (Basingstoke: Palgrave).

Meny, Y. and Knapp, A. (1998) *Government and Politics in Western Europe: Britain, France, Italy, West Germany*, 3rd edn (Oxford and N.Y.: Oxford University Press).

Mernissi, F. (1993) *Islam and Democracy: Fear of the Modern World* (London: Virago).

Mershon, C. (1996) 'The Costs of Coalition: Coalition Theories and Italian Government', *American Political Science Review* (90) 534–54.

Meyer, A. (1983) 'Cultural Revolutions: The Uses of the Concept of Culture in Comparative Communist Studies', *Studies in Comparative Communism* (16) 1–8.

Mezey, M. (1979) *Comparative Legislatures* (Durham, N.C.: Duke University Press).

Mickiewicz, E. (1999) *Changing Channels: Television and the Struggle for Power in Russia* (Durham, N.C.: Duke University Press).

Milbrath, L. and Goel, M. (1977) *Political Participation: How and Why Do People Get Involved in Politics?*, 2nd edn (Chicago, Ill.: Rand McNally).

Mill, J. (1991) 'Considerations on Representative Government' in *Collected Works of John Stuart Mill,* Vol. 19, ed. J. O'Grady and B. Robson (Toronto: University of Toronto Press and London: Routledge) pp. 371–577. First pub. 1861.

Miller, D. (1991) 'Politics', in *Blackwell Encyclopaedia of Political Thought*, ed. V. Bogdanor (Oxford and Cambridge, Mass.: Blackwell) pp. 390–1.

Miller, W. *et al.* (1990) *How Voters Change: The 1987 British Election Campaign in Perspective* (Oxford and N.Y.: Oxford University Press).

Mills, C. Wright (1956) *The Power Elite* (N.Y. and Oxford: Oxford University Press).

Milton, A. (2000) *The Rational Politician: Exploiting the Media in New Democracies* (Aldershot: Ashgate).

Minogue, M., Polidano, C. and Hulne, D. (eds) (1999) *Beyond the New Public Management: Changing Ideas and Practices in Governance* (Cheltenham and Northampton, Maine: Edward Elgar).

Mishra, S. (1994) 'Party Organization and Policy Making in a Changing Environment: The Indian National Congress', in *How Political Parties Work: Perspectives from Within,* ed. K. Lawson (Westport, Conn.: Praeger) pp. 153–79.

Mitrany, D. (1965) *A Working Peace System* (Chicago, Ill.: Quadrangle).

Moe, T. (1980) *The Organization of Interests* (Chicago, Ill.: University of Chicago Press).

Mommsen, H. (1997) 'Cumulative Radicalization and Progressive Self-Destruction as Structural Determinants of the Nazi Dictatorship', in *Stalinism and Nazism: Dictatorships in Comparison*, ed. I. Kershaw and M. Lewin *et al.* (Cambridge and N.Y.: Cambridge University Press) pp. 75–87.

Montesquieu, C.-L. (1949) *The Spirit of the Laws* (N.Y.: Hafner), ed. F. Neumann. First pub. 1748.

Moran, M. (2001) 'The Rise of the Regulatory State in Britain', *Parliamentary Affairs* (54) 19–34.

Morlino, L. (1995) 'Italy's Civic Divide', *Journal of Democracy* (6) 173–7.

Morris, P. (1994) *French Politics Today* (Manchester: Manchester University Press and N.Y.: St. Martin's Press).

Mortimer, E. (1997) 'Prevention Zone', *Financial Times,* 21 September 1997, p. 18.

Morton, F. (1995) 'The Living Constitution', in *Introductory Readings in Canadian Government and Politics,* ed. R. Wagenberg (Mississauga, Ontario: Copp Clark) pp. 41–72.

Mughan, A. (2000) *Media and the Presidentialization of Parliamentary Elections* (Basingstoke: Palgrave).

Mulgan, R. (1997) *Politics in New Zealand*, 2nd edn (Auckland: Auckland University Press).

Müller, W. and Saalfeld, T. (eds) (1997) *Members of Parliament in Western Europe: Roles and Behavior* (London and Portland, Ore.: Frank Cass).

Müller, W., and Strøm, K. (1999) *Policy, Office, or Vote? : How Political Parties in Western Europe Make Hard Decisions* (Cambridge and N.Y.: Cambridge University Press).

Müller, W. and Strøm, K. (1999) 'Party Behaviour and Representative Democracy', in *Policy, Office or Votes?: How Political Parties in Western Europe Make Hard Decisions*, ed. W. Müller and K. Strøm (Cambridge and N.Y.: Cambridge University Press) pp. 279–310.

Munck, R. (1989) *Latin America: The Transition to Democracy* (London and Atlantic Highlands, N.J.: Zed).

Myers, A. (1975) *Parliaments and Estates in Europe to 1789* (London: Thames & Hudson).

Myers, D. and O'Connor, R. (1998) 'Support for Coups in Democratic Political Culture', in *Comparative Politics* (30) 193–212.

Nathan, A., Hong, Z. and Smith, S. (eds) (1999) *Dilemmas of Reform in Jiang Zeming's China* (Boulder, Colo.: Lynne Rienner).

Neumann, F. (1957) *The Democratic and the Authoritarian State: Essays in Political and Legal Theory* (N.Y.: Free Press).

Neustadt, R. (1991) *Presidential Power and the Modern Presidents* (N.Y.: Free Press).

Neustadt, R. (2001) 'The Weakening White House', *British Journal of Political Science* (31) 1–11.

Nigro, L. (ed.) (1984) *Decision Making in the Public Sector* (N.Y.: Marcel Dekker).

Nikolova, K. (1998) 'The Framework for Public Management

Reform in Bulgaria: A View From The Inside', in *Innovations in Public Management: Perspectives from East and West Europe,* ed. T. Verheijen and D. Coombes *et al.* (Cheltenham and Northampton, Mass.: Edward Elgar) pp. 59–102.

Niskanen, W. (1971) *Bureaucracy and Representative Government* (Chicago, Ill.: Aldine Atherton).

Nordlinger, E. (1977) *Soldiers in Politics: Military Coups and Governments* (Englewood Cliffs, N.J.: Prentice Hall).

Norpoth, H. (1996) 'The Economy', in *Elections and Voting in Global Perspective,* ed. L. LeDuc, R. Niemi and P. Norris (Thousand Oaks, Calif. and London: Sage) pp. 299–318.

Norris, P. (1993) 'Comparing Legislative Recruitment', in *Gender and Party Politics,* ed. J. Lovenduski and P. Norris (Thousand Oaks, Calif. and London: Sage) pp. 309–30.

Norris, P. (1995) *Comparative Models of Political Recruitment* (Bordeaux: ECPR Workshop on Political Recruitment).

Norris, P. (1996) 'Legislative Recruitment', in *Elections and Voting in Global Perspective,* ed. R. Niemi and P. Norris (Thousand Oaks, Calif. and London: Sage) pp. 184–215.

Norris, P. (1997) *Electoral Change in Britain since 1945* (Oxford and Cambridge, Mass.: Blackwell).

Norris, P. (1999a) 'The Growth of Critical Citizens and Its Consequences', in *Critical Citizens: Global Support for Democratic Governance,* ed. P. Norris (Oxford and N.Y.: Oxford University Press) pp. 257–72.

Norris, P. (1999b) 'Who Surfs Cafe Europa? Virtual Democracy in the USA and Western Europe', paper presented at the American Political Science Association Annual Meeting, Atlanta, Ga., 1–5 September.

Norris, P. (ed.) *Critical Citizens: Global Support for Democratic Governance* (Oxford and N.Y.: Oxford University Press).

Norton, A. (1991) 'Western European Local Government in Comparative Perspective', in *Local Government in Europe: Trends and Developments,* ed. R. Batley and G. Stoker (Basingstoke: Macmillan) pp. 21–40.

Norton, A. (1994) *International Handbook of Local and Regional Government* (Aldershot and Brookfield, Vt.: Edward Elgar).

Norton, P. (1990a) *Legislatures* (Oxford and N.Y.: Oxford University Press).

Norton, P. (1990b) *Parliaments in Western Europe* (London: Frank Cass).

Norton, P. (1993) *Does Parliament Matter?* (Hemel Hempstead: Harvester Wheatsheaf).

Norton, P. (1997) 'Parliamentary Oversight', in *Developments in British Politics 5,* ed. P. Dunleavy *et al.* (Basingstoke: Macmillan, and N.Y.: St. Martin's) pp. 155–76.

Norton, P. (ed.) (1998) *Parliaments and Governments in Western Europe* (London and Portland, Ore.: Frank Cass).

Norton, P. (2001) *The British Polity,* 4th edn (Harlow and N.Y.: Longman).

Norton, P. and Olson, D. (1996) 'Parliaments in Adolescence' in *The New Parliaments of Central and Eastern Europe,* ed. D. Olson and P. Norton (London and Portland, Ore.: Frank Cass) pp. 231–44.

Norton, P. and Ahmed, N. (eds) (1999) *Parliaments in Asia* (London and Portland, Ore.: Frank Cass).

Nousiainen, J. (1994) 'Finland: Ministerial Autonomy, Constitutional Collectivism and Party Oligarchy', in *Cabinet Ministers and Parliamentary Government,* ed. M. Laver and K. Shepsle (Cambridge and N.Y.: Cambridge University Press) pp. 88–105.

Nugent, N. (1999) *The Government and Politics of the European Union,* 4th edn (Basingstoke: Macmillan).

Nurmi, H. (1990) 'A Theoretical Review of the Finnish Parliamentary and Presidential System', in *Finnish Democracy,* ed. J. Sunberg and S. Berglund (Helsinki: Finnish Political Science Association) pp. 51–64.

Nye, J. (1990) *Bound to Lead: the Changing Nature of America's Power* (N.Y.: Basic Books).

Nye, J., Zelikow, P. and King, D. (eds) (1997) *Why People Don't Trust Government* (Cambridge, Mass.: Harvard University Press).

O'Brien, D. (1993) *Storm Center: The Supreme Court in American Politics* (N.Y.: Norton).

O'Donnell, G. (1973) *Modernization and Bureaucratic Authoritarianism: Studies in South American Politics* (Berkeley, Calif.: California University Press).

O'Donnell, G. (1996) 'Delegative Democracy', in *The Global Resurgence of Democracy,* 2nd edn, ed. L. Diamond and M. Plattner (Baltimore, Maryland and London: Johns Hopkins University Press) pp. 94–110.

O'Donnell, G. and Schmitter, P. (1986a) 'Tentative Conclusions about Uncertain Democracies', in *Transitions from Authoritarian Rule: Prospects for Democracy,* ed. G. O'Donnell, P. Schmitter and L. Whitehead (Baltimore, Md. and London: Johns Hopkins University Press) pp. 1–65.

O'Donnell, G. and Schmitter, P. (1986b) *Transitions from Authoritarian Rule: Tentative Conclusions from Uncertain Democracies* (Berkeley and Los Angeles, Calif.: University of California Press).

O'Donnell, G., Schmitter, P. and Whitehead, L. (eds) (1986) *Transitions from Authoritarian Rule* (Baltimore, Md. and London: Johns Hopkins University Press).

O'Sullivan, N. (1986) *Fascism* (London: Dent).

O'Toole, B. and Chapman, R. (1995) 'Parliamentary Accountability', in *Next Steps: Improving Management in Government?,* ed. B. O'Toole and G. Jordan (Aldershot and Brookfield, Vt.: Dartmouth) pp. 118–41.

O'Toole, B. and Jordan, G. (eds) (1995) *Next Steps: Improving Management in Government?* (Aldershot and Brookfield, Vt.: Dartmouth).

Olson, D. (1994) *Legislative Institutions: A Comparative View* (Armonk, N.Y.: M. E. Sharpe).

Olson, D. and Norton, P. (eds) (1997) *The New Parliaments of Central and Eastern Europe* (London: Frank Cass).

Olson, M. (1968) *The Logic of Collective Action: Public Goods and the Theory of Groups* (N.Y.: Schocken Books).

Olson, M. (1982) *The Rise and Decline of Nations* (New Haven, Conn. and London: Yale University Press).

Olson, M. (2000) *Power and Prosperity: Outgrowing Communist and Capitalist Dictatorships* (N.Y.: Basic Books).

Ong, W. (1982) *Orality and Literacy: The Technologizing of the Word* (London and N.Y.: Methuen).

Opello, W. and Rosow, S. (1999) *The Nation-State and Global Order: A Historical Introduction to Contemporary Politics* (Boulder, Colo. and London: Lynne Rienner).

Osborne, D. and Gaebler, T. (1992) *Reinventing Government:*

How the Entrepreneurial Spirit Is Transforming the Public Sector (N.Y. and London: Penguin).

Ostrogorski, M. (1902) *Democracy and the Organisation of Political Parties* (London: Macmillan).

Padgett, S. (2000) *Organizing Democracy in Eastern Germany: Interest Groups in Post-Communist Society* (Cambridge and N.Y.: Cambridge University Press).

Page, E. (1992) *Political Authority and Bureaucratic Power: A Comparative Analysis*, 2nd edn (Hemel Hempstead: Harvester Wheatsheaf).

Page, E. and Wright, V. (eds) (1999) *Bureaucratic Élites in Western European States: A Comparative Analysis of Top Officials* (Oxford and N.Y.: Oxford University Press).

Palan, R. and Abbott, J. (1996) *State Strategies in the Global Economy* (London and N.Y.: Pinter).

Panebianco, A. (1988) *Political Parties: Organization and Power* (Cambridge and N.Y.: Cambridge University Press).

Parry, G., Moyser, G. and Day, N. (1992) *Political Participation and Democracy in Britain* (Cambridge and N.Y.: Cambridge University Press).

Parsons, T. (1967) 'On the Concept of Political Power', in *Sociological Theory and Modern Society*, ed. T. Parsons (N.Y. and London: Free Press) pp. 286–99.

Parsons, W. (1995) *Public Policy: An Introduction to the Theory and Practice of Policy Analysis* (Brookfield, Vt. and Aldershot: Edward Elgar).

Partridge, H. (1998) *Italian Politics Today* (Manchester: Manchester University Press).

Patterson, S. and Mughan, A. (eds) (1999) *Senates: Bicameralism in the Contemporary World* (Columbus, Ohio: Ohio Sate University Press).

Peele, G. (1984) *Revival and Reaction: The Right in Contemporary America* (Oxford and N.Y.: Clarendon Press).

Peeler, J. (1998) *Building Democracy in Latin America* (Boulder, Col. and London: Lynne Rienner).

Pennings, P., Keman, H. and Kleinnijenhuis, J. (1999) *Doing Research in Political Science: An Introduction to Comparative Methods and Statistics* (Thousand Oaks, Calif. and London: Sage).

Perlmutter, A. (1981) *Modern Authoritarianism* (New Haven, Conn.: Yale University Press).

Perlmutter, A. (1997) *Making the World Safe for Democracy: A Century of Wilsonianism and its Totalitarian Challenges* (Chapel Hill, N.C.: University of North Carolina Press).

Pesic, J. (1994) 'The Cruel Face of Nationalism', in *Nationalism, Ethnic Conflict and Democracy*, ed. L. Diamond and M. Plattner (Baltimore, Md. and London: Johns Hopkins University Press) pp. 132–6.

Petersson, O. (1989) *Maktens Natverk* (Stockholm: Carlssons).

Petracca, M. (1992) 'The Rediscovery of Interest Group Politics', in *The Politics of Interests: Interest Groups Transformed*, ed. M. Petracca (Boulder, Colo. and Oxford: Westview) pp. 3–31.

Petro, N. (1995) *The Rebirth of Russian Democracy: An Interpretation of Political Culture* (Cambridge, Mass. and London: Harvard University Press).

Pharr, S. and Putnam, R. (eds) (2001) *Disaffected Democracies: What's Troubling The Trilateral Countries?* (Princeton, N.J.: Princeton University Press).

Pierson, C. (1998) *Beyond the Welfare State? The New Political Economy of Welfare*, 2nd edn (University Park: Pennsylvania State University Press and Cambridge: Polity).

Pierson, C. (ed.) (2000) *The New Politics of the Welfare State* (Oxford and N.Y.: Oxford University Press).

Pinkney, R. (1990) *Right-Wing Military Government* (London: Pinter).

Polidano, C. (1998) 'Why Bureaucrats Can't Always Do What Ministers Want: Multiple Accountabilities in Westminster Democracies', *Public Policy and Administration* (13) 35–50.

Polsby, N. (1980) *Community Power and Political Theory*, 2nd edn (New Haven, Conn. and London: Yale University Press).

Pomper, G. *et al.* (2001) *The Election of 2000: Reports and Interpretations* (Chatham, N.J.: Chatham House).

Pomper, G. *et al.* (1997) *The Election of 1996: Reports and Interpretations* (Chatham, N.J.: Chatham House).

Porter, B. (1994) *War and the Rise of the Modern State: The Military Foundations of Modern Politics* (N.Y. and London: Free Press).

Potter, D. *et al.* (eds) (1997) *Democratization* (Cambridge: Polity).

Pressman, J. and Wildavsky, A. (1973) *Implementation* (Berkeley, Calif.: University of California Press).

Pridham, G. (1990) 'Political Parties and Consolidation in Southern Europe: Empirical and Theoretical Perspectives', in *Parliament and Democratic Consolidation in Southern Europe*, ed. U. Liebert and M. Cotta (London: Pinter) pp. 225–48.

Pridham, G. (ed.) (1995) *Transitions to Democracy* (Brookfield, Vermont and Aldershot: Dartmouth).

Prillaman, W. (2000) *The Judiciary and Democratic Decay in Latin America: Declining Confidence in the Rule of Law* (Westport, Conn.: Praeger).

Pross, A. (1993) 'Canadian Pressure Groups: Talking Chameleons', in *Pressure Groups*, ed. J. Richardson (Oxford: Oxford University Press) pp. 145–58.

Prosser, T. (1996) 'Understanding the British Constitution', *Political Studies* (44) 473–87.

Prosser, T. and Moran, M. (1994) 'Privatization and Regulatory Change: The Case of Great Britain', in *Privatization and Regulatory Change in Europe*, ed. M. Moran and T. Prosser (Buckingham and Bristol, Pa.: Open Univesity Press) pp. 35–49.

Prunier, G. (1997) *The Rwanda Crisis: History of a Genocide* (London: Hurst).

Przeworski, A. (1991) *Democracy and the Market: Political and Economic Reforms in Eastern Europe and Latin America* (Cambridge and N.Y.: Cambridge University Press).

Przeworski, A. (1995) 'The Role of Theory in Comparative Politics', *World Politics* (48) 16–21.

Przeworski, A., and Teune, H. (1970) *The Logic of Comparative Inquiry* (N.Y.: Wiley).

Putnam, R. (1976) *The Comparative Study of Political Élites* (Englewood Cliffs, N.J.: Prentice Hall).

Putnam, R. (1993) *Making Democracy Work: Civic Traditions in Modern Italy* (Princeton, N.J.: Princeton University Press).

Putnam, R. (1995) 'Bowling Alone: America's Declining Social Capital', *Journal of Democracy* (6) 65–78.

Putnam, R. (1996) 'The Strange Disappearance of Civic America', *Prospect* (6) 66–73.

Putnam, R. (1998) 'Democracy in America at the End of the Twentieth Century', in *Participation and Democracy: Comparisons and Interpretations,* ed. D. Rueschmeyer, M. Rueschmeyer, and B. Wittrock (Armonk, N.Y. and London: M. E. Sharpe) pp. 233–65.

Putnam, R. (2000) *Bowling Alone: The Collapse and Revival of American Community* (N.Y.: Simon & Schuster).

Putzel, J. (1997) 'Why Has Democratization Been a Weaker Impulse in Indonesia and Malaysia than in the Philippines?', in *Democratization,* ed. D. Potter *et al.* (Cambridge: Polity) pp. 240–68.

Pye, L. (1985) *Asian Power and Politics: The Cultural Dimensions of Authority* (Cambridge, Mass.: Harvard University Press).

Pye, L. (1995) 'Political Culture', in *The Encyclopaedia of Democracy,* ed. S. Lipset (London and N.Y.: Routledge) pp. 965–9.

Qualter, T. (1991) 'Public Opinion', in *The Blackwell Encyclopaedia of Political Science,* ed. V. Bogdanor (Oxford and Cambridge, Mass.: Blackwell) p. 511.

Raadschelders, J. and Rutgers, M. (1996) 'The Evolution of Civil Service Systems', in *Civil Service Systems in Comparative Perspective,* ed. H. Bekke, J. Perry and T. Toonen (Bloomington, Ind.: Indiana University Press) pp. 67–99.

Ragin, C. (1994a) 'Introduction to Qualitative Comparative Analysis', in *The Comparative Political Economy of the Welfare State,* ed. T. Janoski and A. Hicks (N.Y. and Cambridge: Cambridge University Press) pp. 299–319.

Ragin, C. (1994b) *Constructing Social Research* (Thousand Oaks, Calif. and London: Sage).

Ragin, C., Berg-Schlosser, D. and de Meur. G. (1996) 'Political Methodology: Qualitative Methods', in *A New Handbook of Political Science,* ed. R. Goodin and H. Klingemann (Oxford and N.Y.: Oxford University Press) pp. 749–68.

Rais, R. (1997) *State, Society and Democratic Change in Pakistan* (Oxford and N.Y.: Oxford University Press).

Rapaczynski, M. (1993) 'Constitutions in Eastern Europe', in *Constitution-making in Eastern Europe,* ed. A. Howard (Washington, D.C.: Woodrow Wilson Center Press) pp. 134–57.

Remmer, K. (1989) *Military Rule in Latin America* (Boston, Mass.: Unwin Hyman).

Reynolds, A. (1994) *Election '94 South Africa: the Campaigns, Results and Future Prospects* (London: James Currey and N.Y.: St. Martin's).

Rhodes, M. (1996) 'Globalization and West European Welfare States: A Critical Review of Recent Debates', *Journal of European Social Policy* (6) 305–27.

Rhodes, R. (1996) 'The New Governance: Governing without Government', *Political Studies* (44) 652–67.

Rhodes, R. (1995) 'The Institutional Approach', in *Theory and Methods in Political Science,* ed. D. Marsh and G. Stoker (Basingstoke: Macmillan) pp. 42–57.

Rhodes, R. (1994) 'State-building Without a Bureaucracy: The Case of the United Kingdom'. in *Developing Democracy: Essays in Honour of J. F. P. Blondel,* ed. I. Budge and D. McKay (Thousand Oaks, Calif. and London: Sage) pp. 165–88.

Rich, P. (ed.) (1994) *The Dynamics of Change in South Africa* (Basingstoke: Macmillan, and N.Y.: St. Martin's).

Richardson, J. (ed.) (1993) *Pressure Groups* (Oxford and N.Y.: Oxford University Press).

Riesman, D. (1950) *The Lonely Crowd* (New Haven: Yale University Press).

Riker, W. (1962) *The Theory of Political Coalitions* (New Haven, Conn. and London: Yale University Press).

Riker, W. (1975) 'Federalism', in *The Handbook of Political Science,* Vol. 5, ed. F. Greenstein and N. Polsby (Reading, Mass: Addison-Wesley) pp. 93–172.

Riker, W. (1996) 'European Federalism: The Lessons of Past Experience', in *Federalizing Europe? The Costs, Benefits and Preconditions of Federal Political Systems,* ed. J. Hesse and V. Wright (Oxford and N.Y.: Oxford University Press) pp. 9–24.

Ripley, R. and Franklin, G. (1991) *Congress, the Bureaucracy and Public Policy,* 5th edn (Homewood Ill.: The Dorsey Press). First pub.1976.

Robinson, A. (1996) 'Kazakhstan: At Last, the Hope of a Secure Future', *Financial Times,* 11 July, p. iii.

Robinson, M. and White, G. (eds) (1998) *The Democratic Developmental State: Political and Institutional Design* (Oxford and N.Y.: Oxford University Press).

Robinson, W. (1996) *Promoting Polyarchy: Globalization, US Intervention and Hegemony* (Cambridge and N.Y.: Cambridge University Press).

Rocher, F. and Smith, M. (eds) (1995) *New Trends in Canadian Federalism* (Peterborough: Broadview Press).

Rogers, E. (1971) *Communication of Innovation: A Cross-cultural Approach* (N.Y.: Free Press).

Rokkan, S. (1970) *Citizens, Elections, Parties* (N.Y.: McKay).

Rose, R. (1976) *The Problem of Party Government* (Harmondsworth: Penguin).

Rose, R. (1989) *Politics in England: Change and Persistence* (Basingstoke: Macmillan).

Rose, R. (1991a) 'Comparing Forms of Comparative Analysis', *Political Studies* (39) 446–62.

Rose, R. (2000) *The Post-Modern President,* 2nd edn (Chatham, N.J.: Chatham House).

Rose, R. (1993) *Lesson-Drawing in Public Policy* (Chatham, N.J.: Chatham House).

Rose, R. (2001) *The Prime Minister in a Shrinking World* (Cambridge: Polity).

Rose, R. and Shin, D. (2001) 'Democratization Backwards: The Problem of Third-Wave Democracies', in *British Journal of Political Science* (31) 331–54.

Rosenau, J. (1989) 'The State in an Era of Cascading Politics: Wavering Concept, Widening Competence, Withering Colossus or Weathering Change?', in *The Elusive State: International and Comparative Perspectives,* ed. J. Caporaso (Thousand Oaks, Calif. and London: Sage) pp. 17–48.

Rosenau, J. (1992) 'Governance, Order and Change in World Politics', in *Governance without Government: Order and Change in World Politics,* ed. J. Rosenau and E.-O. Czempiel (Cambridge and N.Y.: Cambridge University Press) pp. 3–6.

Rosenbluth, F. and Thies, M. (2000) 'Politics in Japan', in *Comparative Politics Today: A World View,* 7th edn, ed. G. Almond *et al.* (N.Y.: Longman) pp. 327–72.

Rosenfeld, M. (ed.) (1994) *Constitutionalism, Identity, Difference and Legitimacy: Theoretical Perspectives* (Durham, N.C. and London: Duke University Press).

Rousseau, D. (1994) 'The Constitutional Judge: Master or Slave of the Constitution?', in *Constitutionalism, Identity, Difference and Legitimacy: Theoretical Perspectives,* ed. M. Rosenfeld (Durham, N.C. and London: Duke University Press) pp. 261–83.

Rueschmeyer, D., Rueschmeyer, M. and Wittrock, B. (eds) (1998) *Participation and Democracy: Comparisons and Interpretations* (Armonk, N.Y. and London: M. E. Sharpe).

Rummel, R. (1997) *Death by Government* (New Brunswick, N.J. and London: Transaction Books).

Russell, M. (2000a) *Reforming the House of Lords: Lessons from Overseas* (Oxford and N.Y.: Oxford University Press).

Russell, M. (2000b) 'A "More Democratic and Representative" Upper House? Some International Comparisons', *Representation* (37) 131–8.

Rustow, D. (1970) 'Transitions to Democracy', *Comparative Politics* (2) 337–63.

Sait, E. (1938) *Political Institutions: A Preface* (N.Y.: Appleton-Century).

Sakwa, R. (1996) *Russian Politics and Society*, 2nd edn (London and N.Y.: Routledge).

Sakwa, R. (2000) 'Russia's Permanent Uninterrupted Elections of 1999–2000', *Journal of Communist and Transition Studies,* (16) 85–112.

Salisbury, R. (1992) *Interests and Institutions: Substance and Structure in American Politics* (Pittsburgh, Pa.: University of Pittsburgh Press).

Sartori, G. (1976) *Parties and Party Systems: A Framework for Analysis* (Cambridge and N.Y.: Cambridge University Press).

Sartori, G. (1993) 'Totalitarianism: Model Mania and Learning from Error', *Journal of Theoretical Politics* (5) 5–22.

Sartori, G. (1994) *Comparative Constitutional Engineering: An Inquiry into Structures, Incentives and Outcomes* (Basingstoke: Macmillan).

Scarrow, H. (1969) *Comparative Pulitical Analysis* (N.Y.: Harper & Row).

Schacht, J. (1964) *An Introduction to Islamic Law* (Oxford and N.Y.: Clarendon Press).

Scharpf, F. (1996) 'Can There Be a Stable Federal Balance in Europe?', in *Federalizing Europe? The Costs, Benefits and Preconditions of Federal Political Systems,* ed. J. Hesse and V. Wright (Oxford and N.Y.: Oxford University Press) pp. 361–73.

Schattschneider, E. (1942) *Party Government* (N.Y.: Farrar & Reinhart).

Schirazi, A. (1998) *The Constitution of Iran: Politics and the State in the Islamic Republic* (London: I.-B. Taurus).

Schmieding, H. (1993) *Europe after Maastricht* (London: Institute of Economic Affairs).

Schmieding, H. (1998) 'From Plan to Market: On the Nature of the Transformation Crisis', *Weltwirtschaftliches Archiv* (129) 216–53.

Schmitter, P. and Lehmbruch, G. (eds) (1979) *Trends Towards Corporatist Intermediation* (Thousand Oaks, Calif. and London: Sage).

Scholzman, K. and Tierney, J. (1986) *Organized Interests and American Democracy* (N.Y.: Harper & Row).

Schöpflin, G. (1990) 'Why Communism Collapsed', *International Affairs* (66) 3–17.

Schöpflin, G. and Hosking, G. (eds) (1997) *Myths and Nationhood* (London: Hurst).

Schubert, G. (1972) 'Judicial Process and Behaviour During the Sixties', *Political Science* (5) 6–15.

Schumpeter, J. (1943) *Capitalism, Socialism and Democracy* (London: Allen & Unwin).

Schwarz, B. (1960) 'The Legend of "the Legend of Maoism"', *China Quarterly* (2) 35–42.

Schwarz, H. (1993) 'The New East European Constitutional Courts', in *Constitution-Making in Eastern Europe,* ed. A. Howard (Washington, D.C.: Woodrow Wilson Center Press).

Scott, S. (1997) 'Australia and International Institutions' in *New Developments in Australian Politics,* ed. B. Galligan, I. McAllister and J. Ravenhill (South Melbourne: Macmillan) pp. 271–90.

Searing, D. (1994) *Westminster's World: Understanding Political Roles* (Cambridge, Mass. and London: Harvard University Press).

Seisselberg, J. (1996) 'Conditions of Success and Political Problems of a "Media-mediated Personality Party": The Case of Forza Italia', *West European Politics* (19) 715–43.

Semetko, H. (1996) 'The Media', in *Comparing Democracies: Elections and Voting in Global Perspective,* ed. L. LeDuc, R. Niemi and P. Norris (Thousand Oaks, Calif. and London: Sage) pp. 254–79.

Senelle, R. (1996) 'The Reform of the Belgian State', in *Federalizing Europe? The Costs, Benefits and Preconditions of Federal Political Systems,* ed. J. Hesse and V. Wright (Oxford and N.Y.: Oxford University Press) pp. 266–324.

Shanks, C., Jackobson, H. and Kaplan, J. (1996) 'Inertia and Change in the Constellation of Intergovernmental Organizations', *International Organization* (50) 593–627.

Shapiro, M. (1990) 'The Supreme Court from Early Burger to Early Rehnquist' in *The New American Political System,* 2nd edn, ed. A. King (Washington, D.C.: American Enterprise Institute) pp. 47–86.

Shapiro, M. and Stone, A. (1994) 'The New Constitutional Politics of Europe', *Comparative Political Studies* (26) 397–420.

Sharlet, R. (1997) 'The Progress of Human Rights', in *Developments in Russian Politics 4,* ed. S. White, A. Pravda and Z. Gitelman (Basingstoke: Macmillan) pp. 129–48.

Shively, W. (1995) *Power and Choice: An Introduction to Political Science,* 4th edn (N.Y. and London: McGraw-Hill).

Shugart, M. and Carey, J. (1992) *Presidents and Assemblies: Constitutional Design and Electoral Dynamics* (Cambridge and N.Y.: Cambridge University Press).

Shugart, M. and Wattenberg, M. (eds) (2000) *Mixed-Member Electoral Systems: The Best of Both Worlds* (Oxford and N.Y.: Oxford University Press).

Siedentop, L. (2000) *Democracy in Europe* (Harmondsworth: Penguin).

Sigmund, P. (1993) 'Christian Democracy, Liberation Theology and Political Culture in Latin America', in *Political Culture and Democracy in Developing Countries,* ed. L. Diamond (Boulder, Colo. and London: Lynne Rienner) pp. 329–46.

Simon, H. (1983) *Reason in Human Affairs* (Oxford and Cambridge, Mass: Blackwell).

Sjolin, M. (1993) *Coalition Politics and Parliamentary Power* (Lund: Lund University Press).

Skocpol, T. (1979) *States and Social Revolutions: A Comparative Analysis of France, Russia and China* (Cambridge and N.Y.: Cambridge University Press).

Smith, B. (1996) *Understanding Third World Politics* (London: Macmillan).

Smith, D. (1970) *Religion and Political Development* (Boston, Mass.: Little Brown).

Smith, D., Solinger, D. and Topik, S. (eds) (1999) *States and Sovereignty in the Global Economy* (London and N.Y.: Routledge).

Smith, G. (1989) *Politics in Western Europe*, 5th edn (Aldershot: Gower).

Smith, G. (1995) *Federalism: The Multiethnic Challenge* (Harlow and N.Y.: Longman).

Smith, G., Paterson, W. and Padgett, S. (eds) (1996) *Developments in German Politics 2* (Basingstoke: Macmillan).

Smith, M. (1995) *Pressure Politics* (Manchester: Baseline Books).

Soley, L. (1998) *Free Radio: Electronic Civil Disobedience* (Boulder, Colo.: Westview Press).

Solomon, P. and Foglesong, T. (2000) *Courts and Transition in Russia: The Challenge of Judicial Reform* (Boulder, Colo. and Oxford: Westview).

Somit, A. (1994) '. . . And Where We Came Out', in *The Victorious Incumbent: A Threat to Democracy?* ed. A. Somit *et al.* (Aldershot and Brookfield, Vt.: Dartmouth) pp. 11–18.

Sorensen, G. (1997) *Democracy and Democratization*, 2nd edn (Boulder, Colo. and Oxford: Westview).

Sorensen, G. (1997) 'An Analysis of Contemporary Statehood: Consequences for Conflict and Cooperation', *Review of International Studies* (23) 253–70.

Splicahl, S. (1999) *Public Opinion: Developments and Controversies in the Twentieth Century* (Lanham, Md.: Rowman & Littlefield).

Spruyt, H. (1994) *The Sovereign State and Its Competitors* (Princeton, N.J.: Princeton University Press).

Stainov, P. (1993) *Durzhava i Chinovnichestvo* (Sofia: Slavianska Beseda).

Steen, A. (1995) *Change of Regime and Political Recruitment: The Parliamentary Elites in the Baltic States* (Bordeaux: ECPR Workshop on Political Recruitment).

Steinbach, P. (1992) 'Reichstag Elections in the Kaiserreich: the Prospects for Electoral Research in the Interdisciplinary Context', in *Elections, Mass Politics and Social Change in Modern Germany: New Perspectives,* ed. L. Jones and J. Retallack (Cambridge and N.Y.: Cambridge University Press) pp. 119–146.

Stepan, A. and Skach, C. (1993) 'Constitutional Frameworks and Democratic Consolidation: Parliamentarism Versus Presidentialism', *World Politics* (46) 1–22.

Stevens, A. (1996) *The Government and Politics of France*, 2nd edn (Basingstoke: Macmillan, and N.Y.: St. Martin's Press).

Stimson, J. (1998) *Public Opinion in America: Moods, Cycles and Swings*, 2nd edn (Boulder, Col. and Oxford: Westview).

Stone, B. (1995) 'Administrative Accountability in the "Westminster" Democracies: Towards a New Conceptual Framework', *Governance* (8) 505–26.

Stouffer, S. (1966) *Communism, Conformity and Civil Liberties* (N.Y.: Wiley).

Strange, S. (1994) *States and Markets* (London and N.Y.: Pinter).

Strom, K. (1990) *Minority Government and Majority Rule* (Cambridge and N.Y.: Cambridge University Press).

Stubbs, R. and Underhill, R. (eds) (1999) *Political Economy and the Changing Global Order*, 2nd edn (Basingstoke: Macmillan).

Sundhaussen, U. (1985) 'The Durability of Military Regimes in South-East Asia', in *Military-Civilian Relations in South-East Asia,* ed. Z. Ahmad and H. Crouch (Singapore and Oxford: Oxford University Press) pp. 269–86.

Sunstein, C. (2001) *Republic.com* (Princeton, N.J.: Princeton University Press).

Taagepera, R. and Shugart, M. (1989) *Seats and Votes: The Effects and Determinants of Electoral Systems* (New Haven, Conn. and London: Yale University Press).

Taras, R. (ed.) (1997) *Postcommunist Presidents* (Cambridge and N.Y.: Cambridge University Press).

Taras, R. (1998) 'The Politics of Leadership', in *Developments in Central and East European Politics 2,* ed. S. White, J. Batt and P. Lewis (Basingstoke: Macmillan) pp. 103–25.

Tarrow, S. (1998) *Power in Movement: Social Movements and Contentious Politics*, 2nd edn (Cambridge and N.Y.: Cambridge University Press).

Tate, C. and Vallinder, T. (eds) (1995) *The Global Expansion of Judicial Power* (N.Y. and London: New York University Press).

Taylor, C. (1993) *Reconciling the Solitudes: Essays on Canadian Federalism and Nationalism* (Montreal and Kingston: McGill-Queen's University Press).

Teune, H. (1995a) 'Preface', *Annals of the American Academy of Political and Social Sciences* (540) 8–10.

Teune, H. (1995b) 'Local Government and Democratic Political Development', *Annals of the American Academy of Political and Social Sciences* (540) 11–23.

Thomas, C. (ed.) (1993) *First World Interest Groups: A Comparative Perspective* (Westport, Conn.: Greenwood Press).

Thomas, C. (1997) 'Globalization and the South', in *Globalization and the South,* ed. C. Thomas and P. Wilkin (Basingstoke: Macmillan) pp. 1–17.

Tismaneanu, V. (ed.) (1995) *Political Culture and Civil Society in Russia and the New States of Eurasia* (N.Y.: M. E. Sharpe).

Tivey, L. (ed.) (1981) *The Nation-State: The Formation of Modern Politics* (London: Martin Robertson).

Tracey, M. (1998) *The Decline and Fall of Public Service Broadcasting* (N.Y. and Oxford: Oxford University Press).

Tsagarousianou, R., Tambini, D. and Bryan, C. (eds) (1997) *Cyberdemocracy: Technology, Cities and Civic Networks* (London and N.Y.: Routledge).

Tsebelis, G. and Money, J. (1997) *Bicameralism* (Cambridge and N.Y.: Cambridge University Press).

Tucker, R. (1990) *Stalin in Power: The Revolution from Above 1928–41* (N.Y. and London: Norton).

Tumarkin, N. (1997) *Lenin Lives! The Lenin Cult in Soviet Russia* (Cambridge, Mass. and London: Harvard University Press).

Turner, F. (1995) 'Reassessing Political Culture', in *Latin America in Comparative Perspective: New Approaches to Methods and Analysis,* ed. P. Smith (Boulder, Colo. and Oxford: Westview) pp. 195–224.

Turner, M. and Hulne, D. (1997) *Governance, Administration and Development* (London: Macmillan).

Ulam, A. (1974) *The Russian Political System* (N.Y.: Random House).

United Nations (1992) *An Agenda for Peace* (Washington, D.C.: United Nations).

United Nations (1995) *Supplement to an Agenda for Peace* (N.Y.: United Nations).

United Nations Development Programme (1999) *Human Development Report 1999* (N.Y. and Oxford: Oxford University Press).

van Creveld, M. (1999) *The Rise and Decline of the State* (Cambridge and N.Y.: Cambridge University Press).

van Eijk, R. (1997) 'The United Nations and the Reconstruction of Collapsed States', *African Journal of International and Comparative Law* (9) 543–72.

van der Meer, F., and Roborgh, R. (1996) ' Civil Servants and Representativeness', in *Civil Service Systems in Comparative Perspective,* ed. H. Bekke, J. Perry and T. Toonen (Bloomington, Ind.: Indiana University Press) pp. 119–33.

Vanhanen, T. (1997) *Prospects of Democracy: A Study of 172 Countries* (London and N.Y.: Routledge).

Vatikiotis, M. (1995) *Political Change in Southeast Asia: Trimming the Banyan Tree* (London and N.Y.: Routledge).

Verba, S. (1987) *Elites and the Idea of Equality: A Comparison of Japan, Sweden and the United States* (Cambridge, Mass. and London: Harvard University Press).

Verba, S. and Nie, N. (1972) *Participation in America: Political Democracy and Social Equality* (N.Y.: Harper & Row).

Verba, S., Scholzman, K. and Brady, H. (1995) *Voice and Equality: Civic Voluntarism in American Politics* (Cambridge, Mass. and London: Harvard University Press).

Vereshchetin, V. (1996) 'New Constitutions and the Old Problem of Relationship between International Law and National Law', *European Journal of International Law* (7) 29–41.

Verheijen, T. (1998) 'NPM Reforms and Other Western Reform Strategies', in *Innovations in Public Management: Perspectives from East and West Europe,* ed. T. Verheijen and D. Coombes (Cheltenham and Northampton, Mass.: Edward Elgar) pp. 407–17.

Verheijen, T. and Coombes, D. (eds) (1998) *Innovations in Public Management: Perspectives from East and West Europe* (Cheltenham and Northampton, Mass.: Edward Elgar).

von Beyme, K. (1985) *Political Parties in Western Democracies* (Aldershot: Gower).

von Mettenheim, K. and Rockman, B. (1997) 'Presidential Institutions, Democracy and Comparative Politics', in *Presidential Institutions and Democratic Politics: Comparing Regional and National Contexts,* ed. K. von Mettenheim (Baltimore, Md. and London: Johns Hopkins University Press) pp. 237–46.

Wachendorfer-Schmidt, U. (ed.) (2000) *Federalism and Political Performance* (London and N.Y.: Routledge).

Waddington, J. and Hoffman, R. (eds) (2001) *Trade Unions in Europe: Facing Challenges and Searching for Solutions* (Brussels: European Trade Union Institute).

Wahlke, J. *et al.* (1962) *The Legislative System* (N.Y.: Wiley).

Walker, D. (1991) 'American Federalism in the 1990s', in *Political Issues in America Today,* ed. P. Davies and F. Waldstein (Manchester and N.Y.: Manchester University Press) pp. 119–32.

Wallerstein, I. (1974, 1979) *The Modern World System* (N.Y.: Academic Press) two vols.

Warwick, P. (1994) *Government Survival in Parliamentary Democracies* (Cambridge and N.Y.: Cambridge University Press).

Waters, M. (2000) *Globalization,* 2nd edn (London and N.Y.: Routledge).

Watt, E. (1982) *Authority* (London: Croom Helm).

Watts, R. (1996) 'Canada: Three Decades of Periodic Federal Crises', *International Political Science Review* (17) 353–72.

Weale, A. (1999) *Democracy* (Basingstoke: Macmillan).

Weaver, R. and Rockman, B. (eds) (1993) *Do Institutions Matter? Government Capabilities in the United States and Abroad* (Washington, D.C.: The Brookings Institution).

Webb, P. (2000) *The Modern British Party System* (London: Sage).

Webber, M. (1997) 'States and Statehood', in *Issues in World Politics,* ed. B. White, R. Little and M. Smith (Basingstoke: Macmillan, and N.Y.: St Martin's) pp. 24–44.

Weber, M. (1957) *The Theory of Economic and Social Organization* (Berkeley, Calif.: University of California Press). First pub. 1922.

Weber, M. (1990) 'The Advent of Plebiscitarian Democracy', in *The West European Party System,* ed. P. Mair (Oxford and N.Y.: Oxford University Press) pp. 31–7. First pub. 1918.

Weigel, G. (1990) 'Catholicism and Democracy: The Other Twentieth Century Revolution' in *The New Democracies: Global Change and U.S. Policy,* ed. B. Roberts (Cambridge, Mass.: MIT Press) pp. 20–25.

Weiler, J. (1994) 'A Quiet Revolution: The European Court of Justice and its Interlocutors', *Comparative Political Studies* (26) 510–34.

Weiss, T. and Gordenker, C. (1996) 'Pluralizing Global Governance', in *Nongovernmental Organizations, the United Nations and Global Governance,* ed. T. Weiss and C. Gordenker (Boulder, Colo. and London: Lynne Rienner) pp. 17–50.

Weissberg, R. (1998) *Political Tolerance: Balancing Community and Diversity* (Thousand Oaks, Calif. and London: Sage).

Weller, P., Bakvis, H. and Rhodes, R. (eds) (1997) *The Hollow Crown: Countervailing Trends in Core Executives* (Basingstoke: Macmillan, and N.Y.: St. Martin's Press).

Westerlund, D. (ed.) (1996) *Questioning the Secular State: The Worldwide Resurgence of Religion in Politics* (London: Hurst).

Wheare K. (1963) *Federal Government,* 4th edn (Oxford and N.Y.: Oxford University Press).

Wheare, K. (1968) *Legislatures* (Oxford: Oxford University Press).

White, S. (1979) *Political Culture and Soviet Politics* (London: Macmillan).

Wilensky, H. (1984) *The Welfare State and Equality* (Berkeley, Calif.: University of California Press).

Williams, C. (1995) 'A Requiem for Canada?', in *Federalism: The Multiethnic Challenge,* ed. G. Smith (Harlow: Longman) pp. 31–72.

Williams, F. (1997) 'Foreign Investment Builds Up', *Financial Times,* 22 September, p. 4.

Williams, R. (1962) *Communications* (Harmondsworth, Middlesex and N.Y.: Penguin).

Williams, R. (1989) *Television: Technology and Cultural Form,* 2nd edn (London and N.Y.: Routledge).

Williamson, P. (1985) *Varieties of Corporatism: A Conceptual Discussion* (London: Macmillan).

Wilson, G. (1990a) *Business and Politics: A Comparative Introduction,* 2nd edn (Basingstoke: Macmillan).

Wilson, G. (1990b) *Interest Groups* (Oxford and Cambridge, Mass.: Blackwell).

Wilson, J. (1973) *Political Organization* (N.Y.: Basic Books).

Wilson, J. (1989) *Bureaucracy: What Government Agencies Do and How They Do It* (N.Y.: Basic Books).

Wilson, J. (1997) *American Government,* 4th edn (Boston, Mass.: Houghton Mifflin).

Wiseman, J. (1985) 'Introduction' in *Democracy and Political Change in Sub-Saharan Africa,* ed. J. Wiseman (London and N.Y.: Routledge) pp. 1–10.

Wiseman, J. (ed.) (1995) *Democracy and Political Change in Sub-Saharan Africa* (London and N.Y.: Routledge).

Wiseman, J. (1996) *The New Struggle for Democracy in Africa* (Aldershot and Brookfield, Vt.: Avebury).

Wolinetz, S. (ed.) (1997) *Political Parties* (Aldershot and Brookfield, Vt.: Ashgate).

Wood, G. (1993) 'Democracy and the American Revolution', in *Democracy: The Unfinished Journey, 508 BC to AD 1993,* ed. J. Dunn (Oxford and N.Y.: Oxford University Press) pp. 91–106.

Woodhouse, D. (1996) 'Politicians and the Judges: A Conflict of Interest', *Parliamentary Affairs* (49) 423–40.

World Bank (1997) *World Development Report: The State in a Changing World* (Oxford and N.Y.: Oxford University Press).

Wright, V. (1989) *The Government and Politics of France,* 3rd edn (London: Unwin Hyman).

Wright, V. (ed.) (1994) *Privatization in Western Europe: Pressures, Problems and Paradoxes* (London and N.Y.: Pinter).

Wright, V. (1997) 'La Fin du Dirigisme?', *Modern and Contemporary France* (5) 151–5.

Wright, V., Guy Peters, B. and Rhodes, R. (eds) (2000) *Administering the Summit: Administration of the Core Executive in Developed Countries* (Basingstoke: Macmillan).

Xia, M. (1999) 'China's National People's Congress: Institutional Transformation in the Process of Regime Transition (1978–98)' in *Parliaments in Asia,* ed. P. Norton and N. Ahmed (London and Portland, Ore.: Frank Cass) pp. 103–30.

Yin, R. (1994) *Case Study Research: Design and Methods,* 2nd edn (Thousand Oaks, Calif. and London: Sage).

Zaller, J. (1992) *The Nature and Origins of Mass Opinion* (N.Y. and Cambridge: Cambridge University Press).

Zariski, R. (1993) 'Italy', in *Politics in Western Europe,* ed. M. Hancock *et al.* (Chatham, N.J.: Chatham House, and Basingstoke: Macmillan) pp. 293–381.

Zartman, I. (ed.) (1995) *Collapsed States: The Disintegration and Restoration of Political Authority* (Boulder, Colo. and London: Lynne Rienner).

Index